`CW00924536`

Oracle Database 12c SQL

Jason Price

New York   Chicago   San Francisco   Athens
London   Madrid   Mexico City   Milan
New Delhi   Singapore   Sydney   Toronto

Library of Congress Cataloging-in-Publication Data

Price, Jason.
    Oracle database 12c SQL / Jason Price.
        pages   cm
Includes index.
ISBN 978-0-07-179935-5 (pbk.)
  1. Oracle (Computer file) 2. SQL (Computer program language) I Title.
  QA76.9.D3P729675 2013
  005.75'85—dc23   2013024724

McGraw-Hill Education books are available at special quantity discounts to use as premiums and sales promotions, or for use in corporate training programs. To contact a representative, please visit the Contact Us page at www.mhprofessional.com.

Oracle Database 12c SQL

1234567890 DOC DOC 109876543

ISBN   978-0-07-179935-5
MHID   0-07-179935-4

Sponsoring Editor Paul Carlstroem	**Technical Editor** Scott Mikolaitis	**Composition** Cenveo Publisher Services
Editorial Supervisor Janet Walden	**Copy Editor** Bill McManus	**Illustration** Cenveo Publisher Services
Project Manager Nidhi Chopra, Cenveo® Publisher Services	**Proofreader** Lisa McCoy	**Art Director, Cover** Jeff Weeks
Acquisitions Coordinator Amanda Russell	**Indexer** Claire Splan	**Cover Designer** Pattie Lee
	Production Supervisor Jean Bodeaux	

This book is dedicated to my family.
Even though you're far away, you are still in my heart.

About the Author

Jason Price is a freelance consultant and former product manager of Oracle Corporation. He has contributed to many of Oracle's products, including the database, the application server, and several of the CRM applications. Jason is an Oracle Certified Database Administrator and Application Developer, and has more than 15 years of experience in the software industry. Jason has written many books on Oracle, Java, and .NET. Jason holds a Bachelor of Science degree in physics from the University of Bristol, England.

Acknowledgments

Thanks to the wonderful people at McGraw-Hill Education/Professional. Thanks also to Scott Mikolaitis and Nidhi Chopra.

Contents at a Glance

Contents

Introduction

Today's database management systems are accessed using a standard language known as *Structured Query Language*, or SQL. Among other things, SQL allows you to retrieve, add, update, and delete information in a database. In this book, you'll learn how to master SQL, and you'll find a wealth of practical examples. You can also get all the scripts and programs featured in this book online (see the last section, "Retrieving the Examples," for details).

With this book, you will perform the following tasks:

- Master standard SQL, as well as the extensions developed by Oracle Corporation for use with the specific features of the Oracle database.
- Explore PL/SQL (Procedural Language/SQL), which enables you to write programs that contain SQL statements.
- Use SQL*Plus to execute SQL statements, scripts, and reports. SQL*Plus is a tool that allows you to interact with the database.
- Execute queries, inserts, updates, and deletes against a database.
- Create database tables, sequences, indexes, views, and users.
- Perform transactions containing multiple SQL statements.
- Define database object types and create object tables to handle advanced data.
- Use large objects to handle multimedia files containing images, music, and movies.
- Perform complex calculations using analytic functions.
- Implement high-performance tuning techniques to make your SQL statements run faster.

- Explore the XML capabilities of the Oracle database.
- Use the latest Oracle Database 12c SQL features.

This book contains 17 chapters and one appendix.

Chapter 1: Introduction
In this chapter, you'll learn about relational databases, be introduced to SQL, see a few simple queries, use SQL*Plus and SQL Developer to execute queries, and briefly examine PL/SQL.

Chapter 2: Retrieving Information from Database Tables
You'll explore how to retrieve information from one or more database tables using SELECT statements, use arithmetic expressions to perform calculations, filter rows using a WHERE clause, and sort the rows retrieved from a table.

Chapter 3: Using SQL*Plus
You'll use SQL*Plus to view a table's structure, edit an SQL statement, save and run scripts, format column output, define and use variables, and create reports.

Chapter 4: Using Simple Functions
You'll learn about some of the Oracle database's built-in functions. A function can accept input parameters and returns an output parameter. Functions allow you to perform tasks such as computing averages and square roots of numbers.

Chapter 5: Storing and Processing Dates and Times
You'll learn how the Oracle database processes and stores dates and times, collectively known as datetimes. You'll also learn about timestamps that allow you to store a specific date and time, and time intervals that allow you to store a length of time.

Chapter 6: Subqueries
You'll learn how to place a SELECT statement within an outer SQL statement. The inner SELECT statement is known as a subquery. You'll learn about the different types of subqueries and see how subqueries allow you to build up very complex statements from simple components.

Chapter 7: Advanced Queries
You'll learn how to perform queries containing advanced operators and functions. The set operators combine rows returned by multiple queries. The TRANSLATE() function converts characters in one string to characters in another string. The DECODE() function searches a set of values for a certain value. The CASE expression performs if-then-else logic. The ROLLUP and CUBE clauses return rows containing subtotals. New for Oracle Database 12c, CROSS APPLY and OUTER APPLY merge rows from two SELECT statements, and LATERAL returns an inline view of data.

Chapter 8: Analyzing Data
You'll learn about the analytic functions that enable you to perform complex calculations such as finding the top-selling product type for each month, the top salespersons, and so on. You'll see how to perform queries against data that is organized into a hierarchy. You'll also explore the MODEL clause, which performs inter-row calculations, and the PIVOT and UNPIVOT clauses,

which are useful for seeing overall trends in large amounts of data. New for Oracle Database 12*c* is the MATCH_RECOGNIZE clause, which enables you to locate patterns in data, and the FETCH FIRST clause, which enables you to perform top-N queries.

Chapter 9: Changing Table Contents

You'll learn how to add, modify, and remove rows using the INSERT, UPDATE, and DELETE statements, and how to make the results of your transactions permanent using the COMMIT statement, or undo their results entirely using the ROLLBACK statement. You'll also learn how an Oracle database can process multiple transactions at the same time.

Chapter 10: Users, Privileges, and Roles

You'll learn about database users and see how privileges and roles are used to enable users to perform specific tasks in the database.

Chapter 11: Creating Tables, Sequences, Indexes, and Views

You'll learn about tables and sequences, which generate a series of numbers, and indexes, which act like an index in a book and allow you quick access to rows. You'll also learn about views, which are predefined queries on one or more tables. Views allow you to hide complexity from a user and implement another layer of security by only allowing a view to access a limited set of data in the tables. You'll also examine flashback data archives, which store changes made to a table over a period of time. New for Oracle Database 12*c* is the ability to define visible and invisible columns in a table.

Chapter 12: Introducing PL/SQL Programming

You'll explore PL/SQL, which is built on top of SQL and enables you to write stored programs in the database that contain SQL statements. PL/SQL contains standard programming constructs.

Chapter 13: Database Objects

You'll learn how to create database object types, which may contain attributes and methods. You'll use object types to define column objects and object tables, and see how to manipulate objects using SQL and PL/SQL.

Chapter 14: Collections

You'll learn how to create collection types, which may contain multiple elements. You'll use collection types to define columns in tables. You'll see how to manipulate collections using SQL and PL/SQL.

Chapter 15: Large Objects

You'll learn about large objects, which can be used to store up to 128 terabytes of character and binary data or point to an external file. You'll also learn about the older LONG types, which are still supported in Oracle Database 12*c* for backward compatibility.

Chapter 16: SQL Tuning

You'll see SQL tuning tips that you can use to shorten the length of time your queries take to execute. You'll learn about the Oracle optimizer and examine how to pass hints to the optimizer. You'll also be introduced to advanced tuning tools.

Chapter 17: XML and the Oracle Database

The Extensible Markup Language (XML) is a general-purpose markup language. XML enables you to share structured data across the Internet, and can be used to encode data and other documents. In this chapter, you'll see how to generate XML from relational data and how to save XML in the database.

Appendix: Oracle Data Types

The appendix shows the data types available in Oracle SQL and PL/SQL.

Intended Audience

This book is suitable for the following readers:

- Developers who need to write SQL and PL/SQL
- Database administrators who need in-depth knowledge of SQL
- Business users who need to write SQL queries to get information from their organization's database
- Technical managers or consultants who need an introduction to SQL and PL/SQL

No prior knowledge of the Oracle database, SQL, or PL/SQL is assumed. Everything you need to know to become an expert is contained in this book.

Retrieving the Examples

All the SQL scripts, programs, and other files used in this book can be downloaded from the Oracle Press website at www.OraclePressBooks.com. The files are contained in a Zip file. Once you've downloaded the Zip file, you need to extract its contents. This will create a directory named `sql_book` that contains the following subdirectories:

- `sample_files` Contains the sample files used in Chapter 15
- `SQL` Contains the SQL scripts used throughout the book, including scripts to create and populate the example database tables
- `xml_files` Contains the XML used in Chapter 17

I hope you enjoy this book!

CHAPTER
1

Introduction

I n this chapter, you will learn about the following:

- Relational databases
- Structured Query Language (SQL), which is used to access a database
- SQL*Plus, Oracle's interactive text-based tool for running SQL statements
- Oracle SQL Developer, which is a graphical tool for database development
- PL/SQL, Oracle's procedural language that contains programming statements

What Is a Relational Database?

The concept of a relational database was originally developed back in 1970 by Dr. E.F. Codd. He developed the theory of relational databases in a paper entitled "A Relational Model of Data for Large Shared Data Banks," published in *Communications of the Association for Computing Machinery*, Vol. 13, No. 6, June 1970.

The basic concepts of a relational database are easy to understand. A *relational database* is a collection of related information that has been organized into *tables*. Each table stores data in *rows*, with the data arranged into *columns*. The tables are stored in database *schemas*, which are areas where users can store their own tables. A user can grant *permissions* to other users so they can access the tables.

Most of us are familiar with data being stored in tables. For example, stock prices and train timetables are sometimes organized into tables. One example table used in this book records the customer information for an imaginary store. The table stores each customer's first name, last name, date of birth (dob), and phone number:

```
FIRST_NAME LAST_NAME  DOB          PHONE
---------- ---------- -----------  ------------
John       Brown      01-JAN-1965  800-555-1211
Cynthia    Green      05-FEB-1968  800-555-1212
Steve      White      16-MAR-1971  800-555-1213
Gail       Black                   800-555-1214
Doreen     Blue       20-MAY-1970
```

This table could be stored in a variety of forms:

- A table in a database
- An HTML file on a web page
- A piece of paper stored in a filing cabinet

An important point to remember is that the information that makes up a database is different from the system used to access that information. The software used to access a database is known as a *database management system*. Example software includes Oracle Database 12c, Microsoft SQL Server, IBM DB2, and open-source MySQL.

Of course, every database must have some way to get data in and out of it, preferably using a common language understood by all databases. Database management systems implement a standard language known as *Structured Query Language*, or SQL. SQL allows you to retrieve, add, modify, and delete information in a database.

Introducing Structured Query Language (SQL)

Structured Query Language (SQL) is the standard language designed to access relational databases. SQL should be pronounced as the letters "S-Q-L."

NOTE
"S-Q-L" is the correct way to pronounce SQL according to the American National Standards Institute. However, the single word "sequel" is frequently used instead.

SQL is based on the groundbreaking work of Dr. E.F. Codd, with the first implementation of SQL being developed by IBM in the mid-1970s. IBM was conducting a research project known as System R, and SQL was born from that project. Later, in 1979, a company then known as Relational Software, Inc. (known today as Oracle Corporation) released the first commercial version of SQL.

SQL became a standard of the American National Standards Institute (ANSI) in 1986, but there are differences between the implementations of SQL from each software company.

SQL uses a simple syntax that is easy to learn and use. You'll see some simple examples of its use in this chapter. There are five types of SQL statements, outlined in the following list:

- **Query statements** retrieve rows stored in database tables. You write a query using the SQL SELECT statement.

- **Data Manipulation Language (DML) statements** modify the contents of tables. There are three DML statements:

  - **INSERT** adds rows to a table.

  - **UPDATE** changes rows.

  - **DELETE** removes rows.

- **Data Definition Language (DDL) statements** define the data structures, such as tables, that make up a database. There are five basic types of DDL statements:

  - **CREATE** creates a database structure. For example, CREATE TABLE is used to create a table. Another example is CREATE USER, which is used to create a database user.

  - **ALTER** modifies a database structure. For example, ALTER TABLE is used to modify a table.

  - **DROP** removes a database structure. For example, DROP TABLE is used to remove a table.

  - **RENAME** changes the name of a table.

  - **TRUNCATE** deletes all the rows from a table.

- **Transaction Control (TC) statements** permanently record row changes or undo row changes. There are three TC statements:

  - `COMMIT` permanently records the row changes.

  - `ROLLBACK` undoes the row changes.

  - `SAVEPOINT` sets a "savepoint" to which you can roll back changes.

- **Data Control Language (DCL) statements** change the permissions on database structures. There are two DCL statements:

  - `GRANT` gives a user access to a specified database structure.

  - `REVOKE` prevents a user from accessing a specified database structure.

Oracle has a program called SQL*Plus that allows you to enter SQL statements and get results back from the database. SQL*Plus also allows you to run scripts containing SQL statements and SQL*Plus commands.

There are other ways to run SQL statements and get results back from the database. For example, Oracle Forms and Oracle Reports allow you to run SQL statements. SQL statements can also be embedded within programs written in programming languages like Java and C#. For details on how to add SQL statements to a Java program, see my book *Oracle9i JDBC Programming* (Oracle Press, 2002). For details on how to add SQL statements to a C# program, see my book *Mastering C# Database Programming* (Sybex, 2003).

Using SQL*Plus

In this section, you'll learn how to start SQL*Plus and run a query.

Starting SQL*Plus

If you're using Windows 7, you can start SQL*Plus by selecting All Programs | Oracle | Application Development | SQL Plus. If you're using Unix or Linux, you start SQL*Plus by running `sqlplus` from the command prompt.

This illustration shows SQL*Plus running on Windows 7.

The illustration shows the `scott` user connecting to the database. The `scott` user is contained in many Oracle database installations. The password for `scott` in my database is `oracle`.

The host string after the @ character tells SQL*Plus which database system to connect to. If you are running the database on your own computer, you'll typically omit the host string. For example, I could enter `scott/oracle` and omit the @ character and the `orcl` string. If the host string is omitted, SQL*Plus attempts to connect to a database on the same computer on which SQL*Plus is running. If the database isn't running on your computer, you should speak with your database administrator (DBA) to get the host string.

If the scott user doesn't exist in your database or is locked, ask your DBA for an alternative user and password. For the examples in the first part of this chapter, you can use any user to connect to the database.

Starting SQL*Plus from the Command Line

You can start SQL*Plus from the command line. To do this, you use the sqlplus command. The full syntax for the sqlplus command is as follows:

```
sqlplus [user_name[/password[@host_string]]]
```

where

- *user_name* specifies the name of the database user.
- *password* specifies the password for the database user.
- *host_string* specifies the database to connect to.

The following examples show sqlplus commands:

```
sqlplus scott/oracle
sqlplus scott/oracle@orcl
```

If you're using SQL*Plus with a Windows operating system, the Oracle installer automatically adds the directory for SQL*Plus to your path. If you're using Unix or Linux, you can do one of the following to run SQL*Plus:

- Change directories using the cd command into the same directory as the sqlplus executable, and then run sqlplus from that directory.
- Add the directory where sqlplus is located to your path, and then run sqlplus. If you need help with setting up a directory path, you should speak with your system administrator.

For security, you can hide the password when connecting to the database. For example, you can enter the following command:

```
sqlplus scott@orcl
```

SQL*Plus then prompts you to enter the password. As you type in the password, it is hidden.
You can also enter the following command:

```
sqlplus
```

SQL*Plus then prompts you for the user name and password. You can specify the host string by adding it to the user name (for example, scott@orcl).

Performing a SELECT Statement Using SQL*Plus

Once you're logged onto the database using SQL*Plus, run the following SELECT statement that returns the current date:

```
SELECT SYSDATE FROM dual;
```

NOTE
In this book, SQL statements shown in **bold** *are statements that you should type in and run if you want to follow along with the examples. Non-bold statements are statements you don't need to type in.*

SYSDATE is a built-in database function that returns the current date. The dual table contains a single dummy row. You'll learn more about the dual table in the next chapter.

NOTE
SQL statements are terminated using a semicolon character (;).

The following illustration shows the date returned by the previous SELECT statement.

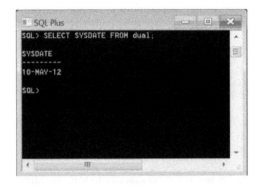

You can edit your last SQL statement in SQL*Plus by entering EDIT. This is useful when you make a mistake or you want to change your SQL statement. On Windows, when you enter EDIT you are taken to the Notepad application. When you exit Notepad and save your statement, the new statement is passed back to SQL*Plus. You can re-execute the statement by entering a forward slash (/). On Linux and Unix, the default editor is ed. To save the statement changes and exit ed, you enter wq.

Resolving the Error When Attempting to Edit Statements

If you encounter error SP2-0110 when trying to edit a statement on Windows, you can run SQL*Plus as an administrator. On Windows 7, you can do that by right-clicking the SQL*Plus shortcut and selecting "Run as administrator." You can permanently set this in Windows 7 by right-clicking the SQL*Plus shortcut and selecting the "Run this program as an administrator" option in the Compatibility tab.

You can also set the directory that SQL*Plus starts in by right-clicking the SQL*Plus shortcut and changing the "Start in" directory in the Shortcut tab. SQL*Plus will use that default directory when saving and retrieving files. For example, you could set the directory to C:\My_SQL_files, and SQL*Plus will store and retrieve files from that directory by default.

On the Windows version of SQL*Plus, you can scroll through previous commands you've run by pressing the UP and DOWN ARROW keys on the keyboard.

You'll learn more about SQL*Plus in Chapter 3.

Using SQL Developer

You can also enter SQL statements using SQL Developer. SQL Developer has a graphical user interface (GUI) through which you can enter SQL statements, examine database tables, run scripts, edit and debug PL/SQL code, and perform other tasks. SQL Developer can connect to Oracle Database version 9.2.0.1 and higher. SQL Developer is available for many operating systems. The following illustration shows SQL Developer running.

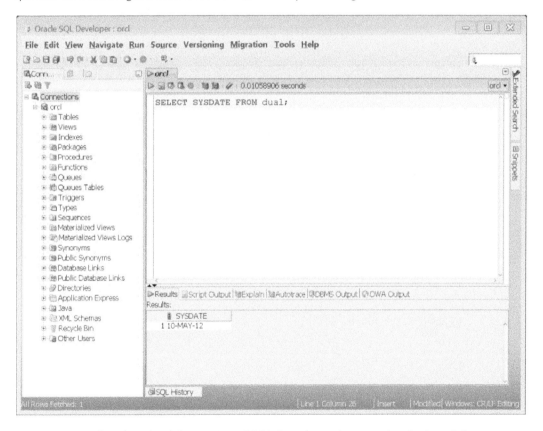

You must either download the version of SQL Developer that contains the Java Software Development Kit (SDK), or already have the correct version of the Java SDK installed on your computer. The Java version required varies depending on the version of SQL Developer, and you should examine the SQL Developer web page on www.oracle.com for details.

After successfully starting SQL Developer, you will need to create a database connection by right-clicking Connections and selecting New Connection. SQL Developer will display a dialog in which you specify the database connection details. The following illustration shows an example dialog with the connection details completed.

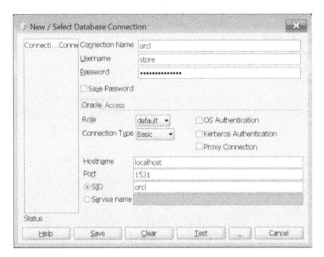

Once you've created a connection and tested it, you can use SQL Developer to examine database tables and run queries. The following illustration shows the columns in a table named `customers`, which is one of the tables used in this book.

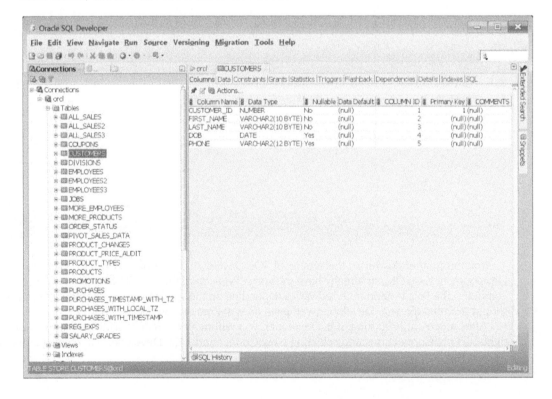

You can also view the data stored in a table by selecting the Data tab, as shown in the following illustration, which shows the rows in the `customers` table.

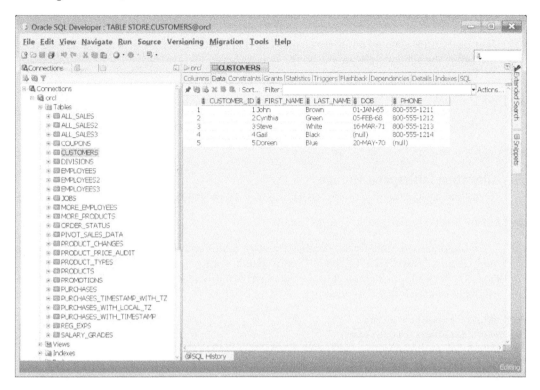

In the next section, you'll learn how to create the `store` schema used in this book.

Creating the Store Schema

The imaginary store sells items such as books, videos, DVDs, and CDs. The database for the store will hold information about the customers, employees, products, and sales. The SQL*Plus script to create the database is named `store_schema.sql`, which is located in the `SQL` directory where you extracted the Zip file for this book. The `store_schema.sql` script contains the DDL and DML statements that create the schema.

Examining the Script

Open the script in an editor and examine the statements in the script. This section introduces the script statements and guides you through any script changes you might need to make. You'll learn more about the script statements later in this chapter.

Dropping and Creating the User

The first executable statement in the `store_schema.sql` script is as follows:

```
DROP USER store CASCADE;
```

The `DROP USER` statement is there so that you don't have to manually drop the `store` user when re-creating the schema later in this book.

The next statement creates the `store` user with a password of `store_password`:

```
CREATE USER store IDENTIFIED BY store_password;
```

The next statement allows the `store` user to connect to the database and create database items:

```
GRANT connect, resource TO store;
```

Allocating Tablespace Storage

The following statement allocates the `store` user 10 megabytes of space in the `users` tablespace:

```
ALTER USER store QUOTA 10M ON users;
```

Tablespaces are used by the database to store tables and other database objects. You'll learn more about tablespaces in Chapter 10. Most databases have a `users` tablespace to store user data. To check this, first connect to the database as a privileged user (for example, the `system` user) and run the following statement:

```
SELECT property_value
FROM database_properties
WHERE property_name = 'DEFAULT_PERMANENT_TABLESPACE';

PROPERTY_VALUE
--------------
USERS
```

This query returns the name of the tablespace to use in the `ALTER USER` statement. In my database, the tablespace is `users`.

If the tablespace returned by the query is different from `users`, then you must replace `users` in the script's `ALTER USER` statement with the one returned by the previous query. For example, if the name of your tablespace is `another_ts`, then change the script statement to:

```
ALTER USER store QUOTA 10M ON another_ts;
```

Setting the Connection

The following statement in the script connects as the `store` user:

```
CONNECT store/store_password;
```

You'll need to modify the `CONNECT` statement in the script if you're connecting to a database on a different computer. For example, if you're connecting to a database named `orcl`, then change the `CONNECT` statement in the script to:

```
CONNECT store/store_password@orcl;
```

Using the Pluggable Database Feature

Pluggable databases are a new feature in Oracle Database 12c. Pluggable databases are created within an outer container database. Pluggable databases save system resources, simplify system administration, and are typically implemented by database administrators. Therefore, a full discussion of pluggable databases is beyond the scope of this book.

If you're using the pluggable database feature, then you'll need to modify the CONNECT statement in the script to include the name of the pluggable database. For example, if your pluggable database name is pdborcl, then change the statement to:

```
CONNECT store/store_password@pdborcl;
```

If you made any changes to the store_schema.sql script, save your modified script.

The remaining statements in the script create the tables and other items required for the example store. You'll learn about those statements later in this chapter.

Running the Script

To create the store schema, you perform the following steps:

1. Start SQL*Plus.

2. Log onto the database as a user with the privileges to create new users, tables, and PL/SQL packages. I run scripts in my database using the system user. This user has all the required privileges.

3. If you're using the pluggable database feature, then you must set the session database container to your pluggable database name. For example, if your pluggable database name is pdborcl, then run the following command:

   ```
   ALTER SESSION SET CONTAINER=pdborcl;
   ```

4. Run the store_schema.sql script using the @ command. The @ command has the following syntax:

   ```
   @ directory\store_schema.sql
   ```

   where directory is the directory where your store_schema.sql script is located.

For example, if your script is located in C:\sql_book\SQL, then you enter the following command:

```
@ C:\sql_book\SQL\store_schema.sql
```

If your script is located in a directory that contains spaces, then you must place the directory and script in quotes after the @ command. For example:

```
@ "C:\Oracle SQL book\sql_book\SQL\store_schema.sql"
```

If you're using Unix or Linux and the script is in a directory named SQL located in tmp, then you enter the following command:

```
@ /tmp/SQL/store_schema.sql
```

NOTE
*Windows uses backslash characters (\) in the directory path. Unix and
Linux use forward slash characters (/).*

When the script has finished running, you'll be connected as the `store` user. The user has a
password of `store_password`.

You'll be asked to run other scripts later in this book. You'll need to perform the steps
described in this section before running each script:

- If your database does not have a `users` tablespace, then you'll need to edit the `ALTER USER` statement in the script.

- If you need to set a host string to connect to a database, then you'll need to edit the `CONNECT` statement in the script.

- If you're using the pluggable database feature, then you'll need to edit the `CONNECT` statement in the script and run the `ALTER SESSION SET CONTAINER` command prior to running the script.

You don't have to edit all of the scripts now. Just remember that you might have to edit each
script before running it.

Examining the Store Data Definition Language Statements

Data Definition Language (DDL) statements are used to create users and tables, plus many other
types of structures in the database. In this section, you'll see the DDL statements used to create
the `store` user and some of the tables.

NOTE
*The SQL statements you'll see in the rest of this chapter are the same
as those contained in the `store_schema.sql` script. You don't have
to type in the statements yourself.*

The next sections describe the following:

- How to create a database user
- The data types commonly used in an Oracle database
- Some of the tables in the imaginary store

Creating a Database User

To create a user in the database, you use the `CREATE USER` statement. The simplified syntax for
the `CREATE USER` statement is as follows:

```
CREATE USER user_name IDENTIFIED BY password;
```

where

- *user_name* is the user name
- *password* is the password for the user

For example, the following CREATE USER statement creates the store user with a password of store_password:

```
CREATE USER store IDENTIFIED BY store_password;
```

If you want the user to be able to work in the database, the user must be granted the necessary *permissions* to do that work. In the case of store, this user must be able to log onto the database (which requires the connect permission) and create items like database tables (which requires the resource permission). Permissions are granted by a privileged user (for example, the system user) using the GRANT statement.

The following example grants the connect and resource permissions to store:

```
GRANT connect, resource TO store;
```

Many of the examples in this book use the store schema. Before I get into the details of the tables in the store schema, you need to know about the commonly used Oracle database types.

The Common Oracle Database Types

There are many types that can be used to handle data in an Oracle database. Some of the commonly used types are shown in Table 1-1. You can see all of the data types in the appendix of this book.

Oracle Type	Description
CHAR(*length*)	CHAR stores a fixed-length string. The *length* parameter specifies the length of the string. If a string of a smaller length is stored, then the string is padded with spaces at the end. For example, CHAR(2) can be used to store a fixed-length string of two characters. If 'C' is stored in a CHAR(2), then a single space is added at the end. 'CA' is stored as is, with no padding necessary.
VARCHAR2(*length*)	VARCHAR2 stores a variable-length string. The *length* parameter specifies the maximum length of the string. For example, VARCHAR2(20) can be used to store a string of up to 20 characters in length. No padding is added at the end of a smaller string.
DATE	DATE stores a date and time. A DATE stores the century, all four digits of a year, the month, the day, the hour (in 24-hour format), the minute, and the second. A DATE can store a date between January 1, 4712 B.C. and December 31, 9999 A.D.
INTEGER	INTEGER stores an integer. An integer is a whole number, such as 1, 10, and 115. An integer doesn't contain a floating point.

(Continued)

Table 1-1   *Commonly Used Oracle Data Types*

Oracle Type	Description
NUMBER (*precision*, *scale*)	NUMBER stores a floating-point number. The *precision* is the maximum number of digits to store. The number of digits includes those digits that appear to the left and right of a decimal point. The maximum precision is 38. The *scale* is the maximum number of digits to the right of a decimal point. If neither *precision* nor *scale* is specified, then any number up to a precision of 38 digits can be stored. Any attempt to store a number that exceeds the specified *precision* is rejected by the database.

Table 1-1   *Commonly Used Oracle Data Types*

The following table shows some NUMBER examples.

Format	Number Supplied	Number Stored
NUMBER	1234.567	1234.567
NUMBER(6, 2)	123.4567	123.46
NUMBER(6, 2)	12345.67	Number exceeds the specified precision and is therefore rejected by the database

Examining the Store Tables

In this section, you'll learn how the tables for the store schema are created. Some of the information held in the store schema includes the following:

■ Customer details
■ Types of products sold
■ Product details
■ A history of the products purchased by the customers
■ Employees of the store
■ Salary grades

The following tables are used to hold the information:

■ **customers** holds the customer details
■ **product_types** holds the types of products sold by the store
■ **products** holds the product details
■ **purchases** holds which products were purchased by which customers
■ **employees** holds the employee details
■ **salary_grades** holds the employee salary grades

In the following sections, you'll see the CREATE TABLE statements in the store_schema. sql script that create the tables.

The customers Table   The customers table holds the details of the customers. The following items are held in this table:

- First name
- Last name
- Date of birth (dob)
- Phone number

Each of these items requires a column in the customers table. The customers table is created by the store_schema.sql script using the following CREATE TABLE statement:

```
CREATE TABLE customers (
  customer_id INTEGER CONSTRAINT customers_pk PRIMARY KEY,
  first_name VARCHAR2(10) NOT NULL,
  last_name VARCHAR2(10) NOT NULL,
  dob DATE,
  phone VARCHAR2(12)
);
```

As you can see, the customers table contains five columns, one for each item in the previous list, and an extra column named customer_id. The columns are as follows:

- **customer_id**   Contains a unique integer for each row in the table. Each table should have a column that uniquely identifies each row. The column is known as the *primary key*. A primary key can consist of multiple columns. The CONSTRAINT clause in the CREATE TABLE statement indicates that the customer_id column is the primary key. A CONSTRAINT clause restricts the values stored in a column, and, for the customer_ id column, the PRIMARY KEY keywords indicate that the customer_id column must contain a unique value for each row. You can also attach an optional name to a constraint, which must immediately follow the CONSTRAINT keyword—for example, customers_pk. You should always name your primary key constraints so that if a constraint error occurs, you can easily find where it happened.

- **first_name**   Contains the first name of the customer. This column is marked as NOT NULL, which means that a value must be supplied for first_name when adding a row. If a NOT NULL constraint is omitted, a user doesn't need to supply a value.

- **last_name**   Contains the last name of the customer. This column is NOT NULL, and therefore a value must be supplied when adding a row.

- **dob**   Contains the date of birth for the customer. No NOT NULL constraint is specified for this column. Therefore, the default NULL is assumed, and a value is optional when adding a row.

- **phone**   Contains the phone number of the customer. No NOT NULL constraint is specified for this column.

The `store_schema.sql` script populates the `customers` table with the following rows:

```
CUSTOMER_ID FIRST_NAME LAST_NAME  DOB        PHONE
----------- ---------- ---------- --------- ------------
          1 John       Brown      01-JAN-65 800-555-1211
          2 Cynthia    Green      05-FEB-68 800-555-1212
          3 Steve      White      16-MAR-71 800-555-1213
          4 Gail       Black                800-555-1214
          5 Doreen     Blue       20-MAY-70
```

Notice that customer #4's date of birth is null, and so is customer #5's phone number.

You can see the rows in the `customers` table for yourself by executing the following SELECT statement using SQL*Plus:

```
SELECT * FROM customers;
```

The asterisk (*) indicates that you want to retrieve all the columns from the `customers` table.

The product_types Table   The `product_types` table holds the names of the product types sold by the store. This table is created by the `store_schema.sql` script using the following CREATE TABLE statement:

```
CREATE TABLE product_types (
  product_type_id INTEGER CONSTRAINT product_types_pk PRIMARY KEY,
  name VARCHAR2(10) NOT NULL
);
```

The `product_types` table contains the following two columns:

- **product_type_id** uniquely identifies each row in the table. The `product_type_id` column is the primary key for this table. Each row in the `product_types` table must have a unique integer value for the `product_type_id` column.
- **name** contains the product type name. It is a NOT NULL column, and therefore a value must be supplied when adding a row.

The `store_schema.sql` script populates the `product_types` table with the following rows:

```
PRODUCT_TYPE_ID NAME
--------------- ----------
              1 Book
              2 Video
              3 DVD
              4 CD
              5 Magazine
```

The `product_types` table holds the names of the product types for the store. Each product sold by the store must be a valid product type.

You can see the rows in the `product_types` table by executing the following SELECT statement using SQL*Plus:

```
SELECT * FROM product_types;
```

The products Table   The `products` table holds the products sold by the store. The following information is held for each product:

- Product type
- Name
- Description
- Price

The `store_schema.sql` script creates the `products` table using the following CREATE TABLE statement:

```
CREATE TABLE products (
  product_id INTEGER CONSTRAINT products_pk PRIMARY KEY,
  product_type_id INTEGER
    CONSTRAINT products_fk_product_types
    REFERENCES product_types(product_type_id),
  name VARCHAR2(30) NOT NULL,
  description VARCHAR2(50),
  price NUMBER(5, 2)
);
```

The columns in the `products` table are as follows:

- **product_id** uniquely identifies each row in the table. This column is the primary key of the table.

- **product_type_id** associates each product with a product type. This column is a reference to the `product_type_id` column in the `product_types` table. This column is known as a *foreign key* because it references a column in another table. The table containing the foreign key (the `products` table) is known as the *detail* or *child* table, and the table that is referenced (the `product_types` table) is known as the *master* or *parent* table. This type of relationship is known as a *master-detail* or *parent-child* relationship. When you add a new product, you associate that product with a type by supplying a matching `product_types.product_type_id` value in the `products.product_type_id` column (you'll see an example later).

- **name** contains the product name. The column is NOT NULL.

- **description** contains an optional description of the product.

- **price** contains an optional price for a product. This column is defined as NUMBER(5, 2). The precision is 5, and therefore a maximum of five digits can be supplied for this number. The scale is 2; therefore, two of those maximum five digits can be to the right of a decimal point.

The following shows the first four rows stored in the `products` table:

```
PRODUCT_ID PRODUCT_TYPE_ID NAME         DESCRIPTION   PRICE
---------- --------------- ------------ ------------ ------
         1               1 Modern       A             19.95
                           Science      description
                                        of modern
                                        science
```

2	1 Chemistry	Introduction to Chemistry	30
3	2 Supernova	A star explodes	25.99
4	2 Tank War	Action movie about a future war	13.95

The first row in the `products` table has a `product_type_id` of 1, which means the product is a book (this `product_type_id` matches the "book" product type in the `product_types` table). The second product is also a book. The third and fourth products are videos (their `product_type_id` is 2, which matches the "video" product type in the `product_types` table).

You can see all the rows in the `products` table by executing the following `SELECT` statement using SQL*Plus:

```
SELECT * FROM products;
```

The purchases Table   The `purchases` table holds the purchases made by a customer. For each purchase made by a customer, the following information is held:

- Product ID
- Customer ID
- Number of units of the product that were purchased by the customer

The `store_schema.sql` script uses the following `CREATE TABLE` statement to create the `purchases` table:

```
CREATE TABLE purchases (
  product_id INTEGER
    CONSTRAINT purchases_fk_products
    REFERENCES products(product_id),
  customer_id INTEGER
    CONSTRAINT purchases_fk_customers
    REFERENCES customers(customer_id),
  quantity INTEGER NOT NULL,
  CONSTRAINT purchases_pk PRIMARY KEY (product_id, customer_id)
);
```

The columns in this table are as follows:

- **product_id** contains the ID of the product that was purchased. This must match a `product_id` column value in the `products` table.
- **customer_id** contains the ID of a customer who made the purchase. This must match a `customer_id` column value in the `customers` table.
- **quantity** contains the number of units of the product that were purchased by the customer.

The `purchases` table has a primary key constraint named `purchases_pk` that consists of two columns: `product_id` and `customer_id`. The combination of the two column values must be unique for each row. When a primary key consists of multiple columns, it is known as a *composite* primary key.

The following shows the first five rows that are stored in the `purchases` table:

```
PRODUCT_ID CUSTOMER_ID   QUANTITY
---------- ----------- ----------
         1           1          1
         2           1          3
         1           4          1
         2           2          1
         1           3          1
```

As you can see, the combination of the values in the `product_id` and `customer_id` columns is unique for each row.

You can see all the rows in the `purchases` table for yourself by executing the following `SELECT` statement using SQL*Plus:

```
SELECT * FROM purchases;
```

The employees Table   The `employees` table holds the details of the employees. The following information is held in the table:

- Employee ID
- The ID of the employee's manager (if applicable)
- First name
- Last name
- Title
- Salary

The `store_schema.sql` script uses the following `CREATE TABLE` statement to create the `employees` table:

```
CREATE TABLE employees (
  employee_id INTEGER CONSTRAINT employees_pk PRIMARY KEY,
  manager_id INTEGER,
  first_name VARCHAR2(10) NOT NULL,
  last_name VARCHAR2(10) NOT NULL,
  title VARCHAR2(20),
  salary NUMBER(6, 0)
);
```

The `store_schema.sql` script populates the `employees` table with the following rows:

```
EMPLOYEE_ID MANAGER_ID FIRST_NAME LAST_NAME   TITLE             SALARY
----------- ---------- ---------- ----------  ------------- ----------
          1            James      Smith       CEO               800000
          2          1 Ron        Johnson     Sales Manager     600000
          3          2 Fred       Hobbs       Salesperson       150000
          4          2 Susan      Jones       Salesperson       500000
```

James Smith is the CEO and he doesn't have a manager.

The salary_grades Table The salary_grades table holds the different salary grades available to employees. The following information is held:

- Salary grade ID
- Low salary boundary for the grade
- High salary boundary for the grade

The store_schema.sql script uses the following CREATE TABLE statement to create the salary_grades table:

```
CREATE TABLE salary_grades (
  salary_grade_id INTEGER CONSTRAINT salary_grade_pk PRIMARY KEY,
  low_salary  NUMBER(6, 0),
  high_salary NUMBER(6, 0)
);
```

The store_schema.sql script populates the salary_grades table with the following rows:

```
SALARY_GRADE_ID LOW_SALARY HIGH_SALARY
--------------- ---------- -----------
              1          1      250000
              2     250001      500000
              3     500001      750000
              4     750001      999999
```

Adding, Modifying, and Removing Rows

In this section, you'll learn how to add, modify, and remove rows in database tables by using the SQL INSERT, UPDATE, and DELETE statements. You can make your row changes permanent in the database by using the COMMIT statement. You can undo your row changes by using the ROLLBACK statement. This section doesn't exhaustively cover all the details of using these statements (you'll learn more about them in Chapter 9).

Adding a Row to a Table

You use the INSERT statement to add new rows to a table. You can specify the following information in an INSERT statement:

- The table into which the row is to be inserted
- A list of columns for which you want to specify column values
- A list of values to store in the specified columns

When adding a row, you need to supply a value for the primary key and all other columns that are defined as NOT NULL. You don't have to specify values for the other columns. Those columns will be automatically set to null if you omit values for them.

You can tell which columns are defined as NOT NULL using the SQL*Plus DESCRIBE command. For example:

```
SQL> DESCRIBE customers
 Name                                      Null?    Type
 ----------------------------------------- -------- ------------
 CUSTOMER_ID                               NOT NULL NUMBER(38)
 FIRST_NAME                                NOT NULL VARCHAR2(10)
 LAST_NAME                                 NOT NULL VARCHAR2(10)
 DOB                                                DATE
 PHONE                                              VARCHAR2(12)
```

The customer_id, first_name, and last_name columns are NOT NULL, meaning that you must supply a value for these columns when adding a row. The dob and phone columns don't require a value. You could omit those values if you wanted, and they would be automatically set to null.

Go ahead and run the following INSERT statement, which adds a row to the customers table. Notice that the order of values in the VALUES list matches the order in which the columns are specified in the column list.

```
SQL> INSERT INTO customers (
  2    customer_id, first_name, last_name, dob, phone
  3  ) VALUES (
  4    6, 'Fred', 'Brown', '01-JAN-1970', '800-555-1215'
  5  );

1 row created.
```

NOTE
*SQL*Plus automatically numbers lines after you press ENTER at the end of each line.*

In the previous example, SQL*Plus responds that one row has been created after the INSERT statement is executed. You can verify this by running the following SELECT statement:

```
SELECT *
FROM customers;

CUSTOMER_ID FIRST_NAME LAST_NAME  DOB       PHONE
----------- ---------- ---------- --------- ------------
          1 John       Brown      01-JAN-65 800-555-1211
          2 Cynthia    Green      05-FEB-68 800-555-1212
          3 Steve      White      16-MAR-71 800-555-1213
          4 Gail       Black                800-555-1214
          5 Doreen     Blue       20-MAY-70
          6 Fred       Brown      01-JAN-70 800-555-1215
```

Notice the new row shown at the end.

By default, the Oracle database displays dates in the format DD-MON-YY, where DD is the day number, MON is the first three characters of the month (in uppercase), and YY is the last two digits of the year. The database actually stores all four digits for the year, but by default, it only displays the last two digits.

When a row is added to the customers table, a unique value for the customer_id column must be given. The Oracle database will prevent you from adding a row with a primary key value that already exists in the table. For example, the following INSERT statement generates an error because a row with a customer_id of 1 already exists:

```
SQL> INSERT INTO customers (
  2     customer_id, first_name, last_name, dob, phone
  3  ) VALUES (
  4     1, 'Lisa', 'Jones', '02-JAN-1971', '800-555-1225'
  5  );

INSERT INTO customers (
*
ERROR at line 1:
ORA-00001: unique constraint (STORE.CUSTOMERS_PK) violated
```

Notice that the name of the constraint is shown in the error (STORE.CUSTOMERS_PK). That's why you should always name your primary key constraints. Otherwise, the Oracle database assigns an unfriendly system-generated name to a constraint, which makes it difficult to locate the problem (for example, SYS_C0011277).

Modifying an Existing Row in a Table

You use the UPDATE statement to change rows in a table. Typically, when you use the UPDATE statement, you specify the following information:

- The table containing the rows that are to be changed
- A WHERE clause that specifies the rows that are to be changed
- A list of column names, along with their new values, which are specified using the SET clause

You can change one or more rows using the same UPDATE statement. If more than one row is specified, then the same change will be made for all the rows. The following example updates customer #2's last_name to Orange:

```
UPDATE customers
SET last_name = 'Orange'
WHERE customer_id = 2;

1 row updated.
```

SQL*Plus confirms that one row was updated.

CAUTION
If you forget to add a WHERE clause, then all the rows will be updated.

The following query shows the updated row:

```
SELECT *
FROM customers
WHERE customer_id = 2;

CUSTOMER_ID FIRST_NAME LAST_NAME  DOB       PHONE
----------- ---------- ---------- --------- -----------
          2 Cynthia    Orange     05-FEB-68 800-555-1212
```

Removing a Row from a Table

You use the DELETE statement to remove rows from a table. You typically use a WHERE clause to limit the rows you wish to delete. If you don't, then *all* of the rows will be deleted from the table.
The following DELETE statement removes customer #6:

```
DELETE FROM customers
WHERE customer_id = 6;

1 row deleted.
```

To undo the changes made to the rows, you use ROLLBACK:

```
ROLLBACK;

Rollback complete.
```

NOTE
You can make changes to rows permanent using COMMIT. You'll see how to do that in Chapter 9.

Connecting to and Disconnecting from a Database

While you're connected to the database, SQL*Plus maintains a database session for you. When you disconnect from the database, your session is ended. You can disconnect from the database and keep SQL*Plus running by entering DISCONNECT:

```
DISCONNECT
```

By default, when you disconnect, a COMMIT is automatically performed for you.
You can reconnect to a database by entering CONNECT. To reconnect to the store schema, you enter store as the user name with a password of store_password:

```
CONNECT store/store_password
```

Quitting SQL*Plus

You use the EXIT command to quit SQL*Plus. The following example quits SQL*Plus using the EXIT command:

```
EXIT
```

By default, when you quit SQL*Plus using EXIT, a COMMIT is automatically performed. If SQL*Plus terminates abnormally—for example, if the computer on which SQL*Plus is running crashes—then a ROLLBACK is automatically performed. You'll learn more about COMMIT and ROLLBACK in Chapter 9.

Introducing Oracle PL/SQL

PL/SQL is Oracle's procedural language. PL/SQL allows you to add programming constructs around SQL statements. PL/SQL is primarily used for creating procedures and functions in a database that contains business logic. PL/SQL contains standard programming constructs such as the following:

- Variable declarations
- Conditional logic (if-then-else)
- Loops
- Procedures and functions

The following CREATE PROCEDURE statement creates a procedure named update_ product_price(). The procedure multiplies the price of a specified product by a supplied factor. If the specified product doesn't exist, then the procedure takes no action. Otherwise, the procedure updates the specified product's price.

> **NOTE**
> *Don't worry about the details of the PL/SQL shown in the following listing. You'll learn all about PL/SQL in Chapter 12. I just want you to get a feel for PL/SQL at this stage.*

```
CREATE PROCEDURE update_product_price(
  p_product_id IN products.product_id%TYPE,
  p_factor     IN NUMBER
) AS
  v_product_count INTEGER;
BEGIN
  -- count the number of products with the
  -- supplied product_id (will be 1 if the product exists)
  SELECT COUNT(*)
  INTO v_product_count
  FROM products
  WHERE product_id = p_product_id;
```

```
  -- if the product exists (v_product_count = 1) then
  -- update that product's price
  IF v_product_count = 1 THEN
    UPDATE products
    SET price = price * p_factor
    WHERE product_id = p_product_id;
    COMMIT;
  END IF;
EXCEPTION
  WHEN OTHERS THEN
    ROLLBACK;
END update_product_price;
/
```

Exceptions are used to handle errors that occur in PL/SQL code. The EXCEPTION block in the previous example performs a ROLLBACK if an exception is thrown in the code.

Summary

In this chapter, you have learned the following:

- A relational database is a collection of related information organized into tables.
- Structured Query Language (SQL) is the standard language for accessing databases.
- SQL*Plus allows you to run SQL statements and SQL*Plus commands.
- SQL Developer is a graphical tool for database development.
- PL/SQL is Oracle's procedural language that contains programming statements.

In the next chapter, you'll learn more about retrieving information from database tables.

CHAPTER
2

Retrieving Information
from Database Tables

I n this chapter, you'll learn how to perform the following tasks:

- Retrieve information using the SELECT statement
- Perform calculations using arithmetic expressions
- Limit the retrieval of rows using the WHERE clause
- Sort the rows retrieved from a table

NOTE
Before continuing, rerun store_schema.sql *to re-create the store tables so that your queries match those in this chapter.*

Performing Single Table SELECT Statements

The SELECT statement retrieves information from database tables. In the SELECT statement's simplest form, you specify the table and columns to retrieve data from. SELECT statements are also known as *queries*.

The following SELECT statement retrieves the customer_id, first_name, last_name, dob, and phone columns from the customers table:

```
SELECT customer_id, first_name, last_name, dob, phone
FROM customers;
```

Immediately after the SELECT keyword, you provide the column names. After the FROM keyword, you provide the table name. The SQL statement is ended using a semicolon (;).

You don't tell the Oracle database software exactly how to access the information you want. You just specify the data you want and let the software retrieve the data.

After you press ENTER at the end of the SQL statement in SQL*Plus, the statement is executed and the results are displayed. For example:

```
CUSTOMER_ID FIRST_NAME LAST_NAME  DOB       PHONE
----------- ---------- ---------- --------- ------------
          1 John       Brown      01-JAN-65 800-555-1211
          2 Cynthia    Green      05-FEB-68 800-555-1212
          3 Steve      White      16-MAR-71 800-555-1213
          4 Gail       Black                800-555-1214
          5 Doreen     Blue       20-MAY-70
```

The rows returned are called a *result set*. Notice the following from the example result set:

- Column names are converted into their uppercase equivalents.
- Character and date columns are left-justified.
- Number columns are right-justified.
- Dates are displayed in the default format DD-MON-YY, where DD is the day number, MON is the first three characters of the month (in uppercase), and YY is the last two digits of the year. The database stores all four digits for the year, but by default it displays only the last two digits.

Although you can specify column names and table names using either lowercase or uppercase text, it is better to stick with one style. The examples in this book use uppercase for reserved keywords, and lowercase for everything else.

Retrieving All Columns from a Table

To retrieve all columns in a table, you can use the asterisk character (*) instead of a list of columns. In the following query, the asterisk is used to retrieve all columns from the `customers` table:

```
SELECT *
FROM customers;
```

```
CUSTOMER_ID FIRST_NAME LAST_NAME  DOB       PHONE
----------- ---------- ---------- --------- ------------
          1 John       Brown      01-JAN-65 800-555-1211
          2 Cynthia    Green      05-FEB-68 800-555-1212
          3 Steve      White      16-MAR-71 800-555-1213
          4 Gail       Black                800-555-1214
          5 Doreen     Blue       20-MAY-70
```

All of the columns in the `customers` table are retrieved.

Limiting Rows to Retrieve Using the WHERE Clause

The WHERE clause limits the rows retrieved. An Oracle database can store vast numbers of rows, and you might be interested in only a small subset of those rows.
You place the WHERE clause after the FROM clause:

```
SELECT list of items
FROM list of tables
WHERE list of conditions;
```

In the following query, the WHERE clause is used to retrieve the row from the `customers` table where the `customer_id` column is equal to 2:

```
SELECT *
FROM customers
WHERE customer_id = 2;
```

```
CUSTOMER_ID FIRST_NAME LAST_NAME  DOB       PHONE
----------- ---------- ---------- --------- ------------
          2 Cynthia    Green      05-FEB-68 800-555-1212
```

Row Identifiers

Each row in an Oracle database has a unique row identifier, or *rowid*, which is used internally by the Oracle database to store the physical location of the row. A rowid is an 18-digit number that is represented as a base-64 number. You can view the rowid for rows in a table by retrieving the ROWID column in a query.

The following query retrieves the ROWID and customer_id columns from the customers table. Notice the base-64 number in the ROWID output.

```
SELECT ROWID, customer_id
FROM customers;
```

```
ROWID               CUSTOMER_ID
------------------  -----------
AAAF4yAABAAAHeKAAA            1
AAAF4yAABAAAHeKAAB            2
AAAF4yAABAAAHeKAAC            3
AAAF4yAABAAAHeKAAD            4
AAAF4yAABAAAHeKAAE            5
```

When you examine a table's definition using the SQL*Plus DESCRIBE command, ROWID doesn't appear in the output from the command because it is used internally by the database. ROWID is known as a *pseudo column*. The following example describes the customers table. Notice ROWID doesn't appear in the output.

```
DESCRIBE customers
 Name                                      Null?    Type
 ----------------------------------------- -------- ------------
 CUSTOMER_ID                               NOT NULL NUMBER(38)
 FIRST_NAME                                NOT NULL VARCHAR2(10)
 LAST_NAME                                 NOT NULL VARCHAR2(10)
 DOB                                                DATE
 PHONE                                              VARCHAR2(12)
```

Row Numbers

Another pseudo column is ROWNUM, which returns the row number in a result set. The first row returned by a query has a row number of 1, the second has a row number of 2, and so on.

The following query includes ROWNUM when retrieving the rows from the customers table:

```
SELECT ROWNUM, customer_id, first_name, last_name
FROM customers;
```

```
    ROWNUM CUSTOMER_ID FIRST_NAME LAST_NAME
---------- ----------- ---------- ----------
         1           1 John       Brown
         2           2 Cynthia    Green
         3           3 Steve      White
         4           4 Gail       Black
         5           5 Doreen     Blue
```

Another example:

```
SELECT ROWNUM, customer_id, first_name, last_name
FROM customers
WHERE customer_id = 3;
```

```
ROWNUM CUSTOMER_ID FIRST_NAME LAST_NAME
---------- ----------- ---------- ----------
         1           3 Steve      White
```

Performing Arithmetic

SQL statements can contain arithmetic expressions. Arithmetic consists of addition, subtraction, multiplication, and division operations. Arithmetic expressions contain two *operands*—numbers or dates—and an arithmetic *operator*. The four arithmetic operators are shown in the following table.

Operator	Description
+	Addition
-	Subtraction
*	Multiplication
/	Division

The following query uses the multiplication operator * to calculate 2 multiplied by 6 (the numbers 2 and 6 are the operands):

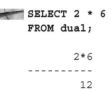
```
SELECT 2 * 6
FROM dual;

       2*6
----------
        12
```

The correct result of 12 is displayed. The use of 2*6 in the query is an example of an *expression*. An expression can contain a combination of columns, literal values, and operators.

Performing Date Arithmetic

Addition and subtraction operators also work with dates. You can add a number—representing a number of days—to a date. The following example adds two days to July 25, 2012, and displays the resulting date:

```
SELECT TO_DATE('25-JUL-2012') + 2
FROM dual;

TO_DATE('
---------
27-JUL-12
```

NOTE
TO_DATE() is a function that converts a string to a date. You'll learn more about dates in Chapter 5.

The dual Table

The `dual` table is often used in conjunction with functions and expressions that return values, without needing to reference a base table in the query. For example, the `dual` table can be used in a query that returns the result from an arithmetic expression, or a query that calls a function like `TO_DATE()`. Of course, if the expression or function call references a column in a base table, then you cannot use the `dual` table in the query.

The following output from the `DESCRIBE` command shows the structure of the `dual` table, which has one `VARCHAR2` column named `dummy`:

```
DESCRIBE dual
 Name                                       Null?    Type
 ------------------------------------------ -------- -----------
 DUMMY                                               VARCHAR2(1)
```

The following query retrieves the single row from the `dual` table, which contains the character `X` in the `dummy` column:

```
SELECT *
FROM dual;


D
-
X
```

The next example subtracts three days from August 2, 2012:

```
SELECT TO_DATE('02-AUG-2012') - 3
FROM dual;

TO_DATE('
---------
30-JUL-12
```

You can also subtract one date from another. The result is the number of days between the two dates. The following example subtracts July 25, 2012, from August 2, 2012:

```
SELECT TO_DATE('02-AUG-2012') - TO_DATE('25-JUL-2012')
FROM dual;

TO_DATE('02-AUG-2012')-TO_DATE('25-JUL-2012')
---------------------------------------------
```

Using Columns in Arithmetic

Operands do not have to be literal numbers or dates. Operands can also be columns from a table. In the following query, the `name` and `price` columns are retrieved from the `products` table. 2 is added to the value in the `price` column to form the expression `price + 2`.

```
SELECT name, price + 2
FROM products;
```

```
NAME                              PRICE+2
------------------------------    ----------
Modern Science                      21.95
Chemistry                              32
Supernova                           27.99
Tank War                            15.95
Z Files                             51.99
2412: The Return                    16.95
Space Force 9                       15.49
From Another Planet                 14.99
Classical Music                     12.99
Pop 3                               17.99
Creative Yell                       16.99
My Front Line                       15.49
```

You can combine more than one operator in an expression. In the following query, the `price` column is multiplied by 3, and then 1 is added to the resulting value:

```
SELECT name, price * 3 + 1
FROM products;
```

```
NAME                              PRICE*3+1
------------------------------    ----------
Modern Science                      60.85
Chemistry                              91
Supernova                           78.97
Tank War                            42.85
Z Files                            150.97
2412: The Return                    45.85
Space Force 9                       41.47
From Another Planet                 39.97
Classical Music                     33.97
Pop 3                               48.97
Creative Yell                       45.97
My Front Line                       41.47
```

Arithmetic Operator Precedence

The standard rules of arithmetic operator precedence apply in SQL. Multiplication and division are performed first, followed by addition and subtraction. If operators of the same precedence are used, they are performed from left to right.

For example, in the expression `10 * 12 / 3 - 1`, 10 is multiplied by 12, producing a result of 120. Then 120 is divided by 3, producing a result of 40. Finally, 1 is subtracted from 40, producing a result of 39. The following example shows the final result of 39:

```
SELECT 10 * 12 / 3 - 1
FROM dual;
```

```
10*12/3-1
----------
       39
```

You can use parentheses, (...), to specify the order of operator execution. For example:

```
SELECT 10 * (12 / 3 - 1)
FROM dual;
```

```
10*(12/3-1)
-----------
         30
```

In this example, the parentheses specify that `12 / 3 - 1` is calculated first. The result is then multiplied by 10, producing a final result of 30.

Using Column Aliases

When you select a column from a table, the uppercase version of the column name is displayed as the header for the column in the result set. For example, when you select the `price` column, the header in the resulting output is `PRICE`. For an expression, the spaces are removed from the expression and displayed as the header in the output.

You can provide your own header using an *alias*. In the following query, the expression `price * 2` is given the alias `DOUBLE_PRICE`:

```
SELECT price * 2 DOUBLE_PRICE
FROM products;
```

```
DOUBLE_PRICE
------------
        39.9
          60
       51.98
        27.9
       99.98
        29.9
       26.98
       25.98
       21.98
       31.98
       29.98
       26.98
```

To use spaces and preserve the case of alias text, you place the text within double quotation marks. For example:

```
SELECT price * 2 "Double Price"
FROM products;

Double Price
------------
        39.9
...
```

You can include the optional AS keyword before the alias, as shown in the following query:

```
SELECT 10 * (12 / 3 - 1) AS "Computation"
FROM dual;

Computation
-----------
         30
```

Combining Column Output Using Concatenation

You can combine the column values retrieved by a query using concatenation, which allows you to create more friendly and meaningful output. For example, in the customers table, the first_name and last_name columns contain the customer name. You can combine the two names using the concatenation operator | |, as shown in the following query. A single space character separates the first name and last name in the output.

```
SELECT first_name || ' ' || last_name AS "Customer Name"
FROM customers;

Customer Name
-------------------
John Brown
Cynthia Green
Steve White
Gail Black
Doreen Blue
```

In the result set, the first_name and last_name column values are combined together under the Customer Name alias.

Null Values

How does a database represent a value that is unknown? It uses a special value called a *null value*. A null value is not a blank string. A null value is a distinct value. A null value means the value for the column is unknown.

When you retrieve a column that contains a null value, you see nothing in the output for that column. For example:

```
SELECT *
FROM customers;

CUSTOMER_ID FIRST_NAME LAST_NAME  DOB       PHONE
----------- ---------- ---------- --------- ------------
          1 John       Brown      01-JAN-65 800-555-1211
          2 Cynthia    Green      05-FEB-68 800-555-1212
          3 Steve      White      16-MAR-71 800-555-1213
          4 Gail       Black                800-555-1214
          5 Doreen     Blue       20-MAY-70
```

Customer #4 has a null value in the dob column. Customer #5 has a null value in the phone column.

You can check for null values using IS NULL. In the following query, customer #4 is retrieved because the dob value is null:

```
SELECT customer_id, first_name, last_name, dob
FROM customers
WHERE dob IS NULL;

CUSTOMER_ID FIRST_NAME LAST_NAME  DOB
----------- ---------- ---------- ---------
          4 Gail       Black
```

In the next query, customer #5 is retrieved because the phone value is null:

```
SELECT customer_id, first_name, last_name, phone
FROM customers
WHERE phone IS NULL;

CUSTOMER_ID FIRST_NAME LAST_NAME  PHONE
----------- ---------- ---------- ------------
          5 Doreen     Blue
```

How do you tell the difference between a null value and a blank string? You use the NVL() function. NVL() returns another value in place of a null. NVL() accepts two parameters: a column (or, more generally, any expression that results in a value) and the value to be returned if the first parameter is null. In the following query, NVL() returns the string 'Unknown phone number' when the phone column contains a null value:

```
SELECT customer_id, first_name, last_name,
  NVL(phone, 'Unknown phone number') AS PHONE_NUMBER
FROM customers;

CUSTOMER_ID FIRST_NAME LAST_NAME  PHONE_NUMBER
----------- ---------- ---------- --------------------
          1 John       Brown      800-555-1211
          2 Cynthia    Green      800-555-1212
```

```
3 Steve      White      800-555-1213
4 Gail       Black      800-555-1214
5 Doreen     Blue       Unknown phone number
```

You can also use NVL() to convert null numbers and dates. In the following query, NVL() returns the date 01-JAN-2000 when the dob column contains a null value:

```
SELECT customer_id, first_name, last_name,
  NVL(dob, '01-JAN-2000') AS DOB
FROM customers;

CUSTOMER_ID FIRST_NAME LAST_NAME  DOB
----------- ---------- ---------- ---------
          1 John       Brown      01-JAN-65
          2 Cynthia    Green      05-FEB-68
          3 Steve      White      16-MAR-71
          4 Gail       Black      01-JAN-00
          5 Doreen     Blue       20-MAY-70
```

Customer #4's dob is displayed as 01-JAN-00. This customer has a null value in the dob column.

Displaying Distinct Rows

Suppose you wanted to retrieve the list of customers who have purchased products. The following query retrieves the customer_id column from the purchases table:

```
SELECT customer_id
FROM purchases;

CUSTOMER_ID
-----------
          1
          2
          3
          4
          1
          2
          3
          4
          3
```

The customer_id column contains the IDs of customers who have purchased a product. The result set shows that some customers have made more than one purchase and therefore appear twice.

You can suppress the duplicate rows that contain the same customer ID by using the DISTINCT keyword. In the following query, DISTINCT is used to suppress the duplicate rows:

```
SELECT DISTINCT customer_id
FROM purchases;
```

```
CUSTOMER_ID
-----------
          1
          2
          4
          3
```

From this list, it's easier to see that customers #1, #2, #3, and #4 have made purchases.

Comparing Values

The following table lists the operators that compare values.

Operator	Description
=	Equal
<> or !=	Not equal You should use <> because it is the American National Standards Institute (ANSI) standard.
<	Less than
>	Greater than
<=	Less than or equal to
>=	Greater than or equal to
ANY	Compares one value with any value in a list
SOME	Identical to the ANY operator You should use ANY rather than SOME because ANY is more widely used and, in my opinion, more readable.
ALL	Compares one value with all values in a list

Using the Not Equal Operator

The following query uses the not equal operator <> in the WHERE clause to retrieve the rows from the customers table whose customer_id is not equal to 2:

```
SELECT *
FROM customers
WHERE customer_id <> 2;

CUSTOMER_ID FIRST_NAME LAST_NAME  DOB       PHONE
----------- ---------- ---------- --------- ------------
          1 John       Brown      01-JAN-65 800-555-1211
          3 Steve      White      16-MAR-71 800-555-1213
          4 Gail       Black                800-555-1214
          5 Doreen     Blue       20-MAY-70
```

Using the Greater Than Operator

The following query uses the greater than operator > to retrieve the `product_id` and `name` columns from the `products` table where the `product_id` column is greater than 8:

```
SELECT product_id, name
FROM products
WHERE product_id > 8;


PRODUCT_ID  NAME
----------- ----------------
          9 Classical Music
         10 Pop 3
         11 Creative Yell
         12 My Front Line
```

Using the Less Than Or Equal To Operator

The following query uses the ROWNUM pseudo column and the less than or equal to operator <= to retrieve the first three rows from the `products` table:

```
SELECT ROWNUM, product_id, name
FROM products
WHERE ROWNUM <= 3;


    ROWNUM PRODUCT_ID NAME
---------- ---------- --------------
         1          1 Modern Science
         2          2 Chemistry
         3          3 Supernova
```

Using the ANY Operator

The ANY operator compares a value with *any* of the values in a list. You must place an =, <>, <, >, <=, or >= operator before ANY. The following query uses ANY to retrieve rows from the `customers` table where the value in the `customer_id` column is greater than any of the values 2, 3, or 4:

```
SELECT *
FROM customers
WHERE customer_id > ANY (2, 3, 4);


CUSTOMER_ID FIRST_NAME LAST_NAME  DOB       PHONE
----------- ---------- ---------- --------- ------------
          3 Steve      White      16-MAR-71 800-555-1213
          4 Gail       Black                800-555-1214
          5 Doreen     Blue       20-MAY-70
```

Using the ALL Operator

The `ALL` operator compares a value with *all* of the values in a list. You must place an =, <>, <, >, <=, or >= operator before `ALL`. The following query uses `ALL` to retrieve rows from the `customers` table where the value in the `customer_id` column is greater than all of the values 2, 3, and 4:

```
SELECT *
FROM customers
WHERE customer_id > ALL (2, 3, 4);

CUSTOMER_ID FIRST_NAME LAST_NAME  DOB       PHONE
----------- ---------- ---------- --------- ------------
          5 Doreen     Blue       20-MAY-70
```

Only customer #5 is returned because 5 is greater than 2, 3, and 4.

Using the SQL Operators

The SQL operators allow you to limit rows based on pattern matching of strings, lists of values, ranges of values, and null values. The SQL operators are listed in the following table.

Operator	Description
LIKE	Matches patterns in strings
IN	Matches lists of values
BETWEEN	Matches a range of values
IS NULL	Matches null values
IS NAN	Matches the `NAN` special value, which means "not a number"
IS INFINITE	Matches infinite `BINARY_FLOAT` and `BINARY_DOUBLE` values

`NOT` reverses the meaning of an operator:

- NOT LIKE
- NOT IN
- NOT BETWEEN
- IS NOT NULL
- IS NOT NAN
- IS NOT INFINITE

You'll learn about the `LIKE`, `IN`, and `BETWEEN` operators in the following sections.

Using the LIKE Operator

The `LIKE` operator searches a string for a pattern. Patterns are specified using a combination of normal characters and the following two wildcard characters:

- **Underscore (_)** matches one character in a specified position.
- **Percent (%)** matches any number of characters beginning at the specified position.

For example, consider the following pattern:

```
'_o%'
```

The underscore _ matches any one character in the first position. The o matches an o character in the second position. The percent % matches any characters following the o character.

The following query uses the LIKE operator to search the first_name column of the customers table for the pattern '_o%':

```
SELECT *
FROM customers
WHERE first_name LIKE '_o%';

CUSTOMER_ID FIRST_NAME LAST_NAME  DOB       PHONE
----------- ---------- ---------- --------- ------------
          1 John       Brown      01-JAN-65 800-555-1211
          5 Doreen     Blue       20-MAY-70
```

Two rows are returned because the strings John and Doreen both have o as the second character.

The next query uses NOT LIKE to retrieve the rows not retrieved by the previous query:

```
SELECT *
FROM customers
WHERE first_name NOT LIKE '_o%';

CUSTOMER_ID FIRST_NAME LAST_NAME  DOB       PHONE
----------- ---------- ---------- --------- ------------
          2 Cynthia    Green      05-FEB-68 800-555-1212
          3 Steve      White      16-MAR-71 800-555-1213
          4 Gail       Black                800-555-1214
```

To search for actual underscore or percent characters in a string, you use the ESCAPE option to identify those characters. For example, consider the following pattern:

```
'%\%%' ESCAPE '\'
```

The characters after ESCAPE indicate how to differentiate between the characters to search for and the wildcards. In the example, the backslash character \ is used. The first percent character % is treated as a wildcard and matches any number of characters. The second % is treated as an actual character to search for. The third % is treated as a wildcard and matches any number of characters.

The following query uses the promotions table, which contains the details for products being discounted by the store. The query uses the LIKE operator to search the name column of the promotions table for the pattern '%\%%' ESCAPE '\'.

```
SELECT name
FROM promotions
WHERE name LIKE '%\%%' ESCAPE '\';
```

```
NAME
------------------------------
10% off Z Files
20% off Pop 3
30% off Modern Science
20% off Tank War
10% off Chemistry
20% off Creative Yell
15% off My Front Line
```

The query returns the rows whose names contain a percent character.

Using the IN Operator

The IN operator checks if a value is in a list of values. The following query uses IN to retrieve rows from the customers table where the customer_id is 2, 3, or 5:

```
SELECT *
FROM customers
WHERE customer_id IN (2, 3, 5);
```

```
CUSTOMER_ID FIRST_NAME LAST_NAME  DOB       PHONE
----------- ---------- ---------- --------- ------------
          2 Cynthia    Green      05-FEB-68 800-555-1212
          3 Steve      White      16-MAR-71 800-555-1213
          5 Doreen     Blue       20-MAY-70
```

The following query uses NOT IN to retrieve the rows not retrieved by IN:

```
SELECT *
FROM customers
WHERE customer_id NOT IN (2, 3, 5);
```

```
CUSTOMER_ID FIRST_NAME LAST_NAME  DOB       PHONE
----------- ---------- ---------- --------- ------------
          1 John       Brown      01-JAN-65 800-555-1211
          4 Gail       Black                800-555-1214
```

An important point to remember is that NOT IN returns false if a value in the list is null. For example, the following query doesn't return any rows because null is included in the list:

```
SELECT *
FROM customers
WHERE customer_id NOT IN (2, 3, 5, NULL);
```

```
no rows selected
```

CAUTION
NOT IN returns false if a value in the list is null. This is important because you can use any expression in the list and not just literal values, and it can be difficult to spot when a null value occurs. You should consider using NVL ( ) with expressions that might return a null value.

Using the BETWEEN Operator

The BETWEEN operator checks if a value is in a range of values. The range is *inclusive*, which means the values at both ends of the range are included. The following query uses BETWEEN to retrieve the rows from the customers table where the customer_id is between 1 and 3:

```
SELECT *
FROM customers
WHERE customer_id BETWEEN 1 AND 3;
```

```
CUSTOMER_ID FIRST_NAME LAST_NAME  DOB       PHONE
----------- ---------- ---------- --------- ------------
          1 John       Brown      01-JAN-65 800-555-1211
          2 Cynthia    Green      05-FEB-68 800-555-1212
          3 Steve      White      16-MAR-71 800-555-1213
```

NOT BETWEEN retrieves the rows not retrieved by BETWEEN:

```
SELECT *
FROM customers
WHERE customer_id NOT BETWEEN 1 AND 3;
```

```
CUSTOMER_ID FIRST_NAME LAST_NAME  DOB       PHONE
----------- ---------- ---------- --------- ------------
          4 Gail       Black                800-555-1214
          5 Doreen     Blue       20-MAY-70
```

Using the Logical Operators

The logical operators limit rows based on logical conditions. The logical operators are listed in the following table.

Operator	Description
x AND y	Returns true when both x and y are true
x OR y	Returns true when either x or y is true
NOT x	Returns true if x is false, and returns false if x is true

Using the AND Operator

The following query uses the AND operator to retrieve the rows from the customers table where *both* of the following conditions are true:

- The dob column is greater than January 1, 1970
- The customer_id column is greater than 3

```
SELECT *
FROM customers
WHERE dob > '01-JAN-1970'
AND customer_id > 3;
```

```
CUSTOMER_ID FIRST_NAME LAST_NAME  DOB       PHONE
----------- ---------- ---------- --------- ------------
          5 Doreen     Blue       20-MAY-70
```

Using the OR Operator

The following query uses the OR operator to retrieve rows from the customers table where *either* of the following conditions is true:

- The dob column is greater than January 1, 1970
- The customer_id column is greater than 3

```
SELECT *
FROM customers
WHERE dob > '01-JAN-1970'
OR customer_id > 3;
```

```
CUSTOMER_ID FIRST_NAME LAST_NAME  DOB       PHONE
----------- ---------- ---------- --------- ------------
          3 Steve      White      16-MAR-71 800-555-1213
          4 Gail       Black                800-555-1214
          5 Doreen     Blue       20-MAY-70
```

You can also use AND and OR to combine expressions in a WHERE clause, as you'll see in the following section.

Logical Operator Precedence

If AND and OR are used in the same expression, AND takes precedence over OR. The comparison operators take precedence over AND. You can override the default precedence using parentheses (...) to indicate the order to execute the expressions.

The following query retrieves the rows from the customers table where *either* of the following two conditions is true:

- The dob column is greater than January 1, 1970
- The customer_id column is less than 2 *and* the phone column has 1211 at the end

```
SELECT *
FROM customers
WHERE dob > '01-JAN-1970'
OR customer_id < 2
AND phone LIKE '%1211';
```

```
CUSTOMER_ID FIRST_NAME LAST_NAME DOB       PHONE
----------- ---------- ---------- --------- ------------
          1 John       Brown      01-JAN-65 800-555-1211
          3 Steve      White      16-MAR-71 800-555-1213
          5 Doreen     Blue       20-MAY-70
```

AND takes precedence over OR, so you can think of the WHERE clause in the previous query as follows:

```
dob > '01-JAN-1970' OR (customer_id < 2 AND phone LIKE '%1211')
```

Customers #1, #3, and #5 are returned by the query.

Sorting Rows Using the ORDER BY Clause

The ORDER BY clause sorts the rows retrieved by a query. The ORDER BY clause can specify one or more columns on which to sort the data. The ORDER BY clause must follow the FROM clause or the WHERE clause.

The following query uses ORDER BY to sort the rows retrieved from the customers table by the last_name:

```
SELECT *
FROM customers
ORDER BY last_name;
```

```
CUSTOMER_ID FIRST_NAME LAST_NAME DOB       PHONE
----------- ---------- ---------- --------- ------------
          4 Gail       Black                800-555-1214
          5 Doreen     Blue       20-MAY-70
          1 John       Brown      01-JAN-65 800-555-1211
          2 Cynthia    Green      05-FEB-68 800-555-1212
          3 Steve      White      16-MAR-71 800-555-1213
```

By default, ORDER BY sorts the columns in ascending order (lower values appear first). You can use the DESC keyword to sort the columns in descending order (higher values appear first). You can use the ASC keyword to explicitly specify an ascending sort. Ascending order is the default, but you can still specify it if you want to make it clear what the order is for the sort.

The next query uses ORDER BY to sort the rows retrieved from the customers table by ascending first_name and descending last_name:

```
SELECT *
FROM customers
ORDER BY first_name ASC, last_name DESC;
```

```
CUSTOMER_ID FIRST_NAME LAST_NAME DOB       PHONE
----------- ---------- ---------- --------- ------------
          2 Cynthia    Green      05-FEB-68 800-555-1212
          5 Doreen     Blue       20-MAY-70
          4 Gail       Black                800-555-1214
          1 John       Brown      01-JAN-65 800-555-1211
          3 Steve      White      16-MAR-71 800-555-1213
```

You can use a column position number in the ORDER BY clause to indicate which column to sort. You use 1 to sort by the first column selected, 2 to sort by the second column selected, and so on. In the following query, column 1 (the customer_id column) is used to sort the rows:

```
SELECT customer_id, first_name, last_name
FROM customers
ORDER BY 1;

CUSTOMER_ID FIRST_NAME LAST_NAME
----------- ---------- ----------
          1 John       Brown
          2 Cynthia    Green
          3 Steve      White
          4 Gail       Black
          5 Doreen     Blue
```

Because the customer_id column is in position 1 after the SELECT keyword, customer_id is the column used in the sort. The result set shows the rows are sorted by customer_id.

Performing SELECT Statements That Use Two Tables

Database schemas typically contain more than one table. For example, the store schema has tables that store information on customers, products, employees, and so on. Up to now, the queries retrieve rows from only one table. You'll often need to retrieve information from multiple tables. For example, you may need to retrieve the name of a product and the name of its product type. In this section, you'll learn how to perform queries that use two tables. Later, you'll see queries that use more than two tables.

You might want to retrieve the name of product #3 and its product type. The name of the product is stored in the name column of the products table. The name of the product type is stored in the name column of the product_types table. The products and product_types tables are related to each other via the foreign key column product_type_id. The product_type_id column (the foreign key) of the products table points to the product_type_id column (the primary key) of the product_types table.

The following query retrieves the name and product_type_id columns from the products table for product #3:

```
SELECT name, product_type_id
FROM products
WHERE product_id = 3;

NAME                            PRODUCT_TYPE_ID
------------------------------- ---------------
Supernova                                     2
```

The next query retrieves the name column from the product_types table for the product_type_id of 2:

```
SELECT name
FROM product_types
WHERE product_type_id = 2;
```

```
NAME
----------
Video
```

Based on the previous results, you can see that product #3 is a video. But, two queries were used.

You can retrieve the product name and its product type name in one query by using a *table join*. To join two tables in a query, you include both tables in the query's FROM clause and include the related columns from each table in the WHERE clause.

The FROM clause is

```
FROM products, product_types
```

The WHERE clause is

```
WHERE products.product_type_id = product_types.product_type_id
AND products.product_id = 3;
```

The first condition in the WHERE clause is the join (products.product_type_id = product_types.product_type_id). Typically, the columns used in the join are a primary key from one table and a foreign key from the other table. The second condition in the WHERE clause (products.product_id = 3) retrieves product #3.

The table names and their column names are included in the WHERE clause. This is because there is a product_type_id column in both the products and product_types tables, and you need to tell the database the table that the column you want to use is in. (If the columns had different names, you could omit the table names, but you should always include them to make it clear where the columns come from.)

The SELECT clause for the query is

```
SELECT products.name, product_types.name
```

Putting everything together, the completed query is

```
SELECT products.name, product_types.name
FROM products, product_types
WHERE products.product_type_id = product_types.product_type_id
AND products.product_id = 3;
```

```
NAME                              NAME
-------------------------------   ----------
Supernova                         Video
```

Perfect! This single query returns the name of the product and the name of the product type.

The next query gets all the products and orders them by the products.name column:

```
SELECT products.name, product_types.name
FROM products, product_types
WHERE products.product_type_id = product_types.product_type_id
ORDER BY products.name;
```

```
NAME                             NAME
------------------------------   ----------
2412: The Return                 Video
Chemistry                        Book
Classical Music                  CD
Creative Yell                    CD
From Another Planet              DVD
Modern Science                   Book
Pop 3                            CD
Space Force 9                    DVD
Supernova                        Video
Tank War                         Video
Z Files                          Video
```

The product with the name "My Front Line" is missing from the result set. The product_type_ id for this product row is null, and the join condition does not return the row. You'll see how to obtain this row later in the "Outer Joins" section.

The join syntax in this section uses Oracle's syntax for joins. This syntax is based on the ANSI SQL/86 standard. In Oracle Database 9*i* and above, the database also implements the ANSI SQL/92 standard syntax for joins. You'll see this new syntax later in the "Performing Joins Using the SQL/92 Syntax" section. You should use the SQL/92 standard in your queries when working with Oracle Database 9*i* and above, and only use SQL/86 queries with Oracle Database 8*i* and below.

Using Table Aliases

In the previous section, you saw the following query:

```
SELECT products.name, product_types.name
FROM products, product_types
WHERE products.product_type_id = product_types.product_type_id
ORDER BY products.name;
```

The products and product_types table names are included in the SELECT and WHERE clauses. You can define table aliases in the FROM clause and then use the aliases when referencing the tables elsewhere in the query.

For example, the following query uses the alias p for the products table and pt for the product_types table. The table aliases are specified in the FROM clause, and the aliases are placed before the columns in the rest of the query.

```
SELECT p.name, pt.name
FROM products p, product_types pt
WHERE p.product_type_id = pt.product_type_id
ORDER BY p.name;
```

Using table aliases reduces the amount of text needed to enter a query, and potentially reduces errors during entry of queries.

Cartesian Products

If a join condition is missing from a query, the Oracle database software will join all rows from one table with all the rows from the other table. The result set is known as a *Cartesian product*.

For example, consider one table containing 50 rows and a second table containing 100 rows. If you select columns from the tables without a join, you would get 5,000 rows. This result happens because each row from table 1 is joined to each row in table 2, which returns 50 rows multiplied by 100 rows, or 5,000 rows.

The following example shows a subset of the rows for a Cartesian product between the product_types and products tables:

```
SELECT pt.product_type_id, p.product_id
FROM product_types pt, products p;

PRODUCT_TYPE_ID PRODUCT_ID
--------------- ----------
              1          1
              1          2
              1          3
              1          4
              1          5
...
              5          8
              5          9
              5         10
              5         11
              5         12

60 rows selected.
```

A total of 60 rows are returned because the product_types and products tables contain 5 and 12 rows, and 5 multiplied by 12 is 60.

In some cases, you might need a Cartesian product for your work. Most often you don't, so include join conditions as needed.

Performing SELECT Statements That Use More than Two Tables

Joins are used in queries to connect tables. The following formula shows the number of joins required in a query's WHERE clause:

Number of joins = number of tables in the query − 1

For example, the following query uses two tables—and therefore one join is used:

```
SELECT p.name, pt.name
FROM products p, product_types pt
WHERE p.product_type_id = pt.product_type_id
ORDER BY p.name;
```

Consider an example that retrieves customer purchase information from four tables:

■ Customer purchases from the purchases table
■ Customer first and last names from the customers table
■ Product name from the products table
■ Product type name from the product_types table

Four tables are used—and therefore three joins are required. The following list shows the required joins:

■ To obtain the customer who made the purchase, join the customers and purchases tables using the customer_id columns.
The join is customers.customer_id = purchases.customer_id.

■ To obtain the product purchased, join the products and purchases tables using the product_id columns.
The join is products.product_id = purchases.product_id.

■ To obtain the product type name for the product, join the products and product_types tables using the product_type_id columns.
The join is products.product_type_id = product_types.product_type_id.

The following query contains the required joins:

```
SELECT c.first_name, c.last_name, p.name AS PRODUCT, pt.name AS TYPE
FROM customers c, purchases pr, products p, product_types pt
WHERE c.customer_id = pr.customer_id
AND p.product_id = pr.product_id
AND p.product_type_id = pt.product_type_id
ORDER BY p.name;
```

FIRST_NAME	LAST_NAME	PRODUCT	TYPE
John	Brown	Chemistry	Book
Cynthia	Green	Chemistry	Book
Steve	White	Chemistry	Book
Gail	Black	Chemistry	Book
John	Brown	Modern Science	Book
Cynthia	Green	Modern Science	Book
Steve	White	Modern Science	Book
Gail	Black	Modern Science	Book
Steve	White	Supernova	Video

The multi-table queries you've seen so far use the equality operator = in the join conditions. These joins are known as *equijoins*. As you'll see in the next section, there are other types of joins.

Join Conditions and Join Types

In this section, you'll examine join conditions and join types that allow you to create more advanced queries.

There are two types of join conditions, which are based on the operator used in the join:

■ **Equijoins** use the equality operator =.
■ **Non-equijoins** use an operator other than the equality operator. For example: <, >, BETWEEN, and so on.

There are three different types of joins:

■ **Inner joins** return a row *only* when the columns in the join contain values that satisfy the join condition. This means that if a row has a null value in one of the columns in the join condition, then that row isn't returned. The examples you've seen so far have been inner joins.
■ **Outer joins** return a row *even when* one of the columns in the join condition contains a null value.
■ **Self joins** return rows joined on the same table.

You'll learn about non-equijoins, outer joins, and self joins next.

Non-equijoins

A non-equijoin uses an operator other than the equality operator = in the join. These operators are not equal <>, less than <, greater than >, less than or equal to <=, greater than or equal to >=, LIKE, IN, and BETWEEN.

For example, you want to get the salary grades for the employees. The following query retrieves the rows from the salary_grades table:

```
SELECT *
FROM salary_grades;

SALARY_GRADE_ID LOW_SALARY HIGH_SALARY
--------------- ---------- -----------
              1          1      250000
              2     250001      500000
              3     500001      750000
              4     750001      999999
```

The next query uses a non-equijoin to retrieve the salary and salary grades for the employees. The salary grade is determined using the BETWEEN operator.

```
SELECT e.first_name, e.last_name, e.title, e.salary, sg.salary_grade_id
FROM employees e, salary_grades sg
WHERE e.salary BETWEEN sg.low_salary AND sg.high_salary
ORDER BY salary_grade_id;

FIRST_NAME LAST_NAME  TITLE              SALARY SALARY_GRADE_ID
---------- ---------- ------------------ ---------- ---------------
Fred       Hobbs      Salesperson        150000               1
Susan      Jones      Salesperson        500000               2
Ron        Johnson    Sales Manager      600000               3
James      Smith      CEO                800000               4
```

The BETWEEN operator returns true if the employee's salary is between the low salary and the high salary for the salary grade. If true is returned for the salary range for that employee, then the salary grade ID for that employee can be located from the salary_grades table.

For example, Fred Hobbs' salary is $150,000. His salary is between the low salary of $1 and the high salary of $250,000 in the salary_grades table, and the salary_grade_id for that salary range is 1. Therefore, Fred Hobbs' salary grade is 1.

Similarly, Susan Jones' salary is $500,000. Her salary is between the low salary of $250,001 and the high salary of $500,000, and the salary_grade_id for that salary range is 2. Therefore, Susan Jones' salary grade is 2.

Finally, Ron Johnson and James Smith have salary grades of 3 and 4, respectively.

Outer Joins

An outer join retrieves a row even when one of the columns in the join contains a null value. You perform an outer join by supplying the outer join operator in the join condition. The Oracle proprietary outer join operator is a plus character in parentheses, (+).

Remember the query earlier that didn't show the "My Front Line" product because its product_type_id is null? You can use an outer join in a query to get that product:

```
SELECT p.name, pt.name
FROM products p, product_types pt
WHERE p.product_type_id = pt.product_type_id (+)
ORDER BY p.name;
```

```
NAME                              NAME
-------------------------------   ----------
2412: The Return                  Video
Chemistry                         Book
Classical Music                   CD
Creative Yell                     CD
From Another Planet               DVD
Modern Science                    Book
My Front Line
Pop 3                             CD
Space Force 9                     DVD
Supernova                         Video
Tank War                          Video
Z Files                           Video
```

Notice that "My Front Line"—the product with the null product_type_id—is now retrieved.

The WHERE clause for the previous query was

```
WHERE p.product_type_id = pt.product_type_id (+);
```

The outer join operator (+) is on the right of the equality operator, and the p.product_type_id column in the product table is on the left of the equality operator. The p.product_type_id column contains the null value.

NOTE
You place the outer join operator (+) on the opposite side of the
equality operator = from the column that contains the null value.

The following query returns the same rows as the previous one, but the outer join operator is on the left of the equality operator and the column with the null is on the right:

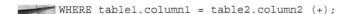

```
SELECT p.name, pt.name
FROM products p, product_types pt
WHERE pt.product_type_id (+) = p.product_type_id
ORDER BY p.name;
```

I've included this example to reinforce the idea that you place the outer join operator on the opposite side of the equality operator from the column that contains the null value.

Left and Right Outer Joins

Outer joins can be split into two types:

- Left outer joins
- Right outer joins

To understand the difference between left and right outer joins, consider the following syntax:

```
SELECT ...
FROM table1, table2
...
```

Assume the tables are to be joined on `table1.column1` and `table2.column2`. Also, assume `table1` contains a row with a null value in `column1`. To perform a left outer join, the WHERE clause is

```
WHERE table1.column1 = table2.column2 (+);
```

NOTE
In a left outer join, the outer join operator (+) is actually on the right
of the equality operator =.

Next, assume `table2` contains a row with a null value in `column2`. To perform a right outer join, you switch the position of the outer join operator to the *left* of the equality operator, and the WHERE clause becomes:

```
WHERE table1.column1 (+) = table2.column2;
```

NOTE
As you'll see, if `table1` and `table2` both contain rows with null
values, you get different results depending on whether you use a left
or right outer join.

Let's take a look at some examples to make left and right outer joins clearer.

An Example of a Left Outer Join   The following query uses a left outer join. The outer join operator appears on the *right* of the equality operator.

```
SELECT p.name, pt.name
FROM products p, product_types pt
WHERE p.product_type_id = pt.product_type_id (+)
ORDER BY p.name;
```

```
NAME                             NAME
-----------------------------    ----------
2412: The Return                 Video
Chemistry                        Book
Classical Music                  CD
Creative Yell                    CD
From Another Planet              DVD
Modern Science                   Book
My Front Line
Pop 3                            CD
Space Force 9                    DVD
Supernova                        Video
Tank War                         Video
Z Files                          Video
```

All the rows from the `products` table are retrieved, including the "My Front Line" row, which has a null value in the `p.product_type_id` column.

An Example of a Right Outer Join   The `product_types` table contains a type of product not referenced in the `products` table (there are no magazines in the `products` table). The magazine product type appears at the end of the following example:

```
SELECT *
FROM product_types;
```

```
PRODUCT_TYPE_ID NAME
--------------- ----------
              1 Book
              2 Video
              3 DVD
              4 CD
              5 Magazine
```

You can retrieve the magazine in a join on the `products` and `product_types` tables by using a right outer join, as shown in the following query. The outer join operator appears on the *left* of the equality operator.

```
SELECT p.name, pt.name
FROM products p, product_types pt
WHERE p.product_type_id (+) = pt.product_type_id
ORDER BY p.name;
```

```
NAME                              NAME
----------------------------      ----------
2412: The Return                  Video
Chemistry                         Book
Classical Music                   CD
Creative Yell                     CD
From Another Planet               DVD
Modern Science                    Book
Pop 3                             CD
Space Force 9                     DVD
Supernova                         Video
Tank War                          Video
Z Files                           Video
                                  Magazine
```

Limitations on Outer Joins

There are limitations when using outer joins. You can only place the Oracle-proprietary outer join operator on one side of the join (not both). If you try to place the outer join operator on both sides, then you get an error. For example:

```
SQL> SELECT p.name, pt.name
  2  FROM products p, product_types pt
  3  WHERE p.product_type_id (+) = pt.product_type_id (+);
WHERE p.product_type_id (+) = pt.product_type_id (+)
                                        *
ERROR at line 3:
ORA-01468: a predicate may reference only one outer-joined table
```

You cannot use an outer join condition with another join using the OR operator:

```
SQL> SELECT p.name, pt.name
  2  FROM products p, product_types pt
  3  WHERE p.product_type_id (+) = pt.product_type_id
  4  OR p.product_type_id = 1;
WHERE p.product_type_id (+) = pt.product_type_id
                                       *
ERROR at line 3:
ORA-01719: outer join operator (+) not allowed in operand of OR or IN
```

NOTE
These are the commonly encountered limitations when using the outer join operator. For all the limitations, read the Oracle Database SQL Reference *manual from Oracle Corporation.*

Self Joins

A self join is a join made on the same table. To perform a self join, you must use a different table alias to identify each reference to the table in the query. Consider an example. The employees table has a manager_id column that contains the employee_id of the manager for each employee. If the employee has no manager, then the manager_id is null.

The `employees` table contains the following rows:

```
EMPLOYEE_ID MANAGER_ID FIRST_NAME LAST_NAME  TITLE           SALARY
----------- ---------- ---------- ---------- ----------- --------
          1            James      Smith      CEO             800000
          2          1 Ron        Johnson    Sales Manager   600000
          3          2 Fred       Hobbs      Salesperson     150000
          4          2 Susan      Jones      Salesperson     500000
```

James Smith—the CEO—has a null value for the `manager_id`, meaning that he doesn't have a manager. Susan Jones and Fred Hobbs are managed by Ron Johnson, and Ron Johnson is managed by James Smith.

You can use a self join to display the names of each employee and their manager. In the following query, the `employees` table is referenced twice, using two aliases w and m. The w alias is used to get the worker name, and the m alias is used to get the manager name. The self join is made between w.`manager_id` and m.`employee_id`:

```
SELECT w.first_name || ' ' || w.last_name || ' works for '||
  m.first_name || ' ' || m.last_name
FROM employees w, employees m
WHERE w.manager_id = m.employee_id
ORDER BY w.first_name;

W.FIRST_NAME||''||W.LAST_NAME||'WORKSFOR'||M.FIRST_NA
----------------------------------------------------
Fred Hobbs works for Ron Johnson
Ron Johnson works for James Smith
Susan Jones works for Ron Johnson
```

Because James Smith's `manager_id` is null, the query does not return that row.

You can perform outer joins in combination with self joins. In the following query, an outer join is used with the self join shown in the previous example to retrieve the row for James Smith. The `NVL()` function in the query provides a string indicating that James Smith works for the shareholders (he's the CEO, so he reports to the store's shareholders).

```
SELECT w.last_name || ' works for ' ||
  NVL(m.last_name, 'the shareholders')
FROM employees w, employees m
WHERE w.manager_id = m.employee_id (+)
ORDER BY w.last_name;

W.LAST_NAME||'WORKSFOR'||NVL(M.LAST_N
-------------------------------------
Hobbs works for Johnson
Johnson works for Smith
Jones works for Johnson
Smith works for the shareholders
```

Performing Joins Using the SQL/92 Syntax

The joins you've seen so far use Oracle's syntax for joins, which is based on the ANSI SQL/86 standard. In Oracle Database 9i and above, the database implements the ANSI SQL/92 standard syntax for joins. You should use SQL/92 joins in your queries. You'll see how to use SQL/92 in this section, including its use in avoiding unwanted Cartesian products.

Performing Inner Joins on Two Tables Using SQL/92

Earlier, you saw the following query that used the SQL/86 standard for performing an inner join:

```
SELECT p.name, pt.name
FROM products p, product_types pt
WHERE p.product_type_id = pt.product_type_id
ORDER BY p.name;
```

SQL/92 introduced the INNER JOIN and ON clauses for performing an inner join. The previous query rewritten to use the INNER JOIN and ON clauses is

```
SELECT p.name, pt.name
FROM products p INNER JOIN product_types pt
ON p.product_type_id = pt.product_type_id
ORDER BY p.name;
```

You can also use non-equijoin operators with the ON clause. Earlier, you saw the following query that used the SQL/86 standard for performing a non-equijoin:

```
SELECT e.first_name, e.last_name, e.title, e.salary, sg.salary_grade_id
FROM employees e, salary_grades sg
WHERE e.salary BETWEEN sg.low_salary AND sg.high_salary
ORDER BY salary_grade_id;
```

The previous query rewritten to use the SQL/92 standard is

```
SELECT e.first_name, e.last_name, e.title, e.salary, sg.salary_grade_id
FROM employees e INNER JOIN salary_grades sg
ON e.salary BETWEEN sg.low_salary AND sg.high_salary
ORDER BY salary_grade_id;
```

Simplifying Joins with the USING Keyword

SQL/92 allows you to further simplify the join condition with the USING clause, but with the following requirements:

- The query must use an equijoin.
- The columns in the equijoin must have the same name.

Equijoins are the most used, and if you always use the same name as the primary key for your foreign keys, then you'll satisfy the requirements.

The following query uses the USING clause instead of ON:

```
SELECT p.name, pt.name
FROM products p INNER JOIN product_types pt
USING (product_type_id);
```

To retrieve the product_type_id, you must provide only this column name on its own without a table name or alias in the SELECT clause. For example:

```
SELECT p.name, pt.name, product_type_id
FROM products p INNER JOIN product_types pt
USING (product_type_id);
```

If you try to provide a table alias with the column, such as p.product_type_id for example, then you'll get an error:

```
SQL> SELECT p.name, pt.name, p.product_type_id
  2  FROM products p INNER JOIN product_types pt
  3  USING (product_type_id);
SELECT p.name, pt.name, p.product_type_id
                        *
ERROR at line 1:
ORA-25154: column part of USING clause cannot have qualifier
```

Only use the column name on its own within the USING clause. For example, if you specify USING (p.product_type_id) in the previous query instead of USING (product_type_id), then you'll get an error:

```
SQL> SELECT p.name, pt.name, p.product_type_id
  2  FROM products p INNER JOIN product_types pt
  3  USING (p.product_type_id);
USING (p.product_type_id)
       *
ERROR at line 3:
ORA-01748: only simple column names allowed here
```

CAUTION
Don't use a table name or alias when referencing columns used in a USING clause. You'll get an error if you do.

Performing Inner Joins on More than Two Tables Using SQL/92

Earlier, you saw the following SQL/86 query that retrieved rows from the customers, purchases, products, and product_types tables:

```
SELECT c.first_name, c.last_name, p.name AS PRODUCT, pt.name AS TYPE
FROM customers c, purchases pr, products p, product_types pt
WHERE c.customer_id = pr.customer_id
AND p.product_id = pr.product_id
AND p.product_type_id = pt.product_type_id
ORDER BY p.name;
```

The following query uses SQL/92. The foreign key relationships are navigated using multiple INNER JOIN and USING clauses.

```
SELECT c.first_name, c.last_name, p.name AS PRODUCT, pt.name AS TYPE
FROM customers c INNER JOIN purchases pr
USING (customer_id)
INNER JOIN products p
USING (product_id)
INNER JOIN product_types pt
USING (product_type_id)
ORDER BY p.name;
```

Performing Inner Joins on Multiple Columns Using SQL/92

If a join uses more than one column from the two tables, then you provide those columns in the ON clause and you use the AND operator. For example, consider two tables named table1 and table2. You want to join these tables using columns named column1 and column2 in both tables. Your query would use the following structure:

```
SELECT ...
FROM table1 INNER JOIN table2
ON table1.column1 = table2.column1
AND table1.column2 = table2.column2;
```

You can simplify the query with the USING clause, but only if you're performing an equijoin and the column names are identical. For example, the following query features the USING clause to simplify the previous query:

```
SELECT ...
FROM table1 INNER JOIN table2
USING (column1, column2);
```

Performing Outer Joins Using SQL/92

Earlier, you saw how to perform outer joins using the outer join operator (+), which is Oracle-proprietary syntax. SQL/92 uses a different syntax for performing outer joins. Instead of using (+), you specify the type of join in the FROM clause using the following syntax:

```
FROM table1 { LEFT | RIGHT | FULL } OUTER JOIN table2
```

where

- *table1* and *table2* are the tables to join.
- LEFT specifies a left outer join.
- RIGHT specifies a right outer join.
- FULL specifies a full outer join. A full outer join uses all rows in *table1* and *table2*, including those that have null values in the columns used in the join. You cannot perform a full outer join using the Oracle join operator (+).

You'll see how to perform left, right, and full outer joins using the SQL/92 syntax in the following sections.

Performing Left Outer Joins Using SQL/92

Earlier, you saw the following query, which performed a left outer join using the Oracle join operator (+):

```
SELECT p.name, pt.name
FROM products p, product_types pt
WHERE p.product_type_id = pt.product_type_id (+)
ORDER BY p.name;
```

Here's the previous query rewritten to use the SQL/92 LEFT OUTER JOIN keywords:

```
SELECT p.name, pt.name
FROM products p LEFT OUTER JOIN product_types pt
USING (product_type_id)
ORDER BY p.name;
```

Performing Right Outer Joins Using SQL/92

Earlier, you saw the following query, which performed a right outer join using the Oracle join operator (+):

```
SELECT p.name, pt.name
FROM products p, product_types pt
WHERE p.product_type_id (+) = pt.product_type_id
ORDER BY p.name;
```

Here's the previous query rewritten to use the SQL/92 RIGHT OUTER JOIN keywords:

```
SELECT p.name, pt.name
FROM products p RIGHT OUTER JOIN product_types pt
USING (product_type_id)
ORDER BY p.name;
```

Performing Full Outer Joins Using SQL/92

A full outer join uses all rows in the joined tables, including those that have null values in either of the columns used in the join. The following query uses the SQL/92 FULL OUTER JOIN keywords:

```
SELECT p.name, pt.name
FROM products p FULL OUTER JOIN product_types pt
USING (product_type_id)
ORDER BY p.name;

NAME                              NAME
--------------------------------- ----------
2412: The Return                  Video
Chemistry                         Book
Classical Music                   CD
Creative Yell                     CD
From Another Planet               DVD
```

```
Modern Science          Book
My Front Line
Pop 3                   CD
Space Force 9           DVD
Supernova               Video
Tank War                Video
Z Files                 Video
                        Magazine
```

Notice that both "My Front Line" from the `products` table and "Magazine" from the `product_types` table are returned. These rows have nulls.

Performing Self Joins Using SQL/92

The following example uses SQL/86 to perform a self join on the `employees` table:

```
SELECT w.last_name || ' works for ' || m.last_name
FROM employees w, employees m
WHERE w.manager_id = m.employee_id;
```

Here's the previous query rewritten to use the SQL/92 INNER JOIN and ON keywords:

```
SELECT w.last_name || ' works for ' || m.last_name
FROM employees w INNER JOIN employees m
ON w.manager_id = m.employee_id;
```

Performing Cross Joins Using SQL/92

Omitting a join condition between two tables produces a Cartesian product. By using the SQL/92 join syntax, you avoid producing a Cartesian product because you must always provide an ON or USING clause to join the tables.

If you really need a Cartesian product, the SQL/92 standard requires the usage of the CROSS JOIN keywords. In the following query, a Cartesian product between the `product_types` and `products` tables is produced using the CROSS JOIN keywords:

```
SELECT *
FROM product_types CROSS JOIN products;
```

Summary

In this chapter, you have learned the following:

- How to perform single and multiple table queries
- How to select all columns from a table using an asterisk (*) in a query
- How a row identifier ROWID is used to store the location of a row
- How to perform arithmetic in SQL
- How to use addition and subtraction operators with dates
- How to reference tables and columns using aliases
- How to merge column output using the concatenation operator ||

■ How nulls are used to represent unknown values

■ How to display distinct rows using the `DISTINCT` operator

■ How to limit the retrieval of rows using the `WHERE` clause

■ How to sort rows using the `ORDER BY` clause

■ How to perform inner, outer, and self joins using the SQL/86 and SQL/92 syntax

In the next chapter, you'll learn about SQL*Plus.

CHAPTER
3

Using SQL*Plus

I n this chapter, you'll learn how to perform the following tasks:

- View the structure of a table
- Edit SQL statements
- Save and run scripts containing SQL statements and SQL*Plus commands
- Format the results returned by SQL*Plus
- Use variables in SQL*Plus
- Create simple reports
- Get help from SQL*Plus
- Automatically generate SQL statements
- Disconnect from a database and exit SQL*Plus

Viewing the Structure of a Table

Knowing the structure of a table is useful because you can use the information to write SQL statements. For example, you can discover the columns you want to retrieve in a query. You use the DESCRIBE command to view the structure of a table.

The following example uses DESCRIBE to view the structure of the customers table. Notice that the semicolon character (;) can be omitted from SQL*Plus commands.

```
SQL> DESCRIBE customers
 Name                      Null?    Type
 ------------------------- -------- --------------
 CUSTOMER_ID               NOT NULL NUMBER(38)
 FIRST_NAME                NOT NULL VARCHAR2(10)
 LAST_NAME                 NOT NULL VARCHAR2(10)
 DOB                                DATE
 PHONE                              VARCHAR2(12)
```

The output from DESCRIBE has three columns that show the structure of the table. These columns are as follows:

- **Name** lists the names of the columns contained in the table. In the example, you can see that the customers table has five columns: customer_id, first_name, last_name, dob, and phone.
- **Null?** indicates whether the column can store null values. If set to NOT NULL, the column cannot store a null value. If blank, the column can store a null value. In the preceding example, you can see that the customer_id, first_name, and last_name columns cannot store null values, but the dob and phone columns can.
- **Type** indicates the type of the column. In the preceding example, you can see that the type of the customer_id column is NUMBER(38) and that the type of the first_name column is VARCHAR2(10).

You can save some typing by shortening the DESCRIBE command to DESC. The following example uses DESC to view the structure of the products table:

```
SQL> DESC products
 Name                     Null?     Type
 -------------------- -------- --------------
 PRODUCT_ID               NOT NULL NUMBER(38)
 PRODUCT_TYPE_ID                   NUMBER(38)
 NAME                     NOT NULL VARCHAR2(30)
 DESCRIPTION                       VARCHAR2(50)
 PRICE                             NUMBER(5,2)
```

Editing SQL Statements

Typing similar SQL statements repeatedly into SQL*Plus becomes tedious, but doing so isn't necessary. SQL*Plus stores your last SQL statement in a buffer. You can then edit the lines stored in the buffer.

Some of the editing commands are listed in the following table. Notice the optional part of each command in square brackets (for example, you can abbreviate the APPEND command to A).

Command	Description
A[PPEND] text	Appends text to the current line.
C[HANGE] /old/new	Changes the text specified by old to new in the current line.
CL[EAR] BUFF[ER]	Clears all lines from the buffer.
DEL	Deletes the current line.
DEL x	Deletes the line specified by the line number x. Line numbers start with 1.
L[IST]	Lists all the lines in the buffer.
L[IST] x	Lists line number x.
R[UN] or /	Runs the statement stored in the buffer. You can also use / to run the statement.
X	Makes the line specified by the line number x the current line.

Let's take a look at some examples of using the SQL*Plus editing commands. The following example shows a query in SQL*Plus:

```
SQL> SELECT customer_id, first_name, last_name
  2  FROM customers
  3  WHERE customer_id = 1;
```

SQL*Plus automatically increments the line number when you press ENTER. You can make line 1 the current line by entering 1 at the prompt:

```
SQL> 1
  1* SELECT customer_id, first_name, last_name
```

SQL*Plus displays the current line and the line number.

The following example uses APPEND to add ", dob" to the end of the line:

```
SQL> APPEND , dob
  1* SELECT customer_id, first_name, last_name, dob
```

The next example uses LIST to show all the lines in the buffer:

```
SQL> LIST
  1  SELECT customer_id, first_name, last_name, dob
  2  FROM customers
  3* WHERE customer_id = 1
```

Notice that the current line has been changed to the last line, as indicated by the asterisk character (*).

The following example uses CHANGE to replace "customer_id = 1" with "customer_id = 2" in the last line:

```
SQL> CHANGE /customer_id = 1/customer_id = 2
  3* WHERE customer_id = 2
```

The next example uses RUN to execute the query:

```
SQL> RUN
  1  SELECT customer_id, first_name, last_name, dob
  2  FROM customers
  3* WHERE customer_id = 2

CUSTOMER_ID FIRST_NAME LAST_NAME  DOB
----------- ---------- ---------- ---------
          2 Cynthia    Green      05-FEB-68
```

You can also use a forward slash character (/) to run the SQL statement. For example:

```
SQL> /

CUSTOMER_ID FIRST_NAME LAST_NAME  DOB
----------- ---------- ---------- ---------
          2 Cynthia    Green      05-FEB-68
```

Saving, Retrieving, and Running Files

SQL*Plus allows you to save, retrieve, and run scripts containing SQL*Plus commands and SQL statements. You've already seen one example of running an SQL*Plus script, which was the store_schema.sql script file that you ran in Chapter 1.

Some of the SQL*Plus file commands are listed in the following table.

Command	Description
SAV[E] *filename* [{ REPLACE | APPEND }]	Saves the contents of the SQL*Plus buffer to a file specified by *filename*. You append the content of the buffer to an existing file using the APPEND option. You overwrite an existing file using the REPLACE option.
GET *filename*	Retrieves the contents of the file specified by *filename* into the SQL*Plus buffer.
STA[RT] *filename*	Retrieves the contents of the file specified by *filename* into the SQL*Plus buffer and then attempts to run the contents of the buffer.
@ *filename*	Same as the START command.
ED[IT]	Copies the contents of the SQL*Plus buffer to a temporary file and then starts the default text editor. When you exit the editor, the contents of the edited file are copied to the SQL*Plus buffer.
ED[IT] *filename*	Same as the EDIT command, but you can specify a file to start editing. You specify the file to edit using the *filename* parameter.
SPO[OL] *filename*	Copies the output from SQL*Plus to the file specified by *filename*. Copying of the output begins after the SPOOL command and ends at the SPOOL OFF command.
SPO[OL] OFF	Stops the copying of output from SQL*Plus to the file and then closes the file.

Let's take a look at some examples of using these SQL*Plus commands. If you want to follow along with the examples, go ahead and enter the following query into SQL*Plus:

```
SQL> SELECT customer_id, first_name, last_name
  2  FROM customers
  3  WHERE customer_id = 1;
```

The following example uses SAVE to save the contents of the SQL*Plus buffer to a file named cust_query.sql in the Windows C:\My_SQL_files directory:

```
SQL> SAVE C:\My_SQL_files\cust_query.sql
```

NOTE
You'll need to create the My_SQL_files *directory before running the example.*

The next example is for Linux:

```
SQL> SAVE /tmp/cust_query.sql
```

The next example uses GET to retrieve the contents of the cust_query.sql file from the Windows C:\My_SQL_files directory:

```
SQL> GET C:\My_SQL_files\cust_query.sql
  1  SELECT customer_id, first_name, last_name
  2  FROM customers
  3* WHERE customer_id = 1
```

The next example is for Linux:

```
SQL> GET /tmp/cust_query.sql
```

The following example runs the query using the forward slash character (/):

```
SQL> /

CUSTOMER_ID FIRST_NAME LAST_NAME
----------- ---------- ----------
          1 John       Brown
```

The next example uses START to load and run the contents of the C:\My_SQL_files\ cust_query.sql file in one step:

```
SQL> START C:\My_SQL_files\cust_query.sql

CUSTOMER_ID FIRST_NAME LAST_NAME
----------- ---------- ----------
          1 John       Brown
```

You can edit the contents of the SQL*Plus buffer using the EDIT command:

```
SQL> EDIT
```

The EDIT command starts the default editor for your operating system. On Windows, the default editor is Notepad. On Linux and Unix, the default editor is ed.

Figure 3-1 shows the contents of the SQL*Plus buffer in Notepad. Notice the SQL statement is terminated using a forward slash character (/) rather than a semicolon.

Resolving the Error When Attempting to Edit Statements

If you encounter error SP2-0110 when trying to edit a statement on Windows, then you can run SQL*Plus as an administrator. On Windows 7, you can do that by right-clicking the SQL*Plus shortcut and selecting "Run as administrator." You can permanently set this in Windows 7 by right-clicking the SQL*Plus shortcut and selecting the "Run this program as an administrator" option in the Compatibility tab.

You can also set the directory that SQL*Plus starts in by right-clicking the SQL*Plus shortcut and changing the "Start in" directory in the Shortcut tab. SQL*Plus will use that default directory when saving and retrieving files. For example, you could set the directory to C:\My_SQL_files, and SQL*Plus will store and retrieve files from that directory by default.

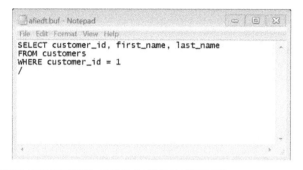

FIGURE 3-1. *Editing the SQL*Plus buffer contents using Notepad*

In your editor, change the WHERE clause to WHERE customer_id = 2, and then save and exit the editor. To save and exit from Windows 7 Notepad, you select File | Exit, and then click Save to save your query. To save and exit from Linux and Unix ed, you enter wq.

SQL*Plus displays the following output containing your modified query:

```
1  SELECT customer_id, first_name, last_name
2  FROM customers
3* WHERE customer_id = 2
```

Changing the Default Editor

You can change the default editor using the SQL*Plus DEFINE command:

```
DEFINE _EDITOR = 'editor'
```

where *editor* is the name of your preferred editor.

For example, the following command sets the default editor to vi, which can be used in Linux:

```
DEFINE _EDITOR = 'vi'
```

You can also change the default editor SQL*Plus uses by adding the line DEFINE _EDITOR = 'editor' to a new file named login.sql, where *editor* is the name of your preferred editor. You can add any SQL*Plus commands you want to this file. SQL*Plus will check the current directory for a login.sql file and execute it when SQL*Plus starts. If there is no login.sql file in the current directory, then SQL*Plus will check all directories (and their subdirectories) in the SQLPATH environment variable for a login.sql file.

On Windows, SQLPATH is defined as a registry entry. For example, on a Windows computer running Oracle Database 12c, SQLPATH might be set to C:\oracle12c\product\12.1.0\dbhome_1\dbs. This is just an example path, and on your computer it might be different. On Linux and Unix, there is no default SQLPATH defined, and you will need to add it as an environment variable.

For further details on setting up a login.sql file, you can read the *SQL*Plus User's Guide and Reference*, published by Oracle Corporation.

You run your modified query using the forward slash character (/):

```
SQL> /

CUSTOMER_ID FIRST_NAME LAST_NAME
----------- ---------- ----------
          2 Cynthia    Green
```

You use the SPOOL command to copy the output from SQL*Plus to a file. The following Windows example spools the output to a file named cust_results.txt, runs the query again, and then turns spooling off by executing SPOOL OFF:

```
SQL> SPOOL C:\My_SQL_files\cust_results.txt
SQL> /

CUSTOMER_ID FIRST_NAME LAST_NAME
----------- ---------- ----------
          2 Cynthia    Green

SQL> SPOOL OFF
```

The cust_results.txt file contains the previous output between the forward slash (/) and SPOOL OFF.

Formatting Columns

You use the COLUMN command to format the display of column headings and column data. The simplified syntax for the COLUMN command is as follows:

```
COL[UMN] {column | alias} [options]
```

where

- column is the column name.
- alias is the column alias to be formatted. In Chapter 2, you saw that you can "rename" a column using a column alias. You can reference an alias in the COLUMN command.
- options are one or more options to be used to format the column or alias.

There are a number of options you can use with the COLUMN command. The following table shows some of these options.

Option	Description
FOR[MAT] format	Sets the format for the display of the column or alias to the format string.
HEA[DING] heading	Sets the heading of the column or alias to the heading string.
JUS[TIFY] [{ LEFT | CENTER | RIGHT }]	Places the column output to the left, center, or right.

Option	Description
WRA[PPED]	Wraps the end of a string onto the next line of output. This option might cause individual words to be split across multiple lines.
WOR[D_WRAPPED]	Similar to the WRAPPED option, except individual words are not split across two lines.
CLE[AR]	Clears any formatting of columns, which sets the formatting back to the default.

The *format* string in the previous table can take a number of formatting parameters. The parameters you specify depend on the data stored in your column:

- If your column contains characters, you use A*x* to format the characters, where *x* specifies the width for the characters. For example, A12 sets the width to 12 characters.

- If your column contains numbers, you can use any of a variety of number formats, which are shown later in Table 4-4 of Chapter 4. For example, $99.99 sets the format to a dollar sign, followed by two digits, the decimal point, plus another two digits.

- If your column contains a date, you can use any of the date formats shown later in Table 5-2 of Chapter 5. For example, MM-DD-YYYY sets the format to a two-digit month (MM), a two-digit day (DD), and a four-digit year (YYYY).

Let's take a look at an example. You'll see how to format the output of a query that retrieves the product_id, name, description, and price columns from the products table. The display requirements, format strings, and COLUMN commands are shown in the following table.

Column	Display As...	Format	COLUMN Command
product_id	Two digits	99	COLUMN product_id FORMAT 99
name	Thirteen-character word-wrapped strings and set the column heading to PRODUCT_NAME	A13	COLUMN name HEADING PRODUCT_NAME FORMAT A13 WORD_WRAPPED
description	Thirteen-character word-wrapped strings	A13	COLUMN description FORMAT A13 WORD_WRAPPED
price	Dollar symbol, with two digits before and after the decimal point	$99.99	COLUMN price FORMAT $99.99

The following example shows the COLUMN commands in SQL*Plus:

```
SQL> COLUMN product_id FORMAT 99
SQL> COLUMN name HEADING PRODUCT_NAME FORMAT A13 WORD_WRAPPED
SQL> COLUMN description FORMAT A13 WORD_WRAPPED
SQL> COLUMN price FORMAT $99.99
```

The next example runs a query to retrieve some rows from the `products` table. Notice the formatting of the columns in the output.

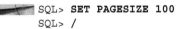

```
SQL> SELECT product_id, name, description, price
  2  FROM products
  3  WHERE product_id < 6;

PRODUCT_ID PRODUCT_NAME  DESCRIPTION      PRICE
---------- ------------- ------------- --------
         1 Modern        A description   $19.95
           Science       of modern
                         science

         2 Chemistry     Introduction    $30.00
                         to Chemistry

         3 Supernova     A star          $25.99
                         explodes

         4 Tank War      Action movie    $13.95

PRODUCT_ID PRODUCT_NAME  DESCRIPTION      PRICE
---------- ------------- ------------- --------
                         about a
                         future war

         5 Z Files       Series on       $49.99
                         mysterious
                         activities
```

This output is readable, but wouldn't it be nice if you could display the headings just once at the top? You do that by setting the page size, as you'll see next.

Setting the Page Size

You set the number of lines in a page using the SET PAGESIZE command. This command sets the number of lines that SQL*Plus considers one "page" of output, after which SQL*Plus will display the headings again.

The following example sets the page size to 100 lines using the SET PAGESIZE command and runs the query again using the forward slash character (/):

```
SQL> SET PAGESIZE 100
SQL> /

PRODUCT_ID PRODUCT_NAME  DESCRIPTION      PRICE
---------- ------------- ------------- --------
         1 Modern        A description   $19.95
           Science       of modern
                         science
```

```
    2 Chemistry     Introduction     $30.00
                    to Chemistry

    3 Supernova     A star           $25.99
                    explodes

    4 Tank War      Action movie     $13.95
                    about a
                    future war

    5 Z Files       Series on        $49.99
                    mysterious
                    activities
```

Notice that the headings are shown only once, at the top, and the resulting output looks better.

NOTE
The maximum number for the page size is 50,000.

The following example sets the page size back to the default of 14:

 SQL> **SET PAGESIZE 14**

Setting the Line Size

You set the number of characters in a line using the SET LINESIZE command. The following example sets the line size to 50 lines and runs another query:

 SQL> **SET LINESIZE 50**
SQL> **SELECT * FROM customers;**

```
CUSTOMER_ID FIRST_NAME LAST_NAME  DOB
----------- ---------- ---------- ---------
PHONE
------------
          1 John       Brown      01-JAN-65
800-555-1211

          2 Cynthia    Green      05-FEB-68
800-555-1212

          3 Steve      White      16-MAR-71
800-555-1213

          4 Gail       Black
800-555-1214

          5 Doreen     Blue       20-MAY-70
```

The lines don't span more than 50 characters.

NOTE
The maximum number for the line size is 32,767.

The following example sets the line size back to the default of 80:

```
SQL> SET LINESIZE 80
```

Clearing Column Formatting

You clear the formatting for a column using the CLEAR option of the COLUMN command. For example, the following COLUMN command clears the formatting for the product_id column:

```
SQL> COLUMN product_id CLEAR
```

You can clear the formatting for all columns using CLEAR COLUMNS. For example:

```
SQL> CLEAR COLUMNS
```

Once you've cleared the columns, the output from the queries will use the default format.

Using Variables

In this section, you'll see how to create variables that can be used in place of actual values in SQL statements. These variables are known as *substitution variables* because they are used as substitutes for values. When you run an SQL statement, you enter values for the variables. The values are then "substituted" into the SQL statement.

There are two types of substitution variables:

- **Temporary variables**   A temporary variable is valid only for the SQL statement in which it is used. A temporary variable doesn't persist.
- **Defined variables**   A defined variable persists until you explicitly remove it, redefine it, or exit SQL*Plus.

You'll learn how to use these types of variables in the following sections.

Temporary Variables

You define a temporary variable using the ampersand character (&), followed by the name you want to call your variable. For example, &v_product_id defines a variable named v_product_id.

When you run the following query, SQL*Plus prompts you to enter a value for v_product_id and then uses that value in the WHERE clause. If you enter the value 2 for v_product_id, then the details for product #2 will be displayed.

```
SQL> SELECT product_id, name, price
  2  FROM products
  3  WHERE product_id = &v_product_id;
Enter value for v_product_id: 2
old   3: WHERE product_id = &v_product_id
```

```
new    3: WHERE product_id = 2
```

```
PRODUCT_ID NAME                                    PRICE
---------- ------------------------------ ----------
         2 Chemistry                                  30
```

In the example, notice that SQL*Plus does the following:

■ Prompts you to enter a value for v_product_id
■ Substitutes the value you entered for v_product_id in the WHERE clause

SQL*Plus shows you the substitution in the old and new lines in the output, along with the line number in the query where the substitution was performed. In the previous example, you can see that the old and new lines indicate that v_product_id is set to 2 in the WHERE clause.

If you rerun the query using the forward slash character (/), SQL*Plus will ask you to enter a new value for v_product_id. For example:

```
SQL> /
Enter value for v_product_id: 3
old    3: WHERE product_id = &v_product_id
new    3: WHERE product_id = 3
```

```
PRODUCT_ID NAME                                    PRICE
---------- ------------------------------ ----------
         3 Supernova                               25.99
```

SQL*Plus echoes the old line of the SQL statement (old 3: WHERE product_id = &v_product_id), followed by the new line containing the variable value you entered (new 3: WHERE product_id = 3).

Why Are Variables Useful?

Variables are useful because they allow you to create scripts that a user who doesn't know SQL can run. Your script would prompt the user to enter the value for a variable and use that value in an SQL statement. Let's take a look at an example.

Suppose you wanted to create a script for a user who doesn't know SQL, but who wants to see the details of a single specified product in the store. To do this, you could hard code the product_id value in the WHERE clause of a query and place it in an SQL*Plus script. For example, the following query retrieves product #1:

```
SELECT product_id, name, price
FROM products
WHERE product_id = 1;
```

This query works, but it only retrieves product #1. What if you wanted to change the product_id value to retrieve a different row? You could modify the script, but this would be tedious. Wouldn't it be great if you could supply a variable for the product_id? You can do that using a substitution variable.

Controlling Output Lines

You can control the output of the old and new lines using the SET VERIFY command. If you
enter SET VERIFY OFF, the old and new lines are suppressed. For example:

```
SQL> SET VERIFY OFF
SQL> /
Enter value for v_product_id: 4

PRODUCT_ID NAME                                   PRICE
---------- ------------------------------ ----------
         4 Tank War                             13.95
```

To turn the echoing of the lines back on, you enter SET VERIFY ON. For example:

```
SQL> SET VERIFY ON
```

Changing the Variable Definition Character

You can use the SET DEFINE command to specify a character other than an ampersand (&) for
defining a variable. The following example shows how to set the variable character to the pound
character (#) and shows a new query:

```
SQL> SET DEFINE '#'
SQL> SELECT product_id, name, price
  2   FROM products
  3   WHERE product_id = #v_product_id;
Enter value for v_product_id: 5
old   3: WHERE product_id = #v_product_id
new   3: WHERE product_id = 5

PRODUCT_ID NAME                                   PRICE
---------- ------------------------------ ----------
         5 Z Files                              49.99
```

The next example uses SET DEFINE to change the character back to an ampersand:

```
SQL> SET DEFINE '&'
```

Substituting Table and Column Names Using Variables

You can use variables to substitute the names of tables and columns. For example, the following
query defines variables for a column name (v_col), a table name (v_table), and a column
value (v_val):

```
SQL> SELECT name, &v_col
  2   FROM &v_table
  3   WHERE &v_col = &v_val;
Enter value for v_col: product_type_id
old   1: SELECT name, &v_col
new   1: SELECT name, product_type_id
```

```
Enter value for v_table: products
old    2: FROM &v_table
new    2: FROM products
Enter value for v_col: product_type_id
Enter value for v_val: 1
old    3: WHERE &v_col = &v_val
new    3: WHERE product_type_id = 1


NAME                            PRODUCT_TYPE_ID
------------------------------  ---------------
Modern Science                                1
Chemistry                                     1
```

You can avoid having to repeatedly enter a variable by using && . For example:

```
SQL> SELECT name, &&v_col
  2    FROM &v_table
  3    WHERE &&v_col = &v_val;
Enter value for v_col: product_type_id
old    1: SELECT name, &&v_col
new    1: SELECT name, product_type_id
Enter value for v_table: products
old    2: FROM &v_table
new    2: FROM products
Enter value for v_val: 1
old    3: WHERE &&v_col = &v_val
new    3: WHERE product_type_id = 1


NAME                            PRODUCT_TYPE_ID
------------------------------  ---------------
Modern Science                                1
Chemistry                                     1
```

Variables give you a lot of flexibility in writing queries that another user can run. You can give the user a script and have them enter the variable values.

Defined Variables

You can define a variable prior to using it in an SQL statement. You can use these variables multiple times within an SQL statement. A defined variable persists until you explicitly remove it, redefine it, or exit SQL*Plus.

You define a variable using the DEFINE command. When you're finished with your variable, you remove it using UNDEFINE. You'll learn about these commands in this section. You'll also learn about the ACCEPT command, which allows you to define a variable and set its data type.

You can also define variables in an SQL*Plus script and pass values to those variables when the script is run. This feature enables you to write generic reports that any user can run—even if they're unfamiliar with SQL. You'll learn how to create simple reports later in the section "Creating Simple Reports."

Defining and Listing Variables Using the DEFINE Command

You use the DEFINE command to both define a new variable and list the currently defined variables. The following example defines a variable named v_product_id and sets its value to 7:

```
SQL> DEFINE v_product_id = 7
```

You can view the definition of a variable using the DEFINE command followed by the name of the variable. The following example displays the definition of v_product_id:

```
SQL> DEFINE v_product_id
DEFINE V_PRODUCT_ID    = "7"  (CHAR)
```

Notice that v_product_id is defined as a CHAR variable.

You can see all your session variables by entering DEFINE on its own. For example:

```
SQL> DEFINE
DEFINE _DATE             = "06-MAY-12"  (CHAR)
DEFINE _CONNECT_IDENTIFIER = "orcl"  (CHAR)
DEFINE _USER             = "STORE"  (CHAR)
DEFINE _PRIVILEGE        = ""  (CHAR)
DEFINE _SQLPLUS_RELEASE  = "1201000001"  (CHAR)
DEFINE _EDITOR           = "vi"  (CHAR)
DEFINE _O_VERSION        = "Oracle Database 12c Enterprise Edition..."  (CHAR)
DEFINE _O_RELEASE        = "1201000001"  (CHAR)
DEFINE 1                 = "employee_id"  (CHAR)
DEFINE 2                 = "="  (CHAR)
DEFINE 3                 = "1"  (CHAR)
DEFINE _RC               = "0"  (CHAR)
DEFINE V_STATEMENT_ID    = "NO_HINT"  (CHAR)
DEFINE V_COL             = "product_type_id"  (CHAR)
DEFINE V_PRODUCT_ID      = "7"  (CHAR)
```

You can use a defined variable to specify an element such as a column value in an SQL statement. For example, the following query uses references v_product_id in the WHERE clause:

```
SQL> SELECT product_id, name, price
  2  FROM products
  3  WHERE product_id = &v_product_id;
old   3: WHERE product_id = &v_product_id
new   3: WHERE product_id = 7

PRODUCT_ID NAME                             PRICE
---------- ------------------------------ ----------
         7 Space Force 9                    13.49
```

You're not prompted for the value of v_product_id because it was set to 7 when the variable was defined earlier.

Defining and Setting Variables Using the ACCEPT Command

The ACCEPT command waits for a user to enter a value for a variable. You can use the ACCEPT command to set an existing variable to a new value or to define a new variable and initialize it with a value. The ACCEPT command also allows you to specify the data type for the variable.

The simplified syntax for the ACCEPT command is as follows:

ACCEPT *variable_name* [*type*] [FORMAT *format*] [PROMPT *prompt*] [HIDE]

where

- *variable_name* is the name of the variable.
- *type* is the data type for the variable. You can use the CHAR, NUMBER, and DATE types. By default, variables are defined using the CHAR type. DATE variables are actually stored as CHAR variables.
- *format* is the format used for the variable. Some examples include A15 (15 characters), 9999 (a four-digit number), and DD-MON-YYYY (a date). You can view the number formats in Table 4-4 of Chapter 4. You can view the date formats in Table 5-2 of Chapter 5.
- *prompt* is the text displayed by SQL*Plus as a prompt to the user to enter the variable's value.
- HIDE means hide the value as it is entered. For example, you might want to hide passwords or other sensitive information.

Let's take a look at some examples of the ACCEPT command. The following example defines a variable named v_customer_id as a two-digit number:

```
SQL> ACCEPT v_customer_id NUMBER FORMAT 99 PROMPT 'Customer id: '
Customer id: 5
```

The next example defines a DATE variable named v_date. The format is DD-MON-YYYY.

```
SQL> ACCEPT v_date DATE FORMAT 'DD-MON-YYYY' PROMPT 'Date: '
Date: 06-MAY-2012
```

The next example defines a CHAR variable named v_password. The value entered is hidden using HIDE.

```
SQL> ACCEPT v_password CHAR PROMPT 'Password: ' HIDE
Password:
```

In Oracle Database 9*i* and below, the value appears as a string of asterisk characters (*) to hide the value as you enter it. In Oracle Database 10*g* and above, nothing is displayed as you type the value.

You can view your variables using the DEFINE command. For example:

```
SQL> DEFINE
...
DEFINE V_PRODUCT_ID    = "7" (CHAR)
DEFINE V_CUSTOMER_ID   =        5 (NUMBER)
DEFINE V_DATE          = "06-MAY-2012" (CHAR)
DEFINE V_PASSWORD      = "1234567" (CHAR)
```

Notice that v_date is stored as a CHAR.

Removing Variables Using the UNDEFINE Command

You remove variables using the UNDEFINE command. The following example uses UNDEFINE to remove v_product_id, v_customer_id, v_date, and v_password:

```
SQL> UNDEFINE v_product_id
SQL> UNDEFINE v_customer_id
SQL> UNDEFINE v_date
SQL> UNDEFINE v_password
```

NOTE
All of your variables are removed when you exit SQL*Plus, even if you don't explicitly remove them using the UNDEFINE *command.*

Creating Simple Reports

You can use variables in a script to create reports that a user can run. The scripts referenced in this section are located in the SQL directory where you extracted the Zip file for this book.

TIP
SQL*Plus was not specifically designed to be a reporting tool. If you have complex reporting requirements, you should use software like Oracle Reports.

Using Temporary Variables in a Script

The following report1.sql script uses a temporary variable named v_product_id in the WHERE clause of a query:

```
-- suppress display of the statements and verification messages
SET ECHO OFF
SET VERIFY OFF

SELECT product_id, name, price
FROM products
WHERE product_id = &v_product_id;
```

The SET ECHO OFF command stops SQL*Plus from displaying the SQL statements and commands in the script. SET VERIFY OFF suppresses display of the verification messages. I put these two commands in to minimize the number of extra lines displayed by SQL*Plus when you run the script.

You can run report1.sql in SQL*Plus using the @ command. For example:

```
SQL> @ C:\sql_book\SQL\report1.sql
Enter value for v_product_id: 2

PRODUCT_ID NAME                                   PRICE
---------- ------------------------------ ----------
         2 Chemistry                                 30
```

You'll need to replace the directory in the example with the directory where you saved the files for this book. Also, if you have spaces in the directory, you'll need to put everything after the @ command in quotes. For example:

```
@ "C:\my directory\sql book\SQL\report1.sql"
```

Using Defined Variables in a Script

The following `report2.sql` script uses the `ACCEPT` command to define a variable named `v_product_id`:

```
SET ECHO OFF
SET VERIFY OFF

ACCEPT v_product_id NUMBER FORMAT 99 PROMPT 'Enter product id: '

SELECT product_id, name, price
FROM products
WHERE product_id = &v_product_id;

-- clean up
UNDEFINE v_product_id
```

A user-friendly prompt is specified for the entry of `v_product_id`, and `v_product_id` is removed at the end of the script.

You can run the `report2.sql` script using SQL*Plus:

```
SQL> @ C:\sql_book\SQL\report2.sql
Enter product id: 4

PRODUCT_ID NAME                                  PRICE
---------- ------------------------------ ----------
         4 Tank War                            13.95
```

Passing a Value to a Variable in a Script

You can pass a value to a variable when you run your script. When you do this, you reference the variable in the script using a number. The following script `report3.sql` shows an example of this. Notice that the variable is identified using `&1`.

```
SET ECHO OFF
SET VERIFY OFF

SELECT product_id, name, price
FROM products
WHERE product_id = &1;
```

When you run `report3.sql`, you supply the variable's value following the script name. The following example passes the value 4 to `report3.sql`:

```
SQL> @ C:\sql_book\SQL\report3.sql 4
PRODUCT_ID NAME                                  PRICE
---------- ------------------------------ ----------
         4 Tank War                            13.95
```

If you have spaces in the directory where you saved the scripts, you'll need to put the directory and script name in quotes. For example:

```
@ "C:\my directory\sql book\SQL\report3.sql" 4
```

You can pass any number of parameters to a script, with each value corresponding to the matching number in the script. The first parameter corresponds to &1, the second to &2, and so on. The following report4.sql script shows an example with two parameters:

```
SET ECHO OFF
SET VERIFY OFF

SELECT product_id, product_type_id, name, price
FROM products
WHERE product_type_id = &1
AND price > &2;
```

The following example run of report4.sql shows the addition of two values for &1 and &2, which are set to 1 and 9.99, respectively:

```
SQL> @ C:\sql_book\SQL\report4.sql 1 9.99

PRODUCT_ID PRODUCT_TYPE_ID NAME                                 PRICE
---------- --------------- ------------------------------ ----------
         1               1 Modern Science                       19.95
         2               1 Chemistry                               30
```

Because &1 is set to 1, the product_type_id column in the WHERE clause is set to 1. Also, because &2 is set to 9.99, the price column in the WHERE clause is set to 9.99. Therefore, rows with a product_type_id of 1 and a price greater than 9.99 are returned.

Adding a Header and Footer

You add a header and footer to a report using the TTITLE and BTITLE commands. The following is an example TTITLE command:

```
TTITLE LEFT 'Run date: ' _DATE CENTER 'Run by the ' SQL.USER ' user'
RIGHT 'Page: ' FORMAT 999 SQL.PNO SKIP 2
```

The following list explains the contents of this command:

- ■ _DATE displays the current date.
- ■ SQL.USER displays the current user.
- ■ SQL.PNO displays the current page (FORMAT is used to format the number).
- ■ LEFT, CENTER, and RIGHT justify the text.
- ■ SKIP 2 skips two lines.

If the example is run on May 6, 2012, by the store user, the example displays the following line:

```
Run date: 06-MAY-12      Run by the STORE user                Page:    1
```

The next example shows a BTITLE command:

```
BTITLE CENTER 'Thanks for running the report' RIGHT 'Page: ' FORMAT 999 SQL
.PNO
```

The previous BTITLE command displays the following line:

```
                         Thanks for running the report            Page:    1
```

The following report5.sql script contains the previous TTITLE and BTITLE commands:

```
TTITLE LEFT 'Run date: ' _DATE CENTER 'Run by the ' SQL.USER ' user'
RIGHT 'Page: ' FORMAT 999 SQL.PNO SKIP 2

BTITLE CENTER 'Thanks for running the report' RIGHT 'Page: '
FORMAT 999 SQL.PNO

SET ECHO OFF
SET VERIFY OFF
SET PAGESIZE 30
SET LINESIZE 70
CLEAR COLUMNS
COLUMN product_id HEADING ID FORMAT 99
COLUMN name HEADING 'Product Name' FORMAT A20 WORD_WRAPPED
COLUMN description HEADING Description FORMAT A30 WORD_WRAPPED
COLUMN price HEADING Price FORMAT $99.99

SELECT product_id, name, description, price
FROM products;

CLEAR COLUMNS
TTITLE OFF
BTITLE OFF
```

The last two lines in the script turn off the header and footer.

The following example shows a run of report5.sql:

```
SQL> @ C:\sql_book\SQL\report5.sql

Run date: 06-MAY-12      Run by the STORE user           Page:    1

 ID Product Name         Description                       Price
 --- -------------------- ------------------------------ -------
  1 Modern Science       A description of modern           $19.95
                         science

  2 Chemistry            Introduction to Chemistry         $30.00
  3 Supernova            A star explodes                   $25.99
  4 Tank War             Action movie about a future       $13.95
                         war
```

```
 5 Z Files              Series on mysterious        $49.99
                        activities

 6 2412: The Return     Aliens return               $14.95
 7 Space Force 9        Adventures of heroes        $13.49
 8 From Another Planet  Alien from another planet   $12.99
                        lands on Earth

 9 Classical Music      The best classical music    $10.99
10 Pop 3                The best popular music      $15.99
11 Creative Yell        Debut album                 $14.99
12 My Front Line        Their greatest hits         $13.49

              Thanks for running the report        Page:    1
```

Computing Subtotals

You can add a subtotal for a column using a combination of the BREAK ON and COMPUTE commands. BREAK ON causes SQL*Plus to break up output based on a change in a column value. COMPUTE causes SQL*Plus to compute a value for a column.

The following report6.sql script shows how to compute a subtotal for products of the same type:

```
BREAK ON product_type_id
COMPUTE SUM OF price ON product_type_id

SET ECHO OFF
SET VERIFY OFF
SET PAGESIZE 50
SET LINESIZE 70

CLEAR COLUMNS
COLUMN price HEADING Price FORMAT $999.99

SELECT product_type_id, name, price
FROM products
ORDER BY product_type_id;

CLEAR COLUMNS
```

The following example shows a run of report6.sql:

```
SQL> @ C:\sql_book\SQL\report6.sql

PRODUCT_TYPE_ID NAME                             Price
--------------- ------------------------------ --------
              1 Modern Science                  $19.95
                Chemistry                       $30.00
***************                                --------
```

```
sum                                              $49.95
              2 Supernova                        $25.99
                Tank War                         $13.95
                Z Files                          $49.99
                2412: The Return                 $14.95
* * * * * * * * * * * * * * *                    --------
sum                                              $104.88
              3 Space Force 9                     $13.49
                From Another Planet              $12.99
* * * * * * * * * * * * * * *                    --------
sum                                              $26.48
              4 Classical Music                   $10.99
                Pop 3                            $15.99
                Creative Yell                    $14.99
* * * * * * * * * * * * * * *                    --------
sum                                              $41.97
                My Front Line                    $13.49
* * * * * * * * * * * * * * *                    --------
sum                                              $13.49
```

In the example output, whenever a new value for `product_type_id` is encountered, SQL*Plus breaks up the output and computes a sum for the `price` columns for the rows with the same `product_type_id`. The `product_type_id` value is shown only once for rows with the same `product_type_id`. For example, "Modern Science" and "Chemistry" are both books and have a `product_type_id` of 1, and 1 is shown once for "Modern Science." The sum of the prices for these two books is $49.95. The other sections of the report contain the sum of the prices for products with different `product_type_id` values.

Getting Help from SQL*Plus

You can get help from SQL*Plus using the `HELP` command. The following example runs `HELP`:

```
SQL> HELP

HELP
----

Accesses this command line help system. Enter HELP INDEX or ? INDEX
for a list of topics.

You can view SQL*Plus resources at
    http://www.oracle.com/technology/tech/sql_plus/
and the Oracle Database Library at
    http://www.oracle.com/technology/documentation/

HELP|? [topic]
```

The next example runs HELP INDEX:

```
SQL> HELP INDEX

Enter Help [topic] for help.

  @              COPY          PAUSE                  SHUTDOWN
  @@             DEFINE        PRINT                  SPOOL
  /              DEL           PROMPT                 SQLPLUS
  ACCEPT         DESCRIBE      QUIT                   START
  APPEND         DISCONNECT    RECOVER                STARTUP
  ARCHIVE LOG    EDIT          REMARK                 STORE
  ATTRIBUTE      EXECUTE       REPFOOTER              TIMING
  BREAK          EXIT          REPHEADER              TTITLE
  BTITLE         GET           RESERVED WORDS (SQL)   UNDEFINE
  CHANGE         HELP          RESERVED WORDS (PL/SQL) VARIABLE
  CLEAR          HOST          RUN                    WHENEVER OSERROR
  COLUMN         INPUT         SAVE                   WHENEVER SQLERROR
  COMPUTE        LIST          SET                    XQUERY
  CONNECT        PASSWORD      SHOW
```

The following example runs HELP EDIT:

```
SQL> HELP EDIT

 EDIT
 ----

 Invokes an operating system text editor on the contents of the
 specified file or on the contents of the SQL buffer. The buffer
 has no command history list and does not record SQL*Plus commands.

 ED[IT] [file_name[.ext]]
```

Automatically Generating SQL Statements

In this section, you'll see how to write SQL statements that produce other SQL statements. This is very useful and can save you a lot of typing when writing SQL statements that are similar.

A simple example is an SQL statement that produces DROP TABLE statements, which remove tables from a database. The following query produces a series of DROP TABLE statements that remove the tables from the store schema:

```
SELECT 'DROP TABLE ' || table_name || ';'
FROM user_tables
ORDER BY table_name;

'DROPTABLE'||TABLE_NAME||';'
---------------------------
DROP TABLE ALL_SALES;
DROP TABLE ALL_SALES2;
```

```
...
DROP TABLE REG_EXPS;
DROP TABLE SALARY_GRADES;
```

I've omitted most of the rows in the result set for brevity. You can spool the generated SQL statements in the result set to a file and run them later.

NOTE
The `user_tables` *view contains the details of the tables in the user's schema. The* `table_name` *column contains names of the tables.*

Disconnecting from the Database and Exiting SQL*Plus

You disconnect from the database by entering DISCONNECT (SQL*Plus also automatically performs a COMMIT when you disconnect).

While you're connected to the database, SQL*Plus maintains the database session. When you disconnect from the database, your session is ended. You can reconnect to a database by entering CONNECT.

To disconnect from the database and quit SQL*Plus, you enter EXIT. You can also enter QUIT.

Summary

In this chapter, you have learned the following:

- DESCRIBE shows the structure of a table.
- EDIT enables the modification of SQL statements.
- SQL*Plus can run scripts containing SQL and SQL*Plus commands.
- Variables can be defined in SQL*Plus.
- Reports can be created and run.
- SQL statements can generate other SQL statements.

For further details on SQL*Plus, you can read the *SQL*Plus User's Guide and Reference,* published by Oracle Corporation.

In the next chapter, you'll learn how to use simple functions.

CHAPTER
4

Using Simple Functions

I n this chapter, you'll learn how to perform the following tasks:

- Operate on rows using functions
- Group blocks of rows together using the GROUP BY clause
- Filter groups of rows using the HAVING clause

Types of Functions

There are two main types of Oracle database functions:

- **Single-row functions** operate on one row at a time and return one row of output for each input row. An example single-row function is CONCAT(x, y), which appends y to x and returns the resulting string.
- **Aggregate functions** operate on multiple rows at the same time and return one row of output. An example aggregate function is AVG(x), which returns the average value of x.

You'll learn about single-row functions first, followed by aggregate functions. You'll see more advanced functions as you progress through this book.

Using Single-Row Functions

A single-row function operates on one row at a time and returns one row of output for each row. There are five main types of single-row functions:

- **Character functions** manipulate strings of characters.
- **Numeric functions** perform calculations.
- **Conversion functions** convert a value from one database type to another.
- **Date functions** process dates and times.
- **Regular expression functions** use regular expressions to search data. These functions were introduced in Oracle Database 10g.

You'll learn about character functions first, followed by numeric functions, conversion functions, and regular expression functions. You'll learn about date functions in the next chapter.

Character Functions

Character functions accept character input, which can come from a column in a table or, more generally, from any expression. This input is processed and a result is returned. An example character function is UPPER(), which converts the letters in an input string to uppercase and returns the new string. Another example is NVL(), which converts a null value to another value.

Table 4-1 shows some of the character functions. In the syntax definitions, x and y represent columns from a table or, more generally, any valid expressions. You'll learn more about some of the functions shown in Table 4-1 in the following sections.

Function	Description
ASCII(*x*)	Returns the ASCII value for the character *x*.
CHR(*x*)	Returns the character with the ASCII value of *x*.
CONCAT(*x*, *y*)	Appends *y* to *x* and then returns the new string.
INITCAP(*x*)	Converts the initial letter of each word in *x* to uppercase and returns the new string.
INSTR(*x*, *find_string* [, *start*] [, *occurrence*])	Searches for *find_string* in *x* and returns the position at which *find_string* occurs. You can provide the following optional parameters:
	■ A *start* position in *x* to begin the search. The first position in *x* is in 1. The *start* position can be a positive number or a negative number. A positive *start* number indicates a position offset from the beginning of *x*. A negative *start* number indicates a position offset from the end of *x*.
	■ An *occurrence* that indicates which occurrence of *find_string* should be returned.
LENGTH(*x*)	Returns the number of characters in *x*.
LOWER(*x*)	Converts the letters in *x* to lowercase and returns the new string.
LPAD(*x*, *width* [, *pad_string*])	Pads *x* with spaces to the left to bring the total length of the string up to *width* characters. You can provide an optional *pad_string*, which specifies a string to be repeated to the left of *x* to fill up the padded space. The resulting padded string is returned.
LTRIM(*x* [, *trim_string*])	Removes characters from the left of *x*. You can provide an optional *trim_string*, which specifies the characters to remove. If no *trim_string* is provided, then spaces are removed by default.
NANVL(*x*, *value*)	Returns *value* if *x* matches the NAN (not a number) special value. Otherwise, *x* is returned. (This function was introduced in Oracle Database 10*g*.)
NVL(*x*, *value*)	Returns *value* if *x* is null. Otherwise, *x* is returned.
NVL2(*x*, *value1*, *value2*)	Returns *value1* if *x* is not null. Otherwise, *value2* is returned.
REPLACE(*x*, *search_string*, *replace_string*)	Searches *x* for *search_string* and replaces it with *replace_string*.
	(Continued)

TABLE 4-1. *Character Functions*

Function	Description
RPAD(x, width [, pad_string])	Pads x with spaces to the right to bring the total length of the string up to width characters. You can provide an optional pad_string, which specifies a string to be repeated to the right of x to fill up the padded space. The resulting padded string is returned.
RTRIM(x [, trim_string])	Removes characters from the right of x. You can provide an optional trim_string, which specifies the characters to remove. If no trim_string is provided, then spaces are removed by default.
SOUNDEX(x)	Returns a string containing the phonetic representation of x. This lets you compare words that sound similar in English but are spelled differently.
SUBSTR(x, start [, length])	Returns a substring of x that begins at the position specified by start. The first position in x is in 1. The start position can be a positive number or a negative number. A positive start number indicates a position offset from the beginning of x. A negative start number indicates a position offset from the end of x. You can provide an optional length for the substring.
TRIM([trim_char FROM) x)	Removes characters from the left and right of x. You can provide an optional trim_char, which specifies the characters to remove. If no trim_char is provided, spaces are removed by default.
UPPER(x)	Converts the letters in x to uppercase and returns the new string.

TABLE 4-1. *Character Functions*

ASCII() and CHR()

ASCII(x) returns the ASCII value for the character x. CHR(x) returns the character with the ASCII value of x.

The following query returns the ASCII value of a, A, z, Z, 0, and 9 using ASCII():

```
SELECT
  ASCII('a'), ASCII('A'), ASCII('z'), ASCII('Z'), ASCII(0), ASCII(9)
FROM dual;

ASCII('A') ASCII('A') ASCII('Z') ASCII('Z')   ASCII(0)   ASCII(9)
---------- ---------- ---------- ---------- ---------- ----------
        97         65        122         90         48         57
```

NOTE
The dual *table is used in this query. As mentioned in Chapter 2, the* dual *table contains a single dummy row.*

The following query returns the characters with the ASCII values of 97, 65, 122, 90, 48, and 57 using CHR():

```
SELECT
   CHR(97), CHR(65), CHR(122), CHR(90), CHR(48), CHR(57)
FROM dual;

C C C C C C
- - - - - -
a A z Z 0 9
```

Notice the characters returned from CHR() in this query are the same as those passed to ASCII() in the previous query. This shows that CHR() and ASCII() have the opposite effect.

CONCAT()

CONCAT(*x*, *y*) appends *y* to *x* and returns the new string. The following query appends last_name to first_name using CONCAT():

```
SELECT CONCAT(first_name, last_name)
FROM customers;

CONCAT(FIRST_NAME,LA
--------------------
JohnBrown
CynthiaGreen
SteveWhite
GailBlack
DoreenBlue
```

NOTE
CONCAT() *is the same as the concatenation operator* || *described in Chapter 2. They are used to join characters together in a continuous string.*

INITCAP()

INITCAP(*x*) converts the initial letter of each word in *x* to uppercase.
   The following query retrieves the product_id and description columns from the products table, and then uses INITCAP() to convert the first letter of each word in description to uppercase:

```
SELECT product_id, INITCAP(description)
FROM products
WHERE product_id < 4;
```

```
PRODUCT_ID INITCAP(DESCRIPTION)
---------- ------------------------------
         1 A Description Of Modern Science
         2 Introduction To Chemistry
         3 A Star Explodes
```

INSTR()

INSTR(*x, find_string* [, *start*] [, *occurrence*]) searches for *find_string* in *x*. INSTR() returns the position at which *find_string* occurs. You can provide the following optional parameters:

- A *start* position in *x* to begin the search. The first position in *x* is in 1. The *start* position can be a positive number or a negative number. A positive *start* number indicates a position offset from the beginning of *x*. A negative *start* number indicates a position offset from the end of *x*.

- An *occurrence* that indicates which occurrence of *find_string* should be returned.

The following query returns the position where the string Science occurs in the name column for product #1:

```
SELECT name, INSTR(name, 'Science')
FROM products
WHERE product_id = 1;

NAME                             INSTR(NAME,'SCIENCE')
-------------------------------- ---------------------
Modern Science                                       8
```

The next query displays the position where the second occurrence of the e character occurs, starting from the beginning of the product name:

```
SELECT name, INSTR(name, 'e', 1, 2)
FROM products
WHERE product_id = 1;

NAME                             INSTR(NAME,'E',1,2)
-------------------------------- -------------------
Modern Science                                    11
```

The second e in Modern Science is the eleventh character.

The next query displays the position where the third occurrence of the e character occurs, starting from the end of the product name:

```
SELECT name, INSTR(name, 'e', -1, 3)
FROM products
WHERE product_id = 1;

NAME                             INSTR(NAME,'E',-1,3)
-------------------------------- -------------------
Modern Science                                     4
```

The third e in Modern Science starting from the end is the fourth character.

You can also use dates with character functions. The following query returns the position where the string JAN occurs in the dob column for customer #1:

```
SELECT customer_id, dob, INSTR(dob, 'JAN')
FROM customers
WHERE customer_id = 1;

CUSTOMER_ID DOB       INSTR(DOB,'JAN')
----------- --------- ----------------
          1 01-JAN-65                4
```

LENGTH()

LENGTH(x) returns the number of characters in x. The following query returns the length of the strings in the name column of the products table using LENGTH():

```
SELECT name, LENGTH(name)
FROM products;

NAME                            LENGTH(NAME)
------------------------------- ------------
Modern Science                            14
Chemistry                                  9
Supernova                                  9
Tank War                                   8
Z Files                                    7
2412: The Return                          16
Space Force 9                             13
From Another Planet                       19
Classical Music                           15
Pop 3                                      5
Creative Yell                             13
My Front Line                             13
```

The next query returns the total number of characters that make up the product price. The decimal point (.) is counted in the number of price characters.

```
SELECT price, LENGTH(price)
FROM products
WHERE product_id < 3;

     PRICE LENGTH(PRICE)
---------- -------------
     19.95             5
        30             2
```

LOWER() and UPPER()

LOWER(x) converts the letters in x to lowercase. UPPER(x) converts the letters in x to uppercase.

The following query converts the strings in the `first_name` column to uppercase using `UPPER()` and the strings in the `last_name` column to lowercase using `LOWER()`:

```
SELECT UPPER(first_name), LOWER(last_name)
FROM customers;

UPPER(FIRS LOWER(LAST
---------- ----------
JOHN       brown
CYNTHIA    green
STEVE      white
GAIL       black
DOREEN     blue
```

LPAD() and RPAD()

The following points describe `LPAD()` and `RPAD()`:

- `LPAD(x, width [, pad_string])` pads x with spaces to the left to bring the total length of the string up to $width$ characters. You can provide an optional pad_string, which specifies a string to be repeated to the left of x to fill up the padded space. The resulting padded string is then returned.
- `RPAD(x, width [, pad_string])` pads x with strings to the right.

The following query retrieves the `name` and `price` columns from the `products` table. The `name` column is right-padded using `RPAD()` to a length of 30 characters, with periods filling up the padded space. The `price` column is left-padded using `LPAD()` to a length of 8, with the string `*+` filling up the padded space.

```
SELECT RPAD(name, 30, '.'), LPAD(price, 8, '*+')
FROM products
WHERE product_id < 4;

RPAD(NAME,30,'.')               LPAD(PRI
------------------------------- --------
Modern Science................. *+*19.95
Chemistry...................... *+*+*+30
Supernova...................... *+*25.99
```

NOTE
This example shows that character functions can use numbers. The `price` *column in the example contains a number that was left-padded by* `LPAD()`.

LTRIM(), RTRIM(), and TRIM()

The following points describe `LTRIM()`, `RTRIM()`, and `TRIM()`:

- `LTRIM(x [, trim_string])` removes characters from the left of x. You can provide an optional $trim\_string$, which specifies the characters to remove. If no $trim\_string$ is provided, spaces are removed by default.

■ RTRIM(*x* [, *trim_string*]) removes characters from the right of *x*.

■ TRIM([*trim_char* FROM) *x*) removes characters from the left and right of *x*. You can provide an optional *trim_char*, which specifies the characters to remove. If no *trim_char* is provided, spaces are removed by default.

The following query uses LTRIM(), RTRIM(), and TRIM():

```
SELECT
  LTRIM('  Hello Kathy Lindsey!'),
  RTRIM('Hi Doreen Oakley!abcabc', 'abc'),
  TRIM('0' FROM '000Hey Steve Button!00000')
FROM dual;

LTRIM('HELLOKATHYLI RTRIM('HIDOREENOA TRIM('0'FROM'000H
-------------------- ------------------ -----------------
Hello Kathy Lindsey! Hi Doreen Oakley! Hey Steve Button!
```

NVL()

NVL() converts a null value to another value. NVL(*x*, *value*) returns *value* if *x* is null. Otherwise, *x* is returned.

The following query retrieves the customer_id and phone columns from the customers table. Null values in the phone column are converted by NVL() to the string Unknown Phone Number.

```
SELECT customer_id, NVL(phone, 'Unknown Phone Number')
FROM customers;

CUSTOMER_ID NVL(PHONE,'UNKNOWNPH
----------- --------------------
          1 800-555-1211
          2 800-555-1212
          3 800-555-1213
          4 800-555-1214
          5 Unknown Phone Number
```

The phone column for customer #5 is converted to Unknown Phone Number because the phone column is null for that row.

NVL2()

NVL2(*x*, *value1*, *value2*) returns *value1* if *x* is not null. Otherwise, *value2* is returned.

The following query retrieves the customer_id and phone columns from the customers table. Non-null values in the phone column are converted to Known, and null values are converted to Unknown.

```
SELECT customer_id, NVL2(phone, 'Known', 'Unknown')
FROM customers;

CUSTOMER_ID NVL2(PH
----------- -------
          1 Known
          2 Known
```

```
3 Known
4 Known
5 Unknown
```

The phone column values are converted to Known for customers #1 through #4 because the phone column values for those rows are not null. For customer #5, the phone column value is converted to Unknown because the phone column is null for that row.

REPLACE()

REPLACE(*x*, *search_string*, *replace_string*) searches *x* for *search_string* and replaces it with *replace_string*.

The following query retrieves the name column from the products table for product #1 (whose name is Modern Science) and replaces the string Science with Physics using REPLACE():

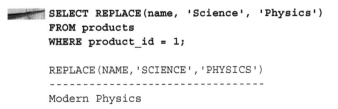

```
SELECT REPLACE(name, 'Science', 'Physics')
FROM products
WHERE product_id = 1;

REPLACE(NAME,'SCIENCE','PHYSICS')
--------------------------------
Modern Physics
```

NOTE
REPLACE() *doesn't modify the actual row in the database.*

SOUNDEX()

SOUNDEX(*x*) returns a string containing the phonetic representation of *x*. This compares words that sound similar in English but are spelled differently.

The following query retrieves the last_name column from the customers table where last_name sounds like "whyte":

```
SELECT last_name
FROM customers
WHERE SOUNDEX(last_name) = SOUNDEX('whyte');

LAST_NAME
----------
White
```

The next query retrieves last names that sound like "bloo":

```
SELECT last_name
FROM customers
WHERE SOUNDEX(last_name) = SOUNDEX('bloo');

LAST_NAME
----------
Blue
```

SUBSTR()

SUBSTR(*x*, *start* [, *length*]) returns a substring of *x* that begins at the position specified by *start*. The first position in *x* is in 1. The *start* position can be a positive number or a negative number. A positive *start* number indicates a position offset from the beginning of *x*. A negative *start* number indicates a position offset from the end of *x*. You can provide an optional *length* for the substring.

The following query uses SUBSTR() to get the seven-character substring starting at position 2 of the name column of the products table:

```
SELECT SUBSTR(name, 2, 7)
FROM products
WHERE product_id < 4;

SUBSTR(
-------
odern S
hemistr
upernov
```

The next query uses SUBSTR() to get the three-character substring starting at position –5 of the name column of the products table:

```
SELECT SUBSTR(name, -5, 3)
FROM products
WHERE product_id < 4;

SUB
---
ien
ist
rno
```

Using Expressions with Functions

You're not limited to using columns in functions. You can provide any valid expression that evaluates to a string. The following query uses the SUBSTR() function to return the substring little from the string Mary had a little lamb:

```
SELECT SUBSTR('Mary had a little lamb', 12, 6)
FROM dual;

SUBSTR
------
little
```

Combining Functions

You can use any valid combination of functions in an SQL statement. The following query combines the UPPER() and SUBSTR() functions. The output from SUBSTR() is passed to UPPER().

```
SELECT name, UPPER(SUBSTR(name, 2, 8))
FROM products
WHERE product_id < 4;
```

```
NAME                               UPPER(SU
----------------------------       --------
Modern Science                     ODERN SC
Chemistry                          HEMISTRY
Supernova                          UPERNOVA
```

NOTE
This ability to combine functions is not limited to character functions.
Any valid combination of functions will work.

Numeric Functions

The numeric functions perform calculations. These functions accept an input number, which can come from a numeric column or any expression that evaluates to a number. A calculation is then performed and a number is returned. An example numeric function is $SQRT(x)$, which returns the square root of x.

Table 4-2 shows some of the numeric functions. In the following sections, you'll learn more about some of the functions shown in Table 4-2.

ABS()

$ABS(x)$ returns the absolute value of x. The absolute value of a number is the number without any positive or negative sign. The absolute value of 10 is 10. The absolute value of –10 is 10. The following query returns the absolute value of 10 and –10:

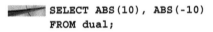

```
SELECT ABS(10), ABS(-10)
FROM dual;
```

```
   ABS(10)    ABS(-10)
---------- ----------
        10          10
```

An input parameter can be a numeric column from a table or, more generally, any valid numeric expression. The following query returns the absolute value of subtracting 30 from the `price` column from the `products` table for the first three products:

```
SELECT product_id, price, price - 30, ABS(price - 30)
FROM products
WHERE product_id < 4;
```

```
PRODUCT_ID      PRICE   PRICE-30 ABS(PRICE-30)
---------- ---------- ---------- -------------
         1      19.95     -10.05         10.05
         2         30          0             0
         3      25.99      -4.01          4.01
```

Function	Description	Examples
ABS(*x*)	Returns the absolute value of *x*.	ABS(10) = 10 ABS(-10) = 10
ACOS(*x*)	Returns the arccosine of *x*.	ACOS(1) = 0 ACOS(-1) = 3.14159265
ASIN(*x*)	Returns the arcsine of *x*.	ASIN(1) = 1.57079633 ASIN(-1) = -1.5707963
ATAN(*x*)	Returns the arctangent of *x*.	ATAN(1) = .785398163 ATAN(-1) = -.78539816
ATAN2(*x*, *y*)	Returns the arctangent of *x* and *y*.	ATAN2(1, -1) = 2.35619449
BITAND(*x*, *y*)	Returns the result of performing a bitwise AND on *x* and *y*.	BITAND(0, 0) = 0 BITAND(0, 1) = 0 BITAND(1, 0) = 0 BITAND(1, 1) = 1 BITAND(1010, 1100) = 64
COS(*x*)	Returns the cosine of *x*, where *x* is an angle in radians.	COS(90 * 3.1415926) = 1 COS(45 * 3.1415926) = -1
COSH(*x*)	Returns the hyperbolic cosine of *x*.	COSH(3.1415926) = 11.5919527
CEIL(*x*)	Returns the smallest integer greater than or equal to *x*.	CEIL(5.8) = 6 CEIL(-5.2) = -5
EXP(*x*)	Returns the result of the number e raised to the power *x*, where e is approximately 2.71828183.	EXP(1) = 2.71828183 EXP(2) = 7.3890561
FLOOR(*x*)	Returns the largest integer less than or equal to *x*.	FLOOR(5.8) = 5 FLOOR(-5.2) = -6
GREATEST(*values*)	Returns the largest value from a list of *values*.	GREATEST(3, 4, 1) = 4 GREATEST(50 / 2, EXP(2)) = 25
LEAST(*values*)	Returns the smallest value from a list of *values*.	LEAST(3, 4, 1) = 1 LEAST(50 / 2, EXP(2)) = 7.3890561

(Continued)

TABLE 4-2.   *Numeric Functions*

Function	Description	Examples
LOG(x, y)	Returns the logarithm in base x of y.	LOG(2, 4) = 2 LOG(2, 5) = 2.32192809
LN(x)	Returns the natural logarithm of x.	LN(2.71828183) = 1
MOD(x, y)	Returns the remainder when x is divided by y.	MOD(8, 3) = 2 MOD(8, 4) = 0
POWER(x, y)	Returns the result of x raised to the power y.	POWER(2, 1) = 2 POWER(2, 3) = 8
ROUND(x [, y])	Returns the result of rounding x to an optional y decimal places. If y is omitted, x is rounded to zero decimal places. If y is negative, x is rounded to the left of the decimal point.	ROUND(5.75) = 6 ROUND(5.75, 1) = 5.8 ROUND(5.75, -1) = 10
SIGN(x)	Returns –1 if x is negative, 1 if x is positive, or 0 if x is zero.	SIGN(-5) = -1 SIGN(5) = 1 SIGN(0) = 0
SIN(x)	Returns the sine of x.	SIN(0) = 0
SINH(x)	Returns the hyperbolic sine of x.	SINH(1) = 1.17520119
SQRT(x)	Returns the square root of x.	SQRT(25) = 5 SQRT(5) = 2.23606798
TAN(x)	Returns the tangent of x.	TAN(0) = 0
TANH(x)	Returns the hyperbolic tangent of x.	TANH(1) = .761594156
TRUNC(x [, y])	Returns the result of truncating x to an optional y decimal places. If y is omitted, x is truncated to zero decimal places. If y is negative, x is truncated to the left of the decimal point.	TRUNC(5.75) = 5 TRUNC(5.75, 1) = 5.7 TRUNC(5.75, -1) = 0

TABLE 4-2. *Numeric Functions*

CEIL()

CEIL (*x*) returns the smallest integer greater than or equal to *x*. The following query uses
CEIL () to return the absolute values of 5.8 and –5.2:

```
SELECT CEIL(5.8), CEIL(-5.2)
FROM dual;

 CEIL(5.8) CEIL(-5.2)
---------- ----------
        6         -5
```

These results show the following:

- The ceiling for 5.8 is 6, because 6 is the smallest integer greater than 5.8.
- The ceiling for –5.2 is –5, because –5.2 is negative, and the smallest integer greater than –5.2 is –5.

FLOOR()

FLOOR (*x*) returns the largest integer less than or equal to *x*. The following query uses FLOOR ()
to return the absolute value of 5.8 and –5.2:

```
SELECT FLOOR(5.8), FLOOR(-5.2)
FROM dual;

FLOOR(5.8) FLOOR(-5.2)
---------- -----------
        5          -6
```

These results show the following:

- The floor for 5.8 is 5, because 5 is the largest integer less than 5.8.
- The floor for –5.2 is –6, because –5.2 is negative, and the largest integer less than –5.2 is –6.

GREATEST()

GREATEST (*values*) returns the largest value from a list of *values*. The following query uses
GREATEST () to return the largest value from the list 3, 4, and 1:

```
SELECT GREATEST(3, 4, 1)
FROM dual;

GREATEST(3,4,1)
---------------
              4
```

The next query uses GREATEST () to return the largest value from the list of values produced
by calculating 50 divided by 2 and EXP (2):

```
SELECT GREATEST(50 / 2, EXP(2))
FROM dual;
```

```
GREATEST(50/2,EXP(2))
--------------------
                  25
```

LEAST()

LEAST(*values*) returns the smallest value from a list of *values*. The following query uses LEAST() to return the smallest value from the list 3, 4, and 1:

```
SELECT LEAST(3, 4, 1)
FROM dual;
```

```
LEAST(3,4,1)
------------
           1
```

The next query uses LEAST() to return the smallest value from the list of values produced by calculating 50 divided by 2 and EXP(2):

```
SELECT LEAST(50 / 2, EXP(2))
FROM dual;
```

```
LEAST(50/2,EXP(2))
------------------
         7.3890561
```

POWER()

POWER(x, y) returns the result of x raised to the power y. The following query uses POWER() to return 2 raised to the power 1 and 3:

```
SELECT POWER(2, 1), POWER(2, 3)
FROM dual;
```

```
POWER(2,1) POWER(2,3)
---------- ----------
         2          8
```

These results show the following:

- When 2 is raised to the power 1, which is equivalent to 2*1, the result is 2.
- When 2 is raised to the power 3, which is equivalent to 2*2*2, the result is 8.

ROUND()

ROUND(x, [y]) returns the result of rounding x to an optional y decimal places. If y is omitted, x is rounded to zero decimal places. If y is negative, x is rounded to the left of the decimal point.

The following query uses ROUND() to return the result of rounding 5.75 to zero, 1, and –1 decimal places:

```
SELECT ROUND(5.75), ROUND(5.75, 1), ROUND(5.75, -1)
FROM dual;
```

```
ROUND(5.75)  ROUND(5.75,1)  ROUND(5.75,-1)
-----------  -------------  --------------
          6            5.8              10
```

These results show the following:

- 5.75 rounded to zero decimal places is 6.
- 5.75 rounded to one decimal place to the right of the decimal point is 5.8.
- 5.75 rounded to one decimal place to the left of the decimal point, as indicated using a negative sign, is 10.

SIGN()

$SIGN(x)$ returns the sign of x. $SIGN()$ returns -1 if x is negative, 1 if x is positive, or 0 if x is zero. The following query returns the sign of -5, 5, and 0:

```
SELECT SIGN(-5), SIGN(5), SIGN(0)
FROM dual;
```

```
 SIGN(-5)     SIGN(5)     SIGN(0)
----------  ----------  ----------
       -1           1           0
```

These results show the following:

- The sign of -5 is -1.
- The sign of 5 is 1.
- The sign of 0 is 0.

SQRT()

$SQRT(x)$ returns the square root of x. The following query returns the square root of 25 and 5:

```
SELECT SQRT(25), SQRT(5)
FROM dual;
```

```
  SQRT(25)      SQRT(5)
----------   ----------
         5   2.23606798
```

TRUNC()

$TRUNC(x, [y])$ returns the result of truncating the number x to an optional y decimal places. If y is omitted, x is truncated to zero decimal places. If y is negative, x is truncated to the left of the decimal point. The following query truncates 5.75 to zero, 1, and -1 decimal places:

```
SELECT TRUNC(5.75), TRUNC(5.75, 1), TRUNC(5.75, -1)
FROM dual;
```

```
TRUNC(5.75)  TRUNC(5.75,1)  TRUNC(5.75,-1)
-----------  -------------  --------------
          5            5.7               0
```

These results show the following:

- 5.75 truncated to zero decimal places is 5.
- 5.75 truncated to one decimal place to the right of the decimal point is 5.7.
- 5.75 truncated to one decimal place to the left of the decimal point, as indicated using a negative sign, is 0.

Conversion Functions

Sometimes you need to convert a value from one data type to another. For example, you might want to reformat the price of a product that is stored as a number (for example, 1346.95) to a string containing dollar signs and commas (for example, $1,346.95). You use a conversion function to convert a value from one data type to another.

Table 4-3 shows some of the conversion functions.

Function	Description
ASCIISTR(x)	Converts x to an ASCII string, where x can be a string in any character set. Non-ASCII characters are converted to the form \xxxx, where xxxx represents a Unicode value. Unicode enables representation of text in a large number of different languages.
BIN_TO_NUM(x)	Converts a binary number x to a NUMBER.
CAST(x AS $type$)	Converts x to a compatible database type specified in $type$.
CHARTOROWID(x)	Converts x to a ROWID. As described in Chapter 2, a ROWID can store the location of a row.
COMPOSE(x)	Converts x to a Unicode string. The returned string uses the same character set as x.
CONVERT(x, $source\_char\_set$, $dest\_char\_set$)	Converts x from $source\_char\_set$ to $dest\_char\_set$.
DECODE(x, $search$, $result$, $default$)	Compares x with the value in $search$. If equal, DECODE() returns the value in $result$. Otherwise, the value in $default$ is returned. You'll learn about DECODE() in Chapter 7.
DECOMPOSE(x)	Converts x to a Unicode string after decomposition of the string into the same character set as x.
HEXTORAW(x)	Converts the character x containing hexadecimal digits (base-16) to a binary number (RAW). The function returns the RAW number.

TABLE 4-3. *Conversion Functions*

Function	Description
NUMTODSINTERVAL(*x*)	Converts the number *x* to an INTERVAL DAY TO SECOND. You'll learn about date and time interval functions in Chapter 5.
NUMTOYMINTERVAL(*x*)	Converts the number *x* to an INTERVAL YEAR TO MONTH.
RAWTOHEX(*x*)	Converts the RAW binary number *x* to a VARCHAR2 string containing the equivalent hexadecimal number.
RAWTONHEX(*x*)	Converts the RAW binary number *x* to an NVARCHAR2 string containing the equivalent hexadecimal number. NVARCHAR2 stores a string using the national character set.
ROWIDTOCHAR(*x*)	Converts the ROWID *x* to a VARCHAR2 string.
ROWIDTONCHAR(*x*)	Converts the ROWID *x* to an NVARCHAR2 string.
TO_BINARY_DOUBLE(*x*)	Converts *x* to a BINARY_DOUBLE. This function was introduced in Oracle Database 10*g*.
TO_BINARY_FLOAT(*x*)	Converts *x* to a BINARY_FLOAT. This function was introduced in Oracle Database 10*g*.
TO_BLOB(*x*)	Converts *x* to a binary large object (BLOB). A BLOB is used to store large amounts of binary data. You'll learn about large objects in Chapter 14.
TO_CHAR(*x* [, *format*])	Converts *x* to a VARCHAR2 string. You can provide an optional *format* that indicates the format of *x*.
TO_CLOB(*x*)	Converts *x* to a character large object (CLOB). A CLOB is used to store large amounts of character data.
TO_DATE(*x* [, *format*])	Converts *x* to a DATE. You'll learn about dates in Chapter 5.
TO_DSINTERVAL(*x*)	Converts the string *x* to an INTERVAL DAY TO SECOND.
TO_MULTI_BYTE(*x*)	Converts the single-byte characters in *x* to their corresponding multi-byte characters. The return type is the same as the type for *x*.
TO_NCHAR(*x*)	Converts *x* in the database character set to an NVARCHAR2 string.
TO_NCLOB(*x*)	Converts *x* to a large object NCLOB. An NCLOB is used to store large amounts of national language character data.
TO_NUMBER(*x* [, *format*])	Converts *x* to a NUMBER. An optional number *format* can also be provided.
TO_SINGLE_BYTE(*x*)	Converts the multi-byte characters in *x* to their corresponding single-byte characters. The return type is the same as the type for *x*.

(Continued)

TABLE 4-3. *Conversion Functions*

Function	Description
TO_TIMESTAMP(x)	Converts the string x to a TIMESTAMP. You'll learn about timestamps in Chapter 5.
TO_TIMESTAMP_TZ(x)	Converts the string x to a TIMESTAMP WITH TIME ZONE.
TO_YMINTERVAL(x)	Converts the string x to an INTERVAL YEAR TO MONTH. You'll learn about time intervals in Chapter 5.
TRANSLATE(x, from_string, to_string)	Converts all occurrences of from_string in x to to_string. You'll learn about TRANSLATE() in Chapter 7.
UNISTR(x)	Converts the characters in x to an NCHAR string. NCHAR stores characters using the national language character set. UNISTR() supports Unicode. You can specify the Unicode value of characters in x. A Unicode value has the form \xxxx, where xxxx is the hexadecimal value of a character in the Unicode format.

TABLE 4-3. *Conversion Functions*

You'll learn more about many of the conversion functions in the following sections. You'll learn about some of the other conversion functions as you progress through this book (those functions use data types that are described in later chapters, and you need to know how to use those data types first).

Some of the conversion functions use national language character sets and Unicode. Unicode enables representation of text in a large number of different languages. For more details, see the *Oracle Database Globalization Support Guide* from Oracle Corporation.

ASCIISTR()

ASCIISTR(x) converts x to an ASCII string, where x can be a string in any character set. Non-ASCII characters are converted to the form \xxxx, where xxxx represents a Unicode value.

The following query uses ASCIISTR() to convert the string 'ABCÄCDE' to an ASCII string. The dots above the A are collectively known as an umlaut. In the example, notice that Ä is converted to \017D, which is the Unicode value for the Ä character.

```
SELECT ASCIISTR('ABC Ä CDE')
FROM DUAL;

ASCIISTR('ABC
-------------
ABC \017D CDE
```

The next query uses ASCIISTR() to convert the characters returned by the CHR() function to their Unicode values. CHR(x) returns the character that has the ASCII value x.

```
SELECT ASCIISTR(CHR(128) || ' ' || CHR(129) || ' ' || CHR(130))
FROM DUAL;
```

```
ASCIISTR(CHR(128)
-----------------
\20AC \0081 \201A
```

BIN_TO_NUM()

BIN_TO_NUM(x) converts a binary number x to a NUMBER.

The following query uses BIN_TO_NUM() to convert various binary numbers to their decimal equivalents:

```
SELECT
  BIN_TO_NUM(1, 0, 1),
  BIN_TO_NUM(1, 1, 0),
  BIN_TO_NUM(1, 1, 1, 0)
FROM dual;

BIN_TO_NUM(1,0,1) BIN_TO_NUM(1,1,0) BIN_TO_NUM(1,1,1,0)
----------------- ----------------- -------------------
                5                 6                  14
```

CAST()

CAST(x AS type) converts x to a compatible database type specified by type. The following table shows the valid type conversions (valid conversions are marked with an X).

To	From BINARY_ FLOAT BINARY_ DOUBLE	CHAR VARCHAR2	NUMBER	DATE TIMESTAMP INTERVAL	RAW	ROWID UROWID	NCHAR NVARCHAR2
BINARY_ FLOAT BINARY_ DOUBLE	X	X	X				X
CHAR VARCHAR2	X	X	X	X	X	X	
NUMBER	X	X	X				X
DATE TIMESTAMP INTERVAL		X		X			
RAW		X			X		
ROWID UROWID		X				X	
NCHAR NVARCHAR2	X		X	X	X	X	X

The following query uses CAST() to convert literal values to specific types:

```
SELECT
  CAST(12345.67 AS VARCHAR2(10)),
  CAST('9A4F' AS RAW(2)),
  CAST('05-JUL-07' AS DATE),
  CAST(12345.678 AS NUMBER(10,2))
FROM dual;
```

```
CAST(12345  CAST CAST('05-  CAST(12345.678ASNUMBER(10,2))
----------  ---- --------- ------------------------------
12345.67    9A4F 05-JUL-07                       12345.68
```

You can also convert column values from one type to another, as shown in the following query:

```
SELECT
  CAST(price AS VARCHAR2(10)),
  CAST(price + 2 AS NUMBER(7,2)),
  CAST(price AS BINARY_DOUBLE)
FROM products
WHERE product_id = 1;

CAST(PRICE CAST(PRICE+2ASNUMBER(7,2)) CAST(PRICEASBINARY_DOUBLE)
---------- -------------------------- --------------------------
19.95                          21.95                  1.995E+001
```

You'll see additional examples in Chapter 5 that show how to use CAST() to convert dates, times, and intervals. Also, Chapter 14 shows how you use CAST() to convert collections of database values.

CHARTOROWID()

CHARTOROWID(*x*) converts *x* to a ROWID. As described in Chapter 2, a ROWID can store the location of a row.

The following example retrieves the rowid for customer #1 and then passes that rowid to CHARTOROWID() to retrieve customer #1:

```
SELECT ROWID
FROM customers
WHERE customer_id = 1;

ROWID
------------------
AAAF4yAABAAAHeKAAA

SELECT *
FROM customers
WHERE ROWID = CHARTOROWID('AAAF4yAABAAAHeKAAA');

CUSTOMER_ID FIRST_NAME LAST_NAME  DOB       PHONE
----------- ---------- ---------- --------- ------------
          1 John       Brown      01-JAN-65 800-555-1211
```

NOTE
If you run the example, your rowid will be different.

COMPOSE()

COMPOSE(*x*) converts *x* to a Unicode string. The returned string uses the same character set as *x*.

The following query uses COMPOSE() to an add an umlaut to an o character (ö) and a circumflex to an e character (ê):

```
SELECT
  COMPOSE('o' || UNISTR('\0308')),
  COMPOSE('e' || UNISTR('\0302'))
FROM DUAL;

C C
- -
ö ê
```

The UNISTR(*x*) function converts the characters in *x* to an NCHAR string. NCHAR stores characters using the national language character set. A Unicode value has the form \xxxx, where xxxx is the hexadecimal value of a character in the Unicode format.

NOTE
Depending on your operating system and database settings, you might see different results from those shown in the example query. You can use SQL Developer to run the query and see the special Unicode characters in the output. This comment applies to the other examples in this chapter that use special characters.

CONVERT()

CONVERT(*x*, *source_char_set*, *dest_char_set*) converts *x* from *source_char_set* to *dest_char_set*.

The following query uses CONVERT() to convert a string from the US7ASCII character set (U.S. 7-bit ASCII) to the WE8ISO8859P1 character set (Western European 8-bit ISO 8859 Part 1):

```
SELECT CONVERT('Ä Ê Í Ó A B C','US7ASCII','WE8ISO8859P1')
FROM DUAL;

CONVERT('ÄEIO
-------------
A E I O A B C
```

DECOMPOSE()

DECOMPOSE(*x*) converts *x* to a Unicode string after decomposition of the string into the same character set as *x*. For example, an o-umlaut (ö) is returned as the o followed by the umlaut.

The following query uses DECOMPOSE() to split out the umlaut from ö and the circumflex from ê:

```
SELECT DECOMPOSE('öê')
FROM DUAL;

DECO
----
o¨e^
```

HEXTORAW()

HEXTORAW (*x*) converts the character *x* containing hexadecimal digits (base-16) to a binary number (RAW). The function returns the RAW number.

The following query uses HEXTORAW () to convert a hexadecimal number to a RAW number:

```
SELECT UTL_RAW.CAST_TO_VARCHAR2(HEXTORAW('41414743'))
FROM DUAL;

UTL_RAW.CAST_TO_VARCHAR2(HEXTORAW('41414743'))
----------------------------------------------
AAGC
```

The UTL_RAW.CAST_TO_VARCHAR2() function converts the RAW number returned by HEXTORAW() to a VARCHAR2 for viewing in SQL*Plus.

RAWTOHEX()

RAWTOHEX (*x*) converts the RAW binary number *x* to a VARCHAR2 string containing the equivalent hexadecimal number.

The following query uses RAWTOHEX() to convert a RAW number to a hexadecimal number:

```
SELECT RAWTOHEX(41414743)
FROM DUAL;

RAWTOHEX(4
----------
C42A2A302C
```

ROWIDTOCHAR()

ROWIDTOCHAR (*x*) converts the ROWID *x* to a VARCHAR2 string.

The following query shows the use of ROWIDTOCHAR() in the WHERE clause:

```
SELECT ROWID, customer_id, first_name, last_name
FROM customers
WHERE ROWIDTOCHAR(ROWID) LIKE '%KAAA%';

ROWID              CUSTOMER_ID FIRST_NAME LAST_NAME
------------------ ----------- ---------- ----------
AAAF4yAABAAAHeKAAA           1 John       Brown
```

NOTE
If you run the example, your rowid will be different.

TO_BINARY_DOUBLE()

TO_BINARY_DOUBLE (*x*) converts *x* to a BINARY_DOUBLE.

The following query uses TO_BINARY_DOUBLE() to convert a number:

```
SELECT TO_BINARY_DOUBLE(1087623)
FROM dual;

TO_BINARY_DOUBLE(1087623)
-------------------------
               1.088E+006
```

TO_BINARY_FLOAT()

TO_BINARY_FLOAT(x) converts x to a BINARY_FLOAT. The following query uses
TO_BINARY_FLOAT() to convert a number:

```
SELECT TO_BINARY_FLOAT(10623)
FROM dual;

TO_BINARY_FLOAT(10623)
----------------------
            1.062E+004
```

TO_CHAR()

TO_CHAR(x [, format]) converts x to a string. You can also provide an optional format that
indicates the format of x. The structure format depends on whether x is a number or date. You'll
learn how to use TO_CHAR() to convert a number to a string in this section, and you'll see how
to convert a date to a string in Chapter 5.

Let's take a look at a couple of simple queries that use TO_CHAR() to convert a number to a
string. The following query converts 12345.67 to a string:

```
SELECT TO_CHAR(12345.67)
FROM dual;

TO_CHAR(1
---------
 12345.67
```

The next query uses TO_CHAR() to convert 12345678.90 to a string and specifies that this
number is to be converted using the format 99,999.99. The string returned by TO_CHAR()
contains a comma to delimit the thousands.

```
SELECT TO_CHAR(12345.67, '99,999.99')
FROM dual;

TO_CHAR(12
----------
 12,345.67
```

The optional format string you can pass to TO_CHAR() has a number of parameters that
affect the string returned by TO_CHAR(). Some of these parameters are listed in Table 4-4.

Parameter	Format Example	Description
9	999	Returns digits in specified positions, with a leading negative sign if the number is negative.
0	0999 9990	0999: Returns a number with leading zeros. 9990: Returns a number with trailing zeros.
.	999.99	Returns a decimal point in the specified position.
,	9,999	Returns a comma in the specified position.
$	$999	Returns a leading dollar sign.
B	B9.99	If the integer part of a fixed-point number is zero, returns spaces for the zeros.
C	C999	Returns the ISO currency symbol in the specified position. The symbol comes from the NLS_ISO_CURRENCY database parameter set by a database administrator.
D	9D99	Returns the decimal point symbol in the specified position. The symbol comes from the NLS_NUMERIC_CHARACTER database parameter (the default is a period character).
EEEE	9.99EEEE	Returns the number using the scientific notation.
FM	FM90.9	Removes leading and trailing spaces from the number.
G	9G999	Returns the group separator symbol in the specified position. The symbol comes from the NLS_NUMERIC_CHARACTER database parameter.
L	L999	Returns the local currency symbol in the specified position. The symbol comes from the NLS_CURRENCY database parameter.
MI	999MI	Returns a negative number with a trailing minus sign. Returns a positive number with a trailing space.
PR	999PR	Returns a negative number in angle brackets < >. Returns a positive number with leading and trailing spaces.
RN rn	RN rn	Returns the number as Roman numerals. RN returns uppercase numerals. rn returns lowercase numerals. The number must be an integer between 1 and 3999.
S	S999 999S	S999: Returns a negative number with a leading negative sign. Returns a positive number with a leading positive sign. 999S: Returns a negative number with a trailing negative sign. Returns a positive number with a trailing positive sign.
TM	TM	Returns the number using the minimum number of characters. The default is TM9, which returns the number using fixed notation unless the number of characters is greater than 64. If greater than 64, the number is returned using scientific notation.

TABLE 4-4. *Numeric Formatting Parameters*

Parameter	Format Example	Description
U	U999	Returns the dual currency symbol (for example, Euro) in the specified position. The symbol comes from the NLS_DUAL_CURRENCY database parameter.
V	99V99	Returns the number multiplied by 10^x, where x is the number of 9 characters after the V. If necessary, the number is rounded.
X	XXXX	Returns the number in hexadecimal. If the number is not an integer, the number is rounded to an integer.

TABLE 4-4. *Numeric Formatting Parameters*

Let's look at some more examples that convert numbers to strings using TO_CHAR(). The following table shows examples of calling TO_CHAR(), along with the output returned.

TO_CHAR() Function Call	Output
TO_CHAR(12345.67, '99999.99')	12345.67
TO_CHAR(12345.67, '99,999.99')	12,345.67
TO_CHAR(-12345.67, '99,999.99')	-12,345.67
TO_CHAR(12345.67, '099,999.99')	012,345.67
TO_CHAR(12345.67, '99,999.9900')	12,345.6700
TO_CHAR(12345.67, '$99,999.99')	$12,345.67
TO_CHAR(0.67, 'B9.99')	.67
TO_CHAR(12345.67, 'C99,999.99')	USD12,345.67
TO_CHAR(12345.67, '99999D99')	12345.67
TO_CHAR(12345.67, '99999.99EEEE')	1.23E+04
TO_CHAR(0012345.6700, 'FM99999.99')	12345.67
TO_CHAR(12345.67, '99999G99')	123,46
TO_CHAR(12345.67, 'L99,999.99')	$12,345.67
TO_CHAR(-12345.67, '99,999.99MI')	12,345.67
TO_CHAR(-12345.67, '99,999.99PR')	12,345.67
TO_CHAR(2007, 'RN')	MMVII
TO_CHAR(12345.67, 'TM')	12345.67
TO_CHAR(12345.67, 'U99,999.99')	$12,345.67
TO_CHAR(12345.67, '99999V99')	1234567

TO_CHAR() returns a string of pound characters (#) if you try to format a number that contains too many digits for the format. For example:

```
SELECT TO_CHAR(12345678.90, '99,999.99')
FROM dual;

TO_CHAR(12
----------
##########
```

Pound characters are returned by TO_CHAR() because the number 12345678.90 has more digits than those allowed in the format 99,999.99.

You can also use TO_CHAR() to convert columns containing numbers to strings. For example, the following query uses TO_CHAR() to convert the price column of the products table to a string:

```
SELECT
    product_id, 'The price of the product is' || TO_CHAR(price, '$99.99')
FROM products
WHERE product_id < 5;

PRODUCT_ID 'THEPRICEOFTHEPRODUCTIS'||TO_CHAR(
---------- ----------------------------------
         1 The price of the product is $19.95
         2 The price of the product is $30.00
         3 The price of the product is $25.99
         4 The price of the product is $13.95
```

TO_MULTI_BYTE()

TO_MULTI_BYTE(x) converts the single-byte characters in x to their corresponding multi-byte characters. The return type is the same as the type for x.

The following query uses TO_MULTI_BYTE() to convert a letter to a multi-byte representation:

```
SELECT TO_MULTI_BYTE('A')
FROM dual;

T
-
A
```

TO_NUMBER()

TO_NUMBER(x [, format]) converts x to a number. You can provide an optional *format* to indicate the format of x. The *format* string can use the same parameters as those listed earlier in Table 4-4.

The following query converts the string 970.13 to a number using TO_NUMBER():

```
SELECT TO_NUMBER('970.13')
FROM dual;
```

```
TO_NUMBER('970.13')
-------------------
             970.13
```

The next query converts the string 970.13 to a number using TO_NUMBER() and then adds 25.5 to that number:

```
SELECT TO_NUMBER('970.13') + 25.5
FROM dual;
```

```
TO_NUMBER('970.13')+25.5
------------------------
                  995.63
```

The next query converts the string -$12,345.67 to a number, passing the format string $99,999.99 to TO_NUMBER():

```
SELECT TO_NUMBER('-$12,345.67', '$99,999.99')
FROM dual;
```

```
TO_NUMBER('-$12,345.67','$99,999.99')
-------------------------------------
                           -12345.67
```

TO_SINGLE_BYTE()

TO_SINGLE_BYTE(x) converts the multi-byte characters in x to their corresponding single-byte characters. The return type is the same as the type for x.

The following query uses TO_SINGLE_BYTE() to convert a letter to a single-byte representation:

```
SELECT TO_SINGLE_BYTE('A')
FROM DUAL;
```

```
T
-
A
```

UNISTR()

UNISTR(x) converts the characters in x to an NCHAR string. NCHAR stores characters using the national language character set. UNISTR() also provides support for Unicode. You can specify the Unicode value of characters in the string. A Unicode value has the form \xxxx, where xxxx is the hexadecimal value of a character in the Unicode format.

The following query uses UNISTR() to display an umlaut and a circumflex:

```
SELECT UNISTR('\0308'), UNISTR('\0302')
FROM DUAL;
```

```
U U
- -
.. ^
```

Regular Expression Functions

In this section, you'll learn about regular expressions and their associated Oracle database functions. These functions allow you to search for a pattern of characters in a string. For example, let's say you want to obtain the years 1965 through 1968 from the following list of years:

```
1964
1965
1966
1967
1968
1969
1970
1971
```

To obtain the years 1965 through 1968, you use the following regular expression:

```
^196[5-8]$
```

The regular expression contains a number of *metacharacters*. In the example, `^`, `[5-8]`, and `$` are the metacharacters:

- `^` matches the beginning position of a string.
- `[5-8]` matches characters between 5 and 8.
- `$` matches the end position of a string.

Therefore, `^196[5-8]$` matches 1965, 1966, 1967, and 1968, which are the years you wanted to get from the list shown earlier.

The next example uses the following string, which contains a quote from Shakespeare's *Romeo and Juliet*:

```
But, soft! What light through yonder window breaks?
```

To obtain the substring `light`, you use the following regular expression:

```
l[[:alpha:]]{4}
```

In this regular expression, `[[:alpha:]]` and `{4}` are the metacharacters:

- `[[:alpha:]]` matches any alphanumeric character from A to Z and a to z.
- `{4}` repeats the previous match four times.

When `l`, `[[:alpha:]]`, and `{4}` are combined, they match a sequence of five letters starting with `l`. Therefore, the regular expression `l[[:alpha:]]{4}` matches `light` in the string.

Table 4-5 lists some of the metacharacters you can use in a regular expression, along with their meaning and an example of their use.

Oracle Database 10g Release 2 introduced a number of Perl-influenced metacharacters, which are shown in Table 4-6.

Metacharacter	Meaning	Examples
\	Matches a special character or a literal or performs a backreference. (A backreference repeats the previous match.)	\n matches the newline character. \\ matches \. \(matches (. \) matches).
^	Matches the position at the start of the string.	^A matches A if A is the first character in the string.
$	Matches the position at the end of the string.	$B matches B if B is the last character in the string.
*	Matches the preceding character zero or more times.	ba*rk matches brk, bark, baark, and so on.
+	Matches the preceding character one or more times.	ba+rk matches bark, baark, and so on, but not brk.
?	Matches the preceding character zero or one time.	ba?rk matches brk and bark only.
{n}	Matches a character exactly n times, where n is an integer.	hob{2}it matches hobbit.
{n,m}	Matches a character at least n times and at most m times, where n and m are both integers.	hob{2,3}it matches hobbit and hobbbit only.
.	Matches any single character except null.	hob.it matches hobait, hobbit, and so on.
(pattern)	A subexpression that matches the specified pattern. You use subexpressions to build up complex regular expressions. You can access the individual matches, known as *captures*, from this type of subexpression.	anatom(y|ies) matches anatomy and anatomies.
x|y	Matches x or y, where x and y are one or more characters.	war|peace matches war or peace.
[abc]	Matches any of the enclosed characters.	[ab]bc matches abc and bbc.
[a-z]	Matches any character in the specified range.	[a-c]bc matches abc, bbc, and cbc.

(Continued)

TABLE 4-5. *Regular Expression Metacharacters*

Metacharacter	Meaning	Examples
[: :]	Specifies a character class and matches any character in that class.	[:alphanum:] matches alphanumeric characters 0 to 9, A to Z, and a to z. [:alpha:] matches alphabetic characters A to Z and a to z. [:blank:] matches a space or tab. [:digit:] matches digits 0 to 9. [:graph:] matches non-blank characters. [:lower:] matches lowercase alphabetic characters a to z. [:print:] is similar to [:graph:] except [:print:] includes the space character. [:punct:] matches punctuation characters .,"', and so on. [:space:] matches all whitespace characters. [:upper:] matches all uppercase alphabetic characters A to Z. [:xdigit:] matches characters permissible in a hexadecimal number 0 to 9, A to F, and a to f.
[..]	Matches one collation element, like a multicharacter element.	No example.
[==]	Specifies equivalence classes.	No example.
\n	This is a backreference to an earlier capture, where n is a positive integer.	(.)\1 matches two consecutive identical characters. The (.) captures any single character except null, and the \1 repeats the capture, matching the same character again, therefore matching two consecutive identical characters.

TABLE 4-5. *Regular Expression Metacharacters*

Metacharacter	Meaning
\d	Digit character
\D	Non-digit character
\w	Word character
\W	Non-word character
\s	Whitespace character
\S	Non-whitespace character
\A	Matches only at the beginning of a string or before a newline character at the end of a string
\Z	Matches only at the end of a string
*?	Matches the preceding pattern element 0 or more times
+?	Matches the preceding pattern element 1 or more times
??	Matches the preceding pattern element 0 or 1 time
{n}	Matches the preceding pattern element exactly n times
{n,}	Matches the preceding pattern element at least n times
{n,m}	Matches the preceding pattern element at least n but not more than m times

TABLE 4-6. *Perl-Influenced Metacharacters*

Table 4-7 shows the regular expression functions. Regular expression functions were introduced in Oracle Database 10g, and additional items were added to Oracle Database 11g, as indicated in the table. You'll learn more about the regular expression functions in the following sections.

REGEXP_LIKE()

REGEXP_LIKE(x, pattern [, match_option]) searches x for the regular expression defined in the *pattern* parameter. You can also provide an optional *match_option* that can be set to one of the following characters:

- 'c', which specifies case-sensitive matching (the default)
- 'I', which specifies case-insensitive matching
- 'n', which allows you to use the match-any-character operator
- 'm', which treats x as a multiple line

Function	Description
`REGEXP_LIKE(x, pattern [, match_option])`	Searches x for the regular expression defined in the `pattern` parameter. You can also provide an optional `match_option`, which can be set to one of the following characters:

- `'c'`, which specifies case-sensitive matching (this is the default)
- `'I'`, which specifies case-insensitive matching
- `'n'`, which allows you to use the match-any-character operator
- `'m'`, which treats x as a multiple line

Function	Description
`REGEXP_INSTR(x, pattern [, start [, occurrence [, return_option [, match_option [, subexp_option]]]]])`	Searches x for `pattern` and returns the position at which `pattern` occurs. You can provide the following optional parameters:

- A `start` position in x to begin the search. The default is 1, which is the first character in x.
- An `occurrence` that indicates which occurrence of `pattern` should be returned. The default is 1, which means the function returns the position of the first occurrence of `pattern` in x.
- A `return_option` that indicates what integer to return. 0 specifies the integer to return is the position of the first character in x. 1 specifies the integer to return is the position of the character in x after the occurrence.
- A `match_option` to change the default matching. Works in the same way as described for `REGEXP_LIKE()`.
- A `subexp_option` (introduced in Oracle Database 11g) works as follows: for a pattern with subexpressions, `subexp_option` is a non-negative integer from 0 to 9 indicating which subexpression in `pattern` is the target of the function. For example, consider the following expression:

  `0123(((abc)(de)f)ghi)45(678)`

  This expression has five subexpressions in the following order: "abcdefghi", "abcdef", "abc", "de", and "678".
  If `subexp_option` is 0, the position of `pattern` is returned. If `pattern` does not have the correct number of subexpressions, then the function returns 0. A null `subexp_option` value returns null. The default value for `subexp_option` is 0.

TABLE 4-7. *Regular Expression Functions*

Function	Description
REGEXP_REPLACE(x, pattern [, replace_string [, start [, occurrence [, match_option]]]])	Searches x for the pattern and replaces it with replace_string. The other options have the same meaning as those described earlier.
REGEXP_SUBSTR(x, pattern [, start [, occurrence [, match_option [, subexp_option]]]])	Returns a substring of x that matches pattern. The search begins at the position specified by start. The other options have the same meaning as described earlier. The subexp_option (introduced in Oracle Database 11g) works in the same way as described for REGEXP_INSTR().
REGEXP_COUNT(x, pattern [, start [, match_option]])	Introduced in Oracle Database 11g. Searches in x for the pattern and returns the number of times the pattern is found in x. You can provide the following optional parameters: ■ A start position in x to begin the search. The default is 1, which is the first character in x. ■ A match_option to change the default matching. Works in the same way as described for REGEXP_LIKE().

TABLE 4-7. *Regular Expression Functions*

The following query retrieves customers whose date of birth is between 1965 and 1968 using REGEXP_LIKE():

```
SELECT customer_id, first_name, last_name, dob
FROM customers
WHERE REGEXP_LIKE(TO_CHAR(dob, 'YYYY'), '^196[5-8]$');

CUSTOMER_ID FIRST_NAME LAST_NAME  DOB
----------- ---------- ---------- ---------
          1 John       Brown      01-JAN-65
          2 Cynthia    Green      05-FEB-68
```

The next query retrieves customers whose first name starts with J or j. The regular expression passed to REGEXP_LIKE() is ^j and the match option is i (i indicates case-insensitive matching, and so in this example ^j matches J or j).

```
SELECT customer_id, first_name, last_name, dob
FROM customers
WHERE REGEXP_LIKE(first_name, '^j', 'i');
```

```
CUSTOMER_ID FIRST_NAME LAST_NAME  DOB
----------- ---------- ---------- ---------
          1 John       Brown      01-JAN-65
```

REGEXP_INSTR()

REGEXP_INSTR(*x*, *pattern* [, *start* [, *occurrence* [, *return_option* [, *match_option*]]]]) searches *x* for *pattern*. The function returns the position at which *pattern* occurs (positions start at 1).

The following query returns the position that matches the regular expression l[[:alpha:]]{4} using REGEXP_INSTR():

```
SELECT
  REGEXP_INSTR('But, soft! What light through yonder window breaks?',
    'l[[:alpha:]]{4}') AS result
FROM dual;

    RESULT
----------
        17
```

17 is the position of the l in light contained in the string.

The next query returns the position of the second occurrence that matches the regular expression s[[:alpha:]]{3} starting at position 1:

```
SELECT
  REGEXP_INSTR('But, soft! What light through yonder window softly breaks?',
    's[[:alpha:]]{3}', 1, 2) AS result
FROM dual;

    RESULT
----------
        45
```

The next query returns the position of the second occurrence that matches the letter o starting the search at position 10:

```
SELECT
  REGEXP_INSTR('But, soft! What light through yonder window breaks?',
    'o', 10, 2) AS result
FROM dual;

    RESULT
----------
        32
```

REGEXP_REPLACE()

REGEXP_REPLACE(*x*, *pattern* [, *replace_string* [, *start* [, *occurrence* [, *match_option*]]]]) searches *x* for *pattern* and replaces it with *replace_string*.

The following query replaces the substring that matches the regular expression l[[:alpha:]] {4} with the string sound using REGEXP_REPLACE():

```
SELECT
  REGEXP_REPLACE('But, soft! What light through yonder window breaks?',
    'l[[:alpha:]]{4}', 'sound') AS result
FROM dual;

RESULT
--------------------------------------------------
But, soft! What sound through yonder window breaks?
```

Notice that light has been replaced by sound.

REGEXP_SUBSTR()

REGEXP_SUBSTR(x, pattern [, start [, occurrence [, match_option]]]) returns a substring of x that matches pattern. The search begins at the position specified by start.

The following query returns the substring that matches the regular expression l[[:alpha:]] {4} using REGEXP_SUBSTR():

```
SELECT
  REGEXP_SUBSTR('But, soft! What light through yonder window breaks?',
    'l[[:alpha:]]{4}') AS result
FROM dual;

RESUL
-----
light
```

REGEXP_COUNT()

REGEXP_COUNT() was introduced in Oracle Database 11g. REGEXP_COUNT(x, pattern [, start [, match_option]]) searches x for pattern and returns the number of times pattern is found in x. You can provide an optional start number to indicate the character in x to begin searching for pattern and an optional match_option string to indicate the match option.

The following query returns the number of times the regular expression s[[:alpha:]] {3} occurs in a string using REGEXP_COUNT():

```
SELECT
  REGEXP_COUNT('But, soft! What light through yonder window softly breaks?',
    's[[:alpha:]]{3}') AS result
FROM dual;

    RESULT
----------
         2
```

2 is returned, which means the regular expression has two matches in the provided string.

Using Aggregate Functions

The functions you've seen so far operate on a single row at a time and return one row of output for each input row. In this section, you'll learn about aggregate functions, which operate on a group of rows and return one row of output.

> **NOTE**
> *Aggregate functions are also known as group functions because they operate on groups of rows.*

Table 4-8 lists some of the aggregate functions, all of which return a NUMBER. Remember the following points when using aggregate functions:

■ Aggregate functions work with any valid expression. For example, you can use the COUNT(), MAX(), and MIN() functions with numbers, strings, and datetimes.

■ Null values are ignored by aggregate functions, because a null value indicates the value is unknown and therefore cannot be used in the aggregate function's calculation.

■ You can use the DISTINCT keyword with an aggregate function to exclude duplicate entries from the aggregate function's calculation.

You'll learn more about some of the aggregate functions shown in Table 4-8 in the following sections.

AVG()

AVG(x) returns the average value of x. The following query returns the average price of the products. The price column from the products table is passed to the AVG() function.

Function	Description
AVG(x)	Returns the average value of x
COUNT(x)	Returns the number of rows returned by a query involving x
MAX(x)	Returns the maximum value of x
MEDIAN(x)	Returns the median value of x
MIN(x)	Returns the minimum value of x
STDDEV(x)	Returns the standard deviation of x
SUM(x)	Returns the sum of x
VARIANCE(x)	Returns the variance of x

TABLE 4-8. *Aggregate Functions*

```
SELECT AVG(price)
FROM products;

AVG(PRICE)
----------
19.7308333
```

Aggregate functions work with any valid expression. For example, the following query passes the expression `price + 2` to `AVG()`, which adds 2 to each row's `price` and then returns the average of those values:

```
SELECT AVG(price + 2)
FROM products;

AVG(PRICE)
----------
21.7308333
```

You can use the `DISTINCT` keyword to exclude identical values from a computation. For example, the following query uses the `DISTINCT` keyword to exclude identical values in the `price` column when computing the average using `AVG()`:

```
SELECT AVG(DISTINCT price)
FROM products;

AVG(DISTINCTPRICE)
------------------
        20.2981818
```

The average returned by this example is slightly higher than the average returned by the first query in this section. This is because the value for product #12 in the `price` column is the same as the value for product #7. This value is a duplicate and excluded from the computation performed by `AVG()`.

COUNT()

`COUNT(x)` returns the number of rows returned by a query. The following query returns the number of rows in the `products` table using `COUNT()`:

```
SELECT COUNT(product_id)
FROM products;

COUNT(PRODUCT_ID)
-----------------
               12
```

TIP
You should avoid using the asterisk character (*) with the COUNT() function, as it might take longer for COUNT() to return the result. Instead, you should use a column in the table or use the ROWID pseudo column, which contains the internal location of a row in the Oracle database.

The following example passes `ROWID` to `COUNT()` and returns the number of rows in the `products` table:

```
SELECT COUNT(ROWID)
FROM products;

COUNT(ROWID)
------------
          12
```

MAX() and MIN()

`MAX(x)` and `MIN(x)` return the maximum and minimum values for x. The following query gets the maximum and minimum values of the `price` column from the `products` table using `MAX()` and `MIN()`:

```
SELECT MAX(price), MIN(price)
FROM products;

MAX(PRICE) MIN(PRICE)
---------- ----------
     49.99      10.99
```

`MAX()` and `MIN()` work with many database types, including strings and dates. When using `MAX()` with strings, the strings are ordered alphabetically with the "maximum" string being at the bottom of a list and the "minimum" string being at the top of the list. For example, the string `Albert` would appear before `Zeb` in such a list.

The following example gets the maximum and minimum `name` strings from the `products` table using `MAX()` and `MIN()`:

```
SELECT MAX(name), MIN(name)
FROM products;

MAX(NAME)                        MIN(NAME)
-------------------------------- ------------------------------
Z Files                          2412: The Return
```

For dates, the "maximum" date occurs at the latest point in time, and the "minimum" date at the earliest point in time. The following query gets the maximum and minimum `dob` from the `customers` table using `MAX()` and `MIN()`:

```
SELECT MAX(dob), MIN(dob)
FROM customers;

MAX(DOB)  MIN(DOB)
--------- ---------
16-MAR-71 01-JAN-65
```

STDDEV()

`STDDEV(x)` returns the standard deviation of x. Standard deviation is a statistical function and is defined as the square root of the variance (you'll learn about variance shortly).

The following query gets the standard deviation of the `price` column values from the `products` table using `STDDEV()`:

```
SELECT STDDEV(price)
FROM products;

STDDEV(PRICE)
-------------
   11.0896303
```

SUM()

`SUM(x)` adds all the values in `x` and returns the total. The following query gets the sum of the `price` column from the `products` table using `SUM()`:

```
SELECT SUM(price)
FROM products;

SUM(PRICE)
----------
    236.77
```

VARIANCE()

`VARIANCE(x)` returns the variance of `x`. Variance is a statistical function and is defined as the spread or variation of a group of numbers in a sample. Variance is equal to the square of the standard deviation.

The following query returns the variance of the `price` column values from the `products` table using `VARIANCE()`:

```
SELECT VARIANCE(price)
FROM products;

VARIANCE(PRICE)
---------------
     122.979899
```

Grouping Rows

You can group blocks of rows in a table and obtain information on those groups of rows. For example, you can obtain the average price for the different types of products in the `products` table.

Using the GROUP BY Clause to Group Rows

The `GROUP BY` clause groups rows into blocks. For example, the following query groups the rows from the `products` table into blocks with the same `product_type_id`:

```
SELECT product_type_id
FROM products
GROUP BY product_type_id;
```

```
PRODUCT_TYPE_ID
---------------
              1

              2
              3
              4
```

There's one row in the result set for each block of rows with the same `product_type_id`. There's one row for products with a `product_type_id` of 1, another for products with a `product_type_id` of 2, and so on. There's a gap between 1 and 2 in the result set, and you'll see why shortly.

There are two rows in the `products` table with a `product_type_id` of 1, four rows with a `product_type_id` of 2, and so on for the other rows in the table. These rows are grouped together into separate blocks by the `GROUP BY` clause, one block for each `product_type_id`. The first block contains two rows, the second block contains four rows, and so on.

The gap between 1 and 2 is caused by a row whose `product_type_id` is null. This row is shown in the following example:

```
SELECT product_id, name, price
FROM products
WHERE product_type_id IS NULL;
```

```
PRODUCT_ID NAME                                   PRICE
---------- ------------------------------- ----------
        12 My Front Line                          13.49
```

Because this row's `product_type_id` is null, the `GROUP BY` clause in the earlier query groups this row into its own block. The row in the result set is blank because the `product_type_id` is null for the block, so there's a gap between 1 and 2.

Using Multiple Columns in a Group

You can specify multiple columns in a `GROUP BY` clause. For example, the following query includes the `product_id` and `customer_id` columns from the `purchases` table in a `GROUP BY` clause:

```
SELECT product_id, customer_id
FROM purchases
GROUP BY product_id, customer_id;
```

```
PRODUCT_ID CUSTOMER_ID
---------- -----------
         1           1
         1           2
         1           3
         1           4
         2           1
         2           2
         2           3
         2           4
         3           3
```

Using Groups of Rows with Aggregate Functions

You can pass blocks of rows to an aggregate function. The aggregate function performs a computation on the group of rows in each block and returns one value per block. For example, to obtain the number of rows with the same product_type_id from the products table:

- Use the GROUP BY clause to group rows into blocks with the same product_type_id.
- Use COUNT(ROWID) to get the number of rows in each block.

The following query contains these items:

```
SELECT product_type_id, COUNT(ROWID)
FROM products
GROUP BY product_type_id
ORDER BY product_type_id;


PRODUCT_TYPE_ID COUNT(ROWID)
--------------- ------------
              1            2
              2            4
              3            2
              4            3
                           1
```

There are five rows in the result set, with each row corresponding to one or more rows in the products table grouped together with the same product_type_id. From the result set, there are two rows with a product_type_id of 1, four rows with a product_type_id of 2, and so on. The last line in the result set shows there is one row with a null product_type_id (this is caused by the "My Front Line" product).

Consider another example. To get the average price for the different types of products in the products table:

- Use the GROUP BY clause to group rows into blocks with the same product_type_id.
- Use AVG(price) to get the average price for each block of rows.

The following query contains these items:

```
SELECT product_type_id, AVG(price)
FROM products
GROUP BY product_type_id
ORDER BY product_type_id;


PRODUCT_TYPE_ID AVG(PRICE)
--------------- ----------
              1     24.975
              2      26.22
              3      13.24
              4      13.99
                     13.49
```

Each group of rows with the same product_type_id is passed to the AVG() function. AVG() then computes the average price for each group. From the result set, the average price for the group of products with a `product_type_id` of 1 is 24.975. Similarly, the average price of the products with a `product_type_id` of 2 is 26.22. The last row in the result set shows an average price of 13.49. This is the price of the "My Front Line" product, the only row with a null `product_type_id`.

You can use any of the aggregate functions with the GROUP BY clause. For example, the following query gets the variance of product prices for each `product_type_id`:

```
SELECT product_type_id, VARIANCE(price)
FROM products
GROUP BY product_type_id
ORDER BY product_type_id;

PRODUCT_TYPE_ID VARIANCE(PRICE)
--------------- ---------------
              1        50.50125
              2         280.8772
              3            .125
              4               7
                             0
```

You don't have to include the columns used in the GROUP BY in the list of columns immediately after the SELECT. For example, the following query is the same as the previous one except `product_type_id` is omitted from the SELECT clause:

```
SELECT VARIANCE(price)
FROM products
GROUP BY product_type_id
ORDER BY product_type_id;

VARIANCE(PRICE)
---------------
       50.50125
        280.8772
           .125
              7
              0
```

You can include an aggregate function call in the ORDER BY clause, as shown in the following query:

```
SELECT VARIANCE(price)
FROM products
GROUP BY product_type_id
ORDER BY VARIANCE(price);

VARIANCE(PRICE)
---------------
              0
           .125
              7
       50.50125
        280.8772
```

Incorrect Usage of Aggregate Function Calls

When your query contains an aggregate function—and retrieves columns not placed within an aggregate function—those columns must be placed in a GROUP BY clause. If you don't do this, you'll see the error ORA-00937: not a single-group group function.

For example, the following query attempts to retrieve the product_type_id column and AVG(price) but omits a GROUP BY clause for product_type_id:

```
SQL> SELECT product_type_id, AVG(price)
  2  FROM products;
SELECT product_type_id, AVG(price)
       *
ERROR at line 1:
ORA-00937: not a single-group group function
```

The error occurs because the database doesn't know what to do with the product_type_id column. The query attempts to use the AVG() aggregate function, which operates on multiple rows, but the query attempts to get the product_type_id column values for each individual row. You cannot do both at the same time. You must provide a GROUP BY clause to tell the database to group multiple rows with the same product_type_id together. Only then can the database successfully pass those groups of rows to the AVG() function.

CAUTION
When a query contains an aggregate function—and retrieves columns not placed within an aggregate function—then those columns must be placed in a GROUP BY clause.

You cannot use an aggregate function to limit rows in a WHERE clause. If you try to do so, you'll see the error ORA-00934: group function is not allowed here. For example:

```
SQL> SELECT product_type_id, AVG(price)
  2  FROM products
  3  WHERE AVG(price) > 20
  4  GROUP BY product_type_id;
WHERE AVG(price) > 20
      *
ERROR at line 3:
ORA-00934: group function is not allowed here
```

The error occurs because you can only use the WHERE clause to filter *individual* rows, not *groups* of rows. To filter groups of rows, you use the HAVING clause.

Using the HAVING Clause to Filter Groups of Rows

You use the HAVING clause to filter groups of rows. The HAVING clause is placed after the GROUP BY clause:

```
SELECT ...
FROM ...
WHERE
```

```
GROUP BY ...
HAVING ...
ORDER BY ...;
```

NOTE
GROUP BY *can be used without* HAVING, *but* HAVING *must be used in conjunction with* GROUP BY.

For example, to view the types of products that have an average price greater than $20:

■ Use the GROUP BY clause to group rows into blocks with the same product_type_id.

■ Use the HAVING clause to limit the returned results to those groups that have an average price greater than $20.

The following query contains these clauses:

```
SELECT product_type_id, AVG(price)
FROM products
GROUP BY product_type_id
HAVING AVG(price) > 20;

PRODUCT_TYPE_ID AVG(PRICE)
--------------- ----------
              1     24.975
              2      26.22
```

Only the groups with an average price greater than $20 are displayed.

Using the WHERE and GROUP BY Clauses Together

You can use the WHERE and GROUP BY clauses together in the same query. When you do this, the WHERE clause first filters the rows returned, and then the GROUP BY clause groups the remaining rows into blocks.

For example, the following query contains:

■ A WHERE clause to filter the rows from the products table to select those whose price is less than $15

■ A GROUP BY clause to group the remaining rows by the product_type_id column

```
SELECT product_type_id, AVG(price)
FROM products
WHERE price < 15
GROUP BY product_type_id
ORDER BY product_type_id;

PRODUCT_TYPE_ID AVG(PRICE)
--------------- ----------
              2      14.45
              3      13.24
              4      12.99
                     13.49
```

Using the WHERE, GROUP BY, and HAVING Clauses Together

You can use the WHERE, GROUP BY, and HAVING clauses together in the same query. The WHERE clause filters the rows, then the GROUP BY clause groups the remaining rows into blocks, and then the HAVING clause filters the row groups.

For example, the following query contains:

- A WHERE clause to filter the rows from the products table to select those whose price is less than $15
- A GROUP BY clause to group the remaining rows by the product_type_id column
- A HAVING clause to filter the row groups to select those whose average price is greater than $13

```
SELECT product_type_id, AVG(price)
FROM products
WHERE price < 15
GROUP BY product_type_id
HAVING AVG(price) > 13
ORDER BY product_type_id;

PRODUCT_TYPE_ID AVG(PRICE)
--------------- ----------
              2      14.45
              3      13.24
                     13.49
```

Compare these results with the previous example. The group of rows with the product_type_id of 4 is filtered out. That's because the group of rows has an average price less than $13.

The following query uses ORDER BY AVG(price) to reorder the results by the average price:

```
SELECT product_type_id, AVG(price)
FROM products
WHERE price < 15
GROUP BY product_type_id
HAVING AVG(price) > 13
ORDER BY AVG(price);

PRODUCT_TYPE_ID AVG(PRICE)
--------------- ----------
              3      13.24
                     13.49
              2      14.45
```

Summary

In this chapter, you have learned the following:

- There are two main groups of functions: single-row functions and aggregate functions.
- Single-row functions operate on one row at a time and return one row of output for each input row.

- There are five main types of single-row functions: character functions, numeric functions, conversion functions, date functions, and regular expression functions.
- Aggregate functions operate on multiple rows and return one row of output.
- Blocks of rows are grouped together using the GROUP BY clause.
- Groups of rows are filtered using the HAVING clause.

In the next chapter, you'll learn about dates and times.

CHAPTER
5

Storing and Processing
Dates and Times

I n this chapter, you'll learn how to perform the following tasks:

- Use a *datetime* to store a date and time. A datetime stores a year, month, day, hour, minute, and second.

- Use a *timestamp* to store a date and time. A timestamp stores a year, month, day, hour, minute, second, fractional second, and time zone.

- Use a *time interval* to store a length of time. An example time interval is 1 year 3 months.

Simple Examples of Storing and Retrieving Dates

A datetime is stored in the database using the DATE type. An example format for the date part is DD-MON-YYYY. The following table describes the format components.

Component	Description	Example
DD	Two-digit day	05
MON	Three-letter month	FEB
YYYY	Four-digit year	1968

Consider an example of adding a row to the customers table, which contains a DATE column named dob. The following INSERT adds a row to the customers table, setting the dob column to 05-FEB-1968:

```
INSERT INTO customers (
  customer_id, first_name, last_name, dob, phone
) VALUES (
  6, 'Fred', 'Brown', '05-FEB-1968', '800-555-1215'
);
```

You can use the DATE keyword to supply a date literal to the database. The date must use the ANSI standard date format YYYY-MM-DD. The following table describes the components in the format.

Component	Description	Example
YYYY	Four-digit year	1972
MM	Two-digit month from 1 to 12	10
DD	Two-digit day	25

October 25, 1972, is specified using DATE '1972-10-25'. The following INSERT adds a row to the customers table, specifying DATE '1972-10-25' for the dob column:

```
INSERT INTO customers (
  customer_id, first_name, last_name, dob, phone
) VALUES (
  7, 'Steve', 'Purple', DATE '1972-10-25', '800-555-1215'
);
```

By default, the database returns dates in the format DD-MON-YY. YY are the last two digits of the year. For example, the following example retrieves rows from the customers table:

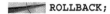

```
SELECT *
FROM customers;
```

```
CUSTOMER_ID FIRST_NAME LAST_NAME  DOB        PHONE
----------- ---------- ---------- ---------  ------------
          1 John       Brown      01-JAN-65  800-555-1211
          2 Cynthia    Green      05-FEB-68  800-555-1212
          3 Steve      White      16-MAR-71  800-555-1213
          4 Gail       Black                 800-555-1214
          5 Doreen     Blue       20-MAY-70
          6 Fred       Brown      05-FEB-68  800-555-1215
          7 Steve      Purple     25-OCT-72  800-555-1215
```

Customer #4's dob is null and is therefore blank in the result set.

The following ROLLBACK undoes the previous INSERT statements:

```
ROLLBACK;
```

NOTE
If you ran the INSERT statements, undo the changes by executing the ROLLBACK. That way, you'll keep the database in its initial state, and the results from your queries will match those in this chapter.

Converting Datetimes Using TO_CHAR() and TO_DATE()

The Oracle database has functions that convert a value in one data type to another. In this section, you'll see how to use the TO_CHAR() and TO_DATE() functions to convert a datetime to a string and vice versa. Table 5-1 summarizes the TO_CHAR() and TO_DATE() functions.

Function	Description
TO_CHAR(x [, format])	Converts x to a string. You can also supply an optional format for x. (You saw how to use TO_CHAR() to convert a number to a string in the previous chapter. In this chapter, you'll see how to convert a datetime to a string.)
TO_DATE(x [, format])	Converts the string x to a DATE.

TABLE 5-1. *TO_CHAR() and TO_DATE() Conversion Functions*

The following section shows how to use TO_CHAR() to convert a datetime to a string. Later, you'll see how to use TO_DATE() to convert a string to a DATE.

Using TO_CHAR() to Convert a Datetime to a String

TO_CHAR(x [, *format*]) converts the datetime x to a string. You can also provide an optional *format* for x. An example format is MONTH DD, YYYY. The following table describes the components in the format.

Component	Description	Example
MONTH	Full name of the month in uppercase	JANUARY
DD	Two-digit day	02
YYYY	Four-digit year	1965

The following query uses TO_CHAR() to convert the dob column from the customers table to a string with the format MONTH DD, YYYY:

```
SELECT customer_id, TO_CHAR(dob, 'MONTH DD, YYYY')
FROM customers;

CUSTOMER_ID TO_CHAR(DOB,'MONTH
----------- ------------------
          1 JANUARY   01, 1965
          2 FEBRUARY  05, 1968
          3 MARCH     16, 1971
          4
          5 MAY       20, 1970
```

The next query gets the current date and time from the database using the SYSDATE function, and then converts the date and time to a string using TO_CHAR() with the format MONTH DD, YYYY, HH24:MI:SS. The time portion indicates that the hours are in 24-hour format and that the minutes and seconds are also included in the string.

```
SELECT TO_CHAR(SYSDATE, 'MONTH DD, YYYY, HH24:MI:SS')
FROM dual;

TO_CHAR(SYSDATE,'MONTHDD,YYY
---------------------------
NOVEMBER  05, 2011, 12:34:36
```

The format passed to TO_CHAR() for converting a datetime to a string has parameters that affect the returned string. Some of these parameters are listed in Table 5-2.

Aspect	Parameter	Description	Example
Century	CC	Two-digit century	21
	SCC	Two-digit century with a negative sign (–) for B.C.	–10
Quarter	Q	One-digit quarter of the year	1
Year	YYYY	All four digits of the year	2008
	IYYY	All four digits of the ISO year (ISO means International Organization for Standardization.)	2008
	RRRR	All four digits of the rounded year, which is determined by the current year (See the section "How Oracle Interprets Two-Digit Years" later in this chapter for details.)	2008
	SYYYY	All four digits of the year with a negative sign (–) for B.C.	–1001
	Y,YYY	All four digits of the year, with a comma after the first digit	2,008
	YYY	Last three digits of the year	008
	IYY	Last three digits of the ISO year	008
	YY	Last two digits of the year	08
	IY	Last two digits of the ISO year	06
	RR	Last two digits of the rounded year, which is determined by the current year (See the section "How Oracle Interprets Two-Digit Years" later in this chapter for details.)	08
	Y	Last digit of the year	8
	I	Last digit of the ISO year	8
	YEAR	Name of the year in uppercase	TWO THOUSAND-EIGHT
	Year	Name of the year with the first letter in uppercase	Two Thousand-Eight
Month	MM	Two-digit month of the year	01
	MONTH	Full name of the month in uppercase, right-padded with spaces to a total length of nine characters	JANUARY

(Continued)

TABLE 5-2. *Datetime Formatting Parameters*

Aspect	Parameter	Description	Example
	Month	Full name of the month with first letter in uppercase, right-padded with spaces to a total length of nine characters	January
	MON	First three letters of the name of the month in uppercase	JAN
	Mon	First three letters of the name of the month with the first letter in uppercase	Jan
	RM	Roman numeral month	The Roman numeral month for the fourth month (April) is IV.
Week	WW	Two-digit week of the year	02
	IW	Two-digit ISO week of the year	02
	W	One-digit week of the month	2
Day	DDD	Three-digit day of the year	103
	DD	Two-digit day of the month	31
	D	One-digit day of the week	5
	DAY	Full name of the day in uppercase	SATURDAY
	Day	Full name of the day with the first letter in uppercase	Saturday
	DY	First three letters of the name of the day in uppercase	SAT
	Dy	First three letters of the name of the day with the first letter in uppercase	Sat
	J	Julian day (The number of days that have passed since January 1, 4713 B.C.)	2439892
Hour	HH24	Two-digit hour in 24-hour format	23
	HH	Two-digit hour in 12-hour format	11
Minute	MI	Two-digit minute	57
Second	SS	Two-digit second	45
	FF[1..9]	Fractional seconds with an optional number of digits to the right of the decimal point (Only applies to timestamps, which you'll learn about in the section "Using Timestamps" later in this chapter)	FF3 rounds 0.123456789 seconds to 0.123 seconds

TABLE 5-2. *Datetime Formatting Parameters*

Aspect	Parameter	Description	Example
	SSSSS	Number of seconds past 12 A.M.	46748
	MS	Millisecond (millionths of a second)	100
	CS	Centisecond (hundredths of a second)	10
Separators	`-/,.;:` `"text"`	Characters that allow you to separate the aspects of a date and time (You can supply freeform text in quotes as a separator.)	For the date December 13, 1969, `DD-MM-YYYY` would produce `12-13-1969`, and `DD/MM/YYYY` would produce `12/13/1969`.
Suffixes	AM or PM	AM or PM as appropriate	AM
	A.M. or P.M.	A.M. or P.M. as appropriate	`P.M.`
	AD or BC	AD or BC as appropriate	AD
	A.D. or B.C.	A.D. or B.C. as appropriate	`B.C.`
	TH	Number suffix (th, st, nd, rd, TH, ST, ND, RD) To make the suffix lowercase, specify the format in lowercase (`th`). To make the suffix uppercase, specify the format in uppercase (`TH`).	For a day number of 28, `ddTH` would produce 28th, and `DDTH` would produce `28TH`. For a day number of 21, `ddTH` would produce 21st, and `DDTH` would produce `21ST`. For a day number of 22, `ddTH` would produce 22nd, and `DDTH` would produce `22ND`. For a day number of 23, `ddTH` would produce 23rd, and `DDTH` would produce `23RD`.

(Continued)

TABLE 5-2. *Datetime Formatting Parameters*

Aspect	Parameter	Description	Example
	SP	Number is spelled out	For a day number of 28, DDSP would produce TWENTY-EIGHT, and ddSP would produce twenty-eight.
	SPTH	Combination of TH and SP	For a day number of 28, DDSPTH would produce TWENTY-EIGHTH, and ddSPTH would produce twenty-eighth.
Era	EE	Full era name for Japanese Imperial, ROC Official, and Thai Buddha calendars	No example
	E	Abbreviated era name	No example
Time zones	TZH	Time zone hour (You'll learn about time zones later in the chapter in the section "Using Time Zones.")	12
	TZM	Time zone minute	30
	TZR	Time zone region	PST
	TZD	Time zone with daylight saving time information	No example

TABLE 5-2. *Datetime Formatting Parameters*

The following table shows examples of strings to format the date February 5, 1968, along with the string returned from a call to TO_CHAR().

Format String Passed to TO_CHAR()	String Returned by TO_CHAR()
MONTH DD, YYYY	FEBRUARY 05, 1968
MM/DD/YYYY	02/05/1968
MM-DD-YYYY	02-05-1968
DD/MM/YYYY	05/02/1968
DAY MON, YY AD	MONDAY FEB, 68 AD

Format String Passed to TO_CHAR()	String Returned by TO_CHAR()
DDSPTH "of" MONTH, YEAR A.D.	FIFTH of FEBRUARY, NINETEEN SIXTY-EIGHT A.D.
CC, SCC	20, 20
Q	1
YYYY, IYYY, RRRR, SYYYY, Y,YYY, YYY, IYY, YY, IY, RR, Y, I, YEAR, Year	1968, 1968, 1968, 1968, 1,968, 968, 968, 68, 68, 68, 8, 8, NINETEEN SIXTY-EIGHT, Nineteen Sixty-Eight
MM, MONTH, Month, MON, Mon, RM	02, FEBRUARY, February, FEB, Feb, II
WW, IW, W	06, 06, 1
DDD, DD, DAY, Day, DY, Dy, J	036, 05, MONDAY, Monday, MON, Mon, 2439892
ddTH, DDTH, ddSP, DDSP, DDSPTH	05th, 05TH, five, FIVE, FIFTH

You can see the results shown in this table by calling TO_CHAR() in a query. For example, the following query converts February 5, 1968, to a string with the format MONTH DD, YYYY:

```
SELECT TO_CHAR(TO_DATE('05-FEB-1968'), 'MONTH DD, YYYY')
FROM dual;

TO_CHAR(TO_DATE('0
------------------
FEBRUARY  05, 1968
```

NOTE
The TO_DATE() *function converts a string to a datetime. You'll learn more about the* TO_DATE() *function shortly.*

The following table shows examples that format the time 19:32:36 (32 minutes and 36 seconds past 7 P.M.)—along with the output returned from a call to TO_CHAR().

Format String	Returned String
HH24:MI:SS	19:32:36
HH.MI.SS AM	7.32.36 PM

Using TO_DATE() to Convert a String to a Datetime

TO_DATE(x [, format]) converts the x string to a datetime. You can provide an optional format string to indicate the format of x. If you omit format, the date must be in the default database format (usually DD-MON-YYYY or DD-MON-YY).

NOTE
The NLS_DATE_FORMAT *database parameter specifies the default date format for the database. As you'll learn later in the section "Setting the Default Date Format,"* NLS_DATE_FORMAT *can be changed.*

The following query uses TO_DATE() to convert the strings 04-JUL-2012 and 04-JUL-12 to the date July 4, 2012. Notice that the final date is displayed in the default format of DD-MON-YY.

```
SELECT TO_DATE('04-JUL-2012'), TO_DATE('04-JUL-12')
FROM dual;

TO_DATE('  TO_DATE('
--------- ---------
04-JUL-12 04-JUL-12
```

Specifying a Datetime Format

You can supply an optional format for a datetime to TO_DATE(). You use the same format parameters as those defined previously in Table 5-2. The following query uses TO_DATE() to convert the string July 4, 2012 to a date, passing the format string MONTH DD, YYYY to TO_DATE():

```
SELECT TO_DATE('July 4, 2012', 'MONTH DD, YYYY')
FROM dual;

TO_DATE('
---------
04-JUL-12
```

The next query passes the format string MM.DD.YY to TO_DATE() and converts the string 7.4.12 to the date July 4, 2012. The final date is displayed in the default format DD-MON-YY.

```
SELECT TO_DATE('7.4.12', 'MM.DD.YY')
FROM dual;

TO_DATE('
---------
04-JUL-12
```

Specifying Times

You can specify a time with a datetime. If you don't supply a time with a datetime, the time part of the datetime defaults to 12:00:00 A.M. You can supply the format for a time using the various formats shown earlier in Table 5-2. One example time format is HH24:MI:SS. The following table describes the components in the format.

Component	Description	Example
HH24	Two-digit hour in 24-hour format from 00 to 23	05
MI	Two-digit minute from 00 to 59	55
SS	Two-digit second from 00 to 59	16

An example time that uses the HH24:MI:SS format is 19:32:36. A full example of a datetime that uses this time is

```
05-FEB-1968 19:32:36
```

and the format for this datetime is

```
DD-MON-YYYY HH24:MI:SS
```

The following TO_DATE() call shows the use of this datetime and format:

```
TO_DATE('05-FEB-1968 19:32:36', 'DD-MON-YYYY HH24:MI:SS')
```

The datetime returned by TO_DATE() in this example is used in the following INSERT that adds a row to the customers table. The dob column for the new row is set to the datetime returned by TO_DATE().

```
INSERT INTO customers (
    customer_id, first_name, last_name,
    dob,
    phone
) VALUES (
    6, 'Fred', 'Brown',
    TO_DATE('05-FEB-1968 19:32:36', 'DD-MON-YYYY HH24:MI:SS'),
    '800-555-1215'
);
```

You can use TO_CHAR() to view the time part of a datetime. For example, the following query retrieves the rows from the customers table and uses TO_CHAR() to convert the dob column values. Customer #6 has the time previously set in the INSERT.

```
SELECT customer_id, TO_CHAR(dob, 'DD-MON-YYYY HH24:MI:SS')
FROM customers;

CUSTOMER_ID TO_CHAR(DOB,'DD-MON-
----------- --------------------
          1 01-JAN-1965 00:00:00
          2 05-FEB-1968 00:00:00
          3 16-MAR-1971 00:00:00
          4
          5 20-MAY-1970 00:00:00
          6 05-FEB-1968 19:32:36
```

The time for the dob column for customers #1, #2, #3, and #5 is 00:00:00 (12 a.m.). This is the default time substituted by the database when no time is explicitly set in a datetime.

The next statement rolls back the addition of the new row:

```
ROLLBACK;
```

NOTE
If you ran the earlier INSERT *statement, undo the change using*
ROLLBACK.

Combining TO_CHAR() and TO_DATE() Calls
You can combine TO_CHAR() and TO_DATE() calls, which allows you to use datetimes in
different formats. For example, the following query combines TO_CHAR() and TO_DATE() to
view the time part of a datetime. The output from TO_DATE() is passed to TO_CHAR().

```
SELECT TO_CHAR(TO_DATE('05-FEB-1968 19:32:36',
  'DD-MON-YYYY HH24:MI:SS'), 'HH24:MI:SS')
FROM dual;

TO_CHAR(
--------
19:32:36
```

Setting the Default Date Format
The default date format is specified in the NLS_DATE_FORMAT database parameter. A database
administrator can change the setting of NLS_DATE_FORMAT by setting the parameter value in
the database's init.ora or spfile.ora file, both of which are read when the database is started.
A database administrator can also set NLS_DATE_FORMAT using the ALTER SYSTEM command.

   You can also set the NLS_DATE_FORMAT parameter for your own SQL*Plus session using the
ALTER SESSION command. For example, the following ALTER SESSION statement sets
NLS_DATE_FORMAT to MONTH-DD-YYYY:

```
ALTER SESSION SET NLS_DATE_FORMAT = 'MONTH-DD-YYYY';

Session altered
```

NOTE
*A session is started when you connect to a database and is ended
when you disconnect.*

   The following query retrieves the dob column for customer #1 and shows the result of the
session date change:

```
SELECT dob
FROM customers
WHERE customer_id = 1;

DOB
-----------------
JANUARY  -01-1965
```

You can also use the new date format when inserting a row in the database. For example, the following `INSERT` adds a new row to the `customers` table. Notice the use of the format `MONTH-DD-YYYY` when supplying the `dob` column's value.

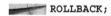

```
INSERT INTO customers (
    customer_id, first_name, last_name, dob, phone
) VALUES (
    6, 'Fred', 'Brown', 'MARCH-15-1970', '800-555-1215'
);
```

When you disconnect from the database and connect again, the date format is back to the default. That's because any changes you make using the `ALTER SESSION` statement last only for that particular session. When you disconnect, you lose the change.

The next statement rolls back the addition of the new row:

```
ROLLBACK;
```

NOTE
If you actually ran the earlier INSERT *statement, make sure you undo the change using* ROLLBACK.

Before continuing, set `NLS_DATE_FORMAT` back to the default of `DD-MON-YY` using the following command:

```
ALTER SESSION SET NLS_DATE_FORMAT = 'DD-MON-YY';
```

```
Session altered
```

How Oracle Interprets Two-Digit Years

An Oracle database stores all four digits of the year. If only two digits are supplied when adding or updating rows, the database software will interpret the century according to whether the `YY` or `RR` format is used.

TIP
You should always specify all four digits of the year. That way, you won't get confused as to which year you mean.

Let's take a look at the `YY` format first, followed by the `RR` format.

Using the YY Format

If a date format uses `YY` for the year and you supply only two digits of a year, then the century for your year is assumed to be the same as the present century currently set on the database server. Therefore, *the first two digits of your supplied year are set to the first two digits of the present year.*

For example, if your supplied year is 15 and the present year is 2012, then your supplied year is set to 2015. Similarly, a supplied year of 75 is set to 2075.

NOTE
If you use the YYYY *format but only supply a two-digit year, then your year is interpreted using the* YY *format.*

Let's take a look at a query that uses the YY format for interpreting the years 15 and 75. In the following query, the input dates 15 and 75 are passed to TO_DATE(), whose output is passed to TO_CHAR(), which then converts the dates to a string using the format DD-MON-YYYY. The YYYY format allows you to see all four digits of the year.

```
SELECT
  TO_CHAR(TO_DATE('04-JUL-15', 'DD-MON-YY'), 'DD-MON-YYYY'),
  TO_CHAR(TO_DATE('04-JUL-75', 'DD-MON-YY'), 'DD-MON-YYYY')
FROM dual;

TO_CHAR(TO_ TO_CHAR(TO_
----------- -----------
04-JUL-2015 04-JUL-2075
```

As expected, the years 15 and 75 are interpreted as 2015 and 2075.

Using the RR Format

If the date format is RR and you supply the last two digits of a year, the first two digits of your year are determined using the two-digit year you supply (your *supplied year*) and the last two digits of the present date on the database server (the *present year*). The rules used to determine the century of your supplied year are as follows:

- **Rule 1**   If your supplied year is between 00 and 49 and the present year is between 00 and 49, then the century is the same as the present century. Therefore, *the first two digits of your supplied year are set to the first two digits of the present year.* For example, if your supplied year is 15 and the present year is 2012, your supplied year is set to 2015.

- **Rule 2**   If your supplied year is between 50 and 99 and the present year is between 00 and 49, then the century is the present century minus 1. Therefore, *the first two digits of your supplied year are set to the present year's first two digits minus 1.* For example, if your supplied year is 75 and the present year is 2012, your supplied year is set to 1975.

- **Rule 3**   If your supplied year is between 00 and 49 and the present year is between 50 and 99, then the century is the present century plus 1. Therefore, *the first two digits of your supplied year are set to the present year's first two digits plus 1.* For example, if your supplied year is 15 and the present year is 2075, your supplied year is set to 2115.

- **Rule 4**   If your supplied year is between 50 and 99 and the present year is between 50 and 99, then the century is the same as the present century. Therefore, *the first two digits of your supplied year are set to the first two digits of the present year.* For example, if your supplied year is 55 and the present year is 2075, your supplied year is set to 2055.

Table 5-3 summarizes these results.

NOTE
If you use the RRRR *format but you supply only a two-digit year, then your year is interpreted using the* RR *format.*

		Two-Digit Supplied Year	
		00–49	**50–99**
Last Two Digits of Present Year	**00–49**	Rule 1: First two digits of supplied year are set to first two digits of present year.	Rule 2: First two digits of supplied year are set to present year's first two digits minus 1.
	50–99	Rule 3: First two digits of supplied year are set to present year's first two digits plus 1.	Rule 4: First two digits of supplied year are set to first two digits of present year.

TABLE 5-3.   *How Two-Digit Years Are Interpreted*

Let's take a look at a query that uses the RR format for interpreting the years 15 and 75. In the following query, assume the present year is 2012.

```
SELECT
  TO_CHAR(TO_DATE('04-JUL-15', 'DD-MON-RR'), 'DD-MON-YYYY'),
  TO_CHAR(TO_DATE('04-JUL-75', 'DD-MON-RR'), 'DD-MON-YYYY')
FROM dual;

TO_CHAR(TO_ TO_CHAR(TO_
----------- -----------
04-JUL-2015 04-JUL-1975
```

As expected from rules 1 and 2, the years 15 and 75 are interpreted as 2015 and 1975.

In the next query, you should assume the present year is 2075 (I changed the system clock on my database server before performing this query):

```
SELECT
  TO_CHAR(TO_DATE('04-JUL-15', 'DD-MON-RR'), 'DD-MON-YYYY'),
  TO_CHAR(TO_DATE('04-JUL-55', 'DD-MON-RR'), 'DD-MON-YYYY')
FROM dual;

TO_CHAR(TO_ TO_CHAR(TO_
----------- -----------
04-JUL-2115 04-JUL-2055
```

As expected from rules 3 and 4, the years 15 and 75 are interpreted as 2115 and 2055.

Using Datetime Functions

The datetime functions process datetimes and timestamps (you'll learn about timestamps later in this chapter). Table 5-4 shows some of the datetime functions. In the table, *x* represents a datetime or a timestamp.

You'll learn more about the functions shown in Table 5-4 in the following sections.

Function	Description
ADD_MONTHS(x, y)	Returns the result of adding y months to x. If y is negative, y months are subtracted from x.
LAST_DAY(x)	Returns the last day of the month part of x.
MONTHS_BETWEEN(x, y)	Returns the number of months between x and y. If x appears before y on the calendar, then the number returned is positive. Otherwise, the number is negative.
NEXT_DAY(x, day)	Returns the datetime of the next day following x. The day is specified as a literal string (SATURDAY, for example).
ROUND(x [, unit])	Rounds x. By default, x is rounded to the beginning of the nearest day. You can supply an optional unit string that indicates the rounding unit. For example, YYYY rounds x to the first day of the nearest year.
SYSDATE	Returns the current datetime set in the database server's operating system.
TRUNC(x [, unit])	Truncates x. By default, x is truncated to the beginning of the day. You can supply an optional unit string that indicates the truncating unit. For example, MM truncates x to the first day of the month.

TABLE 5-4. *Datetime Functions*

ADD_MONTHS()

ADD_MONTHS(x, y) returns the result of adding y months to x. If y is negative, then y months are subtracted from x.

The following example adds 13 months to January 1, 2012:

```
SELECT ADD_MONTHS('01-JAN-2012', 13)
FROM dual;

ADD_MONTH
---------
01-FEB-13
```

The next example subtracts 13 months from January 1, 2012. Notice that –13 months are "added" to this date using ADD_MONTHS():

```
SELECT ADD_MONTHS('01-JAN-2012', -13)
FROM dual;
```

```
ADD_MONTH
---------
01-DEC-10
```

You can provide a time and date to `ADD_MONTHS()`. For example, the following query adds two months to the datetime 7:15:26 P.M. on January 1, 2012:

```sql
SELECT ADD_MONTHS(TO_DATE('01-JAN-2012 19:15:26',
  'DD-MON-YYYY HH24:MI:SS'), 2)
FROM dual;
```

```
ADD_MONTH
---------
01-MAR-12
```

The next query rewrites the previous example to convert the returned datetime from `ADD_MONTHS()` to a string using `TO_CHAR()` with the format `DD-MON-YYYY HH24:MI:SS`:

```sql
SELECT TO_CHAR(ADD_MONTHS(TO_DATE('01-JAN-2012 19:15:26',
  'DD-MON-YYYY HH24:MI:SS'), 2), 'DD-MON-YYYY HH24:MI:SS')
FROM dual;
```

```
TO_CHAR(ADD_MONTHS(T
--------------------
01-MAR-2012 19:15:26
```

NOTE
You can provide a date and time to any of the functions shown earlier in Table 5-4.

LAST_DAY()

`LAST_DAY(x)` returns the date of the last day of the month part of x. The following example displays the last date in January 2012:

```sql
SELECT LAST_DAY('01-JAN-2012')
FROM dual;
```

```
LAST_DAY(
---------
31-JAN-12
```

MONTHS_BETWEEN()

`MONTHS_BETWEEN(x, y)` returns the number of months between x and y. If x occurs before y in the calendar, then the number returned by `MONTHS_BETWEEN()` is negative.

NOTE
The ordering of the dates in a call to `MONTHS_BETWEEN()` *is important. The later date must appear first if you want the result as a positive number.*

The following query returns the number of months between May 25, 2012, and January 15, 2012. Because the later date (May 25, 2012) appears first, the result returned is a positive number.

```
SELECT MONTHS_BETWEEN('25-MAY-2012', '15-JAN-2012')
FROM dual;

MONTHS_BETWEEN('25-MAY-2012','15-JAN-2012')
-------------------------------------------
                                 4.32258065
```

The next query reverses the same dates in the call to MONTHS_BETWEEN(), and therefore the returned result is a negative number of months:

```
SELECT MONTHS_BETWEEN('15-JAN-2012', '25-MAY-2012')
FROM dual;

MONTHS_BETWEEN('15-JAN-2012','25-MAY-2012')
-------------------------------------------
                                 -4.3225806
```

NEXT_DAY()

NEXT_DAY(x, day) returns the date of the next day following x. You specify day as a literal string (for example, SATURDAY).

The following query returns the date of the next Saturday after January 1, 2012:

```
SELECT NEXT_DAY('01-JAN-2012', 'SATURDAY')
FROM dual;

NEXT_DAY(
---------
07-JAN-12
```

ROUND()

ROUND(x [, $unit$]) rounds x, by default, to the beginning of the nearest day. If you supply an optional $unit$ string, x is rounded to that unit. For example, YYYY rounds x to the first day of the nearest year. You can use many of the parameters shown earlier in Table 5-2 to round a datetime.

The following query uses ROUND() to round October 25, 2012, up to the first day in the nearest year, which is January 1, 2013. The date is specified as 25-OCT-2012 and is contained within a call to the TO_DATE() function.

```
SELECT ROUND(TO_DATE('25-OCT-2012'), 'YYYY')
FROM dual;

ROUND(TO_
---------
01-JAN-13
```

The next query rounds May 25, 2012, to the first day in the nearest month, which is June 1, 2012, because May 25 is closer to the beginning of June than it is to the beginning of May:

```
SELECT ROUND(TO_DATE('25-MAY-2012'), 'MM')
FROM dual;

ROUND(TO_
---------
01-JUN-12
```

The next query rounds 7:45:26 P.M. on May 25, 2012, to the nearest hour, which is 8:00 P.M.:

```
SELECT TO_CHAR(ROUND(TO_DATE('25-MAY-2012 19:45:26',
  'DD-MON-YYYY HH24:MI:SS'), 'HH24'), 'DD-MON-YYYY HH24:MI:SS')
FROM dual;

TO_CHAR(ROUND(TO_DAT
--------------------
25-MAY-2012 20:00:00
```

SYSDATE

SYSDATE returns the current datetime set in the database server's operating system. The following query retrieves the current date:

```
SELECT SYSDATE
FROM dual;

SYSDATE
---------
05-NOV-11
```

TRUNC()

TRUNC(x [, unit]) truncates x. By default, x is truncated to the beginning of the day. If you supply an optional unit string, x is truncated to that unit. For example, MM truncates x to the first day in the month. You can use many of the parameters shown earlier in Table 5-2 to truncate a datetime.

The following query uses TRUNC() to truncate May 25, 2012, to the first day in the year, which is January 1, 2012:

```
SELECT TRUNC(TO_DATE('25-MAY-2012'), 'YYYY')
FROM dual;

TRUNC(TO_
---------
01-JAN-12
```

The next query truncates May 25, 2012, to the first day in the month, which is May 1, 2012:

```
SELECT TRUNC(TO_DATE('25-MAY-2012'), 'MM')
FROM dual;

TRUNC(TO_
---------
01-MAY-12
```

The next query truncates 7:45:26 P.M. on May 25, 2012, to the hour, which is 7:00 P.M.:

```
SELECT TO_CHAR(TRUNC(TO_DATE('25-MAY-2012 19:45:26',
 'DD-MON-YYYY HH24:MI:SS'), 'HH24'), 'DD-MON-YYYY HH24:MI:SS')
FROM dual;

TO_CHAR(TRUNC(TO_DAT
--------------------
25-MAY-2012 19:00:00
```

Using Time Zones

Oracle Database 9*i* introduced the ability to use different time zones. A time zone is an offset from the time in Greenwich, England. The time in Greenwich was once known as Greenwich Mean Time (GMT), but is now known as Coordinated Universal Time (UTC, which comes from the initials of the French wording).

You specify a time zone using either an offset from UTC or a geographical region (for example, PST for Pacific Standard Time). When you specify an offset, you use HH:MI prefixed with a plus or minus sign:

```
+|-HH:MI
```

where

- + or – indicates an increase or decrease for the offset from UTC.
- HH:MI specifies the offset in hours and minutes for the time zone.

NOTE
The time zone hour and minute use the format parameters TZH *and* TZR, *shown earlier in Table 5-2.*

The following example shows offsets of 8 hours behind UTC and 2 hours 15 minutes ahead of UTC:

```
-08:00
+02:15
```

You can also specify a time zone using the geographical region. For example, PST indicates Pacific Standard Time, which is 8 hours behind UTC. EST indicates Eastern Standard Time, which is 5 hours behind UTC.

Function	Description
CURRENT_DATE	Returns the current date in the local time zone set for the database session
DBTIMEZONE	Returns the time zone for the database
NEW_TIME(x, time_zone1, time_zone2)	Converts x from time_zone1 to time_zone2 and returns the new datetime
SESSIONTIMEZONE	Returns the time zone for the database session
TZ_OFFSET(time_zone)	Returns the offset for time_zone in hours and minutes

TABLE 5-5.   *Time Zone Functions*

NOTE
The time zone region uses the format parameter TZR, *shown earlier in Table 5-2.*

Time Zone Functions

There are a number of functions that are related to time zones; these functions are shown in Table 5-5. You'll learn more about these functions in the following sections.

The Database Time Zone and Session Time Zone

If you're working for a large, worldwide organization, the database you access may be located in a time zone different from your local time zone. The time zone for the database is known as the *database time zone*, and the time zone set for your database session is known as the *session time zone*. You'll learn about the database and session time zones in the following sections.

The Database Time Zone

The database time zone is controlled using the TIME_ZONE database parameter. A database administrator can change the setting of the TIME_ZONE parameter in the database's init.ora or spfile.ora file, or by using the following command:

```
ALTER DATABASE SET TIME_ZONE = offset | region
```

For example:

```
ALTER DATABASE SET TIME_ZONE = '-8:00'
ALTER DATABASE SET TIME_ZONE = 'PST'
```

You can obtain the database time zone using the DBTIMEZONE function. For example, the following query obtains the time zone for my database:

```
SELECT DBTIMEZONE
FROM dual;
```

```
DBTIME
------
+00:00
```

As you can see, +00:00 is returned. This means my database uses the time zone set in the operating system, which is set to PST on my computer.

NOTE
The Windows operating system typically adjusts the clock for daylight saving time. For California (where I'm located), this means that in the summer the clock is only 7 hours behind UTC, rather than 8 hours. When I wrote this chapter, I set the date to November 5, 2011, which means my clock is 8 hours behind UTC.

The Session Time Zone
The session time zone is the time zone for a particular session. By default, the session time zone is the same as the operating system time zone. You can change your session time zone using the ALTER SESSION statement to set the session TIME_ZONE parameter. For example, the following command sets the local time zone to Pacific Standard Time:

```
ALTER SESSION SET TIME_ZONE = 'PST'
```

You can also set the session TIME_ZONE to LOCAL, which sets the time zone to the one used by the operating system of the computer on which the ALTER SESSION statement was run. You can also set the session TIME_ZONE to DBTIMEZONE, which sets the time zone to the one used by the database.

You can get the session time zone using the SESSIONTIMEZONE function. For example, the following query gets the time zone for my session:

```
SELECT SESSIONTIMEZONE
FROM dual;
```

```
SESSIONTIMEZONE
---------------
-08:00
```

As you can see, my session time zone is 8 hours behind UTC.

Getting the Current Date in the Session Time Zone
The SYSDATE function gets the date from the database. This gives you the date in the database time zone. You can get the date in your session time zone using the CURRENT_DATE function. For example:

```
SELECT CURRENT_DATE
FROM dual;

CURRENT_D
---------
05-NOV-11
```

Obtaining Time Zone Offsets

You can get the time zone offset hours using the `TZ_OFFSET()` function, passing the time zone region name to `TZ_OFFSET()`. For example, the following query uses `TZ_OFFSET()` to get the time zone offset hours for PST, which is 8 hours behind UTC:

```
SELECT TZ_OFFSET('PST')
FROM dual;

TZ_OFFS
-------
-08:00
```

NOTE
In the summer, this will be –7:00 when using Windows, which sets the clock automatically to adjust for daylight saving time.

Obtaining Time Zone Names

You can obtain all the time zone names by selecting all the rows from `v$timezone_names`. To query `v$timezone_names`, you should first connect to the database as the `system` user. The following query shows the first five rows from `v$timezone_names`:

```
SELECT tzname, tzabbrev
FROM v$timezone_names
WHERE ROWNUM <= 5
ORDER BY tzabbrev;

TZNAME              TZABBREV
------------------- --------
Africa/Accra        GHST
Africa/Accra        GMT
Africa/Abidjan      GMT
Africa/Abidjan      LMT
Africa/Accra        LMT
```

You can use any of the `tzname` or `tzabbrev` values for your time zone setting.

NOTE
The `ROWNUM` pseudo column contains the row number. For example, the first row returned by a query has a row number of 1. The second row has a row number of 2, and so on. Therefore, the `WHERE` clause in the previous query causes the query to return the first five rows.

Converting a Datetime from One Time Zone to Another

NEW_TIME() converts a datetime from one time zone to another. For example, the following query uses NEW_TIME() to convert 7:45 P.M. on May 13, 2012, from PST to EST:

```
SELECT TO_CHAR(NEW_TIME(TO_DATE('25-MAY-2012 19:45',
  'DD-MON-YYYY HH24:MI'), 'PST', 'EST'), 'DD-MON-YYYY HH24:MI')
FROM dual;

TO_CHAR(NEW_TIME(
-----------------
25-MAY-2012 22:45
```

EST is 3 hours ahead of PST. Therefore, 3 hours are added to 7:45 P.M. to give 10:45 P.M. (or 22:45 in 24-hour format).

Using Timestamps

Oracle Database 9i introduced the ability to store timestamps. A timestamp stores all four digits of a year, plus a month, day, hour (in 24-hour format), minute, second, fractional second, and time zone. The advantages of a timestamp over a datetime (a DATE) are as follows:

- A timestamp stores a fractional second.
- A timestamp stores a time zone.

The following section describes the timestamp types.

Using the Timestamp Types

There are three timestamp types, which are shown in Table 5-6. You'll learn how to use these timestamp types in the following sections.

Using the TIMESTAMP Type

As with the other types, you can use the TIMESTAMP type to define a column in a table. The following statement creates a table named purchases_with_timestamp that stores customer purchases. This table contains a TIMESTAMP column named made_on to record when a purchase was made. A precision of 4 is set for the TIMESTAMP (this means up to four digits can be stored to the right of the decimal point for the second).

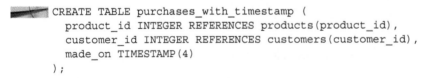
```
CREATE TABLE purchases_with_timestamp (
  product_id INTEGER REFERENCES products(product_id),
  customer_id INTEGER REFERENCES customers(customer_id),
  made_on TIMESTAMP(4)
);
```

NOTE
The purchases_with_timestamp *table is created and populated with rows by the* store_schema.sql *script. You'll see other tables in the rest of this chapter that are also created by the script, so you don't need to type in the CREATE TABLE or any of the INSERT statements shown in this chapter.*

Type	Description

`TIMESTAMP [`
`  (seconds_precision)`
`]`
	Stores all four digits of a year, the month, the day, the hour (in 24-hour format), the minute, and the second.
	You can specify an optional precision for the seconds using `seconds_precision`, which can be an integer from 0 to 9. The default precision is 9, which means you can store up to nine digits to the right of the decimal point for your second.
	If you try to add a row with more digits in the fractional second than the `TIMESTAMP` can store, then the fractional amount is rounded.

`TIMESTAMP [`
`  (seconds_precision)`
`] WITH TIME ZONE`
	Extends `TIMESTAMP` to store a time zone.

`TIMESTAMP [`
`  (seconds_precision)`
`] WITH LOCAL TIME ZONE`
	Extends `TIMESTAMP` to convert a supplied datetime to the local time zone set for the database.
	The process of conversion is known as *normalizing* the datetime.

TABLE 5-6.   *Timestamp Types*

To supply a `TIMESTAMP` literal value to the database, you use the `TIMESTAMP` keyword along with a datetime in the following format:

```
TIMESTAMP 'YYYY-MM-DD HH24:MI:SS.SSSSSSSSS'
```

There are nine S characters after the decimal point, which means you can supply up to nine digits for the fractional second in the literal string. The number of digits you can actually store in a `TIMESTAMP` column depends on how many digits were set for storage of fractional seconds when the column was defined. For example, up to four digits can be stored in the made_on column of the purchases_with_timestamp table. If you try to add a row with more than four fractional second digits, your fractional amount is rounded. For example,

```
2005-05-13 07:15:31.123456789
```

is rounded to

```
2005-05-13 07:15:31.1235
```

The following `INSERT` statement adds a row to the purchases_with_timestamp table. The `TIMESTAMP` keyword supplies a datetime literal.

```
INSERT INTO purchases_with_timestamp (
  product_id, customer_id, made_on
) VALUES (
  1, 1, TIMESTAMP '2005-05-13 07:15:31.1234'
);
```

The following query retrieves the row:

```
SELECT *
FROM purchases_with_timestamp;

PRODUCT_ID CUSTOMER_ID MADE_ON
---------- ----------- -------------------------
         1           1 13-MAY-05 07.15.31.1234 AM
```

Using the TIMESTAMP WITH TIME ZONE Type

The `TIMESTAMP WITH TIME ZONE` type extends `TIMESTAMP` to store a time zone. The following statement creates a table named `purchases_timestamp_with_tz` that stores customer purchases. This table contains a `TIMESTAMP WITH TIME ZONE` column named `made_on` to record when a purchase was made.

```
CREATE TABLE purchases_timestamp_with_tz (
  product_id INTEGER REFERENCES products(product_id),
  customer_id INTEGER REFERENCES customers(customer_id),
  made_on TIMESTAMP(4) WITH TIME ZONE
);
```

To supply a timestamp literal with a time zone to the database, you add the time zone to the `TIMESTAMP`. For example, the following `TIMESTAMP` includes a time zone offset of –07:00:

```
TIMESTAMP '2005-05-13 07:15:31.1234 -07:00'
```

You can supply a time zone region, as shown in the following example that specifies PST as the time zone:

```
TIMESTAMP '2005-05-13 07:15:31.1234 PST'
```

The following example adds two rows to the `purchases_timestamp_with_tz` table:

```
INSERT INTO purchases_timestamp_with_tz (
  product_id, customer_id, made_on
) VALUES (
  1, 1, TIMESTAMP '2005-05-13 07:15:31.1234 -07:00'
);

INSERT INTO purchases_timestamp_with_tz (
  product_id, customer_id, made_on
) VALUES (
  1, 2, TIMESTAMP '2005-05-13 07:15:31.1234 PST'
);
```

The following query retrieves the rows:

```
SELECT *
FROM purchases_timestamp_with_tz;
```

```
PRODUCT_ID CUSTOMER_ID MADE_ON
---------- ----------- ----------------------------------
         1           1 13-MAY-05 07.15.31.1234 AM -07:00
         1           2 13-MAY-05 07.15.31.1234 AM PST
```

Using the TIMESTAMP WITH LOCAL TIME ZONE Type

The TIMESTAMP WITH LOCAL TIME ZONE type extends TIMESTAMP to store a timestamp with the local time zone set for the database. When you supply a timestamp for storage in a TIMESTAMP WITH LOCAL TIME ZONE column, your timestamp is converted—or *normalized*—to the time zone set for the database. When you retrieve the timestamp, it is normalized to the time zone set for your session.

TIP
You should use TIMESTAMP WITH LOCAL TIME ZONE *to store timestamps when your organization has a global system accessed throughout the world. This is because* TIMESTAMP WITH LOCAL TIME ZONE *stores a timestamp using the local time where the database is located, but users see the timestamp normalized to their own time zone.*

My database time zone is PST (PST is 8 hours behind UTC), and I want to store the following timestamp in my database:

```
2005-05-13 07:15:30 EST
```

EST is 5 hours behind UTC, and the difference between PST and EST is 3 hours (8 − 5 = 3). Therefore, to normalize the previous timestamp for PST, 3 hours must be subtracted from it to give the following normalized timestamp:

```
2005-05-13 04:15:30
```

This is the timestamp that would be stored in a TIMESTAMP WITH LOCAL TIME ZONE column in my database.

The following statement creates a table named purchases_with_local_tz that stores customer purchases. This table contains a TIMESTAMP WITH LOCAL TIME ZONE column named made_on to record when a purchase was made.

```
CREATE TABLE purchases_with_local_tz (
  product_id INTEGER REFERENCES products(product_id),
  customer_id INTEGER REFERENCES customers(customer_id),
  made_on TIMESTAMP(4) WITH LOCAL TIME ZONE
);
```

The following INSERT adds a row to the purchases_with_local_tz table with the made_on column set to 2005-05-13 07:15:30 EST:

```
INSERT INTO purchases_with_local_tz (
  product_id, customer_id, made_on
) VALUES (
  1, 1, TIMESTAMP '2005-05-13 07:15:30 EST'
);
```

Although the timestamp for the `made_on` column is set to `2005-05-13 07:15:30 EST`, the actual timestamp stored in my database is `2005-05-13 04:15:30` (the timestamp normalized for PST).

The following query retrieves the row:

```
SELECT *
FROM purchases_with_local_tz;

PRODUCT_ID CUSTOMER_ID MADE_ON
---------- ----------- --------------------------
         1           1 13-MAY-05 04.15.30.0000 AM
```

Because my database time zone and session time zone are both PST, the timestamp returned by the query is for PST.

NOTE
The timestamp returned by the previous query is normalized for PST. If your database time zone or session time zone is not PST, the timestamp returned when you run the query will be different (it will be normalized for your time zone).

If I set the local time zone for my session to EST and repeat the previous query, I get the timestamp normalized for EST:

```
ALTER SESSION SET TIME_ZONE = 'EST';

Session altered.

SELECT *
FROM purchases_with_local_tz;

PRODUCT_ID CUSTOMER_ID MADE_ON
---------- ----------- --------------------------
         1           1 13-MAY-05 07.15.30.0000 AM
```

The timestamp returned by the query is `13-MAY-05 07.15.30.0000 AM`, which is the timestamp normalized for the session time zone of EST. Because EST is 3 hours ahead of PST, 3 hours must be added to `13-MAY-05 04:15:30` (the timestamp stored in the database) to give `13-MAY-05 07.15.30 AM` (the timestamp returned by the query).

The following statement sets the session time zone back to PST:

```
ALTER SESSION SET TIME_ZONE = 'PST';

Session altered.
```

Timestamp Functions

There are a number of functions that allow you to obtain and process timestamps. These functions are shown in Table 5-7. You'll learn more about these functions in the following sections.

Function	Description
`CURRENT_TIMESTAMP`	Returns a `TIMESTAMP WITH TIME ZONE` containing the current date and time for the session, plus the session time zone.

`EXTRACT(`
`{ YEAR | MONTH | DAY |`
`HOUR | MINUTE | SECOND }`
`|`
`{ TIMEZONE_HOUR |`
`TIMEZONE_MINUTE } |`
`{ TIMEZONE_REGION | }`
`TIMEZONE_ABBR }`
`FROM x)`
	Extracts and returns the year, month, day, hour, minute, second, or time zone from *x*. *x* can be a timestamp or a `DATE`.

`FROM_TZ(x, time_zone)`	Converts the `TIMESTAMP` *x* to the time zone specified by *time_zone* and returns a `TIMESTAMP WITH TIMEZONE`. *time_zone* must be specified as a string of the form `+|- HH:MI`. The function basically merges *x* and *time_zone* into one value.
`LOCALTIMESTAMP`	Returns a `TIMESTAMP` containing the current date and time for the session.
`SYSTIMESTAMP`	Returns a `TIMESTAMP WITH TIME ZONE` containing the current date and time for the database, plus the database time zone.
`SYS_EXTRACT_UTC(x)`	Converts the `TIMESTAMP WITH TIMEZONE` *x* to a `TIMESTAMP` containing the date and time in UTC.
`TO_TIMESTAMP(x, [format])`	Converts the string *x* to a `TIMESTAMP`. You can also specify an optional *format* for *x*.
`TO_TIMESTAMP_TZ(x, [format])`	Converts the string *x* to a `TIMESTAMP WITH TIMEZONE`. You can also specify an optional *format* for *x*.

TABLE 5-7. *Timestamp Functions*

CURRENT_TIMESTAMP, LOCALTIMESTAMP, and SYSTIMESTAMP

The following query calls the CURRENT_TIMESTAMP, LOCALTIMESTAMP, and SYSTIMESTAMP functions (my session time zone and database time zone are both PST, which is 8 hours behind UTC):

```
SELECT CURRENT_TIMESTAMP, LOCALTIMESTAMP, SYSTIMESTAMP
FROM dual;
```

```
CURRENT_TIMESTAMP
-----------------------------------
LOCALTIMESTAMP
-----------------------------------
SYSTIMESTAMP
-----------------------------------
05-NOV-11 12.15.32.734000 PM PST
05-NOV-11 12.15.32.734000 PM
05-NOV-11 12.15.32.734000 PM -08:00
```

If I change my session TIME_ZONE to EST and repeat the previous query, I get the following results:

```
ALTER SESSION SET TIME_ZONE = 'EST';

Session altered.

SELECT CURRENT_TIMESTAMP, LOCALTIMESTAMP, SYSTIMESTAMP
FROM dual;

CURRENT_TIMESTAMP
------------------------------------------------------------
LOCALTIMESTAMP
------------------------------------------------------------
SYSTIMESTAMP
------------------------------------------------------------
05-NOV-11 03.19.57.562000 PM EST
05-NOV-11 03.19.57.562000 PM
05-NOV-11 12.19.57.562000 PM -08:00
```

The following statement sets my session time zone back to PST:

```
ALTER SESSION SET TIME_ZONE = 'PST';

Session altered.
```

EXTRACT()

EXTRACT() extracts and returns the year, month, day, hour, minute, second, or time zone from x (x can be a timestamp or a DATE). The following query uses EXTRACT() to get the year, month, and day from a DATE returned by TO_DATE():

```
SELECT
    EXTRACT(YEAR FROM TO_DATE('05-JAN-2012 19:15:26',
      'DD-MON-YYYY HH24:MI:SS')) AS YEAR,
    EXTRACT(MONTH FROM TO_DATE('05-JAN-2012 19:15:26',
      'DD-MON-YYYY HH24:MI:SS')) AS MONTH,
    EXTRACT(DAY FROM TO_DATE('05-JAN-2012 19:15:26',
      'DD-MON-YYYY HH24:MI:SS')) AS DAY
FROM dual;
```

```
    YEAR      MONTH        DAY
---------- ---------- ----------
      2012          1          5
```

The next query uses EXTRACT() to get the hour, minute, and second from a TIMESTAMP returned by TO_TIMESTAMP():

```
SELECT
  EXTRACT(HOUR FROM TO_TIMESTAMP('05-JAN-2012 19:15:26',
    'DD-MON-YYYY HH24:MI:SS')) AS HOUR,
  EXTRACT(MINUTE FROM TO_TIMESTAMP('05-JAN-2012 19:15:26',
    'DD-MON-YYYY HH24:MI:SS')) AS MINUTE,
  EXTRACT(SECOND FROM TO_TIMESTAMP('05-JAN-2012 19:15:26',
    'DD-MON-YYYY HH24:MI:SS')) AS SECOND
FROM dual;
```

```
    HOUR      MINUTE     SECOND
---------- ---------- ----------
      19          15          26
```

The following query uses EXTRACT() to get the time zone hour, minute, second, region, and region abbreviation from a TIMESTAMP WITH TIMEZONE returned by TO_TIMESTAMP_TZ():

```
SELECT
  EXTRACT(TIMEZONE_HOUR FROM TO_TIMESTAMP_TZ(
    '05-JAN-2012 19:15:26 -7:15', 'DD-MON-YYYY HH24:MI:SS TZH:TZM'))
    AS TZH,
  EXTRACT(TIMEZONE_MINUTE FROM TO_TIMESTAMP_TZ(
    '05-JAN-2012 19:15:26 -7:15', 'DD-MON-YYYY HH24:MI:SS TZH:TZM'))
    AS TZM,
  EXTRACT(TIMEZONE_REGION FROM TO_TIMESTAMP_TZ(
    '05-JAN-2012 19:15:26 PST', 'DD-MON-YYYY HH24:MI:SS TZR'))
    AS TZR,
  EXTRACT(TIMEZONE_ABBR FROM TO_TIMESTAMP_TZ(
    '05-JAN-2012 19:15:26 PST', 'DD-MON-YYYY HH24:MI:SS TZR'))
    AS TZA
FROM dual;
```

```
     TZH       TZM TZR                 TZA
---------- ---------- ----------- ----------
      -7       -15 PST                 PST
```

FROM_TZ()

FROM_TZ(x, time_zone) converts the TIMESTAMP x to the time zone specified by time_zone and returns a TIMESTAMP WITH TIMEZONE (time_zone must be specified as a string of the form + | - HH:MI). The function basically merges x and time_zone into one value.

For example, the following query merges the timestamp 2012-05-13 07:15:31.1234 and the time zone offset of -7:00 from UTC:

```
SELECT FROM_TZ(TIMESTAMP '2012-05-13 07:15:31.1234', '-7:00')
FROM dual;
```

```
FROM_TZ(TIMESTAMP'2012-05-1307:15:31.1234','-7:00')
----------------------------------------------------
13-MAY-12 07.15.31.123400000 AM -07:00
```

SYS_EXTRACT_UTC()

SYS_EXTRACT_UTC(x) converts the TIMESTAMP WITH TIMEZONE x to a TIMESTAMP containing the date and time in UTC.

The following query converts 2012-11-17 19:15:26 PST to UTC:

```
SELECT SYS_EXTRACT_UTC(TIMESTAMP '2012-11-17 19:15:26 PST')
FROM dual;

SYS_EXTRACT_UTC(TIMESTAMP'2012-11-1719:15:26PST')
-------------------------------------------------
18-NOV-12 03.15.26.000000000 AM
```

Because PST is 8 hours behind UTC in the winter, the query returns a TIMESTAMP 8 hours ahead of 2012-11-17 19:15:26 PST, which is 18-NOV-12 03.15.26 AM.

For a date in the summer, the returned TIMESTAMP is only 7 hours ahead of UTC:

```
SELECT SYS_EXTRACT_UTC(TIMESTAMP '2012-05-17 19:15:26 PST')
FROM dual;

SYS_EXTRACT_UTC(TIMESTAMP'2012-05-1719:15:26PST')
-------------------------------------------------
18-MAY-12 02.15.26.000000000 AM
```

TO_TIMESTAMP()

TO_TIMESTAMP(x, $format$) converts the string x (which can be a CHAR, VARCHAR2, NCHAR, or NVARCHAR2) to a TIMESTAMP. You can also specify an optional $format$ for x.

The following query converts the string 2012-05-13 07:15:31.1234 with the format YYYY-MM-DD HH24:MI:SS.FF to a TIMESTAMP:

```
SELECT TO_TIMESTAMP('2012-05-13 07:15:31.1234', 'YYYY-MM-DD HH24:MI:SS.FF')
FROM dual;

TO_TIMESTAMP('2012-05-1307:15:31.1234','YYYY-MM-DDHH24:MI:SS.FF')
-----------------------------------------------------------------
13-MAY-12 07.15.31.123400000 AM
```

TO_TIMESTAMP_TZ()

TO_TIMESTAMP_TZ(x, [$format$]) converts x to a TIMESTAMP WITH TIMEZONE. You can specify an optional $format$ for x.

The following query passes the PST time zone (identified using TZR in the format string) to TO_TIMESTAMP_TZ():

```
SELECT TO_TIMESTAMP_TZ('2012-05-13 07:15:31.1234 PST',
  'YYYY-MM-DD HH24:MI:SS.FF TZR')
FROM dual;
```

```
TO_TIMESTAMP_TZ('2012-05-1307:15:31.1234PST','YYYY-MM-DDHH24:MI:SS.FFTZR')
---------------------------------------------------------------------------
13-MAY-12 07.15.31.123400000 AM PST
```

The next query uses a time zone offset of –7:00 from UTC (–7:00 is identified using TZR and TZM in the format string):

```
SELECT TO_TIMESTAMP_TZ('2012-05-13 07:15:31.1234 -7:00',
  'YYYY-MM-DD HH24:MI:SS.FF TZH:TZM')
FROM dual;

TO_TIMESTAMP_TZ('2012-05-1307:15:31.1234-7:00','YYYY-MM-DDHH24:MI:SS.FFTZH
---------------------------------------------------------------------------
13-MAY-12 07.15.31.123400000 AM -07:00
```

Converting a String to a TIMESTAMP WITH LOCAL TIME ZONE

CAST() converts a string to a TIMESTAMP WITH LOCAL TIME ZONE.

You were introduced to CAST() in Chapter 4. CAST(x AS type) converts x to a compatible database type specified by type.

The following query uses CAST() to convert the string 13-JUN-12 to a TIMESTAMP WITH LOCAL TIME ZONE:

```
SELECT CAST('13-JUN-12' AS TIMESTAMP WITH LOCAL TIME ZONE)
FROM dual;

CAST('13-JUN-12'ASTIMESTAMPWITHLOCALTIMEZONE)
---------------------------------------------
13-JUN-12 12.00.00.000000 AM
```

The timestamp returned by this query contains the date June 13, 2012, and the time of 12 A.M.

The next query uses CAST() to convert a more complex string to a TIMESTAMP WITH LOCAL TIME ZONE:

```
SELECT CAST(TO_TIMESTAMP_TZ('2012-05-13 07:15:31.1234 PST',
  'YYYY-MM-DD HH24:MI:SS.FF TZR') AS TIMESTAMP WITH LOCAL TIME ZONE)
FROM dual;

CAST(TO_TIMESTAMP_TZ('2012-05-1307:15:31.1234PST','YYYY-MM-DDHH24:MI:SS.FF
---------------------------------------------------------------------------
13-MAY-12 06.15.31.123400 AM
```

The timestamp returned by this query contains the date May 13, 2012, and the time of 6:15:31.1234 AM PST (PST is the time zone for both my database and session).

The following query does the same thing as the previous one, except this time EST is the time zone:

```
SELECT CAST(TO_TIMESTAMP_TZ('2012-05-13 07:15:31.1234 EST',
  'YYYY-MM-DD HH24:MI:SS.FF TZR') AS TIMESTAMP WITH LOCAL TIME ZONE)
FROM dual;
```

```
CAST(TO_TIMESTAMP_TZ('2012-05-1307:15:31.1234EST','YYYY-MM-DDHH24:MI:SS.FF
-------------------------------------------------------------------------
13-MAY-12 04.15.31.123400 AM
```

The timestamp returned by this query contains the date May 13, 2012 and the time of 4:15:31.1234 AM PST (because PST is 3 hours behind EST, the time returned in the timestamp is 3 hours earlier than the time in the actual query).

Using Time Intervals

Oracle Database 9*i* introduced data types that allow you to store *time intervals*. The following list shows examples of time intervals:

- 1 year 3 months
- 25 months
- −3 days 5 hours 16 minutes
- 1 day 7 hours
- −56 hours

NOTE
Do not confuse time intervals with datetimes or timestamps. A time interval records a length of time (for example, 1 year 3 months). A datetime or timestamp records a specific date and time (for example, 7:32:16 P.M. on October 28, 2006).

For the imaginary online store, you might want to offer limited-time discounts on products. For example, you could give customers a coupon that is valid for a few months, or you could run a special promotion for a few days. You'll see examples that feature coupons and promotions later in this section.

Table 5-8 shows the interval types. You'll learn how to use the time interval types in the following sections.

Using the INTERVAL YEAR TO MONTH Type

INTERVAL YEAR TO MONTH stores a time interval measured in years and months. The following statement creates a table named coupons that stores coupon information. The coupons table contains an INTERVAL YEAR TO MONTH column named duration to record the interval of time for which the coupon is valid. I've provided a precision of 3 for the duration column, which means that up to three digits can be stored for the year.

```
CREATE TABLE coupons (
    coupon_id INTEGER CONSTRAINT coupons_pk PRIMARY KEY,
    name VARCHAR2(30) NOT NULL,
    duration INTERVAL YEAR(3) TO MONTH
);
```

Type	Description
INTERVAL YEAR [(years_precision)] TO MONTH	Stores a time interval measured in years and months. You can specify an optional precision for the years using years_precision, which is an integer from 0 to 9. The default precision is 2, which means you can store two digits for the years in your interval. If you try to add a row with more year digits than the INTERVAL YEAR TO MONTH column can store, you'll get an error. You can store a positive or negative time interval.
INTERVAL DAY [(days_precision)] TO SECOND [(seconds_precision)]	Stores a time interval measured in days and seconds. You can specify an optional precision for the days using days_precision, which is an integer from 0 to 9. The default is 2. You can also specify an optional precision for the fractional seconds using seconds_precision, which is an integer from 0 to 9. The default is 6. You can store a positive or negative time interval.

TABLE 5-8. *Time Interval Types*

To supply an INTERVAL YEAR TO MONTH literal value to the database, you use the following simplified syntax:

```
INTERVAL '[+|-] [y] [-m]' [YEAR[(years_precision)])] [TO MONTH]
```

where

- + or - is an optional indicator that specifies whether the time interval is positive or negative (the default is positive).

- y is the optional number of years for the interval.

- m is the optional number of months for the interval. If you supply years *and* months, you must include TO MONTH in your literal.

- years_precision is the optional precision for the years (the default is 2).

The following table shows some examples of year-to-month interval literals.

Literal	Description
INTERVAL '1' YEAR	Interval of 1 year
INTERVAL '11' MONTH	Interval of 11 months
INTERVAL '14' MONTH	Interval of 14 months (equivalent to 1 year 2 months)
INTERVAL '1-3' YEAR TO MONTH	Interval of 1 year 3 months

Literal	Description
`INTERVAL '0-5' YEAR TO MONTH`	Interval of 0 years 5 months
`INTERVAL '123' YEAR(3) TO MONTH`	Interval of 123 years with a precision of 3 digits
`INTERVAL '-1-5' YEAR TO MONTH`	A negative interval of 1 year 5 months
`INTERVAL '1234' YEAR(3)`	Invalid interval: 1234 contains four digits and therefore contains one too many digits allowed by the precision of 3 (three digits maximum)

The following INSERT statements add rows to the coupons table with the duration column set to some of the intervals shown in the previous table:

```
INSERT INTO coupons (coupon_id, name, duration)
VALUES (1, '$1 off Z Files', INTERVAL '1' YEAR);

INSERT INTO coupons (coupon_id, name, duration)
VALUES (2, '$2 off Pop 3', INTERVAL '11' MONTH);

INSERT INTO coupons (coupon_id, name, duration)
VALUES (3, '$3 off Modern Science', INTERVAL '14' MONTH);

INSERT INTO coupons (coupon_id, name, duration)
VALUES (4, '$2 off Tank War', INTERVAL '1-3' YEAR TO MONTH);

INSERT INTO coupons (coupon_id, name, duration)
VALUES (5, '$1 off Chemistry', INTERVAL '0-5' YEAR TO MONTH);

INSERT INTO coupons (coupon_id, name, duration)
VALUES (6, '$2 off Creative Yell', INTERVAL '123' YEAR(3));
```

If you try to add a row with the duration column set to the invalid interval of INTERVAL '1234' YEAR(3), you'll get an error because the precision of the duration column is 3 and is therefore too small to accommodate the number 1234. The following INSERT shows the error:

```
SQL> INSERT INTO coupons (coupon_id, name, duration)
  2  VALUES (7, '$1 off Z Files', INTERVAL '1234' YEAR(3));
VALUES (7, '$1 off Z Files', INTERVAL '1234' YEAR(3))
                             *
ERROR at line 2:
ORA-01873: the leading precision of the interval is too small
```

The following query retrieves the rows from the coupons table:

```
SELECT *
FROM coupons;
```

```
COUPON_ID NAME                                    DURATION
---------- ----------------------------          --------
         1 $1 off Z Files                         +001-00
         2 $2 off Pop 3                           +000-11
         3 $3 off Modern Science                  +001-02
         4 $2 off Tank War                        +001-03
         5 $1 off Chemistry                       +000-05
         6 $2 off Creative Yell                   +123-00
```

Using the INTERVAL DAY TO SECOND Type

INTERVAL DAY TO SECOND stores time intervals measured in days and seconds. The following statement creates a table named promotions that stores promotion information. The promotions table contains an INTERVAL DAY TO SECOND column named duration to record the interval of time for which the promotion is valid.

```
CREATE TABLE promotions (
  promotion_id INTEGER CONSTRAINT promotions_pk PRIMARY KEY,
  name VARCHAR2(30) NOT NULL,
  duration INTERVAL DAY(3) TO SECOND (4)
);
```

A precision of 3 is set for the day, and a precision of 4 is set for the fractional seconds of the duration column. This means that up to three digits can be stored for the day of the interval and up to four digits to the right of the decimal point for the fractional seconds.

To supply an INTERVAL DAY TO SECOND literal value to the database, you use the following simplified syntax:

```
INTERVAL '[+|-][d] [h[:m[:s]]]' [DAY[(days_precision)]])
[TO HOUR | MINUTE | SECOND[(seconds_precision)]]
```

where

- + or - is an optional indicator that specifies whether the time interval is positive or negative (the default is positive).
- d is the number of days for the interval.
- h is the optional number of hours for the interval. If you supply days and hours, you must include TO HOUR in your literal.
- m is the optional number of minutes for the interval. If you supply days and minutes, you must include TO MINUTES in your literal.
- s is the optional number of seconds for the interval. If you supply days and seconds, you must include TO SECOND in your literal.
- days_precision is the optional precision for the days (the default is 2).
- seconds_precision is the optional precision for the fractional seconds (the default is 6).

The following table shows some examples of day-to-second interval literals.

Literal	Description
INTERVAL '3' DAY	Interval of 3 days.
INTERVAL '2' HOUR	Interval of 2 hours.
INTERVAL '25' MINUTE	Interval of 25 minutes.
INTERVAL '45' SECOND	Interval of 45 seconds.
INTERVAL '3 2' DAY TO HOUR	Interval of 3 days 2 hours.
INTERVAL '3 2:25' DAY TO MINUTE	Interval of 3 days 2 hours 25 minutes.
INTERVAL '3 2:25:45' DAY TO SECOND	Interval of 3 days 2 hours 25 minutes 45 seconds.
INTERVAL '123 2:25:45.12' DAY(3) TO SECOND(2)	Interval of 123 days 2 hours 25 minutes 45.12 seconds. The precision for days is 3 digits, and the precision for the fractional seconds is 2 digits.
INTERVAL '3 2:00:45' DAY TO SECOND	Interval of 3 days 2 hours 0 minutes 45 seconds.
INTERVAL '-3 2:25:45' DAY TO SECOND	Negative interval of 3 days 2 hours 25 minutes 45 seconds.
INTERVAL '1234 2:25:45' DAY(3) TO SECOND	Invalid interval because the number of digits in the days exceeds the specified precision of 3.
INTERVAL '123 2:25:45.123' DAY TO SECOND(2)	Invalid interval because the number of digits in the fractional seconds exceeds the specified precision of 2.

The following INSERT statements add rows to the promotions table:

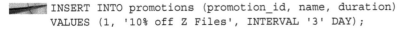

```
INSERT INTO promotions (promotion_id, name, duration)
VALUES (1, '10% off Z Files', INTERVAL '3' DAY);

INSERT INTO promotions (promotion_id, name, duration)
VALUES (2, '20% off Pop 3', INTERVAL '2' HOUR);

INSERT INTO promotions (promotion_id, name, duration)
VALUES (3, '30% off Modern Science', INTERVAL '25' MINUTE);

INSERT INTO promotions (promotion_id, name, duration)
VALUES (4, '20% off Tank War', INTERVAL '45' SECOND);

INSERT INTO promotions (promotion_id, name, duration)
VALUES (5, '10% off Chemistry', INTERVAL '3 2:25' DAY TO MINUTE);

INSERT INTO promotions (promotion_id, name, duration)
VALUES (6, '20% off Creative Yell', INTERVAL '3 2:25:45' DAY TO SECOND);
```

```
INSERT INTO promotions (promotion_id, name, duration)
VALUES (7, '15% off My Front Line',
 INTERVAL '123 2:25:45.12' DAY(3) TO SECOND(2));
```

The following query retrieves the rows from the `promotions` table:

```
SELECT *
FROM promotions;
```

```
PROMOTION_ID NAME                          DURATION
------------ ----------------------------- ------------------
           1 10% off Z Files               +003 00:00:00.0000
           2 20% off Pop 3                 +000 02:00:00.0000
           3 30% off Modern Science        +000 00:25:00.0000
           4 20% off Tank War              +000 00:00:45.0000
           5 10% off Chemistry             +003 02:25:00.0000
           6 20% off Creative Yell         +003 02:25:45.0000
           7 15% off My Front Line         +123 02:25:45.1200
```

Time Interval Functions

There are a number of functions that allow you to get and process time intervals. These functions are shown in Table 5-9. You'll learn more about these functions in the following sections.

NUMTODSINTERVAL()

`NUMTODSINTERVAL(x, interval_unit)` converts the number x to an INTERVAL DAY TO SECOND. The interval for x is specified in `interval_unit`, which can be DAY, HOUR, MINUTE, or SECOND.

For example, the following query converts several numbers to time intervals using `NUMTODSINTERVAL()`:

```
SELECT
  NUMTODSINTERVAL(1.5, 'DAY'),
  NUMTODSINTERVAL(3.25, 'HOUR'),
```

Function	Description
NUMTODSINTERVAL(x, interval_unit)	Converts the number x to an INTERVAL DAY TO SECOND. The interval for x is specified in `interval_unit`, which can be DAY, HOUR, MINUTE, or SECOND.
NUMTOYMINTERVAL(x, interval_unit)	Converts the number x to an INTERVAL YEAR TO MONTH. The interval for x is specified in `interval_unit`, which can be YEAR or MONTH.
TO_DSINTERVAL(x)	Converts the string x to an INTERVAL DAY TO SECOND.
TO_YMINTERVAL(x)	Converts the string x to an INTERVAL YEAR TO MONTH.

TABLE 5-9. *Time Interval Functions*

```
    NUMTODSINTERVAL(5, 'MINUTE'),
    NUMTODSINTERVAL(10.123456789, 'SECOND')
FROM dual;

NUMTODSINTERVAL(1.5,'DAY')
---------------------------------------------
NUMTODSINTERVAL(3.25,'HOUR')
---------------------------------------------
NUMTODSINTERVAL(5,'MINUTE')
---------------------------------------------
NUMTODSINTERVAL(10.123456789,'SECOND')
---------------------------------------------
+000000001 12:00:00.000000000
+000000000 03:15:00.000000000
+000000000 00:05:00.000000000
+000000000 00:00:10.123456789
```

NUMTOYMINTERVAL()

NUMTOYMINTERVAL(*x*, *interval_unit*) converts the number *x* to an INTERVAL YEAR TO MONTH. The interval for *x* is specified in *interval_unit*, which can be YEAR or MONTH.

For example, the following query converts two numbers to time intervals using NUMTOYMINTERVAL():

```
SELECT
    NUMTOYMINTERVAL(1.5, 'YEAR'),
    NUMTOYMINTERVAL(3.25, 'MONTH')
FROM dual;

NUMTOYMINTERVAL(1.5,'YEAR')
---------------------------
NUMTOYMINTERVAL(3.25,'MONTH')
---------------------------
+000000001-06
+000000000-03
```

Summary

In this chapter, you have learned the following:

- A datetime stores all four digits of a year, plus the month, day, hour, minute, and second.
- A datetime is stored using the DATE type.
- A time zone is specified using either an offset from UTC or the name of the region (for example, PST).
- A timestamp stores all four digits of a year, plus the month, day, hour, minute, second, fractional second, and time zone.
- A time interval stores a length of time. An example time interval is 1 year 3 months.

In the next chapter, you'll learn how to place one query within another.

CHAPTER

6

Subqueries

I n this chapter, you'll learn how to perform the following tasks:

■ Place an inner SELECT statement within an outer SQL statement. The inner SELECT is called a *subquery*.

■ Use the different types of subqueries.

■ Create complex statements from simple components.

Types of Subqueries

There are two basic types of subqueries:

■ **Single-row subqueries** return zero rows or one row to the outer SQL statement. There is a special case of a single-row subquery that contains exactly one column. This type of subquery is called a *scalar subquery*.

■ **Multiple-row subqueries** return one or more rows to the outer SQL statement.

In addition, there are three subtypes of subqueries that can return single or multiple rows:

■ **Multiple-column subqueries** return more than one column to the outer SQL statement.

■ **Correlated subqueries** reference one or more columns in the outer SQL statement. These are called *correlated subqueries* because they are related to the outer SQL statement through the same columns.

■ **Nested subqueries** are placed within another subquery.

You'll learn about each of these types of subqueries and how to add them to SELECT, UPDATE, and DELETE statements.

Writing Single-Row Subqueries

A single-row subquery returns zero rows or one row to the outer SQL statement. You can place a subquery in a WHERE clause, a HAVING clause, or a FROM clause of a SELECT statement.

Subqueries in a WHERE Clause

You can place a subquery in the WHERE clause of another query. The following query contains a subquery placed in its WHERE clause. The subquery is placed within parentheses (…).

```
SELECT first_name, last_name
FROM customers
WHERE customer_id =
  (SELECT customer_id
   FROM customers
   WHERE last_name = 'Brown');
```

```
FIRST_NAME LAST_NAME
---------- ----------
John       Brown
```

The example retrieves the `first_name` and `last_name` of the row from the `customers` table whose `last_name` is Brown.

The subquery in the `WHERE` clause is

```
SELECT customer_id
FROM customers
WHERE last_name = 'Brown';
```

The subquery is executed first and returns the `customer_id` for the row whose `last_name` is Brown. The `customer_id` for this row is 1, which is passed to the `WHERE` clause of the outer query. The outer query returns the same result as the following query:

```
SELECT first_name, last_name
FROM customers
WHERE customer_id = 1;
```

Using Other Single-Row Operators

The example shown at the start of the previous section used the equality operator = in the `WHERE` clause. You can also use other comparison operators, such as <>, <, >, <=, and >=, with a single-row subquery.

The following example uses the greater-than operator > in the outer query's `WHERE` clause. The subquery uses the `AVG()` function to get the average price of the products, which is passed to the `WHERE` clause of the outer query. The entire query returns the `product_id`, name, and `price` of products whose price is greater than that average price.

```
SELECT product_id, name, price
FROM products
WHERE price >
  (SELECT AVG(price)
   FROM products);
```

```
PRODUCT_ID NAME                                PRICE
---------- ----------------------------- ----------
         1 Modern Science                     19.95
         2 Chemistry                             30
         3 Supernova                          25.99
         5 Z Files                            49.99
```

Let's examine the details of the example. The subquery executed on its own returns the following results:

```
SELECT AVG(price)
FROM products;
```

```
AVG(PRICE)
----------
19.7308333
```

NOTE
This subquery is an example of a scalar subquery because it returns exactly one row containing one column. The value returned by a scalar subquery is treated as a single scalar value.

The value 19.7308333 returned by the subquery is used in the WHERE clause of the outer query. The query is therefore equivalent to the following:

```
SELECT product_id, name, price
FROM products
WHERE price > 19.7308333;
```

Subqueries in a HAVING Clause

You use the HAVING clause to filter groups of rows. You can place a subquery in the HAVING clause of an outer query. This allows you to filter groups of rows based on the result returned by a subquery.

The following example has a subquery in the HAVING clause of the outer query. The example retrieves the product_type_id and the average price for products whose average price is less than the maximum of the average for the groups of the same product type.

```
SELECT product_type_id, AVG(price)
FROM products
GROUP BY product_type_id
HAVING AVG(price) <
  (SELECT MAX(AVG(price))
   FROM products
   GROUP BY product_type_id)
ORDER BY product_type_id;

PRODUCT_TYPE_ID AVG(PRICE)
--------------- ----------
              1     24.975
              3      13.24
              4      13.99
                     13.49
```

The subquery uses AVG() to first compute the average price for each product type. The result returned by AVG() is passed to MAX(), which returns the maximum of the averages.

Let's break the example down. The following example shows the output from the subquery when it is run on its own:

```
SELECT MAX(AVG(price))
FROM products
GROUP BY product_type_id;

MAX(AVG(PRICE))
---------------
          26.22
```

The value of 26.22 is used in the HAVING clause of the outer query to filter the group's rows to those having an average price less than 26.22. The following query shows a version of the outer query that retrieves the product_type_id and average price of the products grouped by product_type_id:

```
SELECT product_type_id, AVG(price)
FROM products
GROUP BY product_type_id
ORDER BY product_type_id;

PRODUCT_TYPE_ID AVG(PRICE)
--------------- ----------
              1     24.975
              2      26.22
              3      13.24
              4      13.99
                     13.49
```

The groups with a product_type_id of 1, 3, 4, and null have an average price less than 26.22. As expected, these are the same groups returned by the query at the start of this section.

Subqueries in a FROM Clause (Inline Views)

You can place a subquery in the FROM clause of an outer query. These types of subqueries are also known as *inline views* because the subquery provides data in line with the FROM clause.

The following simple example retrieves the products whose product_id is less than 3:

```
SELECT product_id
FROM
   (SELECT product_id
    FROM products
    WHERE product_id < 3);

PRODUCT_ID
----------
         1
         2
```

The subquery returns the rows from the products table whose product_id is less than 3 to the outer query, which then retrieves and displays those product_id values. For the FROM clause of the outer query, the output from the subquery is just another source of data.

The next example is more useful and retrieves the product_id and price from the products table in the outer query. The subquery retrieves the number of times a product has been purchased.

```
SELECT prds.product_id, price, purchases_data.product_count
FROM products prds,
   (SELECT product_id, COUNT(product_id) product_count
    FROM purchases
    GROUP BY product_id) purchases_data
WHERE prds.product_id = purchases_data.product_id;
```

```
PRODUCT_ID     PRICE PRODUCT_COUNT
---------- ---------- -------------
         1     19.95             4
         2        30             4
         3     25.99             1
```

The subquery retrieves the `product_id` and `COUNT(product_id)` from the `purchases` table and returns them to the outer query. The output from the subquery is just another source of data to the `FROM` clause of the outer query.

Errors You Might Encounter

In this section, you'll see some errors you might encounter when writing single-row subqueries. You'll see that a single-row subquery can return a maximum of one row, and that a subquery cannot contain an `ORDER BY` clause.

Single-Row Subqueries May Return a Maximum of One Row

If your subquery returns more than one row, you'll get the following error:

```
ORA-01427: single-row subquery returns more than one row.
```

For example, the subquery in the following statement attempts to pass multiple rows to the equality operator = in the outer query:

```
SQL> SELECT product_id, name
  2  FROM products
  3  WHERE product_id =
  4    (SELECT product_id
  5     FROM products
  6     WHERE name LIKE '%e%');

  (SELECT product_id
    *
ERROR at line 4:
ORA-01427: single-row subquery returns more than one row
```

There are nine rows in the `products` table whose names contain the letter e, and the subquery attempts to pass these rows to the equality operator in the outer query. Because the equality operator can handle only a single row, the query is invalid and an error is returned.

You'll learn how to return multiple rows from a subquery in the upcoming section "Writing Multiple-Row Subqueries."

Subqueries Cannot Contain an ORDER BY Clause

A subquery cannot contain an `ORDER BY` clause. Instead, any ordering must be done in the outer query. For example, the following outer query has an `ORDER BY` clause at the end that sorts the `product_id` values in descending order:

```
SELECT product_id, name, price
FROM products
WHERE price >
  (SELECT AVG(price)
```

```
    FROM products)
ORDER BY product_id DESC;

PRODUCT_ID NAME                              PRICE
---------- --------------------------- ----------
         5 Z Files                          49.99
         3 Supernova                        25.99
         2 Chemistry                           30
         1 Modern Science                   19.95
```

Writing Multiple-Row Subqueries

A multiple-row subquery returns one or more rows to an outer SQL statement. To process the multiple rows returned by a subquery, an outer query can use the IN, ANY, or ALL operators. You can use these operators to see if a column value is contained in a list of values. For example:

```
SELECT product_id, name
FROM products
WHERE product_id IN (1, 2, 3);

PRODUCT_ID NAME
---------- -------------------
         1 Modern Science
         2 Chemistry
         3 Supernova
```

As you'll see in this section, the list of values can come from a subquery.

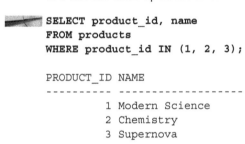

NOTE
You can also use the EXISTS operator to check if a value is in a list returned by a correlated subquery. You'll learn about this later, in the section "Writing Correlated Subqueries."

Using IN with a Multiple-Row Subquery

The IN operator checks if a value is in a list of values. The list of values can come from the results returned by a subquery. NOT IN checks if a value is not in a list of values.

The following simple example uses IN to check if a product_id is in the list of values returned by the subquery. The subquery returns the product_id for products whose name contains the letter e.

```
SELECT product_id, name
FROM products
WHERE product_id IN
  (SELECT product_id
   FROM products
   WHERE name LIKE '%e%');
```

```
PRODUCT_ID NAME
---------- -------------------
         1 Modern Science
         2 Chemistry
         3 Supernova
         5 Z Files
         6 2412: The Return
         7 Space Force 9
         8 From Another Planet
        11 Creative Yell
        12 My Front Line
```

The next example uses NOT IN to retrieve the products that are not in the purchases table:

```
SELECT product_id, name
FROM products
WHERE product_id NOT IN
  (SELECT product_id
   FROM purchases)
ORDER BY product_id;

PRODUCT_ID NAME
---------- -------------------
         4 Tank War
         5 Z Files
         6 2412: The Return
         7 Space Force 9
         8 From Another Planet
         9 Classical Music
        10 Pop 3
        11 Creative Yell
        12 My Front Line
```

Using ANY with a Multiple-Row Subquery

The ANY operator compares one value with any value in a list. You must place an =, <>, <, >, <=, or >= operator before ANY in your query.

The following example uses ANY to retrieve the employees whose salary is less than any of the lowest salaries in the salary_grades table:

```
SELECT employee_id, last_name
FROM employees
WHERE salary < ANY
  (SELECT low_salary
   FROM salary_grades)
ORDER BY employee_id;

EMPLOYEE_ID LAST_NAME
----------- ----------
          2 Johnson
          3 Hobbs
          4 Jones
```

Using ALL with a Multiple-Row Subquery

The ALL operator compares one value with all values in a list. You must place an =, <>, <, >, <=, or >= operator before ALL in your query. The following example uses ALL to get the employees whose salary is greater than all of the highest salaries in the salary_grades table:

```
SELECT employee_id, last_name
FROM employees
WHERE salary > ALL
  (SELECT high_salary
   FROM salary_grades);
```

```
no rows selected
```

No employee has a salary greater than the highest salary.

Writing Multiple-Column Subqueries

A subquery can return multiple columns. The following example retrieves the products with the lowest price for each product type group:

```
SELECT product_id, product_type_id, name, price
FROM products
WHERE (product_type_id, price) IN
  (SELECT product_type_id, MIN(price)
   FROM products
   GROUP BY product_type_id)
ORDER BY product_id;
```

```
PRODUCT_ID PRODUCT_TYPE_ID NAME                               PRICE
---------- --------------- ----------------------------    ----------
         1               1 Modern Science                     19.95
         4               2 Tank War                           13.95
         8               3 From Another Planet                12.99
         9               4 Classical Music                    10.99
```

The subquery returns the product_type_id and the minimum price for each group of products. The product_type_id and minimum price for each group are compared in the outer query's WHERE clause with the product_type_id and price for each product. The products with the lowest price for each product type group are displayed.

Writing Correlated Subqueries

A correlated subquery references one or more columns in the outer SQL statement. These are called *correlated* subqueries because they are related to the outer SQL statement through the same columns.

You typically use a correlated subquery when you need an answer to a question that depends on a value in each row contained in an outer query. For example, you might want to see whether there is a relationship between the data, but you don't care how many rows are returned by the subquery. You just want to check whether *any* rows are returned.

A correlated subquery is run once for each row in the outer query. This is different from a non-correlated subquery, which is run once prior to running the outer query. In addition, a correlated subquery can resolve null values. You'll see examples in the following sections.

A Correlated Subquery Example

The following correlated subquery retrieves the products that have a price greater than the average price for their product type:

```
SELECT product_id, product_type_id, name, price
FROM products outer
WHERE price >
  (SELECT AVG(price)
  FROM products inner
  WHERE inner.product_type_id = outer.product_type_id)
ORDER BY product_id;
```

PRODUCT_ID	PRODUCT_TYPE_ID	NAME	PRICE
2	1	Chemistry	30
5	2	Z Files	49.99
7	3	Space Force 9	13.49
10	4	Pop 3	15.99
11	4	Creative Yell	14.99

I've used the alias outer to label the outer query and the alias inner for the inner subquery. The reference to the product_type_id column in both the inner and outer parts is what makes the inner subquery correlated with the outer query. Also, the subquery returns a single row containing the average price for the product.

In a correlated subquery, each row in the outer query is passed one at a time to the subquery. The subquery reads each row in turn from the outer query and applies it to the subquery until all the rows from the outer query have been processed. The results from the entire query are then returned.

In the previous example, the outer query retrieves each row from the products table and passes it to the inner query. Each row is read by the inner query, which calculates the average price for each product where the product_type_id in the inner query is equal to the product_type_id in the outer query.

Using EXISTS and NOT EXISTS with a Correlated Subquery

You use the EXISTS operator to check for the existence of rows returned by a subquery. Although you can use EXISTS with non-correlated subqueries, EXISTS is typically used with correlated subqueries.

NOT EXISTS does the logical opposite of EXISTS. NOT EXISTS checks if rows do not exist in the results returned by a subquery.

Using EXISTS with a Correlated Subquery

The following example uses EXISTS to retrieve employees who manage other employees. I don't care how many rows are returned by the subquery. I only care whether any rows are returned.

```
SELECT employee_id, last_name
FROM employees outer
WHERE EXISTS
  (SELECT employee_id
   FROM employees inner
   WHERE inner.manager_id = outer.employee_id)
ORDER BY employee_id;

EMPLOYEE_ID LAST_NAME
----------- ----------
          1 Smith
          2 Johnson
```

Because EXISTS checks for the existence of rows returned by the subquery, a subquery doesn't have to return a column—it can just return a literal value. This feature can improve the performance of your query. For example, the following query rewrites the previous example with the subquery returning the literal value 1:

```
SELECT employee_id, last_name
FROM employees outer
WHERE EXISTS
  (SELECT 1
   FROM employees inner
   WHERE inner.manager_id = outer.employee_id)
ORDER BY employee_id;

EMPLOYEE_ID LAST_NAME
----------- ----------
          1 Smith
          2 Johnson
```

As long as the subquery returns one or more rows, EXISTS returns true. If the subquery returns no rows, EXISTS returns false. In the previous example, all I cared about was whether any rows are returned. Because the outer query required at least one column, I specified that the literal value 1 be returned by the subquery in the example.

Using NOT EXISTS with a Correlated Subquery

The following example uses NOT EXISTS to retrieve products that haven't been purchased:

```
SELECT product_id, name
FROM products outer
WHERE NOT EXISTS
  (SELECT 1
   FROM purchases inner
   WHERE inner.product_id = outer.product_id)
ORDER BY product_id;

PRODUCT_ID NAME
---------- ------------------
         4 Tank War
         5 Z Files
```

```
 6 2412: The Return
 7 Space Force 9
 8 From Another Planet
 9 Classical Music
10 Pop 3
11 Creative Yell
12 My Front Line
```

EXISTS and NOT EXISTS Versus IN and NOT IN

The IN operator checks if a value is contained in a list of values. EXISTS is different from IN. EXISTS checks for the existence of rows, whereas IN checks for actual values.

TIP
EXISTS typically offers better performance than IN with subqueries. Therefore, you should use EXISTS rather than IN wherever possible.

There is an important difference between NOT EXISTS and NOT IN: When a list of values contains a null value, NOT EXISTS returns true, but NOT IN returns false. For example, the following query uses NOT EXISTS to retrieve the product types that don't have any products of that type in the products table:

```
SELECT product_type_id, name
FROM product_types outer
WHERE NOT EXISTS
   (SELECT 1
    FROM products inner
    WHERE inner.product_type_id = outer.product_type_id)
ORDER BY product_type_id;

PRODUCT_TYPE_ID NAME
--------------- ----------
              5 Magazine
```

One row is returned by this example.

The next example rewrites the previous query to use NOT IN. Notice that no rows are returned.

```
SELECT product_type_id, name
FROM product_types
WHERE product_type_id NOT IN
   (SELECT product_type_id
    FROM products)
ORDER BY product_type_id;

no rows selected
```

No rows are returned because the subquery returns a list of product_id values, one of which is null (the product_type_id for product #12 is null). Because of this, NOT IN in the outer query returns false, and therefore no rows are returned. You must use the NVL() function to convert nulls to a value. In the following example, NVL() is used to convert null product_type_id values to 0:

```
SELECT product_type_id, name
FROM product_types
WHERE product_type_id NOT IN
  (SELECT NVL(product_type_id, 0)
   FROM products)
ORDER BY product_type_id;


PRODUCT_TYPE_ID NAME
--------------- ----------
              5 Magazine
```

This time the row appears.

> **NOTE**
> *These examples illustrate another difference between correlated and non-correlated subqueries: A correlated subquery can resolve null values.*

Writing Nested Subqueries

You can nest subqueries inside other subqueries. The following example contains a nested subquery. The nested subquery is contained within a subquery, which is itself contained in an outer query.

```
SELECT product_type_id, AVG(price)
FROM products
GROUP BY product_type_id
HAVING AVG(price) <
  (SELECT MAX(AVG(price))
   FROM products
   WHERE product_type_id IN
     (SELECT product_id
      FROM purchases
      WHERE quantity > 1)
   GROUP BY product_type_id)
ORDER BY product_type_id;


PRODUCT_TYPE_ID AVG(PRICE)
--------------- ----------
              1     24.975
              3      13.24
              4      13.99
                     13.49
```

This example is quite complex and contains three queries: a nested subquery, a subquery, and an outer query. These query parts are run in that order. Let's break the example down into the three parts and examine the results returned. The nested subquery is

```
SELECT product_id
FROM purchases
WHERE quantity > 1
```

This nested subquery returns the `product_id` for the products that have been purchased more than once. The rows returned by the nested subquery are

```
PRODUCT_ID
----------
         2
         1
```

The subquery that receives this output is

```
SELECT MAX(AVG(price))
FROM products
WHERE product_type_id IN
   (... output from the nested subquery ...)
GROUP BY product_type_id
```

This subquery returns the maximum average price for the products returned by the nested subquery. The row returned by the subquery is

```
MAX(AVG(PRICE))
---------------
          26.22
```

This row is returned to the following outer query:

```
SELECT product_type_id, AVG(price)
FROM products
GROUP BY product_type_id
HAVING AVG(price) <
   (... output from the subquery ...)
ORDER BY product_type_id;
```

This query returns the `product_type_id` and average price of products that are less than the average price returned by the subquery. The rows returned are

```
PRODUCT_TYPE_ID AVG(PRICE)
--------------- ----------
              1     24.975
              3      13.24
              4      13.99
                     13.49
```

These are the same rows returned by the complete query shown at the start of this section.

Writing UPDATE and DELETE Statements Containing Subqueries

You can place subqueries inside UPDATE and DELETE statements.

Writing an UPDATE Statement Containing a Subquery

In an UPDATE statement, you can set a column to the result returned by a single-row subquery. For example, the following UPDATE sets employee #4's salary to the average of the high salary grades returned by a subquery:

```
UPDATE employees
SET salary =
  (SELECT AVG(high_salary)
   FROM salary_grades)
WHERE employee_id = 4;
```

```
1 row updated.
```

The update increases employee #4's salary from $500,000 to $625,000. ($625,000 is the average of the high salaries from the salary_grades table.)

The next statement rolls back the update:

```
ROLLBACK;
```

NOTE
If you executed the UPDATE statement, remember to execute the ROLLBACK to undo the change. That way, your results will match those shown later in this book.

Writing a DELETE Statement Containing a Subquery

You can use the rows returned by a subquery in the WHERE clause of a DELETE statement. For example, the following DELETE statement removes the employee whose salary is greater than the average of the high salary grades returned by a subquery:

```
DELETE FROM employees
WHERE salary >
  (SELECT AVG(high_salary)
   FROM salary_grades);
```

```
1 row deleted.
```

The DELETE statement removes employee #1.

The next statement rolls back the deletion:

```
ROLLBACK;
```

NOTE
If you executed the DELETE *statement, remember to execute a*
ROLLBACK *to undo the removal of the row.*

Using Subquery Factoring

You can place subqueries inside a WITH clause and reference those subqueries outside of the WITH clause. This is known as subquery factoring.

The following example contains a subquery named customer_purchases inside the WITH clause. The subquery retrieves the customer IDs and the sum total of their purchases. The main query outside of the WITH clause returns the result set from the customer_purchases subquery.

```
WITH
  customer_purchases AS (
    SELECT
      cu.customer_id,
      SUM(pr.price * pu.quantity) AS purchase_total
    FROM customers cu, purchases pu, products pr
    WHERE cu.customer_id = pu.customer_id
    AND pu.product_id = pr.product_id
    GROUP BY cu.customer_id
  )
SELECT *
FROM customer_purchases
ORDER BY customer_id;

CUSTOMER_ID PURCHASE_TOTAL
----------- --------------
          1         109.95
          2           69.9
          3          75.94
          4          49.95
```

The average of these purchase totals is 76.435.

The next example extends the previous example. The customer_purchases subquery retrieves the customer IDs, the sum total of their purchases, and the average of the totals. The main query outside of the WITH clause returns the customer ID and purchase total for the customers whose purchase total is less than the average of the purchase totals.

```
WITH
  customer_purchases AS (
    SELECT
      cu.customer_id,
      SUM(pr.price * pu.quantity) AS purchase_total
    FROM customers cu, purchases pu, products pr
    WHERE cu.customer_id = pu.customer_id
    AND pu.product_id = pr.product_id
    GROUP BY cu.customer_id),
  average_purchase AS (
    SELECT SUM(purchase_total)/COUNT(*) AS average
```

```
        FROM customer_purchases
    )
SELECT *
FROM customer_purchases
WHERE purchase_total < (
  SELECT average
  FROM average_purchase
)
ORDER BY customer_id;

CUSTOMER_ID PURCHASE_TOTAL
----------- --------------
          2           69.9
          3          75.94
          4          49.95
```

The average of the purchase totals is 76.435. Therefore, the result set returned by the example contains the customers whose purchase totals are less than 76.435.

Summary

In this chapter, you have learned the following:

- A subquery is a query placed within a SELECT, UPDATE, or DELETE statement.
- Single-row subqueries return zero or one row.
- Multiple-row subqueries return one or more rows.
- Multiple-column subqueries return more than one column.
- Correlated subqueries reference one or more columns in the outer SQL statement.
- Nested subqueries are subqueries placed within another subquery.
- Subqueries can be placed inside a WITH clause.

In the next chapter, you'll learn about advanced queries.

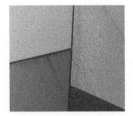

CHAPTER
7

Advanced Queries

I n this chapter, you'll learn how to perform the following tasks:

- Combine rows returned by two or more queries using the set operators
- Translate characters in one string to characters in another string using the TRANSLATE() function
- Search for a value in a set using the DECODE() function
- Perform if-then-else logic using the CASE expression
- Retrieve hierarchical data
- Calculate totals for groups of rows using the ROLLUP and CUBE clauses
- Merge rows from two SELECT statements using CROSS APPLY and OUTER APPLY
- Return an inline view of data using LATERAL

Using the Set Operators

The set operators combine rows returned by two or more queries. Table 7-1 shows the four set operators.

Remember the following restriction when using a set operator: *The number of columns and the column types returned by the queries must match, although the column names can be different.*

You'll learn how to use each of the set operators shown in Table 7-1 shortly, but first let's look at the example tables used in this section.

The Example Tables

The products and more_products tables are created by the store_schema.sql script using the following statements:

```
CREATE TABLE products (
  product_id INTEGER
    CONSTRAINT products_pk PRIMARY KEY,
  product_type_id INTEGER
    CONSTRAINT products_fk_product_types
    REFERENCES product_types(product_type_id),
  name VARCHAR2(30) NOT NULL,
  description VARCHAR2(50),
  price NUMBER(5, 2)
);

CREATE TABLE more_products (
  prd_id INTEGER
    CONSTRAINT more_products_pk PRIMARY KEY,
  prd_type_id INTEGER
    CONSTRAINT more_products_fk_product_types
    REFERENCES product_types(product_type_id),
  name VARCHAR2(30) NOT NULL,
  available CHAR(1)
);
```

Operator	Description
UNION ALL	Returns all the rows retrieved by the queries, including duplicate rows
UNION	Returns all non-duplicate rows retrieved by the queries
INTERSECT	Returns rows that are retrieved by both queries
MINUS	Returns the remaining rows when the rows retrieved by the second query are subtracted from the rows retrieved by the first query

TABLE 7-1. *Set Operators*

The following query retrieves the product_id, product_type_id, and name columns from the products table:

```
SELECT product_id, product_type_id, name
FROM products;

PRODUCT_ID PRODUCT_TYPE_ID NAME
---------- --------------- -------------------
         1               1 Modern Science
         2               1 Chemistry
         3               2 Supernova
         4               2 Tank War
         5               2 Z Files
         6               2 2412: The Return
         7               3 Space Force 9
         8               3 From Another Planet
         9               4 Classical Music
        10               4 Pop 3
        11               4 Creative Yell
        12                 My Front Line
```

The next query retrieves the prd_id, prd_type_id, and name columns from the more_products table:

```
SELECT prd_id, prd_type_id, name
FROM more_products;

    PRD_ID PRD_TYPE_ID NAME
---------- ----------- --------------
         1           1 Modern Science
         2           1 Chemistry
         3             Supernova
         4           2 Lunar Landing
         5           2 Submarine
```

Using the UNION ALL Operator

The UNION ALL operator returns all the rows retrieved by the queries, including duplicate rows. The following query uses UNION ALL:

```
SELECT product_id, product_type_id, name
FROM products
UNION ALL
SELECT prd_id, prd_type_id, name
FROM more_products;
```

```
PRODUCT_ID PRODUCT_TYPE_ID NAME
---------- --------------- ------------------------------
         1               1 Modern Science
         2               1 Chemistry
         3               2 Supernova
         4               2 Tank War
         5               2 Z Files
         6               2 2412: The Return
         7               3 Space Force 9
         8               3 From Another Planet
         9               4 Classical Music
        10               4 Pop 3
        11               4 Creative Yell
        12                 My Front Line
         1               1 Modern Science
         2               1 Chemistry
         3                 Supernova
         4               2 Lunar Landing
         5               2 Submarine

17 rows selected.
```

The result set contains all of the rows from products and more_products, including the duplicate rows.

You can sort the rows using the ORDER BY clause followed by the position of the column. The following example uses ORDER BY 1 to sort the rows by the first column retrieved by the two queries (product_id and prd_id):

```
SELECT product_id, product_type_id, name
FROM products
UNION ALL
SELECT prd_id, prd_type_id, name
FROM more_products
ORDER BY 1;
```

```
PRODUCT_ID PRODUCT_TYPE_ID NAME
---------- --------------- -------------------
         1               1 Modern Science
         1               1 Modern Science
         2               1 Chemistry
```

```
        2                       1 Chemistry
        3                       2 Supernova
        3                         Supernova
        4                       2 Tank War
        4                       2 Lunar Landing
        5                       2 Z Files
        5                       2 Submarine
        6                       2 2412: The Return
        7                       3 Space Force 9
        8                       3 From Another Planet
        9                       4 Classical Music
       10                       4 Pop 3
       11                       4 Creative Yell
       12                         My Front Line
```

```
17 rows selected.
```

Using the UNION Operator

The UNION operator returns only the non-duplicate rows retrieved by the queries. The following example uses UNION:

```
SELECT product_id, product_type_id, name
FROM products
UNION
SELECT prd_id, prd_type_id, name
FROM more_products;
```

```
PRODUCT_ID PRODUCT_TYPE_ID NAME
---------- --------------- -------------------
        1                       1 Modern Science
        2                       1 Chemistry
        3                       2 Supernova
        3                         Supernova
        4                       2 Lunar Landing
        4                       2 Tank War
        5                       2 Submarine
        5                       2 Z Files
        6                       2 2412: The Return
        7                       3 Space Force 9
        8                       3 From Another Planet
        9                       4 Classical Music
       10                       4 Pop 3
       11                       4 Creative Yell
       12                         My Front Line
```

```
15 rows selected.
```

The duplicate "Modern Science" and "Chemistry" rows are not retrieved, so only 15 rows are returned by the example.

Using the INTERSECT Operator

The INTERSECT operator returns only rows that are retrieved by both queries. The following example uses INTERSECT:

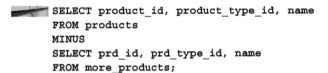

```
SELECT product_id, product_type_id, name
FROM products
INTERSECT
SELECT prd_id, prd_type_id, name
FROM more_products;

PRODUCT_ID PRODUCT_TYPE_ID NAME
---------- --------------- --------------
         1               1 Modern Science
         2               1 Chemistry
```

The "Modern Science" and "Chemistry" rows are returned.

Using the MINUS Operator

The MINUS operator returns the remaining rows when the rows retrieved by the second query are subtracted from the rows retrieved by the first query. The following example uses MINUS:

```
SELECT product_id, product_type_id, name
FROM products
MINUS
SELECT prd_id, prd_type_id, name
FROM more_products;

PRODUCT_ID PRODUCT_TYPE_ID NAME
---------- --------------- -------------------
         3               2 Supernova
         4               2 Tank War
         5               2 Z Files
         6               2 2412: The Return
         7               3 Space Force 9
         8               3 From Another Planet
         9               4 Classical Music
        10               4 Pop 3
        11               4 Creative Yell
        12                 My Front Line

10 rows selected.
```

The rows from more_products are subtracted from products, and the remaining rows are returned by the example.

Combining Set Operators

You can combine more than two queries with multiple set operators, with the returned results from one operator feeding into the next operator. By default, set operators are evaluated from top to bottom, but you should indicate the order using parentheses in case Oracle Corporation changes this default behavior in future software releases.

In the examples in this section, I'll use the following `product_changes` table (created by the `store_schema.sql` script):

```
CREATE TABLE product_changes (
    product_id INTEGER
      CONSTRAINT prod_changes_pk PRIMARY KEY,
    product_type_id INTEGER
      CONSTRAINT prod_changes_fk_product_types
      REFERENCES product_types(product_type_id),
    name VARCHAR2(30) NOT NULL,
    description VARCHAR2(50),
    price NUMBER(5, 2)
);
```

The following query returns the `product_id`, `product_type_id`, and `name` columns from the `product_changes` table:

```
SELECT product_id, product_type_id, name
FROM product_changes;

PRODUCT_ID PRODUCT_TYPE_ID NAME
---------- --------------- --------------
         1               1 Modern Science
         2               1 New Chemistry
         3               1 Supernova
        13               2 Lunar Landing
        14               2 Submarine
        15               2 Airplane
```

The next query does the following:

■ Uses the UNION operator to combine the results from the `products` and `more_products` tables. (The UNION operator returns only the non-duplicate rows retrieved by the queries.)

■ Uses the INTERSECT operator to combine the results from the previous UNION operator with the results from the `product_changes` table. (The INTERSECT operator returns only rows that are retrieved by both queries.)

■ Uses parentheses to indicate the order of evaluation. The UNION is evaluated first, followed by the INTERSECT.

```
(SELECT product_id, product_type_id, name
FROM products
UNION
SELECT prd_id, prd_type_id, name
FROM more_products)
INTERSECT
SELECT product_id, product_type_id, name
FROM product_changes;
```

```
PRODUCT_ID PRODUCT_TYPE_ID NAME
---------- --------------- ---------------
         1               1 Modern Science
```

The following query has the parentheses set so that the INTERSECT is performed first. Different results are returned by the query compared with the previous example.

```
SELECT product_id, product_type_id, name
FROM products
UNION
(SELECT prd_id, prd_type_id, name
FROM more_products
INTERSECT
SELECT product_id, product_type_id, name
FROM product_changes);

PRODUCT_ID PRODUCT_TYPE_ID NAME
---------- --------------- -------------------
         1               1 Modern Science
         2               1 Chemistry
         3               2 Supernova
         4               2 Tank War
         5               2 Z Files
         6               2 2412: The Return
         7               3 Space Force 9
         8               3 From Another Planet
         9               4 Classical Music
        10               4 Pop 3
        11               4 Creative Yell
        12                 My Front Line
```

This concludes the discussion of the set operators.

Using the TRANSLATE() Function

The TRANSLATE(*x*, *from_string*, *to_string*) function converts the occurrences of characters in *from_string* found in *x* to corresponding characters in *to_string*. The easiest way to understand how TRANSLATE() works is to see some examples.

The following example uses TRANSLATE() to shift each character in the string SECRET MESSAGE: MEET ME IN THE PARK by four places to the right. A becomes E, B becomes F, and so on.

```
SELECT TRANSLATE('SECRET MESSAGE: MEET ME IN THE PARK',
   'ABCDEFGHIJKLMNOPQRSTUVWXYZ',
   'EFGHIJKLMNOPQRSTUVWXYZABCD')
FROM dual;

TRANSLATE('SECRETMESSAGE:MEETMEINTH
------------------------------------
WIGVIX QIWWEKI: QIIX QI MR XLI TEVO
```

The next example takes the output of the previous example and shifts the characters four places to the left. E becomes A, F becomes B, and so on.

```
SELECT TRANSLATE('WIGVIX QIWWEKI: QIIX QI MR XLI TEVO',
  'EFGHIJKLMNOPQRSTUVWXYZABCD',
  'ABCDEFGHIJKLMNOPQRSTUVWXYZ')
FROM dual;

TRANSLATE('WIGVIXQIWWEKI:QIIXQIMRXL
----------------------------------
SECRET MESSAGE: MEET ME IN THE PARK
```

You can pass column values to TRANSLATE(). The following example passes the name column from the products table to TRANSLATE(), which shifts the letters in the product name four places to the right:

```
SELECT product_id, TRANSLATE(name,
  'ABCDEFGHIJKLMNOPQRSTUVWXYZabcdefghijklmnopqrstuvwxyz',
  'EFGHIJKLMNOPQRSTUVWXYZABCDefghijklmnopqrstuvwxyzabcd')
FROM products;

PRODUCT_ID TRANSLATE(NAME,'ABCDEFGHIJKLMN
---------- ------------------------------
         1 Qshivr Wgmirgi
         2 Gliqmwxvc
         3 Wytivrsze
         4 Xero Aev
         5 D Jmpiw
         6 2412: Xli Vixyvr
         7 Wtegi Jsvgi 9
         8 Jvsq Ersxliv Tperix
         9 Gpewwmgep Qywmg
        10 Tst 3
        11 Gviexmzi Cipp
        12 Qc Jvsrx Pmri
```

You can use TRANSLATE() to convert numbers. The following example takes the number 12345 and converts 5 to 6, 4 to 7, 3 to 8, 2 to 9, and 1 to 0:

```
SELECT TRANSLATE(12345,
  54321,
  67890)
FROM dual;

TRANS
-----
09876
```

Using the DECODE() Function

The DECODE(*value*, *search_value*, *result*, *default_value*) function compares *value* with *search_value*. If the values are equal, DECODE() returns *result*. Otherwise, *default_value* is returned. DECODE() allows you to perform if-then-else logic in SQL. The parameters to DECODE() can be a column, a literal value, a function, or a subquery.

NOTE
DECODE() is an Oracle-proprietary function. You should use CASE expressions when using Oracle Database 9i and above (you will learn about CASE in the next section). You might encounter the use of DECODE() when using older Oracle databases, and therefore DECODE() is described here for completeness.

The following example uses DECODE() with literal values. DECODE() returns 2 (1 is compared with 1, and because they are equal 2 is returned).

```
SELECT DECODE(1, 1, 2, 3)
FROM dual;

DECODE(1,1,2,3)
---------------
              2
```

The next example uses DECODE() to compare 1 to 2, and because they are not equal 3 is returned:

```
SELECT DECODE(1, 2, 1, 3)
FROM dual;

DECODE(1,2,1,3)
---------------
              3
```

The next example compares the available column in the more_products table. If available equals Y, then the string 'Product is available' is returned. Otherwise, 'Product is not available' is returned.

```
SELECT prd_id, available,
  DECODE(available, 'Y', 'Product is available',
    'Product is not available')
FROM more_products;

    PRD_ID A DECODE(AVAILABLE,'Y','PR
---------- - ------------------------
         1 Y Product is available
         2 Y Product is available
         3 N Product is not available
         4 N Product is not available
         5 Y Product is available
```

You can pass multiple search and result parameters to DECODE(). The following example returns the product_type_id column as the name of the product type:

```
SELECT product_id, product_type_id,
  DECODE(product_type_id,
    1, 'Book',
    2, 'Video',
    3, 'DVD',
    4, 'CD',
    'Magazine')
FROM products;

PRODUCT_ID PRODUCT_TYPE_ID DECODE(P
---------- --------------- --------
         1               1 Book
         2               1 Book
         3               2 Video
         4               2 Video
         5               2 Video
         6               2 Video
         7               3 DVD
         8               3 DVD
         9               4 CD
        10               4 CD
        11               4 CD
        12                 Magazine
```

Notice the following from the result set:

- If product_type_id is 1, then Book is returned.
- If product_type_id is 2, then Video is returned.
- If product_type_id is 3, then DVD is returned.
- If product_type_id is 4, then CD is returned.
- If product_type_id is any other value, then Magazine is returned.

Using the CASE Expression

The CASE expression performs if-then-else logic in SQL and is supported in Oracle Database 9*i* and above. The CASE expression works in a similar way to DECODE(). You should use CASE because it is ANSI-compliant and forms part of the SQL/92 standard. In addition, the CASE expression is easier to read.

There are two types of CASE expressions:

- Simple CASE expressions, which use expressions to determine the returned value
- Searched CASE expressions, which use conditions to determine the returned value

You'll learn about both of these types of CASE expressions next.

Using Simple CASE Expressions

Simple CASE expressions use embedded expressions to determine the value to return. Simple CASE expressions have the following syntax:

```
CASE search_expression
  WHEN expression1 THEN result1
  WHEN expression2 THEN result2
  ...
  WHEN expressionN THEN resultN
  ELSE default_result
END
```

where

- *search_expression* is the expression to be evaluated.
- *expression1, expression2, ..., expressionN* are the expressions to be evaluated against *search_expression*.
- *result1, result2, ..., resultN* are the returned results (one for each possible expression). If *expression1* evaluates to *search_expression*, then *result1* is returned, and similarly for the other expressions.
- *default_result* is returned when no matching expression is found.

The following example shows a simple CASE expression that returns the product types as names:

```
SELECT product_id, product_type_id,
  CASE product_type_id
    WHEN 1 THEN 'Book'
    WHEN 2 THEN 'Video'
    WHEN 3 THEN 'DVD'
    WHEN 4 THEN 'CD'
    ELSE 'Magazine'
  END
FROM products;

PRODUCT_ID PRODUCT_TYPE_ID CASEPROD
---------- --------------- --------
         1               1 Book
         2               1 Book
         3               2 Video
         4               2 Video
         5               2 Video
         6               2 Video
         7               3 DVD
         8               3 DVD
         9               4 CD
        10               4 CD
        11               4 CD
        12                 Magazine
```

Using Searched CASE Expressions

Searched CASE expressions use conditions to determine the returned value. Searched CASE expressions have the following syntax:

```
CASE
   WHEN condition1 THEN result1
   WHEN condition2 THEN result2
   ...
   WHEN conditionN THEN resultN
   ELSE default_result
END
```

where

- condition1, condition2, ..., conditionN are the expressions to be evaluated.

- result1, result2, ..., resultN are the returned results (one for each possible condition). If condition1 is true, then result1 is returned, and similarly for the other expressions.

- default_result is returned when there is no condition that returns true.

The following example illustrates the use of a searched CASE expression:

```
SELECT product_id, product_type_id,
   CASE
     WHEN product_type_id = 1 THEN 'Book'
     WHEN product_type_id = 2 THEN 'Video'
     WHEN product_type_id = 3 THEN 'DVD'
     WHEN product_type_id = 4 THEN 'CD'
     ELSE 'Magazine'
   END
FROM products;

PRODUCT_ID PRODUCT_TYPE_ID CASEPROD
---------- --------------- --------
         1               1 Book
         2               1 Book
         3               2 Video
         4               2 Video
         5               2 Video
         6               2 Video
         7               3 DVD
         8               3 DVD
         9               4 CD
        10               4 CD
        11               4 CD
        12                 Magazine
```

You can use operators in a searched CASE expression. For example:

```
SELECT product_id, price,
  CASE
    WHEN price > 15 THEN 'Expensive'
    ELSE 'Cheap'
  END
FROM products;
```

```
PRODUCT_ID      PRICE CASEWHENP
---------- ---------- ---------
         1      19.95 Expensive
         2         30 Expensive
         3      25.99 Expensive
         4      13.95 Cheap
         5      49.99 Expensive
         6      14.95 Cheap
         7      13.49 Cheap
         8      12.99 Cheap
         9      10.99 Cheap
        10      15.99 Expensive
        11      14.99 Cheap
        12      13.49 Cheap
```

You'll see more advanced examples of CASE expressions later in this chapter.

Hierarchical Queries

Certain data are organized into a hierarchy. Examples include

- Employees in a company
- People in a family tree

In this section, you'll see queries that access a hierarchy of employees who work for the example store.

The Example Data

This section uses a table named more_employees, which is created by the store_schema.sql script using the following statement:

```
CREATE TABLE more_employees (
  employee_id INTEGER
    CONSTRAINT more_employees_pk PRIMARY KEY,
  manager_id INTEGER
    CONSTRAINT more_empl_fk_fk_more_empl
    REFERENCES more_employees(employee_id),
  first_name VARCHAR2(10) NOT NULL,
  last_name VARCHAR2(10) NOT NULL,
  title VARCHAR2(20),
  salary NUMBER(6, 0)
);
```

The manager_id column is a self-reference back to the employee_id column of the more_ employees table. The manager_id column indicates the manager of an employee (if any).
     The following query returns the rows from more_employees:

```
SELECT *
FROM more_employees;
```

```
EMPLOYEE_ID MANAGER_ID FIRST_NAME LAST_NAME  TITLE            SALARY
----------- ---------- ---------- ---------- -------------- ----------
          1            James      Smith      CEO            800000
          2          1 Ron        Johnson    Sales Manager  600000
          3          2 Fred       Hobbs      Sales Person   200000
          4          1 Susan      Jones      Support Manager 500000
          5          2 Rob        Green      Sales Person    40000
          6          4 Jane       Brown      Support Person  45000
          7          4 John       Grey       Support Manager 30000
          8          7 Jean       Blue       Support Person  29000
          9          6 Henry      Heyson     Support Person  30000
         10          1 Kevin      Black      Ops Manager    100000
         11         10 Keith      Long       Ops Person      50000
         12         10 Frank      Howard     Ops Person      45000
         13         10 Doreen     Penn       Ops Person      47000
```

It's difficult to pick out the employee relationships from these results. Figure 7-1 shows the relationships in a graphical form.

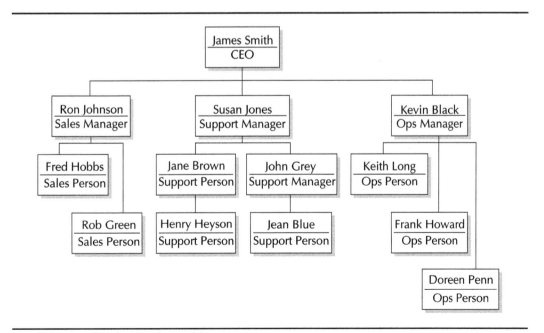

FIGURE 7-1.   *Employee relationships*

In Figure 7-1, the elements—or *nodes*—form a tree. Trees have the following technical terms associated with them:

- **Root node** The root node is the node at the top of the tree. In Figure 7-1, the root node is James Smith, the CEO.

- **Parent node** A parent node is a node that has one or more nodes beneath it. For example, James Smith is the parent to the following nodes: Ron Johnson, Susan Jones, and Kevin Black.

- **Child node** A child node is a node that has one parent node above it. For example, Ron Johnson's parent is James Smith.

- **Leaf node** A leaf node is a node that has no children. For example, Fred Hobbs and Rob Green are leaf nodes.

- **Sibling nodes** Sibling nodes are nodes that have the same parent node. For example, Ron Johnson, Susan Jones, and Kevin Black are sibling nodes whose parent node is James Smith. Also, Jane Brown and John Grey are sibling nodes whose parent node is Susan Jones.

You can use the CONNECT BY and START WITH clauses of a SELECT statement to perform hierarchical queries, as described next. Later, you'll see how to use the WITH clause to perform hierarchical queries using recursive subquery factoring (this feature was introduced in Oracle Database 11g Release 2).

Using the CONNECT BY and START WITH Clauses

The CONNECT BY and START WITH clauses of a SELECT statement have the following syntax:

```
SELECT [LEVEL], column, expression, ...
FROM table
[WHERE where_clause]
[[START WITH start_condition] [CONNECT BY PRIOR prior_condition]];
```

where

- LEVEL is a pseudo column that indicates the level of the tree. LEVEL returns 1 for a root node, 2 for a child of the root, and so on.

- *start_condition* specifies where to start the hierarchical query. An example *start_ condition* is employee_id = 1, which specifies the query starts from employee #1.

- *prior_condition* specifies the relationship between the parent and child rows. An example *prior_condition* is employee_id = manager_id, which specifies the relationship is between the parent employee_id and the child manager_id. This means the child's manager_id points to the parent's employee_id.

The following query uses the START WITH and CONNECT BY PRIOR clauses. The first row contains the details of James Smith (employee #1), the second row contains the details of Ron Johnson, whose manager_id is 1, and so on.

```
SELECT employee_id, manager_id, first_name, last_name
FROM more_employees
START WITH employee_id = 1
CONNECT BY PRIOR employee_id = manager_id;
```

```
EMPLOYEE_ID MANAGER_ID FIRST_NAME LAST_NAME
----------- ---------- ---------- ---------
          1            James      Smith
          2          1 Ron        Johnson
          3          2 Fred       Hobbs
          5          2 Rob        Green
          4          1 Susan      Jones
          6          4 Jane       Brown
          9          6 Henry      Heyson
          7          4 John       Grey
          8          7 Jean       Blue
         10          1 Kevin      Black
         11         10 Keith      Long
         12         10 Frank      Howard
         13         10 Doreen     Penn
```

Using the LEVEL Pseudo Column

The following query includes the LEVEL pseudo column to display the tree level:

```
SELECT LEVEL, employee_id, manager_id, first_name, last_name
FROM more_employees
START WITH employee_id = 1
CONNECT BY PRIOR employee_id = manager_id
ORDER BY LEVEL, employee_id;
```

```
LEVEL EMPLOYEE_ID MANAGER_ID FIRST_NAME LAST_NAME
----- ----------- ---------- ---------- ----------
    1           1            James      Smith
    2           2          1 Ron        Johnson
    2           4          1 Susan      Jones
    2          10          1 Kevin      Black
    3           3          2 Fred       Hobbs
    3           5          2 Rob        Green
    3           6          4 Jane       Brown
    3           7          4 John       Grey
    3          11         10 Keith      Long
    3          12         10 Frank      Howard
    3          13         10 Doreen     Penn
    4           8          7 Jean       Blue
    4           9          6 Henry      Heyson
```

The next query uses the COUNT() function and LEVEL to retrieve the total number of tree levels:

```
SELECT COUNT(DISTINCT LEVEL)
FROM more_employees
START WITH employee_id = 1
CONNECT BY PRIOR employee_id = manager_id;

COUNT(DISTINCTLEVEL)
--------------------
                   4
```

Formatting the Results from a Hierarchical Query

You can format the results from a hierarchical query using `LEVEL` and the `LPAD()` function. `LPAD()` left-pads values with characters.

The following query uses `LPAD(' ', 2 * LEVEL - 1)` to left-pad a total of `2 * LEVEL - 1` spaces. This indents an employee's name with spaces based on their `LEVEL`. `LEVEL` 1 isn't padded, `LEVEL` 2 is padded by two spaces, `LEVEL` 3 by four spaces, and so on.

```
SET PAGESIZE 999
COLUMN employee FORMAT A25
SELECT LEVEL,
  LPAD(' ', 2 * LEVEL - 1) || first_name || ' ' || last_name AS employee
FROM more_employees
START WITH employee_id = 1
CONNECT BY PRIOR employee_id = manager_id;

     LEVEL EMPLOYEE
---------- -----------------
         1 James Smith
         2   Ron Johnson
         3     Fred Hobbs
         3     Rob Green
         2   Susan Jones
         3     Jane Brown
         4       Henry Heyson
         3     John Grey
         4       Jean Blue
         2   Kevin Black
         3     Keith Long
         3     Frank Howard
         3     Doreen Penn
```

The employee relationships are easy to see from these results.

Starting at a Node Other than the Root

You don't have to start at the root node when traversing a tree. You can start at any node using the `START WITH` clause. The following query starts with Susan Jones. Notice that `LEVEL` returns 1 for Susan Jones, 2 for Jane Brown, and so on.

```
SELECT LEVEL,
  LPAD(' ', 2 * LEVEL - 1) || first_name || ' ' || last_name AS employee
FROM more_employees
START WITH last_name = 'Jones'
CONNECT BY PRIOR employee_id = manager_id;

     LEVEL EMPLOYEE
---------- -----------------
         1   Susan Jones
         2     Jane Brown
         3       Henry Heyson
```

```
2      John Grey
3         Jean Blue
```

If the store had more than one employee with the same name, you could use the `employee_id` in the query's `START WITH` clause. For example, the following query uses Susan Jones' `employee_id` of 4:

```
SELECT LEVEL,
  LPAD(' ', 2 * LEVEL - 1) || first_name || ' ' || last_name AS employee
FROM more_employees
START WITH employee_id = 4
CONNECT BY PRIOR employee_id = manager_id;
```

This query returns the same rows as the previous query.

Using a Subquery in a START WITH Clause

You can use a subquery in a `START WITH` clause. The following example uses a subquery to select the `employee_id` whose name is Kevin Black. This `employee_id` is passed to the `START WITH` clause.

```
SELECT LEVEL,
  LPAD(' ', 2 * LEVEL - 1) || first_name || ' ' || last_name AS employee
FROM more_employees
START WITH employee_id = (
  SELECT employee_id
  FROM more_employees
  WHERE first_name = 'Kevin'
  AND last_name = 'Black'
)
CONNECT BY PRIOR employee_id = manager_id;

     LEVEL EMPLOYEE
---------- ---------------
         1 Kevin Black
         2   Keith Long
         2   Frank Howard
         2   Doreen Penn
```

Traversing Upward Through the Tree

You can traverse a tree upward from child to parent. You do this by switching the child and parent columns in the `CONNECT BY PRIOR` clause. For example, `CONNECT BY PRIOR manager_id = employee_id` connects the child's `manager_id` to the parent's `employee_id`.

The following query starts with Jean Blue and traverses upward to James Smith. Notice that `LEVEL` returns 1 for Jean Blue, 2 for John Grey, and so on.

```
SELECT LEVEL,
  LPAD(' ', 2 * LEVEL - 1) || first_name || ' ' || last_name AS employee
FROM more_employees
START WITH last_name = 'Blue'
```

```
CONNECT BY PRIOR manager_id = employee_id;

    LEVEL EMPLOYEE
---------- ------------------
        1  Jean Blue
        2     John Grey
        3        Susan Jones
        4           James Smith
```

Eliminating Nodes and Branches from a Hierarchical Query

You can eliminate a particular node from a query tree using a WHERE clause. The following query eliminates Ron Johnson from the results using WHERE last_name != 'Johnson':

```
SELECT LEVEL,
   LPAD(' ', 2 * LEVEL - 1) || first_name || ' ' || last_name AS employee
FROM more_employees
WHERE last_name != 'Johnson'
START WITH employee_id = 1
CONNECT BY PRIOR employee_id = manager_id;

    LEVEL EMPLOYEE
---------- ------------------
        1 James Smith
        3     Fred Hobbs
        3     Rob Green
        2  Susan Jones
        3     Jane Brown
        4        Henry Heyson
        3     John Grey
        4        Jean Blue
        2  Kevin Black
        3     Keith Long
        3     Frank Howard
        3     Doreen Penn
```

Although Ron Johnson is eliminated from the results, his employees Fred Hobbs and Rob Green are still included.

To eliminate an entire branch of nodes from the results of a query, you add an AND clause to the CONNECT BY PRIOR clause. The following example uses AND last_name != 'Johnson' to eliminate Ron Johnson and all his employees from the results:

```
SELECT LEVEL,
   LPAD(' ', 2 * LEVEL - 1) || first_name || ' ' || last_name AS employee
FROM more_employees
START WITH employee_id = 1
CONNECT BY PRIOR employee_id = manager_id
AND last_name != 'Johnson';
```

```
    LEVEL EMPLOYEE
---------- -------------------
         1  James Smith
         2    Susan Jones
         3      Jane Brown
         4        Henry Heyson
         3      John Grey
         4        Jean Blue
         2    Kevin Black
         3      Keith Long
         3      Frank Howard
         3      Doreen Penn
```

Including Other Conditions in a Hierarchical Query

You can include other conditions in a hierarchical query using a WHERE clause. The following example uses a WHERE clause to show only employees whose salaries are less than or equal to $50,000:

```
SELECT LEVEL,
  LPAD(' ', 2 * LEVEL - 1) || first_name || ' ' || last_name AS employee,
  salary
FROM more_employees
WHERE salary <= 50000
START WITH employee_id = 1
CONNECT BY PRIOR employee_id = manager_id;
```

```
    LEVEL EMPLOYEE                    SALARY
---------- ------------------------- ----------
         3      Rob Green              40000
         3      Jane Brown             45000
         4        Henry Heyson         30000
         3      John Grey              30000
         4        Jean Blue            29000
         3      Keith Long             50000
         3      Frank Howard           45000
         3      Doreen Penn            47000
```

Using Recursive Subquery Factoring to Query Hierarchical Data

Oracle Database 11*g* Release 2 introduced support for recursive subquery factoring, which, among other capabilities, enables you to query hierarchical data. This feature is more powerful than CONNECT BY because it enables depth-first searches and breadth-first searches, and also supports multiple recursive branches.

You place a subquery inside a WITH clause, and reference the subquery outside of the WITH clause. The following example shows the use of recursive subquery factoring, which shows the employee hierarchy and the reporting levels. The example contains a subquery named reporting_hierarchy inside the WITH clause. The main query outside of the WITH clause processes the result set from the reporting_hierarchy subquery.

```
WITH
    reporting_hierarchy (
        employee_id, manager_id, reporting_level, first_name, last_name
    ) AS (
        SELECT
            employee_id, manager_id, 0 reporting_level, first_name, last_name
        FROM more_employees
        WHERE employee_id = 1
        UNION ALL
        SELECT
            e.employee_id, e.manager_id, reporting_level + 1,
            e.first_name, e.last_name
        FROM reporting_hierarchy r, more_employees e
        WHERE r.employee_id = e.manager_id
    )
SELECT
    employee_id, manager_id, reporting_level, first_name, last_name
FROM reporting_hierarchy
ORDER BY employee_id;

EMPLOYEE_ID MANAGER_ID REPORTING_LEVEL FIRST_NAME LAST_NAME
----------- ---------- --------------- ---------- ----------
          1                          0 James      Smith
          2          1              1 Ron        Johnson
          3          2              2 Fred       Hobbs
          4          1              1 Susan      Jones
          5          2              2 Rob        Green
          6          4              2 Jane       Brown
          7          4              2 John       Grey
          8          7              3 Jean       Blue
          9          6              3 Henry      Heyson
         10          1              1 Kevin      Black
         11         10              2 Keith      Long
         12         10              2 Frank      Howard
         13         10              2 Doreen     Penn
```

The first SELECT contains 0 reporting_level, which specifies that the first reporting level has a value of zero. This means that the reporting level for James Smith (the CEO) is set to zero in the result set. The second SELECT contains reporting_level + 1, which adds one to subsequent reporting levels in the hierarchy. This means that the reporting level for Ron Johnson, Susan Jones, and Kevin Black is set to 1 in the result set (those employees report directly to James Smith). The reporting level for the other employees is set according to their position in the reporting hierarchy.

Sibling rows have the same parent row. A depth-first search returns child rows before sibling rows. A breadth-first search returns sibling rows before child rows. The following example performs a depth-first search of the employees and formats the result set to make the reporting hierarchy clear:

```
WITH
    reporting_hierarchy (
        employee_id, manager_id, reporting_level, first_name, last_name
    ) AS (
        SELECT
```

```
      employee_id, manager_id, 0 reporting_level, first_name, last_name
    FROM more_employees
    WHERE manager_id IS NULL
    UNION ALL
    SELECT
      e.employee_id, e.manager_id,
      r.reporting_level + 1 AS reporting_level,
      e.first_name, e.last_name
    FROM reporting_hierarchy r, more_employees e
    WHERE r.employee_id = e.manager_id
  )
SEARCH DEPTH FIRST BY employee_id SET order_by_employee_id
SELECT
  employee_id, manager_id, reporting_level,
  lpad(' ', 2 * reporting_level) || first_name ||
    ' ' || last_name AS name
FROM reporting_hierarchy
ORDER BY order_by_employee_id;
```

```
EMPLOYEE_ID MANAGER_ID REPORTING_LEVEL NAME
----------- ---------- --------------- -------------------------
          1                          0 James Smith
          2          1               1   Ron Johnson
          3          2               2     Fred Hobbs
          5          2               2     Rob Green
          4          1               1   Susan Jones
          6          4               2     Jane Brown
          9          6               3       Henry Heyson
          7          4               2     John Grey
          8          7               3       Jean Blue
         10          1               1   Kevin Black
         11         10               2     Keith Long
         12         10               2     Frank Howard
         13         10               2     Doreen Penn
```

Ron Johnson, Susan Jones, and Kevin Black are sibling rows whose parent row is James Smith. Also, Jane Brown and John Grey are sibling rows whose parent row is Susan Jones.

A breadth-first search returns sibling rows before child rows. The following example performs a breadth-first search of the employees:

```
WITH
  reporting_hierarchy (
    employee_id, manager_id, reporting_level, first_name, last_name
  ) AS (
    SELECT
      employee_id, manager_id, 0 reporting_level, first_name, last_name
    FROM more_employees
    WHERE manager_id IS NULL
    UNION ALL
    SELECT
      e.employee_id, e.manager_id,
```

```
      r.reporting_level + 1 AS reporting_level,
      e.first_name, e.last_name
    FROM reporting_hierarchy r, more_employees e
    WHERE r.employee_id = e.manager_id
  )
SEARCH BREADTH FIRST BY employee_id SET order_by_employee_id
SELECT
  employee_id, manager_id, reporting_level,
  lpad(' ', 2 * reporting_level) || first_name ||
    ' ' || last_name AS name
FROM reporting_hierarchy
ORDER BY order_by_employee_id;

EMPLOYEE_ID MANAGER_ID REPORTING_LEVEL NAME
----------- ---------- --------------- -------------------------
          1                          0 James Smith
          2          1              1   Ron Johnson
          4          1              1   Susan Jones
         10          1              1   Kevin Black
          3          2              2     Fred Hobbs
          5          2              2     Rob Green
          6          4              2     Jane Brown
          7          4              2     John Grey
         11         10              2     Keith Long
         12         10              2     Frank Howard
         13         10              2     Doreen Penn
          8          7              3       Jean Blue
          9          6              3       Henry Heyson
```

The following example retrieves the managers and the number of employees who work for them:

```
WITH
  reporting_hierarchy (
    employee_id, manager_id, first_name, last_name,
    reporting_level, employee_count
  ) AS (
    SELECT
      employee_id, manager_id, first_name, last_name,
      0 reporting_level, 0 employee_count
    FROM more_employees
    UNION ALL
    SELECT
      e.employee_id, e.manager_id, e.first_name, e.last_name,
      r.reporting_level + 1 reporting_level, 1 employee_count
    FROM reporting_hierarchy r, more_employees e
    WHERE e.employee_id = r.manager_id
  )
SEARCH DEPTH FIRST BY employee_id SET order_by_employee_id
SELECT
```

```
  employee_id, manager_id, first_name, last_name,
  SUM(employee_count) AS emp_count,
  MAX(reporting_level) AS rept_level
FROM reporting_hierarchy
GROUP BY employee_id, manager_id, first_name, last_name
HAVING MAX(reporting_level) > 0
ORDER BY employee_id;
```

EMPLOYEE_ID	MANAGER_ID	FIRST_NAME	LAST_NAME	EMP_COUNT	REPT_LEVEL
1		James	Smith	12	3
2	1	Ron	Johnson	2	1
4	1	Susan	Jones	4	2
6	4	Jane	Brown	1	1
7	4	John	Grey	1	1
10	1	Kevin	Black	3	1

You use the CYCLE clause to define cycles in the recursion of the data. The following example uses CYCLE title SET same_title TO 'Y' DEFAULT 'N', which returns Y for an employee who has the same title as a manager above them in the reporting hierarchy:

```
WITH
  reporting_hierarchy (
    employee_id, manager_id, reporting_level,
    first_name, last_name, title
  ) AS (
    SELECT
      employee_id, manager_id, 0 reporting_level,
      first_name, last_name, title
    FROM more_employees
    WHERE manager_id IS NULL
    UNION ALL
    SELECT
      e.employee_id, e.manager_id,
      r.reporting_level + 1 AS reporting_level,
      e.first_name, e.last_name, e.title
    FROM reporting_hierarchy r, more_employees e
    WHERE r.employee_id = e.manager_id
  )
SEARCH DEPTH FIRST BY employee_id SET order_by_employee_id
CYCLE title SET same_title TO 'Y' DEFAULT 'N'
SELECT
  employee_id AS emp_id, manager_id AS mgr_id,
  lpad(' ', 2 * reporting_level) || first_name ||
    ' ' || last_name AS name,
  title, same_title
FROM reporting_hierarchy
ORDER BY order_by_employee_id;
```

```
    EMP_ID    MGR_ID NAME                       TITLE                 S
---------- ---------- ------------------------ -------------------- -
         1            James Smith                CEO                   N
         2         1  Ron Johnson                Sales Manager         N
         3         2    Fred Hobbs               Sales Person          N
         5         2    Rob Green                Sales Person          N
         4         1  Susan Jones                Support Manager       N
         6         4    Jane Brown               Support Person        N
         9         6      Henry Heyson           Support Person        Y
         7         4    John Grey                Support Manager       Y
        10         1  Kevin Black                Ops Manager           N
        11        10    Keith Long               Ops Person            N
        12        10    Frank Howard             Ops Person            N
        13        10    Doreen Penn              Ops Person            N
```

This concludes the discussion of hierarchical queries. In the next section, you'll learn about the ROLLUP and CUBE clauses.

Using the ROLLUP and CUBE Clauses

In this section, you'll learn about the following clauses:

- ROLLUP, which returns a row containing a subtotal for each group of rows, plus a row containing a grand total for all the groups
- CUBE, which returns rows containing a subtotal for all combinations of columns, plus a row containing the grand total

First, let's look at the example tables used in this section.

The Example Tables

The following tables hold more data about the store employees:

- divisions holds the divisions within the store.
- jobs holds the jobs within the store.
- employees2 holds employees.

These tables are created by the store_schema.sql script. The divisions table is created using the following statement:

```
CREATE TABLE divisions (
  division_id CHAR(3)
    CONSTRAINT divisions_pk PRIMARY KEY,
  name VARCHAR2(15) NOT NULL
);
```

The following query retrieves the rows from the divisions table:

```
SELECT *
FROM divisions;
```

```
DIV NAME
--- ----------
SAL Sales
OPE Operations
SUP Support
BUS Business
```

The jobs table is created using the following statement:

```
CREATE TABLE jobs (
  job_id CHAR(3)
    CONSTRAINT jobs_pk PRIMARY KEY,
  name VARCHAR2(20) NOT NULL
);
```

The next query retrieves the rows from the jobs table:

```
SELECT *
FROM jobs;
```

```
JOB NAME
--- ------------
WOR Worker
MGR Manager
ENG Engineer
TEC Technologist
PRE President
```

The employees2 table is created using the following statement:

```
CREATE TABLE employees2 (
  employee_id INTEGER
    CONSTRAINT employees2_pk PRIMARY KEY,
  division_id CHAR(3)
    CONSTRAINT employees2_fk_divisions
    REFERENCES divisions(division_id),
  job_id CHAR(3) REFERENCES jobs(job_id),
  first_name VARCHAR2(10) NOT NULL,
  last_name VARCHAR2(10) NOT NULL,
  salary NUMBER(6, 0)
);
```

The following query retrieves the first five rows from the employees2 table:

```
SELECT *
FROM employees2
WHERE ROWNUM <= 5;
```

```
EMPLOYEE_ID DIV JOB FIRST_NAME LAST_NAME    SALARY
----------- --- --- ---------- ---------- ----------
          1 BUS PRE James      Smith        800000
          2 SAL MGR Ron        Johnson      350000
```

```
3 SAL WOR Fred      Hobbs       140000
4 SUP MGR Susan     Jones       200000
5 SAL WOR Rob       Green       350000
```

Using the ROLLUP Clause

The ROLLUP clause extends GROUP BY to return a row containing a subtotal for each group of rows, plus a row containing a total for all the groups.

GROUP BY groups rows into blocks with a common column value. For example, the following query uses GROUP BY to group the rows from the employees2 table by department_id and uses SUM() to get the sum of the salaries for each division_id:

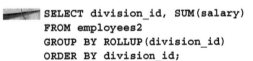

```
SELECT division_id, SUM(salary)
FROM employees2
GROUP BY division_id
ORDER BY division_id;

DIV SUM(SALARY)
--- -----------
BUS    1610000
OPE    1320000
SAL    4936000
SUP    1015000
```

Passing a Single Column to ROLLUP

The following query rewrites the previous example to use ROLLUP. Notice the additional row at the end of the output, which shows the total salaries for all groups.

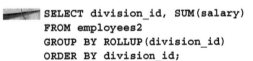

```
SELECT division_id, SUM(salary)
FROM employees2
GROUP BY ROLLUP(division_id)
ORDER BY division_id;

DIV SUM(SALARY)
--- -----------
BUS    1610000
OPE    1320000
SAL    4936000
SUP    1015000
       8881000
```

NOTE
If you need the rows in a specific order, use an ORDER BY clause.
You need to do this in case Oracle Corporation decides to change the
default order of rows returned by ROLLUP.

Passing Multiple Columns to ROLLUP

You can pass multiple columns to ROLLUP, which then groups the rows into blocks with the same column values. The following example passes the division_id and job_id columns of the employees2 table to ROLLUP, which groups the rows by those columns:

```
SELECT division_id, job_id, SUM(salary)
FROM employees2
GROUP BY ROLLUP(division_id, job_id)
ORDER BY division_id, job_id;
```

```
DIV JOB SUM(SALARY)
--- --- -----------
BUS MGR      530000
BUS PRE      800000
BUS WOR      280000
BUS         1610000
OPE ENG      245000
OPE MGR      805000
OPE WOR      270000
OPE         1320000
SAL MGR     4446000
SAL WOR      490000
SAL         4936000
SUP MGR      465000
SUP TEC      115000
SUP WOR      435000
SUP         1015000
            8881000
```

The salaries are summed by division_id and job_id. ROLLUP returns a row with the sum of the salaries in each division_id, plus a grand total of salaries at the end of the result set.

Changing the Position of Columns Passed to ROLLUP

The next example switches division_id and job_id. This causes ROLLUP to calculate the sum of the salaries for each job_id.

```
SELECT job_id, division_id, SUM(salary)
FROM employees2
GROUP BY ROLLUP(job_id, division_id)
ORDER BY job_id, division_id;
```

```
JOB DIV SUM(SALARY)
--- --- -----------
ENG OPE      245000
ENG          245000
MGR BUS      530000
MGR OPE      805000
MGR SAL     4446000
MGR SUP      465000
MGR         6246000
```

```
PRE BUS    800000
PRE        800000
TEC SUP    115000
TEC        115000
WOR BUS    280000
WOR OPE    270000
WOR SAL    490000
WOR SUP    435000
WOR       1475000
          8881000
```

Using Other Aggregate Functions with ROLLUP

You can use any of the aggregate functions with ROLLUP (for a list of the main aggregate functions, see Table 4-8 in Chapter 4). The following example uses AVG() to calculate the average salaries:

```sql
SELECT division_id, job_id, AVG(salary)
FROM employees2
GROUP BY ROLLUP(division_id, job_id)
ORDER BY division_id, job_id;
```

```
DIV JOB AVG(SALARY)
--- --- -----------
BUS MGR 176666.667
BUS PRE    800000
BUS WOR    280000
BUS        322000
OPE ENG    245000
OPE MGR    201250
OPE WOR    135000
OPE     188571.429
SAL MGR 261529.412
SAL WOR    245000
SAL     259789.474
SUP MGR    232500
SUP TEC    115000
SUP WOR    145000
SUP     169166.667
        240027.027
```

Using the CUBE Clause

The CUBE clause extends GROUP BY to return rows containing a subtotal for all combinations of columns, plus a row containing the grand total. The following example passes division_id and job_id to CUBE, which groups the rows by those columns:

```sql
SELECT division_id, job_id, SUM(salary)
FROM employees2
GROUP BY CUBE(division_id, job_id)
ORDER BY division_id, job_id;
```

```
DIV JOB SUM(SALARY)
--- --- -----------
BUS MGR     530000
BUS PRE     800000
BUS WOR     280000
BUS        1610000
OPE ENG     245000
OPE MGR     805000
OPE WOR     270000
OPE        1320000
SAL MGR    4446000
SAL WOR     490000
SAL        4936000
SUP MGR     465000
SUP TEC     115000
SUP WOR     435000
SUP        1015000
    ENG     245000
    MGR    6246000
    PRE     800000
    TEC     115000
    WOR    1475000
            8881000
```

The salaries are summed by `division_id` and `job_id`. CUBE returns a row with the sum of the salaries for each `division_id`, along with the sum of all salaries for each `job_id`. At the end of the output is a row with the grand total of the salaries.

The next example switches `division_id` and `job_id`:

```
SELECT job_id, division_id, SUM(salary)
FROM employees2
GROUP BY CUBE(job_id, division_id)
ORDER BY job_id, division_id;
```

```
JOB DIV SUM(SALARY)
--- --- -----------
ENG OPE     245000
ENG         245000
MGR BUS     530000
MGR OPE     805000
MGR SAL    4446000
MGR SUP     465000
MGR        6246000
PRE BUS     800000
PRE         800000
TEC SUP     115000
TEC         115000
WOR BUS     280000
WOR OPE     270000
WOR SAL     490000
WOR SUP     435000
```

```
WOR          1475000
    BUS      1610000
    OPE      1320000
    SAL      4936000
    SUP      1015000
             8881000
```

Using the GROUPING() Function

The GROUPING() function accepts a column and returns 0 or 1. GROUPING() returns 1 when the column value is null and returns 0 when the column value is non-null. GROUPING() is used only in queries that use ROLLUP or CUBE. GROUPING() is useful when you want to display a value when a null would otherwise be returned.

Using GROUPING() with a Single Column in a ROLLUP

As you saw earlier in the section "Passing a Single Column to ROLLUP," the last row in the example's result set contained a total of the salaries:

```
SELECT division_id, SUM(salary)
FROM employees2
GROUP BY ROLLUP(division_id)
ORDER BY division_id;

DIV SUM(SALARY)
--- -----------
BUS     1610000
OPE     1320000
SAL     4936000
SUP     1015000
        8881000
```

The division_id column for the last row is null.

You can use the GROUPING() function to determine whether this column is null, as shown in the following query. GROUPING() returns 0 for the rows that have non-null division_id values and returns 1 for the last row that has a null division_id.

```
SELECT GROUPING(division_id), division_id, SUM(salary)
FROM employees2
GROUP BY ROLLUP(division_id)
ORDER BY division_id;

GROUPING(DIVISION_ID) DIV SUM(SALARY)
--------------------- --- -----------
                    0 BUS     1610000
                    0 OPE     1320000
                    0 SAL     4936000
                    0 SUP     1015000
                    1         8881000
```

Using CASE to Convert the Returned Value from GROUPING()

You can use the CASE expression to convert the 1 in the previous example to a meaningful value. The following example uses CASE to convert 1 to the string 'All divisions':

```
SELECT
  CASE GROUPING(division_id)
    WHEN 1 THEN 'All divisions'
    ELSE division_id
  END AS div,
  SUM(salary)
FROM employees2
GROUP BY ROLLUP(division_id)
ORDER BY division_id;

DIV            SUM(SALARY)
-------------  -----------
BUS                1610000
OPE                1320000
SAL                4936000
SUP                1015000
All divisions      8881000
```

Using CASE and GROUPING() to Convert Multiple Column Values

The next example replaces null values in a ROLLUP containing multiple columns (division_id and job_id). Null division_id values are replaced with the string 'All divisions', and null job_id values are replaced with 'All jobs'.

```
SELECT
  CASE GROUPING(division_id)
    WHEN 1 THEN 'All divisions'
    ELSE division_id
  END AS div,
  CASE GROUPING(job_id)
    WHEN 1 THEN 'All jobs'
    ELSE job_id
  END AS job,
  SUM(salary)
FROM employees2
GROUP BY ROLLUP(division_id, job_id)
ORDER BY division_id, job_id;

DIV            JOB       SUM(SALARY)
-------------  --------  -----------
BUS            MGR            530000
BUS            PRE            800000
BUS            WOR            280000
BUS            All jobs      1610000
OPE            ENG            245000
OPE            MGR            805000
OPE            WOR            270000
```

```
OPE           All jobs      1320000
SAL           MGR           4446000
SAL           WOR            490000
SAL           All jobs      4936000
SUP           MGR            465000
SUP           TEC            115000
SUP           WOR            435000
SUP           All jobs      1015000
All divisions All jobs      8881000
```

Using GROUPING() with CUBE

You can use the GROUPING() function with CUBE. For example:

```
SELECT
   CASE GROUPING(division_id)
     WHEN 1 THEN 'All divisions'
     ELSE division_id
   END AS div,
   CASE GROUPING(job_id)
     WHEN 1 THEN 'All jobs'
     ELSE job_id
   END AS job,
   SUM(salary)
FROM employees2
GROUP BY CUBE(division_id, job_id)
ORDER BY division_id, job_id;

DIV           JOB       SUM(SALARY)
------------- --------- -----------
BUS           MGR            530000
BUS           PRE            800000
BUS           WOR            280000
BUS           All jobs      1610000
OPE           ENG            245000
OPE           MGR            805000
OPE           WOR            270000
OPE           All jobs      1320000
SAL           MGR           4446000
SAL           WOR            490000
SAL           All jobs      4936000
SUP           MGR            465000
SUP           TEC            115000
SUP           WOR            435000
SUP           All jobs      1015000
All divisions ENG            245000
All divisions MGR           6246000
All divisions PRE            800000
All divisions TEC            115000
All divisions WOR           1475000
All divisions All jobs      8881000
```

Using the GROUPING SETS Clause

You use the GROUPING SETS clause to obtain the subtotal rows. The following example uses GROUPING SETS to obtain the subtotals for salaries by division_id and job_id:

```
SELECT division_id, job_id, SUM(salary)
FROM employees2
GROUP BY GROUPING SETS(division_id, job_id)
ORDER BY division_id, job_id;
```

```
DIV JOB SUM(SALARY)
--- --- -----------
BUS         1610000
OPE         1320000
SAL         4936000
SUP         1015000
    ENG      245000
    MGR     6246000
    PRE      800000
    TEC      115000
    WOR     1475000
```

Only the subtotals for the division_id and job_id columns are returned. The total for all salaries is not returned.

TIP
The GROUPING SETS clause typically offers better performance than CUBE. Therefore, you should use GROUPING SETS rather than CUBE wherever possible.

You'll see how to get the total and subtotals in the next section.

Using the GROUPING_ID() Function

You can use the GROUPING_ID() function to filter rows with a HAVING clause. This allows you to filter rows to those that contain a subtotal or total. The GROUPING_ID() function accepts one or more columns and returns the decimal equivalent of the GROUPING bit vector. The GROUPING bit vector is computed by combining the results of a call to the GROUPING() function for each column in order.

Computing the GROUPING Bit Vector

The GROUPING() function returns 1 when the column value is null and returns 0 when the column value is non-null. For example:

- If both division_id and job_id are non-null, GROUPING() returns 0 for both columns. The result for division_id is combined with the result for job_id, giving a bit vector of 00, whose decimal equivalent is 0. GROUPING_ID() therefore returns 0 when division_id and job_id are non-null.

- If division_id is non-null (the GROUPING bit is 0), but job_id is null (the GROUPING bit is 1), the resulting bit vector is 01 and GROUPING_ID() returns 1.

- If `division_id` is null (the GROUPING bit is 1), but `job_id` is non-null (the GROUPING bit is 0), the resulting bit vector is 10 and `GROUPING_ID()` returns 2.
- If both `division_id` and `job_id` are null (both GROUPING bits are 0), the bit vector is 11 and `GROUPING_ID()` returns 3.

The following table summarizes these results.

division_id	job_id	Bit Vector	GROUPING_ID() Return Value
Non-null	Non-null	00	0
Non-null	Null	01	1
Null	Non-null	10	2
Null	Null	11	3

An Example Query That Illustrates the Use of GROUPING_ID()

The following example passes `division_id` and `job_id` to `GROUPING_ID()`:

```
SELECT
    division_id, job_id,
    GROUPING(division_id) AS DIV_GRP,
    GROUPING(job_id) AS JOB_GRP,
    GROUPING_ID(division_id, job_id) AS grp_id,
    SUM(salary)
FROM employees2
GROUP BY CUBE(division_id, job_id)
ORDER BY division_id, job_id;
```

```
DIV JOB   DIV_GRP    JOB_GRP      GRP_ID SUM(SALARY)
--- ---   ----------  ----------  ---------- -----------
BUS MGR        0          0          0       530000
BUS PRE        0          0          0       800000
BUS WOR        0          0          0       280000
BUS            0          1          1      1610000
OPE ENG        0          0          0       245000
OPE MGR        0          0          0       805000
OPE WOR        0          0          0       270000
OPE            0          1          1      1320000
SAL MGR        0          0          0      4446000
SAL WOR        0          0          0       490000
SAL            0          1          1      4936000
SUP MGR        0          0          0       465000
SUP TEC        0          0          0       115000
SUP WOR        0          0          0       435000
SUP            0          1          1      1015000
    ENG        1          0          2       245000
    MGR        1          0          2      6246000
    PRE        1          0          2       800000
    TEC        1          0          2       115000
    WOR        1          0          2      1475000
               1          1          3      8881000
```

Filtering Rows Using GROUPING_ID() and a HAVING Clause

A useful application of GROUPING_ID() is to filter rows with a HAVING clause. The HAVING clause can exclude rows that don't contain a subtotal or total by checking if GROUPING_ID() returns a value greater than 0. For example:

```
SELECT
  division_id, job_id,
  GROUPING_ID(division_id, job_id) AS grp_id,
  SUM(salary)
FROM employees2
GROUP BY CUBE(division_id, job_id)
HAVING GROUPING_ID(division_id, job_id) > 0
ORDER BY division_id, job_id;
```

```
DIV JOB   GRP_ID SUM(SALARY)
--- ---   ------ -----------
BUS            1     1610000
OPE            1     1320000
SAL            1     4936000
SUP            1     1015000
    ENG        2      245000
    MGR        2     6246000
    PRE        2      800000
    TEC        2      115000
    WOR        2     1475000
               3     8881000
```

Using a Column Multiple Times in a GROUP BY Clause

You can use a column many times in a GROUP BY clause. This allows you to reorganize your data or report on different groupings of data. The following query contains a GROUP BY clause that uses division_id twice, once to group by division_id and again in a ROLLUP:

```
SELECT division_id, job_id, SUM(salary)
FROM employees2
GROUP BY division_id, ROLLUP(division_id, job_id);
```

```
DIV JOB SUM(SALARY)
--- --- -----------
BUS MGR     530000
BUS PRE     800000
BUS WOR     280000
OPE ENG     245000
OPE MGR     805000
OPE WOR     270000
SAL MGR    4446000
SAL WOR     490000
SUP MGR     465000
SUP TEC     115000
```

```
SUP WOR      435000
BUS         1610000
OPE         1320000
SAL         4936000
SUP         1015000
BUS         1610000
OPE         1320000
SAL         4936000
SUP         1015000
```

The last four rows are duplicates of the previous four rows. You can eliminate these duplicates using the GROUP_ID() function, which you'll learn about next.

Using the GROUP_ID() Function

You can use the GROUP_ID() function to remove duplicate rows returned by a GROUP BY clause. If *n* duplicates exist for a particular grouping, GROUP_ID() returns numbers in the range 0 to *n* – 1.

The following example rewrites the query shown in the previous section to include the output from GROUP_ID():

```
SELECT division_id, job_id, GROUP_ID(), SUM(salary)
FROM employees2
GROUP BY division_id, ROLLUP(division_id, job_id);
```

```
DIV JOB GROUP_ID() SUM(SALARY)
--- --- ---------- -----------
BUS MGR          0      530000
BUS PRE          0      800000
BUS WOR          0      280000
OPE ENG          0      245000
OPE MGR          0      805000
OPE WOR          0      270000
SAL MGR          0     4446000
SAL WOR          0      490000
SUP MGR          0      465000
SUP TEC          0      115000
SUP WOR          0      435000
BUS              0     1610000
OPE              0     1320000
SAL              0     4936000
SUP              0     1015000
BUS              1     1610000
OPE              1     1320000
SAL              1     4936000
SUP              1     1015000
```

Notice GROUP_ID() returns 0 for all rows except the last four, which are duplicates of the previous four rows. GROUP_ID() returns 1 for the last four rows.

You can eliminate duplicate rows using a HAVING clause that allows only rows whose GROUP_ID() is 0. For example:

```
SELECT division_id, job_id, GROUP_ID(), SUM(salary)
FROM employees2
GROUP BY division_id, ROLLUP(division_id, job_id)
HAVING GROUP_ID() = 0;
```

```
DIV JOB GROUP_ID() SUM(SALARY)
--- --- ---------- -----------
BUS MGR          0      530000
BUS PRE          0      800000
BUS WOR          0      280000
OPE ENG          0      245000
OPE MGR          0      805000
OPE WOR          0      270000
SAL MGR          0     4446000
SAL WOR          0      490000
SUP MGR          0      465000
SUP TEC          0      115000
SUP WOR          0      435000
BUS              0     1610000
OPE              0     1320000
SAL              0     4936000
SUP              0     1015000
```

This concludes the discussion of the extended GROUP BY clauses.

Using CROSS APPLY and OUTER APPLY

New for Oracle Database 12c are CROSS APPLY and OUTER APPLY, which compare the rows returned by two SELECT statements and return the matching rows in one merged result set.

The examples in the following sections use the divisions and employees3 tables. The following query retrieves the rows from the divisions table:

```
SELECT *
FROM divisions;
```

```
DIV NAME
--- ----------
SAL Sales
OPE Operations
SUP Support
BUS Business
```

Only employees in the Business division are included in the employees3 table. Business division employees have BUS in their division_id column, as shown in the following query:

```
SELECT *
FROM employees3;
```

```
EMPLOYEE_ID DIV JOB FIRST_NAME LAST_NAME      SALARY
----------- --- --- ---------- ---------- ----------
          1 BUS PRE James      Smith          800000
         14 BUS MGR Mark       Smith          155000
         15 BUS MGR Jill       Jones          175000
         19 BUS MGR Tanya      Conway         200000
         37 BUS WOR Damon      Jones          280000
```

There are no Sales, Operations, or Support division employees.

CROSS APPLY

CROSS APPLY returns a merge of the rows from two SELECT statements. Only rows from the outer SELECT that match the rows from the inner SELECT are returned in the result set. The following example retrieves the rows from the `divisions` table and `employees3` table:

```
SELECT *
FROM divisions d
CROSS APPLY
  (SELECT *
   FROM employees3 e
   WHERE e.division_id = d.division_id);
ORDER BY employee_id;
```

```
DIV NAME            EMPLOYEE_ID DIV JOB FIRST_NAME LAST_NAME      SALARY
--- --------------- ----------- --- --- ---------- ---------- ----------
BUS Business                  1 BUS PRE James      Smith          800000
BUS Business                 14 BUS MGR Mark       Smith          155000
BUS Business                 15 BUS MGR Jill       Jones          175000
BUS Business                 19 BUS MGR Tanya      Conway         200000
BUS Business                 37 BUS WOR Damon      Jones          280000
```

The Business division details from the `divisions` table and the matching employee details from the `employees3` table are merged in the result set.

OUTER APPLY

OUTER APPLY returns a merge of the rows from two SELECT statements, including non-matching rows returned by the outer SELECT. The following example retrieves the rows from the `divisions` table and `employees3` table:

```
SELECT *
FROM divisions d
OUTER APPLY
  (SELECT *
   FROM employees3 e
   WHERE e.division_id = d.division_id);
ORDER BY employee_id;
```

```
DIV NAME            EMPLOYEE_ID DIV JOB FIRST_NAME LAST_NAME      SALARY
--- --------------- ----------- --- --- ---------- ---------- ----------
BUS Business                  1 BUS PRE James      Smith          800000
BUS Business                 14 BUS MGR Mark       Smith          155000
```

```
BUS Business            15 BUS MGR Jill      Jones        175000
BUS Business            19 BUS MGR Tanya     Conway       200000
BUS Business            37 BUS WOR Damon     Jones        280000
SAL Sales
SUP Support
OPE Operations
```

The Business employees are included in the result set. In addition, the Operations, Sales, and Support division rows are also included in the result set, even though there are no matching employee rows for those divisions. The additional rows are included because OUTER APPLY includes the non-matching rows returned by the outer SELECT. The columns for the non-matching employees are set to null in the result set.

Using LATERAL

New for Oracle Database 12c is LATERAL, which provides a subquery as an inline view. An inline view retrieves data from one or more tables to produce a temporary table that an outer SELECT can use as a source of data. The following example uses LATERAL:

```
SELECT *
FROM divisions d,
LATERAL
  (SELECT *
   FROM employees3 e
   WHERE e.division_id = d.division_id
  );
ORDER BY employee_id;
```

```
DIV NAME            EMPLOYEE_ID DIV JOB FIRST_NAME LAST_NAME     SALARY
--- --------------- ----------- --- --- ---------- ---------- ----------
BUS Business                  1 BUS PRE James      Smith         800000
BUS Business                 14 BUS MGR Mark       Smith         155000
BUS Business                 15 BUS MGR Jill       Jones         175000
BUS Business                 19 BUS MGR Tanya      Conway        200000
BUS Business                 37 BUS WOR Damon      Jones         280000
```

The Business division details and the employees are returned.

Unlike OUTER APPLY, LATERAL cannot provide null columns for non-matching rows. The following are limitations of using LATERAL:

- LATERAL cannot be used with PIVOT and UNPIVOT in the table reference.
- The LATERAL inline view cannot contain a left correlation to the first table in a right outer join or full outer join.

Summary

In this chapter, you have learned the following:

- The set operators (UNION ALL, UNION, INTERSECT, and MINUS) combine rows returned by two or more queries.
- TRANSLATE() translates characters in one string to characters in another string.

- `CASE` performs if-then-else logic in SQL.
- Queries can be run against data that are organized into a hierarchy.
- `ROLLUP` extends the `GROUP BY` clause to return a row containing a subtotal for each group of rows, plus a row containing a grand total for all the groups.
- `CUBE` extends the `GROUP BY` clause to return rows containing a subtotal for all combinations of columns, plus a row containing the grand total.
- `CROSS APPLY` returns a merge of the rows from two `SELECT` statements.
- `OUTER APPLY` returns a merge of the rows from two `SELECT` statements, including non-matching rows returned by the outer `SELECT`.
- `LATERAL` returns an inline view of data.

In the next chapter, you'll learn about analyzing data.

CHAPTER
8

Analyzing Data

I n this chapter, you'll learn how to perform the following tasks:

- Use analytic functions to perform complex calculations
- Perform inter-row calculations using the MODEL clause
- Use the PIVOT and UNPIVOT clauses, which are useful for finding trends in data
- Perform top-N queries to return the top or bottom N rows from a data set
- Locate patterns in data using the MATCH_RECOGNIZE clause

Using Analytic Functions

Analytic functions enable you to perform complex calculations. For example, analytic functions enable you to find the top-selling product type for each month, the top salespersons, and so on. Analytic functions are organized into the following categories:

- **Ranking functions** calculate ranks, percentiles, and n-tiles (tertiles, quartiles, and so on).
- **Inverse percentile functions** calculate the value that corresponds to a percentile.
- **Window functions** calculate cumulative and moving aggregates.
- **Reporting functions** calculate the market share and so on.
- **Lag and lead functions** obtain a value in a row where that row is a certain number of rows away from the current row.
- **First and last functions** obtain the first and last values in an ordered group.
- **Linear regression functions** fit an ordinary-least-squares regression line to a set of number pairs.
- **Hypothetical rank and distribution functions** calculate the rank and percentile that a new row would have if the row was inserted into a table.

You'll learn about these functions shortly, but first let's examine the all_sales example table.

The Example Table

The all_sales table is used in the following sections. The all_sales table stores the sum of all the sales by dollar amount for a particular year, month, product type, and employee. The all_sales table is created by the store_schema.sql script as follows:

```
CREATE TABLE all_sales (
    year INTEGER NOT NULL,
    month INTEGER NOT NULL,
    prd_type_id INTEGER
      CONSTRAINT all_sales_fk_product_types
      REFERENCES product_types(product_type_id),
    emp_id INTEGER
      CONSTRAINT all_sales_fk_employees2
```

```
    REFERENCES employees2 (employee_id),
  amount NUMBER(8, 2),
  CONSTRAINT all_sales_pk PRIMARY KEY (
    year, month, prd_type_id, emp_id
  )
);
```

The all_sales table contains the following five columns:

- **year** stores the year the sales took place.
- **month** stores the month the sales took place (1 to 12).
- **prd_type_id** stores the product_type_id of the product.
- **emp_id** stores the employee_id of the employee who handled the sales.
- **amount** stores the total dollar amount of the sales.

The following query retrieves the first 12 rows from the all_sales table:

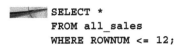

```
SELECT *
FROM all_sales
WHERE ROWNUM <= 12;
```

```
    YEAR    MONTH PRD_TYPE_ID      EMP_ID    AMOUNT
---------- ---------- ----------- ---------- ----------
      2003         1           1         21   10034.84
      2003         2           1         21   15144.65
      2003         3           1         21   20137.83
      2003         4           1         21   25057.45
      2003         5           1         21   17214.56
      2003         6           1         21   15564.64
      2003         7           1         21   12654.84
      2003         8           1         21   17434.82
      2003         9           1         21   19854.57
      2003        10           1         21   21754.19
      2003        11           1         21   13029.73
      2003        12           1         21   10034.84
```

NOTE
*The all_sales table contains a lot more rows, but for brevity they
are not shown here.*

The ranking functions are described next.

Using the Ranking Functions

The ranking functions calculate ranks, percentiles, and *n*-tiles. The ranking functions are shown in Table 8-1.

Let's examine the RANK() and DENSE_RANK() functions first.

Function	Description
RANK()	Returns the rank of items in a group. RANK() leaves a gap in the sequence of rankings in the event of a tie.
DENSE_RANK()	Returns the rank of items in a group. DENSE_RANK() doesn't leave a gap in the sequence of rankings in the event of a tie.
CUME_DIST()	Returns the cumulative distribution of a value in a group of values.
PERCENT_RANK()	Returns the percent rank of a value in a group of values.
NTILE()	Returns n-tiles: tertiles, quartiles, and so on.
ROW_NUMBER()	Returns a number with each row in a group.

TABLE 8-1. *The Ranking Functions*

Using the RANK() and DENSE_RANK() Functions

RANK() and DENSE_RANK() rank items in a group. The difference between these two functions is in the way they handle items that tie: RANK() leaves a gap in the sequence when there is a tie, but DENSE_RANK() leaves no gaps.

For example, when ranking sales by product type and two product types tie for first place, RANK() would put the two product types in first place, but the next product type would be in third place. DENSE_RANK() would also put the two product types in first place, but the next product type would be in second place.

The following query uses RANK() and DENSE_RANK() to obtain the ranking of sales by product type for the year 2003. Notice the use of the keyword OVER when calling the RANK() and DENSE_RANK() functions.

```
SELECT
  prd_type_id, SUM(amount),
  RANK() OVER (ORDER BY SUM(amount) DESC) AS rank,
  DENSE_RANK() OVER (ORDER BY SUM(amount) DESC) AS dense_rank
FROM all_sales
WHERE year = 2003
AND amount IS NOT NULL
GROUP BY prd_type_id
ORDER BY prd_type_id;

PRD_TYPE_ID SUM(AMOUNT)      RANK DENSE_RANK
----------- -----------      ---- ----------
          1   905081.84         1          1
          2   186381.22         4          4
          3   478270.91         2          2
          4   402751.16         3          3
```

The sales for product type #1 are ranked first, sales for product type #2 are ranked fourth, and so on. Because there are no ties, RANK() and DENSE_RANK() return the same ranks.

The `all_sales` table contains nulls in the `amount` column for all rows whose `prd_type_id` column is 5. The previous query omits these rows because of the inclusion of the line "AND amount IS NOT NULL" in the WHERE clause. The next example includes these rows by leaving out the AND line from the WHERE clause:

```
SELECT
  prd_type_id, SUM(amount),
  RANK() OVER (ORDER BY SUM(amount) DESC) AS rank,
  DENSE_RANK() OVER (ORDER BY SUM(amount) DESC) AS dense_rank
FROM all_sales
WHERE year = 2003
GROUP BY prd_type_id
ORDER BY prd_type_id;
```

```
PRD_TYPE_ID SUM(AMOUNT)       RANK DENSE_RANK
----------- ----------- ---------- ----------
          1   905081.84          2          2
          2   186381.22          5          5
          3   478270.91          3          3
          4   402751.16          4          4
          5                      1          1
```

The last row contains null for the sum of the `amount` column, and `RANK()` and `DENSE_RANK()` return 1 for this row. This is because by default `RANK()` and `DENSE_RANK()` assign the highest rank of 1 to null values in descending rankings (that is, DESC is used in the OVER clause) and the lowest rank in ascending rankings (that is, ASC is used in the OVER clause).

Controlling Ranking of Null Values Using the NULLS FIRST and NULLS LAST Clauses   When using an analytic function, you can explicitly control whether nulls are the highest or lowest in a group using NULLS FIRST or NULLS LAST. The following example uses NULLS LAST to specify that nulls are the lowest:

```
SELECT
  prd_type_id, SUM(amount),
  RANK() OVER (ORDER BY SUM(amount) DESC NULLS LAST) AS rank,
  DENSE_RANK() OVER (ORDER BY SUM(amount) DESC NULLS LAST) AS dense_rank
FROM all_sales
WHERE year = 2003
GROUP BY prd_type_id
ORDER BY prd_type_id;
```

```
PRD_TYPE_ID SUM(AMOUNT)       RANK DENSE_RANK
----------- ----------- ---------- ----------
          1   905081.84          1          1
          2   186381.22          4          4
          3   478270.91          2          2
          4   402751.16          3          3
          5                      5          5
```

Using the PARTITION BY Clause with Analytic Functions   You use the PARTITION BY clause with the analytic functions when you need to divide the groups into subgroups. For example, to subdivide the sales amount by month, you use PARTITION BY month, as shown in the following query:

```
SELECT
  prd_type_id, month, SUM(amount),
  RANK() OVER (PARTITION BY month ORDER BY SUM(amount) DESC) AS rank
FROM all_sales
WHERE year = 2003
AND amount IS NOT NULL
GROUP BY prd_type_id, month
ORDER BY prd_type_id, month;
```

PRD_TYPE_ID	MONTH	SUM(AMOUNT)	RANK
1	1	38909.04	1
1	2	70567.9	1
1	3	91826.98	1
1	4	120344.7	1
1	5	97287.36	1
1	6	57387.84	1
1	7	60929.04	2
1	8	75608.92	1
1	9	85027.42	1
1	10	105305.22	1
1	11	55678.38	1
1	12	46209.04	2
2	1	14309.04	4
2	2	13367.9	4
2	3	16826.98	4
2	4	15664.7	4
2	5	18287.36	4
2	6	14587.84	4
2	7	15689.04	3
2	8	16308.92	4
2	9	19127.42	4
2	10	13525.14	4
2	11	16177.84	4
2	12	12509.04	4
3	1	24909.04	2
3	2	15467.9	3
3	3	20626.98	3
3	4	23844.7	2
3	5	18687.36	3
3	6	19887.84	3
3	7	81589.04	1
3	8	62408.92	2
3	9	46127.42	3
3	10	70325.29	3
3	11	46187.38	2
3	12	48209.04	1
4	1	17398.43	3

4	2	17267.9	2
4	3	31026.98	2
4	4	16144.7	3
4	5	20087.36	2
4	6	33087.84	2
4	7	12089.04	4
4	8	58408.92	3
4	9	49327.42	2
4	10	75325.14	2
4	11	42178.38	3
4	12	30409.05	3

Using ROLLUP, CUBE, and GROUPING SETS Operators with Analytic Functions   The
ROLLUP, CUBE, and GROUPING SETS operators can be used with the analytic functions. The
following query uses ROLLUP and RANK() to get the sales rankings by product type ID:

```
SELECT
  prd_type_id, SUM(amount),
  RANK() OVER (ORDER BY SUM(amount) DESC) AS rank
FROM all_sales
WHERE year = 2003
GROUP BY ROLLUP(prd_type_id)
ORDER BY prd_type_id;

PRD_TYPE_ID SUM(AMOUNT)      RANK
----------- -----------  ----------
          1    905081.84          3
          2    186381.22          6
          3    478270.91          4
          4    402751.16          5
          5                       1
               1972485.13         2
```

The next query uses CUBE and RANK() to get all rankings of sales by product type ID and
employee ID:

```
SELECT
  prd_type_id, emp_id, SUM(amount),
  RANK() OVER (ORDER BY SUM(amount) DESC) AS rank
FROM all_sales
WHERE year = 2003
GROUP BY CUBE(prd_type_id, emp_id)
ORDER BY prd_type_id, emp_id;

PRD_TYPE_ID     EMP_ID SUM(AMOUNT)       RANK
----------- ---------- -----------  ----------
          1         21   197916.96          19
          1         22   214216.96          17
          1         23    98896.96          26
          1         24   207216.96          18
          1         25    93416.96          28
```

```
    1      26      93417.04        27
    1             905081.84         9
    2      21      20426.96        40
    2      22      19826.96        41
    2      23      19726.96        42
    2      24      43866.96        34
    2      25      32266.96        38
    2      26      50266.42        31
    2             186381.22        21
    3      21     140326.96        22
    3      22     116826.96        23
    3      23     112026.96        24
    3      24      34829.96        36
    3      25      29129.96        39
    3      26      45130.11        33
    3             478270.91        10
    4      21     108326.96        25
    4      22      81426.96        30
    4      23      92426.96        29
    4      24      47456.96        32
    4      25      33156.96        37
    4      26      39956.36        35
    4             402751.16        13
    5      21                       1
    5      22                       1
    5      23                       1
    5      24                       1
    5      25                       1
    5      26                       1
    5                               1
           21     466997.84        11
           22     432297.84        12
           23     323077.84        15
           24     333370.84        14
           25     187970.84        20
           26     228769.93        16
                 1972485.13         8
```

The next query uses GROUPING SETS and RANK() to get just the sales amount subtotal rankings:

```sql
SELECT
  prd_type_id, emp_id, SUM(amount),
  RANK() OVER (ORDER BY SUM(amount) DESC) AS rank
FROM all_sales
WHERE year = 2003
GROUP BY GROUPING SETS(prd_type_id, emp_id)
ORDER BY prd_type_id, emp_id;
```

```
PRD_TYPE_ID     EMP_ID SUM(AMOUNT)       RANK
----------- ---------- ----------- ----------
          1             905081.84          2
```

```
       2              186381.22         11
       3              478270.91          3
       4              402751.16          6
       5                                 1
                  21   466997.84          4
                  22   432297.84          5
                  23   323077.84          8
                  24   333370.84          7
                  25   187970.84         10
                  26   228769.93          9
```

Using the CUME_DIST() and PERCENT_RANK() Functions

CUME_DIST() calculates the cumulative distribution of a value in a group of values. PERCENT_
RANK() calculates the percent rank of a value in a group of values.

The following query uses CUME_DIST() and PERCENT_RANK() to get the cumulative
distribution and percent rank of sales:

```
SELECT
  prd_type_id, SUM(amount),
  CUME_DIST() OVER (ORDER BY SUM(amount) DESC) AS cume_dist,
  PERCENT_RANK() OVER (ORDER BY SUM(amount) DESC) AS percent_rank
FROM all_sales
WHERE year = 2003
GROUP BY prd_type_id
ORDER BY prd_type_id;
```

```
PRD_TYPE_ID SUM(AMOUNT)   CUME_DIST PERCENT_RANK
----------- -----------   --------- ------------
          1   905081.84        .4          .25
          2   186381.22         1            1
          3   478270.91        .6           .5
          4   402751.16        .8          .75
          5                    .2            0
```

Using the NTILE() Function

NTILE(buckets) calculates *n*-tiles (tertiles, quartiles, and so on). The buckets parameter
specifies the number of "buckets" into which groups of rows are placed. For example:

- NTILE(2) specifies two buckets and therefore divides the rows into two groups of rows.
- NTILE(4) divides the groups into four buckets and therefore divides the rows into four
  groups.

The following query uses NTILE(4) to split the groups of rows into four buckets:

```
SELECT
  prd_type_id, SUM(amount),
  NTILE(4) OVER (ORDER BY SUM(amount) DESC) AS ntile
FROM all_sales
WHERE year = 2003
AND amount IS NOT NULL
GROUP BY prd_type_id
```

```
ORDER BY prd_type_id;
```

```
PRD_TYPE_ID SUM(AMOUNT)      NTILE
----------- -----------  ----------
          1   905081.84           1
          2   186381.22           4
          3   478270.91           2
          4   402751.16           3
```

Using the ROW_NUMBER() Function

ROW_NUMBER() returns a number with each row in a group, starting at 1. The following query uses ROW_NUMBER():

```
SELECT
  prd_type_id, SUM(amount),
  ROW_NUMBER() OVER (ORDER BY SUM(amount) DESC) AS row_number
FROM all_sales
WHERE year = 2003
GROUP BY prd_type_id
ORDER BY prd_type_id;
```

```
PRD_TYPE_ID SUM(AMOUNT) ROW_NUMBER
----------- -----------  ----------
          1   905081.84           2
          2   186381.22           5
          3   478270.91           3
          4   402751.16           4
          5                       1
```

This concludes the discussion of ranking functions.

Using the Inverse Percentile Functions

In the earlier section "Using the CUME_DIST() and PERCENT_RANK() Functions," you saw that CUME_DIST() calculates the position of a value in a group of values, and PERCENT_RANK() calculates the percent rank of a value in a group of values.

In this section, you'll see how to use the inverse percentile functions, which operate in a reverse way to CUME_DIST() and PERCENT_RANK(). There are two inverse percentile functions:

- PERCENTILE_DISC(x) examines the cumulative distribution values in each group until a value is found that is greater than or equal to x.
- PERCENTILE_CONT(x) examines the percent rank values in each group until a value is found that is greater than or equal to x.

The following query uses PERCENTILE_CONT() and PERCENTILE_DISC() to obtain the sum of the amount whose percentile is greater than or equal to 0.6:

```
SELECT
  PERCENTILE_CONT(0.6) WITHIN GROUP (ORDER BY SUM(amount) DESC)
```

```
   AS percentile_cont,
 PERCENTILE_DISC(0.6) WITHIN GROUP (ORDER BY SUM(amount) DESC)
   AS percentile_disc
FROM all_sales
WHERE year = 2003
GROUP BY prd_type_id;


PERCENTILE_CONT PERCENTILE_DISC
--------------- ---------------
     417855.11        402751.16
```

If you compare the sum of the amounts shown in this result set with those shown in the earlier section "Using the CUME_DIST() and PERCENT_RANK() Functions," you'll see that the sums correspond to those whose cumulative distribution and percent rank are 0.6 and 0.75, respectively.

Using the Window Functions

The window functions calculate items like cumulative sums and moving averages within a specified range of rows, a range of values, or an interval of time.

A query returns a set of rows called the result set. The term "window" is used to describe a subset of rows within the result set. The subset of rows "seen" through the window is then processed by the window functions, which return a value. You can define the start and end of the window.

You can use a window with the following functions: SUM(), AVG(), MAX(), MIN(), COUNT(), VARIANCE(), and STDDEV(). These functions were introduced in Chapter 4. You can also use a window with FIRST_VALUE(), LAST_VALUE(), and NTH_VALUE(), which return the first, last, and *n*th values in a window. You'll learn about these functions later in this section, after you see how to perform a cumulative sum, a moving average, and a centered average.

Performing a Cumulative Sum

The following query performs a cumulative sum to compute the cumulative sales amount for 2003, starting with January and ending in December. Notice that each monthly sales amount is added to the cumulative amount, which grows after each month.

```
SELECT
  month, SUM(amount) AS month_amount,
  SUM(SUM(amount)) OVER
    (ORDER BY month ROWS BETWEEN UNBOUNDED PRECEDING AND CURRENT ROW)
    AS cumulative_amount
FROM all_sales
WHERE year = 2003
GROUP BY month
ORDER BY month;


   MONTH MONTH_AMOUNT CUMULATIVE_AMOUNT
---------- ------------ -----------------
       1     95525.55          95525.55
       2     116671.6         212197.15
       3    160307.92         372505.07
       4     175998.8         548503.87
```

5	154349.44	702853.31
6	124951.36	827804.67
7	170296.16	998100.83
8	212735.68	1210836.51
9	199609.68	1410446.19
10	264480.79	1674926.98
11	160221.98	1835148.96
12	137336.17	1972485.13

The query used the following expression to compute the cumulative aggregate:

```
SUM(SUM(amount)) OVER
   (ORDER BY month ROWS BETWEEN UNBOUNDED PRECEDING AND CURRENT ROW)
   AS cumulative_amount
```

Let's break down this expression:

- `SUM(amount)` computes the sum of an amount. The outer `SUM()` computes the cumulative amount.
- `ORDER BY month` orders the rows read by the query by month.
- `ROWS BETWEEN UNBOUNDED PRECEDING AND CURRENT ROW` defines the start and end of the window. The start is set to `UNBOUNDED PRECEDING`, which means the start of the window is fixed at the first row in the result set returned by the query. The end of the window is set to `CURRENT ROW`, which represents the current row in the result set being processed. The end of the window slides down one row after the outer `SUM()` function computes and returns the current cumulative amount.

The entire query computes and returns the cumulative total of the sales amounts, starting at month 1, and then adding the sales amount for month 2, then month 3, and so on, up to and including month 12. The start of the window is fixed at month 1, but the bottom of the window moves down one row in the result set after each month's sales amounts are added to the cumulative total. This continues until the last row in the result set is processed by the window and the `SUM()` functions.

Don't confuse the end of the window with the end of the result set. In the previous example, the end of the window slides down one row in the result set as each row is processed (the sum of the sales amount for that month is added to the cumulative total). In the example, the end of the window starts at the first row, the sum sales amount for that month is added to the cumulative total, and then the end of the window moves down one row to the second row. At this point, the window sees two rows. The sum of the sales amount for that month is added to the cumulative total, and the end of the window moves down one row to the third row. At this point, the window sees three rows. This continues until the 12th row is processed. At this point, the window sees 12 rows.

The following query uses a cumulative sum to compute the cumulative sales amount, starting with June of 2003 (month 6) and ending in December of 2003 (month 12):

```
SELECT
   month, SUM(amount) AS month_amount,
   SUM(SUM(amount)) OVER
      (ORDER BY month ROWS BETWEEN UNBOUNDED PRECEDING AND CURRENT ROW) AS
      cumulative_amount
```

```
FROM all_sales
WHERE year = 2003
AND month BETWEEN 6 AND 12
GROUP BY month
ORDER BY month;
```

```
    MONTH MONTH_AMOUNT CUMULATIVE_AMOUNT
---------- ------------ -----------------
         6    124951.36         124951.36
         7    170296.16         295247.52
         8    212735.68          507983.2
         9    199609.68         707592.88
        10    264480.79         972073.67
        11    160221.98        1132295.65
        12    137336.17        1269631.82
```

Performing a Moving Average

The following query computes the moving average of the sales amount between the current month and the previous three months:

```
SELECT
   month, SUM(amount) AS month_amount,
   AVG(SUM(amount)) OVER
      (ORDER BY month ROWS BETWEEN 3 PRECEDING AND CURRENT ROW)
      AS moving_average
FROM all_sales
WHERE year = 2003
GROUP BY month
ORDER BY month;
```

```
    MONTH MONTH_AMOUNT MOVING_AVERAGE
---------- ------------ --------------
         1     95525.55       95525.55
         2     116671.6      106098.575
         3    160307.92      124168.357
         4     175998.8      137125.968
         5    154349.44       151831.94
         6    124951.36       153901.88
         7    170296.16       156398.94
         8    212735.68       165583.16
         9    199609.68       176898.22
        10    264480.79      211780.578
        11    160221.98      209262.033
        12    137336.17      190412.155
```

The query used the following expression to compute the moving average:

```
AVG(SUM(amount)) OVER
   (ORDER BY month ROWS BETWEEN 3 PRECEDING AND CURRENT ROW)
   AS moving_average
```

Let's break down this expression:

- `SUM(amount)` computes the sum of an amount. The outer `AVG()` computes the average.
- `ORDER BY month` orders the rows read by the query by month.
- `ROWS BETWEEN 3 PRECEDING AND CURRENT ROW` defines the start of the window as including the three rows preceding the current row. The end of the window is the current row being processed.

The entire expression computes the moving average of the sales amount between the current month and the previous three months. Because for the first two months less than the full three months of data are available, the moving average is based on only the months available.

Both the start and the end of the window begin at row #1 read by the query. The end of the window moves down after each row is processed. The start of the window moves down only after row #4 has been processed, and subsequently moves down one row after each row is processed. This continues until the last row in the result set is read.

Performing a Centered Average

The following query computes the moving average of the sales amount centered between the previous and next month from the current month:

```
SELECT
  month, SUM(amount) AS month_amount,
  AVG(SUM(amount)) OVER
    (ORDER BY month ROWS BETWEEN 1 PRECEDING AND 1 FOLLOWING)
    AS moving_average
FROM all_sales
WHERE year = 2003
GROUP BY month
ORDER BY month;
```

```
    MONTH MONTH_AMOUNT MOVING_AVERAGE
---------- ------------ --------------
        1     95525.55     106098.575
        2     116671.6     124168.357
        3    160307.92     150992.773
        4     175998.8     163552.053
        5    154349.44     151766.533
        6    124951.36     149865.653
        7    170296.16     169327.733
        8    212735.68      194213.84
        9    199609.68     225608.717
       10    264480.79      208104.15
       11    160221.98     187346.313
       12    137336.17     148779.075
```

The query used the following expression to compute the moving average:

```
AVG(SUM(amount)) OVER
  (ORDER BY month ROWS BETWEEN 1 PRECEDING AND 1 FOLLOWING)
  AS moving_average
```

Let's break down this expression:

- SUM(amount) computes the sum of an amount. The outer AVG() computes the average.
- ORDER BY month orders the rows read by the query by month.
- ROWS BETWEEN 1 PRECEDING AND 1 FOLLOWING defines the start of the window as including the row preceding the current row being processed. The end of the window is the row following the current row.

The entire expression computes the moving average of the sales amount between the current month and the previous month. Because for the first and last month less than the full three months of data are available, the moving average is based on only the months available.

The start of the window begins at row #1 read by the query. The end of the window begins at row #2 and moves down after each row is processed. The start of the window moves down only once row #2 has been processed. Processing continues until the last row read by the query is processed.

Getting the First and Last Rows Using FIRST_VALUE() and LAST_VALUE()

The FIRST_VALUE() and LAST_VALUE() functions return the first and last rows in a window. The following query uses FIRST_VALUE() and LAST_VALUE() to obtain the previous month's sales amount and the next month's sales amount:

```
SELECT
    month, SUM(amount) AS month_amount,
    FIRST_VALUE(SUM(amount)) OVER
      (ORDER BY month ROWS BETWEEN 1 PRECEDING AND 1 FOLLOWING)
      AS previous_month_amount,
    LAST_VALUE(SUM(amount)) OVER
      (ORDER BY month ROWS BETWEEN 1 PRECEDING AND 1 FOLLOWING)
      AS next_month_amount
FROM all_sales
WHERE year = 2003
GROUP BY month
ORDER BY month;
```

MONTH	MONTH_AMOUNT	PREVIOUS_MONTH_AMOUNT	NEXT_MONTH_AMOUNT
1	95525.55	95525.55	116671.6
2	116671.6	95525.55	160307.92
3	160307.92	116671.6	175998.8
4	175998.8	160307.92	154349.44
5	154349.44	175998.8	124951.36
6	124951.36	154349.44	170296.16
7	170296.16	124951.36	212735.68
8	212735.68	170296.16	199609.68
9	199609.68	212735.68	264480.79
10	264480.79	199609.68	160221.98
11	160221.98	264480.79	137336.17
12	137336.17	160221.98	137336.17

The next query divides the current month's sales amount by the previous month's sales amount (labeled as `curr_div_prev`) and also divides the current month's sales amount by the next month's sales amount (labeled as `curr_div_next`):

```
SELECT
  month, SUM(amount) AS month_amount,
  SUM(amount)/FIRST_VALUE(SUM(amount)) OVER
    (ORDER BY month ROWS BETWEEN 1 PRECEDING AND 1 FOLLOWING)
    AS curr_div_prev,
  SUM(amount)/LAST_VALUE(SUM(amount)) OVER
    (ORDER BY month ROWS BETWEEN 1 PRECEDING AND 1 FOLLOWING)
    AS curr_div_next
FROM all_sales
WHERE year = 2003
GROUP BY month
ORDER BY month;
```

MONTH	MONTH_AMOUNT	CURR_DIV_PREV	CURR_DIV_NEXT
1	95525.55	1	.818755807
2	116671.6	1.22136538	.727796855
3	160307.92	1.37400978	.910846665
4	175998.8	1.09787963	1.14026199
5	154349.44	.876991434	1.23527619
6	124951.36	.809535558	.733729756
7	170296.16	1.36289961	.800505867
8	212735.68	1.24921008	1.06575833
9	199609.68	.93829902	.754722791
10	264480.79	1.3249898	1.65071478
11	160221.98	.605798175	1.16664081
12	137336.17	.857161858	1

Getting the *n*th Row Using NTH_VALUE()

The `NTH_VALUE()` function returns the *n*th row in a window. This function was introduced in Oracle Database 11*g* Release 2. The following query uses `NTH_VALUE()` to obtain the second month's sales, which are retrieved using `NTH_VALUE(SUM(amount), 2)`:

```
SELECT
  month, SUM(amount) AS month_amount,
  NTH_VALUE(SUM(amount), 2) OVER (
    ORDER BY month ROWS BETWEEN
    UNBOUNDED PRECEDING AND UNBOUNDED FOLLOWING
  ) nth_value
FROM all_sales
WHERE year = 2003
GROUP BY month
ORDER BY month;
```

MONTH	MONTH_AMOUNT	NTH_VALUE

```
 1       95525.55    116671.6
 2       116671.6    116671.6
 3      160307.92    116671.6
 4       175998.8    116671.6
 5      154349.44    116671.6
 6      124951.36    116671.6
 7      170296.16    116671.6
 8      212735.68    116671.6
 9      199609.68    116671.6
10      264480.79    116671.6
11      160221.98    116671.6
12      137336.17    116671.6
```

The next query uses NTH_VALUE() to obtain the 24th employee's maximum sales for product types #1, #2, and #3. The 24th employee's maximum sales are contained in the fourth position of the window and are retrieved using NTH_VALUE(MAX(amount), 4).

```
SELECT
  prd_type_id, emp_id, MAX(amount),
  NTH_VALUE(MAX(amount), 4) OVER (
    PARTITION BY prd_type_id ORDER BY emp_id
    ROWS BETWEEN UNBOUNDED PRECEDING AND UNBOUNDED FOLLOWING
  ) nth_value
FROM all_sales
WHERE prd_type_id BETWEEN 1 AND 3
GROUP BY prd_type_id, emp_id
ORDER BY prd_type_id, emp_id;
```

```
PRD_TYPE_ID    EMP_ID MAX(AMOUNT)  NTH_VALUE
-----------  -------- -----------  ---------
          1        21    25057.45  25214.56
          1        22    29057.45  25214.56
          1        23    16057.45  25214.56
          1        24    25214.56  25214.56
          1        25    14057.45  25214.56
          1        26    16754.27  25214.56
          2        21     2754.19   7314.56
          2        22     2657.45   7314.56
          2        23     2357.45   7314.56
          2        24     7314.56   7314.56
          2        25     5364.84   7314.56
          2        26     5434.84   7314.56
          3        21    32754.19   6337.83
          3        22    27264.84   6337.83
          3        23    23264.84   6337.83
          3        24     6337.83   6337.83
          3        25     4364.64   6337.83
          3        26     5457.45   6337.83
```

This concludes the discussion of window functions.

Using the Reporting Functions

The reporting functions perform calculations across groups and partitions within groups.

You can perform reporting with the following functions: SUM(), AVG(), MAX(), MIN(), COUNT(), VARIANCE(), and STDDEV(). You can also use the RATIO_TO_REPORT() function to compute the ratio of a value to the sum of a set of values, and the LISTAGG() function to order the rows within a group and concatenate the set of grouped values.

In this section, you'll see how to perform a report on a sum and use the RATIO_TO_REPORT() and LISTAGG() functions.

Reporting on a Sum

For the first three months of 2003, the following query reports:

- The total sum of all sales for all three months (labeled as total_month_amount)
- The total sum of all sales for all product types (labeled as total_product_type_amount)

```
SELECT
  month, prd_type_id,
  SUM(SUM(amount)) OVER (PARTITION BY month)
    AS total_month_amount,
  SUM(SUM(amount)) OVER (PARTITION BY prd_type_id)
    AS total_product_type_amount
FROM all_sales
WHERE year = 2003
AND month <= 3
GROUP BY month, prd_type_id
ORDER BY month, prd_type_id;
```

MONTH	PRD_TYPE_ID	TOTAL_MONTH_AMOUNT	TOTAL_PRODUCT_TYPE_AMOUNT
1	1	95525.55	201303.92
1	2	95525.55	44503.92
1	3	95525.55	61003.92
1	4	95525.55	65693.31
1	5	95525.55	
2	1	116671.6	201303.92
2	2	116671.6	44503.92
2	3	116671.6	61003.92
2	4	116671.6	65693.31
2	5	116671.6	
3	1	160307.92	201303.92
3	2	160307.92	44503.92
3	3	160307.92	61003.92
3	4	160307.92	65693.31
3	5	160307.92	

The query used the following expression to report the total sum of all sales for all months (labeled as total_month_amount):

```
SUM(SUM(amount)) OVER (PARTITION BY month)
  AS total_month_amount
```

Let's break down this expression:

- `SUM(amount)` computes the sum of an amount. The outer `SUM()` computes the total sum.
- `OVER (PARTITION BY month)` causes the outer `SUM()` to compute the sum for each month.

The previous query also used the following expression to report the total sum of all sales for all product types (labeled as `total_product_type_amount`):

```
SUM(SUM(amount)) OVER (PARTITION BY prd_type_id)
    AS total_product_type_amount
```

Let's break down this expression:

- `SUM(amount)` computes the sum of an amount. The outer `SUM()` computes the total sum.
- `OVER (PARTITION BY prd_type_id)` causes the outer `SUM()` to compute the sum for each product type.

Using the RATIO_TO_REPORT() Function

The `RATIO_TO_REPORT()` function calculates the ratio of a value to the sum of a set of values. For the first three months of 2003, the following query reports:

- The sum of the sales amount by product type for each month (labeled as `prd_type_amount`)
- The ratio of the product type's sales amount to the entire month's sales (labeled as `prd_type_ratio`), which is calculated using `RATIO_TO_REPORT()`

```
SELECT
    month, prd_type_id,
    SUM(amount) AS prd_type_amount,
    RATIO_TO_REPORT(SUM(amount)) OVER (PARTITION BY month) AS prd_type_ratio
FROM all_sales
WHERE year = 2003
AND month <= 3
GROUP BY month, prd_type_id
ORDER BY month, prd_type_id;

    MONTH PRD_TYPE_ID PRD_TYPE_AMOUNT PRD_TYPE_RATIO
---------- ----------- --------------- --------------
        1           1        38909.04      .40731553
        1           2        14309.04     .149792804
        1           3        24909.04     .260757881
        1           4        17398.43     .182133785
        1           5
        2           1         70567.9     .604842138
        2           2         13367.9     .114577155
        2           3         15467.9     .132576394
        2           4         17267.9     .148004313
```

```
2          5
3          1          91826.98          .57281624
3          2          16826.98          .104966617
3          3          20626.98          .128670998
3          4          31026.98          .193546145
3          5
```

The query used the following expression to compute the ratio (labeled as `prd_type_ratio`):

```
RATIO_TO_REPORT(SUM(amount)) OVER (PARTITION BY month) AS prd_type_ratio
```

Let's break down this expression:

- `SUM(amount)` calculates the sum of the sales amount.
- `OVER (PARTITION BY month)` causes the outer `SUM()` to calculate the sum of the sales amount for each month.
- The ratio is calculated by dividing the sum of the sales amount for each product type by the sum of the entire month's sales amount.

Using the LISTAGG() Function

The `LISTAGG()` function orders the rows within a group and concatenates the set of grouped values. This function was introduced in Oracle Database 11g Release 2. The following query retrieves products #1 through #5 from the `products` table, ordered by price and name, and returns the most expensive product:

```
SELECT
    LISTAGG(name, ', ') WITHIN GROUP (ORDER BY price, name) AS "Product List",
    MAX(price) AS "Most Expensive"
FROM products
WHERE product_id <= 5;

Product List                                            Most Expensive
------------------------------------------------------- --------------
Tank War, Modern Science, Supernova, Chemistry, Z Files         49.99
```

The next query retrieves products #1 through #5 from the `products` table and, for each product, uses `LISTAGG()` to display the products with the same `product_type_id` value:

```
SELECT
    product_id, product_type_id, name,
    LISTAGG(name, ', ')
      WITHIN GROUP (ORDER BY name)
      OVER (PARTITION BY product_type_id) AS "Product List"
FROM products
WHERE product_id <= 5
ORDER BY product_id, product_type_id;

PRODUCT_ID PRODUCT_TYPE_ID NAME             Product List
---------- --------------- ---------------- ------------------------------
```

```
1          1 Modern Science   Chemistry, Modern Science
2          1 Chemistry        Chemistry, Modern Science
3          2 Supernova        Supernova, Tank War, Z Files
4          2 Tank War         Supernova, Tank War, Z Files
5          2 Z Files          Supernova, Tank War, Z Files
```

This concludes the discussion of reporting functions.

Using the LAG() and LEAD() Functions

The LAG() and LEAD() functions obtain a value in a row where that row is a certain number of rows away from the current row. The following query uses LAG() and LEAD() to obtain the previous month's sales amount and the next month's sales amount:

```sql
SELECT
  month, SUM(amount) AS month_amount,
  LAG(SUM(amount), 1) OVER (ORDER BY month) AS previous_month_amount,
  LEAD(SUM(amount), 1) OVER (ORDER BY month) AS next_month_amount
FROM all_sales
WHERE year = 2003
GROUP BY month
ORDER BY month;
```

```
    MONTH MONTH_AMOUNT PREVIOUS_MONTH_AMOUNT NEXT_MONTH_AMOUNT
--------- ------------ --------------------- -----------------
        1     95525.55                                 116671.6
        2     116671.6              95525.55           160307.92
        3    160307.92              116671.6            175998.8
        4     175998.8             160307.92           154349.44
        5    154349.44              175998.8           124951.36
        6    124951.36             154349.44           170296.16
        7    170296.16             124951.36           212735.68
        8    212735.68             170296.16           199609.68
        9    199609.68             212735.68           264480.79
       10    264480.79             199609.68           160221.98
       11    160221.98             264480.79           137336.17
       12    137336.17             160221.98
```

The query used the following expressions to obtain the previous month's and next month's sales:

```sql
LAG(SUM(amount), 1) OVER (ORDER BY month) AS previous_month_amount,
LEAD(SUM(amount), 1) OVER (ORDER BY month) AS next_month_amount
```

LAG(SUM(amount), 1) obtains the previous row's sum of the amount.
LEAD(SUM(amount), 1) obtains the next row's sum of the amount.

Using the FIRST and LAST Functions

The FIRST and LAST functions obtain the first and last values in an ordered group. You can use FIRST and LAST with the following functions: MIN(), MAX(), COUNT(), SUM(), AVG(), STDDEV(), and VARIANCE().

The following query uses FIRST and LAST to get the months in 2003 that had the highest and lowest sales:

```
SELECT
  MIN(month) KEEP (DENSE_RANK FIRST ORDER BY SUM(amount))
    AS highest_sales_month,
  MIN(month) KEEP (DENSE_RANK LAST ORDER BY SUM(amount))
    AS lowest_sales_month
FROM all_sales
WHERE year = 2003
GROUP BY month
ORDER BY month;

HIGHEST_SALES_MONTH LOWEST_SALES_MONTH
------------------- ------------------
                  1                 10
```

Using the Linear Regression Functions

The linear regression functions fit an ordinary-least-squares regression line to a set of number pairs. You can use the linear regression functions as aggregate, windowing, or reporting functions.

The following table shows the linear regression functions. In the function syntax, y is interpreted by the functions as a variable that depends on x.

Function	Description
REGR_AVGX (y, x)	Returns the average of x after eliminating x and y pairs where either x or y is null
REGR_AVGY (y, x)	Returns the average of y after eliminating x and y pairs where either x or y is null
REGR_COUNT (y, x)	Returns the number of non-null number pairs that are used to fit the regression line
REGR_INTERCEPT (y, x)	Returns the intercept on the y-axis of the regression line
REGR_R2 (y, x)	Returns the coefficient of determination (R-squared) of the regression line
REGR_SLOPE (y, x)	Returns the slope of the regression line
REGR_SXX (y, x)	Returns REG_COUNT (y, x) * VAR_POP (x)
REGR_SXY (y, x)	Returns REG_COUNT (y, x) * COVAR_POP (y, x)
REGR_SYY (y, x)	Returns REG_COUNT (y, x) * VAR_POP (y)

The following query shows the use of the linear regression functions:

```
SELECT
  prd_type_id,
  REGR_AVGX(amount, month) AS avgx,
  REGR_AVGY(amount, month) AS avgy,
  REGR_COUNT(amount, month) AS count,
  REGR_INTERCEPT(amount, month) AS inter,
```

```
  REGR_R2(amount, month) AS r2,
  REGR_SLOPE(amount, month) AS slope,
  REGR_SXX(amount, month) AS sxx,
  REGR_SXY(amount, month) AS sxy,
  REGR_SYY(amount, month) AS syy
FROM all_sales
WHERE year = 2003
GROUP BY prd_type_id
ORDER BY prd_type_id;
```

```
PRD_TYPE_ID       AVGX        AVGY       COUNT       INTER         R2
----------- ---------- ---------- ---------- ---------- ----------
     SLOPE        SXX         SXY         SYY
---------- ---------- ---------- ----------
          1        6.5 12570.5811          72 13318.4543 .003746289
-115.05741        858   -98719.26 3031902717

          2        6.5 2588.62806          72 2608.11268    .0000508
 -2.997634        858    -2571.97   151767392

          3        6.5 6642.65153          72 2154.23119 .126338815
690.526206        858 592471.485 3238253324

          4        6.5 5593.76611          72 2043.47164 .128930297
546.199149        858  468638.87 1985337488

          5                                 0
```

Using the Hypothetical Rank and Distribution Functions

The hypothetical rank and distribution functions calculate the rank and percentile that a new row would have if the row was inserted into a table. You can perform hypothetical calculations with the following functions: RANK(), DENSE_RANK(), PERCENT_RANK(), and CUME_DIST().

The following query uses RANK() and PERCENT_RANK() to obtain the rank and percent rank of sales by product type for 2003:

```
SELECT
  prd_type_id, SUM(amount),
  RANK() OVER (ORDER BY SUM(amount) DESC) AS rank,
  PERCENT_RANK() OVER (ORDER BY SUM(amount) DESC) AS percent_rank
FROM all_sales
WHERE year = 2003
AND amount IS NOT NULL
GROUP BY prd_type_id
ORDER BY prd_type_id;
```

```
PRD_TYPE_ID SUM(AMOUNT)       RANK PERCENT_RANK
----------- ----------- ---------- ------------
          1   905081.84          1            0
          2   186381.22          4            1
          3   478270.91          2  .333333333
          4   402751.16          3  .666666667
```

The next query shows the hypothetical rank and percent rank of a sales amount of $500,000:

```
SELECT
  RANK(500000) WITHIN GROUP (ORDER BY SUM(amount) DESC)
    AS rank,
  PERCENT_RANK(500000) WITHIN GROUP (ORDER BY SUM(amount) DESC)
    AS percent_rank
FROM all_sales
WHERE year = 2003
AND amount IS NOT NULL
GROUP BY prd_type_id
ORDER BY prd_type_id;

      RANK PERCENT_RANK
---------- ------------
         2          .25
```

The hypothetical rank and percent rank of a sales amount of $500,000 are 2 and .25.
  This concludes the discussion of hypothetical functions.

Using the MODEL Clause

The MODEL clause was introduced with Oracle Database 10g and enables you to perform inter-row calculations. The MODEL clause allows you to access a column in a row like a cell in an array. This provides the ability to perform calculations in a similar manner to spreadsheet calculations. For example, the all_sales table contains sales information for the months in 2003. You can use the MODEL clause to calculate sales in future months based on sales in 2003.

An Example of the MODEL Clause

The easiest way to learn how to use the MODEL clause is to see an example query. The following query retrieves the sales amount for each month in 2003 made by employee #21 for product types #1 and #2 and predicts sales for January, February, and March of 2004 based on sales in 2003:

```
SELECT prd_type_id, year, month, sales_amount
FROM all_sales
WHERE prd_type_id BETWEEN 1 AND 2
AND emp_id = 21
MODEL
PARTITION BY (prd_type_id)
DIMENSION BY (month, year)
MEASURES (amount sales_amount) (
  sales_amount[1, 2004] = sales_amount[1, 2003],
  sales_amount[2, 2004] = sales_amount[2, 2003] + sales_amount[3, 2003],
  sales_amount[3, 2004] = ROUND(sales_amount[3, 2003] * 1.25, 2)
)
ORDER BY prd_type_id, year, month;
```

Let's break down this query:

- PARTITION BY (prd_type_id) specifies that the results are partitioned by prd_type_id.
- DIMENSION BY (month, year) specifies that the dimensions of the array are month and year. This means that a cell in the array is accessed by specifying a month and year.
- MEASURES (amount sales_amount) specifies that each cell in the array contains an amount and that the array name is sales_amount. To access the cell in the sales_amount array for January 2003, you use sales_amount[1, 2003], which returns the sales amount for that month and year.
- After the MEASURES keyword are three lines that calculate the future sales for January, February, and March of 2004:
  - sales_amount[1, 2004] = sales_amount[1, 2003] sets the sales amount for January 2004 to the amount for January 2003.
  - sales_amount[2, 2004] = sales_amount[2, 2003] + sales_amount[3, 2003] sets the sales amount for February 2004 to the amount for February 2003 plus March 2003.
  - sales_amount[3, 2004] = ROUND(sales_amount[3, 2003] * 1.25, 2) sets the sales amount for March 2004 to the rounded value of the sales amount for March 2003 multiplied by 1.25.
- ORDER BY prd_type_id, year, month orders the results returned by the entire query.

The result set from the query is shown in the following listing. Notice the results contain the sales amounts for all months in 2003 for product types #1 and #2, plus the predicted sales amounts for the first three months in 2004 (which I've made bold to make them easier to see):

```
PRD_TYPE_ID       YEAR       MONTH SALES_AMOUNT
----------- ----------- ----------- ------------
          1        2003           1     10034.84
          1        2003           2     15144.65
          1        2003           3     20137.83
          1        2003           4     25057.45
          1        2003           5     17214.56
          1        2003           6     15564.64
          1        2003           7     12654.84
          1        2003           8     17434.82
          1        2003           9     19854.57
          1        2003          10     21754.19
          1        2003          11     13029.73
          1        2003          12     10034.84
          1        2004           1     10034.84
          1        2004           2     35282.48
          1        2004           3     25172.29
          2        2003           1      1034.84
          2        2003           2      1544.65
          2        2003           3      2037.83
```

2	2003	4	2557.45
2	2003	5	1714.56
2	2003	6	1564.64
2	2003	7	1264.84
2	2003	8	1734.82
2	2003	9	1854.57
2	2003	10	2754.19
2	2003	11	1329.73
2	2003	12	1034.84
2	**2004**	**1**	**1034.84**
2	**2004**	**2**	**3582.48**
2	**2004**	**3**	**2547.29**

Using Positional and Symbolic Notation to Access Cells

In the previous example, a cell in an array was accessed using the following notation: sales_amount[1, 2004], where 1 is the month and 2004 is the year. This is referred to as positional notation because the meaning of the dimensions is determined by their position. The first position contains the month and the second position contains the year.

You can also use symbolic notation to explicitly indicate the meaning of the dimensions. For example, sales_amount[month=1, year=2004]. The following query uses symbolic notation:

```
SELECT prd_type_id, year, month, sales_amount
FROM all_sales
WHERE prd_type_id BETWEEN 1 AND 2
AND emp_id = 21
MODEL
PARTITION BY (prd_type_id)
DIMENSION BY (month, year)
MEASURES (amount sales_amount) (
  sales_amount[month=1, year=2004] = sales_amount[month=1, year=2003],
  sales_amount[month=2, year=2004] =
    sales_amount[month=2, year=2003] + sales_amount[month=3, year=2003],
  sales_amount[month=3, year=2004] =
    ROUND(sales_amount[month=3, year=2003] * 1.25, 2)
)
ORDER BY prd_type_id, year, month;
```

When using positional or symbolic notation, be aware of the different way they handle null values in the dimensions. For example, sales_amount[null, 2003] returns the amount whose month is null and year is 2003, but sales_amount[month=null, year=2004] won't access a valid cell because null=null always returns false.

Accessing a Range of Cells Using BETWEEN and AND

You can access a range of cells using the BETWEEN and AND keywords. For example, the following expression sets the sales amount for January 2004 to the rounded average of the sales between January and March 2003:

```
sales_amount[1, 2004] =
  ROUND(AVG(sales_amount)[month BETWEEN 1 AND 3, 2003], 2)
```

The following query shows the use of this expression:

```
SELECT prd_type_id, year, month, sales_amount
FROM all_sales
WHERE prd_type_id BETWEEN 1 AND 2
AND emp_id = 21
MODEL
PARTITION BY (prd_type_id)
DIMENSION BY (month, year)
MEASURES (amount sales_amount) (
  sales_amount[1, 2004] =
    ROUND(AVG(sales_amount)[month BETWEEN 1 AND 3, 2003], 2)
)
ORDER BY prd_type_id, year, month;
```

Accessing All Cells Using ANY and IS ANY

You can access all cells in an array using the ANY and IS ANY predicates. You use ANY with positional notation and IS ANY with symbolic notation. For example, the following expression sets the sales amount for January 2004 to the rounded sum of the sales for all months and years:

```
sales_amount[1, 2004] =
    ROUND(SUM(sales_amount)[ANY, year IS ANY], 2)
```

The following query shows the use of this expression:

```
SELECT prd_type_id, year, month, sales_amount
FROM all_sales
WHERE prd_type_id BETWEEN 1 AND 2
AND emp_id = 21
MODEL
PARTITION BY (prd_type_id)
DIMENSION BY (month, year)
MEASURES (amount sales_amount) (
  sales_amount[1, 2004] =
    ROUND(SUM(sales_amount)[ANY, year IS ANY], 2)
)
ORDER BY prd_type_id, year, month;
```

Getting the Current Value of a Dimension Using CURRENTV()

The CURRENTV() function returns the current value of a dimension. For example, the following expression sets the sales amount for the first month of 2004 to 1.25 times the sales of the same month in 2003. Notice the use of CURRENTV() to get the current month, which is 1.

```
sales_amount[1, 2004] =
    ROUND(sales_amount[CURRENTV(), 2003] * 1.25, 2)
```

The following query shows the use of this expression:

```
SELECT prd_type_id, year, month, sales_amount
FROM all_sales
```

```
WHERE prd_type_id BETWEEN 1 AND 2
AND emp_id = 21
MODEL
PARTITION BY (prd_type_id)
DIMENSION BY (month, year)
MEASURES (amount sales_amount) (
  sales_amount[1, 2004] =
    ROUND(sales_amount[CURRENTV(), 2003] * 1.25, 2)
)
ORDER BY prd_type_id, year, month;
```

The result set returned by this query is shown in the following listing. The values for 2004 are highlighted in bold.

PRD_TYPE_ID	YEAR	MONTH	SALES_AMOUNT
1	2003	1	10034.84
1	2003	2	15144.65
1	2003	3	20137.83
1	2003	4	25057.45
1	2003	5	17214.56
1	2003	6	15564.64
1	2003	7	12654.84
1	2003	8	17434.82
1	2003	9	19854.57
1	2003	10	21754.19
1	2003	11	13029.73
1	2003	12	10034.84
1	**2004**	**1**	**12543.55**
2	2003	1	1034.84
2	2003	2	1544.65
2	2003	3	2037.83
2	2003	4	2557.45
2	2003	5	1714.56
2	2003	6	1564.64
2	2003	7	1264.84
2	2003	8	1734.82
2	2003	9	1854.57
2	2003	10	2754.19
2	2003	11	1329.73
2	2003	12	1034.84
2	**2004**	**1**	**1293.55**

Accessing Cells Using a FOR Loop

You can access cells using a FOR loop. For example, the following expression sets the sales amount for the first three months of 2004 to 1.25 times the sales of the same months in 2003. Notice the use of the INCREMENT keyword, which specifies the amount to increment month by during each iteration of the loop.

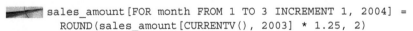

```
sales_amount[FOR month FROM 1 TO 3 INCREMENT 1, 2004] =
  ROUND(sales_amount[CURRENTV(), 2003] * 1.25, 2)
```

The following query shows the use of this expression:

```
SELECT prd_type_id, year, month, sales_amount
FROM all_sales
WHERE prd_type_id BETWEEN 1 AND 2
AND emp_id = 21
MODEL
PARTITION BY (prd_type_id)
DIMENSION BY (month, year)
MEASURES (amount sales_amount) (
  sales_amount[FOR month FROM 1 TO 3 INCREMENT 1, 2004] =
    ROUND(sales_amount[CURRENTV(), 2003] * 1.25, 2)
)
ORDER BY prd_type_id, year, month;
```

The result set returned by this query is shown in the following listing. The values for 2004 are highlighted in bold.

PRD_TYPE_ID	YEAR	MONTH	SALES_AMOUNT
1	2003	1	10034.84
1	2003	2	15144.65
1	2003	3	20137.83
1	2003	4	25057.45
1	2003	5	17214.56
1	2003	6	15564.64
1	2003	7	12654.84
1	2003	8	17434.82
1	2003	9	19854.57
1	2003	10	21754.19
1	2003	11	13029.73
1	2003	12	10034.84
1	**2004**	**1**	**12543.55**
1	**2004**	**2**	**18930.81**
1	**2004**	**3**	**25172.29**
2	2003	1	1034.84
2	2003	2	1544.65
2	2003	3	2037.83
2	2003	4	2557.45
2	2003	5	1714.56
2	2003	6	1564.64
2	2003	7	1264.84
2	2003	8	1734.82
2	2003	9	1854.57
2	2003	10	2754.19
2	2003	11	1329.73
2	2003	12	1034.84
2	**2004**	**1**	**1293.55**
2	**2004**	**2**	**1930.81**
2	**2004**	**3**	**2547.29**

Handling Null and Missing Values

In this section, you'll learn how to handle null and missing values using the MODEL clause.

Using IS PRESENT

IS PRESENT returns true if the row specified by the cell reference existed prior to the execution of the MODEL clause. For example:

```
sales_amount[CURRENTV(), 2003] IS PRESENT
```

will return true if sales_amount[CURRENTV(), 2003] exists.

The following expression sets the sales amount for the first three months of 2004 to 1.25 multiplied by the sales of the same months in 2003:

```
sales_amount[FOR month FROM 1 TO 3 INCREMENT 1, 2004] =
  CASE WHEN sales_amount[CURRENTV(), 2003] IS PRESENT THEN
    ROUND(sales_amount[CURRENTV(), 2003] * 1.25, 2)
  ELSE
    0
  END
```

The following query shows the use of this expression:

```
SELECT prd_type_id, year, month, sales_amount
FROM all_sales
WHERE prd_type_id BETWEEN 1 AND 2
AND emp_id = 21
MODEL
PARTITION BY (prd_type_id)
DIMENSION BY (month, year)
MEASURES (amount sales_amount) (
  sales_amount[FOR month FROM 1 TO 3 INCREMENT 1, 2004] =
    CASE WHEN sales_amount[CURRENTV(), 2003] IS PRESENT THEN
      ROUND(sales_amount[CURRENTV(), 2003] * 1.25, 2)
    ELSE
      0
    END
)
ORDER BY prd_type_id, year, month;
```

The result set returned by this query is the same as the example in the previous section.

Using PRESENTV()

The PRESENTV(*cell*, *expr1*, *expr2*) function returns the expression *expr1* if the row specified by the *cell* reference existed prior to the execution of the MODEL clause. If the row doesn't exist, the expression *expr2* is returned. For example:

```
PRESENTV(sales_amount[CURRENTV(), 2003],
  ROUND(sales_amount[CURRENTV(), 2003] * 1.25, 2), 0)
```

will return the rounded sales amount if `sales_amount[CURRENTV(), 2003]` exists. Otherwise 0 will be returned.

The following query shows the use of this expression:

```
SELECT prd_type_id, year, month, sales_amount
FROM all_sales
WHERE prd_type_id BETWEEN 1 AND 2
AND emp_id = 21
MODEL
PARTITION BY (prd_type_id)
DIMENSION BY (month, year)
MEASURES (amount sales_amount) (
  sales_amount[FOR month FROM 1 TO 3 INCREMENT 1, 2004] =
    PRESENTV(sales_amount[CURRENTV(), 2003],
      ROUND(sales_amount[CURRENTV(), 2003] * 1.25, 2), 0)
)
ORDER BY prd_type_id, year, month;
```

Using PRESENTNNV()

The `PRESENTNNV(cell, expr1, expr2)` function returns the expression `expr1` if the row specified by the `cell` reference existed prior to the execution of the `MODEL` clause and the cell value is not null. If the row doesn't exist or the cell value is null, the expression `expr2` is returned. For example,

```
PRESENTNNV(sales_amount[CURRENTV(), 2003],
  ROUND(sales_amount[CURRENTV(), 2003] * 1.25, 2), 0)
```

will return the rounded sales amount if `sales_amount[CURRENTV(), 2003]` exists and is not null. Otherwise 0 will be returned.

Using IGNORE NAV and KEEP NAV

By default, the `MODEL` clause treats a cell that is missing a value as if it had a null value. A cell with a null value is also treated as a null value. You can change this default behavior by using `IGNORE NAV`, which returns one of the following values:

- 0 for a cell with a missing or null numeric value
- An empty string for a cell with a missing or null string value
- 01-JAN-2000 for a cell with a missing or null date value
- Null for a cell with a missing or null value of any other database type

You can also explicitly specify `KEEP NAV`, which is the default behavior. `KEEP NAV` returns null for a cell with a missing or null value.

The following query shows the use of `IGNORE NAV`:

```
SELECT prd_type_id, year, month, sales_amount
FROM all_sales
WHERE prd_type_id BETWEEN 1 AND 2
AND emp_id = 21
```

```
MODEL IGNORE NAV
PARTITION BY (prd_type_id)
DIMENSION BY (month, year)
MEASURES (amount sales_amount) (
  sales_amount[FOR month FROM 1 TO 3 INCREMENT 1, 2004] =
    ROUND(sales_amount[CURRENTV(), 2003] * 1.25, 2)
)
ORDER BY prd_type_id, year, month;
```

Updating Existing Cells

By default, if the cell referenced on the left side of an expression exists, then it is updated. If the cell doesn't exist, then a new row in the array is created. You can change this default behavior using RULES UPDATE, which specifies that if the cell doesn't exist, a new row will not be created.

The following query shows the use of RULES UPDATE:

```
SELECT prd_type_id, year, month, sales_amount
FROM all_sales
WHERE prd_type_id BETWEEN 1 AND 2
AND emp_id = 21
MODEL
PARTITION BY (prd_type_id)
DIMENSION BY (month, year)
MEASURES (amount sales_amount)
RULES UPDATE (
  sales_amount[FOR month FROM 1 TO 3 INCREMENT 1, 2004] =
    ROUND(sales_amount[CURRENTV(), 2003] * 1.25, 2)
)
ORDER BY prd_type_id, year, month;
```

Because cells for 2004 don't exist and RULES UPDATE is used, no new rows are created in the array for 2004. Therefore, the query doesn't return rows for 2004. The following listing shows the result set returned by the query. Notice there are no rows for 2004.

PRD_TYPE_ID	YEAR	MONTH	SALES_AMOUNT
1	2003	1	10034.84
1	2003	2	15144.65
1	2003	3	20137.83
1	2003	4	25057.45
1	2003	5	17214.56
1	2003	6	15564.64
1	2003	7	12654.84
1	2003	8	17434.82
1	2003	9	19854.57
1	2003	10	21754.19
1	2003	11	13029.73
1	2003	12	10034.84
2	2003	1	1034.84
2	2003	2	1544.65

```
2        2003        3        2037.83
2        2003        4        2557.45
2        2003        5        1714.56
2        2003        6        1564.64
2        2003        7        1264.84
2        2003        8        1734.82
2        2003        9        1854.57
2        2003       10        2754.19
2        2003       11        1329.73
2        2003       12        1034.84
```

Using the PIVOT and UNPIVOT Clauses

The PIVOT and UNPIVOT clauses were introduced in Oracle Database 11*g*. PIVOT rotates rows
into columns in the output from a query and runs an aggregation function on the data. UNPIVOT
does the opposite of PIVOT. UNPIVOT rotates columns into rows.

PIVOT and UNPIVOT are useful to see overall trends in large amounts of data, such as trends
in sales data over a period of time.

A Simple Example of the PIVOT Clause

The easiest way to learn how to use PIVOT is to see an example. The following query shows the
total sales amount of product types #1, #2, and #3 for the first four months in 2003. The cells in
the result set show the sum of the sales amounts for each product type in each month.

```
SELECT *
FROM (
  SELECT month, prd_type_id, amount
  FROM all_sales
  WHERE year = 2003
  AND prd_type_id IN (1, 2, 3)
)
PIVOT (
  SUM(amount) FOR month IN (1 AS JAN, 2 AS FEB, 3 AS MAR, 4 AS APR)
)
ORDER BY prd_type_id;


PRD_TYPE_ID        JAN          FEB          MAR          APR
-----------    ----------   ----------   ----------   ----------
          1     38909.04      70567.9     91826.98     120344.7
          2     14309.04      13367.9     16826.98      15664.7
          3     24909.04      15467.9     20626.98      23844.7
```

Starting with the first line in the result set, you can see the sales were

■ $38,909.04 of product type #1 sold in January

■ $70,567.90 of product type #1 sold in February

■   ...and so on for the rest of the first line

The second line of the result set shows there were

- $14,309.04 of product type #2 sold in January
- $13,367.90 of product type #2 sold in February
- ...and so on for the rest of the output

NOTE
PIVOT *allows you to see trends in sales of types of products over a period of months. Based on such trends, a real store could use the information to alter its sales tactics and formulate new marketing campaigns.*

The previous SELECT statement has the following structure:

```
SELECT *
FROM (
  inner_query
)
PIVOT (
  aggregate_function FOR pivot_column IN (list_of_values)
)
ORDER BY ...;
```

Let's break down the previous example into the structural elements:

- There is an inner and outer query. The inner query gets the month, product type, and amount from the all_sales table and passes the results to the outer query.
- SUM(amount) FOR month IN (1 AS JAN, 2 AS FEB, 3 AS MAR, 4 AS APR) is the line within the PIVOT clause.
  - The SUM() function adds up the sales amounts for the product types in the first four months (the months are listed in the IN part). Instead of returning the months as 1, 2, 3, and 4 in the output, the AS part renames the numbers to JAN, FEB, MAR, and APR to make the months more readable in the output.
  - The month column from the all_sales table is used as the pivot column. This means that the months appear as columns in the output. The rows are rotated—or *pivoted*—to view the months as columns.
- At the very end of the example, the ORDER BY prd_type_id line orders the results by the product type.

Pivoting on Multiple Columns

To pivot on multiple columns, you place the columns in the FOR part of the PIVOT. The following example pivots on both the month and prd_type_id columns, which are referenced in the FOR part. The list of values in the IN part of the PIVOT contains a value for the month and prd_type_id columns.

```
SELECT *
FROM (
  SELECT month, prd_type_id, amount
  FROM all_sales
  WHERE year = 2003
  AND prd_type_id IN (1, 2, 3)
)
PIVOT (
  SUM(amount) FOR (month, prd_type_id) IN (
    (1, 2) AS JAN_PRDTYPE2,
    (2, 3) AS FEB_PRDTYPE3,
    (3, 1) AS MAR_PRDTYPE1,
    (4, 2) AS APR_PRDTYPE2
  )
);


JAN_PRDTYPE2 FEB_PRDTYPE3 MAR_PRDTYPE1 APR_PRDTYPE2
------------ ------------ ------------ ------------
    14309.04      15467.9     91826.98      15664.7
```

The result set shows the sum of the sales amounts for each product type in the specified month (the product type and month to query are placed in the list of values in the IN part). From the result set, the sales were as follows:

- $14,309.04 of product type #2 in January
- $15,467.90 of product type #3 in February
- $91,826.98 of product type #1 in March
- $15,664.70 of product type #2 in April

You can put any values in the IN part to get the values of interest. In the following example, the values of the product types are changed in the IN part to get the sales for those product types for the specified months:

```
SELECT *
FROM (
  SELECT month, prd_type_id, amount
  FROM all_sales
  WHERE year = 2003
  AND prd_type_id IN (1, 2, 3)
)
PIVOT (
  SUM(amount) FOR (month, prd_type_id) IN (
    (1, 1) AS JAN_PRDTYPE1,
    (2, 2) AS FEB_PRDTYPE2,
    (3, 3) AS MAR_PRDTYPE3,
    (4, 1) AS APR_PRDTYPE1
  )
);
```

```
JAN_PRDTYPE1 FEB_PRDTYPE2 MAR_PRDTYPE3 APR_PRDTYPE1
------------ ------------ ------------ ------------
    38909.04      13367.9     20626.98     120344.7
```

From the result set, the sales were as follows:

- $38,909.04 of product type #1 in January
- $13,367.90 of product type #2 in February
- $20,626.98 of product type #3 in March
- $120,344.70 of product type #1 in April

Using Multiple Aggregate Functions in a Pivot

You can use multiple aggregate functions in a pivot. For example, the following query uses SUM() to get the total sales for the product types in January and February and AVG() to get the averages of the sales:

```
SELECT *
FROM (
  SELECT month, prd_type_id, amount
  FROM all_sales
  WHERE year = 2003
  AND prd_type_id IN (1, 2, 3)
)
PIVOT (
  SUM(amount) AS sum_amount,
  AVG(amount) AS avg_amount
  FOR (month) IN (
    1 AS JAN, 2 AS FEB
  )
)
ORDER BY prd_type_id;

PRD_TYPE_ID JAN_SUM_AMOUNT JAN_AVG_AMOUNT FEB_SUM_AMOUNT FEB_AVG_AMOUNT
----------- -------------- -------------- -------------- --------------
          1       38909.04        6484.84        70567.9     11761.3167
          2       14309.04        2384.84        13367.9     2227.98333
          3       24909.04     4151.50667        15467.9     2577.98333
```

The first line in the result set shows the following sales for product type #1:

- A total of $38,909.04 and an average of $6,484.84 sold in January
- A total of $70,567.90 and an average of $11,761.32 sold in February

The second line shows the following sales for product type #2:

- A total of $14,309.04 and an average of $2,384.84 sold in January
- A total of $13,367.90 and an average of $2,227.98 sold in February
- ...and so on for the third line in the result set.

Using the UNPIVOT Clause

The UNPIVOT clause rotates columns into rows. UNPIVOT does the opposite of PIVOT.

The examples in this section use the following table named pivot_sales_data, which is created by the store_schema.sql script:

```
CREATE TABLE pivot_sales_data AS
  SELECT *
  FROM (
   SELECT month, prd_type_id, amount
   FROM all_sales
   WHERE year = 2003
   AND prd_type_id IN (1, 2, 3)
  )
  PIVOT (
    SUM(amount) FOR month IN (1 AS JAN, 2 AS FEB, 3 AS MAR, 4 AS APR)
  )
  ORDER BY prd_type_id;
```

The pivot_sales_data table is populated by a query that returns a pivoted version of the sales data stored in the all_sales table.

The following query retrieves the rows from the pivot_sales_data table:

```
SELECT *
FROM pivot_sales_data;
```

PRD_TYPE_ID	JAN	FEB	MAR	APR
1	38909.04	70567.9	91826.98	120344.7
2	14309.04	13367.9	16826.98	15664.7
3	24909.04	15467.9	20626.98	23844.7

The next query uses UNPIVOT when retrieving the rows from the pivot_sales_data table:

```
SELECT *
FROM pivot_sales_data
UNPIVOT (
  amount FOR month IN (JAN, FEB, MAR, APR)
)
ORDER BY prd_type_id;
```

PRD_TYPE_ID	MON	AMOUNT
1	JAN	38909.04
1	FEB	70567.9
1	MAR	91826.98
1	APR	120344.7
2	JAN	14309.04
2	FEB	13367.9
2	APR	15664.7
2	MAR	16826.98

```
3 JAN    24909.04
3 MAR    20626.98
3 FEB     15467.9
3 APR     23844.7
```

The monthly sales totals are shown vertically in this result set. Compare this result set to the result set from the previous query, in which the monthly sales totals are shown horizontally.

Performing Top-N Queries

A new feature in Oracle Database 12c is native support for performing top-N queries. Top-N queries contain a row-limiting clause. A row-limiting clause allows you to limit the retrieval of rows by specifying the following:

- The number of rows to return, using the FETCH FIRST clause
- An offset, specifying the number of rows to skip before row limiting begins, using the OFFSET clause
- The percentage of the total number of selected rows to return, using the PERCENT clause

You also add one of the following when using a row-limiting clause:

- ONLY, which returns the exact number of rows or percentage of rows specified in the row-limiting clause
- WITH TIES, which includes additional rows with the same sort key value as the last row retrieved (the sort key is the column specified in the ORDER BY clause)

The following sections show examples.

Using the FETCH FIRST Clause

The following query uses FETCH FIRST to retrieve the five employees with the lowest employee_id from the more_employees table:

```
SELECT employee_id, first_name, last_name
FROM more_employees
ORDER BY employee_id
FETCH FIRST 5 ROWS ONLY;

EMPLOYEE_ID FIRST_NAME LAST_NAME
----------- ---------- ----------
          1 James      Smith
          2 Ron        Johnson
          3 Fred       Hobbs
          4 Susan      Jones
          5 Rob        Green
```

This example orders the employees by their employee_id value and returns the five rows with the lowest employee_id values.

The next query retrieves the five employees with the highest employee_id from the more_employees table. This is done by ordering the employees by descending employee_id.

```
SELECT employee_id, first_name, last_name
FROM more_employees
ORDER BY employee_id DESC
FETCH FIRST 5 ROWS ONLY;

EMPLOYEE_ID FIRST_NAME LAST_NAME
----------- ---------- ----------
         13 Doreen     Penn
         12 Frank      Howard
         11 Keith      Long
         10 Kevin      Black
          9 Henry      Heyson
```

The next query uses FETCH FIRST to retrieve the four products with the lowest price from the products table. This is done by ordering the products by their price and returning the four rows with the lowest price.

```
SELECT product_id, name, price
FROM products
ORDER BY price
FETCH FIRST 4 ROWS ONLY;

PRODUCT_ID NAME                                PRICE
---------- ----------------------------------- ----------
         9 Classical Music                     10.99
         8 From Another Planet                 12.99
         7 Space Force 9                       13.49
        12 My Front Line                       13.49
```

Using the OFFSET Clause

You use the OFFSET clause to specify the number of rows to skip before row limiting begins. The following query retrieves employees with employeed_id values starting at 6 and ending at 10 from the more_employees table:

```
SELECT employee_id, first_name, last_name
FROM more_employees
ORDER BY employee_id
OFFSET 5 ROWS FETCH NEXT 5 ROWS ONLY;

EMPLOYEE_ID FIRST_NAME LAST_NAME
----------- ---------- ----------
          6 Jane       Brown
          7 John       Grey
          8 Jean       Blue
          9 Henry      Heyson
         10 Kevin      Black
```

The OFFSET clause in this example is

```
OFFSET 5 ROWS FETCH NEXT 5 ROWS ONLY
```

This means start the row limiting from row #5 and fetch the next five rows after that start position. This causes rows with employeed_id values between 6 and 10 to be retrieved.

The next query uses OFFSET when retrieving products from the products table. The query orders the products by price, starts the row limiting from row #5, and fetches the next four rows after that start position.

```
SELECT product_id, name, price
FROM products
ORDER BY price
OFFSET 5 ROWS FETCH NEXT 4 ROWS ONLY;
```

```
PRODUCT_ID NAME                                    PRICE
---------- ------------------------------- ----------
         6 2412: The Return                        14.95
        11 Creative Yell                           14.99
        10 Pop 3                                   15.99
         1 Modern Science                          19.95
```

Using the PERCENT Clause

You use the PERCENT clause to specify the percentage of the total number of selected rows to return. The following query retrieves the 20 percent of the products with the highest price from the products table:

```
SELECT product_id, name, price
FROM products
ORDER BY price DESC
FETCH FIRST 20 PERCENT ROWS ONLY;
```

```
PRODUCT_ID NAME                                    PRICE
---------- ------------------------------- ----------
         5 Z Files                                 49.99
         2 Chemistry                                  30
         3 Supernova                               25.99
```

The next query retrieves the 10 percent of the employees with the lowest salary from the more_employees table:

```
SELECT employee_id, first_name, last_name, salary
FROM more_employees
ORDER BY salary
FETCH FIRST 10 PERCENT ROWS ONLY;
```

```
EMPLOYEE_ID FIRST_NAME LAST_NAME    SALARY
----------- ---------- ---------- ----------
          8 Jean       Blue         29000
          7 John       Grey         30000
```

Using the WITH TIES Clause

You use `WITH TIES` to include additional rows with the same sort key value as the last row fetched. The sort key is the column specified in the `ORDER BY` clause.

The following query retrieves the 10 percent of the employees with the lowest salary from the `more_employees` table using `WITH TIES`. The sort key is the `salary` column.

```
SELECT employee_id, first_name, last_name, salary
FROM more_employees
ORDER BY salary
FETCH FIRST 10 PERCENT ROWS WITH TIES;
```

```
EMPLOYEE_ID FIRST_NAME LAST_NAME     SALARY
----------- ---------- ---------- ----------
          8 Jean       Blue            29000
          7 John       Grey            30000
          9 Henry      Heyson          30000
```

Compare this result set with the result set returned by the previous example. This result set includes the employee Henry Heyson, who has the same salary as the last row returned by the previous example.

Finding Patterns in Data

A new feature in Oracle Database 12c is native support for finding patterns in data using the `MATCH_RECOGNIZE` clause. Finding patterns in data is useful in a variety of situations. For example, finding patterns in data is useful for finding trends in sales, detecting fraudulent credit card transactions, and discovering network intrusions.

The examples in this section show how to find V-shaped and W-shaped patterns in the sales for a product over a period of days. These patterns could be used, for example, to adjust the timing of marketing campaigns. The examples use the `all_sales2` and `all_sales3` tables, which are created by the `store_schema.sql` script using the following statements:

```
CREATE TABLE all_sales2 (
  product_id INTEGER REFERENCES products(product_id),
  total_amount NUMBER(8, 2),
  sale_date DATE
);

CREATE TABLE all_sales3 (
  product_id INTEGER REFERENCES products(product_id),
  total_amount NUMBER(8, 2),
  sale_date DATE
);
```

The columns in the tables are the same, and are as follows:

- **product_id** is the identifier of the product sold.
- **total_amount** is the total dollar amount of the product sold on the day.
- **sale_date** is the date of the sale.

You'll learn how to find V-shaped and W-shaped data patterns in the following sections.

Finding V-Shaped Data Patterns in the all_sales2 Table

In this section, you'll learn how to find V-shaped data patterns in the `all_sales2` table. For simplicity, the sales for only one product during a ten-day period are stored in the table.

The following query retrieves the rows from the `all_sales2` table. The `total_amount` value rises to a high value on June 3rd, then falls to a low value on June 7th, and then rises to another high value on June 9th. These dates are the start, low point, and end of a V-shape in the sales data (I've highlighted the relevant rows in bold in the result set).

```
SELECT *
FROM all_sales2;

PRODUCT_ID TOTAL_AMOUNT SALE_DATE
---------- ------------ ---------
         1         1000 01-JUN-11
         1         1100 02-JUN-11
         1         1200 03-JUN-11
         1         1100 04-JUN-11
         1         1000 05-JUN-11
         1          900 06-JUN-11
         1          800 07-JUN-11
         1          900 08-JUN-11
         1         1000 09-JUN-11
         1          900 10-JUN-11
```

The following query finds the V-shape and returns the start, low point, and end dates:

```
SELECT *
FROM all_sales2
MATCH_RECOGNIZE (
  PARTITION BY product_id
  ORDER BY sale_date
  MEASURES
    strt.sale_date AS start_v_date,
    down.sale_date AS low_v_date,
    up.sale_date AS end_v_date
  ONE ROW PER MATCH
  AFTER MATCH SKIP TO LAST up
  PATTERN (strt down+ up+)
  DEFINE
    down AS down.total_amount < PREV(down.total_amount),
    up AS up.total_amount > PREV(up.total_amount)
) my_pattern
ORDER BY my_pattern.product_id, my_pattern.start_v_date;

PRODUCT_ID START_V_D LOW_V_DAT END_V_DAT
---------- --------- --------- ---------
         1 03-JUN-11 07-JUN-11 09-JUN-11
```

Let's examine each part of the MATCH_RECOGNIZE clause in this example:

■ PARTITION BY product_id groups the rows retrieved from the all_sales2 table by product_id. Each group of rows contains one product_id value. (The all_sales2 table only contains sales for one product, but real data could contain sales for thousands of different products.)

■ ORDER BY sale_date sorts the rows in each group by sale_date.

■ MEASURES specifies the following items to return in the result set:

■ strt.sale_date AS start_v_date, which is the start date of a V-shape

■ down.sale_date AS low_v_date, which is the date at the low point of a V-shape

■ up.sale_date AS end_v_date, which is the end date of a V-shape

■ ONE ROW PER MATCH generates one row in the result set for each V-shape found in the data. In the example, there is one V-shape, which means the query generates one row in the result set. If there were multiple V-shapes, then the result set would contain one row for each V-shape.

■ AFTER MATCH SKIP TO LAST up causes the search to continue from the row containing the last up in the V-shape. As you'll see shortly, up is a pattern variable specified in the DEFINE clause.

■ PATTERN (strt down+ up+) specifies that the pattern to search for is a V-shape. To see this pattern, consider the pattern variables in the PATTERN clause: strt, down, and up. The order indicates the order to search for the variables. The plus character (+) placed after down and up indicates that at least one row must be found for each variable. In this example, the PATTERN clause searches for a V-shape: a start row strt, which is followed by down rows and up rows.

■ DEFINE defines the following pattern variables:

■ down AS down.total_amount < PREV(down.total_amount), which uses the PREV() function to compare the value in the total_amount column for the current row to the total_amount column value in the previous row; down is found when a row has a total_amount that is less than the previous row; down defines the downward part of the V-shape.

■ up AS up.total_amount > PREV(up.total_amount) defines the upward part of the V-shape.

The following query shows the use of additional MATCH_RECOGNIZE options:

```
SELECT
    sale_date, start_v_date, low_v_date, end_v_date,
    match_variable, up_days, down_days, count_days,
    sales_difference, total_amount
FROM all_sales2
MATCH_RECOGNIZE (
    PARTITION BY product_id
    ORDER BY sale_date
    MEASURES
```

```
      strt.sale_date AS start_v_date,
      FINAL LAST(down.sale_date) AS low_v_date,
      FINAL LAST(up.sale_date) AS end_v_date,
      CLASSIFIER() AS match_variable,
      FINAL COUNT(up.sale_date) AS up_days,
      FINAL COUNT(down.sale_date) AS down_days,
      RUNNING COUNT(sale_date) AS count_days,
      total_amount - strt.total_amount AS sales_difference
    ALL ROWS PER MATCH
    AFTER MATCH SKIP TO LAST up
    PATTERN (strt down+ up+)
    DEFINE
      down AS down.total_amount < PREV(down.total_amount),
      up AS up.total_amount > PREV(up.total_amount)
    ) my_pattern
ORDER BY my_pattern.product_id, my_pattern.start_v_date;
```

```
SALE_DATE START_V_D LOW_V_DAT END_V_DAT MATCH_VARIABLE
--------- --------- --------- --------- ------------------------------
   UP_DAYS   DOWN_DAYS COUNT_DAYS SALES_DIFFERENCE TOTAL_AMOUNT
--------- --------- ---------- ---------------- ------------
03-JUN-11 03-JUN-11 07-JUN-11 09-JUN-11 STRT
         2         4          1                0         1200

04-JUN-11 03-JUN-11 07-JUN-11 09-JUN-11 DOWN
         2         4          2             -100         1100

05-JUN-11 03-JUN-11 07-JUN-11 09-JUN-11 DOWN
         2         4          3             -200         1000

09-JUN-11 03-JUN-11 07-JUN-11 09-JUN-11 UP
         2         4          7             -200         1000

07-JUN-11 03-JUN-11 07-JUN-11 09-JUN-11 DOWN
         2         4          5             -400          800

08-JUN-11 03-JUN-11 07-JUN-11 09-JUN-11 UP
         2         4          6             -300          900

06-JUN-11 03-JUN-11 07-JUN-11 09-JUN-11 DOWN
         2         4          4             -300          900
```

Let's examine the relevant items in the MATCH_RECOGNIZE clause in this example:

- MEASURES specifies the following items to return in the result set:

  - strt.sale_date AS start_v_date, which is the start date of a V-shape.

  - FINAL LAST(down.sale_date) AS low_v_date, which is the date at the low point of a V-shape. The LAST() function returns the last value. Combining FINAL and LAST() for low_v_date causes the rows for each match to have the same date for the low point.

- `FINAL LAST(up.sale_date) AS end_v_date`, which is the end date of a V-shape. Combining `FINAL` and `LAST()` for `end_v_date` causes the rows for each match to have the same date for the end point.

- `CLASSIFIER() AS match_variable`, which is the match variable for each row. In the example query, the match variable is either `strt`, `down`, or `up`. In the result set, the match variable is shown in uppercase.

- `FINAL COUNT(up.sale_date) AS up_days`, which is the number of days matched to the `up` pattern variable for each V-shape.

- `FINAL COUNT(down.sale_date) AS down_days`, which is the number of days matched to the `down` pattern variable for each V-shape.

- `RUNNING COUNT(sale_date) AS count_days`, which is the running total of the days for each period of days in the V-shape.

- `total_amount - strt.total_amount AS sales_difference`, which is each day's difference in the `total_amount` value from the `total_amount` value on the first day of the V-shape.

- `ALL ROWS PER MATCH` generates one row in the result set for each row contained in a V-shape. In the example, there are seven rows in the V-shape, which means the query generates seven rows in the result set.

Finding W-Shaped Data Patterns in the all_sales3 Table

In this section, you'll learn how to find W-shaped patterns in the `all_sales3` table. For simplicity, the sales for only one product during a ten-day period are stored in the table.

The following query retrieves the rows from the `all_sales3` table. The high and low points that form a W-pattern in the `total_amount` column are highlighted in the query's result set. The W-pattern starts on June 2nd and ends on June 9th.

```
SELECT *
FROM all_sales3;
```

PRODUCT_ID	TOTAL_AMOUNT	SALE_DATE
1	1000	01-JUN-11
1	**1100**	**02-JUN-11**
1	900	03-JUN-11
1	**800**	**04-JUN-11**
1	900	05-JUN-11
1	**1000**	**06-JUN-11**
1	900	07-JUN-11
1	**800**	**08-JUN-11**
1	**1000**	**09-JUN-11**
1	900	10-JUN-11

The following query finds the W-shape and returns the start and end dates of the W-shape:

```
SELECT *
FROM all_sales3
MATCH_RECOGNIZE (
  PARTITION BY product_id
  ORDER BY sale_date
  MEASURES
    strt.sale_date AS start_w_date,
    up.sale_date AS end_w_date
  ONE ROW PER MATCH
  AFTER MATCH SKIP TO LAST up
  PATTERN (strt down+ up+ down+ up+)
  DEFINE
    down AS down.total_amount < PREV(down.total_amount),
    up AS up.total_amount > PREV(up.total_amount)
) my_pattern
ORDER BY my_pattern.product_id, my_pattern.start_w_date;

PRODUCT_ID START_W_D END_W_DAT
---------- --------- ---------
         1 02-JUN-11 09-JUN-11
```

Let's examine the relevant parts of the MATCH_RECOGNIZE clause in this example:

- MEASURES specifies the following items to return in the result set:

  - strt.sale_date AS start_w_date, which is the start date of a W-shape

  - up.sale_date AS end_w_date, which is the end date of a W-shape

- PATTERN (strt down+ up+ down+ up+) specifies that the pattern to search for is a W-shape: a start row strt, followed by a series of down rows, up rows, down rows, and up rows.

Finding V-Shaped Data Patterns in the all_sales3 Table

In this section, you'll see how to find V-shaped data patterns in the all_sales3 table and interpret the results. The previous section showed that the all_sales3 table contains a W-shaped pattern. You can think of a W-shape as two V-shapes.

The following query returns the dates for the start, low point, and end of the V-shapes in the all_sales3 table. The query uses ONE ROW PER MATCH to generate one row in the result set for each V-shape found in the data.

```
SELECT *
FROM all_sales3
MATCH_RECOGNIZE (
  PARTITION BY product_id
  ORDER BY sale_date
  MEASURES
    strt.sale_date AS start_v_date,
    down.sale_date AS low_v_date,
```

```
    up.sale_date AS end_v_date
ONE ROW PER MATCH
AFTER MATCH SKIP TO LAST up
PATTERN (strt down+ up+)
DEFINE
  down AS down.total_amount < PREV(down.total_amount),
  up AS up.total_amount > PREV(up.total_amount)
) my_pattern
ORDER BY my_pattern.product_id, my_pattern.start_v_date;


PRODUCT_ID START_V_D LOW_V_DAT END_V_DAT
---------- --------- --------- ---------
         1 02-JUN-11 04-JUN-11 06-JUN-11
         1 06-JUN-11 08-JUN-11 09-JUN-11
```

The result set contains two rows, one for each V-shape found in the data.

The following query uses ALL ROWS PER MATCH, which generates one row in the result set for each row contained in a V-shape:

```
SELECT *
FROM all_sales3
MATCH_RECOGNIZE (
  PARTITION BY product_id
  ORDER BY sale_date
  MEASURES
    strt.sale_date AS start_v_date,
    down.sale_date AS low_v_date,
    up.sale_date AS end_v_date
  ALL ROWS PER MATCH
  AFTER MATCH SKIP TO LAST up
  PATTERN (strt down+ up+)
  DEFINE
    down AS down.total_amount < PREV(down.total_amount),
    up AS up.total_amount > PREV(up.total_amount)
) my_pattern
ORDER BY my_pattern.product_id, my_pattern.start_v_date;


PRODUCT_ID SALE_DATE START_V_D LOW_V_DAT END_V_DAT TOTAL_AMOUNT
---------- --------- --------- --------- --------- ------------
         1 02-JUN-11 02-JUN-11                             1100
         1 03-JUN-11 02-JUN-11 03-JUN-11                    900
         1 04-JUN-11 02-JUN-11 04-JUN-11                    800
         1 05-JUN-11 02-JUN-11 04-JUN-11 05-JUN-11          900
         1 06-JUN-11 02-JUN-11 04-JUN-11 06-JUN-11         1000
         1 06-JUN-11 06-JUN-11                             1000
         1 07-JUN-11 06-JUN-11 07-JUN-11                    900
         1 08-JUN-11 06-JUN-11 08-JUN-11                    800
         1 09-JUN-11 06-JUN-11 08-JUN-11 09-JUN-11         1000
```

The result set contains a total of nine rows. The first five rows are for the first V-shape. The last four rows are for the second V-shape.

This section has shown a useful subset of the pattern matching options. The complete set of options is too extensive for coverage in this book. For full details, see the *Oracle Database Data Warehousing Optimization Guide 12c Release* document, published by Oracle Corporation.

Summary

In this chapter, you have learned the following:

- The analytic functions perform complex calculations.
- The MODEL clause performs inter-row calculations and treats table data as an array.
- The PIVOT and UNPIVOT clauses are useful for finding trends in data.
- Top-N queries return the top or bottom N rows from a data set.
- The MATCH_RECOGNIZE clause is used for locating patterns in data.

In the next chapter, you'll learn about changing the contents of a table.

CHAPTER
9

Changing Table Contents

I n this chapter, you'll learn how to perform the following tasks:

- Add, modify, and remove rows using INSERT, UPDATE, and DELETE statements
- Use database transactions, which can consist of multiple SQL statements
- Make transactions permanent using COMMIT and undo transactions using ROLLBACK
- Use query flashbacks to view rows as they were before changes were made to them

NOTE
Before running any of the examples in this chapter, rerun the store_
schema.sql *script as described in Chapter 1 in the section "Creating the Store Schema." This will ensure the results of your SQL statements match those in this chapter.*

Adding Rows Using the INSERT Statement

The INSERT statement adds rows to a table. You can specify the following information in an INSERT statement:

- The table into which the row is to be inserted
- A list of columns
- A list of values to store in the specified columns

When adding a row, you typically supply a value for the primary key and all other columns that are defined as NOT NULL. If you don't specify values for NULL columns, then they will be set to null.

You can find out which columns are defined as NOT NULL using the SQL*Plus DESCRIBE command. The following example describes the customers table:

```
DESCRIBE customers
 Name                                      Null?    Type
 ----------------------------------------- -------- ------------
 CUSTOMER_ID                               NOT NULL NUMBER(38)
 FIRST_NAME                                NOT NULL VARCHAR2(10)
 LAST_NAME                                 NOT NULL VARCHAR2(10)
 DOB                                                DATE
 PHONE                                              VARCHAR2(12)
```

The customer_id, first_name, and last_name columns are NOT NULL, meaning that a value must be supplied for these columns. The dob and phone columns don't require a value: If you omit these values when adding a row, then the columns would be set to null.

The following INSERT statement adds a row to the customers table. The order of values in the VALUES clause matches the order in which the columns are specified in the column list.

```
INSERT INTO customers (
    customer_id, first_name, last_name, dob, phone
) VALUES (
```

```
    6, 'Fred', 'Brown', '01-JAN-1970', '800-555-1215'
);
```

```
1 row created.
```

SQL*Plus responds that one row has been created. You can verify this by performing the following
SELECT statement:

```
SELECT *
FROM customers;
```

```
CUSTOMER_ID FIRST_NAME LAST_NAME  DOB       PHONE
----------- ---------- ---------- --------- ------------
          1 John       Brown      01-JAN-65 800-555-1211
          2 Cynthia    Green      05-FEB-68 800-555-1212
          3 Steve      White      16-MAR-71 800-555-1213
          4 Gail       Black                800-555-1214
          5 Doreen     Blue       20-MAY-70
          6 Fred       Brown      01-JAN-70 800-555-1215
```

The new row appears in the result set returned by the query.

Omitting the Column List

You can omit the column list when supplying values for every column, as in this example:

```
INSERT INTO customers
VALUES (7, 'Jane', 'Green', '01-JAN-1970', '800-555-1216');
```

When you omit the column list, the order of the values must match the order of the columns
as listed in the output from the DESCRIBE command.

Specifying a Null Value for a Column

You can specify a null value for a column using the NULL keyword. For example, the following
INSERT specifies a null value for the dob and phone columns:

```
INSERT INTO customers
VALUES (8, 'Sophie', 'White', NULL, NULL);
```

When you view this new row using a query, you won't see a value for the dob and phone
columns because they've been set to null values:

```
SELECT *
FROM customers
WHERE customer_id = 8;
```

```
CUSTOMER_ID FIRST_NAME LAST_NAME  DOB       PHONE
----------- ---------- ---------- --------- ------------
          8 Sophie     White
```

The dob and phone column values are blank because they are set to null.

Including Quote Marks in a Column Value

You can include a single quote mark (') as well as a double quote mark (") in a column value. For example, the following INSERT specifies a last name of O'Malley for a new customer. Notice two single quote marks are required after the letter O to indicate that a single quote mark is to be added after the letter O.

```
INSERT INTO customers
VALUES (9, 'Kyle', 'O''Malley', NULL, NULL);
```

The next example specifies the name The "Great" Gatsby for a new product. Notice the use of double quote marks around "Great".

```
INSERT INTO products (
    product_id, product_type_id, name, description, price
) VALUES (
    13, 1, 'The "Great" Gatsby', NULL, 12.99
);
```

Copying Rows from One Table to Another

You can copy rows from one table to another using a query in the place of the column values in an INSERT. The number of columns and the column types in the source and destination must match. The following example uses a SELECT to retrieve the first_name and last_name columns for customer #1 and supplies those columns to an INSERT statement:

```
INSERT INTO customers (customer_id, first_name, last_name)
SELECT 10, first_name, last_name
FROM customers
WHERE customer_id = 1;
```

Notice that the customer_id for the new row is set to 10.

NOTE
The MERGE statement allows you to merge rows from one table into another. MERGE is much more flexible than combining an INSERT and a SELECT to copy rows from one table to another. You'll learn about MERGE later in the section "Merging Rows Using MERGE."

Modifying Rows Using the UPDATE Statement

The UPDATE statement modifies rows in a table. When using UPDATE, you typically specify the following information:

- The table name
- A WHERE clause that specifies the rows to be changed
- A list of column names, along with their new values, specified using the SET clause

You can change one or more rows using the same UPDATE. If more than one row is specified, the same change will be implemented for all of those rows. For example, the following UPDATE sets the last_name column to Orange for the row whose customer_id is 2:

```
UPDATE customers
SET last_name = 'Orange'
WHERE customer_id = 2;
```

```
1 row updated.
```

SQL*Plus confirms that one row was updated. The following query confirms the change was made:

```
SELECT *
FROM customers
WHERE customer_id = 2;
```

```
CUSTOMER_ID FIRST_NAME LAST_NAME DOB       PHONE
----------- ---------- --------- --------- ------------
          2 Cynthia    Orange    05-FEB-68 800-555-1212
```

You can change multiple rows and multiple columns in the same UPDATE statement. For example, the following UPDATE raises the price by 20 percent for all products whose current price is greater than or equal to $20. The UPDATE also changes those products' names to lowercase.

```
UPDATE products
SET
  price = price * 1.20,
  name = LOWER(name)
WHERE
  price >= 20;
```

```
3 rows updated.
```

Three rows are updated by this statement. The following query confirms the change:

```
SELECT product_id, name, price
FROM products
WHERE price >= (20 * 1.20);
```

```
        ID NAME                           PRICE
---------- ------------------------------ ----------
         2 chemistry                         36
         3 supernova                       31.19
         5 z-files                         59.99
```

NOTE
You can also use a subquery with an UPDATE statement. This is described in Chapter 6 in the section "Writing an UPDATE Statement Containing a Subquery."

Returning an Aggregate Function Value Using the RETURNING Clause

Oracle Database 10g introduced the RETURNING clause to return the value from an aggregate function such as AVG(). Aggregate functions were covered in Chapter 4.

The next example performs the following tasks:

- Declares a variable named average_product_price
- Decreases the price column of the rows in the products table and saves the average price in the average_product_price variable using the RETURNING clause
- Prints the value of the average_product_price variable

```
VARIABLE average_product_price NUMBER

UPDATE products
SET price =  price * 0.75
RETURNING AVG(price) INTO :average_product_price;
12 rows updated.

PRINT average_product_price
AVERAGE_PRODUCT_PRICE
--------------------
          16.1216667
```

Removing Rows Using the DELETE Statement

The DELETE statement removes rows from a table. Generally, you should specify a WHERE clause to limit the rows to delete. If you don't, *all* the rows will be deleted.

The following DELETE removes the row from the customers table whose customer_id is 10:

```
DELETE FROM customers
WHERE customer_id = 10;

1 row deleted.
```

SQL*Plus confirms that one row has been deleted.

You can also use a subquery with a DELETE statement. This is described in Chapter 6 in the section "Writing a DELETE Statement Containing a Subquery."

NOTE
If you ran any of the previous statements, rerun the store_schema .sql script to re-create everything. This will ensure that your results match those in the rest of this chapter.

Database Integrity

When you execute a DML statement (an INSERT, UPDATE, or DELETE, for example), the database ensures that the rows in the tables maintain their integrity. This means that any changes made to the rows do not affect the primary key and foreign key relationships for the tables.

Enforcement of Primary Key Constraints

Let's examine some examples that show the enforcement of a primary key constraint. The customers table's primary key is the customer_id column, which means that every value stored in the customer_id column must be unique. If you try to insert a row with a duplicate value for a primary key, the database returns the error ORA-00001, as in this example:

```
SQL> INSERT INTO customers (
  2     customer_id, first_name, last_name, dob, phone
  3  ) VALUES (
  4     1, 'Jason', 'Price', '01-JAN-60', '800-555-1211'
  5  );
INSERT INTO customers (
*
ERROR at line 1:
ORA-00001: unique constraint (STORE.CUSTOMERS_PK) violated
```

If you attempt to update a primary key value to a value that already exists in the table, the database returns the same error:

```
SQL> UPDATE customers
  2   SET customer_id = 1
  3   WHERE customer_id = 2;
UPDATE customers
*
ERROR at line 1:
ORA-00001: unique constraint (STORE.CUSTOMERS_PK) violated
```

Enforcement of Foreign Key Constraints

A foreign key relationship is one in which a column from one table is referenced in another table. For example, the product_type_id column in the products table references the product_type_id column in the product_types table. The product_types table is known as the *parent* table, and the products table is known as the *child* table, which shows the dependence of the product_type_id column in the products table on the product_type_id column in the product_types table.

If you try to insert a row into the products table with a nonexistent product_type_id, the database will return the error ORA-02291. This error indicates the database couldn't find a matching parent key value (the parent key is the product_type_id column of the product_types table). In the following example, the error is returned because there is no row in the product_types table whose product_type_id is 6:

```
SQL> INSERT INTO products (
  2     product_id, product_type_id, name, description, price
  3  ) VALUES (
```

```
  4    13, 6, 'Test', 'Test', NULL
  5  );
INSERT INTO products (
*
ERROR at line 1:
ORA-02291: integrity constraint (STORE.PRODUCTS_FK_PRODUCT_TYPES)
 violated - parent key not found
```

Similarly, if you attempt to update the `product_type_id` of a row in the `products` table to a nonexistent parent key value, the database returns the same error, as in this example:

```
SQL> UPDATE products
  2  SET product_type_id = 6
  3  WHERE product_id = 1;
UPDATE products
*
ERROR at line 1:
ORA-02291: integrity constraint (STORE.PRODUCTS_FK_PRODUCT_TYPES)
 violated - parent key not found
```

Finally, if you attempt to delete a row in the parent table that has dependent child rows, the database returns error ORA-02292. For example, if you attempt to delete the row whose `product_type_id` is 1 from the `product_types` table, the database will return this error because the `products` table contains rows whose `product_type_id` is 1:

```
SQL> DELETE FROM product_types
  2  WHERE product_type_id = 1;
DELETE FROM product_types
*
ERROR at line 1:
ORA-02292: integrity constraint (STORE.PRODUCTS_FK_PRODUCT_TYPES)
 violated - child record found
```

If the database were to allow the deletion, the child rows would be invalid because they wouldn't point to valid values in the parent table.

Using Default Values

You can define a default value for a column. For example, the following statement creates a table named `order_status`. The `status` column has a default setting of `'Order placed'` and the `last_modified` column has a default setting of the date and time returned by SYSDATE.

```
CREATE TABLE order_status (
  order_status_id INTEGER
    CONSTRAINT default_example_pk PRIMARY KEY,
  status VARCHAR2(20) DEFAULT 'Order placed' NOT NULL,
  last_modified DATE DEFAULT SYSDATE
);
```

NOTE
The order_status *table is created by the* store_schema.sql
script. This means you don't type in the previous CREATE TABLE
statement yourself. Also, you don't type in the INSERT *statements*
shown in this section.

When you add a new row to the order_status table but omit values for the status and
last_modified columns, those columns are set to the default values. For example, the following
INSERT statement omits values for the status and last_modified columns:

```
INSERT INTO order_status (order_status_id)
VALUES (1);
```

The status column of the new row is set to the default value of 'Order placed', and the
last_modified column is set to the current date and time.

You can override the defaults by specifying a value for the columns, as shown in the following
example:

```
INSERT INTO order_status (order_status_id, status, last_modified)
VALUES (2, 'Order shipped', '10-JUN-2004');
```

The following query retrieves the rows from the order_status table:

```
SELECT *
FROM order_status;
```

```
ORDER_STATUS_ID STATUS               LAST_MODI
--------------- -------------------- ---------
              1 Order placed         25-JUL-11
              2 Order shipped        10-JUN-04
```

You can set a column back to the default using the DEFAULT keyword in an UPDATE statement.
For example, the following UPDATE sets the status column to the default:

```
UPDATE order_status
SET status = DEFAULT
WHERE order_status_id = 2;
```

The following query shows the change:

```
SELECT *
FROM order_status;
```

```
ORDER_STATUS_ID STATUS               LAST_MODI
--------------- -------------------- ---------
              1 Order placed         25-JUL-11
              2 Order placed         10-JUN-04
```

Merging Rows Using MERGE

The MERGE statement allows you to merge rows from one table into another. For example, you
might want to merge changes to products listed in one table into the products table.

The `store` schema contains a table named `product_changes` that was created using the following CREATE TABLE statement in `store_schema.sql`:

```
CREATE TABLE product_changes (
  product_id INTEGER
    CONSTRAINT prod_changes_pk PRIMARY KEY,
  product_type_id INTEGER
    CONSTRAINT prod_changes_fk_product_types
    REFERENCES product_types(product_type_id),
  name VARCHAR2(30) NOT NULL,
  description VARCHAR2(50),
  price NUMBER(5, 2)
);
```

The following query retrieves the `product_id`, `product_type_id`, `name`, and `price` columns from the `product_changes` table:

```
SELECT product_id, product_type_id, name, price
FROM product_changes;
```

```
PRODUCT_ID PRODUCT_TYPE_ID NAME                              PRICE
---------- --------------- ---------------------------- ----------
         1               1 Modern Science                       40
         2               1 New Chemistry                        35
         3               1 Supernova                         25.99
        13               2 Lunar Landing                     15.99
        14               2 Submarine                         15.99
        15               2 Airplane                          15.99
```

As an example, suppose you want to merge the rows from the `product_changes` table into the `products` table as follows:

- For rows with matching `product_id` values in the two tables, update the existing rows in `products` with the column values from `product_changes`. For example, product #1 has a different price in `product_changes` from the one in `products`. Therefore, product #1's price must be updated in the `products` table. Similarly, product #2 has a different name and price, so both values must be updated in `products`. Finally, product #3 has a different `product_type_id`, so this value must be updated in `products`.

- For new rows in `product_changes`, insert those new rows into the `products` table. Products #13, #14, and #15 are new in `product_changes` and must therefore be inserted into `products`.

The following MERGE statement performs the merge as described in the previous bullet points:

```
MERGE INTO products p
USING product_changes pc ON (
  p.product_id = pc.product_id
)
WHEN MATCHED THEN
```

```
  UPDATE
  SET
    p.product_type_id = pc.product_type_id,
    p.name = pc.name,
    p.description = pc.description,
    p.price = pc.price
WHEN NOT MATCHED THEN
  INSERT (
    p.product_id, p.product_type_id, p.name,
    p.description, p.price
  ) VALUES (
    pc.product_id, pc.product_type_id, pc.name,
    pc.description, pc.price
  );
```

```
6 rows merged.
```

NOTE
You'll find a script named merge_example.sql *in the* SQL
directory. This script contains the previous MERGE *statement, and
saves you from having to type in the* MERGE *statement if you are
following along with the examples.*

Notice the following points about the MERGE statement:

- The MERGE INTO clause specifies the name of the table to merge the rows into. In the example, this is the products table, which is given an alias of p.

- The USING ... ON clause specifies a table join. In the example, the join is made on the product_id columns in the products and product_changes tables. The product_changes table is also given an alias of pc.

- The WHEN MATCHED THEN clause specifies the action to take when the USING ... ON clause is satisfied for a row. In the example, this action is an UPDATE statement that sets the product_type_id, name, description, and price columns of the existing row in the products table to the column values for the matching row in the product_ changes table.

- The WHEN NOT MATCHED THEN clause specifies the action to take when the USING ... ON clause is *not* satisfied for a row. In the example, this action is an INSERT statement that adds a row to the products table, taking the column values from the row in the product_changes table.

If you run the previous MERGE statement, you'll see that it reports six rows are merged. These are the rows with product_id values of 1, 2, 3, 13, 14, and 15. The following query retrieves the six merged rows from the products table:

```
SELECT product_id, product_type_id, name, price
FROM products
WHERE product_id IN (1, 2, 3, 13, 14, 15);
```

```
PRODUCT_ID PRODUCT_TYPE_ID NAME                                PRICE
---------- --------------- ----------------------------  ----------
         1               1 Modern Science                       40
         2               1 New Chemistry                        35
         3               1 Supernova                         25.99
        13               2 Lunar Landing                     15.99
        14               2 Submarine                         15.99
        15               2 Airplane                          15.99
```

The following changes were made to these rows:

■ Product #1 has a new price.

■ Product #2 has a new name and price.

■ Product #3 has a new product type ID.

■ Products #13, #14, and #15 are new.

Now that you've seen how to make changes to the contents of tables, let's move on to database transactions.

Database Transactions

A database *transaction* is a group of SQL statements that perform a *logical unit of work*. A transaction is an inseparable set of SQL statements whose results should be made permanent in the database as a whole (or undone as a whole).

An example of a database transaction is a transfer of money from one bank account to another. One UPDATE statement would subtract from the total amount of money from one account, and another UPDATE would add money to the other account. Both the subtraction and the addition must be permanently recorded in the database; otherwise, money will be lost. If there is a problem with the money transfer, then the subtraction and addition must both be undone. The money transfer example has two UPDATE statements, but a transaction can consist of many INSERT, UPDATE, and DELETE statements.

Committing and Rolling Back a Transaction

To permanently record the results made by SQL statements in a transaction, you perform a COMMIT. To undo the results, you perform a ROLLBACK, which resets all the rows back to what they were before the transaction began.

The following example adds a row to the customers table and then makes the change permanent by performing a COMMIT:

```
INSERT INTO customers
VALUES (6, 'Fred', 'Green', '01-JAN-1970', '800-555-1215');

1 row created.

COMMIT;

Commit complete.
```

The following example updates customer #1 and then undoes the change by performing a ROLLBACK:

```
UPDATE customers
SET first_name = 'Edward'
WHERE customer_id = 1;
```

```
1 row updated.
```

```
ROLLBACK;
```

```
Rollback complete.
```

The following query shows the new row from the COMMIT statement:

```
SELECT *
FROM customers;
```

```
CUSTOMER_ID FIRST_NAME LAST_NAME  DOB        PHONE
----------- ---------- ---------- ---------  ------------
          1 John       Brown      01-JAN-65  800-555-1211
          2 Cynthia    Green      05-FEB-68  800-555-1212
          3 Steve      White      16-MAR-71  800-555-1213
          4 Gail       Black                 800-555-1214
          5 Doreen     Blue       20-MAY-70
          6 Fred       Green      01-JAN-70  800-555-1215
```

Notice that customer #6 has been made permanent by the COMMIT, but the change to customer #1's first name has been undone by the ROLLBACK.

Starting and Ending a Transaction

A transaction is a logical unit of work that enables you to split up your SQL statements. A transaction has a beginning and an end.

A transaction *begins* when one of the following events occurs:

- You connect to the database and perform a DML statement (an INSERT, UPDATE, or DELETE).

- A previous transaction ends and you enter another DML statement.

A transaction *ends* when one of the following events occurs:

- You perform a COMMIT or a ROLLBACK.

- You perform a DDL statement, such as a CREATE TABLE statement, which automatically performs a COMMIT.

- You perform a DCL statement, such as a GRANT statement, which automatically performs a COMMIT. You'll learn about GRANT in the next chapter.

- You disconnect from the database. If you exit SQL*Plus normally, by entering the EXIT command, a COMMIT is automatically performed for you. If SQL*Plus terminates abnormally—for example, if the computer on which SQL*Plus was running were to crash—a ROLLBACK is automatically performed. This applies to any program that accesses a database. For example, if you wrote a Java program that accessed a database and your program crashed, a ROLLBACK would be automatically performed.

■ You perform a DML statement that fails, in which case a ROLLBACK is automatically performed for that individual DML statement.

TIP
It is poor practice not to explicitly commit or roll back your transactions, so perform a COMMIT or ROLLBACK at the end of your transactions.

Savepoints

You can set a *savepoint* at any point within a transaction. This allows you to roll back changes to that savepoint. Savepoints are useful for breaking up very long transactions, because if you make a mistake after you've set a savepoint, you don't have to roll back the transaction all the way to the start. However, you should use savepoints sparingly: it might be better to restructure your transaction into smaller transactions.

You'll see an example of a savepoint shortly, but first let's see the current price for products #4 and #5:

```
SELECT product_id, price
FROM products
WHERE product_id IN (4, 5);

PRODUCT_ID      PRICE
---------- ----------
         4      13.95
         5      49.99
```

The price for product #4 is $13.95, and the price for product #5 is $49.99.
The following UPDATE increases the price of product #4 by 20 percent:

```
UPDATE products
SET price = price * 1.20
WHERE product_id = 4;

1 row updated.
```

The following statement sets a savepoint named save1:

```
SAVEPOINT save1;

Savepoint created.
```

Any DML statements run after this point can be rolled back to the savepoint, and the change made to product #4 will be kept.
The following UPDATE increases the price of product #5 by 30 percent:

```
UPDATE products
SET price = price * 1.30
```

```
WHERE product_id = 5;
```

```
1 row updated.
```

The following query gets the prices of the two products:

```
SELECT product_id, price
FROM products
WHERE product_id IN (4, 5);
```

```
PRODUCT_ID      PRICE
---------- ----------
        4      16.74
        5      64.99
```

Product #4's price is 20 percent greater than its original price, and product #5's price is 30 percent greater than its original price.

The following statement rolls back the transaction to the savepoint established earlier:

```
ROLLBACK TO SAVEPOINT save1;
```

```
Rollback complete.
```

This has undone the price change for product #5, but it has left the price change for product #4 intact. The following query shows this:

```
SELECT product_id, price
FROM products
WHERE product_id IN (4, 5);
```

```
PRODUCT_ID      PRICE
---------- ----------
        4      16.74
        5      49.99
```

As expected, product #4 has kept its increased price, but product #5's price is back to the original.

The following ROLLBACK undoes the entire transaction:

```
ROLLBACK;
```

```
Rollback complete.
```

The ROLLBACK has undone the change made to product #4's price, as is shown by the following query:

```
SELECT product_id, price
FROM products
WHERE product_id IN (4, 5);
```

```
PRODUCT_ID      PRICE
---------- ----------
        4      13.95
        5      49.99
```

ACID Transaction Properties

Earlier, I defined a transaction as a *logical unit of work*, which is a group of related SQL statements that are either *committed* or *rolled back* as one unit. Database theory's more rigorous definition of a transaction states that a transaction has four fundamental properties, known as *ACID* properties (from the first letter of each property in the following list):

- **Atomic**   Transactions are atomic, meaning that the SQL statements contained in a transaction make up a single unit of work.

- **Consistent**   Transactions ensure that the database state remains consistent, meaning that the database is in a consistent state when a transaction begins and the database is in another consistent state when the transaction finishes.

- **Isolated**   Separate transactions should not interfere with each other.

- **Durable**   After a transaction is committed, the database changes are preserved, even if the computer on which the database software is running crashes later.

The Oracle database software handles these ACID properties and has extensive recovery facilities for database restoration after a system crash.

Concurrent Transactions

The Oracle database software supports many users interacting with a database, and each user can run their own transactions at the same time. These transactions are known as *concurrent* transactions.

If users are running transactions that affect the same table, the effects of those transactions are separated from each other until a COMMIT is performed. The following sequence of events, based on two transactions named T1 and T2 that access the customers table, illustrates the separation of transactions:

1. T1 and T2 perform a SELECT that retrieves all the rows from the customers table.
2. T1 performs an INSERT to add a row in the customers table, but T1 doesn't perform a COMMIT.
3. T2 performs another SELECT and retrieves the same rows as those in step 1. T2 doesn't "see" the new row added by T1 in step 2.
4. T1 finally performs a COMMIT to permanently record the new row added in step 2.
5. T2 performs another SELECT and finally "sees" the new row added by T1.

To summarize: T2 doesn't see the changes made by T1 until T1 commits its changes. This is the default level of isolation between transactions, but, as you'll learn later in the section "Transaction Isolation Levels," you can change the level of isolation.

Table 9-1 shows sample SQL statements that further illustrate how concurrent transactions work. The table shows the interleaved order in which the statements are performed by two transactions named T1 and T2. T1 retrieves rows, adds a row, and updates a row in the customers table. T2 retrieves rows from the customers table. T2 doesn't see the changes made by T1 until T1 commits its changes. You can enter the statements shown in Table 9-1 and see their results by starting two separate SQL*Plus sessions and connecting as the store user for both sessions. You enter the statements in the interleaved order shown in the table into the SQL*Plus sessions.

Transaction 1 T1	Transaction 2 T2
(1) `SELECT *` `FROM customers;`	(2) `SELECT *` `FROM customers;`

(3) `INSERT INTO customers (`
  `customer_id, first_name,`
`last_name`
`) VALUES (`
  `7, 'Jason', 'Price'`
`);`	

(4) `UPDATE customers`
`SET last_name = 'Orange'`
`WHERE customer_id = 2;`	

(5) `SELECT *` `FROM customers;` The returned result set contains the new row and the update.	(6) `SELECT *` `FROM customers;` The returned result set doesn't contain the new row or the update made by T1. Instead, the result set contains the original rows retrieved in step 2.
(7) `COMMIT;` This commits the new row and the update.	
	(8) `SELECT *` `FROM customers;` The returned result set contains the new row and the update made by T1 in steps 3 and 4.

TABLE 9-1. *Concurrent Transactions*

Transaction Locking

To support concurrent transactions, the Oracle database software must ensure that the data in the tables remain valid. It does this through the use of *locks*. Consider the following example in which two transactions named T1 and T2 attempt to modify customer #1 in the `customers` table:

1. T1 performs an `UPDATE` to modify customer #1, but T1 doesn't perform a `COMMIT`. T1 is said to have "locked" the row.

2. T2 also attempts to perform an `UPDATE` to modify customer #1, but since this row is already locked by T1, T2 is prevented from getting a lock on the row. T2's `UPDATE` statement has to wait until T1 ends and frees the lock on the row.

3. T1 ends by performing a `COMMIT`, thus freeing the lock on the row.

4. T2 gets the lock on the row and the `UPDATE` is performed. T2 holds the lock on the row until T2 ends.

To summarize: A transaction cannot get a lock on a row while another transaction already holds the lock on that row.

NOTE
The easiest way to understand default locking is as follows: Readers don't block readers, writers don't block readers, and writers only block writers when they attempt to modify the same row.

Transaction Isolation Levels

The *transaction isolation level* is the degree to which the changes made by one transaction are separated from other transactions running concurrently. Before you see the various transaction isolation levels available, you need to understand the types of problems that can occur when current transactions attempt to access the same rows in a table.

There are three types of potential transaction problems when concurrent transactions access the same rows:

- **Phantom reads** Transaction T1 reads a set of rows returned by a specified WHERE clause. Transaction T2 then inserts a new row, which also happens to satisfy the WHERE clause of the query previously used by T1. T1 then reads the rows again using the same query, but now sees the additional row just inserted by T2. This new row is known as a "phantom" because, to T1, this row seems to have magically appeared.

- **Nonrepeatable reads** T1 reads a row, and T2 updates the same row just read by T1. T1 then reads the same row again and discovers that the row it read earlier is now different. This is known as a "nonrepeatable" read, because the row originally read by T1 has been changed.

- **Dirty reads** T1 updates a row but doesn't commit the update. T2 then reads the updated row. T1 then performs a rollback, undoing the previous update. Now the row just read by T2 is no longer valid (it's "dirty") because the update made by T1 wasn't committed when the row was read by T2.

To deal with these potential problems, databases implement various levels of transaction isolation to prevent concurrent transactions from interfering with each other. The SQL standard defines the following transaction isolation levels, shown in order of increasing isolation:

- **READ UNCOMMITTED** Phantom reads, nonrepeatable reads, and dirty reads are permitted.

- **READ COMMITTEED** Phantom reads and nonrepeatable reads are permitted, but dirty reads are not.

- **REPEATABLE READ** Phantom reads are permitted, but nonrepeatable and dirty reads are not.

- **SERIALIZABLE** Phantom reads, nonrepeatable reads, and dirty reads are not permitted.

The Oracle database software supports the READ COMMITTED and SERIALIZABLE transaction isolation levels. It doesn't support the READ UNCOMMITTED and REPEATABLE READ levels.

The default transaction isolation level defined by the SQL standard is SERIALIZABLE, but the default used by the Oracle database is READ COMMITTED, which is acceptable for nearly all applications.

CAUTION
Although you can use SERIALIZABLE with the Oracle database, it can increase the time your SQL statements take to complete. You should only use SERIALIZABLE if you absolutely have to.

You set the transaction isolation level using the SET TRANSACTION statement. For example, the following statement sets the transaction isolation level to SERIALIZABLE:

```
SET TRANSACTION ISOLATION LEVEL SERIALIZABLE;
```

You'll see an example of a transaction that uses the isolation level of SERIALIZABLE next.

A SERIALIZABLE Transaction Example

In this section, you'll see an example that shows the effect of setting the transaction isolation level to SERIALIZABLE.

The example uses two transactions named T1 and T2. T1 has the default isolation level of READ COMMITTED. T2 has a transaction isolation level of SERIALIZABLE. T1 and T2 will read the rows in the customers table, and then T1 will insert a new row and update an existing row in the customers table. Because T2 is SERIALIZABLE, it doesn't see the inserted row or the update made to the existing row made by T1, even *after* T1 commits its changes. That's because reading the inserted row would be a phantom read, and reading the update would be a nonrepeatable read, which are not permitted by SERIALIZABLE transactions.

Table 9-2 shows the SQL statements for T1 and T2 in the interleaved order that the statements are performed.

Transaction 1 T1 (READ COMMITTED)	Transaction 2 T2 (SERIALIZABLE)
	(1) `SET TRANSACTION ISOLATION LEVEL SERIALIZABLE;`
(3) `SELECT * FROM customers;`	(2) `SELECT * FROM customers;`
(4) `INSERT INTO customers ( customer_id, first_name, last_name ) VALUES ( 8, 'Steve', 'Button' );`	
(5) `UPDATE customers SET last_name = 'Yellow' WHERE customer_id = 3;`	
(6) `COMMIT;`	
(7) `SELECT * FROM customers;` The returned result set contains the new row and the update.	(8) `SELECT * FROM customers;` The returned result set *still* doesn't contain the new row or the update made by T1. That's because T2 is SERIALIZABLE.

TABLE 9-2. SERIALIZABLE *Transactions*

Issuing a command that ends a SERIALIZABLE transaction will synchronize the SERIALIZABLE transaction with the READ COMMITTED transaction. For example, issuing a COMMIT in the SERIALIZABLE transaction, even if no row changes have been made by the SERIALIZABLE transaction, will synchronize the SERIALIZABLE transaction with the READ COMMITTED transaction.

Query Flashbacks

If you mistakenly commit changes and you want to view rows as they originally were, you can use a query flashback. You can then use the results of a query flashback to manually change rows back to their original values.

Query flashbacks can be based on a datetime or system change number (SCN). The database uses SCNs to track changes made to data, and you can use them to flash back to a particular SCN in the database.

NOTE
Before continuing, rerun the store_schema.sql *file to ensure that your results match those in this section.*

Granting the Privilege for Using Flashbacks

Flashbacks use the PL/SQL DBMS_FLASHBACK package, for which you must have the EXECUTE privilege to run. The following example connects as the sys user and grants the EXECUTE privilege on DBMS_FLASHBACK to the store user:

```
CONNECT sys/change_on_install AS sysdba
GRANT EXECUTE ON sys.DBMS_FLASHBACK TO store;
```

NOTE
Speak with your database administrator if you are unable to perform these statements. You'll learn about privileges in the next chapter, and you'll learn about PL/SQL packages in Chapter 12.

Time Query Flashbacks

The following example connects as the store user and retrieves the product_id, name, and price columns for the first five rows from the products table:

```
CONNECT store/store_password
SELECT product_id, name, price
FROM products
WHERE product_id <= 5;
```

```
PRODUCT_ID NAME                                     PRICE
---------- -------------------------------- ----------
         1 Modern Science                           19.95
         2 Chemistry                                   30
         3 Supernova                                25.99
```

```
4 Tank War                          13.95
5 Z Files                           49.99
```

The next example reduces the price of these rows, commits the change, and retrieves the rows again to view the new prices:

```
UPDATE products
SET price = price * 0.75
WHERE product_id <= 5;

COMMIT;

SELECT product_id, name, price
FROM products
WHERE product_id <= 5;

PRODUCT_ID NAME                                     PRICE
---------- -------------------------------- ----------
         1 Modern Science                           14.96
         2 Chemistry                                 22.5
         3 Supernova                                19.49
         4 Tank War                                 10.46
         5 Z Files                                  37.49
```

The following statement executes the DBMS_FLASHBACK.ENABLE_AT_TIME() procedure, which performs a flashback to a particular datetime. The DBMS_FLASHBACK.ENABLE_AT_TIME() procedure accepts a datetime. The example passes SYSDATE - 10 / 1440 to the procedure, which is a datetime 10 minutes in the past.

```
EXECUTE DBMS_FLASHBACK.ENABLE_AT_TIME(SYSDATE - 10 / 1440);
```

NOTE
24 hours 60 minutes per hour = 1440 minutes. Therefore, SYSDATE - 10 / 1440 is a datetime 10 minutes in the past.

Any queries you execute now will display the rows as they were 10 minutes ago. Assuming you performed the earlier UPDATE less than 10 minutes ago, the following query will display the prices as they were before you updated them:

```
SELECT product_id, name, price
FROM products
WHERE product_id <= 5;

PRODUCT_ID NAME                                     PRICE
---------- -------------------------------- ----------
         1 Modern Science                           19.95
         2 Chemistry                                   30
         3 Supernova                                25.99
         4 Tank War                                 13.95
         5 Z Files                                  49.99
```

To disable a flashback, you execute DBMS_FLASHBACK.DISABLE(), as shown in the following example:

```
EXECUTE DBMS_FLASHBACK.DISABLE();
```

CAUTION
You must disable a flashback before you can enable it again.

Now when you perform queries, the rows as they currently exist will be retrieved. For example:

```
SELECT product_id, name, price
FROM products
WHERE product_id <= 5;
```

```
PRODUCT_ID NAME                                       PRICE
---------- ------------------------------ ----------
         1 Modern Science                             14.96
         2 Chemistry                                   22.5
         3 Supernova                                  19.49
         4 Tank War                                   10.46
         5 Z Files                                    37.49
```

System Change Number Query Flashbacks

Flashbacks based on system change numbers (SCNs) can be more precise than those based on a time, because the database uses SCNs to track changes made to data. To get the current SCN, you can execute DBMS_FLASHBACK.GET_SYSTEM_CHANGE_NUMBER(), as shown in the following example:

```
VARIABLE current_scn NUMBER

EXECUTE :current_scn := DBMS_FLASHBACK.GET_SYSTEM_CHANGE_NUMBER();

PRINT current_scn

CURRENT_SCN
-----------
     292111
```

The next example adds a row to the products table, commits the change, and retrieves the new row:

```
INSERT INTO products (
  product_id, product_type_id, name, description, price
) VALUES (
  15, 1, 'Physics', 'Textbook on physics', 39.95
);

COMMIT;
```

```
SELECT *
FROM products
WHERE product_id = 15;

PRODUCT_ID PRODUCT_TYPE_ID NAME
---------- --------------- -----------------------------
DESCRIPTION                                          PRICE
---------------------------------------------------- ----------
        15               1 Physics
Textbook on physics                                  39.95
```

The next example executes the following procedure, DBMS_FLASHBACK.ENABLE_AT_
SYSTEM_CHANGE_NUMBER(), which performs a flashback to an SCN. This procedure accepts an
SCN, and then the example passes the current_scn variable to the procedure.

```
EXECUTE DBMS_FLASHBACK.ENABLE_AT_SYSTEM_CHANGE_NUMBER(:current_scn);
```

Any queries you execute now will display the rows as they were at the SCN stored in current_
scn before you performed the INSERT. The following query attempts to get the row with a
product_id of 15. It fails because that new row was added after the SCN stored in current_scn.

```
SELECT product_id
FROM products
WHERE product_id = 15;

no rows selected
```

To disable a flashback, you execute DBMS_FLASHBACK.DISABLE(). For example:

```
EXECUTE DBMS_FLASHBACK.DISABLE();
```

If you perform the previous query again, you'll see the new row that was added by the INSERT:

```
SELECT product_id
FROM products
WHERE product_id = 15;

PRODUCT_ID
----------
        15
```

Summary

In this chapter, you have learned the following:

- The INSERT statement adds rows.
- The UPDATE statement modifies rows.
- The DELETE statement removes rows.
- The database maintains referential integrity through the enforcement of constraints.
- The DEFAULT keyword specifies default values for columns.

- The MERGE statement merges rows from one table into another table.
- A database transaction is a group of SQL statements that comprise a logical unit of work.
- The Oracle database software can process multiple concurrent transactions.
- Query flashbacks are used to view rows as they were before changes were made to them.

In the next chapter, you'll learn about users, privileges, and roles.

CHAPTER
10

Users, Privileges,
and Roles

I n this chapter, you will learn how to perform the following tasks:

- Create users
- See how privileges enable users to access data and perform database tasks
- Explore the two types of privileges: system privileges and object privileges
- Learn how system privileges enable actions such as executing DDL statements
- See how object privileges enable actions such as executing DML statements
- Group privileges together into roles
- Audit the execution of SQL statements

NOTE
Before running any of the examples in this chapter, rerun the `store_` `schema.sql` *script as described in Chapter 1 in the section "Creating the Store Schema." You'll need to type in the SQL statements shown in this chapter if you want to follow the examples.*

A Very Short Introduction to Database Storage

This section contains a very short introduction to the complex and vast subject of database storage. You need to understand the terminology presented in this introduction.

You will see the term *tablespace* used in this chapter. Tablespaces are used by the database to store objects, which can include tables, types, PL/SQL code, and so on. Typically, related objects are grouped together and stored in the same tablespace. For example, you might create an order entry application and store all the objects for that application in one tablespace. You might also create a supply chain application and store the objects for that application in a different tablespace. A user can be assigned a quota of space in a tablespace to store their data.

Tablespaces are stored in *datafiles*, which are files stored in the file system of a database server. A datafile stores data for one tablespace. The Oracle database software creates a datafile for a tablespace by allocating the specified amount of disk space plus the overhead for a file header.

For more details on tablespaces and datafiles, see the *Oracle Database Concepts* manual published by Oracle Corporation.

Users

In this section, you'll learn how to create a user, alter a user's password, and drop a user.

Creating a User

To create a user, you use the CREATE USER statement. The simplified syntax for the CREATE USER statement is as follows:

```
CREATE USER user_name IDENTIFIED BY password
[DEFAULT TABLESPACE default_tablespace]
[TEMPORARY TABLESPACE temporary_tablespace];
```

where

- *user_name* is the name of the database user.
- *password* is the password for the database user.
- *default_tablespace* is the default tablespace where database objects are stored. If you omit a default tablespace, the default SYSTEM tablespace, which always exists in a database, is used.
- *temporary_tablespace* is the default tablespace where temporary objects are stored. These objects include temporary tables that you'll learn about in the next chapter. If you omit a temporary tablespace, the default SYSTEM tablespace is used.

The following example connects as system and creates a user named jason with a password of price:

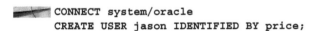

```
CONNECT system/oracle
CREATE USER jason IDENTIFIED BY price;
```

NOTE
If you want to follow along with the examples in this chapter, you'll need to connect to the database as a privileged user. I used the system user in the example, which has a password of oracle in my database.

The next example creates a user named baby and specifies a default and temporary tablespace:

```
CREATE USER baby IDENTIFIED BY nutmeg
DEFAULT TABLESPACE users
TEMPORARY TABLESPACE temp;
```

If your database doesn't have tablespaces named users and temp, then you can skip the previous example. The baby user isn't used elsewhere, and I included the example so that you can see how to specify tablespaces for a user. You can view all of the tablespaces in a database by connecting as the system user and running the query SELECT tablespace_name FROM dba_tablespaces.

If you want a user to be able to perform tasks in the database, then that user must be granted the necessary permissions to perform those tasks. For example, to connect to the database, a user must be granted the permission to create a session, which is the CREATE SESSION system privilege. Permissions are granted by a privileged user (system, for example) using the GRANT statement.

The following example grants the CREATE SESSION permission to jason:

```
GRANT CREATE SESSION TO jason;
```

The jason user will now be able to connect to the database.

The following example creates other users for this chapter and grants the CREATE SESSION privilege to those users:

```
CREATE USER steve IDENTIFIED BY brown;
CREATE USER gail IDENTIFIED BY green;
GRANT CREATE SESSION TO steve, gail;
```

Changing a User's Password

You can change a user's password using the ALTER USER statement. For example, the following statement changes the password for jason to marcus:

```
ALTER USER jason IDENTIFIED BY marcus;
```

You can also change the password for the user you're currently logged in as using the PASSWORD command. After you enter PASSWORD, SQL*Plus prompts you to enter the old password and the new password twice for confirmation. The following example connects as jason and executes PASSWORD. The password itself is hidden using asterisks.

```
CONNECT jason/marcus
PASSWORD
Changing password for JASON
Old password: ******
New password: ******
Retype new password: ******
Password changed
```

Deleting a User

You delete a user using the DROP USER statement. The following example connects as system and uses DROP USER to delete jason:

```
CONNECT system/oracle
DROP USER jason;
```

NOTE
You must add the keyword CASCADE after the user's name in the DROP USER statement if that user's schema contains any tables or other items. However, you should ensure that no other users need access to those objects before doing this.

System Privileges

A *system privilege* allows a user to perform certain actions within the database, such as executing DDL statements. For example, CREATE TABLE allows a user to create a table in their schema. Some of the commonly used system privileges are shown in Table 10-1.

NOTE
You can get the full list of system privileges in the Oracle Database SQL Reference *manual published by Oracle Corporation.*

Privileges can be grouped together into *roles*. Two useful roles to grant to a user are CONNECT and RESOURCE. CONNECT allows a user to connect to the database. RESOURCE allows a user to create various database objects like tables, sequences, PL/SQL code, and so on.

System Privilege	Allows a User to...
CREATE SESSION	Connect to a database.
CREATE SEQUENCE	Create a sequence, which is a series of numbers that is typically used to automatically populate a primary key column. You'll learn about sequences in the next chapter.
CREATE SYNONYM	Create a synonym. A synonym allows you to reference a table in another schema. You'll learn about synonyms later in this chapter.
CREATE TABLE	Create a table in the user's schema.
CREATE ANY TABLE	Create a table in any schema.
DROP TABLE	Drop a table from the user's schema.
DROP ANY TABLE	Drop a table from any schema.
CREATE PROCEDURE	Create a stored procedure.
EXECUTE ANY PROCEDURE	Execute a procedure in any schema.
CREATE USER	Create a user.
DROP USER	Drop a user.
CREATE VIEW	Create a view. A view is a stored query that allows you to access multiple tables and columns. You can then query the view as you would a table. You'll learn about views in the next chapter.

TABLE 10-1.   *Commonly Used System Privileges*

Granting System Privileges to a User

You use GRANT to grant a system privilege to a user. The following example grants some system privileges to steve:

```
GRANT CREATE SESSION, CREATE USER, CREATE TABLE TO steve;
```

You can also use WITH ADMIN OPTION to allow a user to grant a privilege to another user. The following example grants the EXECUTE ANY PROCEDURE privilege with the ADMIN option to steve:

```
GRANT EXECUTE ANY PROCEDURE TO steve WITH ADMIN OPTION;
```

EXECUTE ANY PROCEDURE can then be granted to another user by steve. The following example connects as steve and grants EXECUTE ANY PROCEDURE to gail:

```
CONNECT steve/brown
GRANT EXECUTE ANY PROCEDURE TO gail;
```

You can grant a privilege to all users by granting to PUBLIC. The following example connects as system and grants EXECUTE ANY PROCEDURE to PUBLIC:

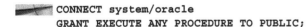

```
CONNECT system/oracle
GRANT EXECUTE ANY PROCEDURE TO PUBLIC;
```

Every user in the database now has the EXECUTE ANY PROCEDURE privilege.

Checking System Privileges Granted to a User

You can check which system privileges a user has by querying user_sys_privs. Table 10-2 describes some of the columns in user_sys_privs.

> **NOTE**
> user_sys_privs *forms part of the Oracle database's data dictionary. The data dictionary stores information about the database itself.*

The following example connects as steve and queries user_sys_privs:

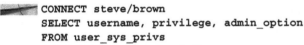

```
CONNECT steve/brown
SELECT username, privilege, admin_option
FROM user_sys_privs
ORDER BY username, privilege;
```

```
USERNAME                         PRIVILEGE                                ADM
-------------------------------- ---------------------------------------- ---
PUBLIC                           EXECUTE ANY PROCEDURE                    NO
STEVE                            CREATE SESSION                           NO
STEVE                            CREATE TABLE                             NO
STEVE                            CREATE USER                              NO
STEVE                            EXECUTE ANY PROCEDURE                    YES
```

The next example connects as gail and queries user_sys_privs:

```
CONNECT gail/green
SELECT username, privilege, admin_option
FROM user_sys_privs
ORDER BY username, privilege;
```

Column	Type	Description
username	VARCHAR2(128)	Name of the current user
privilege	VARCHAR2(40)	The system privilege the user has
admin_option	VARCHAR2(3)	Whether the user is able to grant the privilege to another user (YES or NO)

TABLE 10-2. *Some Columns in* user_sys_privs

```
USERNAME              PRIVILEGE                         ADM
------------------    --------------------------------  ---
GAIL                  CREATE SESSION                    NO
GAIL                  EXECUTE ANY PROCEDURE             NO
PUBLIC                EXECUTE ANY PROCEDURE             NO
```

Making Use of System Privileges

Once a user has been granted a system privilege, they can use it to perform the specified task. For example, steve has the CREATE USER privilege, so he is able to create a user:

```
CONNECT steve/brown
CREATE USER roy IDENTIFIED BY red;
```

If steve attempts to use a system privilege he doesn't have, the database will return the error ORA-01031: insufficient privileges. For example, steve doesn't have the DROP USER privilege, and in the following example steve attempts to drop roy and fails:

```
SQL> DROP USER roy;
DROP USER roy
*
ERROR at line 1:
ORA-01031: insufficient privileges
```

Revoking System Privileges from a User

You remove a system privilege from a user using REVOKE. The following example connects as system and revokes the CREATE TABLE privilege from steve:

```
CONNECT system/oracle
REVOKE CREATE TABLE FROM steve;
```

The next example revokes EXECUTE ANY PROCEDURE from steve:

```
REVOKE EXECUTE ANY PROCEDURE FROM steve;
```

When you revoke EXECUTE ANY PROCEDURE from steve—who has already passed on this privilege to gail—gail still keeps the privilege:

```
CONNECT gail/green
SELECT username, privilege, admin_option
FROM user_sys_privs
ORDER BY username, privilege;
```

```
USERNAME              PRIVILEGE                         ADM
------------------    --------------------------------  ---
GAIL                  CREATE SESSION                    NO
GAIL                  EXECUTE ANY PROCEDURE             NO
PUBLIC                EXECUTE ANY PROCEDURE             NO
```

Object Privileges

An *object privilege* allows a user to perform certain actions on database objects, such as executing DML statements on tables. For example, INSERT ON store.products allows a user to insert rows into the products table of the store schema. Some of the commonly used object privileges are shown in Table 10-3.

NOTE
You can get the full list of system privileges in the Oracle Database SQL Reference *manual published by Oracle Corporation.*

Granting Object Privileges to a User

You use GRANT to grant an object privilege to a user. The following example connects as store and grants the SELECT, INSERT, and UPDATE object privileges on the products table to steve along with the SELECT privilege on the employees table:

```
CONNECT store/store_password
GRANT SELECT, INSERT, UPDATE ON store.products TO steve;
GRANT SELECT ON store.employees TO steve;
```

The next example grants the UPDATE privilege on the last_name and salary columns to steve:

```
GRANT UPDATE (last_name, salary) ON store.employees TO steve;
```

You can also use the GRANT option to enable a user to grant a privilege to another user. The following example grants the SELECT privilege on the customers table with the GRANT option to steve:

```
GRANT SELECT ON store.customers TO steve WITH GRANT OPTION;
```

NOTE
You use the GRANT *option to allow a user to grant an* object privilege *to another user, and you use the* ADMIN *option to allow a user to grant a system privilege to another user.*

Object Privilege	Allows a User to...
SELECT	Perform a select
INSERT	Perform an insert
UPDATE	Perform an update
DELETE	Perform a delete
EXECUTE	Execute a stored procedure

TABLE 10-3. *Commonly Used Object Privileges*

The SELECT ON store.customers privilege can then be granted to another user by steve. The following example connects as steve and grants this privilege to gail:

```
CONNECT steve/brown
GRANT SELECT ON store.customers TO gail;
```

Checking Object Privileges Made

You can check which table object privileges a user has made to other users by querying user_tab_privs_made. Table 10-4 documents some of the columns in user_tab_privs_made.

The following example connects as store and queries user_tab_privs_made. Because there are so many rows, the example limits the retrieved rows to those where table_name is PRODUCTS.

```
CONNECT store/store_password
SELECT grantee, table_name, grantor, privilege, grantable, hierarchy
FROM user_tab_privs_made
WHERE table_name = 'PRODUCTS';

GRANTEE                 TABLE_NAME
--------------------    ------------------------------
GRANTOR                 PRIVILEGE                        GRA HIE
--------------------    ------------------------------   --- ---
STEVE                   PRODUCTS
STORE                   INSERT                           NO  NO

STEVE                   PRODUCTS
STORE                   SELECT                           NO  NO

STEVE                   PRODUCTS
STORE                   UPDATE                           NO  NO
```

You can check which column object privileges a user has made by querying user_col_privs_made. Table 10-5 documents some of the columns in user_col_privs_made.

Column	Type	Description
grantee	VARCHAR2(128)	User to whom the privilege was granted
table_name	VARCHAR2(128)	Name of the object (such as a table) on which the privilege was granted
grantor	VARCHAR2(128)	User who granted the privilege
privilege	VARCHAR2(40)	Privilege on the object
grantable	VARCHAR2(3)	Whether the grantee can grant the privilege to another (YES or NO)
hierarchy	VARCHAR2(3)	Whether the privilege forms part of a hierarchy (YES or NO)

TABLE 10-4. *Some Columns in* user_tab_privs_made

Column	Type	Description
grantee	VARCHAR2(128)	User to whom the privilege was granted
table_name	VARCHAR2(128)	Name of the object on which the privilege was granted
column_name	VARCHAR2(128)	Name of the object on which the privilege was granted
grantor	VARCHAR2(128)	User who granted the privilege
privilege	VARCHAR2(40)	Privilege on the object
grantable	VARCHAR2(3)	Whether the grantee can grant the privilege to another (YES or NO)

TABLE 10-5. *Some Columns in* user_col_privs_made

The following example queries user_col_privs_made:

```
SELECT grantee, table_name, column_name, grantor, privilege, grantable
FROM user_col_privs_made
ORDER BY column_name;

GRANTEE                          TABLE_NAME
------------------------------   -------------
COLUMN_NAME                      GRANTOR
------------------------------   -------------
PRIVILEGE                                  GRA
------------------------------------------ ---
STEVE                            EMPLOYEES
LAST_NAME                        STORE
UPDATE                                     NO

STEVE                            EMPLOYEES
SALARY                           STORE
UPDATE                                     NO
```

Checking Object Privileges Received

You can check which object privileges on a table a user has received by querying the user_tab_privs_recd table. Table 10-6 documents some of the columns in user_tab_privs_recd.

The next example connects as steve and queries user_tab_privs_recd:

```
CONNECT steve/brown
SELECT owner, table_name, grantor, privilege, grantable, hierarchy
FROM user_tab_privs_recd
ORDER BY table_name, privilege;
```

Column	Type	Description
owner	VARCHAR2(128)	User who owns the object
table_name	VARCHAR2(128)	Name of the object on which the privilege was granted
grantor	VARCHAR2(128)	User who granted the privilege
privilege	VARCHAR2(40)	Privilege on the object
grantable	VARCHAR2(3)	Whether the grantee can grant the privilege to another (YES or NO)
hierarchy	VARCHAR2(3)	Whether the privilege forms part of a hierarchy (YES or NO)

TABLE 10-6. *Some Columns in user_tab_privs_recd*

```
OWNER                   TABLE_NAME
-------------------- -----------------------------
GRANTOR                 PRIVILEGE               GRA HIE
-------------------- --------------------- --- ---
STORE                   CUSTOMERS
STORE                   SELECT                  YES NO

STORE                   EMPLOYEES
STORE                   SELECT                  NO  NO

STORE                   PRODUCTS
STORE                   INSERT                  NO  NO

STORE                   PRODUCTS
STORE                   SELECT                  NO  NO

STORE                   PRODUCTS
STORE                   UPDATE                  NO  NO
```

You can check which column object privileges a user has received by querying `user_col_privs_recd`. Table 10-7 documents some of the columns in `user_col_privs_recd`.

The following example queries `user_col_privs_recd`:

```
SELECT owner, table_name, column_name, grantor, privilege, grantable
FROM user_col_privs_recd;
```

```
OWNER                               TABLE_NAME
------------------------------- -------------
COLUMN_NAME                         GRANTOR
------------------------------- -------------
```

Column	Type	Description
owner	VARCHAR2(128)	User who owns the object
table_name	VARCHAR2(128)	Name of the table on which the privilege was granted
column_name	VARCHAR2(128)	Name of the column on which the privilege was granted
grantor	VARCHAR2(128)	User who granted the privilege
privilege	VARCHAR2(40)	Privilege on the object
grantable	VARCHAR2(3)	Whether the grantee can grant the privilege to another (YES or NO)

TABLE 10-7. *Some Columns in* user_col_privs_recd

```
PRIVILEGE                               GRA
--------------------------------------- ---
STORE                         EMPLOYEES
LAST_NAME                     STORE
UPDATE                                  NO

STORE                         EMPLOYEES
SALARY                        STORE
UPDATE                                  NO
```

Making Use of Object Privileges

Once a user has been granted an object privilege, they can use it to perform the specified task. For example, steve has the SELECT privilege on store.customers:

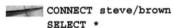

```
CONNECT steve/brown
SELECT *
FROM store.customers;
```

```
CUSTOMER_ID FIRST_NAME LAST_NAME  DOB        PHONE
----------- ---------- ---------- ---------- ------------
          1 John       Brown      01-JAN-65  800-555-1211
          2 Cynthia    Green      05-FEB-68  800-555-1212
          3 Steve      White      16-MAR-71  800-555-1213
          4 Gail       Black                 800-555-1214
          5 Doreen     Blue       20-MAY-70
```

If steve attempts to retrieve from the purchases table—for which he doesn't have any permissions—the database will return the error ORA-00942: table or view does not exist:

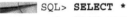

```
SQL> SELECT *
  2  FROM store.purchases;
```

```
FROM store.purchases
            *
ERROR at line 2:
ORA-00942: table or view does not exist
```

Creating Synonyms

In the examples in the previous section, you saw that you can access tables in another schema by specifying the schema name followed by the table. For example, when `steve` retrieved rows from the `customers` table in the `store` schema, he performed a query on `store.customers`. You can avoid having to enter the schema name by creating a *synonym* for a table, which you do by using the `CREATE SYNONYM` statement.

Let's take a look at an example. First, connect as `system` and grant the `CREATE SYNONYM` system privilege to `steve`:

```
CONNECT system/oracle
GRANT CREATE SYNONYM TO steve;
```

Next, connect as `steve` and perform a `CREATE SYNONYM` statement to create a synonym for the `store.customers` table:

```
CONNECT steve/brown
CREATE SYNONYM customers FOR store.customers;
```

To retrieve rows from `store.customers`, all `steve` has to do is reference the `customers` synonym in the `FROM` clause of a `SELECT` statement. For example:

```
SELECT *
FROM customers;
```

```
CUSTOMER_ID FIRST_NAME LAST_NAME  DOB       PHONE
----------- ---------- ---------- --------- ------------
          1 John       Brown      01-JAN-65 800-555-1211
          2 Cynthia    Green      05-FEB-68 800-555-1212
          3 Steve      White      16-MAR-71 800-555-1213
          4 Gail       Black                800-555-1214
          5 Doreen     Blue       20-MAY-70
```

Creating Public Synonyms

You can also create a *public* synonym for a table. When you do this, all the users see the synonym. The following tasks

- Connect as `system`
- Grant the `CREATE PUBLIC SYNONYM` system privilege to `store`
- Connect as `store`
- Create a public synonym named `products` for `store.products`

are performed by the following statements:

```
CONNECT system/oracle
GRANT CREATE PUBLIC SYNONYM TO store;
CONNECT store/store_password
CREATE PUBLIC SYNONYM products FOR store.products;
```

If you connect as steve, who has the SELECT privilege on store.products, you can now retrieve rows from store.products through the products public synonym:

```
CONNECT steve/brown
SELECT *
FROM products;
```

Even though a public synonym has been created for store.products, a user still needs object privileges on that table to actually access the table. For example, gail can see the products public synonym, but gail doesn't have any object privileges on store.products. Therefore, if gail attempts to retrieve rows from products, the database returns the error ORA-00942: table or view does not exist:

```
SQL> CONNECT gail/green
Connected.
SQL> SELECT * FROM products;
SELECT * FROM products
              *
ERROR at line 1:
ORA-00942: table or view does not exist
```

If gail had the SELECT object privilege on the store.products table, then the previous SELECT would succeed.

If a user has other object privileges, that user can exercise those object privileges through a synonym. For example, if gail had the INSERT object privilege on the store.products table, then gail would be able to add a row to store.products through the products synonym.

Revoking Object Privileges

You remove an object privilege using REVOKE. The following example connects as store and revokes the INSERT privilege on the products table from steve:

```
CONNECT store/store_password
REVOKE INSERT ON products FROM steve;
```

The next example revokes the SELECT privilege on the customers table from steve:

```
REVOKE SELECT ON store.customers FROM steve;
```

When you revoke SELECT ON store.customers from steve—who has already passed on this privilege to gail—gail also loses the privilege.

Roles

A *role* is a group of privileges that you can assign to a user or to another role. The following points summarize the benefits of roles:

- Rather than assigning privileges one at a time directly to a user, you can create a role, assign privileges to that role, and then grant that role to multiple users and roles.
- When you add or delete a privilege from a role, all users and roles assigned that role automatically receive or lose that privilege.
- You can assign multiple roles to a user or role.
- You can assign a password to a role.

As you can see from these points, roles can help you manage multiple privileges assigned to multiple users.

Creating Roles

To create a role, you must have the CREATE ROLE system privilege. As you'll see in a later example, the store user also needs the ability to grant the CREATE USER system privilege with the ADMIN option. The following example connects as system and grants the required privileges to store:

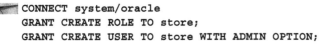

```
CONNECT system/oracle
GRANT CREATE ROLE TO store;
GRANT CREATE USER TO store WITH ADMIN OPTION;
```

You create a role using the CREATE ROLE statement. The example roles to be created for this section are shown in Table 10-8.

The following statements connect as the store user and create the three roles shown in Table 10-8:

```
CONNECT store/store_password
CREATE ROLE product_manager;
CREATE ROLE hr_manager;
CREATE ROLE overall_manager IDENTIFIED by manager_password;
```

Notice that the overall_manager role has a password of manager_password.

Role Name	Has Permissions to...
product_manager	Perform SELECT, INSERT, UPDATE, and DELETE operations on the product_types and products tables.
hr_manager	Perform SELECT, INSERT, UPDATE, and DELETE operations on the salary_grades and employees tables. Also, hr_manager is able to create users.
overall_manager	Perform SELECT, INSERT, UPDATE, and DELETE operations on all the tables shown in the previous roles. To do that, the overall_ manager role will be granted the previous roles.

TABLE 10-8. *Roles to Be Created*

Granting Privileges to Roles

You grant privileges to a role using the GRANT statement. You can grant both system and object privileges to a role as well as grant another role to a role. The following example grants the required privileges to the `product_manager` and `hr_manager` roles and grants these two roles to `overall_manager`:

```
GRANT SELECT, INSERT, UPDATE, DELETE ON product_types TO product_manager;
GRANT SELECT, INSERT, UPDATE, DELETE ON products TO product_manager;
GRANT SELECT, INSERT, UPDATE, DELETE ON salary_grades TO hr_manager;
GRANT SELECT, INSERT, UPDATE, DELETE ON employees TO hr_manager;
GRANT CREATE USER TO hr_manager;
GRANT product_manager, hr_manager TO overall_manager;
```

Granting Roles to a User

The following statements create the users for this section:

```
CONNECT system/oracle
CREATE USER john IDENTIFIED BY brown;
CREATE USER harry IDENTIFIED BY blue;
GRANT CREATE SESSION TO john;
GRANT CREATE SESSION TO harry;
```

You grant a role to a user using GRANT. The following example grants the `hr_manager` role to `john`:

```
GRANT hr_manager TO john;
```

The next example grants the `overall_manager` role to `harry`:

```
GRANT overall_manager TO harry;
```

Checking Roles Granted to a User

You can check which roles have been granted to a user by querying `user_role_privs`. Table 10-9 describes some of the columns in `user_role_privs`.

The following example connects as `john` and queries `user_role_privs`:

```
CONNECT john/brown
SELECT username, granted_role, admin_option, default_role, os_granted
FROM user_role_privs;

USERNAME             GRANTED_ROLE                 ADM DEF OS_
-------------------- ---------------------------- --- --- ---
JOHN                 HR_MANAGER                   NO  YES NO
```

The next example connects as `harry` and queries `user_role_privs`:

```
CONNECT harry/blue
SELECT username, granted_role, admin_option, default_role, os_granted
FROM user_role_privs;
```

Column	Type	Description
username	VARCHAR2(128)	Name of the user to whom the role has been granted
granted_role	VARCHAR2(128)	Name of the role granted to the user
admin_option	VARCHAR2(3)	Whether the user is able to grant the role to another user or role (YES or NO)
default_role	VARCHAR2(3)	Whether the role is enabled by default when the user connects to the database (YES or NO)
os_granted	VARCHAR2(3)	Whether the role was granted by the operating system (YES or NO)

TABLE 10-9. *Some Columns in* user_role_privs

```
USERNAME                GRANTED_ROLE                ADM DEF OS_
----------------        ------------------------    --- --- ---
HARRY                   OVERALL_MANAGER             NO  NO  NO
```

Notice that password-protected roles are disabled. The default_role column in the previous example shows that the overall_manager role is disabled. This role is password protected. Before the user can use the role, the user must enter the role password.

A user who creates a role is granted that role. The following example connects as store and queries user_role_privs:

```
CONNECT store/store_password
SELECT username, granted_role, admin_option, default_role, os_granted
FROM user_role_privs
ORDER BY username, granted_role;

USERNAME                GRANTED_ROLE                ADM DEF OS_
----------------        ------------------------    --- --- ---
STORE                   CONNECT                     NO  YES NO
STORE                   HR_MANAGER                  YES YES NO
STORE                   OVERALL_MANAGER             YES NO  NO
STORE                   PRODUCT_MANAGER             YES YES NO
STORE                   RESOURCE                    NO  YES NO
```

Notice store has the roles CONNECT and RESOURCE in addition to the roles store created earlier.

NOTE
CONNECT and RESOURCE are built-in roles that were granted to store when you ran the store_schema.sql script. As you'll see in the next section, the CONNECT and RESOURCE roles contain multiple privileges.

Column	Type	Description
role	VARCHAR2(128)	Name of the role
privilege	VARCHAR2(40)	System privilege granted to the role
admin_option	VARCHAR2(3)	Whether the privilege was granted with the ADMIN option (YES or NO)

TABLE 10-10. *Some Columns in* `role_sys_privs`

Checking System Privileges Granted to a Role

You can check which system privileges have been granted to a role by querying `role_sys_privs`. Table 10-10 describes some of the columns in `role_sys_privs`.

The following example retrieves the rows from `role_sys_privs` (assuming you're still connected as `store`):

```
SELECT role, privilege, admin_option
FROM role_sys_privs
ORDER BY role, privilege;
```

```
ROLE                        PRIVILEGE                               ADM
--------------------------  --------------------------------------  ---
CONNECT                     CREATE SESSION                          NO
CONNECT                     SET CONTAINER                           NO
HR_MANAGER                  CREATE USER                             NO
RESOURCE                    CREATE CLUSTER                          NO
RESOURCE                    CREATE INDEXTYPE                        NO
RESOURCE                    CREATE OPERATOR                         NO
RESOURCE                    CREATE PROCEDURE                        NO
RESOURCE                    CREATE SEQUENCE                         NO
RESOURCE                    CREATE TABLE                            NO
RESOURCE                    CREATE TRIGGER                          NO
RESOURCE                    CREATE TYPE                             NO
```

Notice that the RESOURCE role has many privileges assigned to it.

NOTE
The previous query was run using Oracle Database 12c. If you are using a different version of the database software, you might get slightly different results.

Checking Object Privileges Granted to a Role

You can check which object privileges have been granted to a role by querying `role_tab_privs`. Table 10-11 describes some of the columns in `role_tab_privs`.

Column	Type	Description
role	VARCHAR2(128)	User to whom the privilege was granted
owner	VARCHAR2(128)	User who owns the object
table_name	VARCHAR2(128)	Name of the object on which the privilege was granted
column_name	VARCHAR2(128)	Name of the column (if applicable)
privilege	VARCHAR2(40)	Privilege on the object
grantable	VARCHAR2(3)	Whether the privilege was granted with the GRANT option (YES or NO)

TABLE 10-11. *Some Columns in* `role_tab_privs`

The following example queries `role_tab_privs` where `role` equals `HR_MANAGER`:

```
SELECT role, owner, table_name, column_name, privilege, grantable
FROM role_tab_privs
WHERE role='HR_MANAGER'
ORDER BY table_name, column_name, privilege;

ROLE                            OWNER
------------------------------  ------------------------------
TABLE_NAME                      COLUMN_NAME
------------------------------  ------------------------------
PRIVILEGE                                          GRA
---------------------------------------------      ---
HR_MANAGER                      STORE
EMPLOYEES
DELETE                                             NO

HR_MANAGER                      STORE
EMPLOYEES
INSERT                                             NO

HR_MANAGER                      STORE
EMPLOYEES
SELECT                                             NO

HR_MANAGER                      STORE
EMPLOYEES
UPDATE                                             NO

HR_MANAGER                      STORE
SALARY_GRADES
DELETE                                             NO
```

```
HR_MANAGER                      STORE
SALARY_GRADES
INSERT                                        NO

HR_MANAGER                      STORE
SALARY_GRADES
SELECT                                        NO

HR_MANAGER                      STORE
SALARY_GRADES
UPDATE                                        NO
```

Making Use of Privileges Granted to a Role

For a non-password-protected role, the user can immediately use the privileges assigned to the role when they connect to the database. For example, the john user has the hr_manager role. The hr_manager role was granted the SELECT, INSERT, UPDATE, and DELETE object privilege on the salary_grades and employees tables. Therefore, john is able to retrieve rows from these tables, as shown in the following example:

```
CONNECT john/brown
SELECT employee_id, last_name
FROM store.employees
WHERE salary < ANY
  (SELECT low_salary
   FROM store.salary_grades)
ORDER BY employee_id;

EMPLOYEE_ID LAST_NAME
----------- ----------
          2 Johnson
          3 Hobbs
          4 Jones
```

For a password-protected role, the user must enter the role password before they can use the role. For example, the harry user has the password-protected overall_manager role. Before harry is able to use the overall_manager role, he must enable the role and provide the role password using the SET ROLE command:

```
CONNECT harry/blue
SET ROLE overall_manager IDENTIFIED BY manager_password;
```

Then, harry can use the privileges granted to the role. For example:

```
SELECT employee_id, last_name
FROM store.employees
WHERE salary < ANY
  (SELECT low_salary
   FROM store.salary_grades)
ORDER BY employee_id;
```

```
EMPLOYEE_ID LAST_NAME
----------- ----------
          2 Johnson
          3 Hobbs
          4 Jones
```

Enabling and Disabling Roles

You can disable a role. You do this by altering a role so that it is no longer a default role using the `ALTER ROLE` statement. The following example connects as `system` and alters `john` so that `hr_manager` is no longer a default role:

```
CONNECT system/oracle
ALTER USER john DEFAULT ROLE ALL EXCEPT hr_manager;
```

The following example connects as `john` and shows that `hr_manager` is no longer a default role:

```
CONNECT john/brown
SELECT username, granted_role, default_role
FROM user_role_privs;
```

```
USERNAME          GRANTED_ROLE               DEF
----------------- -------------------------- ---
JOHN              HR_MANAGER                 NO
```

The following examples show that `john` cannot access the `salary_grades` or the `employees` tables:

```
SQL> SELECT * FROM store.salary_grades;
SELECT * FROM store.salary_grades
                    *
ERROR at line 1:
ORA-00942: table or view does not exist

SQL> SELECT * FROM store.employees;
SELECT * FROM store.employees
                    *
ERROR at line 1:
ORA-00942: table or view does not exist
```

The following example enables the `hr_manager` role using `SET ROLE`:

```
SET ROLE hr_manager;
```

Once the role is set, the privileges granted to that role can be used.

The previous example doesn't set the `hr_manager` role to a default role, which means when `john` logs out and logs back in, the role will be unavailable. The following example makes `hr_manager` a default role, which is preserved after logging out:

```
CONNECT system/oracle
ALTER USER john DEFAULT ROLE hr_manager;
```

You can set the role to NONE, which means no role. For example:

```
CONNECT john/brown
SET ROLE NONE;
```

The following example sets the role to all roles except hr_manager:

```
SET ROLE ALL EXCEPT hr_manager;
```

Revoking a Role

You remove a role from a user using REVOKE. The following example connects as store and revokes the overall_manager role from harry:

```
CONNECT store/store_password
REVOKE overall_manager FROM harry;
```

Revoking Privileges from a Role

You remove a privilege from a role using REVOKE. The following example connects as store and revokes all privileges on the products and product_types tables from product_manager:

```
CONNECT store/store_password
REVOKE ALL ON products FROM product_manager;
REVOKE ALL ON product_types FROM product_manager;
```

Dropping a Role

You drop a role using DROP ROLE. The following example drops the overall_manager, product_manager, and hr_manager roles:

```
CONNECT store/store_password
DROP ROLE overall_manager;
DROP ROLE product_manager;
DROP ROLE hr_manager;
```

Auditing

The Oracle database software contains auditing capabilities that enable you to keep track of database operations. Some operations can be audited at a high level, such as failed attempts to log into the database. Other operations can be audited at a detailed level, such as when a user retrieved rows from a specific table. Typically, your database administrator will be responsible for enabling auditing and monitoring the output for security violations. In this section, you will see some simple examples of auditing. Auditing is performed using the AUDIT statement.

Privileges Required to Perform Auditing

Before a user can issue AUDIT statements, that user must be granted certain privileges:

- For auditing high-level operations, the user must have the AUDIT SYSTEM privilege. An example of a high-level operation is the issuance of *any* SELECT statement, regardless of the table involved.

- For tracking operations on specific database objects, the user must either have the AUDIT ANY privilege or have the database object in their schema. An example of specific database object operation is performing a SELECT statement for a particular table.

The following example connects to the database as the system user and grants the AUDIT SYSTEM and AUDIT ANY privileges to the store user:

```
CONNECT system/oracle
GRANT AUDIT SYSTEM TO store;
GRANT AUDIT ANY TO store;
```

Auditing Examples

The following example connects to the database as the store user and audits CREATE TABLE statements:

```
CONNECT store/store_password
AUDIT CREATE TABLE;
```

As a result of this AUDIT statement, any CREATE TABLE statements will be audited. For example, the following statement creates a table:

```
CREATE TABLE test (
  id INTEGER
);
```

You can view the audit trail of information for the user you are currently logged in as through the user_audit_trail view. The following example shows the audit record generated by the previous CREATE TABLE statement:

```
SELECT username, extended_timestamp
FROM user_audit_trail;

USERNAME
------------------------------
EXTENDED_TIMESTAMP
-----------------------------------
STORE
20-JUN-11 04.13.43.453000 PM -07:00
```

You can also audit the SQL statements performed by a particular user. The following example audits all SELECT statements performed by the store user:

```
AUDIT SELECT TABLE BY store;
```

The next example audits all INSERT, UPDATE, and DELETE statements performed by the store and steve users:

```
AUDIT INSERT TABLE, UPDATE TABLE, DELETE TABLE BY store, steve;
```

You can also audit SQL statements performed on a particular database object. The following example audits all SELECT statements performed on the products table:

```
AUDIT SELECT ON store.products;
```

The next example audits all statements performed on the employees table:

```
AUDIT ALL ON store.employees;
```

You can also use the WHENEVER SUCCESSFUL and WHENEVER NOT SUCCESSFUL options to indicate when auditing should be performed:

■ **WHENEVER SUCCESSFUL** indicates auditing will be performed when the statement executed successfully.

■ **WHENEVER NOT SUCCESSFUL** indicates auditing will be performed when the statement did not execute successfully.

The default is to do both: audit regardless of success.
The following examples use the WHENEVER NOT SUCCESSFUL option:

```
AUDIT UPDATE TABLE BY steve WHENEVER NOT SUCCESSFUL;
AUDIT INSERT TABLE WHENEVER NOT SUCCESSFUL;
```

The next example uses the WHENEVER SUCCESSFUL option to audit the creation and deletion of a user:

```
AUDIT CREATE USER, DROP USER WHENEVER SUCCESSFUL;
```

The next example uses the WHENEVER SUCCESSFUL option to audit the creation and deletion of a user by the store user:

```
AUDIT CREATE USER, DROP USER BY store WHENEVER SUCCESSFUL;
```

You can also use the BY SESSION and BY ACCESS options:

■ **BY SESSION** causes only one audit record to be logged when the same type of statement is issued during the same user database session. A database session starts when the user logs into the database and ends when the user logs out.

■ **BY ACCESS** causes one audit record to be logged every time the same type of statement is issued, regardless of the user session.

The following examples show the use of the `BY SESSION` and `BY ACCESS` options:

```
AUDIT SELECT ON store.products BY SESSION;
AUDIT DELETE ON store.employees BY ACCESS;
AUDIT INSERT, UPDATE ON store.employees BY ACCESS;
```

You use `NOAUDIT` to disable auditing. For example:

```
NOAUDIT SELECT ON store.products;
NOAUDIT DELETE ON store.employees;
NOAUDIT INSERT, UPDATE ON store.employees;
```

You can use `ALL PRIVILEGES` to specify all privileges. For example:

```
AUDIT ALL PRIVILEGES ON store.products BY SESSION;
NOAUDIT ALL PRIVILEGES ON store.employees;
NOAUDIT ALL PRIVILEGES;
```

Oracle Database 11*g* Release 2 introduced the following options:

- **`ALL STATEMENTS`**, which specifies all SQL statements. You can use `ALL STATEMENTS` with `AUDIT` and `NOAUDIT`.
- **`IN SESSION CURRENT`**, which limits auditing to the current database session. You can use `IN SESSION CURRENT` with `AUDIT`.

The following examples show the use of the `ALL STATEMENTS` and `IN SESSION CURRENT` options:

```
AUDIT ALL STATEMENTS;
AUDIT ALL STATEMENTS IN SESSION CURRENT BY ACCESS WHENEVER NOT SUCCESSFUL;
NOAUDIT ALL STATEMENTS;
```

Audit Trail Views

Earlier, you saw the use of the `user_audit_trail` view. This and the other audit trail views are outlined in the following list:

- **`user_audit_object`** displays the audit records for all objects accessible to the current user.
- **`user_audit_session`** displays the audit records for connections and disconnections of the current user.
- **`user_audit_statement`** displays the audit records for `GRANT`, `REVOKE`, `AUDIT`, `NOAUDIT`, and `ALTER SYSTEM` statements issued by the current user.
- **`user_audit_trail`** displays all audit trail entries related to the current user.

You can use these views to examine the contents of the audit trail. There are a number of similarly named views that the database administrator can use to examine the audit trail. These views are named `dba_audit_object`, `dba_audit_session`, `dba_audit_statement`, `dba_audit_trail`, plus others. These views allow the DBA to view audit records across all users. For more details on these views, see the *Oracle Database Reference* manual published by Oracle Corporation.

Summary

In this chapter, you have learned the following:

- A user is created using the CREATE USER statement.
- System privileges allow you to perform certain actions within the database, such as executing DDL statements.
- Object privileges allow you to perform certain actions on database objects, such as executing DML statements on tables.
- You can avoid having to enter the schema name by creating a synonym for a table.
- A role is a group of privileges that you can assign to a user or another role.
- Auditing the execution of SQL statements can be performed using the AUDIT statement.

In the next chapter, you'll learn more about creating tables and see how to create indexes, sequences, and views.

CHAPTER
11

Creating Tables,
Sequences, Indexes,
and Views

I n this chapter, you will learn how to perform the following tasks:

- Create, modify, and drop tables
- Create and use sequences, which generate a series of numbers
- Create and use indexes, which can improve the performance of queries
- Create and use views, which are predefined queries
- Examine flashback data archives, which store row changes made over a period of time

Tables

In this section, you'll learn about creating a table. You'll see how to modify and drop a table as well as how to retrieve information about a table from the data dictionary. The data dictionary contains information about all the database items, such as tables, sequences, indexes, and so on.

Creating a Table

You use the CREATE TABLE statement to create a table. The simplified syntax for the CREATE TABLE statement is as follows:

```
CREATE [GLOBAL TEMPORARY] TABLE table_name (
    column_name type [CONSTRAINT constraint_def DEFAULT default_exp]
    [, column_name type [CONSTRAINT constraint_def DEFAULT default_exp] ...]
)
[ON COMMIT {DELETE | PRESERVE} ROWS]
TABLESPACE tab_space;
```

where

- GLOBAL TEMPORARY specifies that the table's rows are temporary (this type of table is known as a temporary table). The rows in a temporary table are specific to a user session, and how long the rows persist is set using the ON COMMIT clause.
- table_name is the name of the table.
- column_name is the name of a column.
- type is the type of a column.
- constraint_def is a constraint on a column.
- default_exp is an expression to assign a default value to a column.
- ON COMMIT controls the duration of the rows in a temporary table. DELETE specifies that the rows are deleted at the end of a transaction. PRESERVE specifies that the rows are kept until the end of a user session, at which point the rows are deleted. If you omit ON COMMIT for a temporary table, then the default of DELETE is used.
- tab_space is the tablespace for the table. If you omit a tablespace, then the table is stored in the user's default tablespace.

NOTE
The full CREATE TABLE *syntax is more complex than shown here. For details, see the* Oracle Database SQL Reference *manual published by Oracle Corporation.*

The following example connects as the store user and creates a table named order_status2:

```
CONNECT store/store_password
CREATE TABLE order_status2 (
  id INTEGER CONSTRAINT order_status2_pk PRIMARY KEY,
  status VARCHAR2(10),
  last_modified DATE DEFAULT SYSDATE
);
```

NOTE
*If you want to follow along with the examples in this chapter, you'll need to enter and run the SQL statements using SQL*Plus. This will give you a chance to create tables and add rows yourself.*

The next example creates a temporary table named order_status_temp whose rows will be kept until the end of a user session (ON COMMIT PRESERVE ROWS):

```
CREATE GLOBAL TEMPORARY TABLE order_status_temp (
  id INTEGER,
  status VARCHAR2(10),
  last_modified DATE DEFAULT SYSDATE
)
ON COMMIT PRESERVE ROWS;
```

The next example performs the following tasks:

- Adds a row to order_status_temp
- Disconnects from the database to end the session, which causes the row in order_status_temp to be deleted
- Reconnects as store and queries order_status_temp, which shows there are no rows in this table

```
INSERT INTO order_status_temp (
  id, status
) VALUES (
  1, 'New'
);

1 row created.

DISCONNECT
CONNECT store/store_password
```

```
SELECT *
FROM order_status_temp;

no rows selected
```

Getting Information on Tables

You can get information about tables by performing the following tasks:

- Running a DESCRIBE command for the table
- Querying the user_tables view, which forms part of the data dictionary

Table 11-1 describes some of the columns in the user_tables view.
The following example queries user_tables where the table_name is order_status2 or order_status_temp:

```
SELECT table_name, tablespace_name, temporary
FROM user_tables
WHERE table_name IN ('ORDER_STATUS2', 'ORDER_STATUS_TEMP');

TABLE_NAME                      TABLESPACE_NAME                 T
------------------------------- ------------------------------- -
ORDER_STATUS2                   USERS                           N
ORDER_STATUS_TEMP                                               Y
```

Notice the order_status_temp table is temporary, as indicated by the Y in the last column.

NOTE
You can retrieve information on all the tables you have access to by querying the all_tables view.

Getting Information on Columns in Tables

You can retrieve information about the columns in a table from the user_tab_columns view. Table 11-2 describes some of the columns in user_tab_columns.

Column	Type	Description
table_name	VARCHAR2(128)	Name of the table.
tablespace_name	VARCHAR2(30)	Name of the tablespace in which the table is stored. A tablespace is an area used by the database to store objects such as tables.
temporary	VARCHAR2(1)	Whether the table is temporary. This is set to Y if temporary or N if not temporary.

TABLE 11-1. *Some Columns in the user_tables View*

Column	Type	Description
table_name	VARCHAR2(128)	Name of the table
column_name	VARCHAR2(128)	Name of the column
data_type	VARCHAR2(128)	Data type of the column
data_length	NUMBER	Length of the data
data_precision	NUMBER	Precision of a numeric column if a precision was specified
data_scale	NUMBER	Scale of a numeric column

TABLE 11-2.   *Some Columns in the* user_tab_columns *View*

The following example queries user_tab_columns for the products table:

```
COLUMN column_name FORMAT a15
COLUMN data_type FORMAT a10
SELECT column_name, data_type, data_length, data_precision, data_scale
FROM user_tab_columns
WHERE table_name = 'PRODUCTS';

COLUMN_NAME     DATA_TYPE  DATA_LENGTH DATA_PRECISION DATA_SCALE
--------------- ---------- ----------- -------------- ----------
PRODUCT_ID      NUMBER              22                         0
PRODUCT_TYPE_ID NUMBER              22                         0
NAME            VARCHAR2            30
DESCRIPTION     VARCHAR2            50
PRICE           NUMBER              22              5          2
```

NOTE
You can retrieve information on all the columns in tables you have access to by querying the all_tab_columns *view.*

Altering a Table

You alter a table using the ALTER TABLE statement. You can use ALTER TABLE to perform tasks such as the following:

- Adding, modifying, or dropping a column
- Adding or dropping a constraint
- Enabling or disabling a constraint

In the following sections, you'll learn how to use ALTER TABLE to perform each of these tasks. You'll also learn how to obtain information about constraints.

Adding a Column

The following example uses ALTER TABLE to add an INTEGER column named modified_by to the order_status2 table:

```
ALTER TABLE order_status2
ADD modified_by INTEGER;
```

The next example adds a column named initially_created to order_status2:

```
ALTER TABLE order_status2
ADD initially_created DATE DEFAULT SYSDATE NOT NULL;
```

You can verify the addition of the new column by running a DESCRIBE command on order_status2:

```
DESCRIBE order_status2
```

Name	Null?	Type
ID	NOT NULL	NUMBER(38)
STATUS		VARCHAR2(10)
LAST_MODIFIED		DATE
MODIFIED_BY		NUMBER(38)
INITIALLY_CREATED	NOT NULL	DATE

Adding a Virtual Column

Oracle Database 11g introduced virtual columns. A virtual column is a column that refers only to other columns already in the table. For example, the following ALTER TABLE statement adds a virtual column named average_salary to the salary_grades table:

```
ALTER TABLE salary_grades
ADD (average_salary AS ((low_salary + high_salary)/2));
```

Notice that average_salary is set to the average of the low_salary and high_salary values.

The following DESCRIBE command confirms the addition of the average_salary column to the salary_grades table:

```
DESCRIBE salary_grades
```

Name	Null?	Type
SALARY_GRADE_ID	NOT NULL	NUMBER(38)
LOW_SALARY		NUMBER(6)
HIGH_SALARY		NUMBER(6)
AVERAGE_SALARY		NUMBER

The following query retrieves the rows from the salary_grades table:

```
SELECT *
FROM salary_grades;
```

```
SALARY_GRADE_ID LOW_SALARY HIGH_SALARY AVERAGE_SALARY
--------------- ---------- ----------- --------------
              1          1      250000       125000.5
              2     250001      500000       375000.5
              3     500001      750000       625000.5
              4     750001      999999         875000
```

Modifying a Column

The following list shows some of the column aspects you can modify using ALTER TABLE:

- Change the size of a column (if the data type is one whose length may be changed, such as CHAR or VARCHAR2)
- Change the precision of a numeric column
- Change the data type of a column
- Change the default value of a column

You'll see examples of how to change these column aspects for the order_status2 table in the following sections.

Changing the Size of a Column   The following ALTER TABLE statement increases the maximum length of the status column to 15 characters:

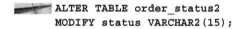

```
ALTER TABLE order_status2
MODIFY status VARCHAR2(15);
```

CAUTION
You can decrease the length of a column only if there are no rows in the table or all the rows contain null values for that column.

Changing the Precision of a Numeric Column   The following ALTER TABLE statement changes the precision of the id column to 5:

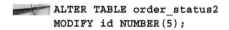

```
ALTER TABLE order_status2
MODIFY id NUMBER(5);
```

CAUTION
You can decrease the precision of a numeric column only if there are no rows in the table or the column contains null values.

Changing the Data Type of a Column   The following ALTER TABLE statement changes the data type of the status column to CHAR:

```
ALTER TABLE order_status2
MODIFY status CHAR(15);
```

If the table is empty or the column contains null values, then you can change the column to any data type (including a data type that is shorter). Otherwise, you can change the data type of a column only to a compatible data type. For example, you can change a VARCHAR2 to CHAR (and vice versa) as long as you don't make the column shorter. You cannot change a DATE to a NUMBER.

Changing the Default Value of a Column   The following ALTER TABLE statement changes the default value for the last_modified column to SYSDATE - 1:

```
ALTER TABLE order_status2
MODIFY last_modified DEFAULT SYSDATE - 1;
```

The default value applies only to new rows added to the table. New rows will get their last_modified column set to the current date minus one day.

Dropping a Column

The following ALTER TABLE statement drops the initially_created column:

```
ALTER TABLE order_status2
DROP COLUMN initially_created;
```

Adding a Constraint

In earlier chapters, you've seen examples of tables with PRIMARY KEY, FOREIGN KEY, and NOT NULL constraints. These constraints, along with the other types of constraints, are summarized in Table 11-3.

Constraint	Constraint Type	Meaning
CHECK	C	The value for a column, or group of columns, must satisfy a certain condition.
NOT NULL	C	The column cannot store a null value. This is actually enforced as a CHECK constraint.
PRIMARY KEY	P	The primary key of a table. A primary key is made up of one or more columns that uniquely identify each row in a table.
FOREIGN KEY	R	A foreign key for a table. A foreign key references a column in another table or a column in the same table (known as a self-reference).
UNIQUE	U	The column, or group of columns, can store only unique values.
CHECK OPTION	V	Changes to the table rows made through a view must pass a check first. (You'll learn about this later in the section "Views.")
READ ONLY	O	The view may only be read from. (You'll learn about this later in the section "Views.")

TABLE 11-3.   *Constraints and Their Meaning*

You'll see how to add some of the constraints shown in Table 11-3 to order_status2 in the following sections.

Adding a CHECK Constraint

The following ALTER TABLE statement adds a CHECK constraint to the order_status2 table:

```
ALTER TABLE order_status2
ADD CONSTRAINT order_status2_status_ck
CHECK (status IN ('PLACED', 'PENDING', 'SHIPPED'));
```

This constraint ensures the status column is always set to PLACED, PENDING, or SHIPPED.

The following INSERT adds a row to the order_status2 table (status is set to PENDING):

```
INSERT INTO order_status2 (
   id, status, last_modified, modified_by
) VALUES (
   1, 'PENDING', '01-JAN-2005', 1
);
```

If you attempt to add a row that doesn't satisfy a constraint, the database returns the error ORA-02290. For example, the following INSERT attempts to add a row whose status is not in the list of valid values:

```
INSERT INTO order_status2 (
   id, status, last_modified, modified_by
) VALUES (
   2, 'CLEARED', '01-JAN-2005', 2
);
INSERT INTO order_status2 (
*
ERROR at line 1:
ORA-02290: check constraint (STORE.ORDER_STATUS2_STATUS_CK) violated
```

Because the constraint is violated, the database rejects the row.

You can use other comparison operators with a CHECK constraint. The following example adds a CHECK constraint that enforces that the id value is greater than zero:

```
ALTER TABLE order_status2
ADD CONSTRAINT order_status2_id_ck CHECK (id > 0);
```

When adding a constraint, the existing rows in the table must satisfy the constraint. For example, if the order_status2 table had rows in it, then the id column for the rows would need to be greater than zero.

NOTE
There are exceptions to the rule requiring that existing rows satisfy the constraint. You can disable a constraint when you initially add it, and you can set a constraint to apply only to new data, by specifying ENABLE NOVALIDATE. *You'll learn more about this later.*

Adding a NOT NULL Constraint

The following ALTER TABLE statement adds a NOT NULL constraint to the status column of the order_status2 table. Notice that you use MODIFY to add a NOT NULL constraint.

```
ALTER TABLE order_status2
MODIFY status CONSTRAINT order_status2_status_nn NOT NULL;
```

The next example adds a NOT NULL constraint to the modified_by column:

```
ALTER TABLE order_status2
MODIFY modified_by CONSTRAINT order_status2_modified_by_nn NOT NULL;
```

The following example adds a NOT NULL constraint to the last_modified column:

```
ALTER TABLE order_status2
MODIFY last_modified NOT NULL;
```

Notice that I didn't supply a name for this constraint. In this case, the database automatically assigns an unfriendly name to the constraint, like SYS_C0010772.

TIP
Always specify a meaningful name to your constraints. That way, when a constraint error occurs, you can easily identify the problem.

Adding a FOREIGN KEY Constraint

Before you see an example of adding a FOREIGN KEY constraint, the following ALTER TABLE statement drops the modified_by column from order_status2:

```
ALTER TABLE order_status2
DROP COLUMN modified_by;
```

The next statement adds a FOREIGN KEY constraint that references the employee_id column of the employees table:

```
ALTER TABLE order_status2
ADD CONSTRAINT order_status2_modified_by_fk
modified_by REFERENCES employees(employee_id);
```

You use the ON DELETE CASCADE clause with a FOREIGN KEY constraint to specify that when a row in the parent table is deleted, any matching rows in the child table are also deleted. The following example drops the modified_by column and includes the ON DELETE CASCADE clause in an ALTER TABLE statement:

```
ALTER TABLE order_status2
DROP COLUMN modified_by;

ALTER TABLE order_status2
ADD CONSTRAINT order_status2_modified_by_fk
modified_by REFERENCES employees(employee_id) ON DELETE CASCADE;
```

When a row is deleted from the employees table, any matching rows in order_status2 are also deleted.

You use the ON DELETE SET NULL clause with a FOREIGN KEY constraint to specify that when a row in the parent table is deleted, the foreign key column for any rows in the child table are set to null. The following example drops the modified_by column from order_status2 and includes the ON DELETE SET NULL clause in an ALTER TABLE statement:

```
ALTER TABLE order_status2
DROP COLUMN modified_by;

ALTER TABLE order_status2
ADD CONSTRAINT order_status2_modified_by_fk
modified_by REFERENCES employees(employee_id) ON DELETE SET NULL;
```

When a row is deleted from the employees table, the modified_by column for any matching rows in order_status2 is set to null.

The following statement drops the modified_by column:

```
ALTER TABLE order_status2
DROP COLUMN modified_by;
```

Adding a UNIQUE Constraint

The following ALTER TABLE statement adds a UNIQUE constraint to the status column:

```
ALTER TABLE order_status2
ADD CONSTRAINT order_status2_status_uq UNIQUE (status);
```

Any existing or new rows must always have a unique value in the status column.

Dropping a Constraint

You drop a constraint using the DROP CONSTRAINT clause of ALTER TABLE. The following example drops the order_status2_status_uq constraint:

```
ALTER TABLE order_status2
DROP CONSTRAINT order_status2_status_uq;
```

Disabling a Constraint

By default, a constraint is enabled when you create it. You can initially disable a constraint by adding DISABLE to the end of the CONSTRAINT clause. The following example adds a constraint to order_status2 but also disables it:

```
ALTER TABLE order_status2
ADD CONSTRAINT order_status2_status_uq UNIQUE (status) DISABLE;
```

You can disable an existing constraint using the DISABLE CONSTRAINT clause of ALTER TABLE. The following example disables the order_status2_status_nn constraint:

```
ALTER TABLE order_status2
DISABLE CONSTRAINT order_status2_status_nn;
```

You can add CASCADE after DISABLE CONSTRAINT to disable all constraints that depend on the specified constraint. You use CASCADE when disabling a primary key or unique constraint that is part of a foreign key constraint of another table.

Enabling a Constraint

You enable an existing constraint using the ENABLE CONSTRAINT clause of ALTER TABLE. The following example enables the order_status2_status_uq constraint:

```
ALTER TABLE order_status2
ENABLE CONSTRAINT order_status2_status_uq;
```

To enable a constraint, all the rows in the table must satisfy the constraint. For example, if the order_status2 table contained rows, then the status column would have to contain unique values.

You can apply a constraint to new data only by specifying ENABLE NOVALIDATE. For example:

```
ALTER TABLE order_status2
ENABLE NOVALIDATE CONSTRAINT order_status2_status_uq;
```

NOTE
The default is ENABLE VALIDATE, *which means existing rows must pass the constraint check.*

Deferring a Constraint

A deferred constraint is one that is enforced when a transaction is committed. You use the DEFERRABLE clause when you initially add the constraint. Once you've added a constraint, you cannot change it to DEFERRABLE. Instead, you must drop and re-create the constraint.

When you add a DEFERRABLE constraint, you can mark it as INITIALLY IMMEDIATE or INITIALLY DEFERRED. Marking as INITIALLY IMMEDIATE specifies that the constraint is checked whenever you add, update, or delete rows from a table (this is the same as the default behavior of a constraint). INITIALLY DEFERRED specifies that the constraint is only checked when a transaction is committed. Let's take a look at an example.

The following statement drops the order_status2_status_uq constraint:

```
ALTER TABLE order_status2
DROP CONSTRAINT order_status2_status_uq;
```

The next example adds the order_status2_status_uq constraint, setting it to DEFERRABLE INITIALLY DEFERRED:

```
ALTER TABLE order_status2
ADD CONSTRAINT order_status2_status_uq UNIQUE (status)
DEFERRABLE INITIALLY DEFERRED;
```

If you add rows to order_status2, the order_status2_status_uq constraint isn't enforced until you perform a COMMIT.

Column	Type	Description
owner	VARCHAR2(128)	Owner of the constraint.
constraint_name	VARCHAR2(128)	Name of the constraint.
constraint_type	VARCHAR2(1)	Constraint type (P, R, C, U, V, or O). See Table 11-3 for the constraint type meanings.
table_name	VARCHAR2(128)	Name of the table on which the constraint is defined.
status	VARCHAR2(8)	Constraint status (ENABLED or DISABLED).
deferrable	VARCHAR2(14)	Whether the constraint is deferrable (DEFERRABLE or NOT DEFERRABLE).
deferred	VARCHAR2(9)	Whether the constraint is enforced immediately or deferred (IMMEDIATE or DEFERRED).

TABLE 11-4. *Some Columns in the* user_constraints *View*

Getting Information on Constraints

You can retrieve information on your constraints by querying the user_constraints view. Table 11-4 describes some of the columns in user_constraints.

The following example queries user_constraints for the order_status2 table:

```
SELECT constraint_name, constraint_type, status, deferrable, deferred
FROM user_constraints
WHERE table_name = 'ORDER_STATUS2'
ORDER BY constraint_name;


CONSTRAINT_NAME                  C STATUS   DEFERRABLE     DEFERRED
-------------------------------- - -------- -------------- ---------
ORDER_STATUS2_ID_CK              C ENABLED  NOT DEFERRABLE IMMEDIATE
ORDER_STATUS2_PK                 P ENABLED  NOT DEFERRABLE IMMEDIATE
ORDER_STATUS2_STATUS_CK          C ENABLED  NOT DEFERRABLE IMMEDIATE
ORDER_STATUS2_STATUS_NN          C DISABLED NOT DEFERRABLE IMMEDIATE
ORDER_STATUS2_STATUS_UQ          U ENABLED  DEFERRABLE     DEFERRED
SYS_C0010772                     C ENABLED  NOT DEFERRABLE IMMEDIATE
```

Notice that all the constraints except one have a helpful name. One constraint has the database-generated name of SYS_C0010772 (this name is automatically generated, and it will be different in your database). This constraint is the one for which I omitted the name when creating it earlier.

NOTE
You can retrieve information on all the constraints you have access to by querying the all_constraints *view.*

Column	Type	Description
owner	VARCHAR2(128)	Owner of the constraint
constraint_name	VARCHAR2(128)	Name of the constraint
table_name	VARCHAR2(128)	Name of the table on which the constraint is defined
column_name	VARCHAR2(4000)	Name of the column on which the constraint is defined

TABLE 11-5. *Some Columns in the* user_cons_columns *View*

Getting Information on the Constraints for a Column

You can retrieve information on the constraints for a column by querying the user_cons_columns view. Table 11-5 describes some of the columns in user_cons_columns.

The following example retrieves the constraint_name and column_name from user_cons_columns for the order_status2 table:

```
COLUMN column_name FORMAT a15
SELECT constraint_name, column_name
FROM user_cons_columns
WHERE table_name = 'ORDER_STATUS2'
ORDER BY constraint_name;

CONSTRAINT_NAME                 COLUMN_NAME
------------------------------- ---------------
ORDER_STATUS2_ID_CK             ID
ORDER_STATUS2_PK                ID
ORDER_STATUS2_STATUS_CK         STATUS
ORDER_STATUS2_STATUS_NN         STATUS
ORDER_STATUS2_STATUS_UQ         STATUS
SYS_C0010772                    LAST_MODIFIED
```

The next query joins user_constraints and user_cons_columns to get the column_name, constraint_name, constraint_type, and status:

```
SELECT
   ucc.column_name, ucc.constraint_name,
   uc.constraint_type, uc.status
FROM user_constraints uc, user_cons_columns ucc
WHERE uc.table_name = ucc.table_name
AND uc.constraint_name = ucc.constraint_name
AND ucc.table_name = 'ORDER_STATUS2'
ORDER BY ucc.constraint_name;
```

```
COLUMN_NAME      CONSTRAINT_NAME                   C STATUS
---------------  --------------------------------  - --------
ID               ORDER_STATUS2_ID_CK               C ENABLED
ID               ORDER_STATUS2_PK                  P ENABLED
STATUS           ORDER_STATUS2_STATUS_CK           C ENABLED
STATUS           ORDER_STATUS2_STATUS_NN           C DISABLED
STATUS           ORDER_STATUS2_STATUS_UQ           U ENABLED
LAST_MODIFIED    SYS_C0010772                      C ENABLED
```

NOTE
You can retrieve information on all the column constraints you have
access to by querying the all_cons_columns *view.*

Renaming a Table

You rename a table using the RENAME statement. The following example renames order_
status2 to order_state:

```
RENAME order_status2 TO order_state;
```

The next example changes the table name back to the original:

```
RENAME order_state TO order_status2;
```

Adding a Comment to a Table

A comment can help you remember what the table or column is used for. You add a comment to
a table or column using the COMMENT statement. The following example adds a comment to the
order_status2 table:

```
COMMENT ON TABLE order_status2 IS
'order_status2 stores the state of an order';
```

The next example adds a comment to the last_modified column:

```
COMMENT ON COLUMN order_status2.last_modified IS
'last_modified stores the date and time the order was modified last';
```

Retrieving Table Comments

You can retrieve the table comments from the user_tab_comments view. For example:

```
SELECT *
FROM user_tab_comments
WHERE table_name = 'ORDER_STATUS2';

TABLE_NAME                      TABLE_TYPE
------------------------------  -----------
COMMENTS
------------------------------------------
ORDER_STATUS2                   TABLE
order_status2 stores the state of an order
```

Retrieving Column Comments

You can retrieve the column comments from the `user_col_comments` view. For example:

```
SELECT *
FROM user_col_comments
WHERE table_name = 'ORDER_STATUS2';

TABLE_NAME                          COLUMN_NAME
----------------------------------  ------------------------------
COMMENTS
----------------------------------------------------------------------
ORDER_STATUS2                       ID

ORDER_STATUS2                       STATUS

ORDER_STATUS2                       LAST_MODIFIED
last_modified stores the date and time the order was modified last
```

Truncating a Table

You truncate a table using the `TRUNCATE` statement. This removes *all* the rows from the table and resets the storage area for the table. The following example truncates `order_status2`:

```
TRUNCATE TABLE order_status2;
```

TIP
If you need to remove all the rows from a table, you should use `TRUNCATE` *rather than* `DELETE`. *This is because* `TRUNCATE` *resets the storage area for a table. A* `TRUNCATE` *statement doesn't require any undo space in the database, and you don't have to run a* `COMMIT` *to make the delete permanent. Undo space is an area that the database software uses to record database changes.*

New for Oracle Database 12*c* is the `CASCADE` clause for `TRUNCATE`, which truncates the specified table, plus any child tables, grandchild tables, and so on. All tables that reference the specified table using an enabled `ON DELETE CASCADE` constraint are truncated. For example, if you had a table named `parent_table`, then `TRUNCATE TABLE parent_table CASCADE` would truncate any child tables, grandchild tables, and so on.

Dropping a Table

You drop a table using the `DROP TABLE` statement. The following example drops the `order_status2` table:

```
DROP TABLE order_status2;
```

Using the BINARY_FLOAT and BINARY_DOUBLE Types

Oracle Database 10*g* introduced two new data types: `BINARY_FLOAT` and `BINARY_DOUBLE`. `BINARY_FLOAT` stores a single-precision, 32-bit, floating-point number. `BINARY_DOUBLE` stores a double-precision, 64-bit, floating-point number. These new data types are based on the IEEE (Institute of Electrical and Electronics Engineers) standard for binary floating-point arithmetic.

Benefits of BINARY_FLOAT and BINARY_DOUBLE

BINARY_FLOAT and BINARY_DOUBLE are intended to complement the existing NUMBER type. BINARY_FLOAT and BINARY_DOUBLE offer the following benefits over NUMBER:

- **Greater range of numbers represented**   BINARY_FLOAT and BINARY_DOUBLE store numbers that are much larger and smaller than can be stored in a NUMBER.

- **Faster performance of operations**   Operations involving BINARY_FLOAT and BINARY_DOUBLE are typically performed faster than NUMBER operations. This is because BINARY_FLOAT and BINARY_DOUBLE operations are typically performed in the hardware, whereas NUMBERs must first be converted using software before operations can be performed.

- **Closed operations**   Arithmetic operations involving BINARY_FLOAT and BINARY_DOUBLE are *closed*, which means that either a number or a special value is returned. For example, if you divide a BINARY_FLOAT by another BINARY_FLOAT, a BINARY_FLOAT is returned.

- **Transparent rounding**   BINARY_FLOAT and BINARY_DOUBLE use binary (base 2) to represent a number, whereas NUMBER uses decimal (base 10). The base used to represent a number affects how rounding occurs for that number. For example, a decimal floating-point number is rounded to the nearest decimal place, but a binary floating-point number is rounded to the nearest binary place.

- **Smaller storage required**   BINARY_FLOAT and BINARY_DOUBLE require 4 and 8 bytes of storage space, respectively, whereas NUMBER can use up to 22 bytes of storage space.

TIP
If you are developing a system that involves a lot of numerical computations, you should use BINARY_FLOAT *and* BINARY_DOUBLE *to represent numbers.*

Using BINARY_FLOAT and BINARY_DOUBLE in a Table

The following statement creates a table named binary_test that contains a BINARY_FLOAT column and a BINARY_DOUBLE column:

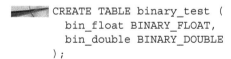

```
CREATE TABLE binary_test (
  bin_float BINARY_FLOAT,
  bin_double BINARY_DOUBLE
);
```

NOTE
You'll find a script named oracle_10g_examples.sql *in the* SQL *directory that creates the* binary_test *table in the* store *schema. The script also performs the* INSERT *statements you'll see in this section. You can run this script if you are using Oracle Database 10*g *or higher.*

The following example adds a row to the `binary_test` table:

```
INSERT INTO binary_test (
  bin_float, bin_double
) VALUES (
  39.5f, 15.7d
);
```

The f character indicates a number is a BINARY_FLOAT. The d character indicates a number is a BINARY_DOUBLE.

Special Values

The following table shows the special values that can be used with a BINARY_FLOAT or BINARY_DOUBLE.

Special Value	Description
BINARY_FLOAT_NAN	Not a number (NaN) for the BINARY_FLOAT type
BINARY_FLOAT_INFINITY	Infinity (INF) for the BINARY_FLOAT type
BINARY_DOUBLE_NAN	Not a number (NaN) for the BINARY_DOUBLE type
BINARY_DOUBLE_INFINITY	Infinity (INF) for the BINARY_DOUBLE type

The following example inserts BINARY_FLOAT_INFINITY and BINARY_DOUBLE_INFINITY into the `binary_test` table:

```
INSERT INTO binary_test (
  bin_float, bin_double
) VALUES (
  BINARY_FLOAT_INFINITY, BINARY_DOUBLE_INFINITY
);
```

The following query retrieves the rows from `binary_test`:

```
SELECT *
FROM binary_test;

 BIN_FLOAT BIN_DOUBLE
---------- ----------
 3.95E+001  1.57E+001
       Inf        Inf
```

Using DEFAULT ON NULL Columns

New for Oracle Database 12*c* is the DEFAULT ON NULL column clause. This clause assigns a default value to a column when an INSERT statement supplies a null value for that column.

The following example creates a table named `purchases_default_null`. The `quantity` column is set to a default value of 1 when a null value is supplied.

```
CREATE TABLE purchases_default_null (
  product_id INTEGER
```

```
    CONSTRAINT purch_default_fk_products
    REFERENCES products(product_id),
  customer_id INTEGER
    CONSTRAINT purch_default_fk_customers
    REFERENCES customers(customer_id),
  quantity INTEGER DEFAULT ON NULL 1 NOT NULL,
  CONSTRAINT purch_default_pk PRIMARY KEY (product_id, customer_id)
);
```

The following INSERT statement adds a row to the table, omitting a value for the quantity column:

```
INSERT INTO purchases_default_null (
  product_id, customer_id
) VALUES (
  5, 4
);
```

The following INSERT statement adds a row to the table, supplying a null value for the quantity column:

```
INSERT INTO purchases_default_null (
  product_id, customer_id, quantity
) VALUES (
  6, 5, NULL
);
```

The following INSERT statement adds a row to the table, supplying a value of 3 for the quantity column:

```
INSERT INTO purchases_default_null (
  product_id, customer_id, quantity
) VALUES (
  7, 2, 3
);
```

The following query retrieves the rows from the table:

```
SELECT *
FROM purchases_default_null
ORDER BY product_id;
```

PRODUCT_ID	CUSTOMER_ID	QUANTITY
5	4	1
6	5	1
7	2	3

The first two rows have the quantity column set to 1, which is the default value set by the DEFAULT ON NULL clause in the table definition. The third row has the quantity column set to 3, which was explicitly supplied in the INSERT statement.

Using Visible and Invisible Columns in a Table

New for Oracle Database 12c is the ability to define visible and invisible columns in a table. You use VISIBLE to indicate that a column is visible, and INVISIBLE to indicate that a column is invisible. If neither is specified for a column, then the column is visible by default.

The following example creates a table named employees_hidden_example. The salary column is set to INVISIBLE. The title column is explicitly set to VISIBLE. The other columns are visible by default.

```
CREATE TABLE employees_hidden_example (
  employee_id INTEGER CONSTRAINT employees_hidden_example PRIMARY KEY,
  manager_id INTEGER,
  first_name VARCHAR2(10) NOT NULL,
  last_name VARCHAR2(10) NOT NULL,
  title VARCHAR2(20) VISIBLE,
  salary NUMBER(6, 0) INVISIBLE
);
```

By default, invisible columns are not shown by the DESCRIBE command. The salary column is not shown in the following example:

```
DESCRIBE employees_hidden_example;
```

Name	Null?	Type
EMPLOYEE_ID	NOT NULL	NUMBER(38)
MANAGER_ID		NUMBER(38)
FIRST_NAME	NOT NULL	VARCHAR2(10)
LAST_NAME	NOT NULL	VARCHAR2(10)
TITLE		VARCHAR2(20)

To view invisible columns with the DESCRIBE command, you use SET COLINVISIBLE ON. To hide invisible columns, you use SET COLINVISIBLE OFF. The default is to hide invisible columns. The following example runs SET COLINVISIBLE ON and describes the employees_hidden_example table:

```
SET COLINVISIBLE ON
DESCRIBE employees_hidden_example;
```

Name	Null?	Type
EMPLOYEE_ID	NOT NULL	NUMBER(38)
MANAGER_ID		NUMBER(38)
FIRST_NAME	NOT NULL	VARCHAR2(10)
LAST_NAME	NOT NULL	VARCHAR2(10)
TITLE		VARCHAR2(20)
SALARY (INVISIBLE)		NUMBER(6)

The salary column is shown in the results.

The following INSERT fails because the salary column is invisible and cannot be implicitly set:

```
INSERT INTO employees_hidden_example VALUES (
  1, 1, 'Jason', 'Price', 'CEO', 250000
);
ERROR at line 1:
ORA-00913: too many values
```

Invisible column values must be explicitly specified in a column list, as shown in the following correct INSERT:

```
INSERT INTO employees_hidden_example (
  employee_id, manager_id, first_name, last_name, title, salary
) VALUES (
  1, 1, 'Jason', 'Price', 'CEO', 250000
);
```

The following query retrieves the row from the table. Notice the salary column is not shown in the result set.

```
SELECT *
FROM employees_hidden_example;

EMPLOYEE_ID MANAGER_ID FIRST_NAME LAST_NAME  TITLE
----------- ---------- ---------- ---------- -----
          1          1 Jason      Price      CEO
```

To view an invisible column in the result set, you explicitly request the column. In the following example, the salary column is explicitly requested at the end of the column list.

```
SELECT employee_id, manager_id, first_name, last_name, title, salary
FROM employees_hidden_example;

EMPLOYEE_ID MANAGER_ID FIRST_NAME LAST_NAME  TITLE     SALARY

----------- ---------- ---------- ---------- ----- ----------


          1          1 Jason      Price      CEO       250000
```

You can alter a table to make visible columns invisible and invisible columns visible. The following example makes the salary column visible and the title column invisible:

```
ALTER TABLE employees_hidden_example MODIFY (
  title INVISIBLE,
  salary VISIBLE
);
```

The following query retrieves the row from the table. Notice the title column is not shown in the result set.

```
SELECT *
FROM employees_hidden_example;
```

```
EMPLOYEE_ID MANAGER_ID FIRST_NAME LAST_NAME       SALARY
----------- ---------- ---------- ---------- ----------
          1          1 Jason      Price          250000
```

As you'll learn later, you can also use visible and invisible columns in views.

This concludes the discussion of tables. In the next section, you'll learn about sequences.

Sequences

A *sequence* is a database item that generates a sequence of integers. You typically use the integers generated by a sequence to populate a numeric primary key column. In this section, you'll learn how to perform the following tasks:

- Create a sequence
- Retrieve information on a sequence from the data dictionary
- Use a sequence in a variety of ways
- Populate a primary key using a sequence
- Specify a default column value using a sequence
- Use an identity column
- Modify a sequence
- Drop a sequence

Creating a Sequence

You create a sequence using the CREATE SEQUENCE statement, which has the following syntax:

```
CREATE SEQUENCE sequence_name
[START WITH start_num]
[INCREMENT BY increment_num]
[ { MAXVALUE maximum_num | NOMAXVALUE } ]
[ { MINVALUE minimum_num | NOMINVALUE } ]
[ { CYCLE | NOCYCLE } ]
[ { CACHE cache_num | NOCACHE } ]
[ { ORDER | NOORDER } ];
```

where

- *sequence_name* is the name of the sequence.
- *start_num* is the integer to start the sequence. The default start number is 1.
- *increment_num* is the integer to increment the sequence by. The default increment number is 1. The absolute value of *increment_num* must be less than the difference between *maximum_num* and *minimum_num*.
- *maximum_num* is the maximum integer of the sequence. The value for *maximum_num* must be greater than or equal to *start_num*, and *maximum_num* must be greater than *minimum_num*.

- NOMAXVALUE specifies the maximum is $10^{28} - 1$ for an ascending sequence or -1 for a descending sequence. NOMAXVALUE is the default.

- *minimum_num* is the minimum integer of the sequence. The value for *minimum_num* must be less than or equal to *start_num*, and *minimum_num* must be less than *maximum_num*.

- NOMINVALUE specifies the minimum is 1 for an ascending sequence or $-(10^{27} - 1)$ for a descending sequence. NOMINVALUE is the default.

- CYCLE specifies the sequence generates integers even after reaching its maximum or minimum value. When an ascending sequence reaches its maximum value, the next value generated is the minimum. When a descending sequence reaches its minimum value, the next value generated is the maximum.

- NOCYCLE specifies the sequence cannot generate any more integers after reaching its maximum or minimum value. NOCYCLE is the default.

- CACHE specifies caching. This pre-allocates integers for the sequence.

- *cache_num* is the number of integers for the sequence to keep in memory. The default number of integers to cache is 20. The minimum number of integers that may be cached is 2. The maximum integers that may be cached is determined by the formula CEIL(*maximum_num* − *minimum_num*)/ABS(*increment_num*).

- NOCACHE specifies no caching. This stops the database from pre-allocating values for the sequence, which prevents numeric gaps in the sequence but reduces performance. Gaps occur because cached values are lost when the database is shut down. If you omit CACHE and NOCACHE, the database caches 20 sequence numbers by default.

- ORDER guarantees the integers are generated in the order of the request. You typically use ORDER when using Oracle Real Application Clusters (RAC). Oracle RAC uses multiple database servers that share the same memory. Oracle RAC can improve performance. Oracle RAC is set up and managed by database administrators.

- NOORDER doesn't guarantee the integers are generated in the order of the request. NOORDER is the default.

The following example connects as the store user and creates a sequence named s_test (I always put s_ at the beginning of sequences):

```
CONNECT store/store_password
CREATE SEQUENCE s_test;
```

Because this CREATE SEQUENCE statement omits the optional parameters, the default values are used. This specifies that *start_num* and *increment_num* are set to the default of 1.

The next example creates a sequence named s_test2 and specifies values for the optional parameters:

```
CREATE SEQUENCE s_test2
START WITH 10 INCREMENT BY 5
MINVALUE 10 MAXVALUE 20
CYCLE CACHE 2 ORDER;
```

The final example creates a sequence named s_test3 that starts at 10 and counts down to 1:

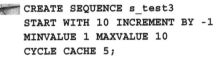
```
CREATE SEQUENCE s_test3
START WITH 10 INCREMENT BY -1
MINVALUE 1 MAXVALUE 10
CYCLE CACHE 5;
```

Retrieving Information on Sequences

You can retrieve information on your sequences from the user_sequences view. Table 11-6 shows some of the columns in user_sequences.

The following example retrieves the details for the sequences from user_sequences:

```
COLUMN sequence_name FORMAT a13
SELECT
  sequence_name, min_value, max_value, increment_by,
  cycle_flag, order_flag, cache_size, last_number
FROM user_sequences
ORDER BY sequence_name;
```

```
SEQUENCE_NAME  MIN_VALUE  MAX_VALUE INCREMENT_BY C O CACHE_SIZE LAST_NUMBER
-------------  ---------- ---------- ------------ - - ---------- -----------
S_TEST                 1 1.0000E+28            1 N N         20           1
S_TEST2               10         20            5 Y Y          2          10
S_TEST3                1         10           -1 Y N          5          10
```

> **NOTE**
> *You can retrieve information on all the sequences you have access to by querying the* all_sequences *view.*

Using a Sequence

A sequence generates a series of numbers. A sequence contains two pseudo columns named CURRVAL and NEXTVAL that you use to get the current value and the next value from the sequence.

Column	Type	Description
sequence_name	VARCHAR2(128)	Name of the sequence
min_value	NUMBER	Minimum value
max_value	NUMBER	Maximum value
increment_by	NUMBER	Number to increment or decrement sequence by
cycle_flag	VARCHAR2(1)	Whether the sequence cycles (Y or N)
order_flag	VARCHAR2(1)	Whether the sequence is ordered (Y or N)
cache_size	NUMBER	Number of sequence values stored in memory
last_number	NUMBER	Last number that was generated or cached by the sequence

TABLE 11-6. *Some Columns in the user_sequences View*

Before retrieving the current value, you must first initialize the sequence by retrieving the next value. When you select s_test.NEXTVAL, the sequence is initialized to 1. For example, the following query retrieves s_test.NEXTVAL. Notice that the dual table is used in the FROM clause:

```
SELECT s_test.NEXTVAL
FROM dual;

  NEXTVAL
----------
        1
```

The first value in the s_test sequence is 1. Once the sequence is initialized, you can get the current value from the sequence by retrieving CURRVAL. For example:

```
SELECT s_test.CURRVAL
FROM dual;

  CURRVAL
----------
        1
```

When you retrieve CURRVAL, NEXTVAL remains unchanged. The value for NEXTVAL only changes when you retrieve NEXTVAL to get the next value. The following example retrieves s_test.NEXTVAL and s_test.CURRVAL. Notice that these values are both 2.

```
SELECT s_test.NEXTVAL, s_test.CURRVAL
FROM dual;

  NEXTVAL    CURRVAL
---------- ----------
        2          2
```

Retrieving s_test.NEXTVAL gets the next value in the sequence, which is 2. The value for s_test.CURRVAL is also 2.

The next example initializes s_test2 by retrieving s_test2.NEXTVAL. Notice that the first value in the sequence is 10.

```
SELECT s_test2.NEXTVAL
FROM dual;

  NEXTVAL
----------
       10
```

The maximum value for s_test2 is 20, and the sequence was created with the CYCLE option, meaning that the sequence will cycle back to 10 once it reaches the maximum of 20:

```
SELECT s_test2.NEXTVAL
FROM dual;
```

```
    NEXTVAL
----------
        15
```

```
SELECT s_test2.NEXTVAL
FROM dual;
```

```
    NEXTVAL
----------
        20
```

```
SELECT s_test2.NEXTVAL
FROM dual;
```

```
    NEXTVAL
----------
        10
```

The s_test3 sequence starts at 10 and counts down to 1:

```
SELECT s_test3.NEXTVAL
FROM dual;
```

```
    NEXTVAL
----------
        10
```

```
SELECT s_test3.NEXTVAL
FROM dual;
```

```
    NEXTVAL
----------
         9
```

```
SELECT s_test3.NEXTVAL
FROM dual;
```

```
    NEXTVAL
----------
         8
```

Populating a Primary Key Using a Sequence

Sequences are useful for populating integer primary key column values. Let's take a look at an example. The following statement re-creates the order_status2 table:

```
CREATE TABLE order_status2 (
    id INTEGER CONSTRAINT order_status2_pk PRIMARY KEY,
    status VARCHAR2(10),
    last_modified DATE DEFAULT SYSDATE
);
```

The following statement creates a sequence named s_order_status2 (this sequence will be used to populate the order_status2.id column shortly):

```
CREATE SEQUENCE s_order_status2 NOCACHE;
```

TIP
When using a sequence to populate a primary key column, you should typically use NOCACHE *to avoid gaps in the sequence of numbers (gaps occur because cached values are lost when the database is shut down). However, using* NOCACHE *reduces performance. If you are absolutely sure that gaps in the primary key values are not a problem for your application, then consider using* CACHE.

The following INSERT statements add rows to order_status2. Notice that the value for the id column is set using s_order_status2.NEXTVAL (returns 1 for the first INSERT and 2 for the second INSERT).

```
INSERT INTO order_status2 (
  id, status, last_modified
) VALUES (
  s_order_status2.NEXTVAL, 'PLACED', '01-JAN-2006'
);

INSERT INTO order_status2 (
  id, status, last_modified
) VALUES (
  s_order_status2.NEXTVAL, 'PENDING', '01-FEB-2006'
);
```

The following query retrieves the rows from order_status2. Notice that the id column is set to the first two values (1 and 2) from the s_order_status2 sequence.

```
SELECT *
FROM order_status2;

        ID STATUS     LAST_MODI
---------- ---------- ---------
         1 PLACED     01-JAN-06
         2 PENDING    01-FEB-06
```

Specifying a Default Column Value Using a Sequence

New for Oracle Database 12c is the ability to specify a default column value using a sequence. The following example creates a sequence named s_default_value_for_column:

```
CREATE SEQUENCE s_default_value_for_column;
```

The following example creates a table named `test_with_sequence` and specifies that the `sequence_value` column's default value is set to the next value from the sequence:

```
CREATE TABLE test_with_sequence (
  id INTEGER CONSTRAINT test_with_sequence_pk PRIMARY KEY,
  sequence_value INTEGER DEFAULT s_default_value_for_column.NEXTVAL
);
```

The following INSERT statements add rows to the table:

```
INSERT INTO test_with_sequence (id) VALUES (1);
INSERT INTO test_with_sequence (id) VALUES (2);
INSERT INTO test_with_sequence (id) VALUES (4);
```

The following query retrieves the rows from the table. Notice that the `sequence_value` column is set to the first three values generated by the sequence, which are 1, 2, and 3.

```
SELECT *
FROM test_with_sequence;

        ID SEQUENCE_VALUE
---------- --------------
         1              1
         2              2
         4              3
```

Remember the following points when using sequences to set a default column value:

■ Users who add rows to the table must have the INSERT privilege on the table and the SELECT privilege on the sequence.

■ If the sequence is dropped, then subsequent INSERT statements will generate an error.

Using Identity Columns

New for Oracle Database 12c are identity columns. An identity column value is specified using a sequence generation statement.

The following example creates a table named `test_with_identity` and specifies that the `identity_value` column's default value is set to the next value from a sequence generation statement:

```
CREATE TABLE test_with_identity (
  id INTEGER CONSTRAINT test_with_identity_pk PRIMARY KEY,
  identity_value INTEGER GENERATED BY DEFAULT AS IDENTITY (
    START WITH 5 INCREMENT BY 2
  )
);
```

The following INSERT statements add rows to the table:

```
INSERT INTO test_with_identity (id) VALUES (1);
INSERT INTO test_with_identity (id) VALUES (2);
INSERT INTO test_with_identity (id) VALUES (4);
```

The following query retrieves the rows from the table. Notice that the `identity_value` column is set to the first three values generated by the sequence, which are 5, 7, and 9.

```
SELECT *
FROM test_with_identity;

        ID IDENTITY_VALUE
---------- --------------
         1              5
         2              7
         4              9
```

Modifying a Sequence

You modify a sequence using the `ALTER SEQUENCE` statement. There are limitations on what you can modify in a sequence:

- You cannot change the start value of a sequence.
- The minimum value cannot be more than the current value of the sequence.
- The maximum value cannot be less than the current value of the sequence.

The following example modifies the sequence `s_test` to increment the sequence of numbers by 2:

```
ALTER SEQUENCE s_test
INCREMENT BY 2;
```

When this is done, the new values generated by `s_test` will be incremented by 2. For example, if `s_test.CURRVAL` is 2, then `s_test.NEXTVAL` is 4. This is shown in the following example:

```
SELECT s_test.CURRVAL
FROM dual;

   CURRVAL
----------
         2

SELECT s_test.NEXTVAL
FROM dual;

   NEXTVAL
----------
         4
```

Dropping a Sequence

You drop a sequence using `DROP SEQUENCE`. The following example drops `s_test3`:

```
DROP SEQUENCE s_test3;
```

This concludes the discussion of sequences. In the next section, you'll learn about indexes.

Indexes

When looking for a particular subject in a book, you can either scan the whole book or use the index to find the location. An index for a database table is similar in concept to a book index, except that database indexes are used to find specific rows in a table. The downside of indexes is that when a row is added to the table, additional time is required to update the index for the new row.

Generally, you should create an index on a column when you are retrieving a small number of rows from a table containing many rows. A simple rule for when to create indexes is

Create an index when a query retrieves <= 10 percent of the total rows in a table.

This means the column for the index should contain a wide range of values. These types of indexes are called *B-tree* indexes, a name that comes from a tree data structure used in computer science. A good candidate for B-tree indexing would be a column containing a unique value for each row (for example, a Social Security number). A poor candidate for B-tree indexing would be a column that contains only a small range of values (for example, N, S, E, W or 1, 2, 3, 4, 5, 6). An Oracle database automatically creates a B-tree index for the primary key of a table and for columns included in a unique constraint. For columns that contain a small range of values, you can use a bitmap index. You'll learn about bitmap indexes shortly.

In this section, you'll learn how to perform the following tasks:

- Create a B-tree index
- Create a function-based index
- Retrieve information on an index from the data dictionary
- Modify an index
- Drop an index
- Create a bitmap index

Creating a B-tree Index

You create a B-tree index using `CREATE INDEX`, which has the following simplified syntax:

```
CREATE [UNIQUE] INDEX index_name ON
table_name(column_name[, column_name ...])
TABLESPACE tab_space;
```

where

- `UNIQUE` specifies that the values in the indexed columns must be unique.
- `index_name` is the name of the index.
- `table_name` is a database table.
- `column_name` is the indexed column. You can create an index on multiple columns (such an index is known as a *composite index*).
- `tab_space` is the tablespace for the index. If you don't provide a tablespace, then the index is stored in the user's default tablespace.

TIP
For performance reasons, you should typically store indexes in a different tablespace from tables. For simplicity, the examples in this chapter use the default tablespace. In a production database, the database administrator should create separate tablespaces for the tables and indexes.

I'll now guide you through an example process you should follow before deciding to create an index. The example will be for creating a B-tree index for the `customers.last_name` column. Assume that the `customers` table contains a large number of rows and that rows are often retrieved using the following type of query:

```
SELECT customer_id, first_name, last_name
FROM customers
WHERE last_name = 'Brown';
```

Also assume that the `last_name` column contains somewhat unique values, so that any query using the `last_name` column in a WHERE clause will return less than 10 percent of the total number of rows in the table. This means the `last_name` column is a good candidate for indexing.

The following CREATE INDEX statement creates an index named `i_customers_last_name` on the `last_name` column of the `customers` table (I always put `i_` at the start of index names):

```
CREATE INDEX i_customers_last_name ON customers(last_name);
```

With an index, the previous query will take less time to complete.

You can enforce uniqueness of column values using a unique index. For example, the following statement creates a unique index named `i_customers_phone` on the `customers.phone` column:

```
CREATE UNIQUE INDEX i_customers_phone ON customers(phone);
```

You can also create a composite index on multiple columns. For example, the following statement creates a composite index named `i_employees_first_last_name` on the `first_name` and `last_name` columns of the `employees` table:

```
CREATE INDEX i_employees_first_last_name ON
employees(first_name, last_name);
```

Creating a Function-Based Index

In the previous section you saw the index `i_customers_last_name`. Let's say you run the following query:

```
SELECT first_name, last_name
FROM customers
WHERE last_name = UPPER('BROWN');
```

Because this query uses a function—UPPER(), in this case—the i_customers_last_name index isn't used. If you want an index to be based on the results of a function, you must create a function-based index, such as:

```
CREATE INDEX i_func_customers_last_name
ON customers(UPPER(last_name));
```

In addition, the database administrator must set the initialization parameter QUERY_REWRITE_ENABLED to true (the default is false) in order to take advantage of function-based indexes. The following example sets QUERY_REWRITE_ENABLED to true:

```
CONNECT system/oracle
ALTER SYSTEM SET QUERY_REWRITE_ENABLED = TRUE;
```

Retrieving Information on Indexes

You can retrieve information on your indexes from the user_indexes view. Table 11-7 describes some of the columns in user_indexes.

The following example connects as the store user and retrieves some of the columns from user_indexes for the customers and employees tables. Notice that the list of indexes includes customers_pk, which is a unique index that is automatically created for the customer_id primary key column of the customers table.

```
CONNECT store/store_password
SELECT index_name, table_name, uniqueness, status
FROM user_indexes
WHERE table_name IN ('CUSTOMERS', 'EMPLOYEES')
ORDER BY index_name;
```

```
INDEX_NAME                      TABLE_NAME            UNIQUENES STATUS
------------------------------  --------------------  --------- ------
CUSTOMERS_PK                    CUSTOMERS             UNIQUE    VALID
EMPLOYEES_PK                    EMPLOYEES             UNIQUE    VALID
I_CUSTOMERS_LAST_NAME           CUSTOMERS             NONUNIQUE VALID
I_CUSTOMERS_PHONE               CUSTOMERS             UNIQUE    VALID
I_EMPLOYEES_FIRST_LAST_NAME     EMPLOYEES             NONUNIQUE VALID
I_FUNC_CUSTOMERS_LAST_NAME      CUSTOMERS             NONUNIQUE VALID
```

Column	Type	Description
index_name	VARCHAR2(128)	Name of the index
table_owner	VARCHAR2(128)	The user who owns the table
table_name	VARCHAR2(128)	The name of the table on which the index was created
uniqueness	VARCHAR2(9)	Whether the index is unique (UNIQUE or NONUNIQUE)
status	VARCHAR2(8)	Whether the index is valid (VALID or INVALID)

TABLE 11-7. *Some Columns in the* user_indexes *View*

Column	Type	Description
index_name	VARCHAR2(128)	Name of the index
table_name	VARCHAR2(128)	Name of the table
column_name	VARCHAR2(4000)	Name of the indexed column

TABLE 11-8.   *Some Columns in the* user_ind_columns *View*

NOTE
*You can retrieve information on all the indexes you have access to by
querying the* all_indexes *view.*

Retrieving Information on the Indexes on a Column

You can retrieve information on the indexes on a column by querying the user_ind_columns
view. Table 11-8 describes some of the columns in user_ind_columns.

The following query retrieves some of the columns from user_ind_columns for the
customers and employees tables:

```
COLUMN table_name FORMAT a15
COLUMN column_name FORMAT a15
SELECT index_name, table_name, column_name
FROM user_ind_columns
WHERE table_name IN ('CUSTOMERS', 'EMPLOYEES')
ORDER BY index_name;

INDEX_NAME                         TABLE_NAME        COLUMN_NAME
---------------------------------  ----------------  ------------
CUSTOMERS_PK                       CUSTOMERS         CUSTOMER_ID
EMPLOYEES_PK                       EMPLOYEES         EMPLOYEE_ID
I_CUSTOMERS_LAST_NAME              CUSTOMERS         LAST_NAME
I_CUSTOMERS_PHONE                  CUSTOMERS         PHONE
I_EMPLOYEES_FIRST_LAST_NAME        EMPLOYEES         LAST_NAME
I_EMPLOYEES_FIRST_LAST_NAME        EMPLOYEES         FIRST_NAME
I_FUNC_CUSTOMERS_LAST_NAME         CUSTOMERS         SYS_NC00006$
```

NOTE
*You can retrieve information on all the indexed columns you have
access to by querying the* all_ind_columns *view.*

Modifying an Index

You modify an index using ALTER INDEX. The following example renames the i_customers_
phone index to i_customers_phone_number:

```
ALTER INDEX i_customers_phone RENAME TO i_customers_phone_number;
```

Dropping an Index

You drop an index using the DROP INDEX statement. The following example drops the i_ customers_phone_number index:

```
DROP INDEX i_customers_phone_number;
```

Creating a Bitmap Index

Bitmap indexes are often used in *data warehouses*, which are databases containing very large amounts of data. Data warehouses are used by organizations for business intelligence analysis, like monitoring sales trends and examining customer behaviors. The data warehouse is typically read using complex queries, but the data are not constantly being updated. The data might only be updated at the end of each day, week, or other scheduled period.

A candidate for a bitmap index is a column that has the following properties:

■ Is referenced in many queries
■ Contains only a small range of values

Example ranges of values include the following:

■ N, S, E, W
■ 1, 2, 3, 4, 5, 6
■ PLACED, PENDING, SHIPPED, REMOVED

An index basically contains a pointer to a row in a table that contains a given index key value. The key value is used to get the rowid for the row in the table. (As discussed in Chapter 2, a rowid is used internally by the database to store the physical location of the row.) In a B-tree index, a list of rowids is stored for each key corresponding to the rows with that key value. In a B-tree index, the database stores a list of key values with each rowid, which enables the database to locate a row in a table.

In a bitmap index, however, a bitmap is used for each key value. The bitmap enables the database to locate a row. Each bit in the bitmap corresponds to a possible rowid. If the bit is set, that means the row with the corresponding rowid contains the key value. A mapping function converts the bit position to a rowid.

Use the following points to guide you when deciding whether to create a bitmap index:

■ A bitmap index is often used in tables containing large amounts of data and whose contents are not modified very often.

■ A bitmap index should only be created on columns that contain a small number of distinct values. If the number of distinct values of a column is less than 1 percent of the number of rows in the table, or if the values in a column are repeated more than 100 times, then the column is a candidate for a bitmap index. For example, if you have a table with 1 million rows, a column with 10,000 distinct values or less is a good candidate for a bitmap index.

■ The column with the bitmap index should be frequently used in a WHERE clause.

The following statement creates a bitmap index on the `status` column of the `order_status` table:

```
CREATE BITMAP INDEX i_order_status ON order_status(status);
```

NOTE
This example is not a real-world example because the `order_status` *table contains few rows.*

You can find more information on bitmap indexes in the *Oracle Database Performance Tuning Guide* and *Oracle Database Concepts* books, both published by Oracle Corporation. These books also contain information about other types of indexes you can use.

This concludes the discussion of indexes. In the next section, you'll learn about views.

Views

A view is a predefined query on one or more tables (known as *base tables*). Retrieving information from a view is done in the same manner as retrieving information from a table: You include the view in the FROM clause of a query. With some views, you can also perform Data Manipulation Language (DML) operations on the base tables.

NOTE
Views don't store rows. Rows are always stored in tables. Views return the rows stored in tables.

You've already seen some examples of retrieving information from views when you selected rows from the data dictionary, which is accessed through views. For example, `user_tables`, `user_sequences`, and `user_indexes` are all views.

Views offer several benefits, such as the following:

■ You can place a complex query into a view and grant users access to the view. This allows you to hide complexity from users.

■ You can stop users from directly querying the base tables by granting them access only to the view.

■ You can allow a view to access only certain rows in the base tables. This allows you to hide rows from an end user.

In this section, you'll learn how to perform the following tasks:

■ Create and use a view
■ Modify a view
■ Drop a view
■ Use visible and invisible columns in a view

Creating and Using a View

You create a view using CREATE VIEW, which has the following simplified syntax:

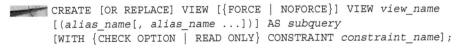

```
CREATE [OR REPLACE] VIEW [{FORCE | NOFORCE}] VIEW view_name
[(alias_name[, alias_name ...])] AS subquery
[WITH {CHECK OPTION | READ ONLY} CONSTRAINT constraint_name];
```

where

- OR REPLACE specifies the view replaces an existing view.
- FORCE specifies the view is to be created even if the base tables don't exist.
- NOFORCE specifies the view is not created if the base tables don't exist. NOFORCE is the default.
- view_name is the name of the view.
- alias_name is the name of an alias for an expression in the subquery. There must be the same number of aliases as there are expressions in the subquery.
- subquery is the subquery that retrieves from the base tables. If you've supplied aliases, you can use those aliases in the list after the SELECT.
- WITH CHECK OPTION specifies that only the rows that would be retrieved by the subquery can be inserted, updated, or deleted. By default, the rows are not checked.
- WITH READ ONLY specifies the rows may only read from the base tables.
- constraint_name is the name of the constraint.

There are two basic types of views:

- Simple views, which contain a subquery that retrieves from one base table
- Complex views, which contain a subquery that
  - Retrieves from multiple base tables
  - Groups rows using a GROUP BY or DISTINCT clause
  - Contains a function call

You'll learn how to create and use views in the following sections.

Granting Privileges for Views

In order to create a view, the user must have the CREATE VIEW privilege. The following example connects as the system user and grants the CREATE VIEW privilege to the store user:

```
CONNECT system/oracle
GRANT CREATE VIEW TO store;
```

Creating and Using Simple Views

Simple views access one base table. The following example connects as the `store` user and creates a view named `cheap_products_view` whose subquery retrieves products only where the price is less than $15:

```
CONNECT store/store_password
CREATE VIEW cheap_products_view AS
SELECT *
FROM products
WHERE price < 15;
```

The next example creates a view named `employees_view` whose subquery retrieves all the columns from the `employees` table except `salary`:

```
CREATE VIEW employees_view AS
SELECT employee_id, manager_id, first_name, last_name, title
FROM employees;
```

Performing a Query on a View

Once you've created a view, you can use it to access the base table. The following query retrieves rows from `cheap_products_view`:

```
SELECT product_id, name, price
FROM cheap_products_view;

PRODUCT_ID NAME                                    PRICE
---------- ------------------------------- ----------
         4 Tank War                                13.95
         6 2412: The Return                        14.95
         7 Space Force 9                           13.49
         8 From Another Planet                     12.99
         9 Classical Music                         10.99
        11 Creative Yell                           14.99
        12 My Front Line                           13.49
```

The next example retrieves rows from `employees_view`:

```
SELECT *
FROM employees_view;

EMPLOYEE_ID MANAGER_ID FIRST_NAME LAST_NAME  TITLE
----------- ---------- ---------- ---------- -------------
          1            James      Smith      CEO
          2          1 Ron        Johnson    Sales Manager
          3          2 Fred       Hobbs      Salesperson
          4          2 Susan      Jones      Salesperson
```

Performing an INSERT Using a View

You can perform DML statements using `cheap_products_view`. The following example performs an `INSERT` using `cheap_products_view` and then retrieves the row:

```
INSERT INTO cheap_products_view (
   product_id, product_type_id, name, price
) VALUES (
   13, 1, 'Western Front', 13.50
);

1 row created.

SELECT product_id, name, price
FROM cheap_products_view
WHERE product_id = 13;

PRODUCT_ID NAME                                 PRICE
---------- ------------------------------- ----------
        13 Western Front                         13.5
```

NOTE
You can perform DML statements only with simple views. Complex views don't support DML.

Because `cheap_products_view` didn't use `WITH CHECK OPTION`, you can insert, update, and delete rows that aren't retrievable by the view. The following example inserts a row whose price is $16.50 (this is greater than $15 and therefore not retrievable by the view):

```
INSERT INTO cheap_products_view (
   product_id, product_type_id, name, price
) VALUES (
   14, 1, 'Eastern Front', 16.50
);

1 row created.

SELECT *
FROM cheap_products_view
WHERE product_id = 14;

no rows selected
```

The `employees_view` contains a subquery that selects every column from `employees` except `salary`. When you perform an `INSERT` using `employees_view`, the `salary` column in the `employees` base table will be set to null. For example:

```
INSERT INTO employees_view (
   employee_id, manager_id, first_name, last_name, title
) VALUES (
```

```
  5, 1, 'Jeff', 'Jones', 'CTO'
);

1 row created.

SELECT employee_id, first_name, last_name, salary
FROM employees
WHERE employee_id = 5;

EMPLOYEE_ID FIRST_NAME LAST_NAME     SALARY
----------- ---------- ---------- ---------
          5 Jeff       Jones
```

The salary column is null.

Creating a View with a CHECK OPTION Constraint

You can specify that DML statements on a view must satisfy the subquery using a CHECK
OPTION constraint. For example, the following statement creates a view named cheap_
products_view2 that has a CHECK OPTION constraint:

```
CREATE VIEW cheap_products_view2 AS
SELECT *
FROM products
WHERE price < 15
WITH CHECK OPTION CONSTRAINT cheap_products_view2_price;
```

The next example attempts to insert a row using cheap_products_view2 with a price of
$19.50. The database returns an error because the row isn't retrievable by the view.

```
INSERT INTO cheap_products_view2 (
  product_id, product_type_id, name, price
) VALUES (
  15, 1, 'Southern Front', 19.50
);
INSERT INTO cheap_products_view2 (
              *
ERROR at line 1:
ORA-01402: view WITH CHECK OPTION where-clause violation
```

Creating a View with a READ ONLY Constraint

You can make a view read-only by adding a READ ONLY constraint to the view. For example, the
following statement creates a view named cheap_products_view3 that has a READ ONLY
constraint:

```
CREATE VIEW cheap_products_view3 AS
SELECT *
FROM products
WHERE price < 15
WITH READ ONLY CONSTRAINT cheap_products_view3_read_only;
```

The following example attempts to insert a row using `cheap_products_view3`. The database returns an error because the view is read-only and doesn't allow DML statements.

```
INSERT INTO cheap_products_view3 (
  product_id, product_type_id, name, price
) VALUES (
  16, 1, 'Northern Front', 19.50
);
  product_id, product_type_id, name, price
  *
ERROR at line 2:
ORA-42399: cannot perform a DML operation on a read-only view
```

Getting Information on View Definitions

You can retrieve information on view definitions using the `DESCRIBE` command. The following example uses `DESCRIBE` with `cheap_products_view3`:

```
DESCRIBE cheap_products_view3
 Name                                      Null?    Type
 ----------------------------------------- -------- ------------
 PRODUCT_ID                                NOT NULL NUMBER(38)
 PRODUCT_TYPE_ID                                    NUMBER(38)
 NAME                                      NOT NULL VARCHAR2(30)
 DESCRIPTION                                        VARCHAR2(50)
 PRICE                                              NUMBER(5,2)
```

You can also retrieve information about your views from the `user_views` view. Table 11-9 describes some of the columns in `user_views`.

To see the entire view definition stored in the `text` column, you use the SQL*Plus command `SET LONG`, which sets the number of characters displayed by SQL*Plus when retrieving `LONG` columns. For example, the following command sets `LONG` to 200:

```
SET LONG 200
```

The following query retrieves the `view_name`, `text_length`, and `text` columns from `user_views`:

```
SELECT view_name, text_length, text
FROM user_views
ORDER BY view_name;

VIEW_NAME                       TEXT_LENGTH
------------------------------- -----------
TEXT
--------------------------------------------------------------
CHEAP_PRODUCTS_VIEW                      97
SELECT "PRODUCT_ID","PRODUCT_TYPE_ID","NAME","DESCRIPTION","PRICE"
FROM products
WHERE price < 15

CHEAP_PRODUCTS_VIEW2                     116
```

Column	Type	Description
view_name	VARCHAR2(128)	Name of the view
text_length	NUMBER	Number of characters in the view's subquery
text	LONG	Text of the view's subquery

TABLE 11-9.   *Some Columns in the* user_views *View*

```
SELECT "PRODUCT_ID","PRODUCT_TYPE_ID","NAME","DESCRIPTION","PRICE"
FROM products
WHERE price < 15
WITH CHECK OPTION

CHEAP_PRODUCTS_VIEW3                      113
SELECT "PRODUCT_ID","PRODUCT_TYPE_ID","NAME","DESCRIPTION","PRICE"
FROM products
WHERE price < 15
WITH READ ONLY

EMPLOYEES_VIEW                            75
SELECT employee_id, manager_id, first_name, last_name, title
FROM employees
```

NOTE
*You can retrieve information on all the indexes you have access to by
querying* all_views.

Retrieving Information on View Constraints

Earlier you saw that you can add CHECK OPTION and READ ONLY constraints to a view. The
view cheap_products_view2 contained a CHECK OPTION constraint to ensure the price was
less than $15. The view cheap_products_view3 contained a READ ONLY constraint to
prevent modifications to the rows in the base table.

    You retrieve information on view constraints from the user_constraints view. For example:

```
SELECT constraint_name, constraint_type, status, deferrable, deferred
FROM user_constraints
WHERE table_name IN ('CHEAP_PRODUCTS_VIEW2', 'CHEAP_PRODUCTS_VIEW3')
ORDER BY constraint_name;

CONSTRAINT_NAME                 C STATUS   DEFERRABLE     DEFERRED
------------------------------- - -------- -------------- ---------
CHEAP_PRODUCTS_VIEW2_PRICE      V ENABLED  NOT DEFERRABLE IMMEDIATE
CHEAP_PRODUCTS_VIEW3_READ_ONLY  O ENABLED  NOT DEFERRABLE IMMEDIATE
```

    The constraint_type for CHEAP_PRODUCTS_VIEW2_PRICE is V, which, as shown
earlier in Table 11-3, corresponds to a CHECK OPTION constraint. The constraint_type for
CHEAP_PRODUCTS_VIEW3_READ_ONLY is O, which corresponds to a READ ONLY constraint.

Creating and Using Complex Views

Complex views contain subqueries that have the following properties:

- Retrieve rows from multiple base tables
- Group rows using a GROUP BY or DISTINCT clause
- Contain a function call

The following example creates a view named products_and_types_view whose subquery performs a full outer join on the products and product_types tables using the SQL/92 syntax:

```
CREATE VIEW products_and_types_view AS
SELECT
  p.product_id, p.name product_name,
  pt.name product_type_name, p.price
FROM products p FULL OUTER JOIN product_types pt
USING (product_type_id)
ORDER BY p.product_id;
```

The following example queries products_and_types_view:

```
SELECT *
FROM products_and_types_view;
```

```
PRODUCT_ID PRODUCT_NAME                            PRODUCT_TY      PRICE
---------- ------------------------------------    ----------   ----------
         1 Modern Science                          Book             19.95
         2 Chemistry                               Book                30
         3 Supernova                               Video            25.99
         4 Tank War                                Video            13.95
         5 Z Files                                 Video            49.99
         6 2412: The Return                        Video            14.95
         7 Space Force 9                           DVD              13.49
         8 From Another Planet                     DVD              12.99
         9 Classical Music                         CD               10.99
        10 Pop 3                                   CD               15.99
        11 Creative Yell                           CD               14.99
        12 My Front Line                                            13.49
        13 Western Front                           Book              13.5
        14 Eastern Front                           Book              16.5
                                                   Magazine
```

The next example creates a view named employee_salary_grades_view whose subquery uses an inner join to retrieve the salary grades for the employees:

```
CREATE VIEW employee_salary_grades_view AS
SELECT
  e.first_name, e.last_name, e.title, e.salary,
  sg.salary_grade_id
```

```
FROM employees e INNER JOIN salary_grades sg
ON e.salary BETWEEN sg.low_salary AND sg.high_salary
ORDER BY sg.salary_grade_id;
```

The following example queries employee_salary_grades_view:

```
SELECT *
FROM employee_salary_grades_view;

FIRST_NAME LAST_NAME  TITLE                    SALARY SALARY_GRADE_ID
---------- ---------- -------------------- ---------- ---------------
Fred       Hobbs      Salesperson              150000               1
Susan      Jones      Salesperson              500000               2
Ron        Johnson    Sales Manager            600000               3
James      Smith      CEO                      800000               4
```

The next example creates a view named product_average_view whose subquery uses the following clauses:

- A WHERE clause to filter the rows from the products table to those whose price is less than $15

- A GROUP BY clause to group the remaining rows by the product_type_id column

- A HAVING clause to filter the row groups to those whose average price is greater than $13

```
CREATE VIEW product_average_view AS
SELECT product_type_id, AVG(price) average_price
FROM products
WHERE price < 15
GROUP BY product_type_id
HAVING AVG(price) > 13
ORDER BY product_type_id;
```

The following example queries product_average_view:

```
SELECT *
FROM product_average_view;

PRODUCT_TYPE_ID AVERAGE_PRICE
--------------- -------------
              1          13.5
              2         14.45
              3         13.24
                        13.49
```

Modifying a View

You can replace a view using CREATE OR REPLACE VIEW. The following example uses CREATE OR REPLACE VIEW to replace product_average_view:

```
CREATE OR REPLACE VIEW product_average_view AS
SELECT product_type_id, AVG(price) average_price
```

```
FROM products
WHERE price < 12
GROUP BY product_type_id
HAVING AVG(price) > 11
ORDER BY product_type_id;
```

You can alter the constraints on a view using ALTER VIEW. The following example uses ALTER VIEW to drop the cheap_products_view2_price constraint from cheap_products_view2:

```
ALTER VIEW cheap_products_view2
DROP CONSTRAINT cheap_products_view2_price;
```

Dropping a View

You delete a view using DROP VIEW. The following example drops cheap_products_view2:

```
DROP VIEW cheap_products_view2;
```

Using Visible and Invisible Columns in a View

New for Oracle Database 12*c* is the ability to define visible and invisible columns in a view. You use VISIBLE to make a column visible, and INVISIBLE to make a column invisible. If neither is specified for a column, then the column is visible by default.

The following example creates a view named employees_hidden_salary_view. The salary column is set to INVISIBLE. The title column is explicitly set to VISIBLE. The other columns are visible by default.

```
CREATE VIEW employees_hidden_salary_view (
   employee_id, manager_id, first_name, last_name,
   title VISIBLE, salary INVISIBLE
) AS
SELECT employee_id, manager_id, first_name, last_name, title, salary
FROM employees;
```

The following query retrieves the rows from the view. Notice the salary column is not shown in the result set.

```
SELECT *
FROM employees_hidden_salary_view;
```

```
EMPLOYEE_ID MANAGER_ID FIRST_NAME LAST_NAME  TITLE
----------- ---------- ---------- ---------- -------------
          1            James      Smith      CEO
          2          1 Ron        Johnson    Sales Manager
          3          2 Fred       Hobbs      Salesperson
          4          2 Susan      Jones      Salesperson
```

To view an invisible column in the result set, you explicitly request the column. In the following example, the salary column is explicitly requested at the end of the column list:

```
SELECT employee_id, manager_id, first_name, last_name, title, salary
FROM employees_hidden_salary_view;
```

```
EMPLOYEE_ID MANAGER_ID FIRST_NAME LAST_NAME  TITLE          SALARY

----------- ---------- ---------- ---------- -------------- ----------

          1            James      Smith      CEO            800000

          2          1 Ron        Johnson    Sales Manager  600000

          3          2 Fred       Hobbs      Salesperson    150000

          4          2 Susan      Jones      Salesperson    500000
```

This concludes the discussion of views. In the next section, you'll learn about flashback data archives.

Flashback Data Archives

Flashback data archives, introduced in Oracle Database 11*g*, store changes made to a table over a period of time and provide you with a full audit trail. Once you've created a flashback archive and added a table to it, you can perform the following tasks:

- View rows as they were at a specific timestamp
- View rows as they were between two timestamps

NOTE
At the time of writing, you cannot create a flashback data archive in a pluggable database. The version of Oracle Database 12c used was 12.1.0.1.0.

You create a flashback archive using the CREATE FLASHBACK ARCHIVE statement. The following example connects as the system user and creates a flashback archive named test_archive:

```
CONNECT system/oracle
CREATE FLASHBACK ARCHIVE test_archive
TABLESPACE example
QUOTA 1 M
RETENTION 1 DAY;
```

Notice the following about the previous example:

- The archive is created in the example tablespace. You can see the full list of tablespaces by running the query SELECT tablespace_name FROM dba_tablespaces.
- test_archive has a quota of 1 megabyte, which means it can store up to 1 megabyte of data in the example tablespace.
- The data in test_archive is retained for one day, after which time the data are purged.

You may alter an existing table to store data in the archive. For example:

```
ALTER TABLE store.products FLASHBACK ARCHIVE test_archive;
```

Any subsequent changes made to the store.products table are now recorded in the archive. The following INSERT statement adds a row to the store.products table:

```
INSERT INTO store.products (
  product_id, product_type_id, name, description, price
) VALUES (
  15, 1, 'Using Linux', 'How to Use Linux', 39.99
);
```

The following query retrieves the new row:

```
SELECT product_id, name, price
FROM store.products
WHERE product_id = 15;
```

```
PRODUCT_ID NAME                                   PRICE
---------- ------------------------------ ----------
        15 Using Linux                            39.99
```

You can view the rows as they were 5 minutes ago using the following query:

```
SELECT product_id, name, price
FROM store.products
AS OF TIMESTAMP
(SYSTIMESTAMP - INTERVAL '5' MINUTE);
```

```
PRODUCT_ID NAME                                   PRICE
---------- ------------------------------ ----------
         1 Modern Science                         19.95
         2 Chemistry                                 30
         3 Supernova                              25.99
         4 Tank War                               13.95
         5 Z Files                                49.99
         6 2412: The Return                       14.95
         7 Space Force 9                          13.49
         8 From Another Planet                    12.99
         9 Classical Music                        10.99
        10 Pop 3                                  15.99
        11 Creative Yell                          14.99
        12 My Front Line                          13.49
        13 Western Front                           13.5
        14 Eastern Front                           16.5
```

Notice that the new row is missing. This is because it was added to the table after the date and time specified in the query (assuming the previous INSERT was run less than 5 minutes ago).

You can also view the rows as they were at a specific timestamp using the following query (if you run this query, you need to change the timestamp to a date and time before you ran the INSERT statement earlier):

```
SELECT product_id, name, price
FROM store.products
AS OF TIMESTAMP
TO_TIMESTAMP('2012-06-15 18:40:00', 'YYYY-MM-DD HH24:MI:SS');
```

The new row will be missing from the results again because it was added to the table after the date and time specified in the query.

You can view the rows as they were between two timestamps using the following query (you need to change the timestamps):

```
SELECT product_id, name, price
FROM store.products VERSIONS BETWEEN TIMESTAMP
TO_TIMESTAMP('2012-06-15 18:40:00', 'YYYY-MM-DD HH24:MI:SS')
AND TO_TIMESTAMP('2012-06-15 18:41:00', 'YYYY-MM-DD HH24:MI:SS');
```

You can view the rows as they were between one timestamp and the present time using the following query (you need to change the timestamp):

```
SELECT product_id, name, price
FROM store.products VERSIONS BETWEEN TIMESTAMP
TO_TIMESTAMP('2012-06-15 18:40:00', 'YYYY-MM-DD HH24:MI:SS')
AND MAXVALUE;
```

You can stop archiving of data for a table using ALTER TABLE. For example:

```
ALTER TABLE store.products NO FLASHBACK ARCHIVE;
```

When you create a table, you can specify a flashback archive for that table. For example:

```
CREATE TABLE store.test_table (
  id INTEGER,
  name VARCHAR2(10)
) FLASHBACK ARCHIVE test_archive;
```

You can view the details for an archive using the following views:

- user_flashback_archive and dba_flashback_archive, which display general information about the flashback archives
- user_flashback_archive_ts and dba_flashback_archive_ts, which display information about the tablespaces containing the flashback archives
- user_flashback_archive_tables and dba_flashback_archive_tables, which display information about the tables that are enabled for flashback archiving

You can alter a flashback archive. For example, the following statement changes the data retention period to two years:

```
ALTER FLASHBACK ARCHIVE test_archive
MODIFY RETENTION 2 YEAR;
```

You can purge the data from a flashback archive before a given timestamp. For example, the following statement purges data older than one day:

```
ALTER FLASHBACK ARCHIVE test_archive
PURGE BEFORE TIMESTAMP(SYSTIMESTAMP - INTERVAL '1' DAY);
```

You can purge all the data in a flashback archive. For example:

```
ALTER FLASHBACK ARCHIVE test_archive PURGE ALL;
```

You can drop a flashback archive. For example:

```
DROP FLASHBACK ARCHIVE test_archive;
```

Summary

In this chapter, you have learned the following:

- A table is created using the CREATE TABLE statement.
- A sequence generates a sequence of integers.
- A database index can speed up access to rows.
- A view is a predefined query on one or more base tables.
- A flashback data archive stores changes made to a table over a period of time.

In the next chapter, you'll learn about PL/SQL programming.

CHAPTER
12

Introducing PL/SQL
Programming

The Oracle database contains a procedural programming language known as PL/SQL (Procedural Language/SQL). PL/SQL enables you to write programs that contain SQL statements.

In this chapter, you'll learn about the following PL/SQL topics:

- Block structure
- Variables and types
- Conditional logic
- Loops
- Cursors, which allow PL/SQL to read the results returned by a query
- Exceptions, which are used to handle errors
- Procedures
- Functions
- Packages, which are used to group procedures and functions together in one unit
- Triggers, which are blocks of code that are run when a certain event occurs in the database

You can use PL/SQL to add business logic to a database application. This centralized business logic can be run by any program that can access the database, including SQL*Plus, Java programs, C# programs, and more.

NOTE
Before continuing, rerun `store_schema.sql` *to re-create the store tables so that your query results match those in this chapter.*

Block Structure

PL/SQL programs are divided up into structures known as *blocks*, with each block containing PL/SQL and SQL statements. A PL/SQL block has the following structure:

```
[DECLARE
    declaration_statements
]
BEGIN
  executable_statements
[EXCEPTION
  exception_handling_statements
]
END;
/
```

where

- *declaration_statements* declare the variables used in the rest of the PL/SQL block. DECLARE blocks are optional.

- *executable_statements* are the actual executable statements, which can include loops, conditional logic, and so on.

- *exception_handling_statements* are statements that handle any execution errors that might occur when the block is run. EXCEPTION blocks are optional.

A PL/SQL block is terminated using the forward slash (/) character.

The following example (contained in the area_example.sql script in the SQL directory) calculates the width of a rectangle given its area and height:

```
SET SERVEROUTPUT ON

DECLARE
  v_width  INTEGER;
  v_height INTEGER := 2;
  v_area   INTEGER := 6;
BEGIN
  -- set the width equal to the area divided by the height
  v_width := v_area / v_height;
  DBMS_OUTPUT.PUT_LINE('v_width = ' || v_width);
EXCEPTION
  WHEN ZERO_DIVIDE THEN
    DBMS_OUTPUT.PUT_LINE('Division by zero');
END;
/
```

The SET SERVEROUTPUT ON command turns on the server output so you can see the lines produced by DBMS_OUTPUT.PUT_LINE() on the screen when you run the script in SQL*Plus. After this initial command comes the PL/SQL block itself, which is divided into the DECLARE, BEGIN, and EXCEPTION blocks.

The DECLARE block contains declarations for three INTEGER variables named v_width, v_height, and v_area (I always put v_ at the start of variable names). The v_height and v_area variables are initialized to 2 and 6, respectively.

The BEGIN block contains three lines. The first line is a comment that contains the text "set the width equal to the area divided by the height." The second line sets v_width to v_area divided by v_height. This means v_width is set to 3 (= 6 / 2). The third line calls DBMS_OUTPUT .PUT_LINE() to display the value of v_width on the screen. DBMS_OUTPUT is a built-in package of code that comes with the Oracle database. Among other items, DBMS_OUTPUT contains procedures that allow you to output values to the screen.

The EXCEPTION block handles any attempts to divide a number by zero. It does this by "catching" the ZERO_DIVIDE exception. In the example, no attempt is actually made to divide by zero, but if you change v_height to 0 and run the script, you'll see the exception.

At the very end of the script, the forward slash character (/) marks the end of the PL/SQL block. The following listing shows the execution of the area_example.sql script in SQL*Plus:

```
SQL> @ C:\sql_book\SQL\area_example.sql
v_width = 3
```

NOTE
If your `area_example.sql` *script is in a different directory, then use your own directory in the previous command. Unix and Linux use forward slash characters in the directory paths.*

Variables and Types

Variables are declared within a `DECLARE` block. As you saw in the previous example, a variable declaration has both a name and a type. For example, the `v_width` variable was declared as follows:

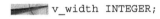
```
v_width INTEGER;
```

NOTE
The PL/SQL types are similar to the database column types. You can see all the types in the appendix.

The following example shows more variable declarations (these variables could be used to store the column values from the `products` table):

```
v_product_id       INTEGER;
v_product_type_id INTEGER;
v_name             VARCHAR2(30);
v_description      VARCHAR2(50);
v_price            NUMBER(5, 2);
```

You can also specify a variable's type using the `%TYPE` keyword, which tells PL/SQL to use the same type as a specified column in a table. The following example uses `%TYPE` to declare a variable of the same type as the `price` column of the `products` table, which is `NUMBER(5, 2)`:

```
v_product_price products.price%TYPE;
```

Conditional Logic

You use the `IF`, `THEN`, `ELSE`, `ELSIF`, and `END IF` keywords to perform conditional logic:

```
IF condition1 THEN
   statements1
ELSIF condition2 THEN
   statements2
ELSE
   statements3
END IF;
```

where

- *condition1* and *condition2* are Boolean expressions that evaluate to true or false.
- *statements1*, *statements2*, and *statements3* are PL/SQL statements.

The conditional logic flows as follows:

- If *condition1* is true, then *statements1* are executed.
- If *condition1* is false but *condition2* is true, then *statements2* are executed.
- If neither *condition1* nor *condition2* is true, then *statements3* are executed.

You can also embed an IF statement within another IF statement, as shown in the following example:

```
IF v_count > 0 THEN
  v_message := 'v_count is positive';
  IF v_area > 0 THEN
    v_message := 'v_count and v_area are positive';
  END IF
ELSIF v_count = 0 THEN
  v_message := 'v_count is zero';
ELSE
  v_message := 'v_count is negative';
END IF;
```

In this example, if v_count is greater than 0, then v_message is set to 'v_count is positive'. If v_count and v_area are greater than 0, then v_message is set to 'v_count and v_area are positive'. The rest of the logic in the example is easy to understand.

Loops

You use a loop to run statements zero or more times. There are three types of loops in PL/SQL:

- **Simple loops** run until you explicitly end the loop.
- **WHILE loops** run until a specified condition occurs.
- **FOR loops** run a predetermined number of times.

You'll learn about these loops in the following sections.

Simple Loops

A simple loop runs until you explicitly end the loop. The syntax for a simple loop is as follows:

```
LOOP
    statements
END LOOP;
```

To end the loop, you use either an EXIT or an EXIT WHEN statement. The EXIT statement ends a loop immediately. The EXIT WHEN statement ends a loop when a specified condition occurs.

The following example shows a simple loop. A variable named v_counter is initialized to 0 prior to the beginning of the loop. The loop adds 1 to v_counter and exits when v_counter is equal to 5 using an EXIT WHEN statement.

```
v_counter := 0;
LOOP
  v_counter := v_counter + 1;
  EXIT WHEN v_counter = 5;
END LOOP;
```

> **NOTE**
> *The EXIT WHEN statement can appear anywhere in the loop code.*

In Oracle Database 11g and above, you can also end the current iteration of a loop using the CONTINUE or CONTINUE WHEN statement. The CONTINUE statement ends the current iteration of the loop unconditionally and continues with the next iteration. The CONTINUE WHEN statement ends the current iteration of the loop when a specified condition occurs and then continues with the next iteration. The following example shows the use of the CONTINUE statement:

```
v_counter := 0;
LOOP
  -- after the CONTINUE statement is executed, control returns here
  v_counter := v_counter + 1;
  IF v_counter = 3 THEN
    CONTINUE; -- end current iteration unconditionally
  END IF;
  EXIT WHEN v_counter = 5;
END LOOP;
```

The next example shows the use of the CONTINUE WHEN statement:

```
v_counter := 0;
LOOP
  -- after the CONTINUE WHEN statement is executed, control returns here
  v_counter := v_counter + 1;
  CONTINUE WHEN v_counter = 3; -- end current iteration when v_counter = 3
  EXIT WHEN v_counter = 5;
END LOOP;
```

> **NOTE**
> *A CONTINUE or CONTINUE WHEN statement cannot cross a procedure, function, or method boundary.*

WHILE Loops

A WHILE loop runs until a specified condition occurs. The syntax for a WHILE loop is as follows:

```
WHILE condition LOOP
  statements
END LOOP;
```

The following example shows a WHILE loop that executes while the v_counter variable is less than 6:

```
v_counter := 0;
WHILE v_counter < 6 LOOP
  v_counter := v_counter + 1;
END LOOP;
```

FOR Loops

A FOR loop runs a predetermined number of times. You set the number of times the loop runs by specifying the *lower* and *upper bounds* for a loop variable. The loop variable is then incremented (or decremented in a reverse loop) each time around the loop. The syntax for a FOR loop is as follows:

```
FOR loop_variable IN [REVERSE] lower_bound..upper_bound LOOP
  statements
END LOOP;
```

where

- *loop_variable* is the loop variable. You can use a variable that already exists as the loop variable, or you can just have the loop create a new variable for you (this occurs if the variable you specify doesn't exist). The loop variable value is increased (or decreased if you use the REVERSE keyword) by 1 each time through the loop.

- REVERSE means that the loop variable value is to be decremented each time through the loop. The loop variable is initialized to the upper boundary, and is decremented by 1 until the loop variable reaches the lower boundary. You must specify the lower boundary before the upper boundary.

- *lower_bound* is the loop's lower boundary. The loop variable is initialized to this lower boundary if REVERSE is not used.

- *upper_bound* is the loop's upper boundary. If REVERSE is used, the loop variable is initialized to this upper boundary.

The following example shows a FOR loop. Notice that the variable v_counter2 isn't explicitly declared—so the FOR loop automatically creates a new INTEGER variable named v_counter2.

```
FOR v_counter2 IN 1..5 LOOP
  DBMS_OUTPUT.PUT_LINE(v_counter2);
END LOOP;
```

The following example uses REVERSE:

```
FOR v_counter2 IN REVERSE 1..5 LOOP
  DBMS_OUTPUT.PUT_LINE(v_counter2);
END LOOP;
```

In this example, v_counter2 starts at 5, is decremented by 1 each time through the loop, and ends at 1.

Cursors

You use a *cursor* to fetch rows returned by a query. You retrieve the rows into the cursor using a query and then fetch the rows one at a time from the cursor. You typically use the following five steps when using a cursor:

1. Declare variables to store the column values for a row.

2. Declare the cursor, which contains a query.

3. Open the cursor.

4. Fetch the rows from the cursor one at a time and store the column values in the variables declared in Step 1. Your PL/SQL code would then do something with those variables, such as display them on the screen, use them in a calculation, and so on.

5. Close the cursor.

You'll learn the details of these five steps in the following sections, and you'll see a simple example that gets the `product_id`, `name`, and `price` columns from the `products` table.

Step 1: Declare the Variables to Store the Column Values

The first step is to declare the variables that will be used to store the column values. These variables must be compatible with the column types.

TIP
Earlier you saw that `%TYPE` can be used to get the type of a column. If you use `%TYPE` when declaring your variables, your variables will automatically be of the correct type.

The following example declares three variables to store the `product_id`, `name`, and `price` columns from the `products` table. Notice that `%TYPE` is used to automatically set the type of the variables to the same type as the columns.

```
DECLARE
    v_product_id products.product_id%TYPE;
    v_name       products.name%TYPE;
    v_price      products.price%TYPE;
```

Step 2: Declare the Cursor

Step 2 is to declare the cursor. A cursor declaration consists of a name that you assign to the cursor and the query you want to execute. The cursor declaration, like all other declarations, is placed in the declaration section. The syntax for declaring a cursor is as follows:

```
CURSOR cursor_name IS
    SELECT_statement;
```

where

- *cursor_name* is the name of the cursor.
- *SELECT_statement* is the query.

The following example declares a cursor named `v_product_cursor` whose query retrieves the `product_id`, `name`, and `price` columns from the `products` table:

```
CURSOR v_product_cursor IS
  SELECT product_id, name, price
  FROM products
  ORDER BY product_id;
```

The query is executed when you open the cursor, as described next.

Step 3: Open the Cursor

Step 3 is to open the cursor. You open a cursor using the OPEN statement, which must be placed in the executable section of the block.

The following example opens `v_product_cursor`, which executes the query:

```
OPEN v_product_cursor;
```

Step 4: Fetch the Rows from the Cursor

Step 4 is to fetch the rows from the cursor, which you do using the FETCH statement. The FETCH statement reads the column values into the variables declared in Step 1. FETCH uses the following syntax:

```
FETCH cursor_name
INTO variable[, variable ...];
```

where

- *cursor_name* is the name of the cursor.
- *variable* is the variable into which a column value from the cursor is stored. You need to provide matching variables for each column value.

The following FETCH example retrieves a row from `v_product_cursor` and stores the column values in the `v_product_id`, `v_name`, and `v_price` variables created earlier in Step 1:

```
FETCH v_product_cursor
INTO v_product_id, v_name, v_price;
```

Because a cursor can contain many rows, you need a loop to read them. To determine when to end the loop, you can use the Boolean variable `v_product_cursor%NOTFOUND`. This variable is true when there are no more rows to read in `v_product_cursor`. The following example shows a loop:

```
LOOP
    -- fetch the rows from the cursor
    FETCH v_product_cursor
    INTO v_product_id, v_name, v_price;

    -- exit the loop when there are no more rows, as indicated by
    -- the Boolean variable v_product_cursor%NOTFOUND (= true when
    -- there are no more rows)
```

```
    EXIT WHEN v_product_cursor%NOTFOUND;

    -- use DBMS_OUTPUT.PUT_LINE() to display the variables
    DBMS_OUTPUT.PUT_LINE(
      'v_product_id = ' || v_product_id || ', v_name = ' || v_name ||
      ', v_price = ' || v_price
    );
  END LOOP;
```

Notice that I've used DBMS_OUTPUT.PUT_LINE() to display the v_product_id, v_name, and v_price variables that were read for each row. In a real application, you might use v_price in a complex calculation.

Step 5: Close the Cursor

Step 5 is to close the cursor using the CLOSE statement. Closing a cursor frees system resources. The following example closes v_product_cursor:

```
CLOSE v_product_cursor;
```

The following section shows a complete script that contains all five steps.

Complete Example: product_cursor.sql

The following product_cursor.sql script is contained in the SQL directory:

```
-- This script displays the product_id, name, and price columns
-- from the products table using a cursor

SET SERVEROUTPUT ON

DECLARE
  -- step 1: declare the variables
  v_product_id products.product_id%TYPE;
  v_name       products.name%TYPE;
  v_price      products.price%TYPE;

  -- step 2: declare the cursor
  CURSOR v_product_cursor IS
    SELECT product_id, name, price
    FROM products
    ORDER BY product_id;
BEGIN
  -- step 3: open the cursor
  OPEN v_product_cursor;

  LOOP
    -- step 4: fetch the rows from the cursor
    FETCH v_product_cursor
    INTO v_product_id, v_name, v_price;

    -- exit the loop when there are no more rows, as indicated by
```

```
   -- the Boolean variable v_product_cursor%NOTFOUND (= true when
   -- there are no more rows)
   EXIT WHEN v_product_cursor%NOTFOUND;

   -- use DBMS_OUTPUT.PUT_LINE() to display the variables
   DBMS_OUTPUT.PUT_LINE(
      'v_product_id = ' || v_product_id || ', v_name = ' || v_name ||
      ', v_price = ' || v_price
   );
 END LOOP;

 -- step 5: close the cursor
 CLOSE v_product_cursor;
END;
/
```

To run this script, follow these steps:

1. Connect to the database as store with the password store_password.

2. Run the product_cursor.sql script using SQL*Plus. For example:

   ```
   SQL> @ C:\sql_book\SQL\product_cursor.sql
   ```

The output from product_cursor.sql is as follows:

```
v_product_id = 1, v_name = Modern Science, v_price = 19.95
v_product_id = 2, v_name = Chemistry, v_price = 30
v_product_id = 3, v_name = Supernova, v_price = 25.99
v_product_id = 4, v_name = Tank War, v_price = 13.95
v_product_id = 5, v_name = Z Files, v_price = 49.99
v_product_id = 6, v_name = 2412: The Return, v_price = 14.95
v_product_id = 7, v_name = Space Force 9, v_price = 13.49
v_product_id = 8, v_name = From Another Planet, v_price = 12.99
v_product_id = 9, v_name = Classical Music, v_price = 10.99
v_product_id = 10, v_name = Pop 3, v_price = 15.99
v_product_id = 11, v_name = Creative Yell, v_price = 14.99
v_product_id = 12, v_name = My Front Line, v_price = 13.49
```

Cursors and FOR Loops

You can use a FOR loop to access the rows in a cursor. When you do this, you don't have to explicitly open and close the cursor—the FOR loop does this automatically for you. The following product_cursor2.sql script uses a FOR loop to access the rows in v_product_cursor:

```
-- This script displays the product_id, name, and price columns
-- from the products table using a cursor and a FOR loop

SET SERVEROUTPUT ON

DECLARE
  CURSOR v_product_cursor IS
    SELECT product_id, name, price
```

```
      FROM products
      ORDER BY product_id;
BEGIN
  FOR v_product IN v_product_cursor LOOP
    DBMS_OUTPUT.PUT_LINE(
       'product_id = ' || v_product.product_id ||
       ', name = ' || v_product.name ||
       ', price = ' || v_product.price
    );
  END LOOP;
END;
/
```

To run the `product_cursor2.sql` script, you issue a command similar to the following:

```
SQL> @ C:\sql_book\SQL\product_cursor2.sql
```

The output from this script is as follows:

```
product_id = 1, name = Modern Science, price = 19.95
product_id = 2, name = Chemistry, price = 30
product_id = 3, name = Supernova, price = 25.99
product_id = 4, name = Tank War, price = 13.95
product_id = 5, name = Z Files, price = 49.99
product_id = 6, name = 2412: The Return, price = 14.95
product_id = 7, name = Space Force 9, price = 13.49
product_id = 8, name = From Another Planet, price = 12.99
product_id = 9, name = Classical Music, price = 10.99
product_id = 10, name = Pop 3, price = 15.99
product_id = 11, name = Creative Yell, price = 14.99
product_id = 12, name = My Front Line, price = 13.49
```

OPEN-FOR Statement

You can also use the OPEN-FOR statement with a cursor, which adds even more flexibility when processing cursors because you can assign the cursor to a different query. This is shown in the following `product_cursor3.sql` script:

```
-- This script displays the product_id, name, and price columns
-- from the products table using a cursor variable and the OPEN-FOR
statement

SET SERVEROUTPUT ON

DECLARE
  -- declare a REF CURSOR type named t_product_cursor
  TYPE t_product_cursor IS
  REF CURSOR RETURN products%ROWTYPE;

  -- declare a t_product_cursor object named v_product_cursor
  v_product_cursor t_product_cursor;
```

```
  -- declare an object to store columns from the products table
  -- named v_product (of type products%ROWTYPE)
  v_product products%ROWTYPE;
BEGIN
  -- assign a query to v_product_cursor and open it using OPEN-FOR
  OPEN v_product_cursor FOR
  SELECT * FROM products WHERE product_id < 5;

  -- use a loop to fetch the rows from v_product_cursor into v_product
  LOOP
    FETCH v_product_cursor INTO v_product;
    EXIT WHEN v_product_cursor%NOTFOUND;
    DBMS_OUTPUT.PUT_LINE(
      'product_id = ' || v_product.product_id ||
      ', name = ' || v_product.name ||
      ', price = ' || v_product.price
    );
  END LOOP;

  -- close v_product_cursor
  CLOSE v_product_cursor;
END;
/
```

In the DECLARE block, the following statement declares a REF CURSOR type named t_
product_cursor (I always put t_ at the start of type names):

```
TYPE t_product_cursor IS
REF CURSOR RETURN products%ROWTYPE;
```

A REF CURSOR is a pointer to a cursor, and is similar to a pointer in the C++ programming
language. The previous statement declares a user-defined type named t_product_cursor, and
returns a row containing the various columns of the products table (this is indicated using
%ROWTYPE). This user-defined type can be used to declare an actual object, as shown in the
following statement, which declares an object named v_product_cursor:

```
v_product_cursor t_product_cursor;
```

The following statement declares an object to store columns from the products table named
v_product (of type products%ROWTYPE):

```
v_product products%ROWTYPE;
```

In the BEGIN block, v_product_cursor is assigned a query and opened by the following
OPEN-FOR statement:

```
OPEN v_product_cursor FOR
SELECT * FROM products WHERE product_id < 5;
```

After this statement is executed, v_product_cursor will be loaded with the first four rows
in the products table. The query assigned to v_product_cursor can be any valid SELECT
statement. This means you can reuse the cursor and assign another query to the cursor later in the
PL/SQL code.

Next, the following loop fetches the rows from v_product_cursor into v_product and displays the row details:

```
LOOP
  FETCH v_product_cursor INTO v_product;
  EXIT WHEN v_product_cursor%NOTFOUND;
  DBMS_OUTPUT.PUT_LINE(
    'product_id = ' || v_product.product_id ||
    ', name = ' || v_product.name ||
    ', price = ' || v_product.price
  );
END LOOP;
```

After the loop, v_product_cursor is closed using the following statement:

```
CLOSE v_product_cursor;
```

To run the product_cursor3.sql script, you issue a command similar to the following:

```
SQL> @ C:\sql_book\SQL\product_cursor3.sql
```

The output from this script is as follows:

```
product_id = 1, name = Modern Science, price = 19.95
product_id = 2, name = Chemistry, price = 30
product_id = 3, name = Supernova, price = 25.99
product_id = 4, name = Tank War, price = 13.95
```

Unconstrained Cursors

The cursors in the previous section all have a specific return type. These cursors are known as *constrained cursors*. The return type for a constrained cursor must match the columns in the query that is run by the cursor. An *unconstrained cursor* has no return type, and can therefore run any query.

The use of an unconstrained cursor is shown in the following unconstrained_cursor.sql script. Notice v_cursor in the code is used to run two different queries.

```
-- This script shows the use of unconstrained cursors

SET SERVEROUTPUT ON

DECLARE
  -- declare a REF CURSOR type named t_cursor (this has no return
  -- type and can therefore run any query)
  TYPE t_cursor IS REF CURSOR;

  -- declare a t_cursor object named v_cursor
  v_cursor t_cursor;

  -- declare an object to store columns from the products table
  -- named v_product (of type products%ROWTYPE)
  v_product products%ROWTYPE;
```

```
  -- declare an object to store columns from the customers table
  -- named v_customer (of type customers%ROWTYPE)
  v_customer customers%ROWTYPE;
BEGIN
  -- assign a query to v_cursor and open it using OPEN-FOR
  OPEN v_cursor FOR
  SELECT * FROM products WHERE product_id < 5;

  -- use a loop to fetch the rows from v_cursor into v_product
  LOOP
    FETCH v_cursor INTO v_product;
    EXIT WHEN v_cursor%NOTFOUND;
    DBMS_OUTPUT.PUT_LINE(
      'product_id = ' || v_product.product_id ||
      ', name = ' || v_product.name ||
      ', price = ' || v_product.price
    );
  END LOOP;

  -- assign a new query to v_cursor and open it using OPEN-FOR
  OPEN v_cursor FOR
  SELECT * FROM customers WHERE customer_id < 3;

  -- use a loop to fetch the rows from v_cursor into v_product
  LOOP
    FETCH v_cursor INTO v_customer;
    EXIT WHEN v_cursor%NOTFOUND;
    DBMS_OUTPUT.PUT_LINE(
      'customer_id = ' || v_customer.customer_id ||
      ', first_name = ' || v_customer.first_name ||
      ', last_name = ' || v_customer.last_name
    );
  END LOOP;

  -- close v_cursor
  CLOSE v_cursor;
END;
/
```

To run the unconstrained_cursor.sql script, you issue a command similar to the following:

```
SQL> @ C:\sql_book\SQL\unconstrained_cursor.sql
```

The output from this script is as follows:

```
product_id = 1, name = Modern Science, price = 19.95
product_id = 2, name = Chemistry, price = 30
product_id = 3, name = Supernova, price = 25.99
product_id = 4, name = Tank War, price = 13.95
customer_id = 1, first_name = John, last_name = Brown
customer_id = 2, first_name = Cynthia, last_name = Green
```

You'll learn more about REF CURSOR variables later in this chapter and more about user-defined types in the next chapter.

Exceptions

Exceptions are used to handle run-time errors in your PL/SQL code. Earlier, you saw the following PL/SQL example that contains an EXCEPTION block:

```
DECLARE
  v_width  INTEGER;
  v_height INTEGER := 2;
  v_area   INTEGER := 6;
BEGIN
  -- set the width equal to the area divided by the height
  v_width := v_area / v_height;
  DBMS_OUTPUT.PUT_LINE('v_width = ' || v_width);
EXCEPTION
  WHEN ZERO_DIVIDE THEN
    DBMS_OUTPUT.PUT_LINE('Division by zero');
END;
/
```

The EXCEPTION block in this example handles an attempt to divide a number by zero. In PL/SQL terminology, the EXCEPTION block *catches* a ZERO_DIVIDE exception that is *raised* in the BEGIN block (although in the example code, ZERO_DIVIDE is never actually raised). The ZERO_DIVIDE exception and the other common exceptions are shown in Table 12-1.

The following sections show examples that raise some of the exceptions shown in Table 12-1.

ZERO_DIVIDE Exception

The ZERO_DIVIDE exception is raised when an attempt is made to divide a number by zero. The following example attempts to divide 1 by 0 in the BEGIN block and therefore raises the ZERO_DIVIDE exception:

```
BEGIN
  DBMS_OUTPUT.PUT_LINE(1 / 0);
EXCEPTION
  WHEN ZERO_DIVIDE THEN
    DBMS_OUTPUT.PUT_LINE('Division by zero');
END;
/

Division by zero
```

When an exception is raised, program control passes to the EXCEPTION block and the WHEN clause is examined for a matching exception; the code inside the matching clause is then executed. In the previous example, the ZERO_DIVIDE exception is raised in the BEGIN block, and program control then passes to the EXCEPTION block. A matching exception is found in the WHEN clause and the code inside the clause is executed.

Exception	Error	Description
ACCESS_INTO_ NULL	ORA-06530	An attempt was made to assign values to the attributes of an uninitialized database object. (You'll learn about objects in Chapter 13.)
CASE_NOT_FOUND	ORA-06592	None of the WHEN clauses of a CASE statement was selected, and there is no default ELSE clause.
COLLECTION_IS_ NULL	ORA-06531	An attempt was made to call a collection method (other than EXISTS) on an uninitialized nested table or varray, or an attempt was made to assign values to the elements of an uninitialized nested table or varray. (You'll learn about collections in Chapter 14.)
CURSOR_ ALREADY_OPEN	ORA-06511	An attempt was made to open an already open cursor. The cursor must be closed before it can be reopened.
DUP_VAL_ON_ INDEX	ORA-00001	An attempt was made to store duplicate values in a column that is constrained by a unique index.
INVALID_CURSOR	ORA-01001	An attempt was made to perform an illegal cursor operation, such as closing an unopened cursor.
INVALID_NUMBER	ORA-01722	An attempt to convert a character string into a number failed because the string does not represent a valid number. Note: In PL/SQL statements, VALUE_ERROR is raised instead of INVALID_NUMBER.
LOGIN_DENIED	ORA-01017	An attempt was made to connect to a database using an invalid user name or password.
NO_DATA_FOUND	ORA-01403	A SELECT INTO statement returned no rows, or an attempt was made to access a deleted element in a nested table or an uninitialized element in an "index by" table.
NOT_LOGGED_ON	ORA-01012	An attempt was made to access a database item without being connected to the database.
PROGRAM_ERROR	ORA-06501	PL/SQL had an internal problem.
ROWTYPE_ MISMATCH	ORA-06504	The host cursor variable and the PL/SQL cursor variable involved in an assignment have incompatible return types. For example, when an open host cursor variable is passed to a stored procedure or function, the return types of the actual and formal parameters must be compatible.

(Continued)

TABLE 12-1. *Predefined Exceptions*

Exception	Error	Description
SELF_IS_NULL	ORA-30625	An attempt was made to call a MEMBER method on a null object. That is, the built-in parameter SELF (which is always the first parameter passed to a MEMBER method) is null.
STORAGE_ERROR	ORA-06500	The PL/SQL module ran out of memory or the memory has been corrupted.
SUBSCRIPT_ BEYOND_COUNT	ORA-06533	An attempt was made to reference a nested table or varray element using an index number larger than the number of elements in the collection.
SUBSCRIPT_ OUTSIDE_LIMIT	ORA-06532	An attempt was made to reference a nested table or varray element using an index number that is outside the legal range (–1 for example).
SYS_INVALID_ ROWID	ORA-01410	The conversion of a character string to a universal rowid failed because the character string does not represent a valid rowid.
TIMEOUT_ON_ RESOURCE	ORA-00051	A timeout occurred while the database was waiting for a resource.
TOO_MANY_ROWS	ORA-01422	A SELECT INTO statement returned more than one row.
VALUE_ERROR	ORA-06502	An arithmetic, conversion, truncation, or size-constraint error occurred.
		For example, when selecting a column value into a character variable, if the value is longer than the declared length of the variable, PL/SQL aborts the assignment and raises VALUE_ERROR.
		Note: In PL/SQL statements, VALUE_ERROR is raised if the conversion of a character string into a number fails. In SQL statements, INVALID_NUMBER is raised instead of VALUE_ERROR.
ZERO_DIVIDE	ORA-01476	An attempt was made to divide a number by zero.

TABLE 12-1. *Predefined Exceptions*

If no matching exception is found, then the exception is propagated to the enclosing block. For example, if the EXCEPTION block was omitted from the previous code, the exception is propagated up to SQL*Plus:

```
BEGIN
  DBMS_OUTPUT.PUT_LINE(1 / 0);
END;
/
BEGIN
```

```
*
ERROR at line 1:
ORA-01476: divisor is equal to zero
ORA-06512: at line 2
```

As you can see from this example, SQL*Plus displays a default error that shows the line numbers, the Oracle error codes, and a simple description.

DUP_VAL_ON_INDEX Exception

The DUP_VAL_ON_INDEX exception is raised when an attempt is made to store duplicate values in a column that is constrained by a unique index.

The following example attempts to insert a row in the customers table with a customer_id of 1. This causes DUP_VAL_ON_INDEX to be raised because the customers table already contains a row with a customer_id of 1.

```
BEGIN
   INSERT INTO customers (
     customer_id, first_name, last_name
   ) VALUES (
     1, 'Greg', 'Green'
   );
EXCEPTION
   WHEN DUP_VAL_ON_INDEX THEN
     DBMS_OUTPUT.PUT_LINE('Duplicate value on an index');
END;
/

Duplicate value on an index
```

INVALID_NUMBER Exception

The INVALID_NUMBER exception is raised when an attempt is made to convert an invalid character string into a number. The following example attempts to convert the string 123X to a number that is used in an INSERT, which causes INVALID_NUMBER to be raised because 123X is not a valid number:

```
BEGIN
   INSERT INTO customers (
     customer_id, first_name, last_name
   ) VALUES (
     '123X', 'Greg', 'Green'
   );
EXCEPTION
   WHEN INVALID_NUMBER THEN
     DBMS_OUTPUT.PUT_LINE('Conversion of string to number failed');
END;
/

Conversion of string to number failed
```

OTHERS Exception

You can use the OTHERS exception to handle all exceptions, as shown in the following example:

```
BEGIN
  DBMS_OUTPUT.PUT_LINE(1 / 0);
EXCEPTION
  WHEN OTHERS THEN
    DBMS_OUTPUT.PUT_LINE('An exception occurred');
END;
/
```

```
An exception occurred
```

Because OTHERS matches all exceptions, you must list it after any specific exceptions in your EXCEPTION block. If you attempt to list OTHERS elsewhere, the database returns the error PLS-00370. For example:

```
SQL> BEGIN
  2    DBMS_OUTPUT.PUT_LINE(1 / 0);
  3  EXCEPTION
  4    WHEN OTHERS THEN
  5      DBMS_OUTPUT.PUT_LINE('An exception occurred');
  6    WHEN ZERO_DIVIDE THEN
  7      DBMS_OUTPUT.PUT_LINE('Division by zero');
  8  END;
  9  /
  WHEN OTHERS THEN
  *
ERROR at line 4:
ORA-06550: line 4, column 3:
PLS-00370: OTHERS handler must be last among the exception handlers of a block
ORA-06550: line 0, column 0:
PL/SQL: Compilation unit analysis terminated
```

Procedures

A procedure contains a group of SQL and PL/SQL statements. Procedures allow you to centralize your business logic in the database and can be used by any program that accesses the database.

In this section, you'll learn how to perform the following tasks:

- Create a procedure
- Call a procedure
- Get information on procedures
- Drop a procedure
- View errors in a procedure

Creating a Procedure

You create a procedure using the CREATE PROCEDURE statement. The simplified syntax for the CREATE PROCEDURE statement is as follows:

```
CREATE [OR REPLACE] PROCEDURE procedure_name
[(parameter_name [IN | OUT | IN OUT] type [, ...])]
{IS | AS}
BEGIN
  procedure_body
END procedure_name;
```

where

- OR REPLACE means replace an existing procedure.

- *procedure_name* is the name of the procedure.

- *parameter_name* is the name of a parameter that is passed to the procedure. You can pass multiple parameters to a procedure.

- IN | OUT | IN OUT is the *mode* of the parameter. You can set one of the following modes for each parameter:

  - IN, which is the default mode for a parameter. An IN parameter must be set to a value when the procedure is run. The value of an IN parameter cannot be changed in the procedure body.

  - OUT, which means the parameter is set to a value in the procedure body.

  - IN OUT, which means the parameter can have a value when the procedure is run, and the value can be changed in the body.

- *type* is the type of the parameter.

- *procedure_body* contains the actual code for the procedure.

The following example creates a procedure named update_product_price(). This procedure, and the other PL/SQL code shown in the rest of this chapter, was created when you ran the store_schema.sql script. The update_product_price() procedure multiplies the price of a product by a factor; the product ID and the factor are passed as parameters to the procedure. If the product exists, the procedure multiplies the product price by the factor and commits the change.

```
CREATE PROCEDURE update_product_price(
  p_product_id IN products.product_id%TYPE,
  p_factor     IN NUMBER
) AS
  v_product_count INTEGER;
BEGIN
  -- count the number of products with the supplied product_id
  -- (the count will be 1 if the product exists)
  SELECT COUNT(*)
  INTO v_product_count
  FROM products
```

```
      WHERE product_id = p_product_id;

      -- if the product exists (v_product_count = 1) then
      -- update that product's price
      IF v_product_count = 1 THEN
        UPDATE products
        SET price = price * p_factor
        WHERE product_id = p_product_id;
        COMMIT;
      END IF;
EXCEPTION
   WHEN OTHERS THEN
      ROLLBACK;
END update_product_price;
/
```

The procedure accepts two parameters named p_product_id and p_factor (I always put p_ at the start of parameter names). Both of these parameters use the IN mode, which means that their values must be set when the procedure is run and that the parameter values cannot be changed in the procedure body.

The declaration section contains an INTEGER variable named v_product_count:

v_product_count INTEGER;

The body of the procedure starts after BEGIN. The SELECT statement in the body gets the number of rows from the products table whose product_id is equal to p_product_id:

```
SELECT COUNT(*)
INTO v_product_count
FROM products
WHERE product_id = p_product_id;
```

NOTE
COUNT(*) *returns the number of rows found.*

If the product is found, then v_product_count will be set to 1. Otherwise, v_product_count will be set to 0. If v_product_count is 1, then the price column is multiplied by p_factor using the UPDATE statement, and the change is committed:

```
IF v_product_count = 1 THEN
   UPDATE products
   SET price = price * p_factor
   WHERE product_id = p_product_id;
   COMMIT;
END IF;
```

The EXCEPTION block performs a ROLLBACK if an exception is raised:

```
EXCEPTION
   WHEN OTHERS THEN
      ROLLBACK;
```

Finally, the END keyword is used to mark the end of the procedure:

```
END update_product_price;
/
```

NOTE
*Repeating the procedure name after the END keyword is not required,
but it is good programming practice to put it in.*

Calling a Procedure

You run (or *call*) a procedure using the CALL statement. The example you'll see in this section will
multiply the price of product #1 by 1.5 using the procedure shown in the previous section. First,
the following query retrieves the price of product #1 so you can compare it with the modified price
later:

```
SELECT price
FROM products
WHERE product_id = 1;

    PRICE
----------
    19.95
```

The following statement calls update_product_price(), passing the parameter values 1
(the product_id) and 1.5 (the factor by which the product price is multiplied):

```
CALL update_product_price(1, 1.5);

Call completed.
```

This statement shows the use of *positional notation* to indicate the values to be passed to the
procedure or function. In positional notation, the position of parameters is used to assign the
values passed to the procedure. In the example, the first value in the call is 1, and this is passed to
the first parameter in the procedure (p_product_id). The second value in the call is 1.5, and
this is passed to the second parameter (p_factor).

The next query retrieves the details for product #1 again. Notice the price has been multiplied
by 1.5.

```
SELECT price
FROM products
WHERE product_id = 1;

    PRICE
----------
    29.93
```

In Oracle Database 11*g* and above, you can pass parameters using named and mixed
notation. In *named notation*, you include the name of the parameter when calling a procedure.
For example, the following statement calls update_product_price() using named notation.

Notice that the values for the p_factor and p_product_id parameters are indicated using the characters =>.

```
CALL update_product_price(p_factor => 1.3, p_product_id => 2);
```

> **TIP**
> *Named notation makes your code easier to read and maintain*
> *because the parameters are explicitly shown.*

In *mixed notation*, you use both positional and named notation. You use positional notation for the first set of parameters and named notation for the last set of parameters. Mixed notation is useful when you have procedures and functions that have both required and optional parameters. You use positional notation for the required parameters and named notation for the optional parameters. The following example uses mixed notation. Notice that positional notation comes before named notation when specifying the parameter values.

```
CALL update_product_price(3, p_factor => 1.7);
```

Getting Information on Procedures

You can get information on your procedures from the user_procedures view. Table 12-2 describes some of the columns in user_procedures.

The following example retrieves the object_name, aggregate, and parallel columns from user_procedures for update_product_price():

```
SELECT object_name, aggregate, parallel
FROM user_procedures
WHERE object_name = 'UPDATE_PRODUCT_PRICE';
```

Column	Type	Description
OBJECT_NAME	VARCHAR2(30)	The object name, which can be a procedure, function, or package name
PROCEDURE_NAME	VARCHAR2(30)	The procedure name
AGGREGATE	VARCHAR2(3)	Whether the procedure is an aggregate function (YES or NO)
IMPLTYPEOWNER	VARCHAR2(30)	The owner of the type (if any)
IMPLTYPENAME	VARCHAR2(30)	The name of the type (if any)
PARALLEL	VARCHAR2(3)	Whether the procedure is enabled for parallel queries (YES or NO)

TABLE 12-2. *Some Columns in the* user_procedures *View*

```
OBJECT_NAME                     AGG PAR
------------------------------  --- ---
UPDATE_PRODUCT_PRICE            NO  NO
```

NOTE
You can get information on all the procedures you have access to using all_procedures.

Dropping a Procedure

You drop a procedure using DROP PROCEDURE. For example, the following statement drops update_product_price():

```
DROP PROCEDURE update_product_price;
```

Viewing Errors in a Procedure

If the database reports an error when you create a procedure, you can view the error using the SHOW ERRORS command. For example, the following CREATE PROCEDURE statement attempts to create a procedure that has a syntax error at line 6 (the parameter should be p_dob, not p_dobs):

```
SQL> CREATE PROCEDURE update_customer_dob (
  2    p_customer_id INTEGER, p_dob DATE
  3  ) AS
  4  BEGIN
  5    UPDATE customers
  6    SET dob = p_dobs
  7    WHERE customer_id = p_customer_id;
  8  END update_customer_dob;
  9  /

Warning: Procedure created with compilation errors.
```

To view the error, you use SHOW ERRORS:

```
SHOW ERRORS
Errors for PROCEDURE UPDATE_CUSTOMER_DOB:

LINE/COL ERROR
-------- -----------------------------------------------
5/3      PL/SQL: SQL Statement ignored
6/13     PL/SQL: ORA-00904: "P_DOBS": invalid identifier
```

Line 5 was ignored because an invalid column name was referenced in line 6. You can fix the error by issuing an EDIT command to edit the CREATE PROCEDURE statement, changing p_dobs to p_dob, and rerunning the statement by entering the forward slash character (/).

Functions

A *function* is similar to a procedure, except that a function must return a value. Together, stored procedures and functions are sometimes referred to as *stored subprograms* because they are small programs.

In this section, you'll learn how to perform the following tasks:

- Create a function
- Call a function
- Get information on functions
- Drop a function

Creating a Function

You create a function using the CREATE FUNCTION statement. The simplified syntax for the CREATE FUNCTION statement is as follows:

```
CREATE [OR REPLACE] FUNCTION function_name
[(parameter_name [IN | OUT | IN OUT] type [, ...])]
RETURN type
{IS | AS}
BEGIN
   function_body
END function_name;
```

where

- OR REPLACE means replace an existing function.
- *function_name* is the name of the function.
- *parameter_name* is the name of a parameter that is passed to the function. You can pass multiple parameters to a function.
- IN |OUT | IN OUT is the mode of the parameter.
- *type* is the type of the parameter.
- *function_body* contains actual code for the function. Unlike a procedure, the body of a function must return a value of the type specified in the RETURN clause.

The following example creates a function named circle_area(), which returns the area of a circle as a NUMBER. The radius of the circle is passed as a parameter named p_radius to circle_area():

```
CREATE FUNCTION circle_area (
   p_radius IN NUMBER
) RETURN NUMBER AS
   v_pi    NUMBER := 3.1415926;
   v_area NUMBER;
BEGIN
   -- circle area is pi multiplied by the radius squared
   v_area := v_pi * POWER(p_radius, 2);
```

```
  RETURN v_area;
END circle_area;
/
```

The next example creates a function named `average_product_price()`, which returns the average price of products whose `product_type_id` equals the parameter value:

```
CREATE FUNCTION average_product_price (
  p_product_type_id IN INTEGER
) RETURN NUMBER AS
  v_average_product_price NUMBER;
BEGIN
  SELECT AVG(price)
  INTO v_average_product_price
  FROM products
  WHERE product_type_id = p_product_type_id;
  RETURN v_average_product_price;
END average_product_price;
/
```

Calling a Function

You call your own functions as you would call any of the built-in database functions, as was described in Chapter 4. You can call a function using a SELECT statement that uses the dual table in the FROM clause. The following example calls `circle_area()`, passing a radius of 2 meters to the function using positional notation:

```
SELECT circle_area
FROM dual;

CIRCLE_AREA(2)
--------------
    12.5663704
```

In Oracle Database 11*g* and above, you can also use named and mixed notation when calling functions. For example, the following query uses named notation when calling `circle_area()`:

```
SELECT circle_area(p_radius => 4)
FROM dual;

CIRCLE_AREA(P_RADIUS=>4)
------------------------
              50.2654816
```

The next example calls `average_product_price()`, passing the parameter value 1 to the function to get the average price of products whose `product_type_id` is 1:

```
SELECT average_product_price(1)
FROM dual;

AVERAGE_PRODUCT_PRICE(1)
------------------------
                  34.465
```

Getting Information on Functions

You can get information on your functions from the `user_procedures` view. This view was covered earlier in the section "Getting Information on Procedures." The following example retrieves the `object_name`, `aggregate`, and `parallel` columns from `user_procedures` for `circle_area()` and `average_product_price()`:

```
SELECT object_name, aggregate, parallel
FROM user_procedures
WHERE object_name IN ('CIRCLE_AREA', 'AVERAGE_PRODUCT_PRICE');

OBJECT_NAME                     AGG PAR
------------------------------- --- ---
AVERAGE_PRODUCT_PRICE           NO  NO
CIRCLE_AREA                     NO  NO
```

Dropping a Function

You drop a function using `DROP FUNCTION`. For example, the following statement drops `circle_area()`:

```
DROP FUNCTION circle_area;
```

Packages

In this section, you'll learn how to group procedures and functions together into *packages*. Packages allow you to encapsulate related functionality into one self-contained unit. By modularizing your PL/SQL code through the use of packages, you build up your own libraries of code that you and other programmers can reuse.

The Oracle database comes with a library of packages that allow you to access external files, manage the database, generate HTML, and much more. To see all the packages, you should consult the *Oracle Database PL/SQL Packages and Types Reference* manual from Oracle Corporation.

Packages are typically made up of two components: a *specification* and a *body*. The package specification lists the available procedures, functions, types, and objects. You can make the items listed in the specification available to all database users, and I refer to these items as being *public*. The specification doesn't contain the code that makes up the procedures and functions. The code is contained in the package body.

Any items in the body that are not listed in the specification are *private* to the package. Private items can be used only inside the package body. By using a combination of public and private items, you can build up a package whose complexity is hidden from the outside world. This is one of the primary goals of all programming: Hide complexity from your users.

Creating a Package Specification

You create a package specification using the `CREATE PACKAGE` statement. The simplified syntax for the `CREATE PACKAGE` statement is as follows:

```
CREATE [OR REPLACE] PACKAGE package_name
{IS | AS}
  package_specification
END package_name;
```

where

- *package_name* is the name of the package.
- *package_specification* lists the public procedures, functions, types, and objects available to your package's users.

The following example creates a specification for a package named product_package:

```
CREATE PACKAGE product_package AS
  TYPE t_ref_cursor IS REF CURSOR;
  FUNCTION get_products_ref_cursor RETURN t_ref_cursor;
  PROCEDURE update_product_price (
    p_product_id IN products.product_id%TYPE,
    p_factor     IN NUMBER
  );
END product_package;
/
```

The t_ref_cursor type is a PL/SQL REF CURSOR type. A REF CURSOR is similar to a pointer in the C++ programming language, and it points to a cursor. As you saw earlier in this chapter, a cursor allows you to read the rows returned by a query.

The get_products_ref_cursor() function returns a t_ref_cursor. As you'll see in the next section, get_products_ref_cursor() returns a cursor that contains the rows retrieved from the products table.

The update_product_price() procedure multiplies the price of a product and commits the change.

Creating a Package Body

You create a package body using the CREATE PACKAGE BODY statement. The simplified syntax for the CREATE PACKAGE BODY statement is as follows:

```
CREATE [OR REPLACE] PACKAGE BODY package_name
{IS | AS}
  package_body
END package_name;
```

where

- *package_name* is the name of the package, which must match the package name in the specification.
- *package_body* contains the code for the procedures and functions.

The following example creates the package body for product_package:

```
CREATE PACKAGE BODY product_package AS
  FUNCTION get_products_ref_cursor
  RETURN t_ref_cursor IS
    v_products_ref_cursor t_ref_cursor;
  BEGIN
    -- get the REF CURSOR
```

```
    OPEN v_products_ref_cursor FOR
      SELECT product_id, name, price
      FROM products;

    -- return the REF CURSOR
    RETURN v_products_ref_cursor;
  END get_products_ref_cursor;

  PROCEDURE update_product_price (
    p_product_id IN products.product_id%TYPE,
    p_factor      IN NUMBER
  ) AS
    v_product_count INTEGER;
  BEGIN
    -- count the number of products with the supplied product_id
    -- (count will be 1 if the product exists)
    SELECT COUNT(*)
    INTO v_product_count
    FROM products
    WHERE product_id = p_product_id;

    -- if the product exists (v_product_count = 1) then
    -- update that product's price
    IF v_product_count = 1 THEN
      UPDATE products
      SET price = price * p_factor
      WHERE product_id = p_product_id;
      COMMIT;
    END IF;
  EXCEPTION
    WHEN OTHERS THEN
      ROLLBACK;
  END update_product_price;
END product_package;
/
```

The `get_products_ref_cursor()` function opens the cursor and retrieves the `product_id`, `name`, and `price` columns from the `products` table. The reference to this cursor (the REF CURSOR) is stored in `v_products_ref_cursor` and returned by the function.

The `update_product_price()` procedure multiplies the price of a product and commits the change. This procedure is identical to the one shown earlier in the section "Creating a Procedure," so I won't go into the details on how it works again.

Calling Functions and Procedures in a Package

When calling functions and procedures in a package, you must include the package name in the call. The following example calls `product_package.get_products_ref_cursor()`, which returns a reference to a cursor containing the `product_id`, `name`, and `price` for the products:

```
SELECT product_package.get_products_ref_cursor
FROM dual;
```

```
GET_PRODUCTS_REF_CUR
--------------------
CURSOR STATEMENT : 1

CURSOR STATEMENT : 1

PRODUCT_ID NAME                                          PRICE
---------- ------------------------------------ ----------
         1 Modern Science                        29.93
         2 Chemistry                                39
         3 Supernova                             44.18
         4 Tank War                              13.95
         5 Z Files                               49.99
         6 2412: The Return                      14.95
         7 Space Force 9                         13.49
         8 From Another Planet                   12.99
         9 Classical Music                       10.99
        10 Pop 3                                 15.99
        11 Creative Yell                         14.99
        12 My Front Line                         13.49
```

The next example calls `product_package.update_product_price()` to multiply product #3's price by 1.25:

```
CALL product_package.update_product_price(3, 1.25);
```

The next query retrieves the details for product #3. Notice that the price has increased.

```
SELECT price
FROM products
WHERE product_id = 3;
```

```
    PRICE
----------
    55.23
```

Getting Information on Functions and Procedures in a Package

You can get information on your functions and procedures in a package from the `user_procedures` view. This view was covered earlier in the section "Getting Information on Procedures." The following example retrieves the `object_name` and `procedure_name` columns from `user_procedures` for `product_package`:

```
SELECT object_name, procedure_name
FROM user_procedures
WHERE object_name = 'PRODUCT_PACKAGE';
```

```
OBJECT_NAME                         PROCEDURE_NAME
----------------------------------- ------------------------------
PRODUCT_PACKAGE                     GET_PRODUCTS_REF_CURSOR
PRODUCT_PACKAGE                     UPDATE_PRODUCT_PRICE
```

Dropping a Package

You drop a package using DROP PACKAGE. For example, the following statement drops product_package:

```
DROP PACKAGE product_package;
```

Triggers

A *trigger* is a procedure that is run (or *fired*) automatically by the database when a specified DML statement (INSERT, UPDATE, or DELETE) is run against a certain database table. Triggers are useful for doing things like advanced auditing of changes made to column values in a table.

When a Trigger Fires

A trigger can fire before or after a DML statement runs. Also, because a DML statement can affect more than one row, the code for the trigger can be run once for every row affected (a *row-level trigger*), or just once for all the rows (a *statement-level trigger*).

For example, if you create a row-level trigger that fires for an UPDATE on a table, and you run an UPDATE statement that modifies ten rows of that table, then that trigger will run ten times. If, however, your trigger is a statement-level trigger, the trigger will fire once for the whole UPDATE statement, regardless of the number of rows affected.

There is another difference between a row-level trigger and a statement-level trigger: A row-level trigger has access to the old and new column values when the trigger fires as a result of an UPDATE statement on that column. The firing of a row-level trigger can also be limited using a trigger *condition*. For example, you could set a condition that limits the trigger to fire only when a column value is less than a specified value.

Setting up the Example Trigger

As mentioned, triggers are useful for doing advanced auditing of changes made to column values. In the next section, you'll see a trigger that records when a product's price is lowered by more than 25 percent. When this occurs, the trigger will add a row to the product_price_audit table. The product_price_audit table is created by the following statement in the store_schema.sql script:

```
CREATE TABLE product_price_audit (
  product_id INTEGER
    CONSTRAINT price_audit_fk_products
    REFERENCES products(product_id),
  old_price  NUMBER(5, 2),
  new_price  NUMBER(5, 2)
);
```

The product_id column of the product_price_audit table is a foreign key to the product_id column of the products table. The old_price column will be used to store the old price of a product prior to the change, and the new_price column will be used to store the new price after the change.

Creating a Trigger

You create a trigger using the CREATE TRIGGER statement. The simplified syntax for the CREATE TRIGGER statement is as follows:

```
CREATE [OR REPLACE] TRIGGER trigger_name
{BEFORE | AFTER | INSTEAD OF | FOR} trigger_event
ON table_name
[FOR EACH ROW]
[{FORWARD | REVERSE} CROSSEDITION]
[{FOLLOWS | PRECEDES} schema.other_trigger}
[{ENABLE | DISABLE}]
[WHEN trigger_condition]]
BEGIN
  trigger_body
END trigger_name;
```

where

- OR REPLACE means replace an existing trigger.

- *trigger_name* is the name of the trigger.

- BEFORE means the trigger fires before the triggering event is performed. AFTER means the trigger fires after the triggering event is performed. INSTEAD OF means the trigger fires instead of performing the triggering event. FOR, which was introduced in Oracle Database 11g, allows you to create a compound trigger consisting of up to four sections in the trigger body.

- *trigger_event* is the event that causes the trigger to fire.

- *table_name* is the table that the trigger references.

- FOR EACH ROW means the trigger is a row-level trigger; that is, the code contained within *trigger_body* is run for each row when the trigger fires. If you omit FOR EACH ROW, the trigger is a statement-level trigger, which means the code within *trigger_body* is run once when the trigger fires.

- {FORWARD | REVERSE} CROSSEDITION was introduced in Oracle Database 11g and will typically be used by database administrators or application administrators. A FORWARD CROSSEDITION trigger is intended to fire when a DML statement makes a change in the database while an online application currently accessing the database is being patched or upgraded (FORWARD is the default). The code in the trigger body must be designed to handle the DML changes when the application patching or upgrade is complete. A REVERSE CROSSEDITION trigger is similar, except it is intended to fire and handle DML changes made after the online application has been patched or upgraded.

- {FOLLOWS | PRECEDES} *schema.other_trigger* was introduced in Oracle Database 11g and specifies whether the firing of the trigger follows or precedes the firing of another trigger specified in *schema.other_trigger*. You can create a series of triggers that fire in a specific order.

- {ENABLE | DISABLE} was introduced in Oracle Database 11g and indicates whether the trigger is initially enabled or disabled when it is created (the default is ENABLE). You enable a disabled trigger by using the ALTER TRIGGER *trigger_name* ENABLE statement or by enabling all triggers for a table using ALTER TABLE *table_name* ENABLE ALL TRIGGERS.

■ *trigger_condition* is a Boolean condition that limits when a trigger actually runs its code.

■ *trigger_body* contains the code for the trigger.

The example trigger you'll see in this section fires before an update of the price column in the products table. Therefore, I've named the trigger before_product_price_update. Also, because I want to use the price column values before and after an UPDATE statement modifies the price column's value, I must use a row-level trigger. Finally, I want to audit a price change when the new price is lowered by more than 25 percent of the old price. Therefore, I specify a trigger condition to compare the new price with the old price. The following statement creates the before_product_price_update trigger:

```
CREATE TRIGGER before_product_price_update
BEFORE UPDATE OF price
ON products
FOR EACH ROW WHEN (new.price < old.price * 0.75)
BEGIN
  dbms_output.put_line('product_id = ' || :old.product_id);
  dbms_output.put_line('Old price = ' || :old.price);
  dbms_output.put_line('New price = ' || :new.price);
  dbms_output.put_line('The price reduction is more than 25%');

  -- insert row into the product_price_audit table
  INSERT INTO product_price_audit (
    product_id, old_price, new_price
  ) VALUES (
    :old.product_id, :old.price, :new.price
  );
END before_product_price_update;
/
```

Notice the following things about the example:

■ BEFORE UPDATE OF price means the trigger fires before an update of the price column.

■ FOR EACH ROW means this is a row-level trigger; that is, the trigger code contained within the BEGIN and END keywords runs once for each row modified by the update.

■ The trigger condition is (new.price < old.price * 0.75), which means the trigger fires only when the new price is less than 75 percent of the old price (that is, when the price is reduced by more than 25 percent).

■ The new and old column values are accessed using the :old and :new aliases in the trigger.

■ The trigger code displays the product_id, the old and new prices, and a message stating that the price reduction is more than 25 percent. The code then adds a row to the product_price_audit table containing the product_id and the old and new prices.

Firing a Trigger

To see the output from the trigger, you need to run the SET SERVEROUTPUT ON command:

```
SET SERVEROUTPUT ON
```

To fire the before_product_price_update trigger, you must reduce a product's price by more than 25 percent. Go ahead and perform the following UPDATE statement to reduce the price of products #5 and #10 by 30 percent (this is achieved by multiplying the price column by .7). The following UPDATE statement causes the before_product_price_update trigger to fire:

```
UPDATE products
SET price = price * .7
WHERE product_id IN (5, 10);

product_id = 5
Old price = 49.99
New price = 34.99
The price reduction is more than 25%
product_id = 10
Old price = 15.99
New price = 11.19
The price reduction is more than 25%

2 rows updated.
```

The trigger fired for products #10 and #5.

You can see that the trigger added two rows to the product_price_audit table containing the product_id values, along with the old and new prices, using the following query:

```
SELECT *
FROM product_price_audit
ORDER BY product_id;

PRODUCT_ID  OLD_PRICE  NEW_PRICE
----------  ---------- ----------
         5      49.99      34.99
        10      15.99      11.19
```

Getting Information on Triggers

You can get information on your triggers from the user_triggers view. Table 12-3 describes some of the columns in user_triggers.

The following example retrieves the details of the before_product_price_update trigger from user_triggers (the output is formatted for clarity):

```
SET LONG 1000
SET PAGESIZE 100
SET LINESIZE 100
SELECT
  trigger_name, trigger_type, triggering_event, table_owner
  base_object_type, table_name, referencing_names, when_clause, status,
```

Column	Type	Description
TRIGGER_NAME	VARCHAR2(128)	Name of the trigger.
TRIGGER_TYPE	VARCHAR2(16)	Type of the trigger.
TRIGGERING_EVENT	VARCHAR2(246)	Event that causes the trigger to fire.
TABLE_OWNER	VARCHAR2(128)	User who owns the table that the trigger references.
BASE_OBJECT_TYPE	VARCHAR2(18)	Type of the object referenced by the trigger.
TABLE_NAME	VARCHAR2(128)	Name of the table referenced by the trigger.
COLUMN_NAME	VARCHAR2(4000)	Name of the column referenced by the trigger.
REFERENCING_NAMES	VARCHAR2(422)	Name of the old and new aliases.
WHEN_CLAUSE	VARCHAR2(4000)	Trigger condition that limits when the trigger runs its code.
STATUS	VARCHAR2(8)	Whether the trigger is enabled or disabled (ENABLED or DISABLED).
DESCRIPTION	VARCHAR2(4000)	Description of the trigger.
ACTION_TYPE	VARCHAR2(11)	Action type of the trigger (CALL or PL/SQL).
TRIGGER_BODY	LONG	Code contained in the trigger body. The LONG type allows storage of large amounts of text. You'll learn about the LONG type in Chapter 15.

TABLE 12-3. *Some Columns in the user_triggers View*

```
   description, action_type, trigger_body
FROM user_triggers
WHERE trigger_name = 'BEFORE_PRODUCT_PRICE_UPDATE';

TRIGGER_NAME                        TRIGGER_TYPE
----------------------------------- ----------------
BEFORE_PRODUCT_PRICE_UPDATE         BEFORE EACH ROW

TRIGGERING_EVENT
----------------
UPDATE

TABLE_OWNER                         BASE_OBJECT_TYPE TABLE_NAME
----------------------------------- ---------------- -----------
STORE                               TABLE            PRODUCTS

REFERENCING_NAMES
-----------------------------------------------------------
```

```
REFERENCING NEW AS NEW OLD AS OLD

WHEN_CLAUSE
------------------------------------------------------------
new.price < old.price * 0.75

STATUS
--------
ENABLED

DESCRIPTION
------------------------------------------------------------
before_product_price_update
BEFORE UPDATE OF
  price
ON
  products
FOR EACH ROW

ACTION_TYPE
-----------
PL/SQL

TRIGGER_BODY
------------------------------------------------------------
BEGIN
  dbms_output.put_line('product_id = ' || :old.product_id);
  dbms_output.put_line('Old price = ' || :old.price);
  dbms_output.put_line('New price = ' || :new.price);
  dbms_output.put_line('The price reduction is more than 25%');

  -- insert row into the product_price_audit table
  INSERT INTO product_price_audit (
    product_id, old_price, new_price
  ) VALUES (
    :old.product_id, :old.price, :new.price
  );
END before_product_price_update;
```

NOTE
You can get information on all the triggers you have access to using
`all_triggers`.

Disabling and Enabling a Trigger

You can stop a trigger from firing by disabling it by using the ALTER TRIGGER statement. The following example disables the before_product_price_update trigger:

```
ALTER TRIGGER before_product_price_update DISABLE;
```

The next example enables the `before_product_price_update` trigger:

```
ALTER TRIGGER before_product_price_update ENABLE;
```

Dropping a Trigger

You drop a trigger using `DROP TRIGGER`. The following example drops the `before_product_price_update` trigger:

```
DROP TRIGGER before_product_price_update;
```

Additional PL/SQL Features

In this section, you'll learn about the following PL/SQL features:

- The `SIMPLE_INTEGER` data type, introduced in Oracle Database 11g
- Support for sequences in PL/SQL, introduced in Oracle Database 11g
- PL/SQL native machine code generation, introduced in Oracle Database 11g
- Ability to use the `WITH` clause in PL/SQL, introduced in Oracle Database 12c

SIMPLE_INTEGER Type

The `SIMPLE_INTEGER` type is a subtype of `BINARY_INTEGER`. The `SIMPLE_INTEGER` type can store the same range as `BINARY_INTEGER`, except `SIMPLE_INTEGER` cannot store a null value. The range of values `SIMPLE_INTEGER` can store is $-2,147,483,647$ to $2,147,483,647$.

Arithmetic overflow is truncated when using `SIMPLE_INTEGER` values. Therefore, calculations don't raise an error when overflow occurs. Because overflow errors are ignored, the values stored in a `SIMPLE_INTEGER` can wrap from positive to negative and from negative to positive, as, for example:

$$2^{30} + 2^{30} = 0x40000000 + 0x40000000 = 0x80000000 = -2^{31}$$

$$-2^{31} + -2^{31} = 0x80000000 + 0x80000000 = 0x00000000 = 0$$

In the first example, two positive values are added, and a negative total is produced. In the second example, two negative values are added, and zero is produced.

Because overflow is ignored and truncated when using `SIMPLE_INTEGER` values in calculations, `SIMPLE_INTEGER` offers much better performance than `BINARY_INTEGER` when a database administrator configures the database to compile PL/SQL to native machine code. Because of this benefit, you should use `SIMPLE_INTEGER` in your PL/SQL code when you don't need to store a `NULL` and you don't care about overflow truncation occurring in your calculations. Otherwise, you should use `BINARY_INTEGER`.

The following `get_area()` procedure shows the use of the `SIMPLE_INTEGER` type. The procedure calculates and displays the area of a rectangle.

```
CREATE PROCEDURE get_area
AS
   v_width  SIMPLE_INTEGER := 10;
   v_height SIMPLE_INTEGER := 2;
```

```
  v_area    SIMPLE_INTEGER := v_width * v_height;
BEGIN
  DBMS_OUTPUT.PUT_LINE('v_area = ' || v_area);
END get_area;
/
```

NOTE
You'll find this example, and the other Oracle Database 11g PL/SQL examples in this section, in a script named plsql_11g_examples. sql *in the* SQL *directory. You can run this script if you are using Oracle Database 11g or above.*

The following example shows the execution of get_area():

```
SET SERVEROUTPUT ON
CALL get_area();
v_area = 20
```

As expected, the calculated area is 20.

Sequences in PL/SQL

In the previous chapter, you saw how to create and use sequences of numbers in SQL. In Oracle Database 11g and above, you can also use sequences in PL/SQL code.

A sequence generates a series of numbers. When you create a sequence in SQL, you can specify its initial value and an increment for the series of subsequent numbers. You use the CURRVAL pseudo column to get the current value in the sequence, and use the NEXTVAL pseudo column to generate the next number. Before you access CURRVAL, you must first use NEXTVAL to generate an initial number.

The following statement creates a table named new_products:

```
CREATE TABLE new_products (
  product_id INTEGER CONSTRAINT new_products_pk PRIMARY KEY,
  name VARCHAR2(30) NOT NULL,
  price NUMBER(5, 2)
);
```

The next statement creates a sequence named s_product_id:

```
CREATE SEQUENCE s_product_id;
```

The following statement creates a procedure named add_new_products, which uses s_product_id to set the product_id column in a row added to the new_products table. Notice the use of the NEXTVAL and CURRVAL pseudo columns in the PL/SQL code (this was introduced in Oracle Database 11g).

```
CREATE PROCEDURE add_new_products
AS
  v_product_id BINARY_INTEGER;
BEGIN
  -- use NEXTVAL to generate the initial sequence number
```

```
v_product_id := s_product_id.NEXTVAL;
DBMS_OUTPUT.PUT_LINE('v_product_id = ' || v_product_id);

-- add a row to new_products
INSERT INTO new_products
VALUES (v_product_id, 'Plasma Physics book', 49.95);

DBMS_OUTPUT.PUT_LINE('s_product_id.CURRVAL = ' || s_product_id.CURRVAL);

-- use NEXTVAL to generate the next sequence number
v_product_id := s_product_id.NEXTVAL;
DBMS_OUTPUT.PUT_LINE('v_product_id = ' || v_product_id);

-- add another row to new_products
INSERT INTO new_products
VALUES (v_product_id, 'Quantum Physics book', 69.95);

DBMS_OUTPUT.PUT_LINE('s_product_id.CURRVAL = ' || s_product_id.CURRVAL);
END add_new_products;
/
```

The following example runs `add_new_products()` and shows the contents of the new_ products table:

```
SET SERVEROUTPUT ON
CALL add_new_products();
v_product_id = 1
s_product_id.CURRVAL = 1
v_product_id = 2
s_product_id.CURRVAL = 2

SELECT * FROM new_products;
PRODUCT_ID NAME                                    PRICE
---------- ------------------------------- ----------
         1 Plasma Physics book                     49.95
         2 Quantum Physics book                    69.95
```

As expected, two rows were added to the table.

PL/SQL Native Machine Code Generation

By default, each PL/SQL program unit is compiled into intermediate-form, machine-readable code. This machine-readable code is stored in the database and interpreted every time the code is run.

With PL/SQL native compilation, the PL/SQL is turned into native code and stored in shared libraries. Native code runs much faster than intermediate code because native code doesn't have to be interpreted before it runs.

In certain versions of the database prior to Oracle Database 11*g*, you can compile PL/SQL code to C code, and then compile the C code into machine code; this is a very laborious and problematic process. In Oracle Database 11*g* and above, the PL/SQL complier can generate native machine code directly.

Setting up the database to generate native machine code should be done only by an experienced database administrator. Because of that, its coverage is beyond the scope of this book. You can read about PL/SQL native machine code generation in the *PL/SQL User's Guide and Reference* manual from Oracle Corporation.

WITH Clause

New for Oracle Database 12c is the ability to use the WITH clause in PL/SQL. The WITH clause enables you to define an embedded PL/SQL function that you can then reference in a query.

The following example calculates the area of a circle:

```
SET SERVEROUTPUT ON
WITH
  FUNCTION circle_area(p_radius NUMBER) RETURN NUMBER IS
    v_pi    NUMBER := 3.1415926;
    v_area NUMBER;
  BEGIN
    v_area := v_pi * POWER(p_radius, 2);
    RETURN v_area;
  END;
SELECT circle_area(3) FROM dual
/

CIRCLE_AREA(3)
--------------
    28.2743334
```

The next example calculates the average product price:

```
WITH
  FUNCTION average_product_price (
    p_product_type_id IN INTEGER
  ) RETURN NUMBER AS
    v_average_product_price NUMBER;
  BEGIN
    SELECT AVG(price)
    INTO v_average_product_price
    FROM products
    WHERE product_type_id = p_product_type_id;
    RETURN v_average_product_price;
  END;
SELECT average_product_price(1) FROM dual
/

AVERAGE_PRODUCT_PRICE(1)
------------------------
                  24.975
```

Because the SELECT in the example passes a parameter value of 1 for the product type to average_product_price(), and the parameter value 1 represents books, the example returns the average product price for books.

Summary

In this chapter, you learned the following:

- PL/SQL programs are divided up into blocks containing PL/SQL and SQL statements.
- A loop, such as a WHILE or FOR loop, runs statements multiple times.
- A cursor allows PL/SQL to read the rows returned by a query.
- Exceptions are used to handle run-time errors that occur in your PL/SQL code.
- A procedure contains a group of statements. Procedures allow you to centralize your business logic in the database and can be run by any program that accesses the database.
- A function is similar to a procedure except that a function must return a value.
- You can group procedures and functions together into packages, which encapsulate related functionality into one self-contained unit.
- A trigger is a procedure that is run automatically by the database when a specific INSERT, UPDATE, or DELETE statement is run.

In the next chapter, you'll learn about database objects.

CHAPTER
13

Database Objects

I n this chapter, you will learn how to perform the following tasks:

- Create object types containing attributes and methods
- Use object types to define column objects and object tables
- Manipulate objects in SQL and PL/SQL
- Create a hierarchy of types
- Define constructors to set the attributes of an object
- Override a method in one type with a method from another type

Introducing Objects

Object-oriented programming languages such as Java, C++, and C# allow you to define classes, and these classes act as templates from which you can create objects. Classes define attributes and methods. Attributes are used to store an object's state, and methods are used to model an object's behaviors.

With the release of Oracle Database 8, objects became available within the database, and object features have been improved upon in subsequent product releases. The availability of objects in the database was a major breakthrough because they enable you to define your own classes, known as *object types*. Like classes in Java and C#, database object types can contain attributes and methods. Object types are also sometimes known as user-defined types.

A simple example of an object type is a type that represents a product. This object type could contain attributes for the product's name, description, price, and, in the case of a product that is perishable, the number of days the product can sit on the shelf before it must be thrown away. This product object type could also contain a method that returns the sell-by date of the product, based on the shelf life of the product and the current date.

Another example of an object type is one that represents a person. This object type could store attributes for the person's first name, last name, date of birth, and address. The person's address could itself be represented by an object type, and it could store things like the street, city, state, and ZIP code.

In this chapter you'll see examples of object types that represent a product, person, and address. You'll also see how to create tables from those object types, populate those tables with actual objects, and manipulate those objects in SQL and PL/SQL.

Running the Script to Create the Object Schema

I've provided in the SQL directory a script named `object_schema.sql`, which creates a user named `object_user` with a password of `object_password`. This script also creates the types and tables, performs the various INSERT statements, and creates the PL/SQL code shown in the first part of this chapter.

You perform the following steps to create the schema:

1. Start SQL*Plus.
2. Log into the database as a user with privileges to create new users, tables, and PL/SQL packages. I run scripts in my database using the system user.
3. Run the object_schema.sql script from within SQL*Plus using the @ command.

For example, if you're using Windows and the script is stored in C:\sql_book\SQL, then you enter the following command:

```
@ C:\sql_book\SQL\object_schema.sql
```

When the script completes, you will be logged in as object_user.

Creating Object Types

You create an object type using the CREATE TYPE statement. The following example uses the CREATE TYPE statement to create an object type named t_address. This object type is used to represent an address and contains four attributes named street, city, state, and zip:

```
CREATE TYPE t_address AS OBJECT (
   street VARCHAR2(15),
   city   VARCHAR2(15),
   state  CHAR(2),
   zip    VARCHAR2(5)
);
/
```

The example shows that each attribute is defined using a database type. For example, street is defined as VARCHAR2(15). As you'll see shortly, the type of an attribute can itself be an object type.

The next example creates an object type named t_person. Notice that t_person has an attribute named address, which is of type t_address.

```
CREATE TYPE t_person AS OBJECT (
   id          INTEGER,
   first_name  VARCHAR2(10),
   last_name   VARCHAR2(10),
   dob         DATE,
   phone       VARCHAR2(12),
   address     t_address
);
/
```

The following example creates an object type named t_product that will be used to represent products. Notice that this type declares a function named get_sell_by_date() using the MEMBER FUNCTION clause.

```
CREATE TYPE t_product AS OBJECT (
   id          INTEGER,
   name        VARCHAR2(15),
```

```
  description VARCHAR2(22),
  price       NUMBER(5, 2),
  days_valid  INTEGER,

  -- get_sell_by_date() returns the date by which the
  -- product must be sold
  MEMBER FUNCTION get_sell_by_date RETURN DATE
);
/
```

Because t_product contains a method declaration, a *body* for t_product must also be created. The body contains the actual code for the method, and the body is created using the CREATE TYPE BODY statement. The following example creates the body for t_product. Notice the body contains the code for the get_sell_by_date() function.

```
CREATE TYPE BODY t_product AS
    -- get_sell_by_date() returns the date by which the
    -- product must be sold
    MEMBER FUNCTION get_sell_by_date RETURN DATE IS
      v_sell_by_date DATE;
    BEGIN
      -- calculate the sell by date by adding the days_valid attribute
      -- to the current date (SYSDATE)
      SELECT days_valid + SYSDATE
      INTO v_sell_by_date
      FROM dual;

      -- return the sell by date
      RETURN v_sell_by_date;
    END;
END;
/
```

The get_sell_by_date() function returns the date by which the product must be sold. The function adds the days_valid attribute to the current date returned by the SYSDATE function.

You can also create a public synonym for a type, which enables all users to see the type and use it to define columns in their own tables. The following example creates a public synonym named t_pub_product for t_product:

```
CREATE PUBLIC SYNONYM t_pub_product FOR t_product;
```

Using DESCRIBE to Get Information on Object Types

You can use the DESCRIBE command to get information on an object type. The following examples show the t_address, t_person, and t_product types:

```
DESCRIBE t_address
 Name                                      Null?    Type
 ----------------------------------------- -------- ------------
 STREET                                             VARCHAR2(15)
 CITY                                               VARCHAR2(15)
```

```
   STATE                                        CHAR(2)
   ZIP                                          VARCHAR2(5)
```

DESCRIBE t_person

```
Name                                   Null?    Type
----------------------------------     -------- -----------
   ID                                            NUMBER(38)
   FIRST_NAME                                    VARCHAR2(10)
   LAST_NAME                                     VARCHAR2(10)
   DOB                                           DATE
   PHONE                                         VARCHAR2(12)
   ADDRESS                                       T_ADDRESS
```

DESCRIBE t_product

```
Name                                   Null?    Type
----------------------------------     -------- -----------
   ID                                            NUMBER(38)
   NAME                                          VARCHAR2(10)
   DESCRIPTION                                   VARCHAR2(22)
   PRICE                                         NUMBER(5,2)
   DAYS_VALID                                    INTEGER

METHOD
------
   MEMBER FUNCTION GET_SELL_BY_DATE RETURNS DATE
```

You can set the depth to which DESCRIBE will show information for embedded types using SET DESCRIBE DEPTH. The following example sets the depth to 2 and then describes t_person again. Notice that the attributes of address are displayed, which is an embedded object of type t_address.

SET DESCRIBE DEPTH 2
DESCRIBE t_person

```
Name                                   Null?    Type
----------------------------------     -------- -----------
   ID                                            NUMBER(38)
   FIRST_NAME                                    VARCHAR2(10)
   LAST_NAME                                     VARCHAR2(10)
   DOB                                           DATE
   PHONE                                         VARCHAR2(12)
   ADDRESS                                       T_ADDRESS
      STREET                                     VARCHAR2(15)
      CITY                                       VARCHAR2(15)
      STATE                                      CHAR(2)
      ZIP                                        VARCHAR2(5)
```

Using Object Types in Database Tables

Now that you've seen how to create object types, let's look at how you use these types in database tables. You can use an object type to define an individual column in a table, and the objects subsequently stored in that column are known as *column objects*. You can also use an object type to define an entire row in a table. The table is then known as an *object table*. Each object in an object table has a unique *object identifier* (OID), which represents the object's location in the database. You can use an *object reference* to access an individual row in an object table. An object reference is similar to a pointer in C++. You'll see examples of column objects, object tables, object identifiers, and object references in this section.

Column Objects

The following example creates a table named `products` that contains a column named `product` of type `t_product`. The table also contains a column named `quantity_in_stock`, which is used to store the number of those products currently in stock.

```
CREATE TABLE products (
  product            t_product,
  quantity_in_stock INTEGER
);
```

When adding a row to this table, you must use a *constructor* to supply the attribute values for the new `t_product` object. As a reminder, the `t_product` type was created using the following statement:

```
CREATE TYPE t_product AS OBJECT (
  id          INTEGER,
  name        VARCHAR2(10),
  description VARCHAR2(22),
  price       NUMBER(5, 2),
  days_valid  INTEGER,

  -- declare the get_sell_by_date() member function,
  -- get_sell_by_date() returns the date by which the
  -- product must be sold
  MEMBER FUNCTION get_sell_by_date RETURN DATE
);
/
```

A constructor is a built-in method for the object type, and it has the same name as the object type. The constructor accepts parameters that are used to set the attributes of the new object. The constructor for the `t_product` type is named `t_product` and accepts five parameters, one to set each of the attributes. For example, `t_product(1, 'pasta', '20 oz bag of pasta', 3.95, 10)` creates a new `t_product` object and sets the object attributes as follows:

- `id` to 1
- `name` to `pasta`
- `description` to `20 oz bag of pasta`
- `price` to `3.95`
- `days_valid` to `10`

The following INSERT statements add two rows to the products table. Notice the use of the t_product constructor to supply the attribute values for the product column objects.

```
INSERT INTO products (
  product,
  quantity_in_stock
) VALUES (
  t_product(1, 'pasta', '20 oz bag of pasta', 3.95, 10),
  50
);

INSERT INTO products (
  product,
  quantity_in_stock
) VALUES (
  t_product(2, 'sardines', '12 oz box of sardines', 2.99, 5),
  25
);
```

The following query retrieves the rows from the products table. Notice that the product column objects' attributes are displayed within a constructor for t_product.

```
SELECT *
FROM products;

PRODUCT(ID, NAME, DESCRIPTION, PRICE, DAYS_VALID)
-----------------------------------------------------------
QUANTITY_IN_STOCK
-----------------
T_PRODUCT(1, 'pasta', '20 oz bag of pasta', 3.95, 10)
              50

T_PRODUCT(2, 'sardines', '12 oz box of sardines', 2.99, 5)
              25
```

You can also retrieve an individual column object from a table. To do this, you must supply a table alias through which you select the object. The following query retrieves product #1 from the products table. Notice the use of the table alias p for the products table, through which the product object's id attribute is specified in the WHERE clause.

```
SELECT p.product
FROM products p
WHERE p.product.id = 1;

PRODUCT(ID, NAME, DESCRIPTION, PRICE, DAYS_VALID)
---------------------------------------------------------
T_PRODUCT(1, 'pasta', '20 oz bag of pasta', 3.95, 10)
```

The next query explicitly includes the `product` object's `id`, `name`, `price`, and `days_valid` attributes in the `SELECT` statement, plus the `quantity_in_stock`:

```
SELECT p.product.id, p.product.name,
 p.product.price, p.product.days_valid, p.quantity_in_stock
FROM products p
WHERE p.product.id = 1;
```

```
PRODUCT.ID PRODUCT.NA PRODUCT.PRICE PRODUCT.DAYS_VALID QUANTITY_IN_STOCK
---------- ---------- ------------- ------------------ -----------------
         1 pasta               3.95                 10                50
```

The `t_product` object type contains a function named `get_sell_by_date()`, which calculates and returns the date by which the product must be sold. The function does this by adding the `days_valid` attribute to the current date, which is obtained from the database using the `SYSDATE` function. You can call the `get_sell_by_date()` function using a table alias, as shown in the following query that uses the table alias `p` for the `products` table:

```
SELECT p.product.get_sell_by_date()
FROM products p;
```

```
P.PRODUCT
---------
19-JUN-12
13-JUN-12
```

If you run this query, your dates will be different. This is because the date calculation uses `SYSDATE`, which returns the current date and time.

The following `UPDATE` statement modifies the description of product #1. Notice that the table alias `p` is used again.

```
UPDATE products p
SET p.product.description = '30 oz bag of pasta'
WHERE p.product.id = 1;
```

```
1 row updated.
```

The following `DELETE` statement removes product #2:

```
DELETE FROM products p
WHERE p.product.id = 2;
```

```
1 row deleted.
```

```
ROLLBACK;
```

NOTE
If you run these UPDATE *and* DELETE *statements, make sure you execute the* ROLLBACK *so that your example data matches that shown in the rest of this chapter.*

Object Tables

You can use an object type to define an entire table, and such a table is known as an object table. The following example creates an object table named `object_products`, which stores objects of type `t_product`. Notice the use of the `OF` keyword to identify the table as an object table of type `t_product`.

```
CREATE TABLE object_products OF t_product;
```

When inserting a row into an object table, you can choose whether to use a constructor to supply attribute values or to supply the values in the same way that you would supply column values in a relational table. The following `INSERT` statement adds a row to the `object_products` table using the constructor for `t_product`:

```
INSERT INTO object_products VALUES (
    t_product(1, 'pasta', '20 oz bag of pasta', 3.95, 10)
);
```

The next `INSERT` statement omits the constructor for `t_product`. Notice that the attribute values for `t_product` are supplied in the same way that columns would be in a relational table.

```
INSERT INTO object_products (
    id, name, description, price, days_valid
) VALUES (
    2, 'sardines', '12 oz box of sardines', 2.99, 5
);
```

The following query retrieves the rows from the `object_products` table:

```
SELECT *
FROM object_products;
```

ID	NAME	DESCRIPTION	PRICE	DAYS_VALID
1	pasta	20 oz bag of pasta	3.95	10
2	sardines	12 oz box of sardines	2.99	5

You can also specify individual object attributes in a query. For example:

```
SELECT id, name, price
FROM object_products op
WHERE id = 1;
```

ID	NAME	PRICE
1	pasta	3.95

Here's another example:

```
SELECT op.id, op.name, op.price
FROM object_products op
WHERE op.id = 1;
```

```
    ID NAME           PRICE
---------- ---------- ----------
         1 pasta        3.95
```

The VALUE() function selects a row from an object table. VALUE() treats the row as an actual object and returns the attributes for the object within a constructor for the object type. VALUE() accepts a parameter containing a table alias, as shown in the following query:

```
SELECT VALUE(op)
FROM object_products op;

VALUE(OP)(ID, NAME, DESCRIPTION, PRICE, DAYS_VALID)
-----------------------------------------------------------
T_PRODUCT(1, 'pasta', '20 oz bag of pasta', 3.95, 10)
T_PRODUCT(2, 'sardines', '12 oz box of sardines', 2.99, 5)
```

You can also add an object attribute after VALUE():

```
SELECT VALUE(op).id, VALUE(op).name, VALUE(op).price
FROM object_products op;

VALUE(OP).ID VALUE(OP). VALUE(OP).PRICE
------------ ---------- ---------------
           1 pasta          3.95
           2 sardines       2.99
```

The following UPDATE statement modifies the description of product #1:

```
UPDATE object_products
SET description = '25 oz bag of pasta'
WHERE id = 1;

1 row updated.
```

The following DELETE statement removes product #2:

```
DELETE FROM object_products
WHERE id = 2;

1 row deleted.
```

```
ROLLBACK;
```

Let's take a look at a more complex object table. The following CREATE TABLE statement creates an object table named object_customers, which stores objects of type t_person:

```
CREATE TABLE object_customers OF t_person;
```

The t_person type contains an embedded t_address object. The t_person type was created using the following statement:

```
CREATE TYPE t_person AS OBJECT (
    id          INTEGER,
```

```
    first_name VARCHAR2(10),
    last_name  VARCHAR2(10),
    dob        DATE,
    phone      VARCHAR2(12),
    address    t_address
);
/
```

The following INSERT statements add two rows into object_customers. The first INSERT uses constructors for t_person and t_address, and the second INSERT omits the t_person constructor:

```
INSERT INTO object_customers VALUES (
    t_person(1, 'John', 'Brown', '01-FEB-1955', '800-555-1211',
      t_address('2 State Street', 'Beantown', 'MA', '12345')
    )
);

INSERT INTO object_customers (
  id, first_name, last_name, dob, phone,
  address
) VALUES (
  2, 'Cynthia', 'Green', '05-FEB-1968', '800-555-1212',
  t_address('3 Free Street', 'Middle Town', 'CA', '12345')
);
```

The following query retrieves these rows from the object_customers table. Notice that the attributes for the embedded address column object are displayed within the t_address constructor.

```
SELECT *
FROM object_customers;

        ID FIRST_NAME LAST_NAME  DOB        PHONE
---------- ---------- ---------- --------- ------------
ADDRESS(STREET, CITY, STATE, ZIP)
--------------------------------------------------------
         1 John       Brown      01-FEB-55 800-555-1211
T_ADDRESS('2 State Street', 'Beantown', 'MA', '12345')

         2 Cynthia    Green      05-FEB-68 800-555-1212
T_ADDRESS('3 Free Street', 'Middle Town', 'CA', '12345')
```

The next query retrieves customer #1 from object_customers. Notice the use of the table alias oc through which the id attribute is specified in the WHERE clause.

```
SELECT *
FROM object_customers oc
WHERE oc.id = 1;
```

```
        ID FIRST_NAME LAST_NAME  DOB        PHONE
---------- ---------- ---------- --------- ------------
ADDRESS(STREET, CITY, STATE, ZIP)
------------------------------------------------------
         1 John       Brown      01-FEB-55 800-555-1211
T_ADDRESS('2 State Street', 'Beantown', 'MA', '12345')
```

In the following query, a customer is retrieved based on the state attribute of the address column object:

```
SELECT *
FROM object_customers oc
WHERE oc.address.state = 'MA';
```

```
        ID FIRST_NAME LAST_NAME  DOB        PHONE
---------- ---------- ---------- --------- ------------
ADDRESS(STREET, CITY, STATE, ZIP)
------------------------------------------------------
         1 John       Brown      01-FEB-55 800-555-1211
T_ADDRESS('2 State Street', 'Beantown', 'MA', '12345')
```

In the next query, the id, first_name, and last_name attributes of customer #1 are explicitly included in the SELECT statement, along with the attributes of the embedded address column object:

```
SELECT
   oc.id, oc.first_name, oc.last_name,
   oc.address.street, oc.address.city, oc.address.state, oc.address.zip
FROM object_customers oc
WHERE oc.id = 1;
```

```
        ID FIRST_NAME LAST_NAME  ADDRESS.STREET  ADDRESS.CITY    AD ADDRE
---------- ---------- ---------- --------------- --------------- -- -----
         1 John       Brown      2 State Street  Beantown        MA 12345
```

Object Identifiers and Object References

Each object in an object table has a unique *object identifier* (OID), and you can retrieve the OID for an object using the REF() function. For example, the following query retrieves the OID for customer #1 in the object_customers table:

```
SELECT REF(oc)
FROM object_customers oc
WHERE oc.id = 1;
```

```
REF(OC)
-------------------------------------------------------------------
0000280209D66AB93F991647649D78D08B267EE44858C7B9989D9D40689FB4DA92820
AFFE2010003280000
```

The long string of numbers and letters is the OID, which identifies the location of the object in the database. You can store an OID in an object reference and later access the object it refers to.

An object reference, which is similar to a pointer in C++, points to an object stored in an object table using the OID. You can use object references to model relationships between object tables, and, as you'll see later, you can use object references in PL/SQL to access objects.

You use the REF type to define an object reference. The following statement creates a table named purchases that contains two object reference columns named customer_ref and product_ref:

```
CREATE TABLE purchases (
  id              INTEGER PRIMARY KEY,
  customer_ref REF t_person  SCOPE IS object_customers,
  product_ref  REF t_product SCOPE IS object_products
);
```

The SCOPE IS clause restricts an object reference to point to objects in a specific table. For example, the customer_ref column is restricted to point to objects in the object_customers table only. Similarly, the product_ref column is restricted to point to objects in the object_ products table only.

As I mentioned earlier, each object has an OID that you can retrieve using the REF() function. For example, the following INSERT statement adds a row to the purchases table. Notice that the REF() function is used in the queries to get the OIDs for customer #1 and product #1 from the object_customers and object_products tables.

```
INSERT INTO purchases (
  id,
  customer_ref,
  product_ref
) VALUES (
  1,
  (SELECT REF(oc) FROM object_customers oc WHERE oc.id = 1),
  (SELECT REF(op) FROM object_products  op WHERE op.id = 1)
);
```

This example records that customer #1 purchased product #1.

The following query selects the row from the purchases table. Notice that the customer_ ref and product_ref columns contain references to the objects in the object_customers and object_products tables.

```
SELECT *
FROM purchases;

        ID
----------
CUSTOMER_REF
----------------------------------------------------------------
PRODUCT_REF
----------------------------------------------------------------
         1
0000220208D66AB93F991647649D78D08B267EE44858C7B9989D9D40689FB4DA92820
AFFE2
0000220208662E2AB4256711D6A1B50010A4E7AE8A662E2AB2256711D6A1B50010A4E
7AE8A
```

You can retrieve the actual objects stored in an object reference using the DEREF() function, which accepts an object reference as a parameter and returns the actual object. For example, the following query uses DEREF() to retrieve customer #1 and product #1 through the customer_ref and product_ref columns of the purchases table:

```
SELECT DEREF(customer_ref), DEREF(product_ref)
FROM purchases;

DEREF(CUSTOMER_REF)(ID, FIRST_NAME, LAST_NAME, DOB, PHONE,
 ADDRESS(STREET, CITY,
-----------------------------------------------------------
DEREF(PRODUCT_REF)(ID, NAME, DESCRIPTION, PRICE, DAYS_VALID)
-----------------------------------------------------------
T_PERSON(1, 'John', 'Brown', '01-FEB-55', '800-555-1211',
 T_ADDRESS('2 State Street', 'Beantown', 'MA', '12345'))
T_PRODUCT(1, 'pasta', '20 oz bag of pasta', 3.95, 10)
```

The next query retrieves the customer's first_name and address.street attributes, plus the product's name attribute:

```
SELECT DEREF(customer_ref).first_name,
 DEREF(customer_ref).address.street, DEREF(product_ref).name
FROM purchases;

DEREF(CUST DEREF(CUSTOMER_ DEREF(PROD
---------- --------------- ----------
John       2 State Street  pasta
```

The following UPDATE statement modifies the product_ref column to point to product #2:

```
UPDATE purchases SET product_ref = (
  SELECT REF(op) FROM object_products op WHERE op.id = 2
) WHERE id = 1;

1 row updated.
```

The following query verifies the modification made by the UPDATE:

```
SELECT DEREF(customer_ref), DEREF(product_ref)
FROM purchases;

DEREF(CUSTOMER_REF)(ID, FIRST_NAME, LAST_NAME, DOB, PHONE,
 ADDRESS(STREET, CITY,
-----------------------------------------------------------
DEREF(PRODUCT_REF)(ID, NAME, DESCRIPTION, PRICE, DAYS_VALID)
-----------------------------------------------------------
T_PERSON(1, 'John', 'Brown', '01-FEB-55', '800-555-1211',
 T_ADDRESS('2 State Street', 'Beantown', 'MA', '12345'))
T_PRODUCT(2, 'sardines', '12 oz box of sardines', 2.99, 5)
```

Comparing Object Values

You can compare the value of two objects in a WHERE clause of a query using the equality operator =. For example, the following query retrieves customer #1 from the object_customers table:

```
SELECT oc.id, oc.first_name, oc.last_name, oc.dob
FROM object_customers oc
WHERE VALUE(oc) =
  t_person(1, 'John', 'Brown', '01-FEB-1955', '800-555-1211',
    t_address('2 State Street', 'Beantown', 'MA', '12345')
  );

        ID FIRST_NAME LAST_NAME  DOB
---------- ---------- ---------- ---------
         1 John       Brown      01-FEB-55
```

The next query retrieves product #1 from the object_products table:

```
SELECT op.id, op.name, op.price, op.days_valid
FROM object_products op
WHERE VALUE(op) = t_product(1, 'pasta', '20 oz bag of pasta', 3.95, 10);

        ID NAME            PRICE DAYS_VALID
---------- ---------- ---------- ----------
         1 pasta           3.95         10
```

You can also use the not equal <> and IN operators in the WHERE clause:

```
SELECT oc.id, oc.first_name, oc.last_name, oc.dob
FROM object_customers oc
WHERE VALUE(oc) <>
  t_person(1, 'John', 'Brown', '01-FEB-1955', '800-555-1211',
    t_address('2 State Street', 'Beantown', 'MA', '12345')
  );

        ID FIRST_NAME LAST_NAME  DOB
---------- ---------- ---------- ---------
         2 Cynthia    Green      05-FEB-68

SELECT op.id, op.name, op.price, op.days_valid
FROM object_products op
WHERE VALUE(op) IN t_product(1, 'pasta', '20 oz bag of pasta', 3.95, 10);

        ID NAME            PRICE DAYS_VALID
---------- ---------- ---------- ----------
         1 pasta           3.95         10
```

If you want to use an operator such as <, >, <=, >=, LIKE, or BETWEEN, you need to provide a map function for the type. A map function must return a single value of one of the built-in types that the database can then use to compare two objects. The value returned by the map function will be different for every object type, and you need to figure out which attribute, or concatenation of attributes, represents an object's value. For example, with the t_product type, I'd return the price attribute; with the t_person type, I'd return a concatenation of the last_name and first_name attributes.

The following statements create a type named t_person2 that contains a map function named get_string(). Notice that get_string() returns a VARCHAR2 string containing a concatenation of the last_name and first_name attributes.

```
CREATE TYPE t_person2 AS OBJECT (
    id          INTEGER,
    first_name  VARCHAR2(10),
    last_name   VARCHAR2(10),
    dob         DATE,
    phone       VARCHAR2(12),
    address     t_address,

    -- declare the get_string() map function,
    -- which returns a VARCHAR2 string
    MAP MEMBER FUNCTION get_string RETURN VARCHAR2
);
/

CREATE TYPE BODY t_person2 AS
    -- define the get_string() map function
    MAP MEMBER FUNCTION get_string RETURN VARCHAR2 IS
    BEGIN
        -- return a concatenated string containing the
        -- last_name and first_name attributes
        RETURN last_name || ' ' || first_name;
    END get_string;
END;
/
```

As you'll see shortly, the database will automatically call get_string() when comparing t_person2 objects.

The following statements create a table named object_customers2 and add rows to it:

```
CREATE TABLE object_customers2 OF t_person2;

INSERT INTO object_customers2 VALUES (
    t_person2(1, 'John', 'Brown', '01-FEB-1955', '800-555-1211',
        t_address('2 State Street', 'Beantown', 'MA', '12345')
    )
);

INSERT INTO object_customers2 VALUES (
    t_person2(2, 'Cynthia', 'Green', '05-FEB-1968', '800-555-1212',
        t_address('3 Free Street', 'Middle Town', 'CA', '12345')
    )
);
```

The following query uses > in the WHERE clause:

```
SELECT oc2.id, oc2.first_name, oc2.last_name, oc2.dob
FROM object_customers2 oc2
WHERE VALUE(oc2) >
  t_person2(1, 'John', 'Brown', '01-FEB-1955', '800-555-1211',
    t_address('2 State Street', 'Beantown', 'MA', '12345')
  );


        ID FIRST_NAME LAST_NAME  DOB
---------- ---------- ---------- ---------
         2 Cynthia    Green      05-FEB-68
```

When the query is executed, the database automatically calls get_string() to compare the objects in the object_customers2 table to the object after the > in the WHERE clause. The get_string() function returns a concatenation of the last_name and first_name attributes of the objects, and because Green Cynthia is greater than Brown John, she is returned by the query.

Using Objects in PL/SQL

You can create and manipulate objects in PL/SQL. In this section, you'll see the use of a package named product_package, which is created when you run the object_schema.sql script. The following methods are contained in product_package:

- A function named get_products() that returns a REF CURSOR that points to the objects in the object_products table

- A procedure named display_product() that displays the attributes of a single object in the object_products table

- A procedure named insert_product() that adds an object to the object_products table

- A procedure named update_product_price() that updates the price attribute of an object in the object_products table

- A function named get_product() that returns a single object from the object_products table

- A procedure named update_product() that updates all the attributes of an object in the object_products table

- A function named get_product_ref() that returns a reference to a single object from the object_products table

- A procedure named delete_product() that deletes a single object from the object_products table

The object_schema.sql script contains the following package specification:

```
CREATE PACKAGE product_package AS
  TYPE t_ref_cursor IS REF CURSOR;
  FUNCTION get_products RETURN t_ref_cursor;
```

```
PROCEDURE display_product(
  p_id IN object_products.id%TYPE
);
PROCEDURE insert_product(
  p_id          IN object_products.id%TYPE,
  p_name        IN object_products.name%TYPE,
  p_description IN object_products.description%TYPE,
  p_price       IN object_products.price%TYPE,
  p_days_valid  IN object_products.days_valid%TYPE
);
PROCEDURE update_product_price(
  p_id     IN object_products.id%TYPE,
  p_factor IN NUMBER
);
FUNCTION get_product(
  p_id IN object_products.id%TYPE
) RETURN t_product;
PROCEDURE update_product(
  p_product t_product
);
FUNCTION get_product_ref(
  p_id IN object_products.id%TYPE
) RETURN REF t_product;
PROCEDURE delete_product(
  p_id IN object_products.id%TYPE
);
END product_package;
/
```

You'll see the methods in the body of product_package in the following sections.

The get_products() Function

The get_products() function returns a REF CURSOR that points to the objects in the object_products table. The get_products() function is defined as follows in the body of product_package:

```
FUNCTION get_products
RETURN t_ref_cursor IS
  -- declare a t_ref_cursor object
  v_products_ref_cursor t_ref_cursor;
BEGIN
  -- get the REF CURSOR
  OPEN v_products_ref_cursor FOR
    SELECT VALUE(op)
    FROM object_products op
    ORDER BY op.id;

  -- return the REF CURSOR
  RETURN v_products_ref_cursor;
END get_products;
```

The following query calls `product_package.get_products()` to retrieve the products from `object_products`:

```
SELECT product_package.get_products
FROM dual;

GET_PRODUCTS
-------------------
CURSOR STATEMENT : 1

CURSOR STATEMENT : 1

VALUE(OP)(ID, NAME, DESCRIPTION, PRICE, DAYS_VALID)
----------------------------------------------------------
T_PRODUCT(1, 'pasta', '20 oz bag of pasta', 3.95, 10)
T_PRODUCT(2, 'sardines', '12 oz box of sardines', 2.99, 5)
```

The display_product() Procedure

The `display_product()` procedure displays the attributes of a single object in the `object_products` table. The `display_product()` procedure is defined as follows in the body of `product_package`:

```
PROCEDURE display_product(
  p_id IN object_products.id%TYPE
) AS
  -- declare a t_product object named v_product
  v_product t_product;
BEGIN
  -- attempt to get the product and store it in v_product
  SELECT VALUE(op)
  INTO v_product
  FROM object_products op
  WHERE id = p_id;

  -- display the attributes of v_product
  DBMS_OUTPUT.PUT_LINE('v_product.id=' ||
    v_product.id);
  DBMS_OUTPUT.PUT_LINE('v_product.name=' ||
    v_product.name);
  DBMS_OUTPUT.PUT_LINE('v_product.description=' ||
    v_product.description);
  DBMS_OUTPUT.PUT_LINE('v_product.price=' ||
    v_product.price);
  DBMS_OUTPUT.PUT_LINE('v_product.days_valid=' ||
    v_product.days_valid);

  -- call v_product.get_sell_by_date() and display the date
  DBMS_OUTPUT.PUT_LINE('Sell by date=' ||
    v_product.get_sell_by_date());
END display_product;
```

The following example calls `product_package.display_product(1)` to retrieve product #1 from the `object_products` table:

```
SET SERVEROUTPUT ON
CALL product_package.display_product(1);
v_product.id=1
v_product.name=pasta
v_product.description=20 oz bag of pasta
v_product.price=3.95
v_product.days_valid=10
Sell by date=25-JUN-12
```

The insert_product() Procedure

The `insert_product()` procedure adds an object to the `object_products` table. The `insert_product()` procedure is defined as follows in the body of `product_package`:

```
PROCEDURE insert_product(
    p_id            IN object_products.id%TYPE,
    p_name          IN object_products.name%TYPE,
    p_description   IN object_products.description%TYPE,
    p_price         IN object_products.price%TYPE,
    p_days_valid    IN object_products.days_valid%TYPE
) AS
    -- create a t_product object named v_product
    v_product t_product :=
      t_product(
        p_id, p_name, p_description, p_price, p_days_valid
      );
BEGIN
    -- add v_product to the object_products table
    INSERT INTO object_products VALUES (v_product);
    COMMIT;
EXCEPTION
    WHEN OTHERS THEN
      ROLLBACK;
END insert_product;
```

The following example calls `product_package.insert_product()` to add a new object to the `object_products` table:

```
CALL product_package.insert_product(3, 'salsa',
  '15 oz jar of salsa', 1.50, 20);
```

The update_product_price() Procedure

The `update_product_price()` procedure updates the `price` attribute of an object in the `object_products` table. The `update_product_price()` procedure is defined as follows in the body of `product_package`:

```
PROCEDURE update_product_price(
    p_id     IN object_products.id%TYPE,
    p_factor IN NUMBER
) AS
```

```
  -- declare a t_product object named v_product
  v_product t_product;
BEGIN
  -- attempt to select the product for update and
  -- store the product in v_product
  SELECT VALUE(op)
  INTO v_product
  FROM object_products op
  WHERE id = p_id
  FOR UPDATE;

  -- display the current price of v_product
  DBMS_OUTPUT.PUT_LINE('v_product.price=' ||
    v_product.price);

  -- multiply v_product.price by p_factor
  v_product.price := v_product.price * p_factor;
  DBMS_OUTPUT.PUT_LINE('New v_product.price=' ||
    v_product.price);

  -- update the product in the object_products table
  UPDATE object_products op
  SET op = v_product
  WHERE id = p_id;
  COMMIT;
EXCEPTION
  WHEN OTHERS THEN
    ROLLBACK;
END update_product_price;
```

The following example calls `product_package.update_product_price()` to update the price of product #3 in the `object_products` table:

```
CALL product_package.update_product_price(3, 2.4);
v_product.price=1.5
New v_product.price=3.6
```

The get_product() Function

The `get_product()` function returns a single object from the `object_products` table. The `get_product()` function is defined as follows in the body of `product_package`:

```
FUNCTION get_product(
  p_id IN object_products.id%TYPE
)
RETURN t_product IS
  -- declare a t_product object named v_product
  v_product t_product;
BEGIN
  -- get the product and store it in v_product
  SELECT VALUE(op)
  INTO v_product
  FROM object_products op
```

```
  WHERE op.id = p_id;

  -- return v_product
  RETURN v_product;
END get_product;
```

The following query calls `product_package.get_product()` to get product #3 from the `object_products` table:

```
SELECT product_package.get_product(3)
FROM dual;

PRODUCT_PACKAGE.GET_PRODUCT(3)(ID, NAME, DESCRIPTION
----------------------------------------------------
T_PRODUCT(3, 'salsa', '15 oz jar of salsa', 3.6, 20)
```

The update_product() Procedure

The `update_product()` procedure updates all the attributes of an object in the `object_products` table. The `update_product()` procedure is defined as follows in the body of `product_package`:

```
PROCEDURE update_product(
  p_product IN t_product
) AS
BEGIN
  -- update the product in the object_products table
  UPDATE object_products op
  SET op = p_product
  WHERE id = p_product.id;
  COMMIT;
EXCEPTION
  WHEN OTHERS THEN
    ROLLBACK;
END update_product;
```

The following example calls `product_package.update_product()` to update product #3 in the `object_products` table:

```
CALL product_package.update_product(t_product(3, 'salsa',
  '25 oz jar of salsa', 2.70, 15));
```

The get_product_ref() Function

The `get_product_ref()` function returns a reference to a single object from the `object_products` table. The `get_product_ref()` function is defined as follows in the body of `product_package`:

```
FUNCTION get_product_ref(
  p_id IN object_products.id%TYPE
)
RETURN REF t_product IS
  -- declare a reference to a t_product
```

```
  v_product_ref REF t_product;
BEGIN
  -- get the REF for the product and
  -- store it in v_product_ref
  SELECT REF(op)
  INTO v_product_ref
  FROM object_products op
  WHERE op.id = p_id;

  -- return v_product_ref
  RETURN v_product_ref;
END get_product_ref;
```

The following query calls `product_package.get_product_ref()` to get the reference to product #3 from the `object_products` table:

```
SELECT product_package.get_product_ref(3)
FROM dual;

PRODUCT_PACKAGE.GET_PRODUCT_REF(3)
--------------------------------------------------------------------------------
000028020956DBE8BEFDEF4D5BA8C806A7B31B49DF916CDB2CAC1B46E9808BA181F9F2760F0100
033D0002
```

The next example calls `product_package.get_product_ref()` again, this time using `DEREF()` to get to the actual product:

```
SELECT DEREF(product_package.get_product_ref(3))
FROM dual;

DEREF(PRODUCT_PACKAGE.GET_PRODUCT_REF(3))(ID, NAME,
----------------------------------------------------
T_PRODUCT(3, 'salsa', '25 oz jar of salsa', 2.7, 15)
```

The delete_product() Procedure

The `delete_product()` procedure deletes a single object from the `object_products` table. The `delete_product()` procedure is defined as follows in the body of `product_package`:

```
PROCEDURE delete_product(
  p_id IN object_products.id%TYPE
) AS
BEGIN
  -- delete the product
  DELETE FROM object_products op
  WHERE op.id = p_id;
  COMMIT;
EXCEPTION
  WHEN OTHERS THEN
    ROLLBACK;
END delete_product;
```

The following example calls `product_package.delete_product()` to delete product #3 from the `object_products` table:

```
CALL product_package.delete_product(3);
```

Now that you've seen all the methods in `product_package`, it's time to see two procedures named `product_lifecycle()` and `product_lifecycle2()` that call the various methods in the package.

The product_lifecycle() Procedure

The `product_lifecycle()` procedure is defined as follows:

```
CREATE PROCEDURE product_lifecycle AS
  -- declare object
  v_product t_product;
BEGIN
  -- insert a new product
  product_package.insert_product(4, 'beef',
   '25 lb pack of beef', 32, 10);

  -- display the product
  product_package.display_product(4);

  -- get the new product and store it in v_product
  SELECT product_package.get_product(4)
  INTO v_product
  FROM dual;

  -- change some attributes of v_product
  v_product.description := '20 lb pack of beef';
  v_product.price := 36;
  v_product.days_valid := 8;

  -- update the product
  product_package.update_product(v_product);

  -- display the product
  product_package.display_product(4);

  -- delete the product
  product_package.delete_product(4);
END product_lifecycle;
/
```

The following example calls `product_lifecycle()`:

```
CALL product_lifecycle();
v_product.id=4
v_product.name=beef
v_product.description=25 lb pack of beef
v_product.price=32
v_product.days_valid=10
```

```
Sell by date=27-JUN-12
v_product.id=4
v_product.name=beef
v_product.description=20 lb pack of beef
v_product.price=36
v_product.days_valid=8
Sell by date=25-JUN-12
```

The product_lifecycle2() Procedure

The product_lifecycle2() procedure uses an object reference to access a product, and is defined as follows:

```
CREATE PROCEDURE product_lifecycle2 AS
  -- declare object
  v_product t_product;

  -- declare object reference
  v_product_ref REF t_product;
BEGIN
  -- insert a new product
  product_package.insert_product(4, 'beef',
   '25 lb pack of beef', 32, 10);

  -- display the product
  product_package.display_product(4);

  -- get the new product reference and store it in v_product_ref
  SELECT product_package.get_product_ref(4)
  INTO v_product_ref
  FROM dual;

  -- dereference v_product_ref using the following query
  SELECT DEREF(v_product_ref)
  INTO v_product
  FROM dual;

  -- change some attributes of v_product
  v_product.description := '20 lb pack of beef';
  v_product.price := 36;
  v_product.days_valid := 8;

  -- update the product
  product_package.update_product(v_product);

  -- display the product
  product_package.display_product(4);

  -- delete the product
  product_package.delete_product(4);
END product_lifecycle2;
/
```

To dereference `v_product_ref`, the procedure contains the following query:

```
SELECT DEREF(v_product_ref)
INTO v_product
FROM dual;
```

The reason this query is used is that you cannot use `DEREF()` directly in PL/SQL code. For example, the following statement won't compile in PL/SQL:

```
v_product := DEREF(v_product_ref);
```

The following example calls `product_lifecycle2()`:

```
CALL product_lifecycle2();
v_product.id=4
v_product.name=beef
v_product.description=25 lb pack of beef
v_product.price=32
v_product.days_valid=10
Sell by date=27-JUN-12
v_product.id=4
v_product.name=beef
v_product.description=20 lb pack of beef
v_product.price=36
v_product.days_valid=8
Sell by date=25-JUN-12
```

Type Inheritance

Oracle Database 9*i* introduced object type *inheritance*, which allows you to define hierarchies of object types. For example, you might want to define a business person object type and have that type inherit the existing attributes from `t_person`. The business person type could extend `t_person` with attributes to store the person's job title and the name of the company they work for. For `t_person` to be inherited from, the `t_person` definition must include the `NOT FINAL` clause:

```
CREATE TYPE t_person AS OBJECT (
    id          INTEGER,
    first_name  VARCHAR2(10),
    last_name   VARCHAR2(10),
    dob         DATE,
    phone       VARCHAR2(12),
    address     t_address,
    MEMBER FUNCTION display_details RETURN VARCHAR2
) NOT FINAL;
/
```

The `NOT FINAL` clause indicates that `t_person` can be inherited from when defining another type. (The default when defining types is `FINAL`, meaning that the object type cannot be inherited from.)

The following statement creates the body for t_person. Notice that the display_details() function returns a VARCHAR2 containing the id and name of the person.

```
CREATE TYPE BODY t_person AS
  MEMBER FUNCTION display_details RETURN VARCHAR2 IS
  BEGIN
    RETURN 'id=' || id || ', name=' || first_name || ' ' || last_name;
  END;
END;
/
```

Running the Script to Create the Second Object Schema

I've provided in the SQL directory an SQL*Plus script named object_schema2.sql, which creates a user named object_user2 with a password of object_password2. This script will run on Oracle Database 9i and above.

You perform the following steps to create the schema:

1. Start SQL*Plus.

2. Log into the database as a user with privileges to create new users, tables, and PL/SQL packages. I run scripts in my database using the system user.

3. Run the object_schema2.sql script from within SQL*Plus using the @ command.

For example, if you're using Windows and the script is stored in C:\sql_book\SQL, then you enter the following command:

```
@ C:\sql_book\SQL\object_schema2.sql
```

When the script completes, you will be logged in as object_user2.

Inheriting Attributes

To have a new type inherit attributes and methods from an existing type, you use the UNDER keyword when defining your new type. Our business person type, which I'll name t_business_person, uses the UNDER keyword to inherit the attributes from t_person:

```
CREATE TYPE t_business_person UNDER t_person (
  title    VARCHAR2(20),
  company VARCHAR2(20)
);
/
```

In this example, t_person is known as the *supertype*, and t_business_person is known as the *subtype*. You can then use t_business_person when defining column objects or object tables. For example, the following statement creates an object table named object_business_customers:

```
CREATE TABLE object_business_customers OF t_business_person;
```

The following INSERT statement adds an object to object_business_customers. Notice that the two additional title and company attributes are supplied at the end of the t_business_person constructor.

```
INSERT INTO object_business_customers VALUES (
  t_business_person(1, 'John', 'Brown', '01-FEB-1955', '800-555-1211',
    t_address('2 State Street', 'Beantown', 'MA', '12345'),
    'Manager', 'XYZ Corp'
  )
);
```

The following query retrieves the object:

```
SELECT *
FROM object_business_customers
WHERE id = 1;
```

```
        ID FIRST_NAME LAST_NAME  DOB        PHONE
---------- ---------- ---------- --------- ------------
ADDRESS(STREET, CITY, STATE, ZIP)
-------------------------------------------------------
TITLE                 COMPANY
--------------------- -------------------
         1 John       Brown      01-FEB-55 800-555-1211
T_ADDRESS('2 State Street', 'Beantown', 'MA', '12345')
Manager               XYZ Corp
```

The following query calls the display_details() function:

```
SELECT o.display_details()
FROM object_business_customers o
WHERE id = 1;
```

```
O.DISPLAY_DETAILS()
---------------------
id=1, name=John Brown
```

When calling a method, the database searches for that method in the subtype first. If it doesn't find the method, it then searches the supertype. In a hierarchy of types, the database will search for the method up the hierarchy. If the database cannot find the method, it will report an error.

Using a Subtype Object in Place of a Supertype Object

In this section you'll see how you can use a subtype object in place of a supertype object. Doing this gives you great flexibility when storing and manipulating related types. In the examples, you'll see how to use a t_business_person object (a subtype object) in place of a t_person object (a supertype object).

SQL Examples

The following statement creates a table named object_customers of type t_person:

```
CREATE TABLE object_customers OF t_person;
```

The following INSERT statement adds a t_person object to this table (the name is Jason Bond):

```
INSERT INTO object_customers VALUES (
    t_person(1, 'Jason', 'Bond', '03-APR-1965', '800-555-1212',
      t_address('21 New Street', 'Anytown', 'CA', '12345')
    )
);
```

There's nothing unusual about the previous statement: The INSERT simply adds a t_person object to the object_customers table. Because the object_customers table stores objects of type t_person, and t_person is a supertype of t_business_person, you can store a t_business_person object in object_customers. The following INSERT shows this, adding a customer named Steve Edwards:

```
INSERT INTO object_customers VALUES (
    t_business_person(2, 'Steve', 'Edwards', '03-MAR-1955', '800-555-1212',
      t_address('1 Market Street', 'Anytown', 'VA', '12345'),
      'Manager', 'XYZ Corp'
    )
);
```

The object_customers table now contains two objects: the t_person object added earlier (Jason Bond) and the new t_business_person object (Steve Edwards). The following query retrieves these two objects. Notice that the title and company attributes for Steve Edwards are missing from the output.

```
SELECT *
FROM object_customers o;

        ID FIRST_NAME LAST_NAME  DOB       PHONE
---------- ---------- ---------- --------- ------------
ADDRESS(STREET, CITY, STATE, ZIP)
-------------------------------------------------------
         1 Jason      Bond       03-APR-65 800-555-1212
T_ADDRESS('21 New Street', 'Anytown', 'CA', '12345')

         2 Steve      Edwards    03-MAR-55 800-555-1212
T_ADDRESS('1 Market Street', 'Anytown', 'VA', '12345')
```

You can get the full set of attributes for Steve Edwards by using VALUE() in the query, as shown in the following example. Notice the different types of the objects for Jason Bond (a t_person object) and Steve Edwards (a t_business_person object) and that the title and company attributes for Steve Edwards now appear in the output:

```
SELECT VALUE(o)
FROM object_customers o;
```

```
VALUE(O)(ID, FIRST_NAME, LAST_NAME, DOB, PHONE,
 ADDRESS(STREET, CITY, STATE, ZIP
-------------------------------------------------------------------
T_PERSON(1, 'Jason', 'Bond', '03-APR-65', '800-555-1212',
 T_ADDRESS('21 New Street', 'Anytown', 'CA', '12345'))

T_BUSINESS_PERSON(2, 'Steve', 'Edwards', '03-MAR-55', '800-555-1212',
 T_ADDRESS('1 Market Street', 'Anytown', 'VA', '12345'),
 'Manager', 'XYZ Corp')
```

PL/SQL Examples

You can also manipulate subtype and supertype objects in PL/SQL. For example, the following procedure named subtypes_and_supertypes() manipulates t_business_person and t_person objects:

```
CREATE PROCEDURE subtypes_and_supertypes AS
  -- create objects
  v_business_person t_business_person :=
    t_business_person(
      1, 'John', 'Brown',
      '01-FEB-1955', '800-555-1211',
      t_address('2 State Street', 'Beantown', 'MA', '12345'),
      'Manager', 'XYZ Corp'
    );
  v_person t_person :=
    t_person(1, 'John', 'Brown', '01-FEB-1955', '800-555-1211',
      t_address('2 State Street', 'Beantown', 'MA', '12345'));
  v_business_person2 t_business_person;
  v_person2 t_person;
BEGIN
  -- assign v_business_person to v_person2
  v_person2 := v_business_person;
  DBMS_OUTPUT.PUT_LINE('v_person2.id = ' || v_person2.id);
  DBMS_OUTPUT.PUT_LINE('v_person2.first_name = ' ||
    v_person2.first_name);
  DBMS_OUTPUT.PUT_LINE('v_person2.last_name = ' ||
    v_person2.last_name);

  -- the following lines will not compile because v_person2
  -- is of type t_person, and t_person does not know about the
  -- additional title and company attributes
  -- DBMS_OUTPUT.PUT_LINE('v_person2.title = ' ||
  --   v_person2.title);
  -- DBMS_OUTPUT.PUT_LINE('v_person2.company = ' ||
  --   v_person2.company);

  -- the following line will not compile because you cannot
  -- directly assign a t_person object to a t_business_person
```

```
    -- object
    -- v_business_person2 := v_person;
END subtypes_and_supertypes;
/
```

The following example shows the result of calling subtypes_and_supertypes():

```
SET SERVEROUTPUT ON
CALL subtypes_and_supertypes();
v_person2.id = 1
v_person2.first_name = John
v_person2.last_name = Brown
```

NOT SUBSTITUTABLE Objects

If you want to prevent the use of a subtype object in place of a supertype object, you can mark an object table or object column as NOT SUBSTITUTABLE. For example, the following statement creates a table named object_customers2:

```
CREATE TABLE object_customers_not_subs OF t_person
NOT SUBSTITUTABLE AT ALL LEVELS;
```

The NOT SUBSTITUTABLE AT ALL LEVELS clause indicates that no objects of a type other than t_person can be inserted into the table. If an attempt is made to add an object of type t_business_person to this table, an error is returned:

```
SQL> INSERT INTO object_customers_not_subs VALUES (
  2     t_business_person(1, 'Steve', 'Edwards', '03-MAR-1955', '800-555-1212',
  3       t_address('1 Market Street', 'Anytown', 'VA', '12345'),
  4       'Manager', 'XYZ Corp'
  5   )
  6 );
  t_business_person(1, 'Steve', 'Edwards', '03-MAR-1955', '800-555-1212',
  *
ERROR at line 2:
ORA-00932: inconsistent datatypes: expected OBJECT_USER2.T_PERSON got
OBJECT_USER2.T_BUSINESS_PERSON
```

You can also mark an object column as NOT SUBSTITUTABLE. For example, the following statement creates a table with an object column named product that can store only objects of type t_product:

```
CREATE TABLE products (
  product              t_product,
  quantity_in_stock INTEGER
)
COLUMN product NOT SUBSTITUTABLE AT ALL LEVELS;
```

Any attempts to add an object not of type t_product to the product column will result in an error.

Other Useful Object Functions

Earlier, you saw the use of the REF(), DEREF(), and VALUE() functions. In this section, you'll see the following additional functions that can be used with objects:

- **IS OF()** checks if an object is of a particular type or subtype.
- **TREAT()** does a run-time check to see if an object's type can be treated as a supertype.
- **SYS_TYPEID()** returns the ID of an object's type.

IS OF()

IS OF() checks whether an object is of a particular type or subtype. For example, the following query uses IS OF() to check whether the objects in the object_business_customers table are of type t_business_person. Because they are, a row is returned by the query.

```
SELECT VALUE(o)
FROM object_business_customers o
WHERE VALUE(o) IS OF (t_business_person);

VALUE(O)(ID, FIRST_NAME, LAST_NAME, DOB, PHONE,
 ADDRESS(STREET, CITY, STATE, ZIP
----------------------------------------------------------------
T_BUSINESS_PERSON(1, 'John', 'Brown', '01-FEB-55', '800-555-1211',
 T_ADDRESS('2 State Street', 'Beantown', 'MA', '12345'),
 'Manager', 'XYZ Corp')
```

You can also use IS OF() to check whether an object is of a subtype of the specified type. For example, the objects in the object_business_customers table are of type t_business_person, which is a subtype of t_person. Therefore, the following query returns the same result as that shown in the previous example:

```
SELECT VALUE(o)
FROM object_business_customers o
WHERE VALUE(o) IS OF (t_person);

VALUE(O)(ID, FIRST_NAME, LAST_NAME, DOB, PHONE,
 ADDRESS(STREET, CITY, STATE, ZIP
----------------------------------------------------------------
T_BUSINESS_PERSON(1, 'John', 'Brown', '01-FEB-55', '800-555-1211',
 T_ADDRESS('2 State Street', 'Beantown', 'MA', '12345'),
 'Manager', 'XYZ Corp')
```

You can include more than one type in IS OF(). For example:

```
SELECT VALUE(o)
FROM object_business_customers o
WHERE VALUE(o) IS OF (t_business_person, t_person);

VALUE(O)(ID, FIRST_NAME, LAST_NAME, DOB, PHONE,
 ADDRESS(STREET, CITY, STATE, ZIP
----------------------------------------------------------------
```

```
T_BUSINESS_PERSON(1, 'John', 'Brown', '01-FEB-55', '800-555-1211',
 T_ADDRESS('2 State Street', 'Beantown', 'MA', '12345'),
 'Manager', 'XYZ Corp')
```

In the earlier section entitled "Using a Subtype Object in Place of a Supertype Object," you saw the addition of a t_person object (Jason Bond) and t_business_person object (Steve Edwards) to the object_customers table. As a reminder, the following query shows these objects:

```
SELECT VALUE(o)
FROM object_customers o;

VALUE(O)(ID, FIRST_NAME, LAST_NAME, DOB, PHONE,
 ADDRESS(STREET, CITY, STATE, ZIP
-----------------------------------------------------------------------
T_PERSON(1, 'Jason', 'Bond', '03-APR-65', '800-555-1212',
 T_ADDRESS('21 New Street', 'Anytown', 'CA', '12345'))

T_BUSINESS_PERSON(2, 'Steve', 'Edwards', '03-MAR-55', '800-555-1212',
 T_ADDRESS('1 Market Street', 'Anytown', 'VA', '12345'),
 'Manager', 'XYZ Corp')
```

Because t_business_person is a subtype of t_person, IS OF (t_person) returns true when a t_business_person object or a t_person object is checked. This is illustrated in the following query that retrieves both Jason Bond and Steve Edwards using IS OF (t_person):

```
SELECT VALUE(o)
FROM object_customers o
WHERE VALUE(o) IS OF (t_person);

VALUE(O)(ID, FIRST_NAME, LAST_NAME, DOB, PHONE,
 ADDRESS(STREET, CITY, STATE, ZIP
-----------------------------------------------------------------------
T_PERSON(1, 'Jason', 'Bond', '03-APR-65', '800-555-1212',
 T_ADDRESS('21 New Street', 'Anytown', 'CA', '12345'))

T_BUSINESS_PERSON(2, 'Steve', 'Edwards', '03-MAR-55', '800-555-1212',
 T_ADDRESS('1 Market Street', 'Anytown', 'VA', '12345'),
 'Manager', 'XYZ Corp')
```

You can also use the ONLY keyword in conjunction with IS OF() to check for objects of a specific type only: IS OF() returns false for objects of another type in the hierarchy. For example, IS OF (ONLY t_person) returns true for objects of type t_person only and returns false for objects of type t_business_person. In this way, you can use IS OF (ONLY t_person) to restrict the object returned by a query against the object_customers table to Jason Bond, as shown in the following example:

```
SELECT VALUE(o)
FROM object_customers o
WHERE VALUE(o) IS OF (ONLY t_person);
```

```
VALUE(O)(ID, FIRST_NAME, LAST_NAME, DOB, PHONE,
 ADDRESS(STREET, CITY, STATE, ZIP
------------------------------------------------------------
T_PERSON(1, 'Jason', 'Bond', '03-APR-65', '800-555-1212',
 T_ADDRESS('21 New Street', 'Anytown', 'CA', '12345'))
```

Similarly, IS OF (ONLY t_business_person) returns true for objects of type t_business_person only and returns false for objects of type t_person. For example, the following query retrieves the t_business_person object only and therefore returns Steve Edwards:

```
SELECT VALUE(o)
FROM object_customers o
WHERE VALUE(o) IS OF (ONLY t_business_person);

VALUE(O)(ID, FIRST_NAME, LAST_NAME, DOB, PHONE,
 ADDRESS(STREET, CITY, STATE, ZIP
----------------------------------------------------------------------
T_BUSINESS_PERSON(2, 'Steve', 'Edwards', '03-MAR-55', '800-555-1212',
 T_ADDRESS('1 Market Street', 'Anytown', 'VA', '12345'),
 'Manager', 'XYZ Corp')
```

You can include multiple types after ONLY. For example, IS OF (ONLY t_person, t_business_person) returns true for t_person and t_business_person objects only. The following query shows this by returning, as expected, both Jason Bond and Steve Edwards:

```
SELECT VALUE(o)
FROM object_customers o
WHERE VALUE(o) IS OF (ONLY t_person, t_business_person);

VALUE(O)(ID, FIRST_NAME, LAST_NAME, DOB, PHONE,
 ADDRESS(STREET, CITY, STATE, ZIP
----------------------------------------------------------------------
T_PERSON(1, 'Jason', 'Bond', '03-APR-65', '800-555-1212',
 T_ADDRESS('21 New Street', 'Anytown', 'CA', '12345'))

T_BUSINESS_PERSON(2, 'Steve', 'Edwards', '03-MAR-55', '800-555-1212',
 T_ADDRESS('1 Market Street', 'Anytown', 'VA', '12345'),
 'Manager', 'XYZ Corp')
```

You can also use IS OF() in PL/SQL. For example, the following procedure named check_types() creates t_business_person and t_person objects and uses IS OF() to check their types:

```
CREATE PROCEDURE check_types AS
    -- create objects
    v_business_person t_business_person :=
      t_business_person(
        1, 'John', 'Brown',
        '01-FEB-1955', '800-555-1211',
        t_address('2 State Street', 'Beantown', 'MA', '12345'),
```

```
        'Manager', 'XYZ Corp'
      );
    v_person t_person :=
      t_person(1, 'John', 'Brown', '01-FEB-1955', '800-555-1211',
        t_address('2 State Street', 'Beantown', 'MA', '12345'));
BEGIN
  -- check the types of the objects
  IF v_business_person IS OF (t_business_person) THEN
    DBMS_OUTPUT.PUT_LINE('v_business_person is of type ' ||
      't_business_person');
  END IF;
  IF v_person IS OF (t_person) THEN
    DBMS_OUTPUT.PUT_LINE('v_person is of type t_person');
  END IF;
  IF v_business_person IS OF (t_person) THEN
    DBMS_OUTPUT.PUT_LINE('v_business_person is of type t_person');
  END IF;
  IF v_business_person IS OF (t_business_person, t_person) THEN
    DBMS_OUTPUT.PUT_LINE('v_business_person is of ' ||
      'type t_business_person or t_person');
  END IF;
  IF v_business_person IS OF (ONLY t_business_person) THEN
    DBMS_OUTPUT.PUT_LINE('v_business_person is of only ' ||
      'type t_business_person');
  END IF;
  IF v_business_person IS OF (ONLY t_person) THEN
    DBMS_OUTPUT.PUT_LINE('v_business_person is of only ' ||
      'type t_person');
  ELSE
    DBMS_OUTPUT.PUT_LINE('v_business_person is not of only ' ||
      'type t_person');
  END IF;
END check_types;
/
```

The following example shows the result of calling `check_types()`:

```
SET SERVEROUTPUT ON
CALL check_types();
v_business_person is of type t_business_person
v_person is of type t_person
v_business_person is of type t_person
v_business_person is of type t_business_person or t_person
v_business_person is of only type t_business_person
v_business_person is not of only type t_person
```

TREAT()

`TREAT()` checks if an object of a subtype can be treated as an object of a supertype. If this is true, `TREAT()` returns an object, and if it's untrue, `TREAT()` returns null. For example, because `t_business_person` is a subtype of `t_person`, a `t_business_person` object can be treated as a t_person object. You saw this earlier in the section "Using a Subtype Object in Place of a Supertype Object," where a t_business_person object (Steve Edwards) was inserted into the object_customers table, which normally holds t_person objects.

The following query uses TREAT() to check that Steve Edwards can be treated as a t_person object:

```
SELECT NVL2(TREAT(VALUE(o) AS t_person), 'yes', 'no')
FROM object_customers o
WHERE first_name = 'Steve' AND last_name = 'Edwards';

NVL
---
yes
```

NVL2() returns yes because TREAT(VALUE(o) AS t_person) returns an object, not a null value. This means that Steve Edwards can be treated as a t_person object.

The next query checks whether Jason Bond (a t_person object) can be treated as a t_business_person object—he cannot, and, therefore, TREAT() returns null and NVL2() returns no:

```
SELECT NVL2(TREAT(VALUE(o) AS t_business_person), 'yes', 'no')
FROM object_customers o
WHERE first_name = 'Jason' AND last_name = 'Bond';

NVL
---
no
```

Because TREAT() returns null for the whole object, all the individual attributes for the object are also null. For example, the following query attempts to access the first_name attribute through Jason Bond—null is returned:

```
SELECT
  NVL2(TREAT(VALUE(o) AS t_business_person).first_name, 'not null', 'null')
FROM object_customers o
WHERE first_name = 'Jason' AND last_name = 'Bond';

NVL2
----
null
```

The next query uses TREAT() to check whether Jason Bond can be treated as a t_person object—he *is* a t_person object and therefore yes is returned:

```
SELECT NVL2(TREAT(VALUE(o) AS t_person).first_name, 'yes', 'no')
FROM object_customers o
WHERE first_name = 'Jason' AND last_name = 'Bond';

NVL
---
yes
```

You can also retrieve an object through the use of TREAT(). For example, the following query retrieves Steve Edwards:

```
SELECT TREAT(VALUE(o) AS t_business_person)
FROM object_customers o
WHERE first_name = 'Steve' AND last_name = 'Edwards';

TREAT(VALUE(O)AST_BUSINESS_PERSON)(ID, FIRST_NAME, LAST_NAME, DOB, PHONE,
 ADDRESS
------------------------------------------------------------------------
T_BUSINESS_PERSON(2, 'Steve', 'Edwards', '03-MAR-55', '800-555-1212',
 T_ADDRESS('1 Market Street', 'Anytown', 'VA', '12345'),
 'Manager', 'XYZ Corp')
```

If you try this query with Jason Bond, then null is returned. Therefore, nothing appears in the output of the following query:

```
SELECT TREAT(VALUE(o) AS t_business_person)
FROM object_customers o
WHERE first_name = 'Jason' AND last_name = 'Bond';

TREAT(VALUE(O)AST_BUSINESS_PERSON)(ID, FIRST_NAME, LAST_NAME, DOB, PHONE,
 ADDRESS
------------------------------------------------------------------------
```

Let's take look at using TREAT() with the object_business_customers table, which contains the t_business_person object John Brown:

```
SELECT VALUE(o)
FROM object_business_customers o;

VALUE(O)(ID, FIRST_NAME, LAST_NAME, DOB, PHONE,
 ADDRESS(STREET, CITY, STATE, ZIP
----------------------------------------------------------------
T_BUSINESS_PERSON(1, 'John', 'Brown', '01-FEB-55', '800-555-1211',
 T_ADDRESS('2 State Street', 'Beantown', 'MA', '12345'),
 'Manager', 'XYZ Corp')
```

The following query uses TREAT() to check whether John Brown can be treated as a t_person object—he can, because t_business_person is a subtype of t_person. Therefore, yes is returned by the query.

```
SELECT NVL2(TREAT(VALUE(o) AS t_person), 'yes', 'no')
FROM object_business_customers o
WHERE first_name = 'John' AND last_name = 'Brown';

NVL
---
yes
```

The following example shows the object returned by TREAT() when querying the object_ business_customers table. Notice that you still get the title and company attributes for John Brown.

```
SELECT TREAT(VALUE(o) AS t_person)
FROM object_business_customers o;
```

```
TREAT(VALUE(O)AST_PERSON)(ID, FIRST_NAME, LAST_NAME, DOB, PHONE,
 ADDRESS(STREET,
-----------------------------------------------------------------
T_BUSINESS_PERSON(1, 'John', 'Brown', '01-FEB-55', '800-555-1211',
 T_ADDRESS('2 State Street', 'Beantown', 'MA', '12345'),
 'Manager', 'XYZ Corp')
```

You can also use TREAT() in PL/SQL. For example, the following procedure named treat_ example() illustrates the use of TREAT() (you should study the comments in the code to understand how TREAT() works in PL/SQL):

```
CREATE PROCEDURE treat_example· AS
  -- create objects
  v_business_person t_business_person :=
    t_business_person(
      1, 'John', 'Brown',
      '01-FEB-1955', '800-555-1211',
      t_address('2 State Street', 'Beantown', 'MA', '12345'),
      'Manager', 'XYZ Corp'
    );
  v_person t_person :=
    t_person(1, 'John', 'Brown', '01-FEB-1955', '800-555-1211',
      t_address('2 State Street', 'Beantown', 'MA', '12345'));
  v_business_person2 t_business_person;
  v_person2 t_person;
BEGIN
  -- assign v_business_person to v_person2
  v_person2 := v_business_person;
  DBMS_OUTPUT.PUT_LINE('v_person2.id = ' || v_person2.id);
  DBMS_OUTPUT.PUT_LINE('v_person2.first_name = ' ||
    v_person2.first_name);
  DBMS_OUTPUT.PUT_LINE('v_person2.last_name = ' ||
    v_person2.last_name);

  -- the following lines will not compile because v_person2
  -- is of type t_person, and t_person does not know about the
  -- additional title and company attributes
  -- DBMS_OUTPUT.PUT_LINE('v_person2.title = ' ||
  --   v_person2.title);
  -- DBMS_OUTPUT.PUT_LINE('v_person2.company = ' ||
  --   v_person2.company);

  -- use TREAT when assigning v_business_person to v_person2
  DBMS_OUTPUT.PUT_LINE('Using TREAT');
  v_person2 := TREAT(v_business_person AS t_person);
```

```
    DBMS_OUTPUT.PUT_LINE('v_person2.id = ' || v_person2.id);
    DBMS_OUTPUT.PUT_LINE('v_person2.first_name = ' ||
      v_person2.first_name);
    DBMS_OUTPUT.PUT_LINE('v_person2.last_name = ' ||
      v_person2.last_name);

    -- the following lines will still not compile because v_person2
    -- is of type t_person, and t_person does not know about the
    -- additional title and company attributes
    -- DBMS_OUTPUT.PUT_LINE('v_person2.title = ' ||
    --    v_person2.title);
    -- DBMS_OUTPUT.PUT_LINE('v_person2.company = ' ||
    --    v_person2.company);

    -- the following lines do compile because TREAT is used
    DBMS_OUTPUT.PUT_LINE('v_person2.title = ' ||
      TREAT(v_person2 AS t_business_person).title);
    DBMS_OUTPUT.PUT_LINE('v_person2.company = ' ||
      TREAT(v_person2 AS t_business_person).company);

    -- the following line will not compile because you cannot
    -- directly assign a t_person object to a t_business_person
    -- object
    -- v_business_person2 := v_person;

    -- the following line throws a run-time error because you cannot
    -- assign a supertype object (v_person) to a subtype object
    -- (v_business_person2)
    -- v_business_person2 := TREAT(v_person AS t_business_person);
END treat_example;
/
```

The following example shows the result of calling `treat_example()`:

```
SET SERVEROUTPUT ON
CALL treat_example();
v_person2.id = 1
v_person2.first_name = John
v_person2.last_name = Brown
Using TREAT
v_person2.id = 1
v_person2.first_name = John
v_person2.last_name = Brown
v_person2.title = Manager
v_person2.company = XYZ Corp
```

SYS_TYPEID()

`SYS_TYPEID()` returns the ID of an object's type. For example, the following query uses `SYS_TYPEID()` to get the ID of the object type in the `object_business_customers` table:

```
SELECT first_name, last_name, SYS_TYPEID(VALUE(o))
FROM object_business_customers o;
```

```
FIRST_NAME LAST_NAME  SY
---------- ---------- --
John       Brown      02
```

You can get details on the types defined by the user through the `user_types` view. The following query retrieves the details of the type with a `typeid` of `'02'` (the ID returned by `SYS_TYPEID()` earlier) and the `type_name` of T_BUSINESS_PERSON:

```
SELECT typecode, attributes, methods, supertype_name
FROM user_types
WHERE typeid = '02'
AND type_name = 'T_BUSINESS_PERSON';
```

```
TYPECODE ATTRIBUTES    METHODS SUPERTYPE_NAME
-------- ---------- ---------- --------------
OBJECT            8          1 T_PERSON
```

From the output of this query, you can see that the supertype of `t_business_person` is `t_person`. Also, `t_business_person` has eight attributes and one method.

NOT INSTANTIABLE Object Types

You can mark an object type as `NOT INSTANTIABLE`, which prevents objects of that type from being created. You might want to mark an object type as `NOT INSTANTIABLE` when you use the type as an abstract supertype only and never create any objects of that type.

For example, you could create a `t_vehicle` abstract type and use it as a supertype for a `t_car` subtype and a `t_motorcycle` subtype; you would then create actual `t_car` and `t_motorcycle` objects, but never `t_vehicle` objects.

The following statement creates a type named `t_vehicle`, which is marked as `NOT INSTANTIABLE`:

```
CREATE TYPE t_vehicle AS OBJECT (
  id    INTEGER,
  make  VARCHAR2(15),
  model VARCHAR2(15)
) NOT FINAL NOT INSTANTIABLE;
/
```

NOTE
The t_vehicle *type is also marked as* NOT FINAL *because a* NOT INSTANTIABLE *type cannot be* FINAL. *If it were* FINAL, *you wouldn't be able to use it as a supertype, which is the whole point of creating it in the first place.*

The next example creates a subtype named `t_car` under the `t_vehicle` supertype. Notice that `t_car` has an additional attribute named `convertible`, which records whether the car has a convertible roof (Y for yes, N for no).

```
CREATE TYPE t_car UNDER t_vehicle (
  convertible CHAR(1)
```

```
);
/
```

The following example creates a subtype named t_motorcycle under the t_vehicle supertype. Notice that t_motorcycle has an additional attribute named sidecar, which will be used to record whether the motorcycle has a sidecar (Y for yes, N for no).

```
CREATE TYPE t_motorcycle UNDER t_vehicle (
   sidecar CHAR(1)
);
/
```

The next example creates tables named vehicles, cars, and motorcycles, which are object tables of the types t_vehicle, t_car, and t_motorcycle, respectively:

```
CREATE TABLE vehicles OF t_vehicle;
CREATE TABLE cars OF t_car;
CREATE TABLE motorcycles OF t_motorcycle;
```

Because t_vehicle is NOT INSTANTIABLE, you cannot add an object to the vehicles table. If you attempt to do so, the database returns an error:

```
SQL> INSERT INTO vehicles VALUES (
  2    t_vehicle(1, 'Toyota', 'MR2', '01-FEB-1955')
  3  );
t_vehicle(1, 'Toyota', 'MR2', '01-FEB-1955')
  *
ERROR at line 2:
ORA-22826: cannot construct an instance of a non instantiable type
```

The following examples add objects to the cars and motorcycles tables:

```
INSERT INTO cars VALUES (
   t_car(1, 'Toyota', 'MR2', 'Y')
);

INSERT INTO motorcycles VALUES (
   t_motorcycle(1, 'Harley-Davidson', 'V-Rod', 'N')
);
```

The following queries retrieve the objects from the cars and motorcycles tables:

```
SELECT *
FROM cars;

        ID MAKE             MODEL            C
---------- ---------------- ---------------- -
         1 Toyota           MR2              Y

SELECT *
FROM motorcycles;
```

```
        ID MAKE            MODEL           S
---------- --------------- --------------- -
         1 Harley-Davidson V-Rod           N
```

User-Defined Constructors

You can define constructors in PL/SQL to initialize a new object. A constructor can programmatically set the attributes of a new object to default values.

The following example creates a type named t_person2 that declares two constructor methods with differing numbers of parameters:

```
CREATE TYPE t_person2 AS OBJECT (
    id          INTEGER,
    first_name VARCHAR2(10),
    last_name  VARCHAR2(10),
    dob         DATE,
    phone       VARCHAR2(12),
    CONSTRUCTOR FUNCTION t_person2(
      p_id          INTEGER,
      p_first_name VARCHAR2,
      p_last_name  VARCHAR2
    ) RETURN SELF AS RESULT,
    CONSTRUCTOR FUNCTION t_person2(
      p_id          INTEGER,
      p_first_name VARCHAR2,
      p_last_name  VARCHAR2,
      p_dob        DATE
    ) RETURN SELF AS RESULT
);
/
```

Notice the following points about the constructor declarations:

- The CONSTRUCTOR FUNCTION keywords are used to identify the constructors.
- The RETURN SELF AS RESULT keywords indicate that the current object being processed is returned by each constructor. SELF represents the current object being processed. This means the constructor returns the new object it creates.
- The first constructor accepts three parameters (p_id, p_first_name, and p_last_name), and the second constructor accepts four parameters (p_id, p_first_name, p_last_name, and p_dob).

The constructor declarations don't contain the actual code definitions for the constructors. The definitions are contained in the type body, which is created by the following statement:

```
CREATE TYPE BODY t_person2 AS
    CONSTRUCTOR FUNCTION t_person2(
      p_id          INTEGER,
      p_first_name VARCHAR2,
      p_last_name  VARCHAR2
```

```
) RETURN SELF AS RESULT IS
BEGIN
  SELF.id := p_id;
  SELF.first_name := p_first_name;
  SELF.last_name := p_last_name;
  SELF.dob := SYSDATE;
  SELF.phone := '555-1212';
  RETURN;
END;
CONSTRUCTOR FUNCTION t_person2(
  p_id          INTEGER,
  p_first_name VARCHAR2,
  p_last_name  VARCHAR2,
  p_dob         DATE
) RETURN SELF AS RESULT IS
BEGIN
  SELF.id := p_id;
  SELF.first_name := p_first_name;
  SELF.last_name := p_last_name;
  SELF.dob := p_dob;
  SELF.phone := '555-1213';
  RETURN;
END;
END;
/
```

Notice the following:

■   The constructors use SELF to reference the new object being created. For example, SELF.id := p_id sets the id attribute of the new object to the value of the p_id parameter passed into the constructor.

■   The first constructor sets the id, first_name, and last_name attributes to the p_id, p_first_name, and p_last_name parameter values passed into the constructor. The dob attribute is set to the current datetime returned by SYSDATE, and the phone attribute is set to 555-1212.

■   The second constructor sets the id, first_name, last_name, and dob attributes to the p_id, p_first_name, p_last_name, and p_dob parameter values passed into the constructor. The phone attribute is set to 555-1213.

Although not shown, the database automatically provides a default constructor that accepts five parameters and sets each attribute to the appropriate parameter value passed into the constructor. You'll see an example of this shortly.

NOTE
The constructors show an example of method overloading, *whereby methods of the same name but different parameters are defined in the same type. A method can be overloaded by providing different numbers of parameters, types of parameters, or ordering of parameters.*

The following example describes t_person2. Notice the constructor definitions in the output.

```
DESCRIBE t_person2
 Name                                          Null?     Type
 ----------------------------------------      --------  --------------------
 ID                                                      NUMBER(38)
 FIRST_NAME                                              VARCHAR2(10)
 LAST_NAME                                               VARCHAR2(10)
 DOB                                                     DATE
 PHONE                                                   VARCHAR2(12)

 METHOD
 ------
 FINAL CONSTRUCTOR FUNCTION T_PERSON2 RETURNS SELF AS RESULT
 Argument Name                    Type                      In/Out Default?
 ----------------------------     ----------------------    ------ --------
 P_ID                             NUMBER                    IN
 P_FIRST_NAME                     VARCHAR2                  IN
 P_LAST_NAME                      VARCHAR2                  IN

 METHOD
 ------
 FINAL CONSTRUCTOR FUNCTION T_PERSON2 RETURNS SELF AS RESULT
 Argument Name                    Type                      In/Out Default?
 ----------------------------     ----------------------    ------ --------
 P_ID                             NUMBER                    IN
 P_FIRST_NAME                     VARCHAR2                  IN
 P_LAST_NAME                      VARCHAR2                  IN
 P_DOB                            DATE                      IN
```

The following statement creates a table of type t_person2:

```
CREATE TABLE object_customers2 OF t_person2;
```

The following INSERT statement adds an object to the table. Notice that three parameters are passed to the t_person2 constructor.

```
INSERT INTO object_customers2 VALUES (
   t_person2(1, 'Jeff', 'Jones')
);
```

Because three parameters are passed to t_person2, the INSERT statement exercises the first constructor. The constructor sets the id, first_name, and last_name attributes of the new object to 1, Jeff, and Jones; the remaining dob and phone attributes are set to the result returned by SYSDATE and the literal 555-1212.

The following query retrieves the new object:

```
SELECT *
FROM object_customers2
WHERE id = 1;
```

```
     ID FIRST_NAME LAST_NAME DOB       PHONE
---------- ---------- ---------- --------- --------
        1 Jeff       Jones      17-JUN-12 555-1212
```

The next INSERT statement adds another object to the table. Notice that four parameters are passed to the t_person2 constructor.

```
INSERT INTO object_customers2 VALUES (
  t_person2(2, 'Gregory', 'Smith', '03-APR-1965')
);
```

Because four parameters are passed to t_person2, the INSERT statement exercises the second constructor. This constructor sets the id, first_name, last_name, and dob attributes of the object to 2, Gregory, Smith, and 03-APR-1965. The phone attribute is set to 555-1213.

The following query retrieves the new object:

```
SELECT *
FROM object_customers2
WHERE id = 2;
```

```
     ID FIRST_NAME LAST_NAME DOB       PHONE
---------- ---------- ---------- --------- --------
        2 Gregory    Smith      03-APR-65 555-1213
```

The next INSERT statement adds another object to the table. Notice that five parameters are passed to the t_person2 constructor.

```
INSERT INTO object_customers2 VALUES (
  t_person2(3, 'Jeremy', 'Hill', '05-JUN-1975', '555-1214')
);
```

Because five parameters are passed to t_person2, this INSERT statement exercises the default constructor. This constructor sets the id, first_name, last_name, dob, and phone attributes to 3, Jeremy, Hill, 05-JUN-1975, and 555-1214.

The following query retrieves the new object:

```
SELECT *
FROM object_customers2
WHERE id = 3;
```

```
     ID FIRST_NAME LAST_NAME DOB       PHONE
---------- ---------- ---------- --------- --------
        3 Jeremy     Hill       05-JUN-75 555-1214
```

Overriding Methods

When you create a subtype under a supertype, you can override a method in the supertype with a method in the subtype. This gives you a very flexible way of defining methods in a hierarchy of types.

The following statements create a supertype named t_person3. Notice that the display_ details() function returns a VARCHAR2 containing the attribute values of the object.

```
CREATE TYPE t_person3 AS OBJECT (
    id          INTEGER,
    first_name VARCHAR2(10),
    last_name  VARCHAR2(10),
    MEMBER FUNCTION display_details RETURN VARCHAR2
) NOT FINAL;
/
CREATE TYPE BODY t_person3 AS
  MEMBER FUNCTION display_details RETURN VARCHAR2 IS
  BEGIN
    RETURN 'id=' || id ||
      ', name=' || first_name || ' ' || last_name;
  END;
END;
/
```

The next set of statements creates a subtype named t_business_person3 under t_ person3. Notice that the display_details() function is overridden using the OVERRIDING keyword and that the function returns a VARCHAR2 containing the original and extended attribute values of the object.

```
CREATE TYPE t_business_person3 UNDER t_person3 (
    title    VARCHAR2(20),
    company VARCHAR2(20),
    OVERRIDING MEMBER FUNCTION display_details RETURN VARCHAR2
);
/
CREATE TYPE BODY t_business_person3 AS
  OVERRIDING MEMBER FUNCTION display_details RETURN VARCHAR2 IS
  BEGIN
    RETURN 'id=' || id ||
      ', name=' || first_name || ' ' || last_name ||
      ', title=' || title || ', company=' || company;
  END;
END;
/
```

The use of the OVERRIDING keyword indicates that display_details() in t_business_ person3 overrides display_details() in t_person3. Therefore, when display_ details() in t_business_person3 is called, it calls display_details() in t_business_ person3, not display_details() in t_person3.

NOTE
In the next section of this chapter, you'll see how you can directly call a method in a supertype from a subtype. This saves you from having to re-create code in the subtype that is already in the supertype. This feature is called generalized invocation.

The following statements create a table named `object_business_customers3` and add an object to this table:

```
CREATE TABLE object_business_customers3 OF t_business_person3;

INSERT INTO object_business_customers3 VALUES (
  t_business_person3(1, 'John', 'Brown', 'Manager', 'XYZ Corp')
);
```

The following example calls `display_details()` using `object_business_customers3`:

```
SELECT o.display_details()
FROM object_business_customers3 o
WHERE id = 1;

O.DISPLAY_DETAILS()
----------------------------------------------------
id=1, name=John Brown, title=Manager, company=XYZ Corp
```

Because the `display_details()` function as defined in `t_business_person3` is called, the `VARCHAR2` returned by the function contains the `id`, `first_name`, and `last_name` attributes, along with the `title` and `company` attributes.

Generalized Invocation

As you saw in the previous section, you can override a method in the supertype with a method in the subtype. *Generalized invocation* was introduced in Oracle Database 11*g* and allows you to call a method in a supertype from a subtype. As you'll see, generalized invocation saves you from having to re-create code in the subtype that is already in the supertype.

Running the Script to Create the Third Object Schema

I've provided in the `SQL` directory an SQL*Plus script named `object_schema3.sql`, which creates a user named `object_user3` with a password of `object_password3`. The script will run on Oracle Database 11*g* and above.

You perform the following steps to create the schema:

1. Start SQL*Plus.
2. Log into the database as a user with privileges to create new users, tables, and PL/SQL packages. I run scripts in my database using the `system` user.
3. Run the `object_schema3.sql` script from within SQL*Plus using the @ command.

For example, if you're using Windows and the script is stored in `C:\sql_book\SQL`, then you enter the following command:

```
@ C:\sql_book\SQL\object_schema3.sql
```

When the script completes, you will be logged in as `object_user3`.

Inheriting Attributes

The following statements create a supertype named t_person. Notice that the display_
details() function returns a VARCHAR2 containing the attribute values.

```
CREATE TYPE t_person AS OBJECT (
    id          INTEGER,
    first_name VARCHAR2(10),
    last_name  VARCHAR2(10),
    MEMBER FUNCTION display_details RETURN VARCHAR2
) NOT FINAL;
/

CREATE TYPE BODY t_person AS
  MEMBER FUNCTION display_details RETURN VARCHAR2 IS
  BEGIN
    RETURN 'id=' || id ||
      ', name=' || first_name || ' ' || last_name;
  END;
END;
/
```

The next set of statements creates a subtype named t_business_person under t_person.
Notice that the display_details() function is overridden using the OVERRIDING keyword.

```
CREATE TYPE t_business_person UNDER t_person (
    title   VARCHAR2(20),
    company VARCHAR2(20),
    OVERRIDING MEMBER FUNCTION display_details RETURN VARCHAR2
);
/

CREATE TYPE BODY t_business_person AS
  OVERRIDING MEMBER FUNCTION display_details RETURN VARCHAR2 IS
  BEGIN
    -- use generalized invocation to call display_details() in t_person
    RETURN (SELF AS t_person).display_details ||
      ', title=' || title || ', company=' || company;
  END;
END;
/
```

As you can see, display_details() in t_business_person overrides display_
details() in t_person. The following line in display_details() uses generalized
invocation to call a method in a supertype from a subtype:

```
RETURN (SELF AS t_person).display_details ||
    ', title=' || title || ', company=' || company;
```

What (SELF AS t_person).display_details does is to treat an object of the
current type (which is t_business_person) as an object of type t_person and then to call

display_details() in t_person. So, when display_details() in t_business_
person is called, it first calls display_details() in t_person (which displays the id,
first_name, and last_name attribute values) and then displays the title and company
attribute values. This meant I didn't have to re-create the code already in t_person.display_
details() in t_business_person.display_details(). If you have more complex
methods in your types, this feature can save a lot of work and make your code easier to maintain.

The following statements create a table named object_business_customers and add an
object to this table:

```
CREATE TABLE object_business_customers OF t_business_person;

INSERT INTO object_business_customers VALUES (
  t_business_person(1, 'John', 'Brown', 'Manager', 'XYZ Corp')
);
```

The following query calls display_details() using object_business_customers:

```
SELECT o.display_details()
FROM object_business_customers o;

O.DISPLAY_DETAILS()
------------------------------------------------------
id=1, name=John Brown, title=Manager, company=XYZ Corp
```

As you can see, the id and name are displayed (which come from display_details() in t_
person), followed by the title and company (which come from display_details() in t_
business_person).

Summary

In this chapter, you have learned the following:

- An object type can contain attributes and methods.
- An object type can be used to define a column object or an object table.
- Objects can be created and manipulated using SQL and PL/SQL.
- An object reference can be used to access a row in an object table.
- Object types can inherit attributes and methods from each other.
- An object type marked as NOT INSTANTIABLE prevents objects of that type from being created.
- A constructor can set a default value for an attribute.
- A method in a supertype can be overridden by a method in a subtype.
- Generalized invocation allows you to call methods in a supertype from a subtype.

In the next chapter, you'll learn about collections.

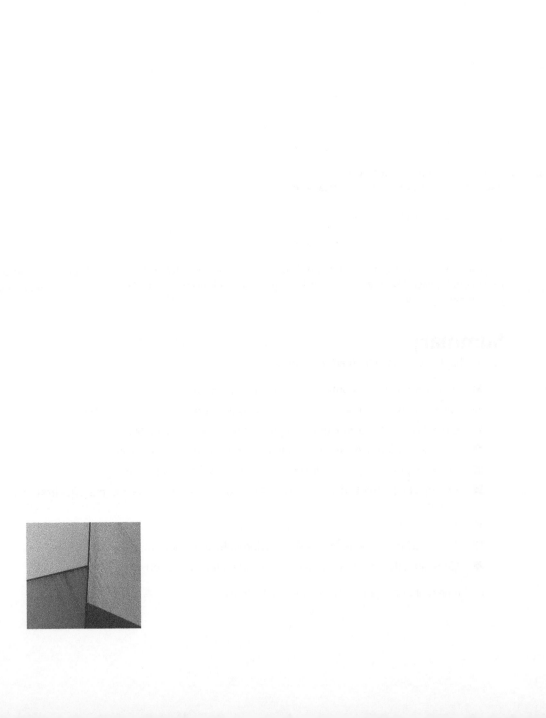

CHAPTER
14

Collections

I n this chapter, you will learn how to perform the following tasks:

- Use collection types to define columns in tables
- Create and manipulate collection data in SQL and PL/SQL
- Embed a collection within a collection

Introducing Collections

Collections allow you to store sets of elements in the database. There are three types of collections:

- **Varrays** A varray is similar to an array in Java and C#. A varray stores an ordered set of elements, and each element has an index that records its position in the array. Elements in a varray can be modified only as a whole, not individually. Even if you want to modify only one element, you must supply all the elements for the varray. A varray has a maximum size that you set when creating it, but you can change the size later.

- **Nested tables** A nested table is a table that is embedded within another table. You can insert, update, and delete individual elements in a nested table. This makes them more flexible than a varray, whose elements can be modified only as a whole. A nested table doesn't have a maximum size, and you can store an arbitrary number of elements in a nested table.

- **Associative arrays (formerly known as index-by tables)** An associative array is similar to a hash table in Java. Introduced in Oracle Database 10*g*, an associative array is a set of key and value pairs. You can get the value from the array using the key (which can be a string) or an integer that specifies the position of the value in the array. An associative array can be used only in PL/SQL and cannot be stored in the database.

You will learn about these collections in this chapter.

Running the Script to Create the Collection Schema

I've provided in the SQL directory a script named collection_schema.sql, which creates a user named collection_user with a password of collection_password.

You perform the following steps to create the schema:

1. Start SQL*Plus.
2. Log into the database as a user with privileges to create new users, tables, and PL/SQL packages. I run scripts in my database using the system user.
3. Run the collection_schema.sql script from within SQL*Plus using the @ command.

For example, if you're using Windows and the script is stored in C:\sql_book\SQL, then you enter the following command:

```
@ C:\sql_book\SQL\collection_schema.sql
```

When the script completes, you will be logged in as collection_user.

Creating Collection Types

In this section, you'll see how to create a varray type and a nested table type.

Creating a Varray Type

A varray stores an ordered set of elements, all of the same type, and the type can be a built-in database type or a user-defined object type. Each element has an index that corresponds to its position in the array, and you can modify elements in the varray only as a whole.

You create a varray type using the CREATE TYPE statement, in which you specify the maximum size and the type of elements stored in the varray. The following example creates a type named t_varray_address that can store up to three VARCHAR2 strings:

```
CREATE TYPE t_varray_address AS VARRAY(3) OF VARCHAR2(50);
/
```

Each VARCHAR2 will be used to represent a different address for a customer of our example store.

In Oracle Database 10g and higher, you can change the maximum number of elements of a varray using the ALTER TYPE statement. For example, the following statement alters the maximum number of elements to ten:

```
ALTER TYPE t_varray_address MODIFY LIMIT 10 CASCADE;
```

The CASCADE option propagates the change to any dependent objects in the database.

Creating a Nested Table Type

A nested table stores an unordered set of any number of elements. You can insert, update, and delete individual elements in a nested table. A nested table doesn't have a maximum size, and you can store an arbitrary number of elements in a nested table.

In this section, you'll see a nested table type that stores t_address object types. You saw the use of t_address in the previous chapter. It represents an address and is defined as follows:

```
CREATE TYPE t_address AS OBJECT (
   street VARCHAR2(15),
   city   VARCHAR2(15),
   state  CHAR(2),
   zip    VARCHAR2(5)
);
/
```

You create a nested table type using the CREATE TYPE statement, and the following example creates a type named t_nested_table_address that stores t_address objects:

```
CREATE TYPE t_nested_table_address AS TABLE OF t_address;
/
```

Notice that you don't specify the maximum size of a nested table. That's because a nested table can store any number of elements.

Using a Collection Type to Define a Column in a Table

Once you've created a collection type, you can use it to define a column in a table. In this section, you'll see how to use the varray type and the nested table type created in the previous section to define a column in a table.

Using a Varray Type to Define a Column in a Table

The following statement creates a table named customers_with_varray, which uses t_varray_address to define a column named addresses:

```
CREATE TABLE customers_with_varray (
  id          INTEGER PRIMARY KEY,
  first_name  VARCHAR2(10),
  last_name   VARCHAR2(10),
  addresses   t_varray_address
);
```

The elements in a varray are stored directly inside the table when the size of the varray is approximately 4,000 bytes or less. Otherwise, the varray is stored outside of the table. When a varray is stored within the table, accessing its elements is faster than accessing elements in a nested table.

Using a Nested Table Type to Define a Column in a Table

The following statement creates a table named customers_with_nested_table, which uses t_nested_table_address to define a column named addresses:

```
CREATE TABLE customers_with_nested_table (
  id          INTEGER PRIMARY KEY,
  first_name  VARCHAR2(10),
  last_name   VARCHAR2(10),
  addresses   t_nested_table_address
)
NESTED TABLE
  addresses
STORE AS
  nested_addresses;
```

The NESTED TABLE clause identifies the name of the nested table column (addresses in the example), and the STORE AS clause specifies the name of the nested table (nested_addresses in the example) where the actual elements are stored. You cannot access the nested table independently of the table in which it is embedded.

Getting Information on Collections

As you'll see in this section, you can use the DESCRIBE command and a couple of user views to get information on your collections.

Getting Information on a Varray

The following example describes t_varray_address:

```
DESCRIBE t_varray_address
 t_varray_address VARRAY(3) OF VARCHAR2(50)
```

The next example describes the customers_with_varray table, whose addresses column is of the t_varray_address type:

```
DESCRIBE customers_with_varray
 Name                                Null?     Type
 --------------------------------    --------  -----------------
 ID                                  NOT NULL  NUMBER(38)
 FIRST_NAME                                    VARCHAR2(10)
 LAST_NAME                                     VARCHAR2(10)
 ADDRESSES                                     T_VARRAY_ADDRESS
```

You can also get information on your varrays from the user_varrays view. Table 14-1 describes some of the columns in user_varrays.

The following example retrieves the details for t_varray_address from user_varrays:

```
SELECT parent_table_name, parent_table_column, type_name
FROM user_varrays
WHERE type_name = 'T_VARRAY_ADDRESS';


PARENT_TABLE_NAME
--------------------
CUSTOMERS_WITH_VARRAY


PARENT_TABLE_COLUMN
------------------
ADDRESSES


TYPE_NAME
---------------
T_VARRAY_ADDRESS
```

Column	Type	Description
parent_table_name	VARCHAR2(128)	Name of the table that contains the varray.
parent_table_column	VARCHAR2(4000)	Name of the column in the parent table containing the varray.
type_owner	VARCHAR2(128)	User who owns the varray type.

(Continued)

TABLE 14-1.   *Some Columns in the user_varrays View*

Column	Type	Description
type_name	VARCHAR2(128)	Name of the varray type.
lob_name	VARCHAR2(128)	Name of the large object (LOB) when the varray is stored in a LOB. You'll learn about LOBs in the next chapter.
storage_spec	VARCHAR2(30)	Storage specification for the varray.
return_type	VARCHAR2(20)	Return type of the column.
element_substitutable	VARCHAR2(25)	Whether or not (Y/N) the varray element is substitutable for a subtype.

TABLE 14-1. *Some Columns in the user_varrays View*

NOTE
You can get information on all the varrays you have access to using the all_varrays *view.*

Getting Information on a Nested Table

You can also use DESCRIBE with a nested table, as shown in the following example that describes t_nested_table_address:

```
DESCRIBE t_nested_table_address
t_nested_table_address TABLE OF T_ADDRESS
Name                                      Null?     Type
----------------------------------------- --------  -----------
STREET                                              VARCHAR2(15)
CITY                                                VARCHAR2(15)
STATE                                               CHAR(2)
ZIP                                                 VARCHAR2(5)
```

The next example describes the customers_with_nested_table table, whose addresses column is of type t_nested_table_address:

```
DESCRIBE customers_with_nested_table
Name                                  Null?     Type
------------------------------------- --------  ---------------------
ID                                    NOT NULL  NUMBER(38)
FIRST_NAME                                      VARCHAR2(10)
LAST_NAME                                       VARCHAR2(10)
ADDRESSES                                       T_NESTED_TABLE_ADDRESS
```

If you set the depth to 2 and describe customers_with_nested_table, you can see the attributes that make up t_nested_table_address:

```
SET DESCRIBE DEPTH 2
DESCRIBE customers_with_nested_table
Name                                      Null?     Type
----------------------------------------- --------  -------------
```

```
ID                                  NOT NULL NUMBER(38)
FIRST_NAME                          VARCHAR2(10)
LAST_NAME                           VARCHAR2(10)
ADDRESSES                           T_NESTED_TABLE_ADDRESS
   STREET                           VARCHAR2(15)
   CITY                             VARCHAR2(15)
   STATE                            CHAR(2)
   ZIP                              VARCHAR2(5)
```

You can also get information on your nested tables from the user_nested_tables view. Table 14-2 describes some of the columns in user_nested_tables.

The following example retrieves the details for the nested_addresses table from user_nested_tables:

```
SELECT table_name, table_type_name, parent_table_name, parent_table_column
FROM user_nested_tables
WHERE table_name = 'NESTED_ADDRESSES';
```

```
TABLE_NAME                          TABLE_TYPE_NAME
--------------------------------    ----------------------
NESTED_ADDRESSES                    T_NESTED_TABLE_ADDRESS

PARENT_TABLE_NAME
--------------------------
CUSTOMERS_WITH_NESTED_TABLE

PARENT_TABLE_COLUMN
-------------------
ADDRESSES
```

Column	Type	Description
table_name	VARCHAR2(128)	Name of the nested table.
table_type_owner	VARCHAR2(128)	User who owns the nested table type.
table_type_name	VARCHAR2(128)	Name of the nested table type.
parent_table_name	VARCHAR2(128)	Name of the parent table that contains the nested table.
parent_table_column	VARCHAR2(4000)	Name of the column in the parent table containing the nested table.
storage_spec	VARCHAR2(30)	Storage specification for the nested table
return_type	VARCHAR2(20)	Return type of the column.
element_substitutable	VARCHAR2(25)	Whether or not (Y/N) the nested table element is substitutable for a subtype.

TABLE 14-2.   *Some Columns in the user_nested_tables View*

> **NOTE**
> *You can get information on all the nested tables you have access to using the* all_nested_tables *view.*

Populating a Collection with Elements

In this section, you'll see how to populate a varray and a nested table with elements using INSERT statements. You don't run the INSERT statements shown in this section. They are executed when you run the collection_schema.sql script.

Populating a Varray with Elements

The following INSERT statements add rows to the customers_with_varray table. Notice the use of the t_varray_address constructor to specify the strings for the elements of the varray.

```
INSERT INTO customers_with_varray VALUES (
  1, 'Steve', 'Brown',
  t_varray_address(
    '2 State Street, Beantown, MA, 12345',
    '4 Hill Street, Lost Town, CA, 54321'
  )
);

INSERT INTO customers_with_varray VALUES (
  2, 'John', 'Smith',
  t_varray_address(
    '1 High Street, Newtown, CA, 12347',
    '3 New Street, Anytown, MI, 54323',
    '7 Market Street, Main Town, MA, 54323'
  )
);
```

The first row has two addresses and the second row has three. Any number of addresses up to the maximum limit for the varray can be stored.

Populating a Nested Table with Elements

The following INSERT statements add rows to customers_with_nested_table. Notice the use of the t_nested_table_address and t_address constructors to specify the elements of the nested table.

```
INSERT INTO customers_with_nested_table VALUES (
  1, 'Steve', 'Brown',
  t_nested_table_address(
    t_address('2 State Street', 'Beantown', 'MA', '12345'),
    t_address('4 Hill Street', 'Lost Town', 'CA', '54321')
  )
);

INSERT INTO customers_with_nested_table VALUES (
  2, 'John', 'Smith',
```

```
  t_nested_table_address(
    t_address('1 High Street', 'Newtown', 'CA', '12347'),
    t_address('3 New Street', 'Anytown', 'MI', '54323'),
    t_address('7 Market Street', 'Main Town', 'MA', '54323')
  )
);
```

The first row has two addresses and the second row has three. Any number of addresses can be stored in a nested table.

Retrieving Elements from Collections

In this section, you'll see how to retrieve elements from a varray and a nested table using queries. The output from the queries has been formatted to make the results more readable.

Retrieving Elements from a Varray

The following query retrieves customer #1 from the `customers_with_varray` table. One row is returned, and it contains the two addresses stored in the varray.

```
SELECT *
FROM customers_with_varray
WHERE id = 1;

        ID FIRST_NAME LAST_NAME
---------- ---------- ----------
ADDRESSES
---------------------------------------------------------
         1 Steve      Brown
T_VARRAY_ADDRESS('2 State Street, Beantown, MA, 12345',
 '4 Hill Street, Lost Town, CA, 54321')
```

The next query specifies the actual column names:

```
SELECT id, first_name, last_name, addresses
FROM customers_with_varray
WHERE id = 1;

        ID FIRST_NAME LAST_NAME
---------- ---------- ----------
ADDRESSES
---------------------------------------------------------
         1 Steve      Brown
T_VARRAY_ADDRESS('2 State Street, Beantown, MA, 12345',
 '4 Hill Street, Lost Town, CA, 54321')
```

These examples all return the addresses in the varray as a single row. Later, in the section "Using TABLE() to Treat a Collection as a Series of Rows," you'll see how you can treat the data stored in a collection as a series of rows.

Retrieving Elements from a Nested Table

The following query retrieves customer #1 from `customers_with_nested_table`. One row is returned, and it contains the two addresses stored in the nested table.

```sql
SELECT *
FROM customers_with_nested_table
WHERE id = 1;

        ID FIRST_NAME LAST_NAME
---------- ---------- ----------
ADDRESSES(STREET, CITY, STATE, ZIP)
--------------------------------------------------------
         1 Steve      Brown
T_NESTED_TABLE_ADDRESS(
 T_ADDRESS('2 State Street', 'Beantown', 'MA', '12345'),
 T_ADDRESS('4 Hill Street', 'Lost Town', 'CA', '54321'))
```

The next query specifies the actual column names:

```sql
SELECT id, first_name, last_name, addresses
FROM customers_with_nested_table
WHERE id = 1;

        ID FIRST_NAME LAST_NAME
---------- ---------- ----------
ADDRESSES(STREET, CITY, STATE, ZIP)
--------------------------------------------------------
         1 Steve      Brown
T_NESTED_TABLE_ADDRESS(
 T_ADDRESS('2 State Street', 'Beantown', 'MA', '12345'),
 T_ADDRESS('4 Hill Street', 'Lost Town', 'CA', '54321'))
```

The next query gets just the `addresses` nested table. As in the previous examples, one row is returned, and it contains the two addresses stored in the nested table.

```sql
SELECT addresses
FROM customers_with_nested_table
WHERE id = 1;

ADDRESSES(STREET, CITY, STATE, ZIP)
--------------------------------------------------------
T_NESTED_TABLE_ADDRESS(
 T_ADDRESS('2 State Street', 'Beantown', 'MA', '12345'),
 T_ADDRESS('4 Hill Street', 'Lost Town', 'CA', '54321'))
```

Using TABLE() to Treat a Collection as a Series of Rows

The previous queries you've seen in this chapter return the contents of a collection as a single row. Sometimes, you might want to treat the data stored in a collection as a series of rows. For example, you might be working with a legacy application that can only use rows. To treat a collection as a series of rows, you use the TABLE() function. In this section, you'll see how to use TABLE() with a varray and a nested table.

Using TABLE() with a Varray

The following query uses TABLE() to retrieve customer #1's two addresses from the customers_with_varray table. Notice that two separate rows are returned.

```
SELECT a.*
FROM customers_with_varray c, TABLE(c.addresses) a
WHERE id = 1;

COLUMN_VALUE
-----------------------------------
2 State Street, Beantown, MA, 12345
4 Hill Street, Lost Town, CA, 54321
```

The Oracle database software automatically adds the column name of COLUMN_VALUE to the rows returned by the query.

COLUMN_VALUE is a pseudo column alias, and it is automatically added when a collection contains data of one of the built-in data types, like VARCHAR2, CHAR, NUMBER, or DATE. Because the example varray contains VARCHAR2 data, the COLUMN_VALUE alias is added. If the varray had contained data of a user-defined object type, then TABLE() would return objects of that type and COLUMN_VALUE would not appear. You'll see an example of this in the next section.

You can also embed an entire SELECT statement inside TABLE(). For example, the following query rewrites the previous example, placing a SELECT inside TABLE():

```
SELECT *
FROM TABLE(
  -- get the addresses for customer #1
  SELECT addresses
  FROM customers_with_varray
  WHERE id = 1
);

COLUMN_VALUE
-----------------------------------
2 State Street, Beantown, MA, 12345
4 Hill Street, Lost Town, CA, 54321
```

The following query shows another example that uses TABLE() to get the addresses:

```
SELECT c.id, c.first_name, c.last_name, a.*
FROM customers_with_varray c, TABLE(c.addresses) a
WHERE id = 1;

        ID FIRST_NAME LAST_NAME
---------- ---------- ----------
COLUMN_VALUE
-----------------------------------
         1 Steve      Brown
```

```
2 State Street, Beantown, MA, 12345

         1 Steve       Brown
4 Hill Street, Lost Town, CA, 54321
```

Using TABLE() with a Nested Table

The following query uses `TABLE()` to retrieve customer #1's two addresses from `customers_with_nested_table`. Notice that two separate rows are returned.

```sql
SELECT a.*
FROM customers_with_nested_table c, TABLE(c.addresses) a
WHERE id = 1;
```

```
STREET           CITY            ST ZIP
---------------  --------------- -- -----
2 State Street   Beantown        MA 12345
4 Hill Street    Lost Town       CA 54321
```

The next query gets the `street` and `state` attributes of the addresses:

```sql
SELECT a.street, a.state
FROM customers_with_nested_table c, TABLE(c.addresses) a
WHERE id = 1;
```

```
STREET           ST
---------------  --
2 State Street   MA
4 Hill Street    CA
```

The following query shows another example that uses `TABLE()` to get the addresses:

```sql
SELECT c.id, c.first_name, c.last_name, a.*
FROM customers_with_nested_table c, TABLE(c.addresses) a
WHERE c.id = 1;
```

```
ID FIRST_NAME LAST_NAME  STREET          CITY            ST ZIP
------ ---------- ---------- --------------- --------------- -- -----
     1 Steve      Brown      2 State Street  Beantown        MA 12345
     1 Steve      Brown      4 Hill Street   Lost Town       CA 54321
```

You'll see an important use of `TABLE()` later in the section "Modifying Elements of a Nested Table."

Modifying Elements of Collections

In this section, you'll see how to modify the elements in a varray and a nested table. You should feel free to run the `UPDATE`, `INSERT`, and `DELETE` statements shown in this section.

Modifying Elements of a Varray

The elements in a varray can be modified only as a whole, which means that even if you want to modify only one element, you must supply all the elements for the varray. The following UPDATE statement modifies the addresses of customer #2 in the customers_with_varray table:

```
UPDATE customers_with_varray
SET addresses = t_varray_address(
  '6 Any Street, Lost Town, GA, 33347',
  '3 New Street, Anytown, MI, 54323',
  '7 Market Street, Main Town, MA, 54323'
)
WHERE id = 2;
```

```
1 row updated.
```

Modifying Elements of a Nested Table

Unlike in a varray, elements in a nested table can be modified individually. You can insert, update, and delete individual elements in a nested table. You'll see how to do all three of these modifications in this section.

The following INSERT statement adds an address to customer #2 in customers_with_nested_table. Notice that TABLE() is used to get the addresses as a series of rows.

```
INSERT INTO TABLE(
  -- get the addresses for customer #2
  SELECT addresses
  FROM customers_with_nested_table
  WHERE id = 2
) VALUES (
  t_address('5 Main Street', 'Uptown', 'NY', '55512')
);
```

```
1 row created.
```

The following UPDATE statement changes the '1 High Street' address of customer #2 to '9 Any Street'. Notice the use of the alias addr in the VALUE clauses when specifying the addresses.

```
UPDATE TABLE(
  -- get the addresses for customer #2
  SELECT addresses
  FROM customers_with_nested_table
  WHERE id = 2
) addr
SET VALUE(addr) =
  t_address('9 Any Street', 'Lost Town', 'VA', '74321')
WHERE VALUE(addr) =
  t_address('1 High Street', 'Newtown', 'CA', '12347');
```

```
1 row updated.
```

The following DELETE statement removes the `'3 New Street...'` address from customer #2:

```
DELETE FROM TABLE(
  -- get the addresses for customer #2
  SELECT addresses
  FROM customers_with_nested_table
  WHERE id = 2
) addr
WHERE VALUE(addr) =
  t_address('3 New Street', 'Anytown', 'MI', '54323');
```

```
1 row deleted.
```

Using a Map Method to Compare the Contents of Nested Tables

You can compare the contents of one nested table with the contents of another. Two nested tables are equal only if the following conditions are true:

- The tables are of the same type.
- The tables have the same number of rows.
- All the table elements contain the same values.

If the elements of the nested table are of a built-in database type, like NUMBER, VARCHAR2, and so on, then the database will automatically compare the contents of the nested tables for you. If, however, the elements are of a user-defined object type, then you must provide a map function that contains code to compare the objects (map functions were shown in the section "Comparing Object Values" of the previous chapter).

The following statements create a type named t_address2 that contains a map function named get_string(). Notice that get_string() returns a VARCHAR2 containing the values for the zip, state, city, and street attributes.

```
CREATE TYPE t_address2 AS OBJECT (
  street VARCHAR2(15),
  city   VARCHAR2(15),
  state  CHAR(2),
  zip    VARCHAR2(5),

  -- declare the get_string() map function,
  -- which returns a VARCHAR2 string
  MAP MEMBER FUNCTION get_string RETURN VARCHAR2
);
/

CREATE TYPE BODY t_address2 AS
  -- define the get_string() map function
```

```
   MAP MEMBER FUNCTION get_string RETURN VARCHAR2 IS
   BEGIN
     -- return a concatenated string containing the
     -- zip, state, city, and street attributes
     RETURN zip || ' ' || state || ' ' || city || ' ' || street;
   END get_string;
END;
/
```

As you'll see shortly, the database will automatically call get_string() when comparing t_address2 objects.

The following statements create a nested table type and a table, and add a row to the table:

```
CREATE TYPE t_nested_table_address2 AS TABLE OF t_address2;
/

CREATE TABLE customers_with_nested_table2 (
   id          INTEGER PRIMARY KEY,
   first_name VARCHAR2(10),
   last_name  VARCHAR2(10),
   addresses  t_nested_table_address2
)
NESTED TABLE
  addresses
STORE AS
  nested_addresses2;

INSERT INTO customers_with_nested_table2 VALUES (
   1, 'Steve', 'Brown',
   t_nested_table_address2(
     t_address2('2 State Street', 'Beantown', 'MA', '12345'),
     t_address2('4 Hill Street', 'Lost Town', 'CA', '54321')
   )
);
```

The following query includes a nested table in the WHERE clause. Notice that the addresses after the equal operator = in the WHERE clause are the same as those in the previous INSERT statement.

```
SELECT cn.id, cn.first_name, cn.last_name
FROM customers_with_nested_table2 cn
WHERE cn.addresses =
  t_nested_table_address2(
    t_address2('2 State Street', 'Beantown', 'MA', '12345'),
    t_address2('4 Hill Street', 'Lost Town', 'CA', '54321')
  );

        ID FIRST_NAME LAST_NAME
---------- ---------- ----------
         1 Steve      Brown
```

When the query is executed, the database automatically calls `get_string()` to compare the `t_address2` objects in `cn.addresses` to the `t_address2` objects after the equal operator = in the WHERE clause. The `get_string()` function returns a VARCHAR2 string containing the `zip`, `state`, `city`, and `street` attributes of the objects, and when the strings are equal for every object, the nested tables are also equal.

The next query returns no rows because the single address after the equal operator = in the WHERE clause matches only one of the addresses in `cn.addresses` (remember: two nested tables are equal only if they are of the same type, *have the same number of rows*, and their elements contain the same values):

```
SELECT cn.id, cn.first_name, cn.last_name
FROM customers_with_nested_table2 cn
WHERE cn.addresses =
  t_nested_table_address2(
    t_address2('4 Hill Street', 'Lost Town', 'CA', '54321')
  );
```

```
no rows selected
```

In Oracle Database 10g and higher, you can use the SUBMULTISET operator to check whether the contents of one nested table are a subset of another nested table. The following query rewrites the previous example and returns a row:

```
SELECT cn.id, cn.first_name, cn.last_name
FROM customers_with_nested_table2 cn
WHERE
  t_nested_table_address2(
    t_address2('4 Hill Street', 'Lost Town', 'CA', '54321')
  )
  SUBMULTISET OF cn.addresses;
```

```
        ID FIRST_NAME LAST_NAME
---------- ---------- ----------
         1 Steve      Brown
```

Because the address in the first part of the WHERE clause is a subset of the addresses in `cn.addresses`, a match is found and a row is returned.

The following query shows another example. This time the addresses in `cn.addresses` are a subset of the addresses after OF in the WHERE clause.

```
SELECT cn.id, cn.first_name, cn.last_name
FROM customers_with_nested_table2 cn
WHERE
  cn.addresses SUBMULTISET OF
  t_nested_table_address2(
    t_address2('2 State Street', 'Beantown', 'MA', '12345'),
    t_address2('4 Hill Street', 'Lost Town', 'CA', '54321'),
    t_address2('6 State Street', 'Beantown', 'MA', '12345')
  );
```

```
        ID FIRST_NAME LAST_NAME
---------- ---------- ----------
         1 Steve      Brown
```

You'll learn more about the SUBMULTISET operator later in this chapter in the section "SUBMULTISET Operator." Also, in the section "Equal and Not-Equal Operators," you'll see how to use the ANSI operators implemented in Oracle Database 10g to compare nested tables.

NOTE
There is no direct mechanism for comparing the contents of varrays.

Using CAST() to Convert Collections from One Type to Another

You can use CAST() to convert a collection of one type to another collection type. In this section, you'll see how to use CAST() to convert a varray to a nested table and vice versa.

Using CAST() to Convert a Varray to a Nested Table

The following statements create and populate a table named customers_with_varray2 that contains an addresses column of type t_varray_address2:

```
CREATE TYPE t_varray_address2 AS VARRAY(3) OF t_address;
/

CREATE TABLE customers_with_varray2 (
  id          INTEGER PRIMARY KEY,
  first_name VARCHAR2(10),
  last_name  VARCHAR2(10),
  addresses  t_varray_address2
);

INSERT INTO customers_with_varray2 VALUES (
  1, 'Jason', 'Bond',
  t_varray_address2(
    t_address('9 Newton Drive', 'Sometown', 'WY', '22123'),
    t_address('6 Spring Street', 'New City', 'CA', '77712')
  )
);
```

The following query uses CAST() to return the varray addresses for customer #1 as a nested table. Notice that the addresses appear in a constructor for the T_NESTED_TABLE_ADDRESS type, indicating the conversion of the elements to this type.

```
SELECT CAST(cv.addresses AS t_nested_table_address)
FROM customers_with_varray2 cv
WHERE cv.id = 1;
```

```
CAST(CV.ADDRESSESAST_NESTED_TABLE_ADDRESS)(STREET, CITY, STATE, ZIP)
-----------------------------------------------------------------
T_NESTED_TABLE_ADDRESS(
 T_ADDRESS('9 Newton Drive', 'Sometown', 'WY', '22123'),
 T_ADDRESS('6 Spring Street', 'New City', 'CA', '77712'))
```

Using CAST() to Convert a Nested Table to a Varray

The following query uses CAST() to return the addresses for customer #1 in customers_with_nested_table as a varray. Notice that the addresses appear in a constructor for T_VARRAY_ADDRESS2.

```
SELECT CAST(cn.addresses AS t_varray_address2)
FROM customers_with_nested_table cn
WHERE cn.id = 1;

CAST(CN.ADDRESSESAST_VARRAY_ADDRESS2)(STREET, CITY, STATE, ZIP)
-----------------------------------------------------------------
T_VARRAY_ADDRESS2(
 T_ADDRESS('2 State Street', 'Beantown', 'MA', '12345'),
 T_ADDRESS('4 Hill Street', 'Lost Town', 'CA', '54321'))
```

Using Collections in PL/SQL

You can use collections in PL/SQL. In this section, you'll see how to perform the following tasks in PL/SQL:

- Manipulate a varray
- Manipulate a nested table
- Use the PL/SQL collection methods to access and manipulate collections

All the packages you'll see in this section are created when you run the collection_schema.sql script. If you performed any of the INSERT, UPDATE, or DELETE statements shown in the earlier sections of this chapter, go ahead and rerun the collection_schema.sql script so that your output matches mine in this section.

Manipulating a Varray

In this section, you'll see a package named varray_package. This package contains the following items:

- A REF CURSOR type named t_ref_cursor
- A function named get_customers(), which returns a t_ref_cursor object that points to the rows in the customers_with_varray table
- A procedure named insert_customer(), which adds a row to the customers_with_varray table

The `collection_schema.sql` script contains the following package specification and body for `varray_package`:

```
CREATE PACKAGE varray_package AS
  TYPE t_ref_cursor IS REF CURSOR;
  FUNCTION get_customers RETURN t_ref_cursor;
  PROCEDURE insert_customer(
    p_id         IN customers_with_varray.id%TYPE,
    p_first_name IN customers_with_varray.first_name%TYPE,
    p_last_name  IN customers_with_varray.last_name%TYPE,
    p_addresses  IN customers_with_varray.addresses%TYPE
  );
END varray_package;
/

CREATE PACKAGE BODY varray_package AS
  -- get_customers() function returns a REF CURSOR
  -- that points to the rows in customers_with_varray
  FUNCTION get_customers
  RETURN t_ref_cursor IS
    --declare the REF CURSOR object
    v_customers_ref_cursor t_ref_cursor;
  BEGIN
    -- get the REF CURSOR
    OPEN v_customers_ref_cursor FOR
      SELECT *
      FROM customers_with_varray;
    -- return the REF CURSOR
    RETURN customers_ref_cursor;
  END get_customers;

  -- insert_customer() procedure adds a row to
  -- customers_with_varray
  PROCEDURE insert_customer(
    p_id         IN customers_with_varray.id%TYPE,
    p_first_name IN customers_with_varray.first_name%TYPE,
    p_last_name  IN customers_with_varray.last_name%TYPE,
    p_addresses  IN customers_with_varray.addresses%TYPE
  ) IS
  BEGIN
    INSERT INTO customers_with_varray
    VALUES (p_id, p_first_name, p_last_name, p_addresses);
    COMMIT;
  EXCEPTION
    WHEN OTHERS THEN
      ROLLBACK;
  END insert_customer;
END varray_package;
/
```

The following example calls `insert_customer()` to add a new row to the `customers_with_varray` table:

```
CALL varray_package.insert_customer(
   3, 'James', 'Red',
   t_varray_address(
     '10 Main Street, Green Town, CA, 22212',
     '20 State Street, Blue Town, FL, 22213'
   )
);

Call completed.
```

The next example calls `get_customers()` to retrieve the rows from `customers_with_varray`:

```
SELECT varray_package.get_customers
FROM dual;

GET_CUSTOMERS
-------------------
CURSOR STATEMENT : 1

CURSOR STATEMENT : 1

        ID FIRST_NAME LAST_NAME
---------- ---------- ----------
ADDRESSES
----------------------------------------------------------
         1 Steve      Brown
T_VARRAY_ADDRESS('2 State Street, Beantown, MA, 12345',
 '4 Hill Street, Lost Town, CA, 54321')

         2 John       Smith
T_VARRAY_ADDRESS('1 High Street, Newtown, CA, 12347',
 '3 New Street, Anytown, MI, 54323',
 '7 Market Street, Main Town, MA, 54323')

         3 James      Red
T_VARRAY_ADDRESS('10 Main Street, Green Town, CA, 22212',
 '20 State Street, Blue Town, FL, 22213')
```

Manipulating a Nested Table

In this section, you'll see a package named `nested_table_package`. This package contains the following items:

- A `REF CURSOR` type named `t_ref_cursor`
- A function named `get_customers()`, which returns a `t_ref_cursor` object that points to the rows in `customers_with_nested_table`

- A procedure named `insert_customer()`, which adds a row to `customers_with_nested_table`

The `collection_schema.sql` script contains the following package specification and body for `nested_table_package`:

```
CREATE PACKAGE nested_table_package AS
  TYPE t_ref_cursor IS REF CURSOR;
  FUNCTION get_customers RETURN t_ref_cursor;
  PROCEDURE insert_customer(
    p_id         IN customers_with_nested_table.id%TYPE,
    p_first_name IN customers_with_nested_table.first_name%TYPE,
    p_last_name  IN customers_with_nested_table.last_name%TYPE,
    p_addresses  IN customers_with_nested_table.addresses%TYPE
  );
END nested_table_package;
/

CREATE PACKAGE BODY nested_table_package AS
  -- get_customers() function returns a REF CURSOR
  -- that points to the rows in customers_with_nested_table
  FUNCTION get_customers
  RETURN t_ref_cursor IS
    -- declare the REF CURSOR object
    v_customers_ref_cursor t_ref_cursor;
  BEGIN
    -- get the REF CURSOR
    OPEN v_customers_ref_cursor FOR
      SELECT *
      FROM customers_with_nested_table;
    -- return the REF CURSOR
    RETURN customers_ref_cursor;
  END get_customers;

  -- insert_customer() procedure adds a row to
  -- customers_with_nested_table
  PROCEDURE insert_customer(
    p_id         IN customers_with_nested_table.id%TYPE,
    p_first_name IN customers_with_nested_table.first_name%TYPE,
    p_last_name  IN customers_with_nested_table.last_name%TYPE,
    p_addresses  IN customers_with_nested_table.addresses%TYPE
  ) IS
  BEGIN
    INSERT INTO customers_with_nested_table
    VALUES (p_id, p_first_name, p_last_name, p_addresses);
    COMMIT;
  EXCEPTION
    WHEN OTHERS THEN
      ROLLBACK;
  END insert_customer;
END nested_table_package;
/
```

The following example calls `insert_customer()` to add a new row to customers_with_nested_table:

```
CALL nested_table_package.insert_customer(
  3, 'James', 'Red',
  t_nested_table_address(
    t_address('10 Main Street', 'Green Town', 'CA', '22212'),
    t_address('20 State Street', 'Blue Town', 'FL', '22213')
  )
);

Call completed.
```

The next example calls `get_customers()` to retrieve the rows from customers_with_nested_table:

```
SELECT nested_table_package.get_customers
FROM dual;

GET_CUSTOMERS
-------------------
CURSOR STATEMENT : 1

CURSOR STATEMENT : 1

        ID FIRST_NAME LAST_NAME
---------- ---------- ----------
ADDRESSES(STREET, CITY, STATE, ZIP)
-----------------------------------------------------------
         1 Steve      Brown
T_NESTED_TABLE_ADDRESS(
 T_ADDRESS('2 State Street', 'Beantown', 'MA', '12345'),
 T_ADDRESS('4 Hill Street', 'Lost Town', 'CA', '54321'))

         2 John       Smith
T_NESTED_TABLE_ADDRESS(
 T_ADDRESS('1 High Street', 'Newtown', 'CA', '12347'),
 T_ADDRESS('3 New Street', 'Anytown', 'MI', '54323'),
 T_ADDRESS('7 Market Street', 'Main Town', 'MA', '54323'))

         3 James      Red
T_NESTED_TABLE_ADDRESS(
 T_ADDRESS('10 Main Street', 'Green Town', 'CA', '22212'),
 T_ADDRESS('20 State Street', 'Blue Town', 'FL', '22213'))
```

Using PL/SQL Collection Methods

In this section, you'll see the PL/SQL methods you can use with collections. Table 14-3 summarizes the collection methods. These methods can be used only in PL/SQL.

Method	Description
COUNT	Returns the number of elements in a collection. Because a nested table can have individual elements that are empty, COUNT returns the number of non-empty elements in a nested table.
DELETE DELETE(*n*) DELETE(*n*, *m*)	Removes elements from a collection. There are three forms of DELETE: ■ DELETE removes all elements. ■ DELETE(*n*) removes element *n*. ■ DELETE(*n*, *m*) removes elements *n* through *m*. Because varrays always have consecutive subscripts, you cannot delete individual elements from a varray (except from the end by using TRIM).
EXISTS(*n*)	Returns true if element *n* in a collection exists: EXISTS returns true for non-empty elements and false for empty elements of nested tables or elements beyond the range of a collection.
EXTEND EXTEND(*n*) EXTEND(*n*, *m*)	Adds elements to the end of a collection. There are three forms of EXTEND: ■ EXTEND adds one element, which is set to null. ■ EXTEND(*n*) adds *n* elements, which are set to null. ■ EXTEND(*n*, *m*) adds *n* elements, which are set to a copy of the *m* element.
FIRST	Returns the index of the first element in a collection. If the collection is completely empty, FIRST returns null. Because a nested table can have individual elements that are empty, FIRST returns the lowest index of a non-empty element in a nested table.
LAST	Returns the index of the last element in a collection. If the collection is completely empty, LAST returns null. Because a nested table can have individual elements that are empty, LAST returns the highest index of a non-empty element in a nested table.
LIMIT	For nested tables, which have no declared size, LIMIT returns null. For varrays, LIMIT returns the maximum number of elements that the varray can contain. You specify the limit in the type definition. The limit is changed when using TRIM and EXTEND, or when you use ALTER TYPE to change the limit.
NEXT(*n*)	Returns the index of the element after *n*. Because a nested table can have individual elements that are empty, NEXT returns the index of a non-empty element after *n*. If there are no elements after *n*, NEXT returns null.
PRIOR(*n*)	Returns the index of the element before *n*. Because a nested table can have individual elements that are empty, PRIOR returns the index of a non-empty element before *n*. If there are no elements before *n*, PRIOR returns null.
TRIM TRIM(*n*)	Removes elements from the end of a collection. There are two forms of TRIM: ■ TRIM removes one element from the end. ■ TRIM(*n*) removes *n* elements from the end.

TABLE 14-3.   *PL/SQL Collection Methods*

The following sections use a package named `collection_method_example`. The examples illustrate the use of the methods shown in the previous table. The package is created by the `collection_schema.sql` script, and you'll see the individual methods defined in this package in the following sections.

COUNT()

`COUNT` returns the number of elements in a collection. Because a nested table can have individual elements that are empty, `COUNT` returns the number of non-empty elements in a nested table. For example, let's say you have a nested table named `v_nested_table` that has its elements set as shown in the following table.

Element Index	Empty/Not Empty
1	Empty
2	Not empty
3	Empty
4	Not empty

Given the configuration for `v_nested_table` shown in the previous table, `v_nested_table.COUNT` returns 2, the number of non-empty elements.

`COUNT` is used in the `get_addresses()` and `display_addresses()` methods of the `collection_method_examples` package. The `get_addresses()` function returns the specified customer's addresses from `customers_with_nested_table`, whose id is passed to the function:

```
FUNCTION get_addresses(
  p_id customers_with_nested_table.id%TYPE
) RETURN t_nested_table_address IS
  -- declare object named v_addresses to store the
  -- nested table of addresses
  v_addresses t_nested_table_address;
BEGIN
  -- retrieve the nested table of addresses into v_addresses
  SELECT addresses
  INTO v_addresses
  FROM customers_with_nested_table
  WHERE id = p_id;

  -- display the number of addresses using v_addresses.COUNT
  DBMS_OUTPUT.PUT_LINE(
    'Number of addresses = '|| v_addresses.COUNT
  );

  -- return v_addresses
  RETURN v_addresses;
END get_addresses;
```

The following example sets the server output on and calls `get_addresses()` for customer #1:

```
SET SERVEROUTPUT ON
SELECT collection_method_examples.get_addresses(1) addresses
FROM dual;

ADDRESSES(STREET, CITY, STATE, ZIP)
-----------------------------------------------------------
T_NESTED_TABLE_ADDRESS(
 T_ADDRESS('2 State Street', 'Beantown', 'MA', '12345'),
 T_ADDRESS('4 Hill Street', 'Lost Town', 'CA', '54321'))

Number of addresses = 2
```

The following `display_addresses()` procedure accepts a parameter named `p_addresses`, which contains a nested table of addresses. The procedure displays the number of addresses in `p_addresses` using COUNT, and then displays those addresses using a loop.

```
PROCEDURE display_addresses(
  p_addresses t_nested_table_address
) IS
  v_count INTEGER;
BEGIN
  -- display the number of addresses in p_addresses
  DBMS_OUTPUT.PUT_LINE(
    'Current number of addresses = '|| p_addresses.COUNT
  );

  -- display the addresses in p_addresses using a loop
  FOR v_count IN 1..p_addresses.COUNT LOOP
    DBMS_OUTPUT.PUT_LINE('Address #' || v_count || ':');
    DBMS_OUTPUT.PUT(p_addresses(v_count).street || ', ');
    DBMS_OUTPUT.PUT(p_addresses(v_count).city || ', ');
    DBMS_OUTPUT.PUT(p_addresses(v_count).state || ', ');
    DBMS_OUTPUT.PUT_LINE(p_addresses(v_count).zip);
  END LOOP;
END display_addresses;
```

You'll see the use of `display_addresses()` shortly.

DELETE()

DELETE removes elements from a collection. There are three forms of DELETE:

- DELETE removes all elements.
- DELETE(n) removes element n.
- DELETE(n, m) removes elements n through m.

For example, let's say you have a nested table named `v_nested_table` that has seven elements, and then `v_nested_table.DELETE(2, 5)` removes elements 2 through 5.

The following `delete_address()` procedure gets the addresses for customer #1 and then uses `DELETE` to remove the address whose index is specified by the `p_address_num` parameter:

```
PROCEDURE delete_address(
  p_address_num INTEGER
) IS
  v_addresses t_nested_table_address;
BEGIN
  v_addresses := get_addresses(1);
  display_addresses(v_addresses);
  DBMS_OUTPUT.PUT_LINE('Deleting address #' || p_address_num);

  -- delete the address specified by p_address_num
  v_addresses.DELETE(p_address_num);

  display_addresses(v_addresses);
END delete_address;
```

The following example calls `delete_address(2)` to remove address #2 from customer #1:

```
CALL collection_method_examples.delete_address(2);
Number of addresses = 2
Current number of addresses = 2
Address #1:
2 State Street, Beantown, MA, 12345
Address #2:
4 Hill Street, Lost Town, CA, 54321
Deleting address #2
Current number of addresses = 1
Address #1:
2 State Street, Beantown, MA, 12345
```

EXISTS()

`EXISTS(n)` returns true if element n in a collection exists: `EXISTS` returns true for non-empty elements, and it returns false for empty elements of nested tables or elements beyond the range of a collection. For example, let's say you have a nested table named `v_nested_table` that has its elements set as shown in the following table.

Element Index	Empty/Not Empty
1	Empty
2	Not empty
3	Empty
4	Not empty

Given the configuration for `v_nested_table` shown in the previous table, `v_nested_table.EXISTS(2)` returns true (because element #2 is not empty), and `v_nested_table.EXISTS(3)` returns false (because element #3 is empty).

The following `exist_addresses()` procedure gets the addresses for customer #1, uses `DELETE` to remove address #1, and then uses `EXISTS` to check whether addresses #1 and #2 exist (#1 does not exist because it has been deleted, #2 does exist):

```
PROCEDURE exist_addresses IS
  v_addresses t_nested_table_address;
BEGIN
  v_addresses := get_addresses(1);
  DBMS_OUTPUT.PUT_LINE('Deleting address #1');
  v_addresses.DELETE(1);

  -- use EXISTS to check if the addresses exist
  IF v_addresses.EXISTS(1) THEN
    DBMS_OUTPUT.PUT_LINE('Address #1 does exist');
  ELSE
    DBMS_OUTPUT.PUT_LINE('Address #1 does not exist');
  END IF;
  IF v_addresses.EXISTS(2) THEN
    DBMS_OUTPUT.PUT_LINE('Address #2 does exist');
  END IF;
END exist_addresses;
```

The following example calls `exist_addresses()`:

```
CALL collection_method_examples.exist_addresses();
Number of addresses = 2
Deleting address #1
Address #1 does not exist
Address #2 does exist
```

EXTEND()

EXTEND adds elements to the end of a collection. There are three forms of `EXTEND`:

- EXTEND adds one element, which is set to null.
- EXTEND(*n*) adds *n* elements, which are set to null.
- EXTEND(*n*, *m*) adds *n* elements, which are set to a copy of the *m* element.

For example, let's say you have a collection named `v_nested_table` that has seven elements, and then `v_nested_table.EXTEND(2, 5)` adds element #5 twice to the end of the collection.

The following `extend_addresses()` procedure gets the addresses for customer #1 into `v_addresses`, and then uses `EXTEND` to copy address #1 twice to the end of `v_addresses`:

```
PROCEDURE extend_addresses IS
  v_addresses t_nested_table_address;
BEGIN
  v_addresses := get_addresses(1);
  display_addresses(v_addresses);
  DBMS_OUTPUT.PUT_LINE('Extending addresses');
```

```
-- copy address #1 twice to the end of v_addresses
v_addresses.EXTEND(2, 1);

display_addresses(v_addresses);
END extend_addresses;
```

The following example calls extend_addresses():

```
CALL collection_method_examples.extend_addresses();
Number of addresses = 2
Current number of addresses = 2
Address #1:
2 State Street, Beantown, MA, 12345
Address #2:
4 Hill Street, Lost Town, CA, 54321
Extending addresses
Current number of addresses = 4
Address #1:
2 State Street, Beantown, MA, 12345
Address #2:
4 Hill Street, Lost Town, CA, 54321
Address #3:
2 State Street, Beantown, MA, 12345
Address #4:
2 State Street, Beantown, MA, 12345
```

FIRST()

FIRST returns the index of the first element in a collection. If the collection is completely empty, FIRST returns null. Because a nested table can have individual elements that are empty, FIRST returns the lowest index of a non-empty element in a nested table. For example, let's say you have a nested table named v_nested_table that has its elements set as shown in the following table.

Element Index	Empty/Not Empty
1	Empty
2	Not empty
3	Empty
4	Not empty

Given the configuration for v_nested_table shown in the previous table, v_nested_table.FIRST returns 2, the lowest index containing a non-empty element.

The following first_address() procedure gets the addresses for customer #1 into v_addresses and then uses FIRST to display the index of the first address in v_addresses. The procedure then deletes address #1 using DELETE and displays the new index returned by FIRST.

```
PROCEDURE first_address IS
  v_addresses t_nested_table_address;
BEGIN
  v_addresses := get_addresses(1);
```

```
  -- display the FIRST address
  DBMS_OUTPUT.PUT_LINE('First address = ' || v_addresses.FIRST);
  DBMS_OUTPUT.PUT_LINE('Deleting address #1');
  v_addresses.DELETE(1);

  -- display the FIRST address again
  DBMS_OUTPUT.PUT_LINE('First address = ' || v_addresses.FIRST);
END first_address;
```

The following example calls first_address():

```
CALL collection_method_examples.first_address();
Number of addresses = 2
First address = 1
Deleting address #1
First address = 2
```

LAST()

LAST returns the index of the last element in a collection. If the collection is completely empty, LAST returns null. Because a nested table can have individual elements that are empty, LAST returns the highest index of a non-empty element in a nested table. For example, let's say you have a nested table named v_nested_table that has its elements set as shown in the following table.

Element Index	Empty/Not Empty
1	Not empty
2	Empty
3	Empty
4	Not empty

Given the configuration for v_nested_table shown in the previous table, v_nested_table.LAST returns 4, the highest index containing a non-empty element.

The following last_address() procedure gets the addresses for customer #1 into v_addresses and then uses LAST to display the index of the last address in v_addresses. The procedure then deletes address #2 using DELETE and displays the new index returned by LAST.

```
PROCEDURE last_address IS
  v_addresses t_nested_table_address;
BEGIN
  v_addresses := get_addresses(1);

  -- display the LAST address
  DBMS_OUTPUT.PUT_LINE('Last address = ' || v_addresses.LAST);
  DBMS_OUTPUT.PUT_LINE('Deleting address #2');
  v_addresses.DELETE(2);

  -- display the LAST address again
  DBMS_OUTPUT.PUT_LINE('Last address = ' || v_addresses.LAST);
END last_address;
```

The following example calls `last_address()`:

```
CALL collection_method_examples.last_address();
Number of addresses = 2
Last address = 2
Deleting address #2
Last address = 1
```

NEXT()

`NEXT(n)` returns the index of the element after n. Because a nested table can have individual elements that are empty, `NEXT` returns the index of a non-empty element after n. If there are no elements after n, `NEXT` returns null. For example, let's say you have a nested table named `v_nested_table` that has its elements set as shown in the following table.

Element Index	Empty/Not Empty
1	Not empty
2	Empty
3	Empty
4	Not empty

Given the configuration for `v_nested_table` shown in the previous table, `v_nested_table.NEXT(1)` returns 4, the index containing the next non-empty element, and `v_nested_table.NEXT(4)` returns null.

The following `next_address()` procedure retrieves the addresses for customer #1 and stores the addresses in `v_addresses`, and then uses `NEXT(1)` to obtain the index of the address after address #1 from `v_addresses`. The procedure then uses `NEXT(2)` to attempt to obtain the index of the address after address #2 (there isn't one, because customer #1 only has two addresses, so null is returned).

```
PROCEDURE next_address IS
  v_addresses t_nested_table_address;
BEGIN
  v_addresses := get_addresses(1);

  -- use NEXT(1) to get the index of the address
  -- after address #1
  DBMS_OUTPUT.PUT_LINE(
    'v_addresses.NEXT(1) = ' || v_addresses.NEXT(1)
  );

  -- use NEXT(2) to attempt to get the index of
  -- the address after address #2 (there isn't one,
  -- so null is returned)
  DBMS_OUTPUT.PUT_LINE(
    'v_addresses.NEXT(2) = ' || v_addresses.NEXT(2)
  );
END next_address;
```

The following example calls `next_address()`. Because `v_addresses.NEXT(2)` is null, no output is shown after the `=` for that element.

```
CALL collection_method_examples.next_address();
Number of addresses = 2
v_addresses.NEXT(1) = 2
v_addresses.NEXT(2) =
```

PRIOR()

`PRIOR(n)` returns the index of the element before `n`. Because a nested table can have individual elements that are empty, `PRIOR` returns the index of a non-empty element before `n`. If there are no elements before `n`, `PRIOR` returns null. For example, let's say you have a nested table named `v_nested_table` that has its elements set as shown in the following table.

Element Index	Empty/Not Empty
1	Not empty
2	Empty
3	Empty
4	Not empty

Given the configuration for `v_nested_table` shown in the previous table, `v_nested_table.PRIOR(4)` returns 1, the index containing the prior non-empty element; `v_nested_table.PRIOR(1)` returns null.

The following `prior_address()` procedure retrieves the addresses for customer #1 and stores the addresses in `v_addresses`, and then uses `PRIOR(2)` to obtain the index of the address before address #2 from `v_addresses`. The procedure then uses `PRIOR(1)` to attempt to obtain the index of the address before address #1 (there isn't one, so null is returned).

```
PROCEDURE prior_address IS
  v_addresses t_nested_table_address;
BEGIN
  v_addresses := get_addresses(1);

  -- use PRIOR(2) to get the index of the address
  -- before address #2
  DBMS_OUTPUT.PUT_LINE(
    'v_addresses.PRIOR(2) = ' || v_addresses.PRIOR(2)
  );

  -- use PRIOR(1) to attempt to get the index of
  -- the address before address #1 (there isn't one,
  -- so null is returned)
  DBMS_OUTPUT.PUT_LINE(
    'v_addresses.PRIOR(1) = ' || v_addresses.PRIOR(1)
  );
END prior_address;
```

The following example calls `prior_address()`. Because `v_addresses.PRIOR(1)` is null, no output is shown after the = for that element.

```
CALL collection_method_examples.prior_address();
Number of addresses = 2
v_addresses.PRIOR(2) = 1
v_addresses.PRIOR(1) =
```

TRIM()

`TRIM` removes elements from the end of a collection. There are two forms of `TRIM`:

- `TRIM` removes one element from the end.
- `TRIM(n)` removes n elements from the end.

For example, let's say you have a nested table named `v_nested_table`, and then `v_nested_table.TRIM(2)` removes two elements from the end.

The following `trim_addresses()` procedure gets the addresses of customer #1, copies address #1 to the end of `v_addresses` three times using `EXTEND(3, 1)`, and then removes two addresses from the end of `v_addresses` using `TRIM(2)`:

```
PROCEDURE trim_addresses IS
  v_addresses t_nested_table_address;
BEGIN
  v_addresses := get_addresses(1);
  display_addresses(v_addresses);
  DBMS_OUTPUT.PUT_LINE('Extending addresses');
  v_addresses.EXTEND(3, 1);
  display_addresses(v_addresses);
  DBMS_OUTPUT.PUT_LINE('Trimming 2 addresses from end');

  -- remove 2 addresses from the end of v_addresses
  -- using TRIM(2)
  v_addresses.TRIM(2);

  display_addresses(v_addresses);
END trim_addresses;
```

The following example calls `trim_addresses()`:

```
CALL collection_method_examples.trim_addresses();
Number of addresses = 2
Current number of addresses = 2
Address #1:
2 State Street, Beantown, MA, 12345
Address #2:
4 Hill Street, Lost Town, CA, 54321
Extending addresses
Current number of addresses = 5
Address #1:
2 State Street, Beantown, MA, 12345
Address #2:
```

```
4 Hill Street, Lost Town, CA, 54321
Address #3:
2 State Street, Beantown, MA, 12345
Address #4:
2 State Street, Beantown, MA, 12345
Address #5:
2 State Street, Beantown, MA, 12345
Trimming 2 addresses from end
Current number of addresses = 3
Address #1:
2 State Street, Beantown, MA, 12345
Address #2:
4 Hill Street, Lost Town, CA, 54321
Address #3:
2 State Street, Beantown, MA, 12345
```

Creating and Using Multilevel Collections

Oracle Database 9*i* and above allows you to create in the database a collection whose elements are also a collection. These "collections of collections" are known as *multilevel collections*. The following list shows the valid multilevel collections:

- A nested table of nested tables
- A nested table of varrays
- A varray of varrays
- A varray of nested tables

The following sections show how to run a script that creates an example schema and how to use multilevel collections.

Running the Script to Create the Second Collection Schema

I've provided an SQL*Plus script named collection_schema2.sql in the SQL directory. This script creates a user named collection_user2, with a password of collection_password2, along with the types and the table shown in this section. You can run this script if you are using Oracle Database 9*i* or higher.

You perform the following steps to create the schema:

1. Start SQL*Plus.
2. Log into the database as a user with privileges to create new users, tables, and PL/SQL packages. I run scripts in my database using the system user.
3. Run the collection_schema2.sql script from within SQL*Plus using the @ command.

For example, if you're using Windows and the script is stored in C:\sql_book\SQL, then you enter the following command:

@ C:\sql_book\SQL\collection_schema2.sql

When the script completes, you will be logged in as collection_user2.

Using Multilevel Collections

Let's say you wanted to store a set of phone numbers for each address of a customer. The following example creates a varray type of three VARCHAR2 strings named t_varray_phone to represent phone numbers:

```
CREATE TYPE t_varray_phone AS VARRAY(3) OF VARCHAR2(14);
/
```

The following example creates an object type named t_address that contains an attribute named phone_numbers, which is of type t_varray_phone:

```
CREATE TYPE t_address AS OBJECT (
  street        VARCHAR2(15),
  city          VARCHAR2(15),
  state         CHAR(2),
  zip           VARCHAR2(5),
  phone_numbers t_varray_phone
);
/
```

The next example creates a nested table type of t_address objects:

```
CREATE TYPE t_nested_table_address AS TABLE OF t_address;
/
```

The following example creates a table named customers_with_nested_table, which contains a column named addresses of type t_nested_table_address:

```
CREATE TABLE customers_with_nested_table (
  id         INTEGER PRIMARY KEY,
  first_name VARCHAR2(10),
  last_name  VARCHAR2(10),
  addresses  t_nested_table_address
)
NESTED TABLE
  addresses
STORE AS
  nested_addresses;
```

So, customers_with_nested_table contains a nested table whose elements contain an address with a varray of phone numbers.

The following INSERT statement adds a row to customers_with_nested_table. Notice the structure and content of the INSERT statement, which contains elements for the nested table of addresses, each of which has an embedded varray of phone numbers.

```
INSERT INTO customers_with_nested_table VALUES (
  1, 'Steve', 'Brown',
  t_nested_table_address(
    t_address('2 State Street', 'Beantown', 'MA', '12345',
      t_varray_phone(
        '(800)-555-1211',
```

```
          '(800)-555-1212',
          '(800)-555-1213'
        )
      ),
      t_address('4 Hill Street', 'Lost Town', 'CA', '54321',
        t_varray_phone(
          '(800)-555-1211',
          '(800)-555-1212'
        )
      )
    )
  )
);
```

You can see that the first address has three phone numbers, while the second address has two. The following query retrieves the row from `customers_with_nested_table`:

```
SELECT *
FROM customers_with_nested_table;

       ID FIRST_NAME LAST_NAME
---------- ---------- ----------
ADDRESSES(STREET, CITY, STATE, ZIP, PHONE_NUMBERS)
----------------------------------------------------------------------
        1 Steve      Brown
T_NESTED_TABLE_ADDRESS(
 T_ADDRESS('2 State Street', 'Beantown', 'MA', '12345',
  T_VARRAY_PHONE('(800)-555-1211', '(800)-555-1212', '(800)-555-1213')),
 T_ADDRESS('4 Hill Street', 'Lost Town', 'CA', '54321',
  T_VARRAY_PHONE('(800)-555-1211', '(800)-555-1212')))
```

You can use `TABLE()` to treat the data stored in the collections as a series of rows, as shown in the following query:

```
SELECT cn.first_name, cn.last_name, a.street, a.city, a.state, p.*
FROM customers_with_nested_table cn,
 TABLE(cn.addresses) a, TABLE(a.phone_numbers) p;

FIRST_NAME LAST_NAME  STREET          CITY          ST COLUMN_VALUE
---------- ---------- --------------- ------------- -- --------------
Steve      Brown      2 State Street  Beantown      MA (800)-555-1211
Steve      Brown      2 State Street  Beantown      MA (800)-555-1212
Steve      Brown      2 State Street  Beantown      MA (800)-555-1213
Steve      Brown      4 Hill Street   Lost Town     CA (800)-555-1211
Steve      Brown      4 Hill Street   Lost Town     CA (800)-555-1212
```

The following UPDATE statement shows how to update the phone numbers for the '2 State Street' address. Notice that TABLE() is used to get the addresses as a series of rows and that a varray containing the new phone numbers is supplied in the SET clause.

```
UPDATE TABLE(
  -- get the addresses for customer #1
  SELECT cn.addresses
```

```
   FROM customers_with_nested_table cn
   WHERE cn.id = 1
) addrs
SET addrs.phone_numbers =
   t_varray_phone(
     '(800)-555-1214',
     '(800)-555-1215'
   )
WHERE addrs.street = '2 State Street';
```

1 row updated.

The following query verifies the change:

```
SELECT cn.first_name, cn.last_name, a.street, a.city, a.state, p.*
FROM customers_with_nested_table cn,
 TABLE(cn.addresses) a, TABLE(a.phone_numbers) p;
```

FIRST_NAME	LAST_NAME	STREET	CITY	ST	COLUMN_VALUE
Steve	Brown	2 State Street	Beantown	MA	(800)-555-1214
Steve	Brown	2 State Street	Beantown	MA	(800)-555-1215
Steve	Brown	4 Hill Street	Lost Town	CA	(800)-555-1211
Steve	Brown	4 Hill Street	Lost Town	CA	(800)-555-1212

Support for multilevel collection types is a very powerful extension to the Oracle database software, and you might want to consider using them in any database designs you contribute to.

Oracle Database 10g Enhancements to Collections

In this section, you'll learn about the following enhancements made to collections, which were introduced in Oracle Database 10g:

- Support for associative arrays
- Ability to change the size or precision of an element type
- Ability to increase the number of elements in a varray
- Ability to use varray columns in temporary tables
- Ability to use a different tablespace for a nested table's storage table
- ANSI support for nested tables

Running the Script to Create the Third Collection Schema

I've provided an SQL*Plus script named collection_schema3.sql in the SQL directory. This script creates a user named collection_user3, with a password of collection_password3, along with the types and the table shown in this section. You can run this script if you are using Oracle Database 10g or higher.

You perform the following steps to create the schema:

1. Start SQL*Plus.

2. Log into the database as a user with privileges to create new users, tables, and PL/SQL packages. I run scripts in my database using the `system` user.

3. Run the `collection_schema3.sql` script from within SQL*Plus using the `@` command.

For example, if you're using Windows and the script is stored in `C:\sql_book\SQL`, then you enter the following command:

```
C:\sql_book\SQL\collection_schema3.sql
```

When the script completes, you will be logged in as `collection_user3`.

Creating Associative Arrays

An associative array is a set of key and value pairs. You can get the value from the array using the key (which can be a string) or an integer that specifies the position of the value in the array. The following example procedure named `customers_associative_array()` illustrates the use of associative arrays:

```
CREATE PROCEDURE customers_associative_array AS
    -- define an associative array type named t_assoc_array;
    -- the value stored in each array element is a NUMBER,
    -- and the index key to access each element is a VARCHAR2
    TYPE t_assoc_array IS TABLE OF NUMBER INDEX BY VARCHAR2(15);

    -- declare an object named v_customer_array of type t_assoc_array;
    -- v_customer_array will be used to store the ages of customers
    v_customer_array t_assoc_array;
BEGIN
    -- assign the values to v_customer_array; the VARCHAR2 key is the
    -- customer name and the NUMBER value is the age of the customer
    v_customer_array('Jason') := 32;
    v_customer_array('Steve') := 28;
    v_customer_array('Fred') := 43;
    v_customer_array('Cynthia') := 27;

    -- display the values stored in v_customer_array
    DBMS_OUTPUT.PUT_LINE(
      'v_customer_array[''Jason''] = ' || v_customer_array('Jason')
    );
    DBMS_OUTPUT.PUT_LINE(
      'v_customer_array[''Steve''] = ' || v_customer_array('Steve')
    );
    DBMS_OUTPUT.PUT_LINE(
      'v_customer_array[''Fred''] = ' || v_customer_array('Fred')
    );
```

```
  DBMS_OUTPUT.PUT_LINE(
    'v_customer_array[''Cynthia''] = ' || v_customer_array('Cynthia')
  );
END customers_associative_array;
/
```

The following example sets the server output on and calls `customers_associative_array()`:

```
SET SERVEROUTPUT ON
CALL customers_associative_array();
v_customer_array['Jason'] = 32
v_customer_array['Steve'] = 28
v_customer_array['Fred'] = 43
v_customer_array['Cynthia'] = 27
```

Changing the Size of an Element Type

You can change the size of an element type in a collection when the element type is one of the character, numeric, or raw types (raw is used to store binary data—you'll learn about this in the next chapter). Earlier in this chapter, you saw the following statement that creates a varray type named `t_varray_address`:

```
CREATE TYPE t_varray_address AS VARRAY(2) OF VARCHAR2(50);
/
```

The following example changes the size of the `VARCHAR2` elements in `t_varray_address` to 60:

```
ALTER TYPE t_varray_address
MODIFY ELEMENT TYPE VARCHAR2(60) CASCADE;
```

```
Type altered.
```

The `CASCADE` option propagates the change to any dependent objects in the database. The `customers_with_varray` table contains a column named `addresses` of type `t_varray_address`. Therefore, the `CASCADE` option in the example propagates the change to the `customers_with_varray` table, because it contains a column of type `t_varray_address`.

You can also use the `INVALIDATE` option to invalidate any dependent objects and immediately recompile the PL/SQL code for the type.

Increasing the Number of Elements in a Varray

You can increase the number of elements in a varray. The following example increases the number of elements in `t_varray_address` to 5:

```
ALTER TYPE t_varray_address
MODIFY LIMIT 5 CASCADE;
```

```
Type altered.
```

Using Varrays in Temporary Tables

You can use varrays in temporary tables, which are tables whose rows are temporary and are specific to a user session. The following example creates a temporary table named `cust_with_varray_temp_table` that contains a varray named `addresses` of type `t_varray_address`:

```
CREATE GLOBAL TEMPORARY TABLE cust_with_varray_temp_table (
  id         INTEGER PRIMARY KEY,
  first_name VARCHAR2(10),
  last_name  VARCHAR2(10),
  addresses  t_varray_address
);
```

Using a Different Tablespace for a Nested Table's Storage Table

By default, a nested table's storage table is created in the same tablespace as the parent table (a tablespace is an area used by the database to store objects such as tables).

In Oracle Database 10g and higher, you can specify a different tablespace for a nested table's storage table. The following example creates a table named `cust_with_nested_table` that contains a nested table named `addresses` of type `t_nested_table_address`. Notice that the tablespace for the `nested_addresses2` storage table is the `users` tablespace.

```
CREATE TABLE cust_with_nested_table (
  id         INTEGER PRIMARY KEY,
  first_name VARCHAR2(10),
  last_name  VARCHAR2(10),
  addresses  t_nested_table_address
)
NESTED TABLE
  addresses
STORE AS
  nested_addresses2 TABLESPACE users;
```

You must have a tablespace named `users` in order for this example to work, and for this reason I've commented out the example in the `collection_schema3.sql` script. You can see all the tablespaces you have access to by performing the following query:

```
SELECT tablespace_name
FROM user_tablespaces;

TABLESPACE_NAME
---------------
SYSTEM
SYSAUX
UNDOTBS1
TEMP
USERS
EXAMPLE
```

If you want to run the previous CREATE TABLE statement, you can edit the example in the collection_schema3.sql script to reference one of your tablespaces and then copy the CREATE TABLE statement into SQL*Plus and run it.

ANSI Support for Nested Tables

The American National Standards Institute (ANSI) specification includes a number of operators that can be used with nested tables. You'll learn about these operators in the following sections.

Equal and Not-Equal Operators

The equal (=) and not-equal (<>) operators compare two nested tables, which are considered equal when they satisfy all of the following conditions:

- The tables are the same type.
- The tables are the same cardinality; that is, they contain the same number of elements.
- All the elements of the table have the same value.

The following equal_example() procedure illustrates the use of the equal and not-equal operators:

```
CREATE PROCEDURE equal_example AS
  -- declare a type named t_nested_table
  TYPE t_nested_table IS TABLE OF VARCHAR2(10);

  -- create t_nested_table objects named v_customer_nested_table1,
  -- v_customer_nested_table2, and v_customer_nested_table3;
  -- these objects are used to store the names of customers
  v_customer_nested_table1 t_nested_table :=
    t_nested_table('Fred', 'George', 'Susan');
  v_customer_nested_table2 t_nested_table :=
    t_nested_table('Fred', 'George', 'Susan');
  v_customer_nested_table3 t_nested_table :=
    t_nested_table('John', 'George', 'Susan');

  v_result BOOLEAN;
BEGIN
  -- use = operator to compare v_customer_nested_table1 with
  -- v_customer_nested_table2 (they contain the same names, so
  -- v_result is set to true)
  v_result := v_customer_nested_table1 = v_customer_nested_table2;
  IF v_result THEN
    DBMS_OUTPUT.PUT_LINE(
      'v_customer_nested_table1 equal to v_customer_nested_table2'
    );
  END IF;

  -- use <> operator to compare v_customer_nested_table1 with
  -- v_customer_nested_table3 (they are not equal because the first
  -- names, 'Fred' and 'John', are different and v_result is set
  -- to true)
```

```
   v_result := v_customer_nested_table1 <> v_customer_nested_table3;
   IF v_result THEN
     DBMS_OUTPUT.PUT_LINE(
       'v_customer_nested_table1 not equal to v_customer_nested_table3'
     );
   END IF;
END equal_example;
/
```

The following example calls equal_example():

```
CALL equal_example();
v_customer_nested_table1 equal to v_customer_nested_table2
v_customer_nested_table1 not equal to v_customer_nested_table3
```

IN and NOT IN Operators

The IN operator checks if the elements of one nested table appear in another nested table. Similarly, NOT IN checks if the elements of one nested table do not appear in another nested table. The following in_example() procedure illustrates the use of IN and NOT IN:

```
CREATE PROCEDURE in_example AS
   TYPE t_nested_table IS TABLE OF VARCHAR2(10);
   v_customer_nested_table1 t_nested_table :=
     t_nested_table('Fred', 'George', 'Susan');
   v_customer_nested_table2 t_nested_table :=
     t_nested_table('John', 'George', 'Susan');
   v_customer_nested_table3 t_nested_table :=
     t_nested_table('Fred', 'George', 'Susan');
   v_result BOOLEAN;
BEGIN
   -- use IN operator to check if elements of v_customer_nested_table3
   -- are in v_customer_nested_table1 (they are, so v_result is
   -- set to true)
   v_result := v_customer_nested_table3 IN
     (v_customer_nested_table1);
   IF v_result THEN
     DBMS_OUTPUT.PUT_LINE(
       'v_customer_nested_table3 in v_customer_nested_table1'
     );
   END IF;

   -- use NOT IN operator to check if the elements of
   -- v_customer_nested_table3 are not in v_customer_nested_table2
   -- (they are not, so v_result is set to true)
   v_result := v_customer_nested_table3 NOT IN
     (v_customer_nested_table2);
   IF v_result THEN
     DBMS_OUTPUT.PUT_LINE(
       'v_customer_nested_table3 not in v_customer_nested_table2'
     );
```

```
    END IF;
END in_example;
/
```

The following example calls `in_example()`:

```
CALL in_example();
v_customer_nested_table3 in v_customer_nested_table1
v_customer_nested_table3 not in v_customer_nested_table2
```

SUBMULTISET Operator

The `SUBMULTISET` operator checks whether the elements of one nested table are a subset of another nested table. The following `submultiset_example()` procedure illustrates the use of `SUBMULTISET`:

```
CREATE PROCEDURE submultiset_example AS
    TYPE t_nested_table IS TABLE OF VARCHAR2(10);
    v_customer_nested_table1 t_nested_table :=
      t_nested_table('Fred', 'George', 'Susan');
    v_customer_nested_table2 t_nested_table :=
      t_nested_table('George', 'Fred', 'Susan', 'John', 'Steve');
    v_result BOOLEAN;
BEGIN
    -- use SUBMULTISET operator to check if elements of
    -- v_customer_nested_table1 are a subset of v_customer_nested_table2
    -- (they are, so v_result is set to true)
    v_result :=
      v_customer_nested_table1 SUBMULTISET OF v_customer_nested_table2;
    IF v_result THEN
      DBMS_OUTPUT.PUT_LINE(
        'v_customer_nested_table1 subset of v_customer_nested_table2'
      );
    END IF;
END submultiset_example;
/
```

The following example calls `submultiset_example()`:

```
CALL submultiset_example();
v_customer_nested_table1 subset of v_customer_nested_table2
```

MULTISET Operator

The `MULTISET` operator returns a nested table whose elements are set to certain combinations of elements from two supplied nested tables. There are three `MULTISET` operators:

- **MULTISET UNION** returns a nested table whose elements are set to the sum of the elements from two supplied nested tables.

- **MULTISET INTERSECT** returns a nested table whose elements are set to the elements that are common to two supplied nested tables.

- **MULTISET EXCEPT** returns a nested table whose elements are in the first supplied nested table but not in the second.

You can also use one of the following options with MULTISET:

- **ALL** indicates that all the applicable elements are in the returned nested table. ALL is the default. For example, MULTISET UNION ALL returns a nested table whose elements are set to the sum of elements from two supplied nested tables, and all elements, including duplicates, are in the returned nested table.

- **DISTINCT** indicates that only the non-duplicate (that is, distinct) elements are in the returned nested table. For example, MULTISET UNION DISTINCT returns a nested table whose elements are set to the sum of elements from two supplied nested tables, but duplicates are removed from the returned nested table.

The following multiset_example() procedure illustrates the use of MULTISET:

```
CREATE PROCEDURE multiset_example AS
  TYPE t_nested_table IS TABLE OF VARCHAR2(10);
  v_customer_nested_table1 t_nested_table :=
    t_nested_table('Fred', 'George', 'Susan');
  v_customer_nested_table2 t_nested_table :=
    t_nested_table('George', 'Steve', 'Rob');
  v_customer_nested_table3 t_nested_table;
  v_count INTEGER;
BEGIN
  -- use MULTISET UNION (returns a nested table whose elements
  -- are set to the sum of the two supplied nested tables)
  v_customer_nested_table3 :=
    v_customer_nested_table1 MULTISET UNION
      v_customer_nested_table2;
  DBMS_OUTPUT.PUT('UNION: ');
  FOR v_count IN 1..v_customer_nested_table3.COUNT LOOP
    DBMS_OUTPUT.PUT(v_customer_nested_table3(v_count) || ' ');
  END LOOP;
  DBMS_OUTPUT.PUT_LINE(' ');

  -- use MULTISET UNION DISTINCT (DISTINCT indicates that only
  -- the non-duplicate elements of the two supplied nested tables
  -- are set in the returned nested table)
  v_customer_nested_table3 :=
    v_customer_nested_table1 MULTISET UNION DISTINCT
      v_customer_nested_table2;
  DBMS_OUTPUT.PUT('UNION DISTINCT: ');
  FOR v_count IN 1..v_customer_nested_table3.COUNT LOOP
    DBMS_OUTPUT.PUT(v_customer_nested_table3(v_count) || ' ');
  END LOOP;
  DBMS_OUTPUT.PUT_LINE(' ');

  -- use MULTISET INTERSECT (returns a nested table whose elements
  -- are set to the elements that are common to the two supplied
  -- nested tables)
  v_customer_nested_table3 :=
```

```
     v_customer_nested_table1 MULTISET INTERSECT
       v_customer_nested_table2;
  DBMS_OUTPUT.PUT('INTERSECT: ');
  FOR v_count IN 1..v_customer_nested_table3.COUNT LOOP
    DBMS_OUTPUT.PUT(v_customer_nested_table3(v_count) || ' ');
  END LOOP;
  DBMS_OUTPUT.PUT_LINE(' ');

  -- use MULTISET EXCEPT (returns a nested table whose
  -- elements are in the first nested table but not in
  -- the second)
  v_customer_nested_table3 :=
     v_customer_nested_table1 MULTISET EXCEPT
       v_customer_nested_table2;
  DBMS_OUTPUT.PUT_LINE('EXCEPT: ');
  FOR v_count IN 1..v_customer_nested_table3.COUNT LOOP
    DBMS_OUTPUT.PUT(v_customer_nested_table3(v_count) || ' ');
  END LOOP;
END multiset_example;
/
```

The following example calls `multiset_example()`:

```
CALL multiset_example();
UNION: Fred George Susan George Steve Rob
UNION DISTINCT: Fred George Susan Steve Rob
INTERSECT: George
EXCEPT:
```

CARDINALITY() Function

The `CARDINALITY()` function returns the number of elements in a collection. The following `cardinality_example()` procedure illustrates the use of `CARDINALITY()`:

```
CREATE PROCEDURE cardinality_example AS
    TYPE t_nested_table IS TABLE OF VARCHAR2(10);
    v_customer_nested_table1 t_nested_table :=
      t_nested_table('Fred', 'George', 'Susan');
    v_cardinality INTEGER;
BEGIN
    -- call CARDINALITY() to get the number of elements in
    -- v_customer_nested_table1
    v_cardinality := CARDINALITY(v_customer_nested_table1);
    DBMS_OUTPUT.PUT_LINE('v_cardinality = ' || v_cardinality);
END cardinality_example;
/
```

The following example calls `cardinality_example()`:

```
CALL cardinality_example();
v_cardinality = 3
```

MEMBER OF Operator

The MEMBER OF operator checks whether an element is in a nested table. The following member_of_example() procedure illustrates the use of MEMBER OF:

```
CREATE PROCEDURE member_of_example AS
   TYPE t_nested_table IS TABLE OF VARCHAR2(10);
   v_customer_nested_table1 t_nested_table :=
     t_nested_table('Fred', 'George', 'Susan');
   v_result BOOLEAN;
BEGIN
   -- use MEMBER OF to check if 'George' is in
   -- v_customer_nested_table1 (he is, so v_result is set
   -- to true)
   v_result := 'George' MEMBER OF v_customer_nested_table1;
   IF v_result THEN
     DBMS_OUTPUT.PUT_LINE('''George'' is a member');
   END IF;
END member_of_example;
/
```

The following example calls member_of_example():

```
CALL member_of_example();
'George' is a member
```

SET() Function

The SET() function first converts a nested table into a set, then removes duplicate elements from the set, and finally returns the set as a nested table. The following set_example() procedure illustrates the use of SET():

```
CREATE PROCEDURE set_example AS
   TYPE t_nested_table IS TABLE OF VARCHAR2(10);
   v_customer_nested_table1 t_nested_table :=
     t_nested_table('Fred', 'George', 'Susan', 'George');
   v_customer_nested_table2 t_nested_table;
   v_count INTEGER;
BEGIN
   -- call SET() to convert a nested table into a set,
   -- remove duplicate elements from the set, and get the set
   -- as a nested table
   v_customer_nested_table2 := SET(v_customer_nested_table1);
   DBMS_OUTPUT.PUT('v_customer_nested_table2: ');
   FOR v_count IN 1..v_customer_nested_table2.COUNT LOOP
     DBMS_OUTPUT.PUT(v_customer_nested_table2(v_count) || ' ');
   END LOOP;
   DBMS_OUTPUT.PUT_LINE(' ');
END set_example;
/
```

The following example calls `set_example()`:

```
CALL set_example();
v_customer_nested_table2: Fred George Susan
```

IS A SET Operator

The `IS A SET` operator checks if the elements in a nested table are distinct. The following `is_a_set_example()` procedure illustrates the use of `IS A SET`:

```
CREATE PROCEDURE is_a_set_example AS
  TYPE t_nested_table IS TABLE OF VARCHAR2(10);
  v_customer_nested_table1 t_nested_table :=
    t_nested_table('Fred', 'George', 'Susan', 'George');
  v_result BOOLEAN;
BEGIN
  -- use IS A SET operator to check if the elements in
  -- v_customer_nested_table1 are distinct (they are not, so
  -- v_result is set to false)
  v_result := v_customer_nested_table1 IS A SET;
  IF v_result THEN
    DBMS_OUTPUT.PUT_LINE('Elements are all unique');
  ELSE
    DBMS_OUTPUT.PUT_LINE('Elements contain duplicates');
  END IF;
END is_a_set_example;
/
```

The following example calls `is_a_set_example()`:

```
CALL is_a_set_example();
Elements contain duplicates
```

IS EMPTY Operator

The `IS EMPTY` operator checks if a nested table doesn't contain elements. The following `is_empty_example()` procedure illustrates the use of `IS EMPTY`:

```
CREATE PROCEDURE is_empty_example AS
  TYPE t_nested_table IS TABLE OF VARCHAR2(10);
  v_customer_nested_table1 t_nested_table :=
    t_nested_table('Fred', 'George', 'Susan');
  v_result BOOLEAN;
BEGIN
  -- use IS EMPTY operator to check if
  -- v_customer_nested_table1 is empty (it is not, so
  -- v_result is set to false)
  v_result := v_customer_nested_table1 IS EMPTY;
  IF v_result THEN
    DBMS_OUTPUT.PUT_LINE('Nested table is empty');
  ELSE
    DBMS_OUTPUT.PUT_LINE('Nested table contains elements');
  END IF;
END is_empty_example;
/
```

The following example calls is_empty_example():

```
CALL is_empty_example();
Nested table contains elements
```

COLLECT() Function

The COLLECT() function returns a nested table from a set of elements. The following query illustrates the use of COLLECT():

```
SELECT COLLECT(first_name)
FROM customers_with_varray;

COLLECT(FIRST_NAME)
-----------------------------------------------
SYSTPfrFhAg+WRJGwW7ma9zy1KA==('Steve', 'John')
```

You can use CAST() to convert the elements returned by COLLECT() to a specific type, as shown in the following query:

```
SELECT CAST(COLLECT(first_name) AS t_table)
FROM customers_with_varray;

CAST(COLLECT(FIRST_NAME)AST_TABLE)
----------------------------------
T_TABLE('Steve', 'John')
```

For your reference, the t_table type used in the previous example is created by the following statement in the collection_schema3.sql script:

```
CREATE TYPE t_table AS TABLE OF VARCHAR2(10);
/
```

POWERMULTISET() Function

The POWERMULTISET() function returns all combinations of elements in a given nested table, as shown in the following query:

```
SELECT *
FROM TABLE(
  POWERMULTISET(t_table('This', 'is', 'a', 'test'))
);

COLUMN_VALUE
----------------------------------
T_TABLE('This')
T_TABLE('is')
T_TABLE('This', 'is')
T_TABLE('a')
T_TABLE('This', 'a')
T_TABLE('is', 'a')
T_TABLE('This', 'is', 'a')
T_TABLE('test')
```

```
T_TABLE('This', 'test')
T_TABLE('is', 'test')
T_TABLE('This', 'is', 'test')
T_TABLE('a', 'test')
T_TABLE('This', 'a', 'test')
T_TABLE('is', 'a', 'test')
T_TABLE('This', 'is', 'a', 'test')
```

POWERMULTISET_BY_CARDINALITY() Function

The `POWERMULTISET_BY_CARDINALITY()` function returns the combinations of elements in a given nested table that have a specified number of elements (or "cardinality"). The following query illustrates the use of `POWERMULTISET_BY_CARDINALITY()`, specifying a cardinality of 3:

```
SELECT *
FROM TABLE(
  POWERMULTISET_BY_CARDINALITY(
    t_table('This', 'is', 'a', 'test'), 3
  )
);

COLUMN_VALUE
-----------------------------
T_TABLE('This', 'is', 'a')
T_TABLE('This', 'is', 'test')
T_TABLE('This', 'a', 'test')
T_TABLE('is', 'a', 'test')
```

Summary

In this chapter, you have learned the following:

- Collections store sets of elements.

- There are three types of collections: varrays, nested tables, and associative arrays.

- A varray stores an ordered set of elements. The elements in a varray are of the same type, and a varray has one dimension. A varray has a maximum size that you set when creating it, but you can change the size later.

- A nested table is a table that is embedded within another table, and you can insert, update, and delete individual elements in a nested table. A nested table doesn't have a maximum size, and you can store an arbitrary number of elements in a nested table.

- An associative array is a set of key and value pairs. You can get the value from the array using the key (which can be a string) or an integer that specifies the position of the value in the array.

- A collection can itself contain embedded collections. Such a collection is known as a multilevel collection.

In the next chapter, you'll learn about large objects.

CHAPTER
15

Large Objects

I n this chapter, you will perform the following tasks:

- Learn about large objects (LOBs)
- See files whose content will be used to populate example LOBs
- Examine the differences between the different types of LOBs
- Create tables containing LOBs
- Use LOBs in SQL and PL/SQL
- Examine the LONG and LONG RAW types
- Explore LOB enhancements

Introducing Large Objects (LOBs)

Today's websites often require multimedia, and databases are now being called upon to store items like music and video. Prior to the release of Oracle Database 8, you had to store large blocks of character data using the LONG database type, and you had to store large blocks of binary data using either the LONG RAW type or the shorter RAW type.

With the release of Oracle Database 8, a new class of database types known as *large objects*, or LOBs for short, was introduced. LOBs can be used to store binary data, character data, and references to files. The binary data can contain images, music, video, documents, executables, and so on. LOBs can store up to 128 terabytes of data, depending on the database configuration.

The Example Files

You'll see the use of the following two files in this chapter:

- textContent.txt   A text file
- binaryContent.doc   A Microsoft Word file

NOTE
These files are contained in the sample_files *directory, which is created when you extract the Zip file for this book. If you want to follow along with the examples, you should copy the* sample_files *directory to the C partition on your database server. If you're using Linux or Unix, you can copy the directory to one of your partitions.*

The file textContent.txt contains an extract from Shakespeare's play *Macbeth*. The following text is the speech made by Macbeth shortly before he is killed:

To-morrow, and to-morrow, and to-morrow,
Creeps in this petty pace from day to day,
To the last syllable of recorded time;
And all our yesterdays have lighted fools

The way to a dusty death. Out, out, brief candle!
Life's but a walking shadow; a poor player,
That struts and frets his hour upon the stage,
And then is heard no more: it is a tale
Told by an idiot, full of sound and fury,
Signifying nothing.

The `binaryContent.doc` file is a Word document that contains the same text as `textContent.txt`. (A Word document is a binary file.) Although a Word document is used in the examples, you can use any binary file. For example, you can use an MP3, DivX, JPEG, MPEG, PDF, or EXE file.

Large Object Types

There are four LOB types:

- **CLOB** The character LOB type, which is used to store character data.
- **NCLOB** The National Character Set LOB type, which is used to store multi-byte character data (typically used for non-English characters). You can learn all about non-English character sets in the *Oracle Database Globalization Support Guide* published by Oracle Corporation.
- **BLOB** The binary LOB type, which is used to store binary data.
- **BFILE** The binary FILE type, which is used to store a pointer to a file. The file can be on a hard disk, CD, DVD, Blu-ray Disc, HD-DVD, or any other device that is accessible through the database server's file system. The file itself is never stored in the database, only a pointer to the file.

Prior to Oracle Database 8, your only choice for storing large amounts of data was to use the `LONG` and `LONG RAW` types. The LOB types have three advantages over these older types:

- A LOB can store up to 128 terabytes of data, depending on the database configuration. This is far more data than you can store in a `LONG` or `LONG RAW` column, which can only store up to 2 gigabytes of data.
- A table can have multiple LOB columns, but a table can have only one `LONG` or `LONG RAW` column.
- LOB data can be accessed in random order. `LONG` and `LONG RAW` data can be accessed only in sequential order.

A LOB consists of two parts:

- **The LOB locator** A pointer that specifies the location of the LOB data
- **The LOB data** The actual character or byte data stored in the LOB

Depending on the amount of data stored in a `CLOB`, `NCLOB`, or `BLOB` column, the data will be stored either inside or outside of the table. If the data is less than 4 kilobytes, the data is stored in the same table; otherwise, the data is stored outside the table. With a `BFILE` column, only the locator is stored in the table—and the locator points to an external file stored in the file system.

Creating Tables Containing Large Objects

You'll see the use of the following three tables in this section:

- The clob_content table, which contains a CLOB column named clob_column
- The blob_content table, which contains a BLOB column named blob_column
- The bfile_content table, which contains a BFILE column named bfile_column

I've provided an SQL*Plus script named lob_schema.sql in the SQL directory. This script can be run using Oracle Database 8 and higher. Open the script using an editor.

The following statement in the script creates a directory object named SAMPLE_FILES_DIR in the Windows file system directory C:\sample_files:

```
CREATE DIRECTORY SAMPLE_FILES_DIR AS 'C:\sample_files';
```

If your sample_files directory is not stored in the C partition, then you need to set the appropriate path in the previous statement.

If you're using Linux or Unix, then you must replace the sample_files directory reference in the script. For example:

```
CREATE DIRECTORY SAMPLE_FILES_DIR AS '/tmp/sample_files';
```

If you made any changes to the script, save the script now.
You must ensure that the following requirements are met:

- The sample_files directory exists in the file system.
- The user account in the operating system that was used to install the Oracle software has read and write permissions on the sample_files directory and on the files inside the directory.

If you're using Windows, you might not need to worry about the second point. The Oracle database software should have been installed using a user account that has administrator privileges, and such a user account has read permission on everything in the file system.

If you're using Linux or Unix, you'll need to grant read and write access on the sample_files directory, and on the files inside the directory, to the appropriate Oracle user account that owns the database. You grant access using the chmod command.

NOTE
If you encounter any file operation errors when running the examples in this chapter, it's probably because you have not granted the correct permissions.

The lob_schema.sql script creates a user named lob_user with a password of lob_password, and it creates the tables and PL/SQL code used in the first part of this chapter. After the script completes, you will be logged in as lob_user.

You perform the following steps to create the schema:

1. Start SQL*Plus.

2. Log into the database as a user with privileges to create new users, tables, and PL/SQL packages. I run scripts in my database using the `system` user.

3. Run the `lob_schema.sql` script from within SQL*Plus using the `@` command.

For example, if you're using Windows and the script is stored in `C:\sql_book\SQL`, then you enter the following command:

```
@ C:\sql_book\SQL\lob_schema.sql
```

When the script completes, you will be logged in as `lob_user`.

The three tables are created using the following statements in the script:

```
CREATE TABLE clob_content (
  id             INTEGER PRIMARY KEY,
  clob_column CLOB NOT NULL
);

CREATE TABLE blob_content (
  id             INTEGER PRIMARY KEY,
  blob_column BLOB NOT NULL
);

CREATE TABLE bfile_content (
  id             INTEGER PRIMARY KEY,
  bfile_column BFILE NOT NULL
);
```

Using Large Objects in SQL

In this section, you'll learn how to use SQL to manipulate large objects. You'll start by examining CLOB and BLOB objects and then move on to BFILE objects.

Using CLOBs and BLOBs

The following sections show how to populate CLOB and BLOB objects with data, retrieve the data, and then modify the data.

Populating CLOBs and BLOBs with Data

The following INSERT statements add two rows to the `clob_content` table. Notice the use of the `TO_CLOB()` function to convert the text to a CLOB.

```
INSERT INTO clob_content (
  id, clob_column
) VALUES (
```

```
  1, TO_CLOB('Creeps in this petty pace')
);

INSERT INTO clob_content (
  id, clob_column
) VALUES (
  2, TO_CLOB(' from day to day')
);
```

The following INSERT statements add two rows to the blob_content table; notice the use of the TO_BLOB() function to convert the numbers to a BLOB (the first statement contains a binary number, and the second contains a hexadecimal number):

```
INSERT INTO blob_content (
  id, blob_column
) VALUES (
  1, TO_BLOB('100111010101011111')
);

INSERT INTO blob_content (
  id, blob_column
) VALUES (
  2, TO_BLOB('A0FFB71CF90DE')
);
```

Retrieving Data from CLOBs

The following query retrieves the rows from the clob_content table:

```
SELECT *
FROM clob_content;

        ID
----------
CLOB_COLUMN
------------------------
         1
Creeps in this petty pace

         2
 from day to day
```

The next query retrieves the rows from the blob_content table:

```
SELECT *
FROM blob_content;

        ID
----------
BLOB_COLUMN
------------------
```

```
         1
100111010101011111

         2
0A0FFB71CF90DE
```

You'll learn more about retrieving the data from a BLOB later in the section "Using Large Objects in PL/SQL."

Modifying the Data in CLOBs and BLOBs

You should feel free to run the UPDATE and INSERT statements shown in this section. The following UPDATE statements show you how to modify the contents of a CLOB and a BLOB:

```
UPDATE clob_content
SET clob_column = TO_CLOB('What light through yonder window breaks')
WHERE id = 1;

UPDATE blob_content
SET blob_column = TO_BLOB('1110011010101011111')
WHERE id = 1;
```

You can also initialize the LOB locator, but not store actual data in the LOB. You do this using the EMPTY_CLOB() function to store an empty CLOB, and EMPTY_BLOB() to store an empty BLOB:

```
INSERT INTO clob_content(
   id, clob_column
) VALUES (
   3, EMPTY_CLOB()
);

INSERT INTO blob_content(
   id, blob_column
) VALUES (
   3, EMPTY_BLOB()
);
```

These statements initialize the LOB locator but set the LOB data to empty.

You can also use EMPTY_CLOB() and EMPTY_BLOB() in UPDATE statements when you want to empty out the LOB data. For example:

```
UPDATE clob_content
SET clob_column = EMPTY_CLOB()
WHERE id = 1;

UPDATE blob_content
SET blob_column = EMPTY_BLOB()
WHERE id = 1;
```

If you ran any of the INSERT and UPDATE statements shown in this section, go ahead and roll back the changes so that your output matches mine in the rest of this chapter:

```
ROLLBACK;
```

Using BFILEs

A BFILE stores a pointer to a file that is accessible through the database server's file system. The important point to remember is that these files are stored outside of the database. A BFILE can point to files located on any media (for example, a hard disk, CD, DVD, Blu-ray Disc, HD-DVD, and so on).

NOTE
A BFILE *contains a pointer to an external file. The actual file itself is never stored in the database; rather, only a pointer to that file is stored. The file must be accessible through the database server's file system.*

Creating a Directory Object

Before you can store a pointer to a file in a BFILE, you must first create a directory object in the database. The directory object stores the directory in the file system where the files are located. You create a directory object using the CREATE DIRECTORY statement, and to run this statement you must have the CREATE ANY DIRECTORY database privilege.

The following example creates a directory object named SAMPLE_FILES_DIR in the Windows file system directory C:\sample_files:

```
CREATE DIRECTORY SAMPLE_FILES_DIR AS 'C:\sample_files';
```

The next example grants read and write permissions on SAMPLE_FILES_DIR to lob_user:

```
GRANT read, write ON DIRECTORY SAMPLE_FILES_DIR TO lob_user;
```

Populating a BFILE Column with a Pointer to a File

Because a BFILE is just a pointer to an external file, populating a BFILE column is very simple. All you have to do is use the Oracle database's BFILENAME() function to populate a BFILE with a pointer to your external file. The BFILENAME() function accepts two parameters: the directory object's name and the name of the file.

For example, the following INSERT adds a row to the bfile_content table. Notice that the BFILENAME() function is used to populate bfile_column with a pointer to the textContent.txt file.

```
INSERT INTO bfile_content (
    id, bfile_column
) VALUES (
    1, BFILENAME('SAMPLE_FILES_DIR', 'textContent.txt')
);
```

The next INSERT adds a row to the bfile_content table. Notice that the BFILENAME() function is used to populate bfile_column with a pointer to the binaryContent.doc file.

```
INSERT INTO bfile_content (
    id, bfile_column
```

```
) VALUES (
  2, BFILENAME('SAMPLE_FILES_DIR', 'binaryContent.doc')
);
```

The following query retrieves the rows from `bfile_content`:

```
SELECT *
FROM bfile_content;

        ID
----------
BFILE_COLUMN
--------------------------------------------------
         1
bfilename('SAMPLE_FILES_DIR', 'textContent.txt')

         2
bfilename('SAMPLE_FILES_DIR', 'binaryContent.doc')
```

You can use PL/SQL to access the content in a BFILE or a BLOB, and you'll learn how to do that next.

Using Large Objects in PL/SQL

In this section, you'll learn how to use LOBs in PL/SQL. You'll start off by examining the methods in the DBMS_LOB package, which comes with the database. Later, you'll see plenty of PL/SQL programs that show how to use the DBMS_LOB methods to read data in a LOB, copy data from one LOB to another, search data in a LOB, copy data from a file to a LOB, copy data from a LOB to a file, and much more.

Table 15-1 summarizes the most commonly used methods in the DBMS_LOB package.

In the following sections, you'll see the details of some of the methods shown in the previous table. You can see all the DBMS_LOB methods in the *Oracle Database PL/SQL Packages and Types Reference* manual published by Oracle Corporation.

Method	Description
APPEND(*dest_lob*, *src_lob*)	Adds the data read from *src_lob* to the end of *dest_lob*.
CLOSE(*lob*)	Closes a previously opened LOB.
COMPARE(*lob1*, *lob2*, *amount*, *offset1*, *offset2*)	Compares the data stored in *lob1* and *lob2*, starting at *offset1* in *lob1* and *offset2* in *lob2*. Offsets always start at 1, which is the position of the first character or byte in the data. The data in the LOBs are compared over a maximum number of characters or bytes (the maximum is specified in *amount*). *(Continued)*

TABLE 15-1. *DBMS_LOB Methods*

Method	Description
CONVERTTOBLOB(*dest_blob*, *src_clob*, *amount*, *dest_offset*, *src_offset*, *blob_csid*, *lang_context*, *warning*)	Converts the character data read from *src_clob* into binary data written to *dest_blob*. The read begins at *src_offset* in *src_clob*, and the write begins at *dest_offset* in *dest_blob*. *blob_csid* is the desired character set for the converted data written to *dest_blob*. You should typically use DBMS_LOB.DEFAULT_CSID, which is the default character set for the database. *lang_context* is the language context to use when converting the characters read from *src_clob*. You should typically use DBMS_LOB.DEFAULT_LANG_CTX, which is the default language context for the database. *warning* is set to DBMS_LOB.WARN_INCONVERTIBLE_CHAR if there was a character that could not be converted.
CONVERTTOCLOB(*dest_clob*, *src_blob*, *amount*, *dest_offset*, *src_offset*, *blob_csid*, *lang_context*, *warning*)	Converts the binary data read from *src_blob* into character data written to *dest_clob*. *blob_csid* is the character set for the data read from *dest_blob*. You should typically use DBMS_LOB.DEFAULT_CSID. *lang_context* is the language context to use when writing the converted characters to *dest_clob*. You should typically use DBMS_LOB.DEFAULT_LANG_CTX. *warning* is set to DBMS_LOB.WARN_INCONVERTIBLE_CHAR if there was a character that could not be converted.
COPY(*dest_lob*, *src_lob*, *amount*, *dest_offset*, *src_offset*)	Copies data from *src_lob* to *dest_lob*, starting at the offsets for a total amount of characters or bytes.
CREATETEMPORARY(*lob*, *cache*, duration)	Creates a temporary LOB in the user's default temporary tablespace.
ERASE(*lob*, *amount*, *offset*)	Erases data from a LOB, starting at the offset for a total amount of characters or bytes.
FILECLOSE(*bfile*)	Closes *bfile*. You should use the newer CLOSE() method instead of FILECLOSE().
FILECLOSEALL()	Closes all previously opened BFILEs.
FILEEXISTS(*bfile*)	Checks if the external file pointed to by *bfile* actually exists.
FILEGETNAME(*bfile*, *directory*, *filename*)	Returns the directory and filename of the external file pointed to by *bfile*.
FILEISOPEN(*bfile*)	Checks if *bfile* is currently open. You should use the newer ISOPEN() method instead of FILEISOPEN().

TABLE 15-1. *DBMS_LOB Methods*

Method	Description
FILEOPEN(*bfile, open_mode*)	Opens *bfile* in the indicated mode, which can be set only to DBMS_LOB.FILE_READONLY, which indicates the file can only be read from and never written to. You should use the newer OPEN() method instead of FILEOPEN().
FREETEMPORARY(*lob*)	Frees a temporary LOB.
GETCHUNKSIZE(*lob*)	Returns the chunk size used when reading and writing the data stored in the LOB. A chunk is a unit of data.
GET_STORAGE_LIMIT()	Returns the maximum allowable size for a LOB.
GETLENGTH(*lob*)	Gets the length of the data stored in the LOB.
INSTR(*lob, pattern, offset, n*)	Returns the starting position of characters or bytes that match the *n*th occurrence of a pattern in the LOB data. The data is read from the LOB starting at the offset.
ISOPEN(*lob*)	Checks if the LOB was already opened.
ISTEMPORARY(*lob*)	Checks if the LOB is a temporary LOB.
LOADFROMFILE(*dest_lob, src_bfile, amount, dest_offset, src_offset*)	Loads the data retrieved via *src_bfile* to *dest_lob*, starting at the offsets for a total amount of characters or bytes; *src_bfile* is a BFILE that points to an external file. LOADFROMFILE() is old, and you should use the higher-performance LOADBLOBFROMFILE() or LOADCLOBFROMFILE() method.
LOADBLOBFROMFILE (*dest_blob, src_bfile, amount, dest_offset, src_offset*)	Loads the data retrieved via *src_bfile* to *dest_blob*, starting at the offsets for a total amount of bytes; *src_bfile* is a BFILE that points to an external file. LOADBLOBFROMFILE() offers improved performance over LOADFROMFILE() when using a BLOB.
LOADCLOBFROMFILE (*dest_clob, src_bfile, amount, dest_offset, src_offset, src_csid, lang_context, warning*)	Loads the data retrieved via *src_bfile* to *dest_clob*, starting at the offsets for a total amount of characters; *src_bfile* is a BFILE that points to an external file. LOADCLOBFROMFILE() offers improved performance over LOADFROMFILE() when using a CLOB/NCLOB.
LOBMAXSIZE	Returns the maximum size for a LOB in bytes (currently 2^{64}).
OPEN(*lob, open_mode*)	Opens the LOB in the indicated mode, which can be set to one of the following values: DBMS_LOB.FILE_READONLY, which indicates the LOB can only be read from. DBMS_LOB.FILE_READWRITE, which indicates the LOB can be read from and written to.

(Continued)

TABLE 15-1. *DBMS_LOB Methods*

Method	Description
`READ(lob, amount, offset, buffer)`	Reads the data from the LOB and stores it in the `buffer` variable, starting at the offset in the LOB for a total amount of characters or bytes.
`SUBSTR(lob, amount, offset)`	Returns part of the LOB data, starting at the offset in the LOB for a total amount of characters or bytes.
`TRIM(lob, newlen)`	Trims the LOB data to the specified shorter length.
`WRITE(lob, amount, offset, buffer)`	Writes the data from the `buffer` variable to the LOB, starting at the offset in the LOB for a total amount of characters or bytes.
`WRITEAPPEND(lob, amount, buffer)`	Writes the data from the `buffer` variable to the end of the LOB, starting at the offset in the LOB for a total amount of characters or bytes.

TABLE 15-1. *DBMS_LOB Methods*

APPEND()

`APPEND()` adds the data in a source LOB to the end of a destination LOB. There are two versions of `APPEND()`:

```
DBMS_LOB.APPEND(
    dest_lob IN OUT NOCOPY BLOB,
    src_lob  IN            BLOB
);

DBMS_LOB.APPEND(
    dest_lob IN OUT NOCOPY CLOB/NCLOB CHARACTER SET ANY_CS,
    src_lob  IN            CLOB/NCLOB CHARACTER SET dest_lob%CHARSET
);
```

where

- *dest_lob* is the destination LOB to which the data is appended.
- *src_lob* is the source LOB from which the data is read.
- `CHARACTER SET ANY_CS` means the data in *dest_lob* can be any character set.
- `CHARACTER SET` *dest_lob*`%CHARSET` is the character set of *dest_lob*.

The following table shows the exception thrown by `APPEND()`.

Exception	Thrown When
`VALUE_ERROR`	Either *dest_lob* or *src_lob* is null.

CLOSE()

CLOSE() closes a previously opened LOB. There are three versions of CLOSE():

```
DBMS_LOB.CLOSE(
   lob IN OUT NOCOPY BLOB
);

DBMS_LOB.CLOSE(
   lob IN OUT NOCOPY CLOB/NCLOB CHARACTER SET ANY_CS
);

DBMS_LOB.CLOSE(
   lob IN OUT NOCOPY BFILE
);
```

where *lob* is the LOB to be closed.

COMPARE()

COMPARE() compares the data stored in two LOBs, starting at the offsets over a total amount of characters or bytes. There are three versions of COMPARE():

```
DBMS_LOB.COMPARE(
   lob1    IN BLOB,
   lob2    IN BLOB,
   amount  IN INTEGER := DBMS_LOB.LOBMAXSIZE,
   offset1 IN INTEGER := 1,
   offset2 IN INTEGER := 1
) RETURN INTEGER;

DBMS_LOB.COMPARE(
   lob1    IN CLOB/NCLOB  CHARACTER SET ANY_CS,
   lob2    IN CLOB/NCLOB  CHARACTER SET lob_1%CHARSET,
   amount  IN INTEGER := DBMS_LOB.LOBMAXSIZE,
   offset1 IN INTEGER := 1,
   offset2 IN INTEGER := 1
) RETURN INTEGER;

DBMS_LOB.COMPARE(
   lob1    IN BFILE,
   lob2    IN BFILE,
   amount  IN INTEGER,
   offset1 IN INTEGER := 1,
   offset2 IN INTEGER := 1
) RETURN INTEGER;
```

where

- *lob1* and *lob2* are the LOBs to compare.
- *amount* is the maximum number of characters to read from a CLOB/NCLOB, or the maximum number of bytes to read from a BLOB/BFILE.

- *offset1* and *offset2* are the offsets in characters or bytes in *lob1* and *lob2* to start the comparison (the offsets start at 1).

COMPARE() returns

- 0 if the LOBs are identical
- 1 if the LOBs aren't identical
- Null if one of the following conditions is true:
  - *amount* < 1
  - *amount* > LOBMAXSIZE (Note: LOBMAXSIZE is the maximum size of the LOB.)
  - *offset1* or *offset2* < 1
  - *offset1* or *offset2* > LOBMAXSIZE

The following table shows the exceptions thrown by COMPARE().

Exception	Thrown When
UNOPENED_FILE	The file hasn't been opened yet.
NOEXIST_DIRECTORY	The directory doesn't exist.
NOPRIV_DIRECTORY	You don't have privileges to access the directory.
INVALID_DIRECTORY	The directory is invalid.
INVALID_OPERATION	The file exists, but you don't have privileges to access the file.

COPY()

COPY() copies data from a source LOB to a destination LOB, starting at the offsets for a total amount of characters or bytes. There are two versions of COPY():

```
DBMS_LOB.COPY(
    dest_lob    IN OUT NOCOPY BLOB,
    src_lob     IN            BLOB,
    amount      IN            INTEGER,
    dest_offset IN            INTEGER := 1,
    src_offset  IN            INTEGER := 1
);

DBMS_LOB.COPY(
    dest_lob    IN OUT NOCOPY CLOB/NCLOB CHARACTER SET ANY_CS,
    src_lob     IN            CLOB/NCLOB CHARACTER SET dest_lob%CHARSET,
    amount      IN            INTEGER,
    dest_offset IN            INTEGER := 1,
    src_offset  IN            INTEGER := 1
);
```

where

- *dest_lob* and *src_lob* are the LOBs to write to and read from, respectively.
- *amount* is the maximum number of characters to read from a CLOB/NCLOB, or the maximum number of bytes to read from a BLOB/BFILE.
- *dest_offset* and *src_offset* are the offsets in characters or bytes in *dest_lob* and *src_lob* to start the copy (the offsets start at 1).

The following table shows the exceptions thrown by COPY().

Exception	Thrown When
VALUE_ERROR	Any of the parameters are null.
INVALID_ARGVAL	Either: ■ *src_offset* < 1 ■ *dest_offset* < 1 ■ *src_offset* > LOBMAXSIZE ■ *dest_offset* > LOBMAXSIZE ■ *amount* < 1 ■ *amount* > LOBMAXSIZE

CREATETEMPORARY()

CREATETEMPORARY() creates a temporary LOB in the user's default temporary tablespace. There are two versions of CREATETEMPORARY():

```
DBMS_LOB.CREATETEMPORARY(
    lob      IN OUT NOCOPY BLOB,
    cache    IN            BOOLEAN,
    duration IN            PLS_INTEGER := DBMS_LOB.SESSION
);
```

```
DBMS_LOB.CREATETEMPORARY (
    lob      IN OUT NOCOPY CLOB/NCLOB CHARACTER SET ANY_CS,
    cache    IN            BOOLEAN,
    duration IN            PLS_INTEGER := DBMS_LOB.SESSION
);
```

where

- *lob* is the temporary LOB to create.
- *cache* indicates whether the LOB should be read into the buffer cache (true for yes, false for no).
- *duration* is a hint (can be set to SESSION, TRANSACTION, or CALL) as to whether the temporary LOB is removed at the end of the session, transaction, or call (the default is SESSION).

The following table shows the exception thrown by CREATETEMPORARY().

Exception	Thrown When
VALUE_ERROR	The *lob* parameter is null.

ERASE()

ERASE() removes data from a LOB, starting at the offset for a total amount of characters or bytes. There are two versions of ERASE():

```
DBMS_LOB.ERASE(
    lob    IN OUT NOCOPY BLOB,
    amount IN OUT NOCOPY INTEGER,
    offset IN            INTEGER := 1
);

DBMS_LOB.ERASE(
    lob    IN OUT NOCOPY CLOB/NCLOB CHARACTER SET ANY_CS,
    amount IN OUT NOCOPY INTEGER,
    offset IN            INTEGER := 1
);
```

where

- *lob* is the LOB to erase.
- *amount* is the maximum number of characters to read from a CLOB/NCLOB, or the number of bytes to read from a BLOB.
- *offset* is the offset in characters or bytes in *lob* to start the erasure (the offset starts at 1).

The following table shows the exceptions thrown by ERASE().

Exception	Thrown When
VALUE_ERROR	Any of the parameters are null.
INVALID_ARGVAL	Either: ■ *amount* < 1 ■ *amount* > LOBMAXSIZE ■ *offset* < 1 ■ *offset* > LOBMAXSIZE

FILECLOSE()

FILECLOSE() closes a BFILE. You should use the newer CLOSE() procedure, as Oracle Corporation does not plan to extend the older FILECLOSE() procedure. I'm only including coverage of FILECLOSE() here so you can understand older programs. There is one version of FILECLOSE():

```
DBMS_LOB.FILECLOSE(
    bfile IN OUT NOCOPY BFILE
);
```

where *bfile* is the BFILE to close.

The following table shows the exceptions thrown by FILECLOSE().

Exception	Thrown When
VALUE_ERROR	The *bfile* parameter is null.
UNOPENED_FILE	The file hasn't been opened yet.
NOEXIST_DIRECTORY	The directory doesn't exist.
NOPRIV_DIRECTORY	You don't have privileges to access the directory.
INVALID_DIRECTORY	The directory is invalid.
INVALID_OPERATION	The file exists, but you don't have privileges to access the file.

FILECLOSEALL()

FILECLOSEALL() closes all BFILE objects.

```
DBMS_LOB.FILECLOSEALL;
```

The following table shows the exception thrown by FILECLOSEALL().

Exception	Thrown When
UNOPENED_FILE	No files have been opened in the session.

FILEEXISTS()

FILEEXISTS() checks if a file exists.

```
DBMS_LOB.FILEEXISTS(
    bfile IN BFILE
) RETURN INTEGER;
```

where *bfile* is a BFILE that points to an external file.

FILEEXISTS() returns

- 0 if the file doesn't exist
- 1 if the file exists

The following table shows the exceptions thrown by `FILEEXISTS()`.

Exception	Thrown When
VALUE_ERROR	The *bfile* parameter is null.
NOEXIST_DIRECTORY	The directory doesn't exist.
NOPRIV_DIRECTORY	You don't have privileges to access the directory.
INVALID_DIRECTORY	The directory is invalid.

FILEGETNAME()

`FILEGETNAME()` returns the directory and filename from a `BFILE`.

```
DBMS_LOB.FILEGETNAME(
    bfile     IN  BFILE,
    directory OUT VARCHAR2,
    filename  OUT VARCHAR2
);
```

where

- *bfile* is the pointer to the file.
- *directory* is the directory where the file is stored.
- *filename* is the name of the file.

The following table shows the exceptions thrown by `FILEGETNAME()`.

Exception	Thrown When
VALUE_ERROR	Any of the input parameters are null or invalid.
INVALID_ARGVAL	Either the *directory* or *filename* parameter is null.

FILEISOPEN()

`FILEISOPEN()` checks if a file is open. You should use the newer `ISOPEN()` procedure to check if a file is open in your own programs, as Oracle Corporation does not plan to extend the older `FILEISOPEN()` method. I'm only including coverage of `FILEISOPEN()` here so you can understand older programs.

```
DBMS_LOB.FILEISOPEN(
    bfile IN BFILE
) RETURN INTEGER;
```

where *bfile* is the pointer to the file.

`FILEISOPEN()` returns

- 0 if the file isn't open
- 1 if the file is open

The following table shows the exceptions thrown by FILEISOPEN().

Exception	Thrown When
NOEXIST_DIRECTORY	The directory doesn't exist.
NOPRIV_DIRECTORY	You don't have privileges to access the directory.
INVALID_DIRECTORY	The directory is invalid.
INVALID_OPERATION	The file doesn't exist or you don't have privileges to access the file.

FILEOPEN()

FILEOPEN() opens a file. You should use the newer OPEN() procedure to open a file in your own programs, as Oracle Corporation does not plan to extend the older FILEOPEN() procedure. I'm only including coverage of FILEOPEN() here so you can understand older programs.

```
DBMS_LOB.FILEOPEN(
   bfile     IN OUT NOCOPY BFILE,
   open_mode IN             BINARY_INTEGER := DBMS_LOB.FILE_READONLY
);
```

where

- *bfile* is the pointer to the file.
- *open_mode* indicates the open mode; the only open mode is DBMS_LOB.FILE_READONLY, which indicates the file can be read from.

The following table shows the exceptions thrown by FILEOPEN().

Exception	Thrown When
VALUE_ERROR	Any of the input parameters are null or invalid.
INVALID_ARGVAL	The *open_mode* is not set to DBMS_LOB.FILE_READONLY.
OPEN_TOOMANY	An attempt was made to open more than SESSION_MAX_OPEN_FILES files, where SESSION_MAX_OPEN_FILES is a database initialization parameter set by a database administrator.
NOEXIST_DIRECTORY	The directory doesn't exist.
INVALID_DIRECTORY	The directory is invalid.
INVALID_OPERATION	The file exists, but you don't have privileges to access the file.

FREETEMPORARY()

FREETEMPORARY() frees a temporary LOB from the default temporary tablespace of the user. There are two versions of FREETEMPORARY():

```
DBMS_LOB.FREETEMPORARY (
   lob IN OUT NOCOPY BLOB
);
```

```
DBMS_LOB.FREETEMPORARY (
  lob IN OUT NOCOPY CLOB/NCLOB CHARACTER SET ANY_CS
);
```

where *lob* is the LOB to be freed.

The following table shows the exception thrown by FREETEMPORARY().

Exception	Thrown When
VALUE_ERROR	Any of the input parameters are null or invalid.

GETCHUNKSIZE()

GETCHUNKSIZE() returns the chunk size when reading and writing LOB data (a chunk is a unit of data). There are two versions of GETCHUNKSIZE():

```
DBMS_LOB.GETCHUNKSIZE(
    lob IN BLOB
) RETURN INTEGER;

DBMS_LOB.GETCHUNKSIZE(
    lob IN CLOB/NCLOB CHARACTER SET ANY_CS
) RETURN INTEGER;
```

where *lob* is the LOB to get the chunk size for.

GETCHUNKSIZE() returns

- The chunk size in bytes for a BLOB
- The chunk size in characters for a CLOB/NCLOB

The following table shows the exception thrown by GETCHUNKSIZE().

Exception	Thrown When
VALUE_ERROR	The *lob* parameter is null.

GETLENGTH()

GETLENGTH() returns the length of the LOB data. There are three versions of GETLENGTH():

```
DBMS_LOB.GETLENGTH(
    lob IN BLOB
) RETURN INTEGER;

DBMS_LOB.GETLENGTH(
    lob IN CLOB/NCLOB CHARACTER SET ANY_CS
) RETURN INTEGER;

DBMS_LOB.GETLENGTH(
    bfile IN BFILE
) RETURN INTEGER;
```

where

- *lob* is the BLOB, CLOB, or NCLOB data to get the length of.
- *bfile* is the BFILE data to get the length of.

GETLENGTH() returns

- The length in bytes for a BLOB or BFILE
- The length in characters for a CLOB or NCLOB

The following table shows the exception thrown by GETLENGTH().

Exception	Thrown When
VALUE_ERROR	The *lob* or *bfile* parameter is null.

GET_STORAGE_LIMIT()

GET_STORAGE_LIMIT() returns the maximum allowable size for a LOB.

```
DBMS_LOB.GET_STORAGE_LIMIT(
   lob IN CLOB CHARACTER SET ANY_CS
) RETURN INTEGER;

DBMS_LOB.GET_STORAGE_LIMIT(
   lob IN BLOB
) RETURN INTEGER;
```

where *lob* is the LOB to get the storage limit for.

INSTR()

INSTR() returns the starting position of characters that match the *n*th occurrence of a pattern in the LOB data, starting at an offset. There are three versions of INSTR():

```
DBMS_LOB.INSTR(
   lob     IN BLOB,
   pattern IN RAW,
   offset  IN INTEGER := 1,
   n       IN INTEGER := 1
) RETURN INTEGER;

DBMS_LOB.INSTR(
   lob     IN CLOB/NCLOB CHARACTER SET ANY_CS,
   pattern IN VARCHAR2 CHARACTER SET lob%CHARSET,
   offset  IN INTEGER := 1,
   n       IN INTEGER := 1
) RETURN INTEGER;

DBMS_LOB.INSTR(
   bfile   IN BFILE,
```

```
    pattern  IN RAW,
    offset   IN INTEGER := 1,
    n        IN INTEGER := 1
) RETURN INTEGER;
```

where

- *lob* is the BLOB, CLOB, or NCLOB to read from.
- *bfile* is the BFILE to read from.
- *pattern* is the pattern to search for in the LOB data; the pattern is a group of RAW bytes for a BLOB or BFILE, and a VARCHAR2 character string for a CLOB; the maximum size of the pattern is 16,383 bytes.
- *offset* is the offset to start reading data from the LOB (the offset starts at 1).
- *n* is the occurrence of the pattern to search the data for.

INSTR() returns

- The offset of the start of the pattern (if found)
- Zero if the pattern isn't found
- Null if one of the following conditions is true:
    - Any of the IN parameters are null or invalid
    - *offset* < 1 or *offset* > LOBMAXSIZE
    - *n* < 1 or *n* > LOBMAXSIZE

The following table shows the exceptions thrown by INSTR().

Exception	Thrown When
VALUE_ERROR	Any of the input parameters are null or invalid.
UNOPENED_FILE	The BFILE isn't open.
NOEXIST_DIRECTORY	The directory doesn't exist.
NOPRIV_DIRECTORY	The directory exists, but you don't have privileges to access the directory.
INVALID_DIRECTORY	The directory is invalid.
INVALID_OPERATION	The file exists, but you don't have privileges to access the file.

ISOPEN()

ISOPEN() checks if the LOB was already opened. There are three versions of ISOPEN():

```
DBMS_LOB.ISOPEN(
    lob IN BLOB
) RETURN INTEGER;
```

```
DBMS_LOB.ISOPEN(
  lob IN CLOB/NCLOB CHARACTER SET ANY_CS
) RETURN INTEGER;

DBMS_LOB.ISOPEN(
  bfile IN BFILE
) RETURN INTEGER;
```

where

- *lob* is the BLOB, CLOB, or NCLOB to check.
- *bfile* is the BFILE to check.

ISOPEN() returns

- 0 if the LOB isn't open
- 1 if the LOB is open

The following table shows the exception thrown by ISOPEN().

Exception	Thrown When
VALUE_ERROR	The *lob* or *bfile* parameter is null or invalid.

ISTEMPORARY()

ISTEMPORARY() checks if the LOB is a temporary LOB. There are two versions of
ISTEMPORARY():

```
DBMS_LOB.ISTEMPORARY(
  lob IN BLOB
) RETURN INTEGER;

DBMS_LOB.ISTEMPORARY (
  lob IN CLOB/NCLOB CHARACTER SET ANY_CS
) RETURN INTEGER;
```

where *lob* is the LOB to check.

ISTEMPORARY() returns

- 0 if the LOB isn't temporary
- 1 if the LOB is temporary

The following table shows the exception thrown by ISTEMPORARY().

Exception	Thrown When
VALUE_ERROR	The *lob* parameter is null or invalid.

LOADFROMFILE()

LOADFROMFILE() loads data retrieved via a BFILE into a CLOB, NCLOB, or BLOB, starting at the offsets for a total amount of characters or bytes. You should use the higher-performance LOADCLOBFROMFILE() or LOADBLOBFROMFILE() procedures in your own programs, and I'm only including coverage of LOADFROMFILE() here so you can understand older programs.

There are two versions of LOADFROMFILE():

```
DBMS_LOB.LOADFROMFILE(
    dest_lob     IN OUT NOCOPY BLOB,
    src_bfile    IN            BFILE,
    amount       IN            INTEGER,
    dest_offset  IN            INTEGER  := 1,
    src_offset   IN            INTEGER  := 1
);

DBMS_LOB.LOADFROMFILE(
    dest_lob     IN OUT NOCOPY CLOB/NCLOB CHARACTER SET ANY_CS,
    src_bfile    IN            BFILE,
    amount       IN            INTEGER,
    dest_offset  IN            INTEGER := 1,
    src_offset   IN            INTEGER := 1
);
```

where

- *dest_lob* is the LOB into which the data is to be written.
- *src_bfile* is the pointer to the file from which the data is to be read.
- *amount* is the maximum number of bytes or characters to read from *src_bfile*.
- *dest_offset* is the offset in bytes or characters in *dest_lob* to start writing data (the offset starts at 1).
- *src_offset* is the offset in bytes in *src_bfile* to start reading data (the offset starts at 1).

The following table shows the exceptions thrown by LOADFROMFILE().

Exception	Thrown When
VALUE_ERROR	Any of the input parameters are null or invalid.
INVALID_ARGVAL	Either: - *src_offset* < 1 - *dest_offset* < 1 - *src_offset* > LOBMAXSIZE - *dest_offset* > LOBMAXSIZE - *amount* < 1 - *amount* > LOBMAXSIZE

LOADBLOBFROMFILE()

LOADBLOBFROMFILE() loads data retrieved via a BFILE into a BLOB. LOADBLOBFROMFILE() offers improved performance over the LOADFROMFILE() method when using a BLOB.

```
DBMS_LOB.LOADBLOBFROMFILE(
   dest_blob    IN OUT NOCOPY BLOB,
   src_bfile    IN            BFILE,
   amount       IN            INTEGER,
   dest_offset  IN OUT        INTEGER := 1,
   src_offset   IN OUT        INTEGER := 1
);
```

where

- *dest_blob* is the BLOB into which the data is to be written.
- *src_bfile* is the pointer to the file from which the data is to be read.
- *amount* is the maximum number of bytes to read from src_bfile.
- *dest_offset* is the offset in bytes in *dest_lob* to start writing data (the offset starts at 1).
- *src_offset* is the offset in bytes in *src_bfile* to start reading data (the offset starts at 1).

The following table shows the exceptions thrown by LOADBLOBFROMFILE().

Exception	Thrown When
VALUE_ERROR	Any of the input parameters are null or invalid.
INVALID_ARGVAL	Either: ■ *src_offset* < 1 ■ *dest_offset* < 1 ■ *src_offset* > LOBMAXSIZE ■ *dest_offset* > LOBMAXSIZE ■ *amount* < 1 ■ *amount* > LOBMAXSIZE

LOADCLOBFROMFILE()

LOADCLOBFROMFILE() loads data retrieved via a BFILE into a CLOB/NCLOB. LOADCLOBFROMFILE() offers improved performance over the LOADFROMFILE() method when using a CLOB/NCLOB. LOADCLOBFROMFILE() also automatically converts binary data to character data.

```
DBMS_LOB.LOADCLOBFROMFILE(
   dest_clob    IN OUT NOCOPY CLOB/NCLOB CHARACTER SET ANY_CS,
   src_bfile    IN            BFILE,
   amount       IN            INTEGER,
   dest_offset  IN OUT        INTEGER,
```

```
    src_offset    IN OUT        INTEGER,
    src_csid      IN            NUMBER,
    lang_context  IN OUT        INTEGER,
    warning       OUT           INTEGER
);
```

where

- *dest_blob* is the CLOB/NCLOB into which the data is to be written.

- *src_bfile* is the pointer to the file from which the data is to be read.

- *amount* is the maximum number of characters to read from *src_bfile*.

- *dest_offset* is the offset in characters in *dest_lob* to start writing data (the offset starts at 1).

- *src_offset* is the offset in characters in *src_bfile* to start reading data (the offset starts at 1).

- *src_csid* is the character set of *src_bfile* (you should typically use DBMS_LOB.DEFAULT_CSID, which is the default character set for the database).

- *lang_context* is the language context to use for the load (you should typically use DBMS_LOB.DEFAULT_LANG_CTX, which is the default language context for the database).

- *warning* is a warning message that contains information if there was a problem with the load; a common problem is that a character in *src_bfile* cannot be converted to a character in *dest_lob* (in which case, *warning* is set to DBMS_LOB.WARN_INCONVERTIBLE_CHAR).

NOTE
You can learn all about character sets, contexts, and how to convert characters from one language to another in the Oracle Database Globalization Support Guide *published by Oracle Corporation.*

The following table shows the exceptions thrown by LOADCLOBFROMFILE().

Exception	Thrown When
VALUE_ERROR	Any of the input parameters are null or invalid.
INVALID_ARGVAL	Either: ■ *src_offset* < 1 ■ *dest_offset* < 1 ■ *src_offset* > LOBMAXSIZE ■ *dest_offset* > LOBMAXSIZE ■ *amount* < 1 ■ *amount* > LOBMAXSIZE

OPEN()

OPEN() opens a LOB. There are three versions of OPEN():

```
DBMS_LOB.OPEN(
    lob        IN OUT NOCOPY BLOB,
    open_mode IN            BINARY_INTEGER
);

DBMS_LOB.OPEN(
    lob        IN OUT NOCOPY CLOB/NCLOB CHARACTER SET ANY_CS,
    open_mode IN            BINARY_INTEGER
);

DBMS_LOB.OPEN(
    bfile      IN OUT NOCOPY BFILE,
    open_mode IN            BINARY_INTEGER := DBMS_LOB.FILE_READONLY
);
```

where

- *lob* is the LOB to open.
- *bfile* is the pointer to the file to open.
- *open_mode* indicates the open mode; the default is DBMS_LOB.FILE_READONLY, which indicates the LOB can only be read from; DBMS_LOB.FILE_READWRITE indicates the LOB can be read from and written to.

The following table shows the exception thrown by OPEN().

Exception	Thrown When
VALUE_ERROR	Any of the input parameters are null or invalid.

READ()

READ() reads data into a buffer from a LOB. There are three versions of READ():

```
DBMS_LOB.READ(
    lob    IN            BLOB,
    amount IN OUT NOCOPY INTEGER,
    offset IN            INTEGER,
    buffer OUT           RAW
);

DBMS_LOB.READ(
    lob    IN            CLOB/NCLOB CHARACTER SET ANY_CS,
    amount IN OUT NOCOPY INTEGER,
    offset IN            INTEGER,
    buffer OUT           VARCHAR2 CHARACTER SET lob%CHARSET
);
```

```
DBMS_LOB.READ(
    bfile  IN               BFILE,
    amount IN OUT NOCOPY INTEGER,
    offset IN               INTEGER,
    buffer OUT              RAW
);
```

where

- *lob* is the CLOB, NCLOB, or BLOB to read from.
- *bfile* is the BFILE to read from.
- *amount* is the maximum number of characters to read from a CLOB/NCLOB, or the maximum number of bytes to read from a BLOB/BFILE.
- *offset* is the offset to start reading (the offset starts at 1).
- *buffer* is the variable where the data read from the LOB is to be stored.

The following table shows the exceptions thrown by READ().

Exception	Thrown When
VALUE_ERROR	Any of the input parameters are null.
INVALID_ARGVAL	Either: ■ *amount* < 1 ■ *amount* > MAXBUFSIZE ■ *amount* > capacity of buffer in bytes or characters ■ *offset* < 1 ■ *offset* > LOBMAXSIZE
NO_DATA_FOUND	The end of the LOB was reached and there are no more bytes or characters to read from the LOB.

SUBSTR()

SUBSTR() returns part of the LOB data, starting at the offset for a total amount of characters or bytes. There are three versions of SUBSTR():

```
DBMS_LOB.SUBSTR(
    lob    IN BLOB,
    amount IN INTEGER := 32767,
    offset IN INTEGER := 1
) RETURN RAW;

DBMS_LOB.SUBSTR (
    lob    IN CLOB/NCLOB CHARACTER SET ANY_CS,
    amount IN INTEGER := 32767,
    offset IN INTEGER := 1
) RETURN VARCHAR2 CHARACTER SET lob%CHARSET;
```

```
DBMS_LOB.SUBSTR (
  bfile  IN BFILE,
  amount IN INTEGER := 32767,
  offset IN INTEGER := 1
) RETURN RAW;
```

where

- *lob* is the BLOB, CLOB, or NCLOB to read from.
- *bfile* is the pointer to the file to read from.
- *amount* is the maximum number of characters read from a CLOB/NCLOB, or the maximum number of bytes to read from a BLOB/BFILE.
- *offset* is the offset to start reading data from the LOB (the offset starts at 1).

SUBSTR() returns the following values:

- RAW data when reading from a BLOB/BFILE
- VARCHAR2 data when reading from a CLOB/NCLOB
- Null if one of the following conditions is true:

  - *amount* < 1
  - *amount* > 32767
  - *offset* < 1
  - *offset* > LOBMAXSIZE

The following table shows the exceptions thrown by SUBSTR().

Exception	Thrown When
VALUE_ERROR	Any of the input parameters are null or invalid.
UNOPENED_FILE	The BFILE isn't open.
NOEXIST_DIRECTORY	The directory doesn't exist.
NOPRIV_DIRECTORY	You don't have privileges on the directory.
INVALID_DIRECTORY	The directory is invalid.
INVALID_OPERATION	The file exists, but you don't have privileges to access the file.

TRIM()

TRIM() trims the LOB data to the specified shorter length. There are two versions of TRIM():

```
DBMS_LOB.TRIM(
  lob    IN OUT NOCOPY BLOB,
  newlen IN            INTEGER
);
```

```
DBMS_LOB.TRIM(
   lob    IN OUT NOCOPY CLOB/NCLOB CHARACTER SET ANY_CS,
   newlen IN            INTEGER
);
```

where

- *lob* is the BLOB, CLOB, or NCLOB to trim.
- *newlen* is the new length (in bytes for a BLOB, or characters for a CLOB/NCLOB).

The following table shows the exceptions thrown by TRIM().

Exception	Thrown When
VALUE_ERROR	The *lob* parameter is null.
INVALID_ARGVAL	Either: - *newlen* < 0 - *newlen* > LOBMAXSIZE

WRITE()

WRITE() writes data from a buffer to a LOB. There are two versions of WRITE():

```
DBMS_LOB.WRITE(
   lob    IN OUT NOCOPY BLOB,
   amount IN            INTEGER,
   offset IN            INTEGER,
   buffer IN            RAW
);

DBMS_LOB.WRITE(
   lob    IN OUT NOCOPY CLOB/NCLOB CHARACTER SET ANY_CS,
   amount IN            INTEGER,
   offset IN            INTEGER,
   buffer IN            VARCHAR2 CHARACTER SET lob%CHARSET
);
```

where

- *lob* is the LOB to write to.
- *amount* is the maximum number of characters to write to a CLOB/NCLOB, or the maximum number of bytes to write to a BLOB.
- *offset* is the offset to start writing data to the LOB (the offset starts at 1).
- *buffer* is the variable that contains the data to be written to the LOB.

The following table shows the exceptions thrown by WRITE().

Exception	Thrown When
VALUE_ERROR	Any of the input parameters are null or invalid.
INVALID_ARGVAL	Either: ■ *amount* < 1 ■ *amount* > MAXBUFSIZE ■ *offset* < 1 ■ *offset* > LOBMAXSIZE

WRITEAPPEND()

WRITEAPPEND() writes data from the buffer to the end of a LOB, starting at the offset for a total amount of characters or bytes. There are two versions of WRITEAPPEND():

```
DBMS_LOB.WRITEAPPEND(
  lob     IN OUT NOCOPY BLOB,
  amount IN            INTEGER,
  buffer IN            RAW
);

DBMS_LOB.WRITEAPPEND(
  lob     IN OUT NOCOPY CLOB/NCLOB CHARACTER SET ANY_CS,
  amount IN            INTEGER,
  buffer IN            VARCHAR2 CHARACTER SET lob%CHARSET
);
```

where

■ *lob* is the BLOB, CLOB, or NCLOB to write to.

■ *amount* is the maximum number of characters to write to a CLOB/NCLOB, or the maximum number of bytes to write to a BLOB.

■ *buffer* is the variable that contains the data to be written to the LOB.

The following table shows the exceptions thrown by WRITEAPPEND().

Exception	Thrown When
VALUE_ERROR	Any of the input parameters are null or invalid.
INVALID_ARGVAL	Either: ■ *amount* < 1 ■ *amount* > MAXBUFSIZE

Example PL/SQL Procedures

In this section, you'll see example PL/SQL procedures that use the various methods described in the previous sections. The example procedures are created when you run the lob_schema.sql script.

Retrieving a LOB Locator

The following get_clob_locator() procedure gets a LOB locator from the clob_content table; get_clob_locator() performs the following tasks:

- Accepts an IN OUT parameter named p_clob of type CLOB; p_clob is set to a LOB locator inside the procedure. Because p_clob is IN OUT, the value is passed out of the procedure.

- Accepts an IN parameter named p_id of type INTEGER, which specifies the id of a row to retrieve from the clob_content table.

- Selects clob_column from the clob_content table into p_clob; this stores the LOB locator of clob_column in p_clob.

```
CREATE PROCEDURE get_clob_locator(
  p_clob IN OUT CLOB,
  p_id   IN INTEGER
) AS
BEGIN
  -- get the LOB locator and store it in p_clob
  SELECT clob_column
  INTO p_clob
  FROM clob_content
  WHERE id = p_id;
END get_clob_locator;
/
```

The following get_blob_locator() procedure does the same thing as the previous procedure, except it gets the locator for a BLOB from the blob_content table:

```
CREATE PROCEDURE get_blob_locator(
  p_blob IN OUT BLOB,
  p_id   IN INTEGER
) AS
BEGIN
  -- get the LOB locator and store it in p_blob
  SELECT blob_column
  INTO p_blob
  FROM blob_content
  WHERE id = p_id;
END get_blob_locator;
/
```

These two procedures are used in the code shown in the following sections.

Reading Data from CLOBs and BLOBs

The following read_clob_example() procedure reads the data from a CLOB and displays the data on the screen; read_clob_example() performs the following tasks:

- Calls get_clob_locator() to get a locator and stores it in v_clob
- Uses READ() to read the contents of v_clob into a VARCHAR2 variable named v_char_buffer

■   Displays the contents of `v_char_buffer` on the screen

```
CREATE PROCEDURE read_clob_example(
  p_id IN INTEGER
) AS
  v_clob CLOB;
  v_offset INTEGER := 1;
  v_amount INTEGER := 50;
  v_char_buffer VARCHAR2(50);
BEGIN
  -- get the LOB locator and store it in v_clob
  get_clob_locator(v_clob, p_id);

  -- read the contents of v_clob into v_char_buffer, starting at
  -- the v_offset position and read a total of v_amount characters
  DBMS_LOB.READ(v_clob, v_amount, v_offset, v_char_buffer);

  -- display the contents of v_char_buffer
  DBMS_OUTPUT.PUT_LINE('v_char_buffer = ' || v_char_buffer);
  DBMS_OUTPUT.PUT_LINE('v_amount = ' || v_amount);
END read_clob_example;
/
```

The following example turns the server output on and calls `read_clob_example()`:

```
SET SERVEROUTPUT ON
CALL read_clob_example(1);
v_char_buffer = Creeps in this petty pace
v_amount = 25
```

The following `read_blob_example()` procedure reads the data from a BLOB; read_ blob_example() performs the following tasks:

■   Calls `get_blob_locator()` to get the locator and stores it in `v_blob`
■   Calls `READ()` to read the contents of `v_blob` into a RAW variable named `v_binary_ buffer`
■   Displays the contents of `v_binary_buffer` on the screen

```
CREATE PROCEDURE read_blob_example(
  p_id IN INTEGER
) AS
  v_blob BLOB;
  v_offset INTEGER := 1;
  v_amount INTEGER := 25;
  v_binary_buffer RAW(25);
BEGIN
  -- get the LOB locator and store it in v_blob
  get_blob_locator(v_blob, p_id);
```

```
                 -- read the contents of v_blob into v_binary_buffer, starting at
                 -- the v_offset position and read a total of v_amount bytes
                 DBMS_LOB.READ(v_blob, v_amount, v_offset, v_binary_buffer);

                 -- display the contents of v_binary_buffer
                 DBMS_OUTPUT.PUT_LINE('v_binary_buffer = ' || v_binary_buffer);
                 DBMS_OUTPUT.PUT_LINE('v_amount = ' || v_amount);
               END read_blob_example;
               /
```

The following example calls `read_blob_example()`:

```
CALL read_blob_example(1);
v_binary_buffer = 100111010101011111
v_amount = 9
```

Writing to a CLOB

The following `write_example()` procedure writes a string in `v_char_buffer` to `v_clob`
using `WRITE()`. Notice that the `SELECT` statement in the procedure uses the `FOR UPDATE`
clause, which is used because the `CLOB` is written to using `WRITE()`.

```
CREATE PROCEDURE write_example(
  p_id IN INTEGER
) AS
  v_clob CLOB;
  v_offset INTEGER := 7;
  v_amount INTEGER := 6;
  v_char_buffer VARCHAR2(10) := 'pretty';
BEGIN
  -- get the LOB locator into v_clob for update (for update
  -- because the LOB is written to using WRITE() later)
  SELECT clob_column
  INTO v_clob
  FROM clob_content
  WHERE id = p_id
  FOR UPDATE;

  -- read and display the contents of the CLOB
  read_clob_example(p_id);

  -- write the characters in v_char_buffer to v_clob, starting
  -- at the v_offset position and write a total of v_amount characters
  DBMS_LOB.WRITE(v_clob, v_amount, v_offset, v_char_buffer);

  -- read and display the contents of the CLOB
  -- and then rollback the write
  read_clob_example(p_id);
  ROLLBACK;
END write_example;
/
```

The following example calls `write_example()`:

```
CALL write_example(1);
v_char_buffer = Creeps in this petty pace
v_amount = 25
v_char_buffer = Creepsprettyis petty pace
v_amount = 25
```

Appending Data to a CLOB

The following `append_example()` procedure uses `APPEND()` to copy the data from `v_src_clob` to the end of `v_dest_clob`:

```
CREATE PROCEDURE append_example AS
  v_src_clob CLOB;
  v_dest_clob CLOB;
BEGIN
  -- get the LOB locator for the CLOB in row #2 of
  -- the clob_content table into v_src_clob
  get_clob_locator(v_src_clob, 2);

  -- get the LOB locator for the CLOB in row #1 of
  -- the clob_content table into v_dest_clob for update
  -- (for update because the CLOB will be added to using
  -- APPEND() later)
  SELECT clob_column
  INTO v_dest_clob
  FROM clob_content
  WHERE id = 1
  FOR UPDATE;

  -- read and display the contents of CLOB #1
  read_clob_example(1);

  -- use APPEND() to copy the contents of v_src_clob to v_dest_clob
  DBMS_LOB.APPEND(v_dest_clob, v_src_clob);

  -- read and display the contents of CLOB #1
  -- and then rollback the change
  read_clob_example(1);
  ROLLBACK;
END append_example;
/
```

The following example calls `append_example()`:

```
CALL append_example();
v_char_buffer = Creeps in this petty pace
v_amount = 25
v_char_buffer = Creeps in this petty pace from day to day
v_amount = 41
```

Comparing the Data in Two CLOBs

The following `compare_example()` procedure compares the data in `v_clob1` and `v_clob2` using `COMPARE()`:

```
CREATE PROCEDURE compare_example AS
    v_clob1 CLOB;
    v_clob2 CLOB;
    v_return INTEGER;
BEGIN
    -- get the LOB locators
    get_clob_locator(v_clob1, 1);
    get_clob_locator(v_clob2, 2);

    -- compare v_clob1 with v_clob2 (COMPARE() returns 1
    -- because the contents of v_clob1 and v_clob2 are different)
    DBMS_OUTPUT.PUT_LINE('Comparing v_clob1 with v_clob2');
    v_return := DBMS_LOB.COMPARE(v_clob1, v_clob2);
    DBMS_OUTPUT.PUT_LINE('v_return = ' || v_return);

    -- compare v_clob1 with v_clob1 (COMPARE() returns 0
    -- because the contents are the same)
    DBMS_OUTPUT.PUT_LINE('Comparing v_clob1 with v_clob1');
    v_return := DBMS_LOB.COMPARE(v_clob1, v_clob1);
    DBMS_OUTPUT.PUT_LINE('v_return = ' || v_return);
END compare_example;
/
```

The following example calls `compare_example()`:

```
CALL compare_example();
Comparing v_clob1 with v_clob2
v_return = 1
Comparing v_clob1 with v_clob1
v_return = 0
```

Notice that `v_return` is 1 when comparing `v_clob1` with `v_clob2`, which indicates the LOB data is different; `v_return` is 0 when comparing `v_clob1` with `v_clob1`, which indicates the LOB data is the same.

Copying Data from One CLOB to Another

The following `copy_example()` procedure copies some characters from `v_src_clob` to `v_dest_clob` using `COPY()`:

```
CREATE PROCEDURE copy_example AS
    v_src_clob CLOB;
    v_dest_clob CLOB;
    v_src_offset INTEGER := 1;
    v_dest_offset INTEGER := 7;
    v_amount INTEGER := 5;
BEGIN
    -- get the LOB locator for the CLOB in row #2 of
```

```
  -- the clob_content table into v_dest_clob
  get_clob_locator(v_src_clob, 2);

  -- get the LOB locator for the CLOB in row #1 of
  -- the clob_content table into v_dest_clob for update
  -- (for update because the CLOB will be added to using
  -- COPY() later)
  SELECT clob_column
  INTO v_dest_clob
  FROM clob_content
  WHERE id = 1
  FOR UPDATE;

  -- read and display the contents of CLOB #1
  read_clob_example(1);

  -- copy characters to v_dest_clob from v_src_clob using COPY(),
  -- starting at the offsets specified by v_dest_offset and
  -- v_src_offset for a total of v_amount characters
  DBMS_LOB.COPY(
    v_dest_clob, v_src_clob,
    v_amount, v_dest_offset, v_src_offset
  );

  -- read and display the contents of CLOB #1
  -- and then rollback the change
  read_clob_example(1);
  ROLLBACK;
END copy_example;
/
```

The following example calls copy_example():

```
CALL copy_example();
v_char_buffer = Creeps in this petty pace
v_amount = 25
v_char_buffer = Creeps fromhis petty pace
v_amount = 25
```

Using Temporary CLOBs

The following temporary_lob_example() procedure illustrates the use of a temporary CLOB:

```
CREATE PROCEDURE temporary_lob_example AS
  v_clob CLOB;
  v_amount INTEGER;
  v_offset INTEGER := 1;
  v_char_buffer VARCHAR2(17) := 'Juliet is the sun';
BEGIN
  -- use CREATETEMPORARY() to create a temporary CLOB named v_clob
  DBMS_LOB.CREATETEMPORARY(v_clob, TRUE);
```

```
-- use WRITE() to write the contents of v_char_buffer to v_clob
v_amount := LENGTH(v_char_buffer);
DBMS_LOB.WRITE(v_clob, v_amount, v_offset, v_char_buffer);

-- use ISTEMPORARY() to check if v_clob is temporary
IF (DBMS_LOB.ISTEMPORARY(v_clob) = 1) THEN
  DBMS_OUTPUT.PUT_LINE('v_clob is temporary');
END IF;

-- use READ() to read the contents of v_clob into v_char_buffer
DBMS_LOB.READ(
  v_clob, v_amount, v_offset, v_char_buffer
);
DBMS_OUTPUT.PUT_LINE('v_char_buffer = ' || v_char_buffer);

-- use FREETEMPORARY() to free v_clob
DBMS_LOB.FREETEMPORARY(v_clob);
END temporary_lob_example;
/
```

The following example calls `temporary_lob_example()`:

```
CALL temporary_lob_example();
v_clob is temporary
v_char_buffer = Juliet is the sun
```

Erasing Data from a CLOB

The following `erase_example()` procedure erases part of a CLOB using `ERASE()`:

```
CREATE PROCEDURE erase_example IS
  v_clob CLOB;
  v_offset INTEGER := 2;
  v_amount INTEGER := 5;
BEGIN
  -- get the LOB locator for the CLOB in row #1 of
  -- the clob_content table into v_dest_clob for update
  -- (for update because the CLOB will be erased using
  -- ERASE() later)
  SELECT clob_column
  INTO v_clob
  FROM clob_content
  WHERE id = 1
  FOR UPDATE;

  -- read and display the contents of CLOB #1
  read_clob_example(1);

  -- use ERASE() to erase a total of v_amount characters
  -- from v_clob, starting at v_offset
  DBMS_LOB.ERASE(v_clob, v_amount, v_offset);
```

```
-- read and display the contents of CLOB #1
-- and then rollback the change
read_clob_example(1);
ROLLBACK;
END erase_example;
/
```

The following example calls `erase_example()`:

```
CALL erase_example();
v_char_buffer = Creeps in this petty pace
v_amount = 25
v_char_buffer = C      in this petty pace
v_amount = 25
```

Searching the Data in a CLOB

The following `instr_example()` procedure uses `INSTR()` to search the character data stored in a CLOB:

```
CREATE PROCEDURE instr_example AS
    v_clob CLOB;
    v_char_buffer VARCHAR2(50) := 'It is the east and Juliet is the sun';
    v_pattern VARCHAR2(5);
    v_offset INTEGER := 1;
    v_amount INTEGER;
    v_occurrence INTEGER;
    v_return INTEGER;
BEGIN
    -- use CREATETEMPORARY() to create a temporary CLOB named v_clob
    DBMS_LOB.CREATETEMPORARY(v_clob, TRUE);

    -- use WRITE() to write the contents of v_char_buffer to v_clob
    v_amount := LENGTH(v_char_buffer);
    DBMS_LOB.WRITE(v_clob, v_amount, v_offset, v_char_buffer);

    -- use READ() to read the contents of v_clob into v_char_buffer
    DBMS_LOB.READ(v_clob, v_amount, v_offset, v_char_buffer);
    DBMS_OUTPUT.PUT_LINE('v_char_buffer = ' || v_char_buffer);

    -- use INSTR() to search v_clob for the second occurrence of is,
    -- and INSTR() returns 27
    DBMS_OUTPUT.PUT_LINE('Searching for second ''is''');
    v_pattern := 'is';
    v_occurrence := 2;
    v_return := DBMS_LOB.INSTR(v_clob, v_pattern, v_offset, v_occurrence);
    DBMS_OUTPUT.PUT_LINE('v_return = ' || v_return);

    -- use INSTR() to search v_clob for the first occurrence of Moon,
    -- and INSTR() returns 0 because Moon doesn't appear in v_clob
    DBMS_OUTPUT.PUT_LINE('Searching for ''Moon''');
```

```
   v_pattern := 'Moon';
   v_occurrence := 1;
   v_return := DBMS_LOB.INSTR(v_clob, v_pattern, v_offset, v_occurrence);
   DBMS_OUTPUT.PUT_LINE('v_return = ' || v_return);

   -- use FREETEMPORARY() to free v_clob
   DBMS_LOB.FREETEMPORARY(v_clob);
END instr_example;
/
```

The following example calls instr_example():

```
CALL instr_example();
v_char_buffer = It is the east and Juliet is the sun
Searching for second 'is'
v_return = 27
Searching for 'Moon'
v_return = 0
```

Copying Data from a File into a CLOB and a BLOB

The following copy_file_data_to_clob() procedure shows how to read text from a file and store it in a CLOB:

```
CREATE PROCEDURE copy_file_data_to_clob(
  p_clob_id INTEGER,
  p_directory VARCHAR2,
  p_file_name VARCHAR2
) AS
  v_file UTL_FILE.FILE_TYPE;
  v_chars_read INTEGER;
  v_dest_clob CLOB;
  v_amount INTEGER := 32767;
  v_char_buffer VARCHAR2(32767);
BEGIN
  -- insert an empty CLOB
  INSERT INTO clob_content(
    id, clob_column
  ) VALUES (
    p_clob_id, EMPTY_CLOB()
  );

  -- get the LOB locator of the CLOB
  SELECT clob_column
  INTO v_dest_clob
  FROM clob_content
  WHERE id = p_clob_id
  FOR UPDATE;

  -- open the file for reading of text (up to v_amount characters per line)
  v_file := UTL_FILE.FOPEN(p_directory, p_file_name, 'r', v_amount);
```

```
  -- copy the data from the file into v_dest_clob one line at a time
  LOOP
    BEGIN
      -- read a line from the file into v_char_buffer;
      -- GET_LINE() does not copy the newline character into
      -- v_char_buffer
      UTL_FILE.GET_LINE(v_file, v_char_buffer);
      v_chars_read := LENGTH(v_char_buffer);

      -- append the line to v_dest_clob
      DBMS_LOB.WRITEAPPEND(v_dest_clob, v_chars_read, v_char_buffer);

      -- append a newline to v_dest_clob because v_char_buffer;
      -- the ASCII value for newline is 10, so CHR(10) returns newline
      DBMS_LOB.WRITEAPPEND(v_dest_clob, 1, CHR(10));
    EXCEPTION
      -- when there is no more data in the file then exit
      WHEN NO_DATA_FOUND THEN
        EXIT;
    END;
  END LOOP;

  -- close the file
  UTL_FILE.FCLOSE(v_file);

  DBMS_OUTPUT.PUT_LINE('Copy successfully completed.');
END copy_file_data_to_clob;
/
```

There are a number of points to note about this procedure:

- UTL_FILE is a package included with the database and contains methods and types that enable you to read and write files. For example, UTL_FILE.FILE_TYPE is an object type used to represent a file.

- The v_amount variable is set to 32767, which is the maximum number of characters that can be read from a file during each read operation.

- The v_char_buffer variable is used to store the results read from the file before they are appended to v_dest_clob. The maximum length of v_char_buffer is set to 32767; this length is large enough to store the maximum number of characters read from the file during each read operation.

- UTL_FILE.FOPEN(*directory*, *file_name*, *open_mode*, *amount*) opens a file; *open_mode* can be set to one of the following modes:

  - r to read text

  - w to write text

  - a to append text

- rb to read bytes

- wb to write bytes

- ab to append bytes

- UTL_FILE.GET_LINE(v_file, v_char_buffer) gets a line of text from v_file into v_char_buffer. GET_LINE() does not add the newline to v_char_buffer; because I want the newline, I add it using DBMS_LOB.WRITEAPPEND(v_dest_clob, 1, CHR(10)).

The following example calls copy_file_data_to_clob() to copy the contents of the file textContent.txt to a new CLOB with an id of 3:

```
CALL copy_file_data_to_clob(3, 'SAMPLE_FILES_DIR', 'textContent.txt');
Copy successfully completed.
```

The following copy_file_data_to_blob() procedure shows how to read binary data from a file and store it in a BLOB. Notice that a RAW array is used to store the binary data read from the file.

```
CREATE PROCEDURE copy_file_data_to_blob(
    p_blob_id INTEGER,
    p_directory VARCHAR2,
    p_file_name VARCHAR2
) AS
    v_file UTL_FILE.FILE_TYPE;
    v_bytes_read INTEGER;
    v_dest_blob BLOB;
    v_amount INTEGER := 32767;
    v_binary_buffer RAW(32767);
BEGIN
    -- insert an empty BLOB
    INSERT INTO blob_content(
        id, blob_column
    ) VALUES (
        p_blob_id, EMPTY_BLOB()
    );

    -- get the LOB locator of the BLOB
    SELECT blob_column
    INTO v_dest_blob
    FROM blob_content
    WHERE id = p_blob_id
    FOR UPDATE;

    -- open the file for reading of bytes (up to v_amount bytes at a time)
    v_file := UTL_FILE.FOPEN(p_directory, p_file_name, 'rb', v_amount);

    -- copy the data from the file into v_dest_blob
    LOOP
```

```
  BEGIN
    -- read binary data from the file into v_binary_buffer
    UTL_FILE.GET_RAW(v_file, v_binary_buffer, v_amount);
    v_bytes_read := LENGTH(v_binary_buffer);

    -- append v_binary_buffer to v_dest_blob
    DBMS_LOB.WRITEAPPEND(v_dest_blob, v_bytes_read/2,
      v_binary_buffer);
  EXCEPTION
    -- when there is no more data in the file then exit
    WHEN NO_DATA_FOUND THEN
      EXIT;
  END;
END LOOP;

-- close the file
UTL_FILE.FCLOSE(v_file);

DBMS_OUTPUT.PUT_LINE('Copy successfully completed.');
END copy_file_data_to_blob;
/
```

The following example calls copy_file_data_to_blob() to copy the contents of the file binaryContent.doc to a new BLOB with an id of 3:

```
CALL copy_file_data_to_blob(3, 'SAMPLE_FILES_DIR', 'binaryContent.doc');
Copy successfully completed.
```

Of course, copy_file_data_to_blob() can be used to write any binary data contained in a file to a BLOB. The binary data can contain music, video, images, executables, and so on. Go ahead and try this using your own files.

TIP
You can also bulk-load data into a LOB using the Oracle SQL*Loader and Data Pump utilities; see the Oracle Database Large Objects Developer's Guide *published by Oracle Corporation for details.*

Copying Data from a CLOB and a BLOB to a File

The following copy_clob_data_to_file() procedure shows how to read text from a CLOB and save it to a file:

```
CREATE PROCEDURE copy_clob_data_to_file(
  p_clob_id INTEGER,
  p_directory VARCHAR2,
  p_file_name VARCHAR2
) AS
  v_src_clob CLOB;
  v_file UTL_FILE.FILE_TYPE;
  v_offset INTEGER := 1;
```

```
   v_amount INTEGER := 32767;
   v_char_buffer VARCHAR2(32767);
BEGIN
  -- get the LOB locator of the CLOB
  SELECT clob_column
  INTO v_src_clob
  FROM clob_content
  WHERE id = p_clob_id;

  -- open the file for writing of text (up to v_amount characters at a time)
  v_file := UTL_FILE.FOPEN(p_directory, p_file_name, 'w', v_amount);

  -- copy the data from v_src_clob to the file
  LOOP
    BEGIN
      -- read characters from v_src_clob into v_char_buffer
      DBMS_LOB.READ(v_src_clob, v_amount, v_offset, v_char_buffer);

      -- copy the characters from v_char_buffer to the file
      UTL_FILE.PUT(v_file, v_char_buffer);

      -- add v_amount to v_offset
      v_offset := v_offset + v_amount;
    EXCEPTION
      -- when there is no more data in the file then exit
      WHEN NO_DATA_FOUND THEN
        EXIT;
    END;
  END LOOP;

  -- flush any remaining data to the file
  UTL_FILE.FFLUSH(v_file);

  -- close the file
  UTL_FILE.FCLOSE(v_file);

  DBMS_OUTPUT.PUT_LINE('Copy successfully completed.');
END copy_clob_data_to_file;
/
```

The following example calls copy_clob_data_to_file() to copy the contents of CLOB #3 to a new file named textContent2.txt:

```
CALL copy_clob_data_to_file(3, 'SAMPLE_FILES_DIR', 'textContent2.txt');
Copy successfully completed.
```

If you look in the C:\sample_files directory, you will find the new textContent2.txt file. This file contains identical text to textContent.txt.

The following `copy_blob_data_to_file()` procedure shows how to read binary data from a BLOB and save it to a file:

```
CREATE PROCEDURE copy_blob_data_to_file(
    p_blob_id INTEGER,
    p_directory VARCHAR2,
    p_file_name VARCHAR2
) AS
    v_src_blob BLOB;
    v_file UTL_FILE.FILE_TYPE;
    v_offset INTEGER := 1;
    v_amount INTEGER := 32767;
    v_binary_buffer RAW(32767);
BEGIN
    -- get the LOB locator of the BLOB
    SELECT blob_column
    INTO v_src_blob
    FROM blob_content
    WHERE id = p_blob_id;

    -- open the file for writing of bytes (up to v_amount bytes at a time)
    v_file := UTL_FILE.FOPEN(p_directory, p_file_name, 'wb', v_amount);

    -- copy the data from v_src_blob to the file
    LOOP
      BEGIN
        -- read characters from v_src_blob into v_binary_buffer
        DBMS_LOB.READ(v_src_blob, v_amount, v_offset, v_binary_buffer);

        -- copy the binary data from v_binary_buffer to the file
        UTL_FILE.PUT_RAW(v_file, v_binary_buffer);

        -- add v_amount to v_offset
        v_offset := v_offset + v_amount;
      EXCEPTION
        -- when there is no more data in the file then exit
        WHEN NO_DATA_FOUND THEN
          EXIT;
      END;
    END LOOP;

    -- flush any remaining data to the file
    UTL_FILE.FFLUSH(v_file);

    -- close the file
    UTL_FILE.FCLOSE(v_file);

    DBMS_OUTPUT.PUT_LINE('Copy successfully completed.');
END copy_blob_data_to_file;
/
```

The following example calls `copy_blob_data_to_file()` to copy the contents of BLOB #3 to a new file named `binaryContent2.doc`:

```
CALL copy_blob_data_to_file(3, 'SAMPLE_FILES_DIR', 'binaryContent2.doc');
Copy successfully completed.
```

If you look in the `C:\sample_files` directory, you will find the new `binaryContent2.doc` file. This file contains identical text to `binaryContent.doc`.

Of course, `copy_blob_data_to_file()` can be used to write any binary data contained in a BLOB to a file. The binary data can contain music, video, images, executables, and so on.

Copying Data from a BFILE to a CLOB and a BLOB

The following `copy_bfile_data_to_clob()` procedure shows how to read text from a BFILE and save it to a CLOB:

```
CREATE PROCEDURE copy_bfile_data_to_clob(
  p_bfile_id INTEGER,
  p_clob_id INTEGER
) AS
  v_src_bfile BFILE;
  v_directory VARCHAR2(200);
  v_filename VARCHAR2(200);
  v_length INTEGER;
  v_dest_clob CLOB;
  v_amount INTEGER := DBMS_LOB.LOBMAXSIZE;
  v_dest_offset INTEGER := 1;
  v_src_offset INTEGER := 1;
  v_src_csid INTEGER := DBMS_LOB.DEFAULT_CSID;
  v_lang_context INTEGER := DBMS_LOB.DEFAULT_LANG_CTX;
  v_warning INTEGER;
BEGIN
  -- get the locator of the BFILE
  SELECT bfile_column
  INTO v_src_bfile
  FROM bfile_content
  WHERE id = p_bfile_id;

  -- use FILEEXISTS() to check if the file exists
  -- (FILEEXISTS() returns 1 if the file exists)
  IF (DBMS_LOB.FILEEXISTS(v_src_bfile) = 1) THEN
    -- use OPEN() to open the file
    DBMS_LOB.OPEN(v_src_bfile);

    -- use FILEGETNAME() to get the name of the file and the directory
    DBMS_LOB.FILEGETNAME(v_src_bfile, v_directory, v_filename);
    DBMS_OUTPUT.PUT_LINE('Directory = ' || v_directory);
    DBMS_OUTPUT.PUT_LINE('Filename = ' || v_filename);
```

```
  -- insert an empty CLOB
  INSERT INTO clob_content(
    id, clob_column
  ) VALUES (
    p_clob_id, EMPTY_CLOB()
  );

  -- get the LOB locator of the CLOB (for update)
  SELECT clob_column
  INTO v_dest_clob
  FROM clob_content
  WHERE id = p_clob_id
  FOR UPDATE;

  -- use LOADCLOBFROMFILE() to get up to v_amount characters
  -- from v_src_bfile and store them in v_dest_clob, starting
  -- at offset 1 in v_src_bfile and v_dest_clob
  DBMS_LOB.LOADCLOBFROMFILE(
    v_dest_clob, v_src_bfile,
    v_amount, v_dest_offset, v_src_offset,
    v_src_csid, v_lang_context, v_warning
  );

  -- check v_warning for an inconvertible character
  IF (v_warning = DBMS_LOB.WARN_INCONVERTIBLE_CHAR) THEN
    DBMS_OUTPUT.PUT_LINE('Warning! Inconvertible character.');
  END IF;

  -- use CLOSE() to close v_src_bfile
  DBMS_LOB.CLOSE(v_src_bfile);
  DBMS_OUTPUT.PUT_LINE('Copy successfully completed.');
ELSE
  DBMS_OUTPUT.PUT_LINE('File does not exist');
END IF;
END copy_bfile_data_to_clob;
/
```

The following example calls copy_bfile_data_to_clob() to copy the contents of BFILE #1 to a new CLOB with an id of 4:

```
CALL copy_bfile_data_to_clob(1, 4);
Copy successfully completed.
```

The next example calls copy_clob_data_to_file() to copy the contents of CLOB #4 to a new file named textContent3.txt:

```
CALL copy_clob_data_to_file(4, 'SAMPLE_FILES_DIR', 'textContent3.txt');
Copy successfully completed.
```

If you look in the C:\sample_files directory, you will find the new textContent3.txt file. This file contains identical text to textContent.txt.

The following `copy_bfile_data_to_blob()` procedure shows how to read binary data from a BFILE and save it to a BLOB:

```
CREATE PROCEDURE copy_bfile_data_to_blob(
    p_bfile_id INTEGER,
    p_blob_id INTEGER
) AS
    v_src_bfile BFILE;
    v_directory VARCHAR2(200);
    v_filename VARCHAR2(200);
    v_length INTEGER;
    v_dest_blob BLOB;
    v_amount INTEGER := DBMS_LOB.LOBMAXSIZE;
    v_dest_offset INTEGER := 1;
    v_src_offset INTEGER := 1;
BEGIN
    -- get the locator of the BFILE
    SELECT bfile_column
    INTO v_src_bfile
    FROM bfile_content
    WHERE id = p_bfile_id;

    -- use FILEEXISTS() to check if the file exists
    -- (FILEEXISTS() returns 1 if the file exists)
    IF (DBMS_LOB.FILEEXISTS(v_src_bfile) = 1) THEN
      -- use OPEN() to open the file
      DBMS_LOB.OPEN(v_src_bfile);

      -- use FILEGETNAME() to get the name of the file and
      -- the directory
      DBMS_LOB.FILEGETNAME(v_src_bfile, v_directory, v_filename);
      DBMS_OUTPUT.PUT_LINE('Directory = ' || v_directory);
      DBMS_OUTPUT.PUT_LINE('Filename = ' || v_filename);

      -- insert an empty BLOB
      INSERT INTO blob_content(
        id, blob_column
      ) VALUES (
        p_blob_id, EMPTY_BLOB()
      );

      -- get the LOB locator of the BLOB (for update)
      SELECT blob_column
      INTO v_dest_blob
      FROM blob_content
      WHERE id = p_blob_id
      FOR UPDATE;

      -- use LOADBLOBFROMFILE() to get up to v_amount bytes
      -- from v_src_bfile and store them in v_dest_blob, starting
      -- at offset 1 in v_src_bfile and v_dest_blob'
```

```
    DBMS_LOB.LOADBLOBFROMFILE(
      v_dest_blob, v_src_bfile,
      v_amount, v_dest_offset, v_src_offset
    );

    -- use CLOSE() to close v_src_bfile
    DBMS_LOB.CLOSE(v_src_bfile);
    DBMS_OUTPUT.PUT_LINE('Copy successfully completed.');
  ELSE
    DBMS_OUTPUT.PUT_LINE('File does not exist');
  END IF;
END copy_bfile_data_to_blob;
/
```

The following example calls copy_bfile_data_to_blob() to copy the contents of BFILE #2 to a new BLOB with an id of 4:

```
CALL copy_bfile_data_to_blob(2, 4);
Copy successfully completed.
```

The next example calls copy_blob_data_to_file() to copy the contents of BLOB #4 to a new file named binaryContent3.doc:

```
CALL copy_blob_data_to_file(4, 'SAMPLE_FILES_DIR', 'binaryContent3.doc');
Copy successfully completed.
```

If you look in the C:\sample_files directory, you will find the new binaryContent3 .doc file. This file contains identical text to binaryContent.doc.

This is the end of the coverage on large objects. In the next section, you'll learn about the LONG and LONG RAW types.

LONG and LONG RAW Types

I mentioned at the start of this chapter that LOBs are the preferred storage type for large blocks of data, but you might encounter databases that still use the following types:

- **LONG**   Used to store up to 2 gigabytes of character data
- **LONG RAW**   Used to store up to 2 gigabytes of binary data
- **RAW**   Used to store up to 32,767 bytes of binary data

In this section, you'll learn how to use LONG and LONG RAW types. RAW is used in the same way as a LONG RAW, so I've omitted coverage of RAW.

The Example Tables

In this section, you'll see the use of the following two tables:

- **long_content**   Contains a LONG column named long_column
- **long_raw_content**   Contains a LONG RAW column named long_raw_column

These two tables are created by the `lob_schema.sql` script using the following statements:

```
CREATE TABLE long_content (
  id            INTEGER PRIMARY KEY,
  long_column LONG NOT NULL
);

CREATE TABLE long_raw_content (
  id                INTEGER PRIMARY KEY,
  long_raw_column LONG RAW NOT NULL
);
```

Adding Data to LONG and LONG RAW Columns

The following INSERT statements add rows to the `long_content` table:

```
INSERT INTO long_content (
  id, long_column
) VALUES (
  1, 'Creeps in this petty pace'
);

INSERT INTO long_content (
  id, long_column
) VALUES (
  2, ' from day to day'
);
```

The following INSERT statements add rows to the `long_raw_content` table (the first INSERT contains a binary number, the second a hexadecimal number):

```
INSERT INTO long_raw_content (
  id, long_raw_column
) VALUES (
  1, '100111010101011111'
);

INSERT INTO long_raw_content (
  id, long_raw_column
) VALUES (
  2, 'A0FFB71CF90DE'
);
```

In the next section, you'll see how to convert LONG and LONG RAW columns to LOBs.

Converting LONG and LONG RAW Columns to LOBs

You can convert a LONG to a CLOB using the TO_LOB() function. For example, the following statement converts long_column to a CLOB using TO_LOB() and stores the results in the clob_content table:

```
INSERT INTO clob_content
SELECT 10 + id, TO_LOB(long_column)
FROM long_content;
```

```
2 rows created.
```

You can convert a LONG RAW to a BLOB using the TO_LOB() function. For example, the following statement converts long_raw_column to a BLOB using TO_LOB() and stores the results in the blob_content table:

```
INSERT INTO blob_content
SELECT 10 + id, TO_LOB(long_raw_column)
FROM long_raw_content;
```

```
2 rows created.
```

You can also use the ALTER TABLE statement to convert LONG and LONG RAW columns directly. For example, the following statement converts long_column to a CLOB:

```
ALTER TABLE long_content MODIFY (long_column CLOB);
```

The next example converts long_raw_column to a BLOB:

```
ALTER TABLE long_raw_content MODIFY (long_raw_column BLOB);
```

Once a LONG or LONG RAW column is converted to a LOB, you can use the rich PL/SQL methods described earlier to access the LOB.

Oracle Database 10g Enhancements to Large Objects

In this section, you'll learn about the following enhancements made to large objects in Oracle Database 10g:

- Implicit conversion between CLOB and NCLOB objects
- Use of the :new attribute when using LOBs in a trigger

I've provided an SQL*Plus script named lob_schema2.sql in the SQL directory. This script can be run using Oracle Database 10g and higher. The script creates a user named lob_user2 with a password of lob_password2 and creates the tables and PL/SQL code used in this section. After the script completes, you will be logged in as lob_user2.

You perform the following steps to create the schema:

1. Start SQL*Plus.
2. Log into the database as a user with privileges to create new users, tables, and PL/SQL packages. I run scripts in my database using the `system` user.
3. Run the `lob_schema2.sql` script from within SQL*Plus using the `@` command.

For example, if you're using Windows and the script is stored in `C:\sql_book\SQL`, then you enter the following command:

```
@ C:\sql_book\SQL\lob_schema2.sql
```

When the script completes, you will be logged in as `lob_user2`.

Implicit Conversion Between CLOB and NCLOB Objects

In today's global business environment, you might have to deal with conversions between Unicode and a national language character set. Unicode is a universal character set that enables you to store text that can be converted into almost any language; it does this by providing a unique code for every character, regardless of the language. A national character set stores text in a specific language.

In versions of the database below Oracle Database 10g, you have to explicitly convert between Unicode text and the national character set text using the `TO_CLOB()` and `TO_NCLOB()` functions. `TO_CLOB()` allows you to convert text stored in a VARCHAR2, NVARCHAR2, or NCLOB to a CLOB. Similarly, `TO_NCLOB()` allows you to convert text stored in a VARCHAR2, NVARCHAR2, or CLOB to an NCLOB.

Oracle Database 10g and higher implicitly converts Unicode text and national character set text in CLOB and NCLOB objects, which saves you from using `TO_CLOB()` and `TO_NCLOB()`. You can use this implicit conversion for IN and OUT variables in queries and DML statements, as well as for PL/SQL method parameters and variable assignments.

Let's take a look at an example. The following statement creates a table named `nclob_content` that contains an NCLOB column named `nclob_column`:

```
CREATE TABLE nclob_content (
  id INTEGER PRIMARY KEY,
  nclob_column NCLOB
);
```

The following `nclob_example()` procedure shows the implicit conversion of a CLOB to an NCLOB, and vice versa:

```
CREATE PROCEDURE nclob_example
AS
  v_clob CLOB := 'It is the east and Juliet is the sun';
  v_nclob NCLOB;
BEGIN
  -- insert v_clob into nclob_column; this implicitly
  -- converts the CLOB v_clob to an NCLOB, storing
  -- the contents of v_clob in the nclob_content table
```

```
   INSERT INTO nclob_content (
     id, nclob_column
   ) VALUES (
     1, v_clob
   );

   -- select nclob_column into v_clob; this implicitly
   -- converts the NCLOB stored in nclob_column to a
   -- CLOB, retrieving the contents of nclob_column
   -- into v_clob
   SELECT nclob_column
   INTO v_clob
   FROM nclob_content
   WHERE id = 1;

   -- display the contents of v_clob
   DBMS_OUTPUT.PUT_LINE('v_clob = ' || v_clob);
END nclob_example;
/
```

The following example turns the server output on and calls `nclob_example()`:

```
SET SERVEROUTPUT ON
CALL nclob_example();
v_clob = It is the east and Juliet is the sun
```

Use of the :new Attribute When Using LOBs in a Trigger

In Oracle Database 10g and higher, you can use the :new attribute when referencing LOBs in a BEFORE UPDATE or BEFORE INSERT row-level trigger. The following example creates a trigger named before_clob_content_update. The trigger fires when the clob_content table is updated and displays the length of the new data in clob_column. In the example trigger, notice that :new is used to access the new data in clob_column.

```
CREATE TRIGGER before_clob_content_update
BEFORE UPDATE
ON clob_content
FOR EACH ROW
BEGIN
  DBMS_OUTPUT.PUT_LINE('clob_content changed');
  DBMS_OUTPUT.PUT_LINE(
    'Length = ' || DBMS_LOB.GETLENGTH(:new.clob_column)
  );
END before_clob_content_update;
/
```

The following example updates the `clob_content` table, causing the trigger to be fired:

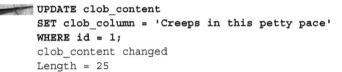

```
UPDATE clob_content
SET clob_column = 'Creeps in this petty pace'
WHERE id = 1;
clob_content changed
Length = 25
```

Oracle Database 11g Enhancements to Large Objects

In this section, you'll learn about the following enhancements that were made to large objects in Oracle Database 11g:

- Encryption of BLOB, CLOB, and NCLOB data, which prevents unauthorized viewing and modification of the data
- Compression to squeeze BLOB, CLOB, and NCLOB data
- De-duplication of BLOB, CLOB, and NCLOB data to automatically detect and remove repeated data

Encrypting LOB Data

You can disguise your data using encryption so that unauthorized users cannot view or modify it. You should encrypt sensitive data such as credit card numbers, Social Security numbers, and so on.

Before you can encrypt data, either you or a database administrator needs to set up a "wallet" to store security details. The data in a wallet includes a private key for encrypting and decrypting data. In this section, you'll see how to create a wallet, encrypt LOB data, and encrypt regular column data.

Creating a Wallet

To create a wallet, you perform the following tasks:

1. Create a directory named `wallet` in the directory `$ORACLE_BASE\admin\$ORACLE_SID`. `ORACLE_BASE` is the base directory in which the Oracle database software is installed. `ORACLE_SID` is the system identifier for the database in which the wallet is to be created. For example, on a computer running Windows, you might create a directory named `wallet` in `C:\oracle12c\admin\orcl`. In Linux, you might create the `wallet` directory in `/u01/app/oracle12c/admin/orcl`.

2. Edit your `sqlnet.ora` file located in the Oracle `NETWORK\ADMIN` directory (for example, `C:\oracle12c\product\12.1.0\dbhome_1\NETWORK\ADMIN`) and add a line at the end of the file to reference your `wallet` directory. For example:
   `ENCRYPTION_WALLET_LOCATION=(SOURCE=(METHOD=FILE)(METHOD_DATA=(DIRECTORY=C:\oracle12c\admin\orcl\wallet)))`

3. Restart the Oracle database.

4. Run SQL*Plus, connect to the database using a privileged user account (for example, `system`), and run the following `ALTER SYSTEM` command to set the password for the wallet encryption key:

```
ALTER SYSTEM SET ENCRYPTION KEY IDENTIFIED BY "testpassword123";
```

Once you have performed these tasks, a file called `ewallet.p12` appears in the `wallet` directory. The encryption key password is stored in the wallet, and is used to encrypt and decrypt the data.

I've provided an SQL*Plus script named `lob_schema3.sql` in the `SQL` directory. This script can be run using Oracle Database 11*g* and higher. The script creates a user named `lob_user3` with a password of `lob_password3` and creates the tables and PL/SQL code used in this section. After the script completes, you will be logged in as `lob_user3`.

You perform the following steps to create the schema:

1. Start SQL*Plus.
2. Log into the database as a user with privileges to create new users, tables, and PL/SQL packages. I run scripts in my database using the `system` user.
3. Run the `lob_schema3.sql` script from within SQL*Plus using the @ command.

For example, if you're using Windows and the script is stored in `C:\sql_book\SQL`, then you enter the following command:

```
@ C:\sql_book\SQL\lob_schema3.sql
```

When the script completes, you will be logged in as `lob_user3`.

Encrypting LOB Data

You can encrypt the data stored in a `BLOB`, `CLOB`, or `NCLOB` to prevent unauthorized access to that data. You cannot encrypt a `BFILE`, because the file itself is stored outside the database.

You can use the following algorithms to encrypt data:

■ **3DES168**   The Triple-DES (Data Encryption Standard) algorithm with a key length of 168 bits.

■ **AES128**   The Advanced Encryption Standard algorithm with a key length of 128 bits. The AES algorithms were developed to replace the older algorithms based on DES.

■ **AES192**   The Advanced Encryption Standard algorithm with a key length of 192 bits.

■ **AES256**   The Advanced Encryption Standard algorithm with a key length of 256 bits. AES256 is the most secure encryption algorithm supported by the Oracle database.

The following statement creates a table with a `CLOB` whose contents are to be encrypted using the AES128 algorithm. Notice the use of the `ENCRYPT` and `SECUREFILE` keywords, which are required when encrypting data.

```
CREATE TABLE clob_content (
  id INTEGER PRIMARY KEY,
  clob_column CLOB ENCRYPT USING 'AES128'
) LOB(clob_column) STORE AS SECUREFILE (
  CACHE
);
```

As you can see, the contents of `clob_column` will be encrypted using the AES128 algorithm. If you omit the `USING` keyword and the algorithm, then the default AES192 algorithm is used.

The `CACHE` keyword in the `CREATE TABLE` statement indicates that the database places data from the LOB into the buffer cache for faster access. The options you can use for buffer caching are as follows:

- **CACHE READS** Use when the LOB data will be frequently read but written only once or occasionally.
- **CACHE** Use when the LOB data will be frequently read and frequently written.
- **NOCACHE** Use when the LOB data will be read once or occasionally and written once or occasionally. This is the default option.

LOBs that are defined using the `SECUREFILE` keyword are known as *SecureFiles* LOBs, which is the official Oracle Corporation name.

NOTE
SecureFiles LOBs can only be created in a tablespace that is configured using Automatic Segment Space Management (ASSM). If you are having difficulties creating SecureFiles LOBs, you should speak with your database administrator.

The following `INSERT` statements add two rows to the `clob_content` table:

```
INSERT INTO clob_content (
  id, clob_column
) VALUES (
  1, TO_CLOB('Creeps in this petty pace')
);

INSERT INTO clob_content (
  id, clob_column
) VALUES (
  2, TO_CLOB(' from day to day')
);
```

The data supplied to `clob_column` in these statements are automatically encrypted by the database.

The following query retrieves the rows from the `clob_content` table:

```
SELECT *
FROM clob_content;

        ID
----------
CLOB_COLUMN
------------------------
         1
Creeps in this petty pace

         2
 from day to day
```

When the data is retrieved, it is automatically decrypted by the database and then returned to SQL*Plus for display.

As long as the wallet is open, you can store and retrieve encrypted data. When the wallet is closed, you cannot store or retrieve the encrypted data. Let's see an example of what happens when the wallet is closed. The following statements connect as the `system` user and close the wallet:

```
CONNECT system/oracle
ALTER SYSTEM SET WALLET CLOSE IDENTIFIED BY "testpassword123";
```

If you now attempt to connect as `lob_user3` and retrieve `clob_column` from the `clob_content` table, then you get the error `ORA-28365: wallet is not open`:

```
CONNECT lob_user3/lob_password3
SELECT clob_column
FROM clob_content;
ORA-28365: wallet is not open
```

You can still retrieve and modify the contents of unencrypted columns. For example, the following query retrieves the `id` column from the `clob_content` table:

```
SELECT id
FROM clob_content;

        ID
----------
         1
         2
```

The following statements connect as the `system` user and reopen the wallet:

```
CONNECT system/oracle
ALTER SYSTEM SET WALLET OPEN IDENTIFIED BY "testpassword123";
```

After the wallet is opened, you can retrieve and modify the encrypted contents of `clob_column` from the `clob_content` table.

Encrypting Column Data

You can also encrypt regular column data. This feature was introduced in Oracle Database 10*g* Release 2. For example, the following statement creates a table named `credit_cards` with an encrypted column named `card_number`:

```
CREATE TABLE credit_cards (
    card_number NUMBER(16, 0) ENCRYPT,
    first_name  VARCHAR2(10),
    last_name   VARCHAR2(10),
    expiration  DATE
);
```

You can use the same algorithms to encrypt a column as for a LOB: 3DES168, AES128, AES192 (the default), and AES256. Because I didn't specify an algorithm after the `ENCRYPT` keyword for the `card_number` column, the default AES192 algorithm is used.

The following `INSERT` statements add two rows to the `credit_cards` table:

```
INSERT INTO credit_cards (
  card_number, first_name, last_name, expiration
) VALUES (
  1234, 'Jason', 'Bond', '03-FEB-2008'
);

INSERT INTO credit_cards (
  card_number, first_name, last_name, expiration
) VALUES (
  5768, 'Steve', 'Edwards', '07-MAR-2009'
);
```

As long as the wallet is open, you can retrieve and modify the contents of the `card_number` column. If the wallet is closed, then you get the error `ORA-28365: wallet is not open`. You saw examples that illustrate these concepts in the previous section, so I won't repeat similar examples here.

Accessing data in an encrypted column introduces additional overhead. The overhead for encrypting or decrypting a column is estimated by Oracle Corporation to be about 5 percent, which means that a `SELECT` or an `INSERT` takes about 5 percent more time to complete. The total overhead depends on the number of encrypted columns and their frequency of access. Therefore, you should only encrypt columns that contain sensitive data.

NOTE
If you are interested in learning more about wallets and database security, you can read the Oracle Database Advanced Security Administrator's Guide *published by Oracle Corporation.*

Compressing LOB Data

You can compress the data stored in a `BLOB`, `CLOB`, or `NCLOB` to reduce storage space. For example, the following statement creates a table with a `CLOB` whose contents are to be compressed. Notice the use of the `COMPRESS` keyword.

```
CREATE TABLE clob_content3 (
  id           INTEGER PRIMARY KEY,
  clob_column CLOB
) LOB(clob_column) STORE AS SECUREFILE (
  COMPRESS
  CACHE
);
```

NOTE
Even though the table does not contain encrypted data, the SECUREFILE *keyword is used.*

When you add data to the LOB, it will be automatically compressed by the database. Similarly, when you read data from a LOB, it will be automatically decompressed. You can use

COMPRESS HIGH for maximum data compression. The default is COMPRESS MEDIUM, and the MEDIUM keyword is optional. The higher the compression, the higher the overhead when reading and writing LOB data. Oracle Database 11g Release 2 introduced the COMPRESS LOW option, which compresses the LOB data to its smallest possible size.

Removing Duplicate LOB Data

You can configure a BLOB, CLOB, or NCLOB so that any duplicate data supplied to it is automatically removed. This process is known as de-duplicating data and can save storage space. For example, the following statement creates a table with a CLOB whose contents are to be de-duplicated. Notice the use of the DEDUPLICATE LOB keywords.

```
CREATE TABLE clob_content2 (
    id          INTEGER PRIMARY KEY,
    clob_column CLOB
) LOB(clob_column) STORE AS SECUREFILE (
    DEDUPLICATE LOB
    CACHE
);
```

Any duplicate data added to the LOB will be automatically removed by the database. The database uses the SHA1 secure hash algorithm to detect duplicate data.

Oracle Database 12c Enhancement to Large Objects

By default, in Oracle Database 12c, LOBs are stored as SecureFiles LOBs. This is equivalent to specifying the SECUREFILE option for LOBs in earlier versions of the Oracle database software. If you do not want a LOB to be stored as a SecureFiles LOB in Oracle Database 12c, then you specify the BASICFILE option. These types of LOBs are known as *BasicFiles* LOBs, which is the official Oracle Corporation name.

For example, the following statement creates a table with a BASICFILE CLOB:

```
CREATE TABLE clob_content_basicfile (
    id          INTEGER PRIMARY KEY,
    clob_column CLOB
) LOB(clob_column) STORE AS BASICFILE;
```

A database administrator can control how LOBs are created using the following two database control parameters, which are stored in the database init.ora file:

- **compatible** specifies the release with which Oracle must maintain compatibility (for example, 12.0.0.0.0, for the earliest version of Oracle Database 12c).

- **db_securefile** specifies how to handle SecureFiles LOBs (for example, PREFERRED, which means that SecureFiles LOBs are created by default when possible).

When the compatible parameter is set to a valid Oracle Database 12c version number, the default value for db_securefile is PREFERRED. A database administrator can change these parameters to control how LOBs are created.

The valid values for `db_securefile` are as follows:

- **PREFERRED** specifies that SecureFiles LOBs are created by default when possible. This option is new for Oracle Database 12c.

- **PERMITTED** specifies that SecureFiles LOBs can be created.

- **NEVER** prevents SecureFiles LOBs from being created. Any LOBs that are specified as SecureFiles LOBs are created as BasicFiles LOBs instead. If you try to specify any SecureFiles LOB options, such as compress, encrypt, or de-duplicate, then an error is returned by the database.

- **ALWAYS** attempts to create SecureFiles LOBs. Any LOBs that are not in an Automatic Segment Space Management (ASSM) tablespace are created as BasicFiles LOBs instead, unless you explicitly specify `SECUREFILE` for the LOB.

- **IGNORE** prevents SecureFiles LOBs from being created. The `SECUREFILE` keyword and all SecureFiles LOB options are ignored.

In addition, the LOB storage behavior is affected by the `compatible` parameter as follows:

- When set to a valid Oracle Database 10g version number, the LOB storage behavior is identical to that of Oracle Database 10g. Oracle Database 10g only allows BasicFiles LOBs, and the `BASICFILE` and `SECUREFILE` keywords are not valid.

- When set to a valid Oracle Database 11g version number, SecureFiles and BasicFiles LOBs are allowed. If `compatible` is not set to 11.1 or higher, then the LOBs are not treated as SecureFiles LOBs (they are instead treated as BasicFiles LOBs).

- When set to a valid Oracle Database 12c version number, you must explicitly specify the `BASICFILE` option to use the BasicFiles LOB storage type. Otherwise, a `CREATE TABLE` statement will create a SecureFiles LOB by default.

You can learn more about large objects in the *Oracle Database SecureFiles and Large Objects Developer's Guide* published by Oracle Corporation.

Summary

In this chapter, you have learned the following:

- LOBs can store binary data, character data, and references to external files.
- LOBs can store up to 128 terabytes of data.
- There are four LOB types: `CLOB`, `NCLOB`, `BLOB`, and `BFILE`.
- A `CLOB` stores character data.
- An `NCLOB` stores multi-byte character data.
- A `BLOB` stores binary data.
- A `BFILE` stores a pointer to a file located in the file system.
- The `DBMS_LOB` PL/SQL package contains methods for accessing LOBs.

In the next chapter, you'll learn about SQL tuning.

CHAPTER
16

SQL Tuning

I n this chapter, you will perform the following tasks:

- Examine SQL tuning
- See SQL tuning tips that you can use to shorten the length of time your queries take to execute
- Learn about the Oracle optimizer
- See how to compare the cost of performing queries
- Examine optimizer hints
- Learn about some additional tuning tools

Introducing SQL Tuning

One of the main strengths of SQL is that you don't have to tell the database exactly how to obtain the data requested. You simply run a query specifying the information you want, and the database software figures out the best way to get it.

Sometimes, you can improve the performance of your SQL statements by "tuning" them. In the following sections, you'll see tuning tips that can make your queries run faster; later, you'll see more advanced tuning techniques. The examples in this chapter use the store schema.

Use a WHERE Clause to Filter Rows

Many novices retrieve all the rows from a table when they only want one row (or a few rows). This is very wasteful. A better approach is to add a WHERE clause to a query. That way, you restrict the rows retrieved to just those actually needed.

For example, say you want the details for customers #1 and #2. The following query retrieves all the rows from the customers table (wasteful):

```
-- BAD (retrieves all rows from the customers table)
SELECT *
FROM customers;

CUSTOMER_ID FIRST_NAME LAST_NAME  DOB       PHONE
----------- ---------- ---------- --------- ------------
          1 John       Brown      01-JAN-65 800-555-1211
          2 Cynthia    Green      05-FEB-68 800-555-1212
          3 Steve      White      16-MAR-71 800-555-1213
          4 Gail       Black                800-555-1214
          5 Doreen     Blue       20-MAY-70
```

The next query adds a WHERE clause to the previous example to just get customers #1 and #2:

```
-- GOOD (uses a WHERE clause to limit the rows retrieved)
SELECT *
FROM customers
WHERE customer_id IN (1, 2);
```

```
CUSTOMER_ID FIRST_NAME LAST_NAME  DOB        PHONE
----------- ---------- ---------- --------- ------------
          1 John       Brown      01-JAN-65 800-555-1211
          2 Cynthia    Green      05-FEB-68 800-555-1212
```

Use Table Joins Rather than Multiple Queries

If you need information from multiple related tables, you should use join conditions rather than multiple queries. In the following bad example, two queries are used to get the product name and the product type name for product #1 (using two queries is wasteful). The first query gets the name and product_type_id column values from the products table for product #1. The second query then uses that product_type_id to get the name column from the product_types table.

```
-- BAD (two separate queries when one would work)
SELECT name, product_type_id
FROM products
WHERE product_id = 1;
```

```
NAME                            PRODUCT_TYPE_ID
------------------------------- ---------------
Modern Science                                1
```

```
SELECT name
FROM product_types
WHERE product_type_id = 1;
```

```
NAME
----------
Book
```

Instead of using the two queries, you should write one query that uses a join between the products and product_types tables. The following good query shows this:

```
-- GOOD (one query with a join)
SELECT p.name, pt.name
FROM products p, product_types pt
WHERE p.product_type_id = pt.product_type_id
AND p.product_id = 1;
```

```
NAME                            NAME
------------------------------- ----------
Modern Science                  Book
```

This query results in the same product name and product type name being retrieved as in the first example, but the results are obtained using one query. One query is generally more efficient than two.

You should choose the join order in your query so that you join fewer rows to tables later in the join order. For example, say you were joining three related tables named tab1, tab2, and tab3. Assume tab1 contains 1,000 rows, tab2 100 rows, and tab3 10 rows. You should join tab1 with tab2 first, followed by tab2 and tab3.

Also, avoid joining complex views in your queries, because doing so causes the queries for the views to be run first, followed by your actual query. Instead, write your query using the tables rather than the views.

Use Fully Qualified Column References When Performing Joins

Always include table aliases in your queries and use the alias for each column in your query (this is known as "fully qualifying" your column references). That way, the database doesn't have to search for each column in the tables used in your query.

The following bad example uses the aliases p and pt for the products and product_types tables, respectively, but the query doesn't fully qualify the description and price columns:

```
-- BAD (description and price columns not fully qualified)
SELECT p.name, pt.name, description, price
FROM products p, product_types pt
WHERE p.product_type_id = pt.product_type_id
AND p.product_id = 1;
```

```
NAME                            NAME
------------------------------- ----------
DESCRIPTION                                                PRICE
---------------------------------------------------------- ----------
Modern Science                  Book
A description of modern science                            19.95
```

This example works, but the database has to search both the products and product_types tables for the description and price columns; that's because there's no alias that tells the database which table those columns are in. The extra time spent by the database having to do the search is wasted time.

The following good example includes the table alias p to fully qualify the description and price columns:

```
-- GOOD (all columns are fully qualified)
SELECT p.name, pt.name, p.description, p.price
FROM products p, product_types pt
WHERE p.product_type_id = pt.product_type_id
AND p.product_id = 1;
```

```
NAME                            NAME
------------------------------- ----------
DESCRIPTION                                                PRICE
---------------------------------------------------------- ----------
Modern Science                  Book
A description of modern science                            19.95
```

Because all references to columns include a table alias, the database doesn't have to waste time searching the tables for the columns.

Use CASE Expressions Rather than Multiple Queries

Use CASE expressions rather than multiple queries when you need to perform many calculations on the same rows in a table. The following bad example uses multiple queries to count the number of products within various price ranges:

```
-- BAD (three separate queries when one CASE statement would work)
SELECT COUNT(*)
FROM products
WHERE price < 13;

  COUNT(*)
----------
        2

SELECT COUNT(*)
FROM products
WHERE price BETWEEN 13 AND 15;

  COUNT(*)
----------
        5

SELECT COUNT(*)
FROM products
WHERE price > 15;

  COUNT(*)
----------
        5
```

Rather than using three queries, you should write one query that uses CASE expressions. This is shown in the following good example:

```
-- GOOD (one query with a CASE expression)
SELECT
  COUNT(CASE WHEN price < 13 THEN 1 ELSE null END) low,
  COUNT(CASE WHEN price BETWEEN 13 AND 15 THEN 1 ELSE null END) med,
  COUNT(CASE WHEN price > 15 THEN 1 ELSE null END) high
FROM products;

       LOW        MED       HIGH
---------- ---------- ----------
         2          5          5
```

Notice that the counts of the products with prices less than $13 are labeled as low, products between $13 and $15 are labeled med, and products greater than $15 are labeled high.

NOTE
You can, of course, use overlapping ranges and different functions in your CASE expressions.

Add Indexes to Tables

When looking for a particular topic in a book, you can either scan the whole book or use the index to find the location. An index for a database table is similar in concept to a book index, except that database indexes are used to find specific rows in a table. The downside of indexes is that when a row is added to the table, additional time is required to update the index for the new row.

Normally, a database administrator is responsible for creating indexes. However, as an application developer, you'll be able to provide the database administrator with feedback on which columns are good candidates for indexing, because you might know more about the application than the database administrator.

Chapter 11 described the following types of indexes:

- B-tree indexes
- Bitmap indexes

The following sections summarize the recommendations for when to use these types of indexes. Chapter 11 contains full details.

When to Create a B-Tree Index

Generally, you should create a b-tree index on a column when you are retrieving a small number of rows from a table containing many rows. The following simple rule shows when to create a b-tree index:

Create a b-tree index when a query retrieves <= 10 percent of the total rows in a table

This means the column for the b-tree index should contain a wide range of values. A good candidate for b-tree indexing would be a column containing a unique value for each row (for example, a Social Security number). A poor candidate for b-tree indexing would be a column that contains only a small range of values (for example, N, S, E, W or 1, 2, 3, 4, 5, 6). The Oracle database software automatically creates a b-tree index for the primary key of a table and for columns included in a unique constraint.

In addition, if your database is accessed using a lot of hierarchical queries (that is, a query containing a CONNECT BY), you should add b-tree indexes to the columns referenced in the START WITH and CONNECT BY clauses (see Chapter 7 for details on hierarchical queries).

When to Create a Bitmap Index

For a column that contains a small range of values and is frequently used in the WHERE clause of queries, you should consider adding a bitmap index to that column. Bitmap indexes are typically used in data warehouses, which are databases containing very large amounts of data. The data in a data warehouse is typically read using many queries, but the data is not modified by many concurrent transactions.

Use WHERE Rather than HAVING

You use the WHERE clause to filter rows; you use the HAVING clause to filter groups of rows. Because the HAVING clause filters groups of rows *after* they have been grouped together (which takes some time to do), you should first filter rows using a WHERE clause whenever possible. That way, you avoid the time taken to group the filtered rows together in the first place.

The following bad query retrieves the `product_type_id` and average price for products whose `product_type_id` is 1 or 2. To do this, the query performs the following:

- It uses the `GROUP BY` clause to group rows into blocks with the same `product_type_id`.
- It uses the `HAVING` clause to filter the returned results to those groups that have a `product_type_id` in 1 or 2 (this is bad, because a `WHERE` clause would work).

```
-- BAD (uses HAVING rather than WHERE)
SELECT product_type_id, AVG(price)
FROM products
GROUP BY product_type_id
HAVING product_type_id IN (1, 2);

PRODUCT_TYPE_ID AVG(PRICE)
--------------- ----------
              1     24.975
              2      26.22
```

The following good query rewrites the previous example to use `WHERE` rather than `HAVING` to first filter the rows to those whose `product_type_id` is 1 or 2:

```
-- GOOD (uses WHERE rather than HAVING)
SELECT product_type_id, AVG(price)
FROM products
WHERE product_type_id IN (1, 2)
GROUP BY product_type_id;

PRODUCT_TYPE_ID AVG(PRICE)
--------------- ----------
              1     24.975
              2      26.22
```

Use UNION ALL Rather than UNION

You use `UNION ALL` to get all the rows retrieved by two queries, including duplicate rows; you use `UNION` to get all non-duplicate rows retrieved by the queries. Because `UNION` removes duplicate rows (which takes some time to do), you should use `UNION ALL` whenever possible.

The following bad query uses `UNION` (bad because `UNION ALL` would work) to get the rows from the `products` and `more_products` tables. Notice that all non-duplicate rows from `products` and `more_products` are retrieved.

```
-- BAD (uses UNION rather than UNION ALL)
SELECT product_id, product_type_id, name
FROM products
UNION
SELECT prd_id, prd_type_id, name
FROM more_products;
```

```
PRODUCT_ID PRODUCT_TYPE_ID NAME
---------- --------------- -------------------
         1               1 Modern Science
         2               1 Chemistry
         3               2 Supernova
         3                 Supernova
         4               2 Lunar Landing
         4               2 Tank War
         5               2 Submarine
         5               2 Z Files
         6               2 2412: The Return
         7               3 Space Force 9
         8               3 From Another Planet
         9               4 Classical Music
        10               4 Pop 3
        11               4 Creative Yell
        12                 My Front Line
```

The following good query rewrites the previous example to use UNION ALL. Notice that all the rows from `products` and `more_products` are retrieved, including duplicates.

```
-- GOOD (uses UNION ALL rather than UNION)
SELECT product_id, product_type_id, name
FROM products
UNION ALL
SELECT prd_id, prd_type_id, name
FROM more_products;
```

```
PRODUCT_ID PRODUCT_TYPE_ID NAME
---------- --------------- -----------------------------
         1               1 Modern Science
         2               1 Chemistry
         3               2 Supernova
         4               2 Tank War
         5               2 Z Files
         6               2 2412: The Return
         7               3 Space Force 9
         8               3 From Another Planet
         9               4 Classical Music
        10               4 Pop 3
        11               4 Creative Yell
        12                 My Front Line
         1               1 Modern Science
         2               1 Chemistry
         3                 Supernova
         4               2 Lunar Landing
         5               2 Submarine
```

Use EXISTS Rather than IN

You use IN to check if a value is contained in a list. You use EXISTS to check for the existence of rows returned by a subquery. EXISTS is different from IN: EXISTS just checks for the existence of rows, whereas IN checks actual values. EXISTS typically offers better performance than IN with subqueries. Therefore, you should use EXISTS rather than IN whenever possible.

You should refer back to the section entitled "Using EXISTS and NOT EXISTS with a Correlated Subquery" in Chapter 6 for full details on when you should use EXISTS with a correlated subquery (an important point to remember is that correlated subqueries can resolve null values).

The following bad query uses IN (bad because EXISTS would work) to retrieve products that have been purchased:

```
-- BAD (uses IN rather than EXISTS)
SELECT product_id, name
FROM products
WHERE product_id IN
  (SELECT product_id
   FROM purchases);

PRODUCT_ID NAME
---------- ---------------------------
         1 Modern Science
         2 Chemistry
         3 Supernova
```

The following good query rewrites the previous example to use EXISTS:

```
-- GOOD (uses EXISTS rather than IN)
SELECT product_id, name
FROM products outer
WHERE EXISTS
  (SELECT 1
   FROM purchases inner
   WHERE inner.product_id = outer.product_id);

PRODUCT_ID NAME
---------- ---------------------------
         1 Modern Science
         2 Chemistry
         3 Supernova
```

Use EXISTS Rather than DISTINCT

You can suppress the display of duplicate rows using DISTINCT. You use EXISTS to check for the existence of rows returned by a subquery. Whenever possible, you should use EXISTS rather than DISTINCT, because DISTINCT sorts the retrieved rows before suppressing the duplicate rows.

The following bad query uses DISTINCT (bad because EXISTS would work) to retrieve products that have been purchased:

```
-- BAD (uses DISTINCT when EXISTS would work)
SELECT DISTINCT pr.product_id, pr.name
FROM products pr, purchases pu
```

```
WHERE pr.product_id = pu.product_id;

PRODUCT_ID NAME
---------- ----------------------------
         1 Modern Science
         2 Chemistry
         3 Supernova
```

The following good query rewrites the previous example to use `EXISTS` rather than `DISTINCT`:

```
-- GOOD (uses EXISTS rather than DISTINCT)
SELECT product_id, name
FROM products outer
WHERE EXISTS
  (SELECT 1
   FROM purchases inner
   WHERE inner.product_id = outer.product_id);

PRODUCT_ID NAME
---------- ----------------------------
         1 Modern Science
         2 Chemistry
         3 Supernova
```

Use GROUPING SETS Rather than CUBE

The `GROUPING SETS` clause typically offers better performance than `CUBE`. Therefore, you should use `GROUPING SETS` rather than `CUBE` wherever possible. This is fully covered in the section entitled "Using the GROUPING SETS Clause" in Chapter 7.

Use Bind Variables

The Oracle database software caches SQL statements; a cached SQL statement is reused if an identical statement is submitted to the database. When an SQL statement is reused, the execution time is reduced. However, the SQL statement must be *absolutely identical* in order for it to be reused. This means

- All characters in the SQL statement must be the same.
- All letters in the SQL statement must be in the same case.
- All spaces in the SQL statement must be the same.

If you need to supply different column values in a statement, you can use bind variables instead of literal column values. You'll see examples that clarify these ideas next.

Non-Identical SQL Statements

In this section, you'll see some non-identical SQL statements. The following non-identical queries retrieve products #1 and #2:

```
SELECT * FROM products WHERE product_id = 1;
SELECT * FROM products WHERE product_id = 2;
```

These queries are not identical because the value 1 is used in the first statement but the value 2 is used in the second.

The following non-identical queries have spaces in different positions:

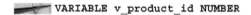

```
SELECT * FROM  products  WHERE  product_id = 1;
SELECT * FROM products WHERE product_id = 1;
```

The following non-identical queries use a different case for some of the characters:

```
select * from products where product_id = 1;
SELECT * FROM products WHERE product_id = 1;
```

Now that you've seen some non-identical statements, let's take a look at identical SQL statements that use bind variables.

Identical SQL Statements That Use Bind Variables

You can ensure that a statement is identical by using bind variables to represent column values. You create a bind variable using the SQL*Plus VARIABLE command. For example, the following command creates a variable named v_product_id of type NUMBER:

```
VARIABLE v_product_id NUMBER
```

NOTE
You can use the types shown in Table A-1 of the appendix to define the type of a bind variable.

You reference a bind variable in an SQL or PL/SQL statement using a colon followed by the variable name (such as :v_product_id). For example, the following PL/SQL block sets v_product_id to 1:

```
BEGIN
   :v_product_id := 1;
END;
/
```

The following query uses v_product_id to set the product_id column value in the WHERE clause. Because v_product_id was set to 1 in the previous PL/SQL block, the query retrieves the details of product #1.

```
SELECT * FROM products WHERE product_id = :v_product_id;

PRODUCT_ID PRODUCT_TYPE_ID NAME
---------- --------------- -----------------------------
DESCRIPTION                                           PRICE
--------------------------------------------------- ----------
         1               1 Modern Science
A description of modern science                       19.95
```

The next example sets `v_product_id` to 2 and repeats the query:

```
BEGIN
  :v_product_id := 2;
END;
/
SELECT * FROM products WHERE product_id = :v_product_id;

PRODUCT_ID PRODUCT_TYPE_ID NAME
---------- --------------- -----------------------------
DESCRIPTION                                              PRICE
-------------------------------------------------- ----------
        2               1 Chemistry
Introduction to Chemistry                                  30
```

Because the query used in this example is identical to the previous query, the cached query is reused and there's an improvement in performance.

TIP
You should typically use bind variables if you're performing the same query many times. Also, in the example, the bind variables are session specific and need to be reset if the session is lost.

Listing and Printing Bind Variables

You list bind variables in SQL*Plus using the `VARIABLE` command. For example:

```
VARIABLE
variable    v_product_id
datatype    NUMBER
```

You display the value of a bind variable in SQL*Plus using the `PRINT` command. For example:

```
PRINT v_product_id
V_PRODUCT_ID
-------------
           2
```

Using a Bind Variable to Store a Value Returned by a PL/SQL Function

You can also use a bind variable to store returned values from a PL/SQL function. The following example creates a bind variable named `v_average_product_price` and stores the result returned by the function `average_product_price()` (this function, described in Chapter 12, calculates the average product price for the supplied `product_type_id`):

```
VARIABLE v_average_product_price NUMBER
BEGIN
  :v_average_product_price := average_product_price(1);
END;
```

```
/
PRINT v_average_product_price

V_AVERAGE_PRODUCT_PRICE
-----------------------
                 24.975
```

Using a Bind Variable to Store Rows from a REFCURSOR

You can also use a bind variable to store returned values from a REFCURSOR (a pointer to a list of rows). The following example creates a bind variable named v_products_refcursor and stores the result returned by the function product_package.get_products_ref_cursor() (this function, introduced in Chapter 12, returns a pointer to the rows in the products table):

```
VARIABLE v_products_refcursor REFCURSOR
BEGIN
  :v_products_refcursor := product_package.get_products_ref_cursor();
END;
/
PRINT v_products_refcursor

PRODUCT_ID NAME                                   PRICE
---------- ------------------------------ ----------
         1 Modern Science                         19.95
         2 Chemistry                                 30
         3 Supernova                              25.99
         4 Tank War                               13.95
         5 Z Files                                49.99
         6 2412: The Return                       14.95
         7 Space Force 9                          13.49
         8 From Another Planet                    12.99
         9 Classical Music                        10.99
        10 Pop 3                                  15.99
        11 Creative Yell                          14.99
        12 My Front Line                          13.49
```

Comparing the Cost of Performing Queries

The Oracle database software uses a subsystem known as the *optimizer* to generate the most efficient path to access the data stored in the tables. The path generated by the optimizer is known as an *execution plan*. Oracle Database 10g and above automatically gathers statistics about the data in your tables and indexes in order to generate the best execution plan (this is known as *cost-based* optimization).

Comparing the execution plans generated by the optimizer allows you to judge the relative cost of one SQL statement versus another. You can use the results to improve your SQL statements. In this section, you'll learn how to view and interpret a couple of example execution plans.

NOTE
Database versions prior to Oracle Database 10g don't automatically gather statistics, and the optimizer automatically defaults to rule-based optimization. Rule-based optimization uses syntactic rules to generate the execution plan. Cost-based optimization is typically better than rule-based optimization because the former uses actual information gathered from the data in the tables and indexes. If you're using Oracle Database 9i or below, you can gather statistics yourself (you'll learn how to do that later in the section "Gathering Table Statistics").

Examining Execution Plans

The optimizer generates an execution plan for an SQL statement. You can examine the execution plan using the SQL*Plus EXPLAIN PLAN command. The EXPLAIN PLAN command populates a table named `plan_table` with the SQL statement's execution plan (`plan_table` is often referred to as the "plan table"). You can then examine that execution plan by querying the plan table. The first thing you must do is check if the plan table currently exists in the database.

Checking If the Plan Table Currently Exists in the Database

To check if the plan table currently exists in the database, you should connect to the database as the `store` user and run the following DESCRIBE command:

```
DESCRIBE plan_table
```

Name	Null?	Type
STATEMENT_ID		VARCHAR2(30)
PLAN_ID		NUMBER
TIMESTAMP		DATE
REMARKS		VARCHAR2(4000)
OPERATION		VARCHAR2(30)
OPTIONS		VARCHAR2(255)
OBJECT_NODE		VARCHAR2(128)
OBJECT_OWNER		VARCHAR2(128)
OBJECT_NAME		VARCHAR2(128)
OBJECT_ALIAS		VARCHAR2(261)
OBJECT_INSTANCE		NUMBER(38)
OBJECT_TYPE		VARCHAR2(30)
OPTIMIZER		VARCHAR2(255)
SEARCH_COLUMNS		NUMBER
ID		NUMBER(38)
PARENT_ID		NUMBER(38)
DEPTH		NUMBER(38)
POSITION		NUMBER(38)
COST		NUMBER(38)
CARDINALITY		NUMBER(38)
BYTES		NUMBER(38)
OTHER_TAG		VARCHAR2(255)
PARTITION_START		VARCHAR2(255)
PARTITION_STOP		VARCHAR2(255)

PARTITION_ID	NUMBER(38)
OTHER	LONG
OTHER_XML	CLOB
DISTRIBUTION	VARCHAR2(30)
CPU_COST	NUMBER(38)
IO_COST	NUMBER(38)
TEMP_SPACE	NUMBER(38)
ACCESS_PREDICATES	VARCHAR2(4000)
FILTER_PREDICATES	VARCHAR2(4000)
PROJECTION	VARCHAR2(4000)
TIME	NUMBER(38)
QBLOCK_NAME	VARCHAR2(30)

If you get a table description similar to these results, you have the plan table already. If you get an error, then you need to create the plan table.

Creating the Plan Table

If you don't have the plan table, you or your database administrator must create it. To do this, you run the SQL*Plus script `utlxplan.sql`, which is located in the `RDBMS\ADMIN` directory. On a Windows computer, the script might be located in the directory `C:\oracle12c\product\12.1.0\dbhome_1\RDBMS\ADMIN`. On a Linux computer, the script might be located in the directory `/u01/app/oracle12c/product/12.1.0/dbhome_1/rdbms/admin`.

The following example shows the SQL*Plus command to run the `utlxplan.sql` script:

```
@ C:\oracle12c\product\12.1.0\dbhome_1\RDBMS\ADMIN\utlxplan.sql
```

NOTE
You'll need to replace the directory path with the path for your environment.

The most important columns in the plan table are shown in Table 16-1.

Creating a Central Plan Table

A database administrator can create one central plan table. That way, individual users don't have to create their own plan tables. To do this, a database administrator performs the following steps:

1. Creates the plan table in a schema of their choice by running the `utlxplan.sql` script.
2. Creates a public synonym for the plan table.
3. Grants access on the plan table to the public role.

Here is an example of these steps:

```
@ C:\oracle12c\product\12.1.0\dbhome_1\RDBMS\ADMIN\utlxplan.sql
CREATE PUBLIC SYNONYM plan_table FOR plan_table;
GRANT SELECT, INSERT, UPDATE, DELETE ON plan_table TO PUBLIC;
```

Column	Description
statement_id	Name you assign to the execution plan.
operation	Database operation performed, which can be one of the following: ■ Scanning a table ■ Scanning an index ■ Accessing rows from a table by using an index ■ Joining two tables together ■ Sorting a row set For example, the operation for accessing a table is TABLE ACCESS.
options	Name of the option used in the operation. For example, the option for a complete scan is FULL.
object_name	Name of the database object referenced in the operation.
object_type	Attribute of object. For example, a unique index has the attribute of UNIQUE.
id	Number assigned to this operation in the execution plan.
parent_id	Parent number for the current step in the execution plan. The parent_id value relates to an id value from a parent step.
position	Processing order for steps that have the same parent_id.
cost	Estimate of units of work for the operation. Cost-based optimization uses disk I/O, CPU usage, and memory usage as units of work. Therefore, the cost is an estimate of the number of disk I/Os and the amount of CPU and memory used in performing an operation.

TABLE 16-1. *Plan Table Columns*

Generating an Execution Plan

Once you have a plan table, you can use the EXPLAIN PLAN command to generate an execution plan for an SQL statement. The syntax for the EXPLAIN PLAN command is as follows:

```
EXPLAIN PLAN SET STATEMENT_ID = statement_id FOR sql_statement;
```

where

- *statement_id* is the name you want to call the execution plan. This can be any alphanumeric text.
- *sql_statement* is the SQL statement you want to generate an execution plan for.

The following example generates the execution plan for a query that retrieves all rows from the customers table (notice that the statement_id is set to 'CUSTOMERS'):

```
EXPLAIN PLAN SET STATEMENT_ID = 'CUSTOMERS' FOR
SELECT customer_id, first_name, last_name FROM customers;
Explained
```

After the command completes, you can examine the execution plan stored in the plan table. You'll see how to do that next.

NOTE
The query in the EXPLAIN PLAN *statement doesn't return rows from the* customers *table. The* EXPLAIN PLAN *statement simply generates the execution plan that would be used if the query was run.*

Querying the Plan Table

For querying the plan table, I have provided an SQL*Plus script named explain_plan.sql in the SQL directory. The script prompts you for the statement_id and then displays the execution plan for that statement.

The explain_plan.sql script is as follows:

```
-- Displays the execution plan for the specified statement_id

UNDEFINE v_statement_id;

SELECT
  id ||
  DECODE(id, 0, '', LPAD(' ', 2*(level - 1))) || ' ' ||
  operation || ' ' ||
  options || ' ' ||
  object_name || ' ' ||
  object_type || ' ' ||
  DECODE(cost, NULL, '', 'Cost = ' || position)
AS execution_plan
FROM plan_table
CONNECT BY PRIOR id = parent_id
AND statement_id = '&&v_statement_id'
START WITH id = 0
AND statement_id = '&v_statement_id';
```

An execution plan is organized into a hierarchy of database operations similar to a tree; the details of these operations are stored in the plan table. The operation with an id of 0 is the root of the hierarchy, and all the other operations in the plan stem from this root. The query in the script retrieves the details of the operations, starting with the root operation and then navigating the tree from the root.

The following example shows how to run the explain_plan.sql script in SQL*Plus to retrieve the 'CUSTOMERS' plan created earlier:

```
@ C:\sql_book\sql\explain_plan.sql
Enter value for v_statement_id: CUSTOMERS
old  12:    statement_id = '&&v_statement_id'
new  12:    statement_id = 'CUSTOMERS'
old  14:    statement_id = '&v_statement_id'
new  14:    statement_id = 'CUSTOMERS'
```

```
EXECUTION_PLAN
---------------------------------------------
0 SELECT STATEMENT      Cost = 3
1    TABLE ACCESS FULL CUSTOMERS TABLE Cost = 1
```

The operations shown in the EXECUTION_PLAN column are executed in the following order:

- The rightmost indented operation is executed first, followed by any parent operations above it.

- For operations with the same indentation, the topmost operation is executed first, followed by any parent operations above it.

Each operation feeds its results back up the chain to its immediate parent operation, and the parent operation is then executed. In the EXECUTION_PLAN column, the operation ID is shown on the far left. In the example execution plan, operation 1 is run first, with the results of that operation being passed to operation 0.

The following example illustrates the ordering for a more complex example:

```
0 SELECT STATEMENT      Cost = 6
1    MERGE JOIN     Cost = 1
2       TABLE ACCESS BY INDEX ROWID PRODUCT_TYPES TABLE Cost = 1
3          INDEX FULL SCAN PRODUCT_TYPES_PK INDEX (UNIQUE) Cost = 1
4       SORT JOIN     Cost = 2
5          TABLE ACCESS FULL PRODUCTS TABLE Cost = 1
```

The order in which the operations are executed in this example is 3, 2, 5, 4, 1, and 0.

Now that you've seen the order in which operations are executed, it's time to move onto what the operations actually do. The execution plan for the 'CUSTOMERS' query was

```
0 SELECT STATEMENT      Cost = 3
1    TABLE ACCESS FULL CUSTOMERS TABLE Cost = 1
```

Operation 1 is run first, with the results of that operation being passed to operation 0. Operation 1 involves a full table scan—indicated by the string TABLE ACCESS FULL—on the customers table. Here's the original command used to generate the 'CUSTOMERS' query:

```
EXPLAIN PLAN SET STATEMENT_ID = 'CUSTOMERS' FOR
SELECT customer_id, first_name, last_name FROM customers;
```

A full table scan is performed because the SELECT statement specifies that all the rows from the customers table are to be retrieved.

The total cost of the query is three work units, as indicated in the cost part shown to the right of operation 0 in the execution plan (0 SELECT STATEMENT Cost = 3). A work unit is the amount of processing the software has to do to perform a given operation. The higher the cost, the more work the database software has to do to complete the SQL statement.

NOTE
If you're using a version of the database prior to Oracle Database 10g, then the output for the overall statement cost can be blank. That's because earlier database versions don't automatically collect table statistics. In order to gather statistics, you have to use the ANALYZE command. You'll learn how to do that later in the section "Gathering Table Statistics."

Generating Execution Plans Involving Table Joins

Execution plans for queries with table joins are more complex. The following example generates the execution plan for a query that joins the products and product_types tables:

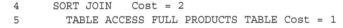
```
EXPLAIN PLAN SET STATEMENT_ID = 'PRODUCTS' FOR
SELECT p.name, pt.name
FROM products p, product_types pt
WHERE p.product_type_id = pt.product_type_id;
```

The execution plan for this query is shown in the following example:

```
@ C:\sql_book\sql\explain_plan.sql
Enter value for v_statement_id: PRODUCTS

EXECUTION_PLAN
-------------------------------------------------------------
0 SELECT STATEMENT     Cost = 6
1   MERGE JOIN     Cost = 1
2     TABLE ACCESS BY INDEX ROWID PRODUCT_TYPES TABLE Cost = 1
3       INDEX FULL SCAN PRODUCT_TYPES_PK INDEX (UNIQUE) Cost = 1
4     SORT JOIN     Cost = 2
5       TABLE ACCESS FULL PRODUCTS TABLE Cost = 1
```

NOTE
If you run the examples in this chapter, you might get slightly different execution plans depending on the version of the database you are using and on the settings of the parameters in the database's init.ora configuration file.

The previous execution plan is more complex, and you can see the hierarchical relationships between the various operations. The execution order of the operations is 3, 2, 5, 4, 1, and 0. Table 16-2 describes each operation in the order they are performed.

Gathering Table Statistics

If you're using a version of the database prior to Oracle Database 10g, then you'll have to gather table statistics yourself using the ANALYZE command. By default, if no statistics are available, then rule-based optimization is used. Rule-based optimization isn't usually as good as cost-based optimization.

Operation ID	Description
3	Full scan of the index `product_types_pk` (which is a unique index) to obtain the addresses of the rows in the `product_types` table. The addresses are in the form of `ROWID` values, which are passed to operation 2.
2	Access the rows in the `product_types` table using the list of `ROWID` values passed from operation 3. The rows are passed to operation 1.
5	Access the rows in the `products` table. The rows are passed to operation 4.
4	Sort the rows passed from operation 5. The sorted rows are passed to operation 1.
1	Merge the rows passed from operations 2 and 5. The merged rows are passed to operation 0.
0	Return the rows from operation 1 to the user. The total cost of the query is 6 work units.

TABLE 16-2.   *Execution Plan Operations*

The following examples use the `ANALYZE` command to gather statistics for the `products` and `product_types` tables:

```
ANALYZE TABLE products COMPUTE STATISTICS;
ANALYZE TABLE product_types COMPUTE STATISTICS;
```

Once the statistics have been gathered, cost-based optimization will be used rather than rule-based optimization.

Comparing Execution Plans

By comparing the total cost shown in the execution plan for different SQL statements, you can determine the value of tuning your SQL. In this section, you'll see how to compare two execution plans and see the benefit of using `EXISTS` rather than `DISTINCT` (a tip I gave earlier). The following example generates an execution plan for a query that uses `EXISTS`:

```
EXPLAIN PLAN SET STATEMENT_ID = 'EXISTS_QUERY' FOR
SELECT product_id, name
FROM products outer
WHERE EXISTS
  (SELECT 1
   FROM purchases inner
   WHERE inner.product_id = outer.product_id);
```

The execution plan for this query is shown in the following example; notice the cost is 5 work units:

```
@ C:\sql_book\sql\explain_plan.sql
Enter value for v_statement_id: EXISTS_QUERY
```

```
EXECUTION_PLAN
-------------------------------------------------------------
0 SELECT STATEMENT Cost = 5
1   MERGE JOIN SEMI Cost = 1
2     TABLE ACCESS BY INDEX ROWID PRODUCTS TABLE Cost = 1
3       INDEX FULL SCAN PRODUCTS_PK INDEX (UNIQUE) Cost = 1
4     SORT UNIQUE Cost = 2
5       INDEX FAST FULL SCAN PURCHASES_PK INDEX (UNIQUE) Cost = 1
```

The next example generates an execution plan for a query that uses DISTINCT:

```
EXPLAIN PLAN SET STATEMENT_ID = 'DISTINCT_QUERY' FOR
SELECT DISTINCT pr.product_id, pr.name
FROM products pr, purchases pu
WHERE pr.product_id = pu.product_id;
```

The execution plan for this query is shown in the following example; notice the cost is 6 work units:

```
@ C:\sql_book\sql\explain_plan.sql
Enter value for v_statement_id: DISTINCT_QUERY


EXECUTION_PLAN
-------------------------------------------------------------
0 SELECT STATEMENT Cost = 6
1   HASH UNIQUE Cost = 1
2     MERGE JOIN SEMI Cost = 1
3       TABLE ACCESS BY INDEX ROWID PRODUCTS TABLE Cost = 1
4         INDEX FULL SCAN PRODUCTS_PK INDEX (UNIQUE) Cost = 1
5       SORT UNIQUE    Cost = 2
6         INDEX FAST FULL SCAN PURCHASES_PK INDEX (UNIQUE) Cost = 1
```

This query is more costly than the earlier query that used EXISTS, which had a slightly lower total cost of 5. These results show that it is better to use EXISTS than DISTINCT.

Passing Hints to the Optimizer

You can pass hints to the optimizer. A hint is an optimizer directive that influences the optimizer's choice of execution plan. The correct hint can improve the performance of an SQL statement. You can check the effectiveness of a hint by comparing the cost in the execution plan of an SQL statement with and without the hint.

In this section, you'll see an example query that uses one of the more useful hints: the FIRST_ROWS(n) hint. The FIRST_ROWS(n) hint tells the optimizer to generate an execution plan that will minimize the time taken to return the first n rows in a query. This hint can be useful when you don't want to wait around too long before getting *some* rows back from your query, but you still want to see all the rows.

The following example generates an execution plan for a query that uses FIRST_ROWS(2). Notice that the hint is placed within the strings /*+ and */.

```
EXPLAIN PLAN SET STATEMENT_ID = 'HINT' FOR
SELECT /*+ FIRST_ROWS(2) */ p.name, pt.name
```

```
FROM products p, product_types pt
WHERE p.product_type_id = pt.product_type_id;
```

CAUTION
Your hint must use the exact syntax shown—otherwise, the hint will be ignored. The syntax is: /+ followed by one space, the hint, followed by one space, and */.*

The execution plan for this query is shown in the following example; notice that the cost is 4 work units:

```
@ C:\sql_book\sql\explain_plan.sql
Enter value for v_statement_id: HINT


EXECUTION_PLAN
-----------------------------------------------------------------
0 SELECT STATEMENT     Cost = 4
1    NESTED LOOPS
2       NESTED LOOPS     Cost = 1
3          TABLE ACCESS FULL PRODUCTS TABLE Cost = 1
4          INDEX UNIQUE SCAN PRODUCT_TYPES_PK INDEX (UNIQUE) Cost = 2
5       TABLE ACCESS BY INDEX ROWID PRODUCT_TYPES TABLE Cost = 2
```

The next example generates an execution plan for the same query without the hint:

```
EXPLAIN PLAN SET STATEMENT_ID = 'NO_HINT' FOR
SELECT p.name, pt.name
FROM products p, product_types pt
WHERE p.product_type_id = pt.product_type_id;
```

The execution plan for the query is shown in the following example; notice the cost is 6 work units (higher than the query with the hint):

```
@ C:\sql_book\sql\explain_plan.sql
Enter value for v_statement_id: NO_HINT


EXECUTION_PLAN
-----------------------------------------------------------------
0 SELECT STATEMENT     Cost = 6
1    MERGE JOIN     Cost = 1
2       TABLE ACCESS BY INDEX ROWID PRODUCT_TYPES TABLE Cost = 1
3          INDEX FULL SCAN PRODUCT_TYPES_PK INDEX (UNIQUE) Cost = 1
4       SORT JOIN     Cost = 2
5          TABLE ACCESS FULL PRODUCTS TABLE Cost = 1
```

These results show that the inclusion of the hint reduces the cost of running the query by 2 work units.

There are many hints, and this section has merely given you a taste of the subject. You should use hints very sparingly because Oracle Corporation provides a number of excellent performance tuning tools that are easier to use than hints, and are typically more effective. You'll be introduced to these tools in the following section.

Additional Tuning Tools

In this final section, I'll mention some other tuning tools. Full coverage of these tools, and detailed database tuning, is a very large subject and well beyond the scope of this humble book. For full coverage, you can read the *Oracle Database Performance Tuning Guide* and the *Oracle Database SQL Tuning Guide*, both published by Oracle Corporation.

Oracle Enterprise Manager

Oracle Enterprise Manager contains a number of performance analysis components, which capture operating system, middle tier, and application performance data, as well as database performance data. Oracle Enterprise Manager analyzes this performance data and displays the results graphically. A database administrator can also configure Oracle Enterprise Manager to alert them immediately of performance problems via e-mail or page. Oracle Enterprise Manager also includes software guides to help resolve performance problems.

Automatic Database Diagnostic Monitor

The Automatic Database Diagnostic Monitor (ADDM) is a self-diagnostic module built into the Oracle database software. ADDM enables a database administrator to monitor the database for performance problems by analyzing system performance over a long period of time. The database administrator can view the performance information generated by ADDM in Oracle Enterprise Manager. When ADDM finds performance problems, it will suggest solutions for corrective action. Some example ADDM suggestions include

- Hardware changes—for example, adding CPUs to the database server
- Database configuration—for example, changing the database initialization parameter settings
- Application changes—for example, using the cache option for sequences or using bind variables
- Use other advisors—for example, running the SQL Tuning Advisor and SQL Access Advisor on SQL statements that are consuming the most database resources to execute

SQL Tuning Advisor

SQL Tuning Advisor allows a developer or database administrator to tune an SQL statement using the following items:

- The text of the SQL statement
- The SQL identifier of the statement (obtained from the V$SQL_PLAN view, which is one of the views available to a database administrator)
- The range of snapshot identifiers
- The SQL Tuning Set name

An SQL Tuning Set is a set of SQL statements with their associated execution plan and execution statistics. SQL Tuning Sets are analyzed to generate SQL Profiles that help the optimizer to choose the optimal execution plan. SQL Profiles contain collections of information that enable optimization of the execution plan.

SQL Access Advisor

SQL Access Advisor provides you with performance advice on materialized views, indexes, and materialized view logs. SQL Access Advisor examines space usage and query performance and recommends the most cost-effective configuration of new and existing materialized views and indexes.

SQL Performance Analyzer

SQL Performance Analyzer enables you to examine the effect of system changes on SQL performance by identifying SQL statements whose performance has regressed, improved, or remained unchanged.

Database Replay

Database Replay enables you to capture the database workload on a production system. Later, you can replay that identical workload on a test system with the same timing and concurrency as the production system for comparison. You can replay the workload on the same release or a newer release of the Oracle database software.

Real-Time SQL Monitoring

Real-Time SQL Monitoring enables you to monitor the performance of SQL statements while they are executing. By default, SQL monitoring automatically starts when an SQL statement runs parallel, or when it has consumed at least 5 seconds of CPU time or input/output time in a single execution.

SQL Plan Management

SQL Plan Management records and evaluates SQL execution plans over time. The database creates a set of baseline SQL execution plans. If the same SQL statement runs repeatedly, and if the optimizer generates a new plan that differs from the baseline, then the database compares the new plan with the baseline plan and uses the most efficient one.

Summary

In this chapter, you have learned the following:

- Tuning is the process of making your SQL statements run faster.
- The optimizer is a subsystem of the Oracle database software that generates an execution plan, which is a set of operations used to perform a particular SQL statement.
- Hints can be passed to the optimizer to influence the generated execution plan for an SQL statement.
- There are a number of additional tuning tools.

In the next chapter, you'll learn about XML in the database.

CHAPTER
17

XML and the
Oracle Database

This chapter provides a brief introduction to XML, and then shows you how to perform the following tasks:

- Generate XML from relational data
- Save XML in the database

Introducing XML

The Extensible Markup Language (XML) is a general-purpose markup language. XML enables you to share structured data across the Internet, and can be used to encode data and other documents. Some advantages of XML include the following:

- XML can be read by humans and computers, and is stored as plain text.
- XML is platform independent.
- XML supports Unicode, which means it can store information written in many human languages.
- XML uses a self-documenting format that contains the document structure, element names, and element values.

Because of these advantages, XML is widely used for document storage and processing, and it is used by many organizations to send data between their computer systems. For example, many suppliers allow their customers to send purchase orders as XML files over the Internet.

The following list shows a brief history of XML in the Oracle database:

- Oracle Database 9*i* introduced the ability to store XML in the database, along with extensive functionality for manipulating and processing XML.
- Oracle Database 10*g* Release 2 added more XML-generating functions.
- Oracle Database 11*g* added capabilities like Java and C processing of binary XML. Binary XML provides more efficient storage and manipulation of XML in the database.
- Oracle Database 12*c* further expands the XML functionality to include additional PL/SQL packages for XML support, XQuery API for Java (XQJ) support, and other features. Also, in Oracle Database 12*c*, the Oracle XML DB feature cannot be uninstalled.

This chapter focuses on a useful subset of the XML capabilities in the Oracle database. If you are new to XML, you will find a wealth of information at the following websites:

- www.w3.org/XML
- www.wikipedia.org/wiki/XML

Generating XML from Relational Data

The Oracle database contains a number of SQL functions you can use for generating XML, and in this section you'll see how to generate XML from relational data using some of these functions.

XMLELEMENT()

The XMLELEMENT() function generates XML elements from relational data. You supply a name for the element, plus the column you wish to retrieve to XMLELEMENT(), and it returns the elements as XMLType objects. XMLType is a built-in Oracle database type that is used to represent XML data.

The following example connects as the store user and gets the customer_id column values as XMLType objects:

```
CONNECT store/store_password
SELECT XMLELEMENT("customer_id", customer_id)
AS xml_customers
FROM customers;

XML_CUSTOMERS
----------------------------
<customer_id>1</customer_id>
<customer_id>2</customer_id>
<customer_id>3</customer_id>
<customer_id>4</customer_id>
<customer_id>5</customer_id>
```

As you can see from these results, XMLELEMENT("customer_id", customer_id) returns the customer_id values within a customer_id tag. You can use whatever tag name you want, as shown in the following example, which uses the tag "cust_id":

```
SELECT XMLELEMENT("cust_id", customer_id)
AS xml_customers
FROM customers;

XML_CUSTOMERS
--------------------
<cust_id>1</cust_id>
<cust_id>2</cust_id>
<cust_id>3</cust_id>
<cust_id>4</cust_id>
<cust_id>5</cust_id>
```

The next example gets the first_name and dob values for customer #2:

```
SELECT XMLELEMENT("first_name", first_name) || XMLELEMENT("dob", dob)
AS xml_customer
FROM customers
WHERE customer_id = 2;

XML_CUSTOMER
-------------------------------------------------------
<first_name>Cynthia</first_name><dob>1968-02-05</dob>
```

The following example uses the TO_CHAR() function to change the date format for the dob value:

```
SELECT XMLELEMENT("dob", TO_CHAR(dob, 'MM/DD/YYYY'))
AS xml_dob
FROM customers
WHERE customer_id = 2;

XML_DOB
--------------------
<dob>02/05/1968</dob>
```

The next example embeds two calls to XMLELEMENT() within an outer call to XMLELEMENT(). Notice that the returned customer_id and name elements are contained within an outer customer element.

```
SELECT XMLELEMENT(
    "customer",
    XMLELEMENT("customer_id", customer_id),
    XMLELEMENT("name", first_name || ' ' || last_name)
)
AS xml_customers
FROM customers
WHERE customer_id IN (1, 2);

XML_CUSTOMERS
------------------------------
<customer>
  <customer_id>1</customer_id>
  <name>John Brown</name>
</customer>

<customer>
  <customer_id>2</customer_id>
  <name>Cynthia Green</name>
</customer>
```

NOTE
I've added some line breaks and spaces in the XML returned by this query to make the XML easier to read. I've done the same thing in some of the other examples in this chapter. When you perform the queries, you'll typically see the XML on one line without any breaks.

You can retrieve regular relational data as well as XML, as shown in the following example, which retrieves the customer_id column as a regular relational result and the first_name and last_name columns concatenated together as XML elements:

```
SELECT customer_id,
    XMLELEMENT("customer", first_name || ' ' || last_name) AS xml_customer
FROM customers;
```

```
CUSTOMER_ID XML_CUSTOMER
----------- ------------------------------------
          1 <customer>John Brown</customer>
          2 <customer>Cynthia Green</customer>
          3 <customer>Steve White</customer>
          4 <customer>Gail Black</customer>
          5 <customer>Doreen Blue</customer>
```

You can generate XML for database objects, as shown in the next example, which connects as object_user and gets the id and address columns for customer #1 in the object_customers table (the address column stores an object of type t_address):

```
CONNECT object_user/object_password
SELECT XMLELEMENT("id", id) || XMLELEMENT("address", address)
AS xml_object_customer
FROM object_customers
WHERE id = 1;

XML_OBJECT_CUSTOMER
------------------------------------
<id>1</id>
<address>
  <T_ADDRESS>
    <STREET>2 State Street</STREET>
    <CITY>Beantown</CITY>
    <STATE>MA</STATE>
    <ZIP>12345</ZIP>
  </T_ADDRESS>
</address>
```

You can generate XML for collections, as shown in the next example, which connects as collection_user and gets the id and addresses columns for customer #1 stored in customers_with_nested_table (the addresses column stores an object of type t_nested_table_address, which is a nested table of t_address objects):

```
CONNECT collection_user/collection_password
SELECT XMLELEMENT("id", id) || XMLELEMENT("addresses", addresses)
AS xml_customer
FROM customers_with_nested_table
WHERE id = 1;

XML_CUSTOMER
----------------------------------------------------------
<id>1</id>
<addresses>
  <T_NESTED_TABLE_ADDRESS>
    <T_ADDRESS>
      <STREET>2 State Street</STREET><CITY>Beantown</CITY>
      <STATE>MA</STATE><ZIP>12345</ZIP>
    </T_ADDRESS>
    <T_ADDRESS>
```

```
        <STREET>4 Hill Street</STREET>
        <CITY>Lost Town</CITY>
        <STATE>CA</STATE>
        <ZIP>54321</ZIP>
      </T_ADDRESS>
    </T_NESTED_TABLE_ADDRESS>
</addresses>
```

XMLATTRIBUTES()

XMLATTRIBUTES() is used in conjunction with XMLELEMENT() to specify the attributes for the XML elements retrieved by XMLELEMENT(). The following example connects as the store user and uses XMLATTRIBUTES() to set attribute names for the customer_id, first_name, last_name, and dob elements:

```
CONNECT store/store_password
SELECT XMLELEMENT(
  "customer",
  XMLATTRIBUTES(
    customer_id AS "id",
    first_name || ' ' || last_name AS "name",
    TO_CHAR(dob, 'MM/DD/YYYY') AS "dob"
  )
)
AS xml_customers
FROM customers
WHERE customer_id IN (1, 2);


XML_CUSTOMERS
-----------------------------------------------------------------
<customer id="1" name="John Brown" dob="01/01/1965"></customer>
<customer id="2" name="Cynthia Green" dob="02/05/1968"></customer>
```

Notice that the id, name, and dob attributes are returned inside customer.

XMLFOREST()

XMLFOREST() generates a "forest" of XML elements. XMLFOREST() concatenates XML elements together without you having to use the concatenation operator || with multiple calls to XMLELEMENT(). The following example uses XMLFOREST() to get the customer_id, phone, and dob for customers #1 and #2:

```
SELECT XMLELEMENT(
  "customer",
  XMLFOREST(
    customer_id AS "id",
    phone AS "phone",
    TO_CHAR(dob, 'MM/DD/YYYY') AS "dob"
  )
)
AS xml_customers
FROM customers
WHERE customer_id IN (1, 2);
```

```
XML_CUSTOMERS
----------------------------
<customer>
  <id>1</id>
  <phone>800-555-1211</phone>
  <dob>01/01/1965</dob>
</customer>

<customer>
  <id>2</id>
  <phone>800-555-1212</phone>
  <dob>02/05/1968</dob>
</customer>
```

The following command sets the SQL*Plus LONG parameter to 500, so you can see all the XML returned by subsequent queries (LONG controls the maximum length of text data displayed by SQL*Plus):

```
SET LONG 500
```

The following query places the customer name inside the customer element tag using XMLATTRIBUTES():

```
SELECT XMLELEMENT(
  "customer",
  XMLATTRIBUTES(first_name || ' ' || last_name AS "name"),
  XMLFOREST(phone AS "phone", TO_CHAR(dob, 'MM/DD/YYYY') AS "dob")
)
AS xml_customers
FROM customers
WHERE customer_id IN (1, 2);
```

```
XML_CUSTOMERS
------------------------------
<customer name="John Brown">
  <phone>800-555-1211</phone>
  <dob>01/01/1965</dob>
</customer>

<customer name="Cynthia Green">
  <phone>800-555-1212</phone>
  <dob>02/05/1968</dob>
</customer>
```

XMLAGG()

XMLAGG() generates a forest of XML elements from a collection of XML elements. XMLAGG() is typically used for grouping XML together into a common list of items underneath one parent or for retrieving data from collections. You use the GROUP BY clause of a query to group the retuned set of rows into multiple groups, and you can use an ORDER BY clause of XMLAGG() to sort the rows.

By default, ORDER BY sorts the results in ascending order, but you can add DESC after the list of columns to sort the rows in descending order. You can add ASC to explicitly indicate an ascending sort. You can also add NULLS LAST to put any null values at the end of the results.

The following example retrieves the customer first_name and last_name values and returns them in a list named customer_list. Notice that ORDER BY is used with XMLAGG() to sort the results by the first_name column. I've added ASC to explicitly indicate an ascending sort.

```sql
SELECT XMLELEMENT(
  "customer_list",
  XMLAGG(
    XMLELEMENT("customer", first_name || ' ' || last_name)
    ORDER BY first_name ASC
  )
)
AS xml_customers
FROM customers
WHERE customer_id IN (1, 2);

XML_CUSTOMERS
------------------------------------
<customer_list>
  <customer>Cynthia Green</customer>
  <customer>John Brown</customer>
</customer_list>
```

The next example retrieves the product_type_id and average price for each group of products. Notice that the products are grouped by product_type_id using the GROUP BY clause of the query, and NULLS LAST is used in the ORDER BY clause of XMLAGG() to place the row with the null product_type_id at the end of the returned results.

```sql
SELECT XMLELEMENT(
  "product_list",
  XMLAGG(
    XMLELEMENT(
      "product_type_and_avg", product_type_id || ' ' || AVG(price)
    )
    ORDER BY product_type_id NULLS LAST
  )
)
AS xml_products
FROM products
GROUP BY product_type_id;

XML_PRODUCTS
-------------------------------------------------------
<product_list>
  <product_type_and_avg>1 24.975</product_type_and_avg>
  <product_type_and_avg>2 26.22</product_type_and_avg>
  <product_type_and_avg>3 13.24</product_type_and_avg>
  <product_type_and_avg>4 13.99</product_type_and_avg>
  <product_type_and_avg> 13.49</product_type_and_avg>
</product_list>
```

NOTE
You can also place the null row first by specifying NULLS FIRST *in the* ORDER BY *clause of* XMLAGG().

The next example retrieves the product_type_id and name for the products with product_type_id values of 1 and 2, and the products are grouped by product_type_id:

```
SELECT XMLELEMENT(
  "products_in_group",
  XMLATTRIBUTES(product_type_id AS "prd_type_id"),
  XMLAGG(
    XMLELEMENT("name", name)
  )
)
AS xml_products
FROM products
WHERE product_type_id IN (1, 2)
GROUP BY product_type_id;

XML_PRODUCTS
------------------------------------
<products_in_group prd_type_id="1">
  <name>Modern Science</name>
  <name>Chemistry</name>
</products_in_group>

<products_in_group prd_type_id="2">
  <name>Supernova</name>
  <name>2412: The Return</name>
</products_in_group>
```

The next example connects as collection_user and retrieves the addresses for customer #1 from customers_with_nested_table:

```
CONNECT collection_user/collection_password
SELECT XMLELEMENT("customer",
  XMLAGG(
    XMLELEMENT("addresses", addresses)
  )
)
AS xml_customer
FROM customers_with_nested_table
WHERE id = 1;

XML_CUSTOMER
---------------------------------------
<customer>
  <addresses>
    <T_NESTED_TABLE_ADDRESS>
      <T_ADDRESS>
```

```
      <STREET>2 State Street</STREET>
      <CITY>Beantown</CITY>
      <STATE>MA</STATE>
      <ZIP>21345</ZIP>
    </T_ADDRESS>
    <T_ADDRESS>
      <STREET>4 Hill Street</STREET>
      <CITY>Lost Town</CITY>
      <STATE>CA</STATE>
      <ZIP>54321</ZIP>
    </T_ADDRESS>
  </T_NESTED_TABLE_ADDRESS>
 </addresses>
</customer>
```

XMLCOLATTVAL()

XMLCOLATTVAL() creates an XML fragment and then expands the resulting XML. Each XML fragment has the name of the column along with the attribute name. You can use the AS clause to change the attribute name.

The following example connects as the store user and retrieves the customer_id, dob, and phone values for customers #1 and #2:

```
CONNECT store/store_password
SELECT XMLELEMENT(
  "customer",
  XMLCOLATTVAL(
    customer_id AS "id",
    dob AS "dob",
    phone AS "phone"
  )
)
AS xml_customers
FROM customers
WHERE customer_id IN (1, 2);

XML_CUSTOMERS
-----------------------------------------------
<customer>
  <column name = "id">1</column>
  <column name = "dob">1965-01-01</column>
  <column name = "phone">800-555-1211</column>
</customer>

<customer>
  <column name = "id">2</column>
  <column name = "dob">1968-02-05</column>
  <column name = "phone">800-555-1212</column>
</customer>
```

XMLCONCAT()

XMLCONCAT() concatenates a series of elements for each row. The following example concatenates the XML elements for first_name, last_name, and phone values for customers #1 and #2:

```
SELECT XMLCONCAT(
  XMLELEMENT("first name", first_name),
  XMLELEMENT("last name", last_name),
  XMLELEMENT("phone", phone)
)
AS xml_customers
FROM customers
WHERE customer_id IN (1, 2);

XML_CUSTOMERS
-------------------------------
<first name>John</first name>
<last name>Brown</last name>
<phone>800-555-1211</phone>

<first name>Cynthia</first name>
<last name>Green</last name>
<phone>800-555-1212</phone>
```

XMLPARSE()

XMLPARSE() parses and generates XML from the evaluated result of an expression. The expression must resolve to a string. If the expression resolves to null, then XMLPARSE() returns null. You must specify one of the following items before the expression:

- CONTENT, which means the expression must resolve to a valid XML value
- DOCUMENT, which means the expression must resolve to a singly rooted XML document

You can also add WELLFORMED after the expression, which means you are guaranteeing that your expression resolves to a well-formed XML document. This also means that the database will not perform validity checks on your expression.

The following example parses an expression containing the details for a customer:

```
SELECT XMLPARSE(
  CONTENT
  '<customer><customer_id>1</customer_id><name>John Brown</name></customer>'
  WELLFORMED
)
AS xml_customer
FROM dual;

XML_CUSTOMER
-----------------------------
<customer>
  <customer_id>1</customer_id>
  <name>John Brown</name>
</customer>
```

NOTE
You can read more about well-formed XML documents and values at
www.w3.org/TR/REC-xml.

XMLPI()

XMLPI() generates an XML processing instruction. You typically use a processing instruction to provide an application with information that is associated with XML data. The application can then use the processing instruction to determine how to process the XML data.

The following example generates a processing instruction for an order status:

```
SELECT XMLPI(
  NAME "order_status",
  'PLACED, PENDING, SHIPPED'
)
AS xml_order_status_pi
FROM dual;

XML_ORDER_STATUS_PI
-----------------------------------------
<?order_status PLACED, PENDING, SHIPPED?>
```

The next example generates a processing instruction to display an XML document using a cascading style sheet file named example.css:

```
SELECT XMLPI(
  NAME "xml-stylesheet",
  'type="text/css" href="example.css"'
)
AS xml_stylesheet_pi
FROM dual;

XML_STYLESHEET_PI
-----------------------------------------------------
<?xml-stylesheet type="text/css" href="example.css"?>
```

XMLCOMMENT()

XMLCOMMENT() generates an XML comment, which is a text string placed within <!-- and -->. For example:

```
SELECT XMLCOMMENT(
  'An example XML Comment'
)
AS xml_comment
FROM dual;

XML_COMMENT
-----------------------------
<!--An example XML Comment-->
```

XMLSEQUENCE()

XMLSEQUENCE() generates an XMLSequenceType object, which is a varray of XMLType objects. Because XMLSEQUENCE() returns a varray, you can use it in the FROM clause of a query. For example:

```
SELECT VALUE(list_of_values).GETSTRINGVAL() order_values
FROM TABLE(
  XMLSEQUENCE(
    EXTRACT(
      XMLType('<A><B>PLACED</B><B>PENDING</B><B>SHIPPED</B></A>'),
      '/A/B'
    )
  )
) list_of_values;

ORDER_VALUES
--------------
<B>PLACED</B>
<B>PENDING</B>
<B>SHIPPED</B>
```

Let's break down this example. The call to XMLType() is as follows:

```
XMLType('<A><B>PLACED</B><B>PENDING</B><B>SHIPPED</B></A>')
```

This creates an XMLType object containing the XML as follows:

```
<A><B>PLACED</B><B>PENDING</B><B>SHIPPED</B></A>.
```

The call to the EXTRACT() function is as follows:

```
EXTRACT(
  XMLType('<A><B>PLACED</B><B>PENDING</B><B>SHIPPED</B></A>'),
  '/A/B'
)
```

EXTRACT() extracts the XML data from the XMLType object returned by the call to XMLType(). The second parameter to EXTRACT() is an XPath string. XPath is a language that allows you to access specific elements in XML data. For example, in the previous call to EXTRACT(), the second parameter '/A/B' returns all the B elements that are children of the A elements, and so the EXTRACT() function returns the following:

```
<B>PLACED</B>
<B>PENDING</B>
<B>SHIPPED</B>
```

The call to XMLSEQUENCE() in the example simply returns a varray containing the elements returned by EXTRACT(). TABLE() converts the varray into a table of rows and applies the alias list_of_values to the table. The SELECT statement retrieves the string value of the rows in the table using GETSTRINGVAL().

You'll see more examples of EXTRACT() and XPath later in this chapter.

XMLSERIALIZE()

`XMLSERIALIZE()` generates a string or LOB (large object) representation of XML data from the evaluated result of an expression. You must specify one of the following items before the expression:

- CONTENT, which means the expression must resolve to a valid XML value
- DOCUMENT, which means the expression must resolve to a singly rooted XML document

The following example uses `XMLSERIALIZE()` with `CONTENT` to generate an XML value:

```
SELECT XMLSERIALIZE(
  CONTENT XMLType('<order_status>SHIPPED</order_status>')
)
AS xml_order_status
FROM DUAL;

XML_ORDER_STATUS
------------------------------------
<order_status>SHIPPED</order_status>
```

The next example uses `XMLSERIALIZE()` with `DOCUMENT` to generate an XML document, with the document returned as a CLOB (character large object):

```
SELECT XMLSERIALIZE(
  DOCUMENT XMLType('<description>Description of a product</description>')
  AS CLOB
)
AS xml_product_description
FROM DUAL;

XML_PRODUCT_DESCRIPTION
---------------------------------------------------
<description>Description of a product</description>
```

A PL/SQL Example That Writes XML Data to a File

In this section, you'll see a complete PL/SQL example that writes customer names to an XML file. First, you need to connect as a privileged user (for example, the `system` user) and grant the `CREATE ANY DIRECTORY` privilege to the `store` user:

```
CONNECT system/oracle;
GRANT CREATE ANY DIRECTORY TO store;
```

Next, you need to connect as the `store` user and create a directory object. For example:

```
CONNECT store/store_password;
CREATE DIRECTORY TEMP_FILES_DIR AS 'C:\temp_files';
```

The directory in the previous example uses a Windows path, and is set to `C:\temp_files`. You'll also need to create a directory named `temp_files` in the Windows C partition. If you're using Linux or Unix, you can create the directory on one of your partitions and use an appropriate

CREATE DIRECTORY command with the correct path. Also, ensure you grant write permissions on the directory to the Oracle user account that you used to install the database software.

Next, you need to run the `xml_examples.sql` script located in the SQL directory. For example:

```
@ C:\sql_book\SQL\xml_examples.sql
```

CAUTION
You might notice there is a script named `xml_schema.sql` *in the* SQL *directory. Do not run* `xml_schema.sql` *yet.*

The `xml_examples.sql` script creates two procedures. The one you'll see in this section is named `write_xml_data_to_file()`, which retrieves the customer names and writes them to an XML file. The `write_xml_data_to_file()` procedure is defined as follows:

```
CREATE PROCEDURE write_xml_data_to_file(
  p_directory VARCHAR2,
  p_file_name VARCHAR2
) AS
  v_file UTL_FILE.FILE_TYPE;
  v_amount INTEGER := 32767;
  v_xml_data XMLType;
  v_char_buffer VARCHAR2(32767);
BEGIN
  -- open the file for writing of text (up to v_amount
  -- characters at a time)
  v_file := UTL_FILE.FOPEN(p_directory, p_file_name, 'w', v_amount);

  -- write the starting line to v_file
  UTL_FILE.PUT_LINE(v_file, '<?xml version="1.0"?>');

  -- retrieve the customers and store them in v_xml_data
  SELECT
    EXTRACT(
      XMLELEMENT(
        "customer_list",
        XMLAGG(
          XMLELEMENT("customer", first_name || ' ' || last_name)
          ORDER BY last_name
        )
      ),
      '/customer_list'
    )
  AS xml_customers
  INTO v_xml_data
  FROM customers;

  -- get the string value from v_xml_data and store it in v_char_buffer
  v_char_buffer := v_xml_data.GETSTRINGVAL();
```

```
-- copy the characters from v_char_buffer to the file
UTL_FILE.PUT(v_file, v_char_buffer);

-- flush any remaining data to the file
UTL_FILE.FFLUSH(v_file);

-- close the file
UTL_FILE.FCLOSE(v_file);
END write_xml_data_to_file;
/
```

The following statement calls `write_xml_data_to_file()`:

```
CALL write_xml_data_to_file('TEMP_FILES_DIR', 'customers.xml');
```

After you run this statement, you'll find a file named `customers.xml` in `C:\temp_files`, or whichever directory you used when using the `CREATE DIRECTORY` command earlier. The content in the `customers.xml` file is as follows:

```
<?xml version="1.0"?>
<customer_list><customer>Gail Black</customer><customer>Doreen Blue
</customer><customer>John Brown</customer><customer>Cynthia Green
</customer><customer>Steve White</customer></customer_list>
```

You can modify the `write_xml_data_to_file()` procedure to retrieve any relational data from the database and write it out to an XML file.

XMLQUERY()

`XMLQUERY()` constructs XML or queries XML. You pass an XQuery expression to `XMLQUERY()`. XQuery is a query language that allows you to construct and query XML. `XMLQUERY()` returns the result of evaluating the XQuery expression.

The following simple example illustrates the use of `XMLQUERY()`:

```
SELECT XMLQUERY(
   '(1, 2 + 5, "d", 155 to 161, <A>text</A>)'
   RETURNING CONTENT
)
AS xml_output
FROM DUAL;

XML_OUTPUT
-------------------------------------------
1 7 d 155 156 157 158 159 160 161<A>text</A>
```

Here are some notes for the example:

- The string passed to `XMLQUERY()` is the XQuery expression, which is `(1, 2 + 5, "d", 155 to 161, <A>text</A>)`. 1 is an integer literal, 2 + 5 is an arithmetic expression, d is a string literal, 155 to 161 is a sequence of integers, and `<A>text</A>` is an XML element.

- Each of the items in the XQuery is evaluated in turn. For example, 2 + 5 is evaluated, and 7 is returned. Similarly, 155 to 161 is evaluated and 155 156 157 158 159 160 161 is returned.

- RETURNING CONTENT means an XML fragment is returned. The XML fragment is a single XML element with any number of "children," which can themselves be of any XML element type, including text elements. The XML fragment also conforms to the extended Infoset data model. Infoset is a specification describing an abstract data model of an XML document. (You can learn more about Infoset at www.w3.org/TR/xml-infoset.)

Let's explore a more complex example. The following statement (contained in the xml_ examples.sql script) creates a procedure named create_xml_resources(). This procedure creates XML strings for products and product types. The procedure uses methods in the PL/SQL DBMS_XDB package to delete and create XML resource files in the Oracle XML DB Repository. The XML DB Repository is a storage area for XML data within the database. The create_xml_ resources() procedure is as follows:

```
CREATE PROCEDURE create_xml_resources AS
  v_result BOOLEAN;

  -- create string containing XML for products
  v_products VARCHAR2(300) :=
    '<?xml version="1.0"?>' ||
    '<products>' ||
      '<product product_id="1" product_type_id="1" name="Modern Science"'
      || ' price="19.95"/>' ||
      '<product product_id="2" product_type_id="1" name="Chemistry"' ||
      ' price="30"/>' ||
      '<product product_id="3" product_type_id="2" name="Supernova"' ||
      ' price="25.99"/>' ||
    '</products>';

  -- create string containing XML for product types
  v_product_types VARCHAR2(300) :=
    '<?xml version="1.0"?>' ||
    '<product_types>' ||
      '<product_type product_type_id="1" name="Book"/>' ||
      '<product_type product_type_id="2" name="Video"/>' ||
    '</product_types>';
BEGIN
  -- create resource for products
  v_result := DBMS_XDB.CREATERESOURCE('/public/products.xml',
    v_products);

  -- create resource for product types
  v_result := DBMS_XDB.CREATERESOURCE('/public/product_types.xml',
    v_product_types);
END create_xml_resources;
/
```

The DBMS_XDB.CREATERESOURCE() function creates an XML resource in the database and returns a Boolean `true` or `false` value indicating whether the operation was successful. The two calls to this function create resources for the products and product types in `/public`, which is the absolute path to store the resources.

The following statement calls `create_xml_resources()`:

```
CALL create_xml_resources();
```

The following query uses XMLQUERY() to retrieve the products from the `/public/products.xml` resource:

```
SELECT XMLQUERY(
    'for $product in doc("/public/products.xml")/products/product
    return <product name="{$product/@name}"/>'
    RETURNING CONTENT
)
AS xml_products
FROM DUAL;

XML_PRODUCTS
-----------------------------------------
<product name="Modern Science"></product>
<product name="Chemistry"></product>
<product name="Supernova"></product>
```

The XQuery expression inside XMLQUERY() in the previous example is as follows:

```
for $product in doc("/public/products.xml")/products/product
return <product name="{$product/@name}"/>
```

Let's break down the XQuery expression:

- The `for` loop iterates over the products in `/public/products.xml`.
- `$product` is a binding variable that is bound to the sequence of products returned by `doc("/public/products.xml")/products/product`. The fragment `doc("/public/products.xml")` returns the `products.xml` document stored in `/public`. With each iteration of the loop, `$product` is set to each product in `products.xml`, one product after another.
- The `return` part of the expression returns the product name in `$product`.

The next query retrieves the product types from the `/public/product_types.xml` resource:

```
SELECT XMLQUERY(
    'for $product_type in
    doc("/public/product_types.xml")/product_types/product_type
    return <product_type name="{$product_type/@name}"/>'
    RETURNING CONTENT
)
```

```
AS xml_product_types
FROM DUAL;

XML_PRODUCT_TYPES
-------------------------------------------
<product_type name="Book"></product_type>
<product_type name="Video"></product_type>
```

The following query retrieves the products whose price is greater than 20, along with their product type:

```
SELECT XMLQUERY(
  'for $product in doc("/public/products.xml")/products/product
  let $product_type :=
    doc("/public/product_types.xml")//product_type[@product_type_id =
      $product/@product_type_id]/@name
  where $product/@price > 20
  order by $product/@product_id
  return <product name="{$product/@name}"
    product_type="{$product_type}"/>'
  RETURNING CONTENT
)
AS xml_query_results
FROM DUAL;

XML_QUERY_RESULTS
-----------------------------------------------------------
<product name="Chemistry" product_type="Book"></product>
<product name="Supernova" product_type="Video"></product>
```

Let's break down the XQuery expression in this example:

- Two binding variables are used: $product and $product_type. These variables are used to store the products and product types.

- The let part of the expression sets $product_type to the product type retrieved from $product. The expression on the right-hand side of the "set equal to" operator := performs a join using the product_type_id value stored in $product_type and $product. The // characters mean "retrieve all elements."

- The where part retrieves only products whose price is greater than 20.

- The order by part orders the results by the product ID (in ascending order by default).

The next example shows the use of the following XQuery functions:

- count(), which counts the number of objects passed to it.

- avg(), which calculates the average of the numbers passed to it.

- integer(), which truncates a number and returns the integer. The integer() function is in the xs namespace. (The count() and avg() functions are in the fn namespace, which is automatically referenced by the database, thereby allowing omission of this namespace when calling the functions.)

The following example returns the product type name, the number of products in each product type, and the average price of the products in each product type (truncated to an integer):

```
SELECT XMLQUERY(
    'for $product_type in
    doc("/public/product_types.xml")/product_types/product_type
    let $product :=
        doc("/public/products.xml")//product[@product_type_id =
            $product_type/@product_type_id]
    return
        <product_type name="{$product_type/@name}"
        num_products="{count($product)}"
        average_price="{xs:integer(avg($product/@price))}"
        />'
    RETURNING CONTENT
)
AS xml_query_results
FROM DUAL;

XML_QUERY_RESULTS
--------------------------------------------------------------
<product_type name="Book" num_products="2" average_price="24">
</product_type>

<product_type name="Video" num_products="1" average_price="25">
</product_type>
```

As you can see from the values in num_products, there are two books and one video. The average prices for the books and videos are $24 and $25, as shown in average_price.

NOTE
You can read more about functions at www.w3.org/TR/xquery-operators.

Saving XML in the Database

In this section, you'll see how to store an XML document in the database and retrieve information from the stored XML.

The Example XML File

You'll see the use of a file named purchase_order.xml, which is an XML file that contains a purchase order. This file is contained in the xml_files directory, which is created when you extracted the Zip file for this book.

The content of the purchase_order.xml file is as follows:

```
<?xml version="1.0"?>
<purchase_order>
    <customer_order_id>176</customer_order_id>
    <order_date>2007-05-17</order_date>
```

```
<customer_name>Best Products 456 Inc.</customer_name>
<street>10 Any Street</street>
<city>Any City</city>
<state>CA</state>
<zip>94440</zip>
<phone_number>555-121-1234</phone_number>
<products>
  <product>
    <product_id>1</product_id>
    <name>Supernova video</name>
    <quantity>5</quantity>
  </product>
  <product>
    <product_id>2</product_id>
    <name>Oracle SQL book</name>
    <quantity>4</quantity>
  </product>
</products>
</purchase_order>
```

In a real-world example, the purchase order could be sent via the Internet to an online store, which would then dispatch the requested items to the customer.

If you want to follow along with the examples, you should copy the `xml_files` directory to the C partition on your database server. If you're using Linux or Unix, you can copy the directory to one of your partitions. Write down the location where you copy the file.

In the following sections, you'll see how to store the content of the XML file in the database.

Creating the Example XML Schema

I've provided a script named `xml_schema.sql` in the SQL directory. The script creates a user named `xml_user` with a password of `xml_password`, and it creates the items used in the rest of this chapter. Don't run this script yet, because you might need to edit it. I'll describe what is in the script first, then I'll tell you what to edit.

The script contains statements that create the following items in the database:

- An object type named `t_product`, which is used to represent products
- A nested table type named `t_nested_table_product`, which is used to represent a nested table of products
- A table named `purchase_order` to hold the purchase order

The following listing shows the statements in `xml_schema.sql` that create the items described in the previous list:

```
CREATE TYPE t_product AS OBJECT (
  product_id INTEGER,
  name VARCHAR2(15),
  quantity INTEGER
);
/
```

```
CREATE TYPE t_nested_table_product AS TABLE OF t_product;
/

CREATE TABLE purchase_order (
  purchase_order_id INTEGER CONSTRAINT purchase_order_pk PRIMARY KEY,
  customer_order_id INTEGER,
  order_date DATE,
  customer_name VARCHAR2(25),
  street VARCHAR2(15),
  city VARCHAR2(15),
  state VARCHAR2(2),
  zip VARCHAR2(5),
  phone_number VARCHAR2(12),
  products t_nested_table_product,
  xml_purchase_order XMLType
)
NESTED TABLE products
STORE AS nested_products;
```

Notice that the xml_purchase_order column is of type XMLType, which is a built-in Oracle database type that allows you to store XML data.

The xml_schema.sql script also contains the following statement that creates a directory object named XML_FILES_DIR:

```
CREATE OR REPLACE DIRECTORY XML_FILES_DIR AS 'C:\xml_files';
```

You'll need to modify this line if you copied the xml_files directory to a location different from C, or if you are using Linux or Unix. If you need to modify this line, go ahead and do it now and then save the script.

The following INSERT statement (also contained in the script) adds a row to the purchase_order table:

```
INSERT INTO purchase_order (
  purchase_order_id,
  xml_purchase_order
) VALUES (
  1,
  XMLType(
    BFILENAME('XML_FILES_DIR', 'purchase_order.xml'),
    NLS_CHARSET_ID('AL32UTF8')
  )
);
```

As you can see from the INSERT, the XMLType() constructor accepts two parameters. The first parameter is a BFILE, which is a pointer to an external file. The second parameter is the character set for the XML text in the external file. In the INSERT, the BFILE points to the purchase_order.xml file, and the character set is AL32UTF8, which is standard UTF-8 encoding. When the INSERT is run, the XML from the purchase_order.xml file is read and then stored in the database in the xml_purchase_order column of the purchase_order table.

NOTE
When working with XML files written in English, you should typically use the AL32UTF8 character set. You can find more information about different character sets in the Oracle Database Globalization Support Guide *published by Oracle Corporation.*

The `INSERT` does not specify values for the `customer_order_id`, `order_date`, `customer_name`, `street`, `city`, `state`, `zip`, `phone_number`, or `products` columns. The data for these columns can be extracted from the XML stored in the `xml_purchase_order` column. Later in this chapter, you'll see a PL/SQL procedure that reads the XML, extracts the values, and sets the other columns to the extracted values.

Go ahead and run the `xml_schema.sql` script as a privileged user using SQL*Plus. For example:

```
CONNECT system/oracle
@ C:\sql_book\SQL\xml_schema.sql
```

After the script completes, you will be logged in as `xml_user`.

Retrieving Information from the Example XML Schema

In this section, you'll see how to retrieve information from the `xml_user` schema.

The following example retrieves the row from the `purchase_order` table:

```
SET LONG 1000
SET PAGESIZE 500
SELECT purchase_order_id, xml_purchase_order
FROM purchase_order;

PURCHASE_ORDER_ID
-----------------
XML_PURCHASE_ORDER
--------------------------------------------------------
                1
<?xml version="1.0"?>
<purchase_order>
  <customer_order_id>176</customer_order_id>
  <order_date>2007-05-17</order_date>
  <customer_name>Best Products 456 Inc.</customer_name>
  <street>10 Any Street</street>
  <city>Any City</city>
  <state>CA</state>
  <zip>94440</zip>
  <phone_number>555-121-1234</phone_number>
  <products>
    <product>
      <product_id>1</product_id>
      <name>Supernova video</name>
      <quantity>5</quantity>
    </product>
```

```
    <product>
      <product_id>2</product_id>
      <name>Oracle SQL book</name>
      <quantity>4</quantity>
    </product>
  </products>
</purchase_order>
```

The next query uses the EXTRACT() function to extract the customer_order_id, order_date, customer_name, and phone_number from the XML stored in the xml_purchase_order column:

```
SELECT
  EXTRACT(xml_purchase_order,
    '/purchase_order/customer_order_id') cust_order_id,
  EXTRACT(xml_purchase_order, '/purchase_order/order_date') order_date,
  EXTRACT(xml_purchase_order, '/purchase_order/customer_name') cust_name,
  EXTRACT(xml_purchase_order, '/purchase_order/phone_number') phone_number
FROM purchase_order
WHERE purchase_order_id = 1;

CUST_ORDER_ID
------------------------------------------
ORDER_DATE
----------------------------------
CUST_NAME
-------------------------------------------------
PHONE_NUMBER
-----------------------------------------
<customer_order_id>176</customer_order_id>
<order_date>2007-05-17</order_date>
<customer_name>Best Products 456 Inc.</customer_name>
<phone_number>555-121-1234</phone_number>
```

The EXTRACT() function returns the values as XMLType objects.

You can use the EXTRACTVALUE() function to get the values as strings. For example, the following query extracts the values as strings using the EXTRACTVALUE() function:

```
SELECT
  EXTRACTVALUE(xml_purchase_order,
    '/purchase_order/customer_order_id') cust_order_id,
  EXTRACTVALUE(xml_purchase_order,
    '/purchase_order/order_date') order_date,
  EXTRACTVALUE(xml_purchase_order,
    '/purchase_order/customer_name') cust_name,
  EXTRACTVALUE(xml_purchase_order,
    '/purchase_order/phone_number') phone_number
FROM purchase_order
WHERE purchase_order_id = 1;
```

```
CUST_ORDER_ID
--------------------
ORDER_DATE
--------------------
CUST_NAME
--------------------
PHONE_NUMBER
--------------------
176
2007-05-17
Best Products 456 Inc.
555-121-1234
```

The next query extracts and converts `order_date` to a DATE using the `TO_DATE()` function. Notice that the format for the date as stored in the XML is supplied using the second parameter to `TO_DATE()` and that `TO_DATE()` returns the date in the default date format used by the database (DD-MON-YY).

```sql
SELECT
  TO_DATE(
    EXTRACTVALUE(xml_purchase_order, '/purchase_order/order_date'),
    'YYYY-MM-DD'
  ) AS ord_date
FROM purchase_order
WHERE purchase_order_id = 1;

ORD_DATE
---------
17-MAY-07
```

The following query retrieves all the products from `xml_purchase_order` as XML using `EXTRACT()`. Notice the use of the characters `//` to get all of the products.

```sql
SELECT
  EXTRACT(xml_purchase_order, '/purchase_order//products') xml_products
FROM purchase_order
WHERE purchase_order_id = 1;

XML_PRODUCTS
--------------------------------
<products>
  <product>
    <product_id>1</product_id>
    <name>Supernova video</name>
    <quantity>5</quantity>
  </product>
  <product>
    <product_id>2</product_id>
    <name>Oracle SQL book</name>
    <quantity>4</quantity>
  </product>
</products>
```

The next query retrieves product #2 from `xml_purchase_order`. Notice that `product[2]` returns product #2.

```
SELECT
  EXTRACT(
    xml_purchase_order,
    '/purchase_order/products/product[2]'
  ) xml_product
FROM purchase_order
WHERE purchase_order_id = 1;

XML_PRODUCT
---------------------------------
<product>
  <product_id>2</product_id>
  <product>Oracle SQL book</name>
  <quantity>4</quantity>
</product>
```

The following query retrieves the "Supernova video" product from `xml_purchase_order`. Notice that the name of the product to retrieve is placed inside square brackets, `[name="Supernova video"]`.

```
SELECT
  EXTRACT(
    xml_purchase_order,
    '/purchase_order/products/product[name="Supernova video"]'
  ) xml_product
FROM purchase_order
WHERE purchase_order_id = 1;

XML_PRODUCT
------------------------------
<product>
  <product_id>1</product_id>
  <name>Supernova video</name>
  <quantity>5</quantity>
</product>
```

You use the `EXISTSNODE()` function to check if an XML element exists in the database. `EXISTSNODE()` returns 1 if the element exists. Otherwise, `EXISTSNODE()` returns 0. For example, the following query returns the string `'Exists'` because product #1 exists in the database:

```
SELECT 'Exists' AS "EXISTS"
FROM purchase_order
WHERE purchase_order_id = 1
AND EXISTSNODE(
  xml_purchase_order,
  '/purchase_order/products/product[product_id=1]'
) = 1;
```

```
EXISTS
------
Exists
```

The next query returns no rows because product #3 does not exist in the database:

```
SELECT 'Exists'
FROM purchase_order
WHERE purchase_order_id = 1
AND EXISTSNODE(
  xml_purchase_order,
  '/purchase_order/products/product[product_id=3]'
) = 1;
```

```
no rows selected
```

The following query retrieves the products as a varray of XMLType objects using the XMLSEQUENCE() function. Notice the use of product.* to retrieve all of the products and their XML elements.

```
SELECT product.*
FROM TABLE(
  SELECT
    XMLSEQUENCE(EXTRACT(xml_purchase_order, '/purchase_order//product'))
  FROM purchase_order
  WHERE purchase_order_id = 1
) product;
```

```
COLUMN_VALUE
-----------------------------
<product>
  <product_id>1</product_id>
  <name>Supernova video</name>
  <quantity>5</quantity>
</product>

<product>
  <product_id>2</product_id>
  <name>Oracle SQL book</name>
  <quantity>4</quantity>
</product>
```

The next query retrieves the product_id, name, and quantity for the products as strings using the EXTRACTVALUE() function:

```
SELECT
  EXTRACTVALUE(product.COLUMN_VALUE, '/product/product_id') AS product_id,
  EXTRACTVALUE(product.COLUMN_VALUE, '/product/name') AS name,
  EXTRACTVALUE(product.COLUMN_VALUE, '/product/quantity') AS quantity
FROM TABLE(
  SELECT
```

```
    XMLSEQUENCE(EXTRACT(xml_purchase_order, '/purchase_order//product'))
  FROM purchase_order
  WHERE purchase_order_id = 1
) product;


PRODUCT_ID
-------------
PRODUCT
---------------
QUANTITY
---------------
1
Supernova video
5

2
Oracle SQL book
4
```

Updating Information in the Example XML Schema

The customer_order_id, order_date, customer_name, street, city, state, zip, phone_number, and products columns in the purchase_order table are empty. The data for these columns will be extracted from the XML stored in the xml_purchase_order column.

In this section, you'll see a PL/SQL procedure named update_purchase_order() that extracts the values from the XML and sets the columns in the purchase_order table to the extracted values.

The most complex part of update_purchase_order() is reading the products from the XML and storing them in the products column of the purchase_order table. To do that, the procedure performs the following steps:

1. A cursor reads the products from the XML stored in the xml_purchase_order column.

2. The XML is converted to strings using EXTRACTVALUE().

3. The strings are stored in the products column, which is a nested table. The nested table stores the multiple products for the order.

The following statement (contained in the xml_schema.sql script) creates the update_purchase_order() procedure:

```
CREATE PROCEDURE update_purchase_order(
  p_purchase_order_id IN purchase_order.purchase_order_id%TYPE
) AS
  v_count INTEGER := 1;

  -- declare a nested table to store products
  v_nested_table_products t_nested_table_product :=
    t_nested_table_product();

  -- declare a type to represent a product record
  TYPE t_product_record IS RECORD (
```

```
    product_id INTEGER,
    name VARCHAR2(15),
    quantity INTEGER
);

-- declare a REF CURSOR type to point to product records
TYPE t_product_cursor IS REF CURSOR RETURN t_product_record;

-- declare a cursor
v_product_cursor t_product_cursor;

-- declare a variable to store a product record
v_product t_product_record;
BEGIN
  -- open v_product_cursor to read the product_id, name, and quantity for
  -- each product stored in the XML of the xml_purchase_order column
  -- in the purchase_order table
  OPEN v_product_cursor FOR
  SELECT
    EXTRACTVALUE(product.COLUMN_VALUE, '/product/product_id')
      AS product_id,
    EXTRACTVALUE(product.COLUMN_VALUE, '/product/name') AS name,
    EXTRACTVALUE(product.COLUMN_VALUE, '/product/quantity') AS quantity
  FROM TABLE(
    SELECT
      XMLSEQUENCE(EXTRACT(xml_purchase_order, '/purchase_order//product'))
    FROM purchase_order
    WHERE purchase_order_id = p_purchase_order_id
  ) product;

  -- loop over the contents of v_product_cursor
  LOOP
    -- fetch the product records from v_product_cursor and exit when there
    -- are no more records found
    FETCH v_product_cursor INTO v_product;
    EXIT WHEN v_product_cursor%NOTFOUND;

    -- extend v_nested_table_products so that a product can be stored in it
    v_nested_table_products.EXTEND;

    -- create a new product and store it in v_nested_table_products
    v_nested_table_products(v_count) :=
      t_product(v_product.product_id, v_product.name, v_product.quantity);

    -- display the new product stored in v_nested_table_products
    DBMS_OUTPUT.PUT_LINE('product_id = ' ||
      v_nested_table_products(v_count).product_id);
    DBMS_OUTPUT.PUT_LINE('name = ' ||
      v_nested_table_products(v_count).name);
    DBMS_OUTPUT.PUT_LINE('quantity = ' ||
      v_nested_table_products(v_count).quantity);
```

```
    -- increment v_count ready for the next iteration of the loop
    v_count := v_count + 1;
  END LOOP;

  -- close v_product_cursor
  CLOSE v_product_cursor;

  -- update the purchase_order table using the values extracted from the
  -- XML stored in the xml_purchase_order column (the products nested
  -- table is set to v_nested_table_products already populated by the
  -- previous loop)
  UPDATE purchase_order
  SET
    customer_order_id =
      EXTRACTVALUE(xml_purchase_order,
        '/purchase_order/customer_order_id'),
    order_date =
      TO_DATE(EXTRACTVALUE(xml_purchase_order,
        '/purchase_order/order_date'), 'YYYY-MM-DD'),
    customer_name =
      EXTRACTVALUE(xml_purchase_order, '/purchase_order/customer_name'),
    street =
      EXTRACTVALUE(xml_purchase_order, '/purchase_order/street'),
    city =
      EXTRACTVALUE(xml_purchase_order, '/purchase_order/city'),
    state =
      EXTRACTVALUE(xml_purchase_order, '/purchase_order/state'),
    zip =
      EXTRACTVALUE(xml_purchase_order, '/purchase_order/zip'),
    phone_number =
      EXTRACTVALUE(xml_purchase_order, '/purchase_order/phone_number'),
    products = v_nested_table_products
  WHERE purchase_order_id = p_purchase_order_id;

  -- commit the transaction
  COMMIT;
END update_purchase_order;
/
```

The following example sets the server output on and calls update_purchase_order() to update purchase order #1:

```
SET SERVEROUTPUT ON
CALL update_purchase_order(1);
product_id = 1
name = Supernova video
quantity = 5
product_id = 2
name = Oracle SQL book
quantity = 4
```

The following query retrieves the columns from purchase order #1:

```
SELECT purchase_order_id, customer_order_id, order_date, customer_name,
   street, city, state, zip, phone_number, products
FROM purchase_order
WHERE purchase_order_id = 1;

PURCHASE_ORDER_ID CUSTOMER_ORDER_ID  ORDER_DAT  CUSTOMER_NAME
----------------- -----------------  ---------  ----------------------
STREET          CITY             ST  ZIP     PHONE_NUMBER
--------------- ---------------- --  -----   ------------
PRODUCTS(PRODUCT_ID, NAME, QUANTITY)
------------------------------------
                1            176  17-MAY-07  Best Products 456 Inc.
10 Any Street   Any City         CA  94440   555-121-1234
T_NESTED_TABLE_PRODUCT(
 T_PRODUCT(1, 'Supernova video', 5),
 T_PRODUCT(2, 'Oracle SQL book', 4)
)
```

The `products` nested table contains the same data as stored in the XML product elements in the `xml_purchase_order` column. I've added some line breaks to separate the products in the example's result set to make them easier to read.

Summary

In this chapter, you have learned how to do the following:

- Generate XML from existing data stored in the database
- Save XML in the database

You can find more information about XML in the *Oracle XML DB Developer's Guide* and the *Oracle XML Developer's Kit Programmer's Guide*, both published by Oracle Corporation.

Apart from the final appendix, you have reached the end of this book. I hope you've found it useful and interesting.

APPENDIX

Oracle Data Types

This appendix documents the main Oracle SQL and PL/SQL data types.

Oracle SQL Types

Table A-1 shows the main Oracle SQL types.

Type	Description
CHAR[(length [BYTE | CHAR])][1]	Fixed-length character data of *length* bytes or characters. The contents of a CHAR are padded with trailing spaces. Maximum length is 2,000 bytes.
VARCHAR2(length [BYTE | CHAR])[1]	Variable-length character data of up to *length* bytes or characters. Maximum length is 32,767 bytes.
NCHAR[(length)]	Fixed-length Unicode character data of *length* characters. Number of bytes stored is 2 multiplied by *length* for AL16UTF16 encoding and 3 multiplied by *length* for UTF8 encoding. Maximum length is 2,000 bytes.
NVARCHAR2(length)	Variable-length Unicode character data of *length* characters. Number of bytes stored is 2 multiplied by *length* for AL16UTF16 encoding and 3 multiplied by *length* for UTF8 encoding. Maximum length is 32,767 bytes.
BINARY_FLOAT	Introduced in Oracle Database 10g, stores a single-precision 32-bit floating-point number. Operations involving BINARY_FLOAT are typically performed faster than operations using NUMBER values.
BINARY_DOUBLE	Introduced in Oracle Database 10g, stores a double-precision 64-bit floating-point number. Operations involving BINARY_DOUBLE are typically performed faster than operations using NUMBER values.
NUMBER(precision, scale) and NUMERIC(precision, scale)	Variable-length number. *precision* is the maximum number of digits that may be used for the number. The digits counted include those to the left and right of a decimal point, if a decimal point is present. The maximum precision supported is 38. *scale* is the maximum number of digits to the right of a decimal point, if a decimal point is specified in the number. *scale* can be between −84 and 127. If neither *precision* nor *scale* is specified, then a number with up to a precision and scale of 38 digits may be supplied. This means that you can supply a number with up to 38 digits, and any of those 38 digits can be to the right or left of the decimal point.
DEC and DECIMAL	Subtype of NUMBER. A fixed-point decimal number with up to 38 digits of decimal precision.
DOUBLE PRECISION and FLOAT	Subtype of NUMBER. A floating-point number with up to 38 digits of precision.
REAL	Subtype of NUMBER. A floating-point number with up to 18 digits of precision.
INT, INTEGER, and SMALLINT	Subtype of NUMBER. An integer with up to 38 digits of decimal precision.
DATE	Date and time with the century. All four digits of year, month, day, hour (in 24-hour format), minute, and second are stored. Can be used to store a date and time between January 1, 4712 B.C. and December 31, 9999 A.D.

[1]The BYTE and CHAR keywords work only with Oracle Database 9*i* and above. If neither BYTE nor CHAR is specified, the default is BYTE.

TABLE A-1. *Oracle SQL Types*

Type	Description
INTERVAL YEAR[(*years_precision*)] TO MONTH	Time interval measured in years and months.
	years_precision specifies the precision for the years, which may be an integer from 0 to 9 (default is 2).
	Can be used to represent a positive or negative time interval by supplying a negative sign.
INTERVAL DAY[(*days_precision*)] TO SECOND[(*seconds_precision*)]	Time interval measured in days and seconds.
	days_precision specifies the precision for the days, which is an integer from 0 to 9 (default is 2).
	seconds_precision specifies the precision for the fractional part of the seconds, which is an integer from 0 to 9 (default is 6).
	Can be used to represent a positive or negative time interval by supplying a negative sign.
TIMESTAMP[(*seconds_precision*)]	Date and time with the century. All four digits of year, month, day, hour (in 24-hour format), minute, and second are stored.
	seconds_precision specifies the number of digits for the fractional part of the seconds, which can be an integer from 0 to 9 (default is 6).
TIMESTAMP[(*seconds_precision*)] WITH TIME ZONE	Extends TIMESTAMP to store a time zone.
	The time zone can be an offset from UTC, such as -8:0, or a region name, such as US/Pacific or PST.
TIMESTAMP[(*seconds_precision*)] WITH LOCAL TIME ZONE	Extends TIMESTAMP to convert a supplied datetime to the local time zone set for the database. The process of conversion is known as *normalizing* the datetime.
CLOB	Variable-length single-byte character data of up to 128 terabytes, depending on the block size for the database.
NCLOB	Variable-length Unicode national character set data of up to 128 terabytes, depending on the block size for the database.
BLOB	Variable-length binary data of up to 128 terabytes, depending on the block size for the database.
BFILE	Pointer to an external file. The external file is not stored in the database. The maximum supported file size is 4 gigabytes.
LONG	Variable-length character data of up to 2 gigabytes. Superseded by the CLOB and NCLOB types, but LONG is supported for backwards compatibility.
RAW(*length*)	Variable-length binary data of up to *length* bytes. Maximum length is 32,767 bytes. Superseded by the BLOB type, but RAW is supported for backwards compatibility.
LONG RAW	Variable-length binary data of up to 2 gigabytes. Superseded by the BLOB type, but LONG RAW is supported for backwards compatibility.
ROWID	Base-64 string representing a row address.
UROWID[(*length*)]	Base-64 string representing the logical address of a row of an index-organized table.
	length specifies the number of bytes. Maximum length is 4,000 bytes (also the default length if none is specified).
REF *object_type*	Reference to an object type. Similar to a pointer in the C++ programming language.
VARRAY	Variable-length array. A varray is a composite type that stores an ordered set of elements.
NESTED TABLE	Nested table. A nested table is a composite type that stores an unordered set of elements.
XMLType	Stores XML data.
User-defined object type	A user-defined object type. You can define your own object type and create objects of that type. See Chapter 13 for details.

TABLE A-1. *Oracle SQL Types*

Oracle PL/SQL Types

Oracle PL/SQL supports all the types previously shown in Table A-1, plus the additional Oracle PL/SQL–specific types shown in Table A-2.

Type	Description
BOOLEAN	Boolean value. The value can be TRUE, FALSE, or NULL.
BINARY_INTEGER	Integer between –2,147,483,647 and 2,147,483,647.
NATURAL	Subtype of BINARY_INTEGER. A non-negative integer between 0 and 2,147,483,647 inclusive.
NATURALN	Subtype of BINARY_INTEGER. A non-negative integer between 0 and 2,147,483,647 inclusive. The value cannot be NULL.
POSITIVE	Subtype of BINARY_INTEGER. A positive integer between 1 and 2,147,483,647 inclusive.
POSITIVEN	Subtype of BINARY_INTEGER. A positive integer between 1 and 2,147,483,647 inclusive. The value cannot be NULL.
SIGNTYPE	Subtype of BINARY_INTEGER. An integer value that can be set to –1, 0, or 1.
PLS_INTEGER	Identical to BINARY_INTEGER.
SIMPLE_INTEGER	Introduced in Oracle Database 11g, a subtype of BINARY_INTEGER. SIMPLE_INTEGER can store the same range of values as BINARY_INTEGER, except for NULL values, which cannot be stored in a SIMPLE_INTEGER. Also, arithmetic overflow does not cause an error when using SIMPLE_INTEGER values. Instead, the result is simply truncated.
STRING	Identical to VARCHAR2.
RECORD	Composite of a group of other types. Similar to a structure in the C++ programming language.
REF CURSOR	Pointer to a set of rows.

TABLE A-2. *Oracle PL/SQL Types*

Index

D

Q

R

T

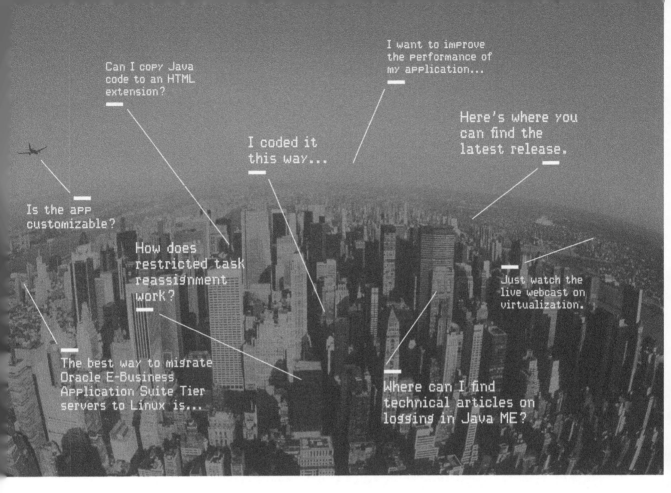

Oracle Technology Network. It's code for sharing expertise.

Come to the best place to collaborate with other IT professionals.

Oracle Technology Network is the world's largest community of developers, administrators, and architects using industry-standard technologies with Oracle products.

Sign up for a free membership and you'll have access to:

- Discussion forums and hands-on labs
- Free downloadable software and sample code
- Product documentation
- Member-contributed content

Take advantage of our global network of knowledge.

JOIN TODAY ▷ Go to: oracle.com/technetwork

ORACLE®
TECHNOLOGY NETWORK

ORACLE®

Reach More than 700,000 Oracle Customers with Oracle Publishing Group

Connect with the Audience that Matters Most to Your Business

Oracle Magazine
The Largest IT Publication in the World
Circulation: 550,000
Audience: IT Managers, DBAs, Programmers, and Developers

Profit
Business Insight for Enterprise-Class Business Leaders to
Help Them Build a Better Business Using Oracle Technology
Circulation: 100,000
Audience: Top Executives and Line of Business Managers

Java Magazine
The Essential Source on Java Technology, the Java
Programming Language, and Java-Based Applications
Circulation: 125,000 and Growing Steady
Audience: Corporate and Independent Java Developers,
Programmers, and Architects

For more information
or to sign up for a FREE
subscription:
Scan the QR code to visit
Oracle Publishing online.

Lightning Source UK Ltd.
Milton Keynes UK
UKHW031332040419
340487UK00005B/270/P